The Louisiana Purchase Bicentennial Series in Louisiana History

Glenn R. Conrad, General Editor

VOLUME I
THE FRENCH EXPERIENCE IN LOUISIANA

VOLUME II
THE SPANISH PRESENCE IN LOUISIANA, 1763 - 1803

VOLUME X
A REFUGE FOR ALL AGES:
IMMIGRATION IN LOUISIANA HISTORY

The Louisiana Purchase Bicentennial Series in Louisiana History

VOLUME II

THE SPANISH PRESENCE IN LOUISIANA 1763 - 1803

EDITED BY

GILBERT C. DIN

CENTER FOR LOUISIANA STUDIES
UNIVERSITY OF SOUTHWESTERN LOUISIANA
LAFAYETTE, LOUISIANA
1996

Endsheets:

Bernardo de Gálvez at the siege of Pensacola
Courtesy Special Collections, University of West Florida

Library of Congress Catalog Number: 96-084494
ISBN Number: 1-887366-03-2

Published by The Center for Louisiana Studies
P.O. Box 40831
University of Southwestern Louisiana
Lafayette, LA 70504-0831

CONTENTS

PART V ECONOMICS

PART VI NATIVE AMERICANS AND IMMIGRATION

PART VII SLAVERY AND FREE AFRICANS

PART VIII ARTS, ENTERTAINMENT, AND MEDICINE

ABOUT THE EDITOR

Gilbert C. Din, editor of **Volume II: The Spanish Presence in Louisiana, 1763-1803**, is today an independent historian. Dr. Din, whose Ph. D. is from the University of Madrid, lectured in history for many years at Fort Lewis College in Colorado. He is presently Professor Emeritus. In 1988 Dr. Din was awarded the L. Kemper Williams Prize for his book *The Canary Islanders of Louisiana.* In 1994 he was a winner of a Certificate of Commendation from the American Association for State and Local History for his book *Francisco Bouligny: A Bourbon Soldier in Spanish Louisiana.* He is the author of other books and many scholarly articles. He was the 1994 recipient of the Garnie W. McGinty Lifetime Meritorious Service Award.

ABOUT THE SERIES

It was in the spring of 1992 that first thought was given to the matter of how best the Center for Louisiana Studies might commemorate the bicentennial of the Louisiana Purchase in 2003. For the next few months the Center's staff and members of its Advisory Council intermittently discussed the possible project, but no concensus was forthcoming. Perhaps the reason being that the Purchase looms so monumentally in United States history there are seemingly few memorials of proper proportion to commemorate the event's bicentennial.

Nevertheless, as time passed the outlines of a project began to take shape. To properly mark the occasion the Center for Louisiana Studies should produce a lasting tribute not only to the people who crafted the Louisiana Purchase but also to the people who, during the last two hundred years, have had a role in transforming that vast wilderness into the heartland of America. But the Center's focus is not mid America for all practical purposes, it is Louisiana, the state that took its name from the Purchase territory. Therefore, the Center's project would concentrate on a Purchase bicentennial memorial that embraced the full range of Louisiana history.

There was another reason for this decision. In March of 1999 the Gulf Coast and the Mississippi Valley will mark the tricentennial of the founding of the French colony of Louisiana and the beginning of the region's historical era. Thus, if the Center's endeavor for the Purchase bicentennial was to be a history of Louisiana, then it should tell not only about the American experience in the area but also the Native American, French, Spanish, African, British and other influences that helped to lay the foundations for the present-day state.

Questions arose: Will the Center's Purchase bicentennial memorial be yet another history of Louisiana? If so, should it be another survey or should it be a more detailed account? Who would write this account of our times and those of our forebears? What interpretation would emerge from such a monograph? Who was expert enough to incorporate a harmonious blend of the political, economic, and social ingredients of our society?

Another year slipped by while we pondered these and other questions concerning the Center's memorial to the Purchase bicentennial and the tricentennial of the founding of the colony. After more discussion, there began to emerge a collective concept that was at once imaginative, exciting, and, above all, challenging. As a fitting memorial for the Louisiana Purchase bicentennial, the Center would organize and direct the publication of a major historical series. Marking the anniversaries, however, should not be the only reason for such an endeavor.

As discussion of the nature of the series evolved, it became obvious that there was an overriding reason for it. The series, to be known as the LOUISIANA PURCHASE BICENTENNIAL SERIES IN LOUISIANA HISTORY, would be a fine sampling of twentieth-century scholarship, particularly the scholarship of the last half of the century which embraced new methodologies leading to broader interpretations of the state's history. Here, in a multi-volume series the student of Louisiana history would be exposed to a wide range of scholarship reflecting multiple interpretations of historical events.

Thus, the decision was made; the Series would bring together in one place the very best articles, essays, and book parts that have been published about Louisiana in the twentieth century, particularly the latter half of the century. Its focus would be to inform scholars, teachers, students, and laypersons on far-ranging topics of Louisiana history drawn from a great resevoir of scholarship found in media ranging from scholarly to popular to obscure.

Most important to the development of such a series, however, was the person or persons who would select the "very best" to incorporate into the Series. The answer came quickly, only widely recognized experts, acting as volume editors, would determine from the broad spectrum of sources those essays which reflect the best in research, writing, and interpretation on topics in Louisiana history.

Initially, nineteen broad topics of Louisiana history were identified, and the Center plans to publish these nineteen volumes between 1995 and 2003. There may be additional volumes, if they are warranted. It should be noted, however, proper presentation of some topics in Louisiana history cannot be confined to a single book; hence, some volumes may incorporate several parts in order to present the full spectrum of scholarship on the subject. Finally, the volumes will not be published in sequential order, although Volume I, *The French Experience in Louisiana* will be the first to appear. All parts of a volume will be published simultaneously. Each volume will be announced upon publication.

THE LOUISIANA PURCHASE BICENTENNIAL SERIES IN LOUISIANA HISTORY will be a great source of information for anyone interested in the history of the colony and the state. It will be, however, an appropriate memorial to the men and women who shaped the colony and state down to the dawn of the twenty-first century.

Glenn R. Conrad, General Editor

INTRODUCTION AND ACKNOWLEDGMENTS

Most readers of Louisiana's colonial history are probably unaware that the state's Spanish period belongs to a larger historical field. Often persons who investigate and publish their work of this era in Louisiana come from Spanish colonial and Latin American history. Because of their background, they are generally interested in events in Louisiana from a wider perspective than just state history. Early in this century, the study of that part of the United States which once belonged to the Spanish Empire in the New World, the Borderlands, took a new turn. This was mostly the work of Herbert Eugene Bolton.

The beginning of Spanish Louisiana as a field of historical inquiry belongs more to the twentieth than to the nineteenth century. As the writing of Louisiana's history developed in the last century, only Charles Gayarré among state historians reached out to write a better history about the Spanish period. He acquired copies of documents from archives in Spain and used them in volumes II and III of his four-volume history of the state.[1] For decades his study of Spanish Louisiana was more accurate and detailed than any other. Indeed, the colonial period interested Gayarré more than the national era because only in his final volume did he focus on the American period. Even then he examined only the first years of the nineteenth century.

Early in the twentieth century, Bolton, who was a professor of history at the University of California, Berkeley, began to interest students in Borderland studies. Because he recognized the importance of primary documentation, he encouraged graduate students to consult foreign archives. Both Bolton and many of his students published translations of documents. While he did not coin the term "borderlands," Bolton is the scholar most associated with the word because of the books and articles he published. His students often followed in his footsteps and wrote widely on the subject. Bolton, however, largely ignored Louisiana. Only his edited work, *Athanase de Mézières and the Louisiana-Texas Frontier, 1768-1780*,[2] touched on the province, and his interest focused on the Natchitoches resident De Mézières and his work among the Indians. Several of Bolton's students, however, devoted more attention to Louisiana under the Spaniards.

Among them were David Bjork, Lawrence Kinnaird, Abraham P. Nasatir, and John Walton Caughey.[3] Of them Nasatir published more about the province, but his primary interest was upper Louisiana.[4]

In his 1921 work, *The Spanish Borderlands: A Chronicle of Old Florida and the Southwest*,[5] Bolton tied the Southeast and Southwest Borderlands together, and he was probably the first historian to do so. Because little—and perhaps nothing would be more accurate—had been published on the Spaniards in Louisiana after Gayarré, Bolton's chapter on the province in this book was general, even inferior to Gayarré's work. During Bolton's lifetime, no one else sought to improve or update his 1921 volume.

Only in 1970, nearly half a century following publication of *The Spanish Borderlands* and seventeen years after Bolton's death, did one of his most prolific students, John Francis Bannon, publish a new work on the same subject, *The Spanish Borderlands Frontier, 1513-1821*. One chapter in this work, "Luisiana, a Quasi-Borderland, 1762-1800," examines the Spanish province.[6] But inexplicably Bannon relied mainly on Nasatir's works on fur and Indian traders in the upper colony and all but ignored lower Louisiana. Bannon failed to employ the studies produced by Bjork, Kinnaird, Caughey, and others. Far more on Spanish Louisiana could still be found in Gayarré's century-old third volume of his state history than in Bannon's new study. Bannons' contribution disappointed persons interested in Spanish Louisiana as a field of historical inquiry.

In 1992 a third-generation Boltonian, David J. Weber, published *The Spanish Frontier in North America*.[7] In it he follows the tradition of Bolton and Bannon in tying both the Southwest and the Southeast Borderlands together. Weber is magisterial in his approach and links the Borderlands to other Spanish colonies (the Borderlands never existed by themselves and were vitally connected with other and more important Spanish poss-essions). Weber touches on numerous new topics that historians of the past ignored. He employs the writings of many recent historians on Spanish Louisiana, among them Eric Beerman, William S. Coker, Light Townsend Cummins, Gilbert C. Din, Jack D. L. Holmes, Daniel H. Usner, Jr., and Thomas D. Watson. Weber's selected bibliography is sixty-three pages long, and it reveals the vastness of Borderlands scholarship, including Spanish Louisiana. The publishers of Weber's book wisely included a vast assortment of impressive illustrations and maps that depict exploration, Indian locations, white settlements, and claims to territory by rival empires. The Southwest Borderlands that extend from Texas to California, however, continued to attract many more students than either Louisiana or Florida in the Southeast. The sections in Weber's volume dealing with Louisiana are excellent starting points for persons interested in the colony under the Spaniards. He uses extensive notes to guide individuals to the better historical literature.

Of the one-volume state histories about Louisiana, one is worthy of comment. Edwin Adams Davis's *Louisiana, A Narrative History*,[8] offers a wider variety of information on the colony than the other state histories. Besides looking at political, economic, and diplomatic issues, he also is interested in the social and cultural life of the colony. He explores topics not generally found in other works such as the smaller settlements, public health, home furnishings, clothing, and entertainment. He covers these subjects in five chapters and fifty-eight pages in the 1971 edition of his work. Louisiana State University graduate students enrolled in Davis' seminars assisted him in locating much of the information he used.

The purpose of *The Spanish Presence in Louisiana, 1763-1803*, is to present a representative sampling of the better research on Spanish Louisiana published during the past half century. Several selections are more than fifty years old, but many others are more recent. The volume also includes three previously unpublished essays. The readings vary widely from diplomacy, governors, administration and law, economics, war, immigration, Indians, slavery, the Catholic Church, to the arts and entertainment. Despite the seeming exhaustion of many topics by earlier researchers, there are probably as many topics yet to be done. In some cases, there is a need to revise earlier studies through the inclusion of documents from the Spanish archives. That task is becoming easier as Louisiana research centers acquire microfilm copies of documentation from European archives. Nevertheless, working Louisiana's colonial past presents more of a challenge to researchers than studying the history of other colonies. Investigators need to know both the Spanish and French languages and be able to decipher handwriting that is often a skill in itself. To cite one example where documents from foreign repositories could have helped write a better history: Had Caroline Maude Burson used the documentation in the Spanish archives, instead of the indices of documents she found in Louisiana, her biography of Esteban Miró[9] would have been infinitely richer. Unfortunately, no one yet has used the Spanish documentation now in Louisiana to write a better biography of Miró.

The first selections in *The Spanish Presence* are on diplomacy, a topic that interested historians in the 1920s. Arthur S. Aiton, a Bolton student, examines the forces that drove France to part with Louisiana and Spain to accept it. Samuel Flagg Bemis discusses how Spain under Minister of State Manuel Godoy in 1795 came to accept American terms in the Treaty of San Lorenzo (Pinckney's Treaty). Arthur Preston Whitaker explains why Spain decided to dispose of the province within a few years after negotiating the 1795 treaty. For the Spanish royal family, to echo Bemis, concerns in Europe outweighed the importance of colonies in America.

The next section on "Governors" examines four Louisiana top administrators in different ways. John Preston Moore explains causes that led to the 1768 revolt that ousted Antonio de Ulloa. Lawrence Kinnaird, a Bolton student in the 1920s, briefly surveys

Alejandro O'Reilly's work as governor during the six months he served in the colony. In a previously unpublished piece, Gilbert C. Din scrutinizes Bernardo de Gálvez's administration. He suggests that Gálvez was not as experienced and disinterested as many historians have asserted and that his administration of Louisiana had flaws. It is revisionist history, about which little has been done partly because few historians have worked on Spanish Louisiana topics. In a selection drawn from his biography of the governor, Jack D. L. Holmes examines the administration of Manuel Gayoso de Lemos and the different problems he faced.

In the section on "Administration and Law," Duvon Clough Corbitt, who spent many years in Cuba as a missionary and wrote history based on documents in the Cuban archives, looks at Spanish governance in "The Administrative System in the Floridas, 1781-1821," which includes Louisiana. Initially when Spain acquired the colony, it was not placed in the hands of the Ministry of the Indies but under the Ministry of State. After Alejandro O'Reilly firmly established Spanish rule following the French Creole revolt of 1768, he introduced Spanish law and institutions in all areas. The Louisiana governor was immediately under the captain general of Cuba and beyond him under the Ministry of the Indies in Spain. Only when Bernardo de Gálvez was viceroy of Mexico, as Corbitt shows, did this official serve as a superior to the Louisiana governor. Mexico City was too far out of the way for New Orleans to communicate there first and then with Spain. It delayed official correspondence and decision-making. Gálvez, who was given the captaincy-general of Louisiana and the Floridas as virtually his personal property, was the only viceroy to enjoy this power. Upon his death, the chain of command returned to what it had been earlier.

Morris S. Arnold, a federal court of appeals judge, meanwhile deals with administration within Louisiana. He examines how O'Reilly established the governor's authority over the outposts, Arkansas Post in this case, and how law functioned there. Gilbert C. Din looks at the city government of New Orleans under the Spaniards in "The Offices and Functions of the New Orleans *Cabildo*." The *cabildo* had no counterpart in the English colonies because it was both a city government and had officials (*alcaldes ordinarios*) who were judges. The *cabildo* was not an independent governing body inasmuch as a governor was present in New Orleans, and all its acts needed that official's approval. The *cabildo* was the first city government of New Orleans, and it led the way in establishing precedents in urban government. In "Do It! Don't Do It!: Spanish Laws on Sex and Marriage," Jack D. L. Holmes examines Spanish statutes that covered these important areas in colonial life. He illustrates his discussion with many examples of the problems that complicated the lives of eighteenth-century people.

Almost midway through Spain's tenure of Louisiana, war erupted during the governorship of Bernardo de Gálvez. Light Townsend Cummins explains that when the

English colonies in North America rebelled, the Spanish government wanted to know if the revolt was genuine or if the colonies might quickly make peace with England and then jointly turn on Spain. The Iberian nation, which lost most wars to England in the eighteenth century, did not want to repeat the humiliating defeat it sustained in the Seven Years' War. Eric Beerman, in "Victory on the Mississippi, 1779," shows that Gálvez had anticipated the war and, rather than wait for the British to attack him, he assaulted them first. He achieved the first Spanish victories in the war. Albert W. Haarmann, in "The Spanish Conquest of British West Florida, 1779-1781," follows up by describing how the Louisiana governor led forces that conquered both Mobile and Pensacola.

In the section on "Economics," Arthur Preston Whitaker describes, in "The Commerce of Louisiana and the Floridas at the End of the Eighteenth Century," laws that governed Louisiana's trade with Spain, Spanish colonies, and foreign nations. Restrictions limited commerce in the 1760s and 1770s, but freedom to trade grew in the 1780s and 1790s. Brian E. Coutts, in "Boom and Bust: The Rise and Fall of the Tobacco Industry in Spanish Louisiana, 1770-1790," discusses the importance of tobacco in Louisiana's economy. Because the Spanish and Mexican markets were not big enough to absorb Louisiana's tobacco, they soon stopped buying it, which doomed its production. The United States became the principal nation to benefit from trade with Louisiana in the 1790s. Whitaker examines this decade through an American trading firm in "Reed and Forde: Merchant Adventurers of Philadelphia: Their Trade with Spanish New Orleans." Finally, John G. Clark looks at the New Orleans and Louisiana economies in the 1790s, when they were growing rapidly and changing tremendously from what they had been at the start of the Spanish period.

In the section "Native Americans and Immigration," F. Todd Smith, in an essay written for this volume describes how Spain won over the Caddo Indians through the use of Frenchmen and trade. When trade goods declined in the late Spanish period, however, the Caddos became disaffected and welcomed United States' acquisition of the colony. Daniel H. Usner, Jr., shows in his article that Indians were in New Orleans throughout the Spanish period, although often they were invisible because many writers failed to mention them. Thomas D. Watson, in "A Scheme Gone Awry: Bernardo de Gálvez, Gilberto Antonio de St. Maxent, and the Southern Indian Trade," examines how Governor Gálvez favored his father-in-law St. Maxent in the Indian trade. But for reasons beyond their control, their plans failed, and St. Maxent spent his last years living with the accusation of smuggler. Gilbert C. Din in two articles describes the changes that the Spaniards made in allowing white immigrants into the colony. Although earlier the government paid for the settlement of Acadians, Canary Islanders, and Malagueños, it did not have sufficient funds to continue to do so. Therefore, it tried to get the right kind of settlers, preferably monarchists and Catholics, from both the Western Hemisphere and Europe.

In the next section on "Slavery and Free Africans," although Alejandro O'Reilly banned the further enslavement of Indians in 1769, he left those already in bondage with their owners who could not part with them except to free them. Stephen Webre, in an award-winning article, "The Problem of Indian Slavery in Spanish Louisiana, 1769-1803," details what happened to that policy and those Indians who were all but forgotten. Hans Baade, in "The Law of Slavery in Spanish *Luisiana*, 1769-1803," explains that Spain introduced its own slave laws in Louisiana. He contradicts the long-held tradition which claimed that O'Reilly only modified the French *Code Noir*. In "A Privilege and Honor to Serve: The Free Black Militia of Spanish New Orleans," Kimberly S. Hanger shows that the Spaniards used free blacks, both *pardos* and *morenos* (mulattoes and blacks), in the militia. They served in the American Revolution under Governor Gálvez, chased runaway slaves, and saw duty when danger threatened the colony. In "'Almost All Have Callings': Free Blacks at Work in Spanish New Orleans," Hanger examines the economic contributions of the free people of color in New Orleans. Through the use of Spanish slave law, many blacks obtained their freedom and worked in diverse fields, some of them quite successfully.

Alfred E. Lemmon contributes an unpublished essay, "Music and Art in Spanish Colonial Louisiana," in the next section. Usually these important aspects of cultural development are forgotten in describing the growth of the colony. Architect Samuel Wilson, Jr., writes on the buildings philanthropist Andrés de Almonester y Roxas had constructed in New Orleans. Some of them still stand in the city, tangible reminders of the Spanish presence. Civic philanthropy was a virtue many well-to-do Spaniards aspired to in both Spain and the colonies, and Almonester was an excellent example of that urban spirit. Jack D. L. Holmes, in an essay that uses data obtained from diverse sources and numerous legajos in the Papeles de Cuba of the Archivo General de Indias, shows how the Spaniards attempted to regulate the sale and consumption of alcoholic beverages. Ronald R. Morazán, in "Quadroon Balls in the Spanish Period," basing himself on historical documentation rather than myth or tradition, writes on a popular topic that has long fascinated readers. Finally, Jo Ann Carrigan explains that life in New Orleans was dangerous in the colonial period. She describes the first recognized outbreak of yellow fever in the city of 1796.

The final section, "The Catholic Church in Spanish Louisiana," has three selections on different topics. Alfred E. Lemmon surveys Spanish religious policy and the work of different church leaders in the colony. Light Townsend Cummins examines a number of church law suits and policy when marriages had clearly failed. While divorce existed at that time, it was in no way similar to what it is today. Richard E. Greenleaf studies the inquisition in colonial Louisiana which, however, was present only briefly.

It is hoped that publication of these essays will provide a deeper insight into life in Spanish Louisiana. Although the study of Louisiana under the Spaniards has advanced significantly beyond what it was seventy-five years ago when Bolton published *The Spanish Borderlands*, much still remains to be done.[10] Perhaps several of the authors included in this volume who are actively engaged in research and writing, together with individuals who have yet to begin their careers as historians, will heed Clio's call and produce new studies in the field of Spanish Louisiana. Then the people and events of two hundred years ago, when for four decades Louisiana formed part of the Spanish Empire, will be better understood. Publication of books is never done alone and several individuals who helped to put this one together must be mentioned. First of all, I am grateful to the general editor of this series, Glenn R. Conrad, for selecting me as editor of this volume, and for providing a model through the publication of his book in this series, *The French Experience in Louisiana.* Glenn's assistance made my work infinitely easier. I wish to thank F. Todd Smith and Alfred E. Lemmon for contributing original essays. Their studies on Spanish Indian policy and the arts helped to broaden topics in this book. Finally but by no means lastly, Regina M. LaBiche, editorial assistant at the Center for Louisiana Studies, assisted in numerous ways to make publication of this volume a reality. Above all, she accepted changes and revisions in good cheer.

Notes for "Introduction and Acknowledgments"

[1]There are many editions of Charles Gayarré's *History of Louisiana*. His third volume, subtitled *The Spanish Domination*, appeared in 1854.

[2]Herbert Eugene Bolton, ed. and trans., *Athanase de Mézières and the Louisiana-Texas Frontier, 1768-1780*, 2 vols. (Cleveland, 1914).

[3]Bolton's students honored him with two *Festschrifts*. The second of these, *Greater America—Essays in Honor of Herbert Eugene Bolton* (Berkeley, CA, 1945), contains a bibliography of the publications of his master and doctoral students to 1945.

[4]A list of Nasatir's publications about the Spaniards in the Mississippi Valley to 1968 can be found in C. Harvey Gardiner, "The Mexican Archives and the Historiography of the Mississippi Valley in the Spanish Period," in *The Spanish in the Mississippi Valley, 1762-1804*, ed. John Francis McDermott (Urbana, IL, 1974), 44n. From his visits to the French and Spanish archives, Nasatir collected an impressive number of documents on the upper province that perhaps totaled two hundred thousand pages. A fire in 1985 destroyed Nasatir's home in San Diego, California. Many books, journals, and documents were lost. But possibly the main part of his documentary collection, which was kept in his office at San Diego State University when the author worked with Nasatir, escaped destruction.

[5]Herbert Eugene Bolton, *The Spanish Borderlands: A Chronicle of Old Florida and the Southwest* (New Haven, 1921). It is Volume 23 of the *Chronicles of America* series.

[6]John Francis Bannon, *The Spanish Borderlands Frontier, 1513-1821* (New York, 1970). The chapter on Louisiana is found on pages 190-205.

[7]David J. Weber, *The Spanish Frontier in North America* (New Haven, 1992). Weber studied under Donald Cutter, a Berkeley graduate, at the University of New Mexico.

[8]Edwin A. Davis, *Louisiana, A Narrative History*, 3rd ed. (Baton Rouge, 1971).

[9]Caroline Maude Burson, *The Stewardship of Don Esteban Miró, 1782-1792* (New Orleans, 1940).

[10]Persons wishing to learn what has been published on Spanish Louisiana should consult Jack D. L. Holmes, *A Guide to Spanish Louisiana, 1762-1806* (New Orleans, 1970); Light Townsend Cummins, "Spanish Louisiana," in *A Guide to the History of Louisiana*, eds., Light Townsend Cummins and Glen Jeansonne (Westport, CT, 1982), 17-25; Sylvia L. Hilton, "El Misisipí y la Luisiana colonial en la historiografía española, 1940-1989," *Revista de Indias*, 50 (1990): 195-212; and Kimberly S. Hanger, "Spanish Louisiana: An Update," Louisiana Library Association *Bulletin*, 55 (1992): 30-36. Additional information can be gleaned from Gardiner, "Mexican Archives," 38-49; Charles Edwards O'Neill, S. J., "The State of Studies on Spanish Colonial Louisiana," in *The Spanish in the Mississippi Valley, 1762-1804*, ed. John Francis McDermott (Urbana, IL, 1974), 16-25; and Weber, *Spanish Frontier*, 491-553.

PART I

DIPLOMACY

THE DIPLOMACY OF THE LOUISIANA CESSION*

Arthur S. Aiton[1]

It has long been the custom of writers of American history to refer to Louisiana, at the time of its transfer by France to Spain, as a colonial "white elephant." It has been equally conventional to describe the cession of this province as a compensation for the loss of Florida by Spain in the peace preliminaries of 1762. A more complete survey of the materials bearing upon this important episode casts some doubt on the validity of these conclusions, adds two years to the story, and brings to light new facts. An attempt at restatement seems, therefore, to be justified.[2]

From the days immediately preceding the outbreak of the Seven Years' War, France used every lure and blandishment at her disposal to secure the support of Spain in the impending maritime war against England. Ferdinand VI and his ministers refused to be turned from their cherished policy of peace. This monarch's death on August 10, 1759, brought his half brother, the king of Naples, to the Spanish throne as Charles III. Charles saw the safety of Spain's colonial empire threatened by the complete destruction of French naval and colonial power at the hands of England and, from the outset, spoke encouragingly of Spanish aid to France. His promises, however, failed to take definite shape until the signing of the Family Compact in 1761. In the interim His Catholic Majesty exasperated the French minister, Choiseul, by futile peace overtures in London and by memorials addressed to England that seemed designed rather to win concessions from that court as the price of continued Spanish neutrality than to promote the success of France in her duel with Pitt's great war machine.

Louisiana began to play a rôle in these negotiations for Spanish aid in the diplomatic dispatches of the Bourbon powers, in 1754, on the eve of the outbreak of the Seven Years' War.[3] Minorca was the prize held out to Spain for military assistance up to 1760 and Louisiana was merely pointed out as a menace to the safety of Mexico if it were captured by England.[4] That Spain had any desire to possess Louisiana, aside from an old claim never officially renounced, or valued it above some of her own possessions, was

*This article first appeared in the *American Historical Review*, 36 (1931): 701-20. It is reprinted here with the kind permission of the American Historical Association.

not realized. In 1760 the trading value of this colony was brought home to the French government in dramatic fashion. Charles III, in a private discussion with the French ambassador, the marquis d'Ossun, concerning a Spanish order barring French vessels en route to Louisiana from the harbor of Havana, suddenly broached the subject. During the course of the conversation he had made the significant remark, "I do believe, as you do, that we are natural and necessary allies; our states adjoin each other in the two continents and we have the same enemies to fear." This seemed to be an isolated, even if interesting, observation, when, near the end of the audience, he abruptly stated his ambition to acquire the province. "I must arrange with France after the peace for Louisiana by means of some exchange." The marquis d'Ossun, startled and somewhat at a loss, replied that perhaps the Spanish part of Santo Domingo would be a good equivalent but added that this was a personal view as he lacked instructions and had no information as to the relative importance of the two possessions. The king of Spain confessed a similar lack of knowledge and ended the interview with the remark "Nevertheless, sir, I believe I know enough to state that the transaction indicated would be advantageous to France."[5]

This suggestion came at the difficult time before the death of the peace-loving queen of Spain, when it seemed, despite the many assurances of Charles III, that Spain was merely using France to gain her own ends and had no sincere intention of helping that power. The idea, for this reason, met with an immediate and curt refusal. In fact, Choiseul could find little in the proposal save another attempt to take advantage of French weakness coming, as it did, on the heels of a definite refusal of a loan of 12,000,000 piasters to France, and a vigorous Spanish claim to the neutral West Indian islands, St. Vincent, Tobago, Dominica, and St. Lucia, which had been regarded as French. He voiced his suspicions and questioned Spain's good faith in a letter to D'Ossun. The conduct of Spain, in his estimation, under the guise of friendship for France and enmity toward England, had in reality for its object the satisfaction of her own political ambitions. Spain's extravagant claim to the right to fish off the Newfoundland Banks, her bid for the neutral islands, he declared, all confirmed this opinion and now, as a climax, "the Catholic King himself has made the first approach to you on his desire to obtain Louisiana by an exchange with us."[6]

This pessimistic view of the intentions of the neighbor kingdom was short-lived. The queen's adverse influence was removed by death, Charles reported his first active step against the English whom he said had been driven from Campeche by force, and better still, statements of Spanish military and naval preparations were more reassuring. Furthermore, every evidence pointed to a firm reply from Pitt to the latest Spanish demands presented in London by De Fuentes, which would leave the Spanish monarch with little excuse for longer delay. At the same time, Choiseul heard of the total loss of Canada. Either Spanish aid must be secured or France would be obliged to seek the best possible peace terms from England immediately. Choiseul preferred, if feasible, to try the test of arms again in an effort to wrest more advantageous terms from his adversary and to this end he plunged wholeheartedly into a diplomatic campaign for Spanish support. No time was wasted. The opening gun was fired with the presentation of Louis XV's note of condolence to Charles III on the death of his queen, October 17, 1760. D'Ossun took full advantage of this splendid opportunity and played all the stops in a veritable anthem of appeal for the union of the two crowns.[7]

In the subsequent conversations, chiefly by use of the threat of a separate French peace, Charles was manoeuvred into the definite statement that he was favorably disposed toward a system of union with France, and finally, into asking that drafts of the proposed treaties of union be submitted to him.[8] With this step taken the long negotiation of the Family Compact was definitely under way. In the exchange of views which ensued Spain constantly recurred to the question of the boundaries of Louisiana, which had never been definitely marked out, because Spain had refused to abandon her claim to the area. This question had been a source of worry and annoyance in the past and was regarded as sufficiently important by the Spaniards to warrant inclusion in the proposed treaties. Indeed, the history of Franco-Spanish relations in this region had been far from tranquil since the days of La Salle, and constitutes another "Half Century of Conflict" that was only to terminate with the cession to Spain and consequent removal of Spanish fear of French overland extension into Texas and New Mexico.[9] New Orleans and Mobile were, in addition, ports from which French clandestine trade could sail to Mexico and the Caribbean colonies of Spain and, in case of war, raiders from these harbors could easily intercept Spanish commerce. Hence, Charles III was most solicitous that the eastern boundary of the province be drawn sufficiently to the north to prevent the even more dangerous English nation from acquiring these gulf ports in case she retained Canada in the peace.[10] In return for recognition of French rights in Louisiana, Spain wanted the treaties of union to include a clear settlement of the Louisiana boundaries.[11] Counter-projects of cession of Louisiana in return for a money loan or for an immediate declaration of war against England prevented the inclusion of this article in the treaties of union, signed on August 15, 1761.

These counterprojects, initiated before the Family Compact was signed, were kept alive well into the autumn of 1761, when it appeared that Spain would drift into the war at her own time and that no further considerable money aid could be expected. It was then that Choiseul conceived other uses for the province.[12] Three separate set of negotiations were conducted simultaneously in Paris and Madrid, and in each, Louisiana was the prize proffered in return for favors. Through D'Ossun in Madrid Choiseul sought two things in separate negotiations: first, an early entry of Spain into the war; second, a large loan to finance the continuance of the French military effort. The third negotiation was carried on directly between Choiseul and the Spanish minister, Grimaldi, in Paris and constituted a third offer of Louisiana with the same object in view, namely, and immediate Spanish declaration of war. All were conditioned on the successful completion of the Bourbon alliance, then in its final stages of preparation, and looked beyond it to the period of cooperation between the two powers in bringing the war to a successful conclusion.[13] In order to avoid confusion the Madrid and Paris *démarches* will be treated separately and, since Louisiana occupied the center of the stage throughout, the account of their progress will be given in some detail.

If the alliance of France and Spain were to be successful, financial assistance as well as military aid was vital. Naturally, in this connection, Choiseul thought of Spain's earlier expression of a desire to acquire Louisiana. With the secret convention and the Family Compact practically ready to receive signature, Spain would be in a propitious mood to listen to overtures. Louisiana was something coveted by Spain which France still possessed. The cession of Louisiana might induce Spain to grant one or both of the French demands—a considerable loan and an advancement of the date of her entry into the conflict, which had been fixed in the draft of the convention at the disappointingly late date of May 1, 1762.[14] So Louisiana had to serve as the *quid pro quo* of two requests as France had little else to offer. Accordingly, on July 13, 1761, two weeks before the alliance was cemented, Choiseul empowered D'Ossun to offer the colony to Spain in exchange for a prompt Spanish declaration of war against England. "We ask Spain to declare herself earlier rather than later," he wrote, "and, at the moment of her declaration we shall propose an arrangement relative to Louisiana." The following day, as there was no time to await results from this first overture, he began a second negotiation in Madrid by authorizing the ambassador to offer the cession of Louisiana to the Spanish minister of finance, Squillace, in return for a large loan to France. D'Ossun was strictly enjoined, in his instructions, to inform no other Spanish minister of the offer as Choiseul wished to keep this second negotiation under cover until Spain reached a decision on the first offer.[15] In Paris, a day later, he injected the same proposals into the conversations on war, peace, and the alliance then under way with the Spanish minister Grimaldi, and on September 13 was still offering a Louisiana "cession with widest boundaries" in return for prompt entry of Spain into the war.[16] By these measures Choiseul, always a facile opportunist, undoubtedly hoped to take advantage of Wall's request for an inclusion of a boundary settlement for Louisiana in the treaties of alliance, and by the cession of Louisiana to solve the pressing questions of finance and war aid.

Despite these energetic and well-timed proposals of Choiseul the happy moment of the signing of the pact and the convention, August 15, 1761, passed without the insertion of an article ceding Louisiana to Spain and consequently without the concomitant advancement of the date of Spain's intervention in the war. The fate of the loan was likewise deferred until after the safe conclusion of the alliance. Louisiana then became the sacrifice which might secure these ends, beyond the terms of the signed and sealed articles of alliance.

In Madrid, the marquis d'Ossun made no progress against Spain's professed inability to wage war before the date agreed on in the convention. The even more important matter of financial aid gave rise to a long negotiation which caused him an infinite amount of trouble and anxiety before he was able to write finis. On the receipt of his instructions he took it on himself to postpone any approach to Squillace as he feared a premature step might jeopardize the success of the alliance between the two powers. He reasoned that it was unwise to expose the desperate state of the French treasury to her prospective ally until the union was consummated and, even then, he anticipated a rebuff in view of the sum asked, the long credit, and the onerous terms accorded Spain. Furthermore, he averred that Charles III, on the eve of waging war himself, would not care to see so much money drawn from his reserves. But his instructions were positive. Therefore, after a brief delay, fearful that he was exceeding his powers, he agreed to make the request, using the Louisiana offer to render it more attractive to Spain. Apparently, begging for money was distasteful to the ambassador and accounted both for his delay and his sudden desire to conclude the unpleasant task as rapidly as possible. He wrote, August 17, 1761, that the full amount, 3,600,000 piasters, with which it was proposed to finance the war in 1762 and 1763—a period regarded as long enough to ruin English credit—had been requested of Squillace. D'Ossun put the case in the best possible light, dwelling on the great resources of France, her exactitude in meeting her obligations, the security of the king's word, and the relative insignificance of the sum required when compared with the assets of his country. Above all, he stressed the temporary nature of French financial stringency as due primarily to the hoarding and draining off of gold and silver during the war. The money would be used to sustain currency circulation and to stiffen French credit. When he perceived that Squillace was still unimpressed, he adroitly insinuated that France was also willing to cede Louisiana as a token of appreciation. Squillace then showed some signs of interest, but he was firm in the opinion that nothing could be done until the silver fleet arrived from America and the treaties of union assumed stability. D'Ossun left the interview with some hope for the success of his enterprise.[17]

Choiseul, still glowing with the success of his policy of union with Spain, wrote to D'Ossun in high good humor, August 25, 1761, that he need delay no longer as both pact and convention were signed. But he insisted with utmost force that the loan must be secured.

> It is [he emphasized] of extreme importance that our propositions on this subject succeed. You seem to be of the opinion that the signature of our treaties would facilitate their success. Therefore, sir, the king expects through your zeal, your talents, and the confidence you have so justly acquired at the Court of Spain, that you will succeed in securing a realization of the necessity that we procure this assistance. The use we desire to make of it had for object the common advantage of the two crowns in maintaining their glory and interest. Moreover, the service we expect from the relationship, friendship, and alliance that so intimately unite His Majesty to His Catholic Majesty, is not gratuitous and I have already confided to you what the king is disposed to do for Spain in addition to the exact reimbursement of the sum advanced to us. You can not, sir, at the present moment render a more essential service to the finances, and consequently to the political and military operations of His Majesty, than to conduct the negotiation, with which you have been entrusted under this head, to a successful conclusion.[18]

But one success worked against another. As Spain moved nearer to war the possibility of drawing on her treasury diminished. Squillace, aware of this, refused to consider the French loan until the silver fleet arrived. In desperation, D'Ossun asked for half the amount of the original request and reduced the term of the loan to one year, but Squillace was adamantine. The silver fleet, object of so much concern (Pitt fell from power in England at this time partly because his desire to intercept it involved an immediate break with Spain), arrived safely in home waters on September 12, 1761. The French ambassador determined to take advantage of the joyful event and ask Charles III for 1,800,000 piasters. But the most that he secured was a loan of 900,000, payable in six installments in the first half of 1762 and to be repaid in similar installments in the last half of the year at an interest rate of 5 percent. The home government, which had been making D'Ossun's path difficult by its simultaneous effort to push the king of Spain into war at an early date, was so well pleased with this result that it granted the ambassador a gratification and suggested only minor changes in the stipulations of the loan contract. But, in view of Spain's professed inability to hasten her entry into the war, and as the loan from Spain was much smaller than asked, Louisiana was not ceded. All hope of additional monetary aid from Spain was to vanish entirely by March of the following year when Spain, taxed to the limit of her ability in waging her own war with England, had no money to lend.[19]

In the meantime, at Paris, Choiseul had been negotiating independently with Grimaldi. Louisiana was an important counter in the *pourparlers* as well, first, in 1761, as a reward for early entry into the war, next, as a possible nucleus about which to rebuild the French colonial empire, and lastly, in 1762, when new and final peace negotiations were opened, as a bribe to secure Spanish consent to an early peace. In order to understand fully these changing purposes one must go back to June, 1761, and follow Choiseul's policy as the vicissitudes of the war and the possibilities of peace forced alterations in his course. That month found Choiseul in the midst of the discussion of pact and convention which were to unite the two Bourbon powers, and with the De Bussy-Stanley peace conferences under way, looking toward a separate peace with England. In their progress it soon developed that England was not in a generous mood and would not consider the German conquests of France as an equivalent for the return of Canada. This alarmed Grimaldi, who kept his court constantly informed as to the proposed boundaries between Canada and Louisiana.[20] Nor was Choiseul's attitude particularly reassuring. That wily diplomat was still playing a desperate game that necessitated a nice balance between war and peace. On one hand, he wished "to keep up the negotiation with England in such a situation that if it did not succeed this time it would serve as a base for the genuine negotiation which must take place if Pitt fell before the influence of Bute"; on the other, he planned to tie Spain to France so that that Crown would support him in the peace or, if that failed, in the war. A successful war would recoup French losses, while defeat would be less costly since "the losses of Spain would lighten those which France might suffer."[21]

At first Choiseul was far from eager for peace and, in the face of what Grimaldi regarded as reasonable and even liberal terms, spoiled any chance of their success by joining the French counterproposals for peace with the Spanish grievances against England. To do this Choiseul had to override strong opposition in the French council, which was clamoring for peace. In addition, Spain was willing to present her case separately rather than have France lose the peace. It was a bold move that Choiseul made to win Spanish confidence, yet little calculated to secure peace from Pitt![22] Choiseul's policy was successful. By combining the French and Spanish negotiations in London he convinced Charles III of French sincerity but drew from the wrathful Pitt a haughty ultimatum. This humiliating document Choiseul used to whip the recalcitrant French council into line[23] and, with characteristic energy, turned to Spain for military and financial aid to sustain a new campaign, made necessary by what he termed England's unreasonable attitude toward the union of their cases. The notes of his decisive memorial on Pitt's ultimatum, which elicited applause when read to the king's council on August 1, 1761, and practically assured the continuation of the war, indicate a full return to his belligerent attitude of 1759. After roundly condemning the individual items of the English offer as being "in content and form more laws dictated by a conqueror than articles of negotiation between equal powers," he turned to Louis XV and declared:

> My opinion, Sire, is not to accept the proposals of England, but, to make a soft answer to gain time, which answer I will submit to your council Sunday; to send Spain England's reply . . . to propose to the king of Spain that he take Minorca in deposit as we can use the troops stationed there and relieve ourselves of that expense; to ask the king of Spain if he wishes to buy Louisiana, and, if the purchase pleases him, to make a banking arrangement with him to this end, which will be necessary to provide funds for the next and the succeeding campaigns.[24]

Choiseul realized that to fight successfully allies must have a preconcerted plan of unified action. He therefore sought to secure agreement upon a common scheme for a general offensive, involving a descent on England, and tried to persuade Spain to break with London in the autumn of 1761. He believed that this move would hamper the English Parliament in raising funds and that it might cause the fall from office of his redoubtable adversary Pitt. A sudden and well-timed entry would also surprise Portugal and force her to alliance or certain defeat. His plan included a Spanish occupation of Minorca and the dispatch of the French troops from there to Santo Domingo on Spanish ships before war was declared, on the pretext of conveying them to France. He feared an English conquest of Florida and Louisiana and offered to supply troops for the defense of the latter colony if Spain would provide transportation and supplies. The colony could then become Spanish or French as the two powers found most convenient. If all this were done, in his estimation, one brief campaign would suffice to bring England to her knees and Spain could strike off the chains of commercial slavery to that power by revoking all past commercial treaties.

The offer of Louisiana to Spain was repeated in September when France, convinced of the futility of the existing peace negotiations with England, nevertheless continued them in order to cover her ally's military unreadiness. Choiseul assured Grimaldi that his concessions to England's pretensions to an enlarged Canada were not serious, as Louisiana remained larger than they could possibly cultivate or populate, and that in any case his original offer of "cession with widest boundaries," in return for prompt entry of Spain into the war, still held good. Ricardo Wall, writing on September 23, 1761, was pleased with this generous attitude, and said that France and Spain were now so united that the former could not, without an open breach of faith, sign a peace unless the latter received satisfaction. But he was unprepared to send a Spanish garrison to Minorca, or to send an ultimatum to Portugal or, in brief, to enter the war as yet. Even the Spanish eagerness to acquire Minorca failed to stimulate that power to attempt to provision the island.[25] This lack of enterprise was not due to a lack of willingness but to very real deficiencies in the Spanish military establishment.

Choiseul, it is clear, had used Louisiana to the fullest extent in the foregoing negotiations, and had fallen short of his aims. He now, under the provocation of a *mémoire* on the colony furnished by D'Ossun, developed a high regard for Louisiana. It suddenly became the nucleus about which France would rebuild her colonial empire in America after the peace. Fired with enthusiasm, he wrote to the ambassador on December 15:

> It is certain that this colony merits a closer attention than has been accorded it up to the present. I am informed as to its fertility, and the mildness and healthfulness of the climate, and when circumstances permit, I shall neglect none of the advantages that a colony so useful can produce. We have already thought of emigration from Canada to Louisiana, but this emigration can not take place until after the peace. You will appreciate all the reasons political and economic for this. Your are informed that we intend to send aid to Louisiana. It is ready to leave and will be there certainly in the month of January.[26]

England's declaration of war on Spain, January 2, 1762, ended all discussion of Louisiana as a "war bribe" or reward for a loan. Spain was in the war and her own expenditures absorbed all her funds. But it was a hopelessly ineffective Spain from which no great victories could be expected to justify Choiseul's last desperate gamble to secure a better peace from Albion. He soon perceived the hopelessness of fighting on, especially after the fall of Pitt from power, and with Bute's government as well as the young George III anxious for peace. It was a situation that might be commuted into an advantage for France if it were written into a treaty of peace without loss of time. The return of Pitt to power in England would mean the inexorable exaction of the full penalty of defeat. With his usual foresight Choiseul prepared for the contingency. Through the intermediary of the Sardinian ambassadors, Count de Viri in London, and the Bailli de Solar in Paris, he had, in anticipation, established an undercover negotiation with Lord Egremont representing England.[27] By April, 1762, the secret *pourparlers* had reached the point where direct negotiation could be begun. Spanish consent had been gained in the meantime by adroit and seemingly frank methods. As early as January 10, 1762, after the conversations had been going on a month, and one day before Spain declared war on England, Choiseul intimated to Grimaldi that he had received vague hints of England's anxiety to make peace but that

> . . . he had replied to all these indirect hints that France could now neither hear nor enter into the slightest discussion without the concurrence of His Catholic Majesty, that he was persuaded that the two monarchs had no desire to perpetuate the war, but in case England found herself disposed to end it in a reasonable manner, he did not believe she should work for it by indirect methods, emissaries, or even words. England ought to make her propositions clearly to both courts, as France had when she thought peace was necessary.[28]

The release of Count d'Estaing, held a prisoner by the British, furnished a good pretext for bringing the negotiation into the light of day. A letter from Lord Egremont to the French government, dated February 28, 1762, concerning the return of this prisoner, enabled Choiseul to direct Spanish attention to these peace overtures as something new. Soon British peace proposals arrived in Paris in the dispatch bags of Count de Viri to Bailli de Solar. Notes of these, submitted to Spain, forced her to countenance the opening of negotiations. This consent was not given, however, until France agreed to inform Vienna and to secure that court's agreement to a separate peace between France and England. It was one thing to get Charles III to agree to consider preliminaries of peace, quite another to get him to sign them. Charles had barely entered the conflict and, unable to realize that the chance for a victorious invasion of Portugal had passed, he felt that the military successes of Spain might bring him the glory of ending the long war. He could then dictate the terms of its triumphant conclusion. In Spain the negotiation was regarded askance as the pernicious result of Sardinian meddling and, as such, a development which must be delayed as circumstances permitted. In so far as the immediate proposal of England was concerned, Spain was primarily interested in preventing any shrinkage of the boundaries of Louisiana and in seeing that a neutral zone be placed between it and Canada.[29]

But the high hopes of Spain were doomed to disappointment. Choiseul, with an acceptable peace in sight, now used every artifice to get that power's consent of the close of hostilities, as he had done previously in urging Spain's entry into the war. Spanish participation had not swung the balance in favor of the Bourbon house. At any moment the war party might return to power in England and the changing fortunes of the Continental war against Prussia were not such as to encourage continued fighting. In particular, the withdrawal of Russia from an active part in the war on May 5, 1762, definitely ended all hope of subduing Prussia, and Austria was added to the nations desiring peace. Choiseul, worthy successor of the great ministers of state who for two centuries had directed French foreign policy, albeit in office at a disastrous hour, saw the implications of this event and could not quickly enough initiate a peace conference with England. Even the assassination of the Czar Peter failed to restore the situation or entirely to recall Russia from "indecent attitude." Faced with irremediable Russian disaffection, Choiseul instructed his ambassador in Spain to urge Charles III to agree to an immediate peace for the sake of France, as the situation was hopeless and England's present peace terms were reasonable. Charles, in his reply, stated that for him the war had just begun and that he expected to conquer Portugal. Nevertheless, for the sake of his ally, he would consent to an immediate formal peace negotiation.[30]

This direct peace negotiation between France, Spain, and England brought Louisiana into prominence again.[31] Choiseul was willing to lose Canada in order to regain the sugar islands, Martinique and Guadaloupe, if he could also retain the right to fish off Newfoundland and in the Gulf of St. Lawrence with proper *abri.* In addition, he was willing to sacrifice Louisiana east of the Mississippi if he could retain the island of St. Lucia, which would secure the defense of the sugar islands and provide a windward fleet base in the West Indies.[32] With characteristic facility he evolved a new colonial policy to meet the new situation. Making a virtue of necessity, he rationalized the loss of the continental colonies of France into a positive benefit.

> I do not think, as formerly held here [he wrote], that it is good to have many colonies. I am the sworn enemy of the American system of colonies for France because I believe it to be pernicious for France, and esteem it to be more essential to cultivate grain and vines in this kingdom and to support its manufactures than to export sugar, coffee, and indigo. But, at the same time, as coffee, sugar, and indigo, are necessary in France, I believe that a great power ought not to let money flow out of its realm for these commodities which have become necessities; rather, one of the elements essential to the welfare of such a state lies in the possession of sufficient American territory to take care of needs of this sort, but not in having more territory than necessary for these needs.[33]

As Choiseul now considered Martinique and Guadaloupe necessary to France, Bute proposed a formula for their return, giving Britain compensation by extending Canada to include eastern Louisiana to the Mississippi River.[34] Accord was reached on all save one point, the island of St. Lucia. Choiseul would not yield here and said he preferred to continue the war rather than lose the island.[35] To secure it he sacrificed Spain's interest, for he had to yield eastern Louisiana with the Mississippi boundary, which would give England territory on the Gulf of Mexico. Spain had agreed to the peace negotiation with the distinct understanding that this concession would not be made. Choiseul felt certain that Spain would object to the arrangement, but nevertheless accepted the English offer without informing his ally. He believed that too vehement Spanish opposition could be quieted by an exchange of Spanish Florida for the balance of Louisiana and was prepared to propose this transaction when news of the loss of Havana was to make necessary an entirely new propitiatory offer.[36] England accepted these terms with one addition, the right to free navigation of the main channel of the Mississippi River. Choiseul ran the boundary along the river through what he termed its eastern mouth by way of the Iberville River and Lakes Pontchartrain and Maurepas to the gulf, but the English were dubious as to the navigability of this outlet.[37] By this clever stroke Choiseul gained the island of New Orleans, which he was able to represent to Spain later as an unexpected diplomatic triumph.

Spain proved to be quite difficult to lead to a French peace. Choiseul was even forced to request the English plenipotentiary, Bedford, to conceal the French cession of eastern Louisiana from the Spanish plenipotentiary, Grimaldi. Bedford wrote home: "I find they are much embarrassed with regard to that court, and very apprehensive of M. Grimaldi being informed of the note they had sent about the Mobile and the navigation they have offered us, through the River Iberville and the lakes, into the Gulf of Mexico, I told them that the navigation as offered by them, was not sufficiently satisfactory to us, and would equally give umbrage to the Spaniards, as *that* we expect to have in common with them." Grimaldi he pictured as an arrogant fool, who at the bare mention of the possibility of the English on the gulf had "monté sur ses grands chevaux," and who, despite *carte blanche* given the king of France by his cousin of Spain, might break off the negotiation unless, as Choiseul suggested, both France and England humored him.[38]

As a matter of solid fact, Grimaldi had the firm backing of his court in his objection. As early as June 18, 1762, he had rejected the idea that the cession of Mobile to England would not harm Spanish interests.[39] Promised by France that England could never navigate from the little tongue of land that the Iberville River boundary gave them, he yielded on that point but not without misgivings.[40] The home government sought to avoid even this concession, and, in its determination to bar the English from the gulf, dug up the old and outworn claims of Spain both to Louisiana and Georgia. In return for Spanish recognition of these colonies as legitimate settlements, it was proposed that the South Carolina boundary be extended westward to the Mississippi as the line between the French and English possessions, keeping the area south of the line to the gulf as a neutral zone. It had required a personal letter from Louis XV to Charles III begging for peace, to secure on August 25, 1762, the necessary powers for Grimaldi.[41] But while yielding to this extent, Spain refused to recognize what Choiseul had already offered England, namely, possession of the shore of the Gulf of Mexico between Florida and the island of New Orleans. France became so impatient at this obstinacy that she offered to cede or evacuate all of Louisiana if Spain would come to a decision and not force her ally to miss the proffered peace.[42] At the same time Choiseul offered England a new article, at least new to Spain, granting to England the Mississippi boundary with free navigation of the river, but, apparently to propitiate Spain, reserving New Orleans to France. As he had already conceded this to England without consulting Spain, and as Great Britain had already agreed to the exclusion of New Orleans from eastern Louisiana, provided the right to navigate the main river were accorded in case the Iberville channel proved unnavigable, Choiseul's double dealing is evident. This concession, on the surface wrung from a reluctant England, naturally failed to satisfy Grimaldi. So Choiseul put the treaty article before the Spanish government. War and peace hinged on Spain's acceptance, he said. Which did the Spanish government want?[43]

Before Spain's reply of September 29, 1762, was received, positive news of the capitulation of Havana changed the entire complexion of the negotiation.[44] It had been thought that this key position in the West Indies was impregnable and rumors of English success had been scoffed at by Spanish officialdom. England could now demand better terms and the elation which swept the nation made it difficult for the English peace party to avoid a continuation of the war. Spain, stung by this loss, wished to fight on.

At this juncture France came forward with a definite offer to cede Louisiana to Spain. Louis XV again wrote a personal letter to his cousin in which he deplored the loss of Havana and offered Louisiana to Spain so that his ally would lose nothing in the peace. Louisiana could be used, he explained, to exchange for the restitution of Havana or kept to offset the loss of other Spanish territory which the English might demand for the return of that port.[45] Choiseul instructed the French ambassador, in an accompanying letter, to play up the value of Louisiana as a sacrifice worthy of French gratitude to Spain for her aid in the war and, by inference, her assent to an immediate peace.[46]

A decision was soon reached. Spain regarded Florida as the least valuable of her possessions and its loss as decidedly less harmful than English acquisition of Louisiana with its danger of smuggling into Mexico and its threat of an overland advance by the English into that treasure house of overseas Spain.[47] Grimaldi was ordered to sign the preliminaries of peace on October 23, 1762, and, at the same time, to accept Louisiana as just recompense for Spanish aid in the war.[48]

On the morning of November 3, 1762, Choiseul, Grimaldi, and Bedford signed the preliminaries of peace. All agreed that the terms were harsh but that further resistance was futile. On the same day, fulfilling his earlier promise, Louis XV signed the document ceding Louisiana, west of the new British boundary, to Spain. The cession was accepted by Grimaldi subject to the approval of his court.[49] Choiseul on the same day instructed D'Ossun anew to stress the importance of the gift and ordered the commercial *chargé*, the Abbé Beliardi, to initiate propaganda among the Spanish merchants with a view of magnifying the generosity of France.[50]

News of the gift was received by Charles III on the evening of November 10, 1762, as he came in from hunting. At first he said that he could not accept such a sacrifice. But, after some persuasion "against his own wishes and solely to defer to the desires of the King his cousin," and because of the good effect it would have on the Spanish nation, he agreed to accept. The formal acceptance by Charles III took place three days later, when he signed the act of cession in the presence of the French ambassador. The king's attitude thoroughly justified Choiseul's *beau geste*. Charles, quite moved, cried: "I say, no, no, my cousin is losing altogether too much; I do not want him to lose anything in addition for my sake, and would to heaven I could do yet more for him."[51] D'Ossun reported that both the peace and the cession pleased the Spaniards but that above all they were delighted with the ". . . unasked cession of Louisiana and New Orleans; this *démarche,* dictated by a dexterous policy, will justify to the Spanish nation the part taken by His Catholic Majesty in coming to the aid of France."[52]

Grimaldi, filled with the idea that he had signed a bad peace but had kept a good union, went to Versailles on November 21, 1762, and thanked Louis XV in the name of his king for the cession and explained that monarch's motives in accepting. On the following day Louis XV confirmed his deed of gift, and Charles, when this preliminary formality was accomplished, promptly wrote a personal letter of thanks couched in polite terms of reluctant assent to such a sacrifice. Almost immediately France laid plans for releasing Louisiana to Spain, and French officials and information were placed freely at the disposal of her ally.[53] But Spain moved slowly, and 1764 found her still preparing to occupy the colony. Governor Antonio de Ulloa finally took possession in March, 1766, but because of revolt in 1768, Spanish authority was not definitely established until Alejandro O'Reilly overawed the local elements of resistance in 1769. This was a full year after the two powers had originally planned to open their war of retaliation against England.

A study of the intricate diplomacy consummated with the success of O'Reilly's military mission leads to certain conclusions concerning this important transfer of American territory. That Louisiana had not paid dividends to France is quite clear,[54] but that it was regarded as worse than valueless by both France and Spain is not substantiated by the record. France rejected Spanish efforts to acquire the colony in 1760 and only the desperate financial and military fortunes of the war drove Choiseul to the final step of cession. To justify its loss to France he had to treat it as a burden of which it was fortunate to be rid. At the same time, to impress Spain with the sincerity of French adhesion to the Family Compact, he was forced to magnify the importance of Louisiana. A superficial view seems to justify regarding Louisiana as simply a compensation for the loss of Florida. In reality, the cession was a peace bribe proffered by France in order to win the consent of the king of Spain to an immediate signing of preliminaries of a peace that promised all that France could hope for under the circumstances. The little island of St. Lucia was the pivotal point of the peace. To secure it Choiseul was willing to give up Louisiana east of the Mississippi despite solemn promises to Spain that Canada would not be allowed to extend to the Gulf of Mexico; without it he was willing to continue the war. Louisiana was viewed as not too great a price to pay for the return of the sugar islands, St. Lucia, and the continuance of a close alliance between the two Bourbon courts. The cession was given all the appearance of an impulsive, generous, even quixotic gesture, but it was a calculated move of selfish national policy, carefully staged by a statesman intent on deriving every ounce of advantage for his own country.

Notes for "The Diplomacy of the Louisiana Cession"

[1]The manuscript materials used in the preparation of this article were secured by the writer while serving as Fellow of the Social Science Research Council, and are included in a larger group of documents which form the basis of a forthcoming volume on *The Rôle of America in French-Spanish Diplomacy, 1759-1779.*

[2]W. R. Shepherd's admirable article, "The Cession of Louisiana to Spain," *Political Science Quarterly,* 19 (1904): 439-58, has been a standard authority on the subject of the Louisiana transfer since its appearance in 1904. He is the only American writer on the subject to make extensive use of the Spanish archives, but relied entirely on French secondary accounts and ignored the British peace papers. In the interval since he wrote many new publications in the field have made contributions to the problem. Some of these works are: Louis Blart, *Les Rapports de la France et l'Espagne après le Pacte de Famille* (Paris, 1915); Alfred Bourguet, *Le Duc de Choiseul et l'Alliance Espagnole* (Paris, 1906), and *Études sur la Politique Étrangère du Duc de Choiseul* (Paris, 1907); Sir Julian S. Corbett, *England in the Seven Years' War* (London, 1907); Kate Hotblack, *The Peace of Paris, 1763,* in Royal Historical Society, *Transactions* (London, 1908), series 3, vol. 2:235-267, and *Chatham's Colonial Policy* (London, 1917); François Rousseau, *Règne de Charles III. d'Espagne,* 2 vols. (Paris, 1907); Francis P. Renaut, *Le Pacte de Famille et l'Amérique* (Paris, 1922); Roger H. Soltau, *The Duke de Choiseul* (Oxford, 1909).

[3]Archivo General de Simancas, Estado, legajo 1709, packet 4521, Duras to Wall, Oct. 26, 1754, and other letters warn Spain that if Canada falls, the *Chemin du Méxique* through Louisiana will be opened to the British. (This repository will be referred to hereafter as Simancas, with the legajo and packet numbers following.)

[4]Ibid., 1710, 4527, Masones de Lima to Wall, Mar. 12, 1756; 1713, 4535, Wall to Masones de Lima, June 9, 1758, and supporting papers in this legajo.

[5]Archives des Affaires Étrangères, Correspondance Politique, Espagne, D'Ossun to Choiseul, July 4, 1760.

[6]Ibid., Choiseul to D'Ossun, July 15; D'Ossun to Choiseul, April 21, 24; Choiseul to D'Ossun, Aug. 19.

[7]Ibid., D'Ossun to Choiseul, Sept. 15, Dec. 29; Bibliothèque Nationale, Salle des MSS., Espagne, 10,764, Beliardi to De Berryer, Oct. 13, Dec. 8; Arch. Aff. Étr., Corr. Pol., Espagne, Choiseul to D'Ossun, Oct. 13; D'Ossun to Choiseul, Oct. 17.

[8]Ibid., D'Ossun to Choiseul, Jan. 12, 1761; Choiseul to D'Ossun, Feb. 17.

[9]*Cf.* Herbert E. Bolton, *Texas in the Middle Eighteenth Century* (1915; New York, 1962); William E. Dunn, *Spanish and French Rivalry in the Gulf Region of the United States, 1678-1702* (Austin, 1917).

[10]Choiseul, early in the year, had warned of this danger. He wrote to D'Ossun: "*La Louisiane, depuis que nous avons perdu le Canada, n'est plus une barrière pour le Nouveau Méxique, et il ne faut q'un port dans le Golphe de cette dernière province pour mettre les Anglois en état d'intercepter toute communication entre les différents pays de la domination Espagnole en Amérique.*" Arch. Aff. Étr., Corr. Pol., Espagne, Choiseul to D'Ossun, Jan. 27, 1761. Choiseul's argument was to be used against him in 1762 when he endeavored to persuade Spain that eastern Louisiana in English possession would be quite harmless.

[11]The Spanish minister, Ricardo Wall, urged this course with great persistence. In reply to D'Ossun's argument that the matter had better be postponed until after the peace, he said "*. . .qu'on pourroit au moins insérer dans le traité que Sa Majesté Catholique cède à la France tous les droits qu'elle peut avoir sur la Louisiane à condition qu'il sera procédé, dans un terme indiqué et par des commissaires respectifs, au réglement des limites de cette colonie.*" Ibid., D'Ossun to Choiseul, July 16, 1761.

[12]Ibid., Choiseul to D'Ossun, Dec. 15. By this time he contemplated a transfer of the French population of Canada to Louisiana after the peace. He had already made provision for the possibility in a *mémoire* to England in September, in which he stipulated that in yielding Canada an eighteen-month period for sale and emigration should be provided. *Cf.* Simancas, 1716, 4545, Mémoire de France sur la Réponse d'Angleterre.

[13]The rôle of Louisiana in the story of the conclusion and first months of the existence of the Family Compact has been ignored by writers on the subject.

[14]In the previous year, before Charles had proposed the Louisiana exchange, the influence of Queen Amelia had frustrated two French efforts to secure a loan. Arch. Aff. Étr., Corr. Pol., Espagne, D'Ossun to Choiseul, Feb. 27, 1760. Subsequently, France had received secret aid from Spain in the form of a special privilege to

export a specified sum of Spanish specie through the banking house of M. de la Borde of Bayonne. M. de la Borde, as court banker, used this specie to bolster French paper issues. The amount of specie thus exported had been fixed at 150,000 piasters a month and the privilege had been renewable annually. Squillace, the Spanish minister of finance, had extended this favor through the *Real Giro* (Royal Exchange). When the negotiations for the Family Compact were opened, Feb. 10, 1761, he, on assurance of complete secrecy, had increased the monthly amount to 600,000 piasters. Ibid., Choiseul to D'Ossun, Feb. 10, 1761; D'Ossun to Choiseul, Feb. 27. In addition, extraordinary facilities had been accorded France in the colonies such as permission to enter the port of Havana, and, soon after the accession of Charles, New Orleans had been provisioned from Campeche with supplies purchased with Spanish money. Simancas, 1713, 4536, Memorial; Arch. Aff. Étr., Corr. Pol., Espagne, D'Ossun to Choiseul, Jan. 8, 1760.

[15]Ibid., Choiseul to D'Ossun, July 30, 31, 1761.

[16]Simancas, 1716, 4544, notes of Choiseul enclosed with (dispatch no. 3) Grimaldi to Wall, August 1, 2.

[17]Arch. Aff. Étr., Corr. Pol., Espagne, D'Ossun to Choiseul, August 17.

[18]Ibid., Choiseul to D'Ossun, August 25.

[19]Ibid., D'Ossun to Choiseul, September 7, 13, 17, 21, 28, October 3, 13, March 15, 1762.

[20]Simancas, 1715, 4543, De Bussy to Choiseul, June 11, 1761. De Bussy saw little hope of regaining Canada and thought ". . .*que les limites de la Louisiane, qui n'est pas entamée, pourront se régler par les eaux pendantes sur les côtes de chacune.*" Pitt, however, refused to consider the Ohio country as other than English.

[21]Corbett, 2:185.

[22]Simancas, 1715, 4543, Grimaldi to De Fuentes, July 1, 7, 1761. The union of the French and Spanish cases also spoiled any chance of keeping the union of the two nations a secret from Pitt.

[23]Ibid., 1716, 4544, Aug. 1. England's demands were regarded as "insolent and extraordinary" by the most timid ministers and Grimaldi informed his government, "*ya es positiva aqui la continuacion de la guerra, si no mudan las proposiciones de la Inglaterra, como ya es casi evidente que no sucedera.*"

[24]*Supra*, note 16.

[25]Simancas, 1716, 4545, Grimaldi to Wall, Sept. 13, 1761; Wall to Grimaldi, Sept. 23, Oct. 12; 1717, 4547, French "office," Dec. 25.

[26]Arch. Aff. Étr., Corr. Pol., Espagne, Choiseul to D'Ossun, Dec. 15.

[27]Corbett, 2:286.

[28]Simancas, 1717, 4549. Grimaldi to Wall, Jan 11, 1762.

[29]Ibid., Dictámen de Su Magestad; Reflexiones sobre el Dictámen de Su Magestad; Wall to Grimaldi, Apr. 23, 1762; Grimaldi to Wall, April 18.

[30]Id., Feb. 1, 18, Mar. 1; Arch. Aff. Étr., Corr, Pol., Espagne, Choiseul to D'Ossun, May 17, 29; D'Ossun to Choiseul, May 31.

[31]Professor Shepherd's discussion introduces Louisiana for the first time at this point.

[32]*Infra*, note 36; *cf.* Corbett, 2:339-43, for a statement of the value of St. Lucia. *Cf.* also George Louis Beer, *British Colonial Policy, 1754-1765* (New York, 1907), ch. 8, and F. W. Pitman, *The Development of the British West Indies, 1700-1763* (1917; reprint ed., Hamden, CN, 1967), ch. 14, for the story of the influence of the West Indies sugar interest on the return of Martinique and Guadaloupe.

[33]Shelburne, MSS., Vol. 4, W. L. Clements Library, Choiseul to Solar, May 28, 1762.

[34]Bute proposed that instead of restoring Martinique in return for the cession of Guadaloupe or Louisiana ". . . the restoring [to the French] both Martinique and Guadaloupe, with Marygalante, we retaining the neutral

islands and the Grenada, and that to prevent all further disputes, the Mississippi should be the boundary between the two nations. . . " Bute to Bedford, May 1, 1762, *Correspondence of John, Fourth Duke of Bedford,* Lord John Russell, ed. 3:76.

[35]"*Il ne nous est possible de céder Ste. Lucie . . . je crois que sans Ste. Lucie, la France n'aura pas de possessions de première nécessité qui lui sont indispensable en Amérique.*" Shelburne MSS., vol 9, Choiseul to Solar, May 27, 1762. So important was the point that Solar wrote, "*Si les réponses que nous attendons sont favorables surtout à l'égard de l'isle de Ste. Lucie, je regarde la paix comme faite.*" Ibid., vol. 10, Solar to Viri, June 14. England's awareness of the importance attached to this island is indicated when Egremont wrote, "*Ste. Lucie, est, on dit, si necessaire à la France que le vaste pais de St. Dominque et la Martinique, et la Guadaloupe ne suffisent pas sans elle.*" Ibid., Mémoire with letter of Viri, June 26.

[36]"*Jamais nous n'aurions consenti l'année Passée à la cession de la Mobille et à l'arrêté des limites de la Louisianne tel que nous l'offrons; c'est presque céder la Louisianne entière qui d'après ces limites n' a plus de communication avec la Floride; nous sentons le prix de cette cession, qui entraine la perte de notre colonie, mais nous sentons en même tems qu'il faut que nous la perdions; l'Espagne fera peutêtre des difficultés sur cet article à cause de sa colonie de la Floride; mais nous lui ferons entendre raison; et si elle manque de l'humeur; nous lui proposerons d'échanger la Floride, dont j'ignore ce que nous pourrons faire, avec ce qui nous restera de la Louisianne.*" Ibid., vol. 9, Choiseul to Solar, May 28.

[37]This extraordinary bit of *chicane* is often overlooked. Choiseul had the effrontery, after granting the Mississippi as a boundary, to declare that he meant the easternmost mouth, or the above unnavigable waterway. Egremont, while accepting it as a boundary, insisted on free navigation by the main channel to the sea. Ibid., Mémoire, with Viri to Solar, June 26; Egremont to Bedford, Sept. 7.

[38]Ibid., Bedford to Egremont, Sept. 12.

[39]Simancas, 1718, 4551, Grimaldi to Wall, June 28; Arch. Aff. Étr., Corr. Pol., Espagne, Choiseul to D'Ossun, June 29.

[40]"*Que esta cession la querian absolutamente los Ingleses segun lo havian explicado tambien de palabra al conde de Viry; que les valia à ellos Sta. Lucia que les era muy importante, que de no concederla les faltaria la paz. . . .* " Simancas, 1718, 4551, Grimaldi to Wall, July 13. This boundary was not approved by Wall until Sept. 5. Ibid., Wall to Grimaldi, Sept. 5.

[41]Ibid., Minuta; Louis XV to Charles III, Aug. 9; Arch. Aff. Étr., Corr. Pol., Espagne, D'Ossun to Choiseul, Aug. 2.

[42]Arch. Aff. Étr., Corr. Pol., Espagne, Choiseul to D'Ossun, Sept. 20.

[43]Ibid.

[44]Rumors of the capitulation of Havana arrived in Paris on August 27, but were not believed. Throughout September the accuracy of the report was questioned in Paris. In Spain the fatal news was not confirmed until Grimaldi forwarded a report sent to him from London, on October 3. Simancas, 1718, 4551, Grimaldi to Wall, Oct.3

[45]Arch. Aff. Étr., Corr. Pol., Espagne, Louis XV to Charles III, Oct. 9. This letter constitutes the "diplomatic overture" that Shepherd found to be lacking ("Cession of Louisiana to Spain," 449). Bedford explained to his court that the delay in signing the preliminaries was due to the fact that Grimaldi's plenary powers of August 25 and September 29 did not permit him to sign away territory without special orders from his government. Shelburne MSS., vol. 12, Bedford to Egremont, Oct. 11.

[46]Arch. Aff. Étr., Corr. Pol., Espagne, Choiseul to D'Ossun, Oct. 14.

[47]Simancas, 1718, 4551, Minuta of Wall.

[48]Grimaldi's powers of August 25 conferred the right to sign a treaty that excluded the English from the Gulf of Mexico. Grimaldi in the first meetings with Bedford refused to sign preliminaries which included the

presence of the English on the gulf as "an innovation." The home government approved his stand but, pressed hard by France, extended his powers on September 29, and authorized him to sign after holding off as long as possible. The additional cession required by England for the return of Havana necessitated a new reference to the home government. Wall's letter of October 23, ordered Grimaldi to sign and to accept Louisiana as Spain's just due. Simancas, 1719, 4552, Wall to Grimaldi, Oct. 23.

[49]Ibid., Louis XV to Charles III, Nov. 3 Grimaldi wrote to his home government that he had kept France in suspense up to the last minute with the fear that Spain would prefer to go on with the war. Ibid., Grimaldi to Wall, Nov. 3.

[50]Arch. Aff. Étr., Corr. Pol., Espagne, Choiseul to D'Ossun, Nov. 3.

[51]Simancas, 1719, 4552, Wall to Grimaldi, Nov. 13, quoted in Shepherd, "Cession of Louisiana to Spain," 451.

[52]Arch. Aff. Étr., Corr. Pol., Espagne, D'Ossun to Choiseul, Nov. 15.

[53]Simancas, 1719, 4552, Girmaldi to Wall, Nov. 24; Charles III to Louis XV, Dec. 2. M. de Vilement entered Spanish service, and numerous Frenchmen, including former Governor Kerlérec drew up memorials for Spanish use.

[54]Cf. Shephard, "Cession of Louisiana to Spain," 439, 452.

PINCKNEY'S TREATY: AMERICA'S ADVANTAGE FROM EUROPE'S DISTRESS, 1783-1800*

Samuel Flagg Bemis

It is unlikely that any treaty ever agreed to by the United States, aside from that of peace and independence, has been accepted with more general satisfaction and approval by the country than that of San Lorenzo. Since we have spent so much time and space in explaining the history of the negotiations which led to this treaty, we are justified in a somewhat detailed analysis of its articles,[1] and comment thereon.

After the declaration of amity in Article I, it is stipulated in Article II that the southern boundary of the United States "shall be designated by a line beginning on the River Mississippi at the Northernmost part of the thirty first degree of latitude North of the Equator, which from thence shall be drawn due East to the middle of the River Apalachicola or Catahouche, thence along the middle thereof to the Atlantic Occean." All garrisons and troops of either party within the territory of the other should be evacuated within six months or sooner after the ratification of the treaty, they being permitted to take with them all their "goods and effects." This stipulation coincided exactly with the connection of the United States for the boundary line of the Anglo-American treaty of 1783. It must be regarded as a great Spanish concession, for the claim of Spain to territory south of the line of the Yazoo was stronger than that of the United States. It was a complete recognition of one of the principal American issues.

The joint survey of this line, to be undertaken within six months of the ratification by surveyors to meet at Natchez, and to be escorted if desired by joint military detachments of equal strength, was provided for by Article III.

The Mississippi navigation article (Article IV), which was phrased only after much study and labor, must be quoted entire:

*First published as the "Conclusion" in Samuel Flagg Bemis, *Pinckney's Treaty: America's Advantage from Europe's Distress, 1783-1800* (New Haven, CT: © Yale University Press, 1960), 294-314.

> It is likewise agreed that the Western boundary of the United States which separates them from the Spanish Colony of Louissiana, is in the middle of the channel or bed of the River Mississippi from the Northern boundary of the said States to the completion of the thirty first degree of latitude North of the Equator; and his Catholic Majesty has likewise agreed that the navigation of the said River in its whole breadth from its source to the Occean shall be free only to his Subjects, and the Citizens of the United States, unless he should extend this privilege to the Subjects of other Powers by special convention.

Was this a recognition of right or a grant by the king of Spain to the United States? The language in itself is fairly clear as stipulating a restricted grant. We have observed how Charles Pinckney strove in vain to insert another formula devised to reserve the contention of the United States to a right to navigation of the river. He was not able to insist upon the sentence which he had proposed: "It is nevertheless agreed, that nothing contained in this article shall be construed or interpreted, to communicate the right of navigating this river to other nations or persons, than to the subjects of His Catholic Majesty, and to the citizens of the United States." This would not have denied the claim by other nations or persons to the navigation of the river by virtue of other treaties or circumstances, merely denying such right to flow from the Treaty of San Lorenzo. That Pinckney tried to get such a qualification and failed, that he subsequently accepted the article above quoted, is sufficient evidence to the impartial investigator that he gave up a claim to a right and accepted a grant. Timothy Pickering, secretary of state, made a weak argument in 1797, that the use of the words "His Catholic Majesty has likewise agreed," without repetition of the words, "The United States *and* His Catholic Majesty," as agreeing together, made Spain the *sole party* to the *excluding clause*;[2] but though Pinckney may possibly have comforted himself with mental reservations when accepting this phraseology, it is not impressive. The article as accepted was a direct stultification, as Godoy later correctly argued, of the American argument on which the claim to the navigation of the Mississippi was originally founded, and a contravention of Article VIII of the Treaty of Peace, which had stipulated that the "navigation of the River Mississippi, from its source to the ocean, shall *forever*[3] remain free and open to the subjects of Great Britain and the citizens of the United States"; and of Article III in Jay's Treaty, which repeated the stipulation with the additional provision that all ports and places on the eastern side of the river, to whichsoever party belonging, could be freely resorted to by both parties. To enforce the provision of Pinckney's Treaty, the last signed, and presumably therefore the governing one, would have placed an estoppel on the Mississippi article of Jay's Treaty. Pinckney knew that well enough. He had been privy to all the details of Jay's Treaty. He even showed Godoy the sentence of Jay's Treaty saying that nothing in it should be construed or operate contrary to any former or existing treaty. It was not open dealing. But then Godoy himself was not noted for open dealing.

John Jay when in London had not succeeded in putting into his treaty an article which he had drafted obligating each party not to make political connections with the Indians dwelling within the territories of the other; and to restrain its Indians from hostilities against the other, and to make common cause, in case of the other party's being engaged in hostilities with its own Indians, to the extent of prohibiting and preventing any supplies of ammunition or arms from being given or sold even by Indian traders to such belligerent tribe or tribes or to any individuals therein.[4] Pinckney succeeded in putting a somewhat similar article (V) into his treaty, with even stronger provisions: both Spain and the United States agreed "to restrain by force all hostilities on the part of the Indian Nations living within their boundaries: so that Spain will not suffer her Indians to attack Citizens of the United States, nor the Indians inhabiting their territory; nor will the United States permit these last mentioned Indians to commence hostilities against the Subjects of His Catholic Majesty, or his Indians, in any manner whatever." This later provision assumed great significance in subsequent Florida history.

Articles VI, VII, VIII, IX, X, and XI contained the conventional provisions for protection of vessels of the one party in the territorial waters of the other; protection against embargo or detention for public or private purposes of ships of one party within the jurisdiction of the other; against seizure for debts or crimes without due process of law (an article which assumed importance a century later in the Cuban insurrection); protection of vessels of the one party forced to take refuge in the ports of the other; restoration of property of citizens or subjects of the one party taken by the other party from pirates; mutual assistance to shipwrecked vessels and mariners; disposition of estates of citizens or subjects of one party in the domains of the other. Article XII provided for official descriptive sea-letters and certificates establishing identity of ship and cargo in case of war in which one party should be neutral, the other belligerent. Article XIII, taken from the treaty of 1785 between the United States and Prussia, stipulated that in case of war between the two parties, merchants of one residing within the jurisdiction of the other should be allowed one year in which to collect and transport, inviolate, their merchandise. Article XIV, modeled on all the earlier American treaties, forbade subjects or citizens of the one party to take out privateering commissions from any prince or state with which the other party should be at war.

One of the most interesting portions of the treaty was that containing the articles on neutral rights—Articles XV, XVI, XVII, XVIII. They adopted the principles of the Armed Neutrality, which were mainly also those of the previous treaties of the United States, excepting that just signed with Great Britain which while not relinquishing the principles in theory nevertheless acquiesced for the duration of the war in the British contrary practice. Pinckney, fully cognizant of the articles of Jay's Treaty and their heavy concessions on these points, now put into the Spanish treaty articles conformable to the old creed: free ships make free goods; neutral ships may trade freely from port to port of the enemy, except in contraband of war or to a really blockaded or besieged enemy port—a repudiation of the British Rule of 1756; and a carefully stipulated list of contraband strictly limited to enumerated warlike implements. The contraband article studiously and elaborately listed non-contraband, including as such especially naval stores and provisions, and all else not mentioned in the enumerated list of contraband. Article XVIII restricted the right of search of neutral ships by belligerent cruisers to small boarding parties and provided that the neutral ship should be equipped with sea letters and certificates, a form for which was declared to be annexed to the treaty.[5]

These were traditionally American articles going back to the model treaty plan of the Continental Congress, the "plan of 1776" and the elaborations on it in the treaties with France (1778), the Netherlands (1782), Sweden (1783), and Prussia (1785), and so inconsistently and purposely omitted from Jay's Treaty of 1794 with Great Britain.

"Consuls shall be reciprocally established with the privileges and powers which those of the most favored Nations enjoy in the Ports where their consuls reside, or are permitted to be." So said Article XIX in toto. This shut out American consuls from Spain's colonial dominions. As to commerce, it was left out except for the provision in the first paragraph of Article XXII which provided that the two parties "will in future give to their mutual commerce all the extension and favor which the advantage of both Countries may require." This not only excluded citizens of the United States along with the subjects of all other countries from Spain's American colonies, but did not even provide for the most-favored-nation commercial privileges which were a feature of all other American treaties. American commerce thus remained at the mercy of any sudden change in Spanish municipal law; so, reciprocally, did Spanish commerce with the United States. Because of the one-sidedness of the trade this article was of greater advantage to Spain than to the United States. This was one of the reasons why William Short did not approve of the treaty. Another was because no entrance for American trade into any of the Spanish colonies was granted—which Short believed could have been secured; and still another objection which he had was that no specific rules for adjudication were laid down to govern the mixed commission for judgment on spoliations by Spanish ships of war on American neutral shipping. By Article XXI this mixed commission, set up according to the machinery for such established by Jay's Treaty, was to decide "according to the merits of the several cases, and to justice, equity, and the laws of Nations."[6] Unlike the rule of the British-American treaty spoliation mixed commission, cases brought before this tribunal did not require to have exhausted the ordinary course of judicial proceedings. This was a distinct advantage for the United States. If Godoy was negligent in overlooking this point, he was even more careless in not detecting a perfectly good opportunity to place before the same mixed commission the spoliations on Spanish vessels in 1793 by French privateers illegally fitted out in American harbors. Pinckney could hardly have refused to make such an article reciprocal.[7]

The second sentence of Article XXII covered the entrepôt provision. When the compromise concerning this was reached at the eleventh hour of the final negotiation Pinckney wrote Short that "we have agreed upon N. Orleans for 3 years paying only storage, but this permission to be continued unless an equal establishment is assigned elsewhere on the Mississippi." As actually worded this part of the article read:

> His Catholic Majesty will permit the Citizens of the United States for the space of three years from this time to deposit their merchandize and effects in the Port of New Orleans and to export them from thence without paying any other duty than a fair price for the hire of the stores, and his Majesty promises either to continue this permission if he finds during that time that it is not prejudicial to the interests of Spain, or if he should not agree to continue it there, he will assign to them on another part of the banks of the Mississippi an equivalent establishment.

Did the terms of this sentence reserve the right to the king of Spain to revoke the entrepôt *altogether* at the expiration of three years, if he found during those three years it had been prejudicial to the interest of Spain? The reader may see for himself, by consulting the original English and Spanish texts of the treaty that it was somewhat ambiguous on this point.

Finally, the last article (XXIII), concerning ratification, should be noticed. Pinckney's powers authorized him to sign and to send the treaty to the United States for ratification by the president by and with the advice and consent of the Senate. This article textually ignored the Senate: "The present treaty shall not be in force untill ratified by the contracting Parties, and the ratifications shall be exchanged in six months, or sooner if possible."

A treaty such as this encountered no opposition in the Senate! It was immediately and unanimously ratified, as soon as submitted, and returned forthwith to Spain, where ratifications were exchanged, April 25, 1796, barely within the allowed six months.

The treaty was not so promptly executed. The history of the long, unpleasant, and highly involved chapter of bickerings over its execution must be told very briefly. The delay was due principally to two things: Governor Carondelet's pursuit of the Wilkinson intrigue; and the incompatibility of the terms of Jay's British treaty with those of Pinckney's Spanish one, together with the realization in Spain that after all the terms of Jay's Treaty were on the whole comparatively innocuous, so far as that monarchy was concerned.

When it became known in Louisiana that direct negotiations on the Mississippi and boundary questions had been resumed at Madrid, Carondelet was influenced, largely by Gayoso de Lemos, to take up again Wilkinson's project. That Spanish vassal and American officer had accepted from President Washington a commission as lieutenant colonel, from which he soon advanced to brigadier general and second in command of the army of the United States, then operating against the western Indians. He was, early in 1792, apprised that the king of Spain at length had formally decided in favor of his pension of $2,000 a year, long since solicited, considerable arrears of which already had accumulated.[8] After the French war and American popular sympathy for it became evident, Carondelet realizing the fluctuating allegiance of the Indians and the precarious military defenses of the frontier—at the most he could muster no more than 2,800 men for the defense of Louisiana and the Floridas, half of these raw militia and half-breed hunters[9]—turned with increasing eagerness to Wilkinson and his fellow plotters. The latter had proved his usefulness to his paymasters by sending information of George Rogers Clark's project for an attack in 1793-1794, with French backing, of Kentucky riflemen on New Orleans.[10] Incidentally he sent in a bill for $8,640, in addition to his pension arrears, for expenses incurred in frustrating Clark's project. A copious secret ciphered correspondence quickly developed with Wilkinson, at United States army headquarters, and with his coterie in Kentucky.[11]

In the transmission of this note the Spanish fort at Nogales where Gayoso de Lemos commanded proved a valuable listening-post for Kentucky, as well as an advanced defense for Louisiana. Wilkinson now advised the cultivation of Kentucky "notables," through heavy subventions to be distributed through his own fingers, and the promise of Spanish gunboats, arms, and ammunition to assist the independence of that state. Carondelet approved the huge estimates. They included $200,000 for bribes, 20 field pieces, 10,000 stand of arms, and two Spanish regiments to garrison the upper river forts of Spain. The governor requested his court forthwith to sanction this expenditure.[12] To his disappointment the grants were not made. They must have caused amazement at Madrid. The annual expenses of the government of Louisiana were already ten times the annual revenue,[13] and Carondelet was asking for other big sums for necessary fortifications and for annuities for the Indians. Godoy and his associates did not for a moment think of diverting such masses of money to a profitless province, any more than they approved the repeated recommendations of Louisiana governors for resurrecting the prosperity of the colony through the opening of unrestricted trade with Europe and America.

Carondelet's new projects for Kentucky were carefully considered by the Council of State on July 25, 1794. At this meeting extracts from Wilkinson's letters were read. They did not alter the decision to propose alliance to the United States. Godoy allowed the governor of Louisiana to continue to cultivate Wilkinson and his friends while the president's answer to the new proposals (of July 26, 1794) was pending. As we have seen, this remained pending much longer than expected. During that time, 1794-1795, Carondelet zealously pursued his intrigues. Upon Wilkinson's advice, he occupied Chickasaw Bluffs,[14] the next high spot of ground above Nogales, 255 miles up the river, as the crow flies from Natchez, and 355 miles north of 31°. Here as an outpost for Nogales, the new fort was erected from which a helping hand might be reached out to Kentucky insurrectionists. In the winter of 1795-1796, Benjamin Sebastian was attracted by way of Nogales and Natchez down the river to New Orleans,[15] bringing with him a paper purporting to give full powers from leading notables of Kentucky who had in secret convention at the house of George Nicholas resolved on a treaty with Spain. The credential was signed by George Nicholas, Harry Innes, William Murray, and by Sebastian himself.

These too are the signatories of the unsigned letter of the "secret committee of correspondence of the west," who had also been in contact with Jaudenes during the Whiskey Rebellion. Sebastian was actually at New Orleans with his "full power" in January, 1796. Carondelet was then anxiously waiting for instruction to permit him to sign a treaty with them.[16] Before his requests could be answered he received, in February, 1796, a copy of the treaty signed with Pinckney. With it were orders to suspend all activities at the new post. Even this treaty did not completely destroy his hope of seducing Kentucky. Sebastian thought that if it could be shown in Kentucky that the Atlantic states had any undue advantage in the treaty, his friends would still go ahead with their movement for independence. Carondelet persuaded him to wait at New Orleans until news should arrive as to the attitude of Kentucky toward the treaty, meanwhile "to agree between us on the means of achieving the desired end while circumstances are preparing for it."[17]

Sebastian lingered a while at New Orleans, but in the spring departed for Kentucky via Philadelphia. With him went a special agent of Carondelet. This was one Thomas Power, whose business it was to proceed to the Ohio country to deliver ten thousand dollars to Wilkinson and to stir up any discoverable sentiment for revolt. He appealed to that treacherous personality now to step forward and become the "Washington of the West." Power had authority from Carondelet to state that Spain did not intend to carry out the terms of the treaty. The mission proved unprofitable, except to Wilkinson.[18]

Godoy allowed Carondelet to continue this intrigue.[19] It was unsuccessful: first, because Wilkinson and his followers never represented the overwhelming sentiment of Kentucky loyalty to the Union; and secondly, because the text of the treaty of 1795 secured for the men of the western waters everything they could desire.

We have noted that Pinckney's Treaty and Jay's Treaty conflicted in regard to maritime principles. In 1796 Spain resumed her traditional diplomacy and became, fatally, the ally of France—now under the less delirious rule of the Directory—and the enemy of Great Britain. Though the published text of Jay's Treaty did not reveal the dreaded Anglo-American understanding or alliance which Godoy had feared, it was highly repugnant to the liberal maritime principles which the United States had pledged itself, both before and after signing that instrument, to observe in its dealing with France and Spain respectively.[20] Spain also felt rightfully concerned at the third (Mississippi) article of Jay's Treaty. That had stated that the river should "according to the treaty of peace be entirely open to both parties." Pinckney's Treaty contained an agreement by the king of Spain to open the river only to citizens of the United States and subjects of the king of Spain. Which treaty should be supreme on this subject? Spanish diplomatists might flatter themselves that the later treaty had undone the earlier, just as Jay's Treaty in some respects was alleged to have undone the earlier Franco-American treaty of 1778. Subsequent to the Spanish treaty, however, the United States ratified, in 1796, an additional article to Jay's Treaty. This contained the provision "that no stipulations in any treaty subsequently [to Jay's Treaty] concluded by either of the contracting parties, with any other state or nation, or with any Indian tribe, can be understood to derogate in any manner, from the rights of free intercourse and commerce, secured by the aforesaid third article." The purpose of this explanatory article had been to remove an inconsistency between Jay's Treaty and the Treaty of Greenville of August 3, 1795, with the northwestern Indians. This purpose could have been achieved perfectly without the inclusive phrase "any other state or nation." Spain had quite proper reason for protesting, as she did, this additional article. She had equally good reason, and her ally France even more,[21] to object to the maritime provision of Jay's Treaty.[22]

A period of several years' disagreeable dispute over the execution of the treaty was the result of these conflicts of obligations on the part of the United States. American officers appeared promptly at Natchez to arrange for the details of evacuation and joint survey of the boundary. In the spring of 1797 strategic reasons impelled the Spanish officials to evacuate their garrison at Chickasaw Bluffs, after razing the works which had been erected there. The guns, munitions, and most of the troops were taken up the river to St. Louis, on the western side. Fort Confederación on the Tombigbee was also relinquished at the same time, its garrison being moved down the river to Fort St. Stephens, at tidewater about ninety miles above Mobile, and still north of the recently agreed boundary line of the United States.[23] Numerous good excuses were found to delay further the evacuation of the remaining posts on the east side of the Mississippi, Nogales and Natchez, while the protests against alleged American violation of the treaty were being presented at Philadelphia by the new minister, Yrujo. The Blount intrigue in Tennessee in 1797, by which British agents conceived the possibility of duplicating, with more success, Genêt's old project of recruiting western frontiersmen to attack Spanish provinces—for Great Britain was now the enemy of Spain and France—presented a valid reason for holding the river posts as necessary defenses against a British invasion from Canada across American soil by *force majeure*, with or without the assistance of lawless American western citizens.[24]

Despite dissatisfaction with the hastily concluded treaty of 1795 and good excuses for refusing to execute it, Spain was induced to do so by circumstances of a European nature. In 1797 relations between the United States and France as a consequence of Jay's Treaty became so strained as to make war likely. France now proposed to Spain joint diplomatic protests to the United States against Jay's Treaty.[25] Before this could be done, diplomatic relations between the two republics had been ruptured. The Prince of the Peace feared that Spain might become involved, as France's new ally, in a war with the United States. In such a conflict Spain had Louisiana and perhaps more to lose, France nothing in America.[26] This was the reason for Spain's ultimate, full execution of the treaty of 1795.

Again the wars of Europe had come to the aid of the United States. A royal order for the evacuation of the forts north of the new American boundary was issued September 22, 1797. Nogales, Natchez, and St. Stephens were given up in 1798.[27] A fine irony of fate caused them to be delivered to subalterns of Brigadier General James Wilkinson, at the time commander of the army of the United States! The joint survey of the boundary was commenced. Scarcely had it been completed, in 1800, before Louisiana was secretly ceded by Spain to France, and that chapter of American expansion which led to the Louisiana Purchase, a chapter made so familiar and so vivid to readers of American history by the genius and the pen of the late Henry Adams, had already begun. It was to end with the Florida purchase, the carrying of the boundary between the United States and Spain to the Pacific Ocean, and presently thereafter by the disappearance forever, in the contemporaneous revolutions of the South American colonies, of the sovereignty of Spain from the American continents. Those revolutions, let it be noted, were themselves the result of the Napoleonic wars which followed the French Revolution, and which were so profoundly consequential in American diplomatic history. The procession of events which resulted in all this history is bound up inseparably with the European balance of power and the wars of the French Revolution.

Thomas Jefferson's reliance on the quarrels of Europe to solve the predicaments of American diplomacy had justified itself after all. The treaty to which Thomas Pinckney succeeded in affixing Godoy's signature at a psychological moment was one of the greatest successes in American diplomacy. From it flowed almost immeasurable consequences for the future territorial expansion of the United States. Issues arising over this document led to the negotiation which brought, at the profit of European imbroglios imperfectly understood across the Atlantic, the extension of American territory to the Gulf of Mexico and to the Pacific Ocean. If it had not been for the right of deposit and the necessity of protecting it, it is extremely unlikely that President Jefferson's diplomatists in 1803 would have been suing at the Court of Napoleon for the purchase of the island of New Orleans at the very time when larger issues unbeknownst to Jefferson, constrained that despot to sell all of Louisiana. What then would have been the destiny of that great region? A second Canada?[28]

Spanish historians condemn Godoy and the treaty as the beginning of the end of Spain's vast colonial empire in America. So it was. It was due to no particular merit or deserved victory of American diplomacy. Godoy capitulated, perhaps unnecessarily, to circumstances in Europe which argued to him the necessity above all of protecting Spain at home, of sacrificing a small portion of expansive overseas dominions and rights for the better security of the remainder. That it would have been wiser for Spain under Godoy's guidance to have maintained after 1795 her neutrality in the great European cataclysm which ended by destroying her empire, does not concern us here. The French Revolution had engulfed Europe in a series of mighty conflicts which already had impelled Great Britain, in order to keep her much needed navy nearer home and to preserve her best customer at a time when money was needed to finance a great war, to sign Jay's Treaty with the United States. Godoy, fearful of the dominance of England after the destruction of French seapower, possibly of Anglo-American cooperation, and threatened by the invasion of French armies, signed a separate peace with France. The youthful Prince of the Peace allowed himself to be overawed by the anticipated wrath of a disappointed ally. Here his nervous imagination ran away with him. When Spain deserted the alliance

England did not declare war. At a time when his other allies were dropping away from him Pitt had enough to confront the French problem without adding to his difficulties. But Godoy feared England. Jay's Treaty, with the subsequent failure at the Basle negotiations to secure a French alliance and even the hoped-for triple alliance with the United States, convinced Godoy that it was indispensably necessary to sign with Pinckney in order that Britain's wrath should not be strengthened by an American alliance which would snatch away from Spain her American colonies then and there. This was Godoy's first mistake. The next, and the greatest, the colossal mistake of all Spanish diplomacy, was his renewal of the French alliance in the secret treaty of San Ildefonso of the following year. Without that Spain might still have had peace with Great Britain and stood aside, at least for several years, perhaps altogether, from the raging whirlpool of Europe soon to be stirred to its depths by the sword of the conquering Corsican.

Notes for "Pinckney's Treaty: America's Advantage from Europe's Distress, 1783-1800"

[1]For the official English and Spanish text of the treaty, see Appendix V to Samuel Flagg Bemis, *Pinckney's Treaty: America's Advantage from Europe's Distress, 1783-1800* (rev. ed., New Haven, 1960).

[2]American State Papers, Foreign Relations (hereafter cited as ASP,FR), 2:16.

[3]Italics inserted.

[4]Samuel Flagg Bemis, *Jay's Treaty: A Study in Commerce and Diplomacy* (New York, 1923), 288.

[5]The forms of ships' passports were conspicuously omitted from both the signed and ratified texts of the treaty. Each government then issued a form of its own; but in 1797 Secretary Pickering and the Marqués de Casa Yrujo agreed on forms for the ships of each nation, respectively. A copy of the American form exists in the archives of the Department of State; and one of the Spanish forms is printed in *Colección de los tratados de paz, alianza, comercio, etc.* (Madrid, 1801), 3:429-31. I am indebted to Mr. Hunter Miller, former Treaty Editor of the Department of State, for this information.

[6]See Appendix IV to Bemis, *Pinckney's Treaty.*

[7]That Godoy permitted these points to escape him is another very strong argument to show that he could not have known the text of Jay's Treaty.

[8]Gayoso de Lemos to Floridablanca, January 7, 1792, Serrano y Sanz, *El Brigadier Jaime Wilkinson and sus tratos con España para la independencia del Kentucky* (Madrid, 1915), 37. See ibid., 42, for Gayoso's memorandum on "The Political Status of Louisiana," July 5, 1792, printed in English in J. A. Robertson's *Louisiana under Spain, France, and the United States,* 2 vols. (Cleveland, OH, 1911), 1:269. See account rendered by Brigadier General James Wilkinson, U.S.A. to Spain, entitled "Quenta de W," in requesting payment for his services as a Spanish vassal and pensioner in stirring up sedition in the American West. Archivo Histórico Nacional, Madrid., Sección de Estado, Legajo (hereinafter cited as AHN, est. leg.), 3886. A photograph of this document is opposite page 348 of the first edition of Bemis, *Pinckney's Treaty* (1926).

[9]Carondelet and Gayoso de Lemos to Las Casas, New Orleans, October 20, 1793, in Las Casas's compendious report of November 21, 1793, Archivo General Central, Simancas, Spain, Sección de Estado, Legajo, (hereafter cited as AGC, est. leg.), 7235. These documents are to the transcripts in the Library of Congress (hereafter cited as L.C. trans.).

[10]Serrano y Sanz, *El Brigadier Jaime Wilkinson*, 117.

[11]Las Casas (Governor-General of Cuba and Louisiana) to Del Campo de Alange (Minister for War), Nos. 398, 415, 444, 452, 453, 454, 1793-1794. These voluminous documents contain copious enclosures relating to the Kentucky intrigue in 1793-1794 and to Spanish efforts to counteract Genêt's projects. AGC, est. leg., 7235. (L.C. trans.)

[12]See AHN, est. leg., 3886, and Actas de la Suprema Junta de Estado, May 2, July 25, August 1, 1794, AHN., est.

[13]Charles Gayarré, *History of Louisiana,* 4 vols. (New York, 1867), 371; According to Gayarré, the expenses in 1795 were $864,126, and customs income $57,506. In 1790 the revenue from all sources was $66,163. Miró, Carondelet, and Gayoso in vain requested free trade with European countries and American ports as a means of reviving the drooping prosperity of the province. All that they could secure was the ordinance of June 9, 1793, allowing Spanish subjects of Louisiana to trade freely with all friendly nations who had treaties of commerce with Spain, through the ports of New Orleans, Pensacola, and St. Augustine, and providing they first stopped at a designated port in Spain to secure license. The commerce of Louisiana did not revive until after the discovery of profitable sugar-making in 1795. How much the removal of restriction on trade to Europe contributed to this is still to be determined.

[14]Chickasaw Bluffs had been variously denominated Écores à Margot, and Barrancas de Margot. The fort was called San Fernando de las Barrancas. It was located near the present site of Memphis. See Carondelet to Alcudia, July 1, 1795, Serrano y Sanz, op. cit., 95.

[15]For secret ciphered correspondence between Carondelet and Wilkinson, in July, 1795, arranging for this negotiation, and promises by Carondelet to negotiate a satisfactory treaty in "less than a month," see Papeles de Cuba, Leg., 2374. See Luis Marino Perez's *Guide to the Materials for American History in Cuban Archives* (Washington, DC, 1907). At my request Dr. A. P. Whitaker kindly had this correspondence photographed for me.

[16]Carondelet to Alcudia, Nos. 67 and 69, January 9 and 30, 1796, ibid., 74. The enclosures referred to but not included in No. 67, may be found in AHN, est. leg., 3886, including Wilkinson's financial account rendered by himself, January 1, 1796.

[17]Carondelet's No. 73 to the Prince of the Peace, February 10, 1796, AHN, est. leg., 3886.

[18]Gayarré, *History of Louisiana,* 3:355-66.

[19]Godoy's instruction of (precise date unknown), 1796, in answer to Carondelet's despatches of January 9 and 30, and February 10, 1796. AHN, est. leg., 3886.

[20]With France by the treaty of 1778, with Spain by the treaty of 1795.

[21]The principles of Jay's Treaty repudiating free ships free goods and the old definition of contraband, etc., applied only to the duration of the war in which Great Britain was *then* engaged, namely the war with France which did not end until 1801. Spain had since made peace with her former enemy France, and thus temporarily withdrawn from that war. Therefore while Spain remained in a brief interim of neutrality, in which Pinckney's Treaty was signed, it did not technically conflict with Jay's Treaty, the maritime provisions of which did not govern relations between the United States and Spain. But Spain soon became engaged in the same old war in which England was a belligerent against France, though now as an ally of France. In this war the English prize courts governed themselves by the provisions of Jay's Treaty. By Jay's Treaty British cruisers could take Spanish property from neutral American decks, while Pinckney's Treaty denied analogous rights to a belligerent Spain.

[22]For notes passed between Secretary Pickering and Yrujo on this, see State Dept., Notes, Spain, Vol. 1A. See also ASP,FR, 2:68, 69, 98, where a few of the most essential notes are printed. Yrujo's energetic notes were so distasteful to Pickering that President Adams requested his recall by Spain. But Yrujo cultivated the good graces of the Jeffersonians and the Spanish Government managed to delay his recall until after the election of 1800, when it became unnecessary. For Yrujo's despatches, 1796-1800, see AHN, est. leg, 3896 *bis*, 3897.

[23]For Spanish correspondence relating to this, see confidential despatches of Morales, Intendant at New Orleans, to Department of Finance, December 31, 1796-May 4, 1797, containing despatches and enclosures explaining evacuation of the upper points and cessation of the movement at Nogales and Natchez, because of

the Blount affair and fear of a British attack from Canada. This is in the *expediente* entitled "Correspondence of Spanish Governors and Officials in Louisiana relating to the Disputed Boundary 1789-1799," AHN, est. leg., 3902. See also, for American correspondence, *Seventh Annual Report* of the Director of the Department of Archives of the State of Mississippi, and *Journal* of Andrew Ellicott, the United States official surveyor. For account of Sir William Dunbar, official Spanish surveyor, see *Publications of Miss. Hist. Soc.* (1901), 3:185-207.

[24]We recall that at the time of the Nootka Crisis of 1790, the deliberations of Washington's Cabinet show that the United States would not have attempted by force to prevent a passage of British troops from Canada across American soil against Louisiana in case of war between Great Britain and Spain. For documents relating to the Blount affair, published by Prof. F. J. Turner, see *American Historical Review*, 10 (1904-05), 574.

[25]See endorsements on Yrujo's despatch No. 4, of September 8, 1796, and documents associated with No. 4, relating to French proposals for joint diplomatic action, AHN, est. leg., 3896.

[26]Prince of the Peace to Yrujo, January 27, August 14, December 31, 1796, Spanish Legation, Vol. 205.

[27]For details of the final evacuation, see Serrano y Sanz, op. cit., 76-77; *Seventh Annual Report* of Director of Archives of Mississippi, and *Journal* of Andrew Ellicott. A great deal of attention has been devoted to the history of these years of border bickering and delay in the execution of the treaty. See B. A. Hinsdale, "Establishment of the First Southern Boundary of the United States," *American Historical Association*, Annual Report, 1893, 331-65; F. R. Riley, "Spanish Policy in Mississippi after the Treaty of San Lorenzo," ibid., 1897, 177-82; I. J. Cox, *West Florida Controversy, 1798-1813: A Study in American Diplomacy* (Gloucester, Mass., 1918).

[28]For some highly stimulating conjectures on this, see Edward Channing, *History of the United States,* 6 vols. (New York, 1932), 4:334.

THE RETROCESSION OF LOUISIANA IN SPANISH POLICY*

Arthur P. Whitaker[1]

If Henry Adam's *History of the United States* had ended instead of beginning with 1800, he might have written a very different account of Spain's retrocession of Louisiana to France in that year. As it is, his *History* coincides almost precisely with the most humiliating period in the history of the Spanish monarchy, a period in which Napoleon first bent Charles IV to his will and then broke him. Less familiar with the events preceding the treaty of San Ildefonso than with those which followed, Adam's view of that episode was inevitably colored by the melancholy sequel. If not every American schoolboy, at least every American historian has read his graphic story of the negotiation, and remembers how the impatient Napoleon, returning to Paris flushed with the victory of Marengo and finding the retrocession still uncompleted by the reluctant Spaniards, directed his ambassador at Madrid to make them stand and deliver; how the ambassador, Alquier, with an arrogance worthy of his master, transmitted the order to the Spanish minister of foreign affairs; and how the latter meekly made a reply which measures the degradation of Spain: "Eh! Who told you that I would not give you Louisiana?" and proceeded forthwith to the surrender.[2]

A better knowledge of Spanish policy toward Louisiana in the decade before 1800 would have led Adams to suspect the truth of this story, which he drew from a French source. This suspicion in turn would have prompted him to examine the Spanish sources with equal care. From these he would have learned that the dispatches of his informant, Ambassador Alquier, are altogether misleading, partly because the ambassador yielded to the temptation, which all diplomats feel and few can resist, to enhance the merit of success by magnifying the difficulty of his mission, and partly because he simply did not know what was going on behind the scenes.[3] He may really have believed that his bullying forced the spineless submission of the Spanish minister to his demand for

*This article first appeared in the *American Historical Review*, 39 (1934): 454-76. Reprinted here with the kind permission of the publisher.

Louisiana; but as a matter of fact the Spaniard, declaring that the province "costs us more than it is worth," had already taken the initiative in proposing the cession through a confidential agent in Paris, and Talleyrand, for reasons of his own had concealed the offer from Alquier. Writers since Adams have added a great deal to our knowledge of the negotiation, but only a little to our understanding of Spanish policy. This can be explained both by the fact that French, not Spanish, policy was the principal object of interest with them, and also by the persistent belief that Spain was unwilling throughout the series of negotiations from 1795 to 1800 to part with Louisiana.[4] Under the circumstances, it seems worthwhile to tell the story again in light of the more ample documentation which has been made available since Adams's day.[5]

The retrocession of Louisiana to France is directly traceable to Spain's treaty of 1795 with the United States. As is well known, Spain had once set great store by the province. Its acquisition from France at the end of the Seven Years' War was indeed a notable feature of Spain's defensive expansion in North America under Charles III—an expansion which also carried the Spanish flag several hundred miles farther northward in California. Eagerly accepting France's offer to cede Louisiana,[6] the court planned to make the province an integral part of the empire, transform it into a colony of the standard Spanish type, and, by promoting its commerce and agriculture, convert it into an impenetrable barrier against the British colonies. By 1795, however, experience had shown that this ambitious plan could never succeed, and the court abandoned it, concluding the Treaty of San Lorenzo, which gave the United States a part of the territory that Spain had hoped to keep, rendered the peaceful penetration of the remainder by the Americans a certainty, and put them in a position to conquer not only Louisiana but also Florida if they were not content with peaceful penetration.

The Treaty of San Lorenzo marked the reversal of the court's policy toward Louisiana, for it was made in tacit recognition of the fact that Spain's position in the Mississippi Valley had become untenable, and it contained stipulations which were sure to hasten the inevitable withdrawal. Louisiana had been valued by Spain primarily as a barrier against the Anglo-Americans, and it no longer served that purpose. Henceforth the province was regarded by the court in the same way that, according to recent French writers, it was regarded by the Directory, namely, as a *monnaie d'échange* of the foreign office.[7] Useless as a colony, it might still have great value as a diplomatic pawn. If there was any French bullying in the Louisiana negotiation of the next five years, France wasted its energy, for bullying was not necessary and at that stage it could not be effective. All France needed to do was to offer a good price, and if that were not done Spain still had strength enough and pride enough to resist intimidation. The key to the retrocession of Louisiana is not French bullying but Spanish bargaining.

Any account of Spanish policy toward Louisiana in this period must begin and end with Manuel de Godoy, Prince of the Peace. Whether as minister of foreign affairs, a position which he held from 1793 to 1798, or as the chief favorite of the queen, who raised him to power, and of the king, who kept him there, Godoy had more influence upon Spanish policy than any other person at court, and his correspondence and memoirs show that he was deeply interested in Louisiana. His policy in regard to it cannot be understood apart from the context of world politics. That he took a comprehensive view of imperial problems and that he appreciated their extreme gravity and attempted to find a solution for them can hardly be doubted. In the period with which we are concerned he was not yet the pudgy, self-complacent courtier of Goya's well-known portrait, but an energetic young *arriviste* striving hard to prove himself worthy of fortune's favors. His equipment for the task of saving the Spanish empire was by no means ideal. Speaking of his linguistic accomplishments, one of the French agents at Madrid said, "He knows about as much French as an Algonquin"; and he was notoriously vain, pretentious, and grasping. The latter vice, however, might become a virtue if put to the service of his country, and with all his failings he possessed an uncommon share of intelligence and pertinacity, and courage of a sort. It was obvious that by serving Spain he would serve himself, for evidences of statesmanship would fortify him in the position which he had won through personal charm.

The result of his labors in the crisis confronting Spain in 1795 was a diplomatic revolution. His coming to power had been signalized by the conclusion of the alliance of 1793 with Great Britain and the beginning of war with the French regicides. The British alliance was not his own idea, but was inherited from Floridablanca, first minister of state of Charles III and Charles IV from 1777 to 1792. Another inheritance from his distinguished predecessor was Eugenio de Llaguno, a savant of some note and secretary of the *Suprema Junta de Estado* in Floridablanca's time, who had been assigned as political mentor to the youthful minister. By the end of 1794 Godoy had had enough of this tutelage. No longer content merely to hold the helm, he resolved to put the ship of state on a new course that he himself had plotted. The old policy had resulted in a disastrous war with France, a dangerous controversy with the United States, a highly unsatisfactory alliance with Great Britain, and widespread unrest in Spain, and a thorough renovation seemed imperative. It also seemed feasible. By making peace with France he would protect Spain from its most formidable enemy in Europe. By preserving peace with the United States he would neutralize one of the two powers that could do Spain the greatest injury in America. The other power, Great Britain, might indeed take Spain's desertion of the alliance of 1793 as a cause for war, but Godoy had come to the conclusion that even alliance with the British was no guaranty against their aggression; and he had reason to believe that if they were prevented from getting the cooperation of the United States, they would be unable to carry out any extensive campaign against Spanish America.[8]

Louisiana played an important part in his plans at this juncture; in short, it was cast for a sacrificial rôle. The wolves were closing in on the imperial sleigh, one of the children must be thrown to them, and none could be spared with less regret than the adopted daughter, Louisiana. An outlying province which had cost nothing to get and a great deal to keep, it could not be assimilated to the traditional type of Spanish colony, had become a corridor for smuggling with other Spanish colonies, and involved Spain not only in costly competition with the American frontier but also in many dangerous controversies with the governments of the United States and Great Britain.[9] Fortunately for Godoy, Louisiana could be made to serve his purpose both with France, which had begun to clamor for the retrocession of the province, and with the United States, which was threatening to go to war unless Spain granted its citizens certain concessions in the Mississippi Valley. The Americans would be satisfied with the territory north of the thirty-first parallel and east of the Mississippi, and with the free navigation of that river and a place of deposit at New Orleans. These concessions would still leave intact the Louisiana ceded to Spain by France a generation earlier, which was all that France could reasonably expect to recover; and the retrocession would carry out Floridablanca's plan of enlisting another European power in support of Spain's resistance to the American advance toward the Gulf of Mexico and the silver mines of New Spain.

The first step was to put an end to the war with France. Accordingly the envoys of the two powers met at Basel in May, 1795, and began a negotiation which was concluded in July. Spain had been beaten and must pay for peace with a territorial cession. France was determined that this should be Louisiana; Spain, that it should be Santo Domingo. Badly as it needed peace, the Spanish court put up such firm resistance that France finally gave in, accepted the latter colony, and signed the treaty.

Godoy's stubborn refusal to gratify the French on this occasion arose not from unwillingness to part with Louisiana but from the determination to keep it until he had used it to effect the second stage of his diplomatic revolution by coming to a good understanding with the United States. The mere avoidance of war was not enough—that might have been accomplished by ceding Louisiana to France at Basel. What his policy required was a positively friendly arrangement. He even hoped for an alliance, and when he found that that was out of the question, he played the part of generous benefactor of the Americans, conceding virtually all they asked for in the Mississippi Valley and throwing in for good measure some very liberal clauses on the subject of neutral rights. The result was the Treaty of San Lorenzo (October 28, 1795), which he thought would keep the Americans neutral and make their neutrality benevolent in case England should declare war on Spain.

That done, he was through with Louisiana. Two months after he signed the Treaty of San Lorenzo he showed his true opinion of the colony by reopening the negotiation with France with the offer to cede Louisiana in return for Santo Domingo, which he had just given the French at Basel in order to be able to keep the continental colony.[10] The time had come for Spain to withdraw from the Mississippi Valley, and the only question was whether it could get a good price for a province it could not afford to keep. Unfortunately for Godoy, the Directory too was engaged in bargain hunting. It welcomed the revival of its cherished project, but refused to consider the proposed exchange, declaring that in the hands of France Louisiana would become an effective screen for the Spanish colonies and that Spain needed no other compensation.

In spite of this unfavorable beginning, it looked for a time as if Godoy's plan might work out to perfection. As soon as he had obtained the formal ratification of the Treaty of San Lorenzo and an emphatic expression of approval from the king in a full meeting of the council of state (May 27, 1796), and had dispatched orders to Louisiana regarding its execution (June 1), he immediately obtained the signature of the French plenipotentiary to a treaty (June 27) which provided for the retrocession of Louisiana. In return, Spain was to receive Gibraltar, which it was believed in some quarters could be taken without great difficulty, and France also agreed to make every effort to obtain fishing rights at Newfoundland for the Spaniards.[11] Though the Directory refused ratification on the ground that its agent had exceeded his powers and had given Spain the better of the bargain, this treaty nevertheless furnishes conclusive proof that Godoy was acting in good faith when he reopened the negotiation in December, 1795, and that as soon as he had conciliated the Americans by giving them a part of Louisiana and by burdening the rest of the province with onerous commercial concessions, he was ready to sell the burdened remnant to France. Only the negative of the French government itself prevented the conclusion of a treaty of retrocession in 1796.[12]

Whatever disappointment the Spanish court may have felt at this rebuff was allayed a few weeks later by the conclusion of another treaty, which provided for an alliance between the two powers and left the Louisiana business for further negotiation. Since the treaty also contained a blanket guaranty by France of all of Spain's possessions, and since the benevolent neutrality of the United States had, Godoy thought, been bought and paid for, Spain's American dominions had apparently been given the maximum degree of security against British aggression. The court could now proceed without undue haste to haggle over the price of Louisiana.

Two unexpected developments soon wrecked the plan so carefully elaborated by the young minister. The first was the conclusion of an "explanatory article" by Great Britain and the United States which purported to clarify the meaning of certain portions of Jay's Treaty of 1794. The article gave great offense to the Spanish court, for it reaffirmed the British right to the navigation of the Mississippi River and thereby undid what Godoy considered an important part of his work at San Lorenzo, namely, the insertion in that treaty of a clause so worded as, in his opinion, to restrict the right of navigating the river to the United States and Spain. Since the Treaty of San Lorenzo was posterior to Jay's Treaty, by which Great Britain and the United States had each guaranteed to the other the free navigation of the Mississippi, Godoy thought his clever wording of the article in question would not only destroy the British claim but also sow discord between the British and American governments. Then came the explanatory article of 1796 which, since it was of later date than the Treaty of San Lorenzo, turned the tables on Spain.[13]

Godoy's resentment at what he regarded at the duplicity of the American government was sharpened by personal pique. Posing as a man of broad general culture and eager to prove himself abreast of the fashionable thought of the times, he found it difficult to squeeze much of the current liberalism into the narrow framework of Spanish orthodoxy and identified himself rather with the romantic school. His private letters to the king and queen abound in noble thoughts, the jargon of sentiment, and echoes of the cult of nature. He spoke of himself as a man of "sensibility," and on one occasion, when he felt that he no longer fully enjoyed the king's confidence, wrote the queen that he was about to retire to his private estate, where, he said, "solitude and crumbling walls shall be my delight." He carried out the plan, and some months later wrote, again to the queen: "Given up on solitude, I am surrounded by books in which I am reminded of the lives of men who have been useful to their country and whose lessons teach me how to live."[14]

Such a man would naturally share the widespread romantic belief that the Americans, nurtured in the ennobling solitude of the New World, were a singularly virtuous people, and therefore most deserving; and Godoy seems to have shared it to the full, until he was enlightened by experience. Though he had read reams of dispatches from the governors of Louisiana which described the western Americans as predatory semi-savages, he was sure that these backwoodsmen were not representative of the mass of their countrymen, who lived on the Atlantic coast and were, as every European philosopher knew, an amiable and upright race. As recently as 1794 his esteem for the American people had been strengthened by dispatches from the Spanish agents at Philadelphia telling him how the United States government had befriended Spain by breaking up Genêt's expeditions against Louisiana. To a Spaniard such conduct would naturally indicate the possession of moral qualities of a high order. So it was that, though Godoy's predecessors had taken a more realistic view of American character and policy and though he himself was soon to return to that view, in 1795 he still held the romantic opinion of the United States once prevalent in France. When he negotiated the Treaty of San Lorenzo with the American minister, Thomas Pinckney, he seems to have regarded himself as a second Vergennes patronizing simple republican virtue; but he suffered a Vergennes's disillusionment, for as Franklin was followed by Adams and Jay, so Pinckney soon gave way to Pickering and Hamilton.

The explanatory article was signed at Philadelphia in May, 1796, by Secretary of State Timothy Pickering for the United States and Phineas Bond for Great Britain. The unwelcome news reached Madrid in September. Though it came direct from Spain's own minister at Philadelphia, Godoy interpreted it in the light of information and advice from Paris. The conclusion he reached was, on the one hand, that the American government's agreement to the article proved its subservience to Great Britain; and, on the other hand, that the American people were devoted to France and indignant at the devious course taken by their Anglophile government. Unwarrantedly confident that he could count upon the wholehearted support of France, which was egging him on, Godoy determined to have it out with Pitt's minions at Philadelphia.

The result was the issuance of an order dated October 29, 1796, which suspended the execution of the Treaty of San Lorenzo by directing the governor of Louisiana to retain until further notice several posts on the eastern bank of the Mississippi despite the fact that the treaty stipulated their immediate surrender to the United States.[15] It was evidently

Godoy's expectation that, in the course of the controversy which his order was sure to provoke, one of two things would happen: the American government would either be forced to give unmistakable proof of its subserviency to Great Britain, whereupon it would be overthrown by the exasperated American people, or else it would have to disavow the explanatory article of May, 1796, in which case the Anglo-American entente would be destroyed. He was highly satisfied with his plan, which seemed a clever way of meeting the crisis caused by the conclusion of the explanatory article and the subsequent outbreak of war between Great Britain and Spain.

A bitter disappointment was in store for him. Since foreign influence in the United States was not decisive, as recent advices from Paris had led him to believe, it was impossible for him to execute the maneuver which he had planned on that assumption. Neither did he create a rift between the people and government of the United States, nor destroy the Anglo-American entente, such as it was. On the contrary, his conduct increased the probability of cooperation between the two English-speaking peoples and played into the hands of Spain's worst enemies in the United States—those elements who were soon to rally around Alexander Hamilton in his projected invasion of Spanish America. This danger in turn became one of the chief obstacles to the completion of the Louisiana business.

The other unfavorable development of this distressing winter was Godoy's discovery that, despite the recently concluded treaty of alliance, Spain could expect little aid from France in America. This disillusionment too came in the course of the crisis caused by his order relating to the border posts. France, though partly responsible for that step and consequently for the ensuing controversy with the United States, refused to support Spain when Godoy tardily remembered that it might be well to have a written pledge of such support before going any further. Instead of giving the pledge, unsympathetic Paris declared that the crisis in the court's relations with the United States was merely another proof that Spain ought in self-defense to effect the immediate and gratuitous retrocession of Louisiana.[16] This was the beginning of Godoy's alienation from the Directory, which was to become much more pronounced before the end of the year.

His double disappointment was not followed by any abrupt change of policy toward either France or the United States. His position at court was not so secure that he could afford to defy France, and he was slow to believe that the American people would not repudiate their government at the behest of France and Spain. He still professed himself ready to cede Louisiana to France, and he still refused to let the United States have the border posts on the Mississippi. If we are to believe the French ambassador, Godoy admitted as late as May, 1797, that in its own interests Spain ought to conclude the negotiation on the terms proposed by France, that is, by surrendering Louisiana immediately and without compensation. But the now wary Spaniard had no difficulty in finding pretexts for evading retrocession on any terms. The unenlightened mass of his countrymen, he said, would never tolerate the cession of Louisiana in return for an equivalent which would benefit the royal family alone and not the Spanish people themselves.[17] This was an allusion to the proposed aggrandizement of the House of Parma, which was the compensation ultimately accepted by Charles IV three years later; but in 1797 the Parma project was open to other objections as well, one of which was that France was not sufficiently strong in Italy to guarantee the execution of its part of the bargain. Since it was even less likely that the French would be able to deliver an equivalent which would benefit the Spanish people, such as Gibraltar or Newfoundland fishing rights, one gets the impression that Godoy was demanding impossible terms in order to block a negotiation which it would not have been prudent for him to break off. He no longer had any desire to conclude this important business with so unreliable a government as the Directory had proved to be.

In July, 1797, as the result of an upheaval at Paris, Talleyrand took over the French foreign office and with it the tedious Louisiana negotiation. His conduct of it was neither original nor successful. He employed the arguments already elaborated by his predecessors, and the world situation was not such as to make his repetition of their hackneyed phrases convincing. If he took at their face value the protestations of the Spanish court, which was still doing lip service to the French alliance, he probably anticipated success. Godoy, however, liked the reconstructed Directory no better than the old one, and he was very far from being subservient to France. Apropos of the crisis in Franco-American relations which was soon to culminate in the XYZ affair, he wrote Minister Irujo at Philadelphia in August, 1797, that if France increased its diplomatic pressure on the United States, Spain would do the same; that if France composed its differences with the United States, Spain would not break with the latter power; but that in case France should go to war with the United States, Spain would either join its ally or take the position of mediator, according to its own interests.[18]

The ominous note of independence in the concluding passage of this letter can probably be explained by recent developments which had destroyed Godoy's small remnant of faith in the Directory. During the spring and summer of 1797 France and Great Britain had been engaged in peace negotiations in the course of which some of the French envoys expressed a willingness to give Louisiana to Great Britain in return for British acquiescence in the territorial gains made by France on the Continent. That would have been a gross betrayal of Spain, since from the very beginning of the Louisiana negotiation in 1795 France had promised to maintain the province as a barrier between New Spain and the Anglo-Americans, or, as Talleyrand put it, "a wall of brass forever impenetrable to the combined efforts of England and America." Whether or not the Spanish court knew the full extent of France's perfidy, it was offended and alarmed by the secretiveness of its ally in regard to the negotiation with Great Britain.[19] This episode seems to have completed Godoy's alienation from France. At any rate, he was henceforth, whether openly or secretly, the principal opponent of the Directory in Spain.

Talleyrand soon found that the Spanish minister was not made of modeling clay. On September 18, 1797, he took up the threadbare Louisiana negotiation, presenting the court with a carefully prepared memoir on the subject. Besides renewing the demand for

Louisiana, on the ground that the Blount conspiracy in the United States and the progress of revolutionary sentiment at New Orleans proved the impossibility of Spain's holding the province much longer, he also urged the court to retain the border posts on the Mississippi until the restoration of general peace in Europe, and in the meanwhile to mollify the Americans by executing the article in the Treaty of San Lorenzo relating to the free navigation of the Mississippi. His eloquence was wasted on Godoy, whose reply evaded the demand for Louisiana and ignored the rest of the memoir.[20] As a matter of fact, Spain had long since executed the article relating to the free navigation of the Mississippi; and as for the disputed border posts, Godoy had just issued the final order for their delivery to the United States.[21] He was not so eager to please France that he would reverse himself for the third time by again ordering their retention.

France's first knowledge of the existence of the order came from the news that the posts had been evacuated. So well had the court kept its own counsel that the information reached Paris by way of the United States, where the French consul general obtained it from a newspaper. Though Godoy, who was responsible for the measure, had been forced out of office by this time, Talleyrand nevertheless protested to Spain against its flagrant disregard of the wishes of its ally. In June, 1798, he presented the court with another memorial, in which he catalogued various French grievances, and among these the surrender of the border posts occupied a prominent place.[22] Saavedra, Godoy's successor, replied through Ambassador Azara, who told Talleyrand that "the treaty which we made with the Colonies [the United States] and the cession of the forts on the left bank of the Mississippi are one of those irremediable errors of policy which it is useless to regret, and we should rather direct our attention to discovering means to correct its ill effects."[23]

If, as one might infer, Azara was here hinting at the possibility of an early cession of Louisiana, he was not following instructions from Madrid, for his government had just informed him in the most unequivocal terms that for the present it would not listen to any proposal relating to the alienation of the province. Late in May, 1798, Azara had informed Saavedra of an interview in which Talleyrand had suggested that France might force Portugal to give Spain a slice of Brazil on condition that Spain should cede Louisiana to France. In support of his proposal Talleyrand had delivered a long disquisition on the uselessness of Louisiana to Spain, asserting that in the present state of affairs England with the aid of the United States was carrying on a vast contraband trade through New Orleans with Mexico and other Spanish possessions on the Gulf, and that he had documents proving that this trade amounted to two million pounds sterling a year. Replying to Azara on June 4, Saavedra rejected the offer unconditionally. "On no account whatever," he wrote, "must the cession of Louisiana, the Floridas, or any other portion of our dominions be involved in the proposed peace with Portugal. These jewels, whether they bring us advantages or disadvantages—and on this point there is a great deal to be said—must in any event be kept for the end of the play when the question of compensations arises. Otherwise we shall be involved in a futile discussion and perhaps also in a disagreeable dispute with the Anglo-Americans [the United States] at a time when we are trying to accommodate existing differences and not to raise new ones."[24]

Though Saavedra disagreed with Godoy on many points, he prudently adhered to his predecessor's policy of conciliating the Americans. This involved the further postponement of the Louisiana negotiation with France, for the Spanish minister at Philadelphia warned his government again and again in 1797 and 1798 that the United States, under the influence of Hamilton, Pickering, and their anti-French associates, would almost certainly go to war rather than permit France to acquire the province. In June of the latter year the imminence of the danger was brought home to Saavedra by a startling piece of intelligence which came to him through the French government itself. Reporting another interview with Talleyrand, Azara wrote: "I found him very much disturbed by letters from North America which he was reading. They inform him that Pitt's gold and intrigues have won Congress over, that the plan of campaign is to begin by an attack on Spanish Louisiana and Florida, which they [the United States] expect to take without resistance. . . . This information is authoritative, for Talleyrand showed me the letters of the French consul in Philadelphia, in which he states that the Vice President of Congress [Thomas Jefferson], who is a friend of the French and consequently hostile to the English party, told him of this in great secrecy. Talleyrand assures me that the directory is determined to leave no stone unturned to avoid this rupture, but that he does not know if they will be in time. He urged me strongly to warn your Excellency of it in order that all possible precautions may be taken; but neither of us knows what they might be."[25]

Talleyrand once more demonstrated his lack of understanding of Spanish policy, for, in the evident expectation that his warning would frighten the court into ceding him the threatened border province, he now sent a new minister to Madrid for the express purpose of obtaining Louisiana. Azara obligingly admitted that Spain derived "fort peu de profit" from the possession of it;[26] but the court knew that, if news of the cession leaked out, it would almost certainly provoke the United States to a war of conquest which would not stop with Louisiana and Florida. Godoy was still determined to get a good price if the cession should be made, and Talleyrand soon found that to drive him from office was not to drive him from power. Harassed by domestic as well as foreign complications, the incompetent Directory was unable to offer Charles IV sufficient inducement to disregard the advice of his favorite. Even if Spain had been willing to strike a bargain at this time, it was beyond the power of the French to make an acceptable offer. They were not strong enough in Italy to create the desired kingdom for the House of Parma. Gibraltar and Newfoundland fishing rights were even further beyond their grasp. The slice of Brazil which was the one equivalent they might have been able to deliver had been disdainfully rejected by the court. Its motive power exhausted for the time being, the negotiation came to a full stop, and no further progress was made in it for the next two years.

By June, 1800, the situation had changed completely. Now the Spanish court had an incentive to negotiate and a new and more satisfactory government at Paris to deal with. Napoleon's victorious progress in Italy was reviving the royal family's hope that something might really be done for their cousin of Parma, and in these early days Spain found the Consulate far more congenial than it ever had the Directory. Charles IV indeed regarded the First Consul with an admiration bordering on hero worship and endeavored to identify himself as closely as possible with the great man, speaking with proprietary pride of the progress of "our arms" in Italy.[27] Spain's reluctance to make the retrocession had abated somewhat since the open break between President Adams and the war party in the United States, which greatly diminished the danger of reprisals in that quarter.

Under these favorable circumstances the Parma negotiation was resumed in April, 1800, but it was not coupled with Louisiana until the latter part of June. That the retrocession project was then revived and linked with Parma was due to the initiative not of France but of Spain. The French government indeed seemed to have forgotten Louisiana, which it was not making any effort to recover at this time.[28] In the early stages the conversations about Parma were conducted through an agent of the Spanish treasury in Paris, José Martínez de Hervas. As late as June 11, Hervas reported the results of long conferences about Parma without even mentioning Louisiana. He had been authorized to pay a bribe of as much as three million dollars for the erection of the Italian kingdom, and, though Charles IV had never stated his terms precisely, Hervas believed that the business could be arranged to his satisfaction. Talleyrand had said, however, that Spain's terms must be made known at once, since the treaty could not be postponed until the end of the war. "You will observe from this expression," commented Hervas, "that the general peace is not so near at hand as is generally believed, and you will decide whether, in view of the uncertainty of the final result, it is worth while making great sacrifices before the general peace, and whether, in case the arrangement is made now, we are likely to be able to procure its continuance without alteration."

Talleyrand had urged him, said Hervas, to keep the negotiation a profound secret, and to conceal it not only from Múzquiz, the Spanish ambassador at Paris, but also from Alquier, the French ambassador at Madrid. The Frenchman explained his strange request by asserting that someone close to the Spanish court was abusing its confidence, but the real reason was doubtless his desire to reduce the number of participants in the negotiation in order to increase his own share of the three million dollar *pot de vin* offered by Spain. Though Hervas promised to keep the secret, he immediately communicated it to Múzquiz, for he feared that Talleyrand might try to play a double game.[29]

Hervas's letter was addressed to Mariano Luis de Urquijo, the new Spanish minister for foreign affairs. On June 22 Urquijo replied in two letters, as Hervas had requested, one of them confidential, the other to be shown to Talleyrand. The letter stated that the peace terms desired by Spain extended only to the recovery of Trinidad and Minorca and to a livelihood for the Duke of Parma. The confidential letter approved of Hervas communicating the secret to Múzquiz, in whom the court had "unlimited confidence" and to whom a copy of the letter was sent; but as for Alquier, said Urquijo, "I will leave him in the most complete ignorance of all this." He then proceeded to introduce Louisiana into the negotiation for the first time, devoting to it a passage which, though lengthy, is of such prime importance for the understanding of Spanish policy that it must be quoted in full.[30] The passage reads:

> I wish to call your attention to only one important point in connection with the general peace. . . . I can never believe that the French will make such sacrifices for us, in spite of its importance to them, as to demand that Minorca and Trinidad be restored to us, although the treaty of alliance stipulates a mutual guaranty of our possessions, without which peace must not be made. Never, I repeat, can I believe that they will have these restored to us free of charge, for the English will interpose a thousand obstacles to it in the general peace, unless we make some sacrifice. You know that the memoirs written by Carnot in Hamburg show that the former Directory thought at one time of demanding Louisiana of us. *Between ourselves, this* [province, Louisiana] *costs us more than it is worth*, and while the cession of it to the French is open to the objection that they would use it to carry on a smuggling trade with Mexico, the English are already doing so by means of the Americans; and it would be a great advantage to us to interpose between the latter and ourselves a barrier against their ambitious plans of conquest, especially if that barrier were raised by such a nation as France, which has neither an active colonizing spirit nor, in view of its absorption in European affairs, the resources for colonization. *Above all, I repeat, this would be an advantage to us because of the recent treaty* [the Treaty of San Lorenzo] *by which we granted the free navigation of the Mississippi and the principal points that served us as a barrier to the Gulf of Mexico—a concession the ultimate consequences of which you can foresee.* Therefore I say that if the French arrange a peace for us in which we obtain Trinidad and Minorca and the House of Parma obtains, in addition to its present possessions, the Legations, Modena, and Reggio or the Milanese, we could not only give the three million to B[onaparte] and T[alleyrand] but also Louisiana and many thanks into the bargain, and we could flatter ourselves that such a treaty had never before been obtained. But this must be understood for the general peace, since otherwise the Americans, who know how important it is that Louisiana should remain in our hands, would prevent the cession and transfer and would even go to the point of declaring war on us, as they have already threatened to do on another occasion when they suspected it [the retrocession of Louisiana], and nothing would be accomplished but to turn the world upside down again and expose us to a mortal blow in the Americas. On the other hand, if this were arranged at the general peace, the Americans would find themselves without any power to aid them in their designs.

That Urquijo was writing in all sincerity can hardly be questioned, for the letter was a highly confidential communication addressed to trusted agents in a secret negotiation. His statement of policy is important for two reasons: first, because it contains an explicit recognition of the fact that the Treaty of San Lorenzo, by making Spain's position in Louisiana untenable, was directly responsible for the retrocession; and second, because it disposes conclusively of the assumption that Napoleon extorted the retrocession from a reluctant Spanish court. When, several weeks later, Napoleon spoiled Talleyrand's game by putting the negotiation in Alquier's hands and the latter presented his abrupt demand for Louisiana,[31] it was only natural that Urquijo should reply, "Eh! Who told you that I would not give it to you?" Since he himself had violated Talleyrand's injunction of secrecy by informing Múzquiz of the negotiation in progress through Hervas, he would naturally assume that the French government had communicated it to Alquier. Misunderstanding the motive behind Talleyrand's request, he had taken this step as a protection against double-dealing on the part of France; and he had no reason to believe that Talleyrand had neglected to take similar precautions against Spanish finesse. His reply to Alquier expressed not submission to French bullying, but surprise that the French ambassador could be so ill informed as to think bullying necessary.

It is true that Urquijo was finally forced to accept less favorable terms than those which he had proposed at the outset; but that is the common lot of negotiators. The most important concession that Bonaparte got from him was his consent to the immediate settlement of the question, whereas Urquijo wished to postpone it to the general peace. Even this concession, however, was not the result of spineless submission, for the treaty was framed in such a way as to meet the principal objections which he had urged against it. These objections were that if the Americans learned of the retrocession, they might go to war to defeat it, and that the prospect of general peace was so remote and the final success of France so problematical that Spain might never receive the price of Louisiana. The first objection was obviated by keeping the treaty secret, and the second by making it contingent—for it was provided that Louisiana should not actually be delivered to France until the House of Parma had been put in full possession of the benefits stipulated in the treaty.

Much as Godoy disliked Urquijo and distrusted France, he could not withhold his approval of the retrocession. It was not merely as a supple courtier that he spoke in favor of it. No one knew better than he the ardent desire of the king and queen to promote the welfare of the closely related House of Parma, but that alone might not have been enough, for Godoy had shown more than once that he could speak his mind quite freely to them. It was at this very time that he dared to raise his voice against the chorus of adulation with which the court, echoing the king and queen, was hailing Bonaparte. "Well, Manuel," said Charles on the morrow of Marengo, "what do you think of Bonaparte?" "Sire," replied the imperturbable Godoy, "we must wait and see how Bonaparte ends. What has happened is a great misfortune for these poor Italians."[32] If on the present occasion he gave his royal masters the counsel they desired, it was probably because he believed the arrangement was advantageous to Spain. It must not be forgotten that he was committed to the principle of retrocession by the treaty which he himself had signed in 1796, and which had failed of adoption only because the Directory refused to pay his price. If the compensation about to be accepted was one which would benefit the royal family alone and not the nation, the change was justified by altered circumstances, for by 1800 it was evident that France could deliver a kingdom in Italy and could not deliver Gibraltar and fishing rights.

He approached the negotiation of 1800 in the same bargaining spirit when his advice was sought by the king. His written reply,[33] which took the form of answers to a questionnaire, lends further support to the thesis that by this time Louisiana was regarded by the Spanish court simply as a piece of merchandise, or, if one prefers, as a diplomatic pawn. There were eleven questions. To ten of them he returned answers which were decidedly favorable to the proposed retrocession. Did Spain derive any advantage from Louisiana? No, he replied. Spanish merchants, who rarely ventured to New Orleans, were coldly received when they did go there; and Louisiana had never repaid the Spanish treasury for the cost of its government, and probably would not do so for a long time to come. Would Louisiana be useful to Spain for the protection of Mexico? If well defended by numerous troops it would doubtless serve as a convenient outpost, but it was not essential for that purpose. Would Louisiana in the hands of France be a valuable barrier between New Spain and the United States? Yes, for Spain could count upon the effective coöperation of France in America after the cession. And so on. But to the eleventh question—Was the price offered by France high enough?—he answered roundly, No! Spain must have assurance that the succession to the Italian kingdom would be vested in the Spanish dynasty, that Spanish commerce with Louisiana would be given preferential treatment, and that France would never alienate Louisiana. This closefisted son of Extremadura was a born bargainer. Though he could not completely stifle his distrust of the French, neither could he resist the temptation to haggle with them over the sale of a province which was no longer of any use to Spain.

The ingenuous king did not share Godoy's suspicions, and after the failure of Bonaparte's eleventh-hour effort to make Spain give him Florida as well as Louisiana, the treaty was concluded at San Ildefonso (October 1, 1800), without the safeguards recommended by his favorite.[34] However regrettable from the point of view of the Bourbons, the omission was fortunate for Godoy, since it stamped the treaty as the work of Urquijo and made it easier for the favorite to procure the dismissal of his rival from office, as he did less than three months later. Yet Urquijo had not done his work so badly. As already stated, the treaty was a secret one and it made the cession of Louisiana contingent upon the previous establishment and recognition of the Italian kingdom. The total consideration given by Spain—this included, besides Louisiana, six ships of the line and the bribe for Bonaparte and Talleyrand—was not disproportionately large. In effect, the king was giving up a colony of fifty thousand inhabitants on the Mississippi in order that his son-in-law might have a kingdom of a million inhabitants on the Arno; and if the cession of Louisiana meant the abandonment of Charles III's expansionist policy in North America, it also meant the resumption of the far more venerable Spanish policy of aggrandizement in Italy. If it be objected that his operation despoiled the Spanish empire for the benefit of the House of Bourbon, we need only recall that the colonies in America were the property not of the Spanish nation but of the Crown, and that, as Urquijo said,[35] Louisiana, in view of the mode of its acquisition, was more completely at the king's personal disposal than any of the rest of his dominions. Whether we consider the question from the national or the dynastic point of view, it can hardly be denied that Spain's experience with Louisiana justified the alienation of the province—and the justification was even greater in 1800 than when Godoy agreed to part with it in 1796.[36] When Urquijo said that it "costs us more than it is worth," he erred, if at all, on the side of understatement. Louisiana was not only an expensive luxury but had actually become a heavy liability, and Urquijo might well consider it an achievement that he had persuaded France to pay for the privilege of having the burden transferred to its shoulders. There is no more indication of Spanish subservience in the terms of the treaty than in the manner of its negotiation.

It is true that in the interval between the conclusion of the Treaty of San Ildefonso and the delivery of Louisiana to France three years later there are evidences of Spanish reluctance and French intimidation, and perhaps Adams read these back into the negotiation of 1800. Spain's reluctance, however, still arose not from attachment to Louisiana but from the growing suspicion that France would not pay the full purchase price; and French intimidation was made easier by the Peace of Amiens in the spring of 1802. As long as the war lasted, France was restrained from abusing Charles IV's abundant good nature by the fear that if the Spaniards were pushed too far they would make a separate peace with England. That restraint was removed by the Peace of Amiens, and Bonaparte immediately gave Spain to understand that Louisiana would have to be handed over to him whether he kept his part of the agreement or not. When hostilities broke out again between France and England a year later, Spain did not have the same advantage as in the earlier war, for the court's eagerness to remain at peace was well known to Bonaparte, who made the most of his knowledge. So it was that even though Bonaparte, violating his treaty obligations, withheld the purchase price, and, breaking his pledge not to alienate Louisiana, sold it to the United States, Spain nevertheless transferred the province to his representative on November 30, 1803, in the face of the certainty that France in turn would deliver it to the United States.[37]

Even in these later phases of the negotiation it was evident that Spain had little or no desire to keep Louisiana. It is not surprising that this was so, for once more Spanish policy was completely dominated by Godoy. Soon tiring of the delights of solitude and crumbling walls, he returned to court and in December, 1800, obtained Urquijo's dismissal and the appointment of his own henchman and relative, Pedro Cevallos, as secretary of state for foreign affairs. Committed as he was to the retrocession of Louisiana, Godoy was not the man to undo the work of San Ildefonso. He soon showed what might be expected of him on that score, for on March 21, 1801, he and Lucien Bonaparte signed the Convention of Aranjuez, which confirmed the existing agreement with regard to Louisiana.[38] It is true that a few months later, in a moment of exasperation at Bonaparte's misconduct in regard to Parma, he said to the queen in a private letter, "The French forced us to give them Louisiana, but we ought to draw back, reject their demands, regard the treaties as annulled, and return to the situation that existed before the revolution";[39] but it was a patent absurdity for the man who had voluntarily revived the Louisiana negotiation in 1795, signed a treaty of retrocession in 1796, approved of retrocession in 1800 and confirmed it in 1801, now to speak of the sale of

Louisiana as if it had been a rape. If his history was bad, his counsel was worse—so bad, indeed, that he can hardly have meant it to be taken seriously. He wrote apparently not as an official submitting a studied opinion to his queen, but as a man of sensibility unburdening himself to an intimate friend. However that may be, the cause of his irritation was not the loss of Louisiana but the miscarriage of his plans for Parma.

Since even men of sensibility may have sober second thoughts, Godoy wisely contented himself with seeking to obtain the guaranties which he had recommended in 1800. Here he met with some success. Among other things, he persuaded the French government to promise through its ambassador (July, 1802) that it would never alienate Louisiana. The pledge was dearly bought, however, for in return Spain had to agree to execute the cession without waiting for France to perform its treaty obligations in regard to the Italian kingdom. Accordingly the king issued an order dated October 15, 1802, directing the governor of Louisiana to deliver the province to Bonaparte's representative.

When war clouds began to gather again early in 1803, it was too late for the court to retrace its steps. Godoy for one had no desire to do so, for just at this time occurred an incident which gave fresh proof that Louisiana was a heavy liability to Spain. In October, 1802, the American deposit at New Orleans was closed under secret orders from the king. The loss of this valuable institution provoked a great outburst of indignation throughout the United States, which was of course reported at once by Minister Irujo. By the beginning of March, 1803, the court knew that it must either immediately restore the deposit, though the privilege had been scandalously abused by the Americans, or else prepare for a ruinous war with the United States. Never was the utter untenability of Spain's position in Louisiana more strikingly demonstrated, for Spanish interests and Spanish pride made it impossible to accept either alternative. As a stop-gap measure, orders were sent to New Orleans by way of the United States directing the immediate reopening of the deposit; and then, publicly washing his hands of Louisiana, Godoy informed the American minister, Charles Pinckney, who was trying to buy New Orleans for his government, that France was now the owner of Louisiana and the Americans would have to do their business in Paris. "I never dared to give this reply before," Godoy told the queen, "but on this occasion it was absolutely necessary to do so."[40]

Officially communicated to Pinckney by Secretary Cevallos, this disclaimer of Spanish sovereignty over Louisiana proved most useful to the United States in the subsequent controversy over the validity of the Louisiana Purchase; but it is unlikely that Godoy ever regretted giving it. When, just after the purchase, it was believed at court that Spain would recover Louisiana by ceding the Floridas to the United States and he was advised to seize the opportunity, he coolly rejected the proposal. "There is a good deal of difference of opinion on this subject," he said, "and not everyone gives so much preference to Louisiana." The defensive expansion of the empire in the preceding reign had been too ambitious. It soon became necessary to surrender some of the ground thus gained, and all the circumstances decreed that Spain's possessions in the Mississippi Valley should be chosen for the sacrifice. The Treaty of San Lorenzo marked the beginning of this retreat, which was continued in the inevitable sequel, Spain's withdraw from Louisiana.

Notes for "The Retrocession of Louisiana in Spanish Policy"

[1]The present article was written during the preparation of the book, *The Mississippi Question, 1795-1803* (New York, 1934). The writer was aided by a grant from the Guggenheim Memorial Foundation in 1929.

[2]Henry Adams, *History of the United States* (New York, 1889), 1:363-65.

[3]Speaking of Alquier's picturesque dispatches from Madrid, André Fugier, the best authority on the subject, says, "Mais il est véritablement difficile d'ajouter la moindre foi à ses racontars vraiment insensés, d'autant qu'Alquier dissimule á peine l'hostilité dont il était animé à l'égard de l'Espagne," *Napoléon et l'Espagne, 1799-1808*, 2 vols. (Paris, 1930), 1:96. This work is indispensable to the student of diplomatic relations between France and Spain in the period covered, but its author does not attempt to settle the principal question raised in the present article.

[4]Only Jerónimo Bécker, *Historia de las relaciones exteriores de España en el siglo XIX* (Madrid, 1924-1926), gives the Spanish side of the Louisiana business, and his account throws no light on the antecedents of the treaty of 1800. Fugier, *Napoléon*, 1:29, states erroneously that the Directory rejected the treaty of June 27, 1796, because it did not provide for the retrocession of Louisiana. Francis P. Renaut, "La question de la Lousiane, 1796-1806," *Revue de l'histoire des colonies françaises*, 6 (1918): 129 ff., states the facts regarding that treaty correctly (149-51); but he was apparently unaware of the existence of Urquijo's letter to Hervas of June 22, 1800 (see below, n. 30), and gives a misleading account of the negotiation of that year (187-189). Raymond Guyot, *Le Directoire et la paix de l'Europe* (Paris, 1911), was so intent upon proving his *monnaie d'échange* thesis that he has little to say about Spanish policy; and he passes very lightly over some important phases of the negotiation in the period 1795-1799. Frederick Jackson Turner, "The Policy of France toward the Mississippi Valley in the Period of Washington and Adams," *American Historical Review*, 10 (1904-1905): 269, says in regard to the negotiation of 1796, "Godoy resolutely refused to give up Louisiana." Edward Channing, *A History of the United States*, 6 vols. (New York, 1905), 4:303-7, points out that Spain was willing to part with Louisiana, and yet he finds it necessary to speak of Bonaparte's putting "intense pressure" on Spain in 1800; and it is difficult to see why he says that the "first effective impulse to the rebuilding of the French colonial empire in North America was given by Talleyrand and may be dated, well enough, from the year 1798."

[5]Attention should be called to the fact that an important group of documents relating to this question, which once existed in the Spanish archives but apparently has never been used by any historian, has disappeared. It was called the *expediente de la Luisiana*, and there are several references to it in the correspondence of the period preserved in the Sección de Estado of the Archivo Histórico Nacional at Madrid; but Sr. Campillo, who has long been the chief of that section and is now director of the archives as well, states that after a long and careful search he has been unable to find it. The present writer also searched for it on two occasions (1929 and 1933), but with no better success. He believes, however, that the discovery of the lost *expediente* would not require any material alteration of the present account of the retrocession.

[6]An excellent article by Arthur S. Aiton, "The Diplomacy of the Louisiana Cession," *American Historical Review*, 36 (1930-1931): 701-20, shows that, contrary to the opinion long held by historians, France surrendered Louisiana with reluctance and Spain was eager to acquire it.

[7]See the works of Guyot and Renaut cited above, note 4.

[8]Archivo Histórico Nacional (Madrid), Sección de Estado, MS. volume entitled "Actas del Supremo Consejo de Estado," entry for December 29, 1794. These archives will hereafter be referred to as AHN, Est. See also Arthur Preston Whitaker, *The Spanish-American Frontier, 1783-1795* (Boston, 1927), chapters 12-14.

[9]Ibid., 216-20.

[10]Dhermand to Delacroix, Madrid, December 21, 1795, deciphered copy, Archives du ministère des Affaires étrangères (Paris), Correspondance politique, Espagne, vol. 638, ff. 267-269; Roume's reflections on the proposed exchange, Madrid, December 20, 1795, ibid., États-Unis, Supplément, vol. 7, ff. 28-30.

[11]Renaut, "La question," 149, 150, and 211 (text of the article relating to Louisiana); Guyot, *Le Directoire*, 239-43.

[12]See note 4 references to Turner and Fugier.

[13]Arthur P. Whitaker, "Godoy's Knowledge of the Terms of Jay's Treaty," *American Historical Review*, 35 (1929-1930): 804-10. See also Samuel Flagg Bemis, *Pinckney's Treaty* (Baltimore, 1926), 333-35, 348.

[14]Godoy to the Queen, September 26, 1798, August 2, 1799, and May 3, 1801; to the king, October 29, 1798, AHN, Est., legajo 2821. This *legajo* contains a valuable series of private letters from Godoy to the king and queen, most of them belonging to the period 1798-1808.

[15]Article cited in note 13 above.

[16]Pérignon to Godoy, January 1, 1797, with a marginal note by Godoy dated January 3, 1797, AHN, Est., legajo 3891, *expediente* no. 3; Godoy to Pérignon, January 5, 1797, draft, ibid., legajo 3896 bis.

[17]Pérignon to the minister of foreign affairs, Aranjuez, May 24, 1797, Arch. Aff. Étr., États-Unis, sup., vol.7, f. 75; the Prince of the Peace to the French ambassador, Aranjuez, March 11, 1797, copy ibid., Espagne, sup., vol. 18, f. 114.

[18]Letter dated San Ildefonso, August 14, 1797, no. 37 (transcript in the Library of Congress), Archivo del ministerio de estado (Madrid).

[19]Pérignon to Delacroix, Madrid, July 20, 1797, enclosing a copy of a note from Godoy dated July 19, Arch. Aff. Étr., Espagne, sup., vol. 18, f. 152; Guyot, *Le Directoire*, 409-29.

[20]Draft of a memoir by Talleyrand, Paris, September 18, 1797, Arch. Aff., Espagne, sup., vol. 18, f. 184; memoir by the Prince of the Peace, September 29, 1797, ibid., f. 195.

[21]For the purpose of the present article it is not necessary to inquire into Godoy's reasons for surrendering the posts. This question, together with others alluded to in the text, will be discussed in the forthcoming book mentioned above, note 1.

[22]Talleyrand to Truguet, April 21, 1798, draft, Arch. Aff. Étr., États-Unis, sup., vol. 7, f. 105; report by Talleyrand to the Directory , ibid., Espagne, vol. 652, f. 203. Talleyrand's memorial is in AHN, Est., legajo 4018.

[23]Saavedra to Azara, Madrid, July 2, 1798, ibid., Azara to Talleyrand, Paris, July 20, 1798, Arch. Aff. Étr., Espagne, vol. 653, f. 126.

[24]Azara to Saavedra, Paris, May 27, 1798, no. 2; Saavedra to Azara, Aranjuez, June 4, 1798, draft, AHN, Est., legajo 4018.

[25]June 19, 1798, dispatch no. 15, ibid.

[26]Azara to Talleyrand, Paris, August 10, 1798, Arch. Aff. Étr., Espagne., vol. 653, f. 243.

[27]Fugier, *Napoléon*, 1:108.

[28]At any rate, the writer has not found any evidence of such an effort in the French diplomatic correspondence for January-June, 1800, though he was aided in his search by N. M. Miller Surrey's useful *Calendar of Manuscripts in Paris Archives and Libraries relating to the History of the Mississippi Valley to 1803* (Washington, DC, 1926-1928).

[29]Hervas to Urquijo, two secret letters, both dated Paris, June 11, 1800, one relating to a loan and the other to Parma, AHN, Est., legajo 3963. For Hervas's mission to Paris, see Fugier, *Napoléon,* 1:99-109.

[30]Urquijo to Múzquiz, Aranjuez, June 22, 1800, copy, inclosing copies of the two letters of the same date to Hervas, AHN, Est., legajo 3963. Portions of the confidential letter to Hervas have been published in Andrés Muriel, *Historia de Carlos IV* (Madrid, 1894), 6:69, 70, and (in French translation) in Fugier, 1:109, but the English translation given in the text of the present article is the first publication of the whole passage relating to Louisiana. The italics are inserted. Henry Adams, whose book was published five years before Muriel's, was apparently unaware of the existence of the letter. Muriel accepts it as a sincere statement of Spanish policy (as does Fugier), but argues that Urquijo was mistaken in saying that Louisiana cost Spain more than it was worth.

[31]Alquier's report of the interview is in Arch. Aff. Étr., Espagne, vol. 659, ff. 244-47, dispatch no. 53, San Ildefonso, August 7, 1800. France's reasons for shifting the negotiation from Paris to Madrid, thus eliminating Hervas, do not fall within the scope of this paper.

[32]Alquier to Talleyrand, Madrid, July 3, 1800, deciphered copy, ibid., f. 133-34. Although Alquier was an unreliable gossip, this story is probably true, for Godoy's private letters to the king and queen (see above, n. 14) show that the favorite's technique consisted of a judicious mixture of flattery and plain speaking.

[33]Manuel Godoy, *Cuenta dada de su vida política* (Madrid, 1909), 3:53-62. This is the Spanish version of Godoy's well-known memoirs, which have also been published in French and English. The present writer has not found the original manuscript of his opinion on the treaty, but that is not surprising, since his subsequent arrest and exile led to the disappearance of many of his papers. There seems to be no good reason to doubt the authenticity of the report, which is not questioned by Henry Adams. In the first place, if it were a fabrication, Godoy would probably have sought to make it more creditable to himself by pretending that he had opposed the retrocession unconditionally. In the second place, as stated in the text, the report is in harmony with his policy as set forth in documents of unquestionable authenticity.

[34]The text has been published several times. Perhaps it can be consulted most conveniently in Renaut, "La question," 217-18.

[35]Urquijo to Berthier, San Ildefonso, September 26, 1800, Arch. Att. Étr., États-Unis, sup., vol. 7, ff. 144-151.

[36]This point is developed at length in the book mentioned above, note 1. *Cf.* Channing, *History of the United States*, 4:310-11.

[37]The transfer of Louisiana to France took place at New Orleans on November 30, 1803. The Spanish commissioners appointed to effect it had not received any order on the subject from the court since the sale of Louisiana by France; but, informed that the United States would seize the province by force if Spain attempted to keep it, they assumed the responsibility of delivering it to France under the authority conferred on them by the royal order of October 15, 1802, as follows: "The king has decided to renounce all right to protest against the sale of Louisiana made by France to the United States of America, and it is therefore his royal will that you direct the commissioners for the delivery of the said province to execute it without any protest whatever" (Archivo de Indias, Seville, Papeles de Cuba, legajo 1737).

[38]Fugier, *Napoléon*, 1:129; Renaut, "La question," 259-60. Adams erroneously states that the sixth article of this convention "provided that the retrocession of Louisiana should be carried out," Channing, *History of the United States*, 1:372.

[39]Godoy to the Queen, Madrid, October 11, 1801, AHN, Est., legajo 2821.

[40]Godoy to the Queen, April 30, 1803, ibid.

PART II
Spanish Governors of Louisiana

"THE GOOD WINE OF BORDEAUX": ANTONIO DE ULLOA*

John Preston Moore

"For myself, I am of the opinion that at all times, one great portion of the events of the world are attributable to very general facts, and another to special influences. These two kinds of causes are always in operation, their proportion only varies."[1] Although Alexis de Tocqueville's dichotomy of causal relationships still has validity, a revolution, even though abortive or incomplete, is a far more complex and intricate phenomenon. It is rather the result of a totality of forces operating in the past, some more obvious than others. The revolt of the French colonists in October, 1768, was a great degree the culmination of two clearly distinguishable elements: an adverse reaction by a majority of the population to unsatisfactory conditions and the activities of a small but determined group of merchant-planters.

The roots of popular disaffection were numerous. There was a malaise that the colony had developed in the process of adjustment to the sovereignty of another power. A sentimental attachment to France remained despite amiable overtures by the Spanish authorities. English observers in West Florida remarked on more than one occasion on the hostility of Frenchmen toward Spaniards.[2] This suspicion of foreigners was strengthened by the natural individualism of the frontiersmen, accentuated by neglect by the French Crown during the Seven Years' War.[3] The widespread unpopularity of the Spanish governor was another intangible factor in the situation, and the state of the economy contributed to the dissatisfaction. Trade declined owing to the uncertainties of foreign markets. Inflation, caused by shortages of consumer goods and an unsound currency, flourished unchecked. As in all periods of economic recession, these conditions bore most heavily on the lowest strata of society. The inability of the Spanish regime to meet its debts dimmed the prospect of a brighter future. In sum, a climate highly propitious to the formation of an anti-Spanish plot had developed in the colony.

But unfavorable political and economic conditions are generally not sufficient to bring about a revolution. Crane Brinton discards the theory of "spontaneous growth" as a

*Reprinted by permission of Louisiana State University Press from *Revolt in Louisiana: The Spanish Occupation, 1766-1770*, by John Preston Moore.

complete explanation. His analogy of the garden and the gardener incorporates both the environment and the planner: We must "hold that revolutions do grow from seeds sown by men who want change, and that these men do a lot of skillful gardening, but that the gardeners are not working against Nature, but rather in a soil and climate propitious to their work; and that the final fruits represent a collaboration between men and Nature."[4]

In the uprising of 1768 the catalytic element was the stance of a powerful, discontented group of traders and landowners. Eventually, they reached the conclusion that their economic interests were imperiled by the assimilation of Louisiana into the Spanish mercantile system. The decrees of September, 1766, and March, 1768, foreshadowed a limitation on both legal and illegal trade. Although Louisiana received some exemptions, it would be difficult for the colony to sell its produce on the Spanish markets and to import from the mother country the manufactured articles necessary for existence. Governor Ulloa's efforts to put the lid on contraband were well known. From time to time members of this clique had protested against the decrees and acts of the Spanish regime. Convinced that their status was threatened, they favored force as a means of changing the direction of Spanish policy. Their program of action, basically economic in motivation, would be ostensibly defended on the respectable grounds of Spanish injustice and of flagrant violation of the laws and mores of the province.

The ringleaders of the cabal that might have charted a new destiny for Louisiana were two prominent colonial figures, the commissary [Denis-Nicolas] Foucault and the attorney general [Nicolas Chauvin de] La Frénière. It would be difficult to assess the proportionate contribution of each to the uprising. As a former French official, Foucault had considerable prestige among the officers of the old regime and among those engaged in commercial activities. Knowing the interests of the merchants, he worked to preserve their prosperity by retaining the ties to France and the French islands. Like previous French colonial officials, he had selfish interests which would suffer in the decline and collapse of the economy. If Spanish accusations were correct, he had profited by countenancing smuggling and by taking bribes in the purchase of supplies for French officials. He stood to gain greatly by the redemption of the paper currency at par value. Having luxurious tastes, he maintained a well-appointed establishment in the capital, but, since his income did not match his desires, his indebtedness was considerable at the time of O'Reilly's arrival in the colony.[5] Shrewd, energetic, but unprincipled, he was an indispensable part of the leadership.

Popular with the crowd because of his handsome appearance and his eloquence at public gatherings, La Frénière was likewise an essential element in the leadership. His personality, unlike that of Foucault, had a charismatic quality. Judging by his speeches and his actions, there was some idealism in his makeup. It is possible that some of the thinking of the Enlightenment directed his conduct. He had a sympathy for the rights of colonists, which, he believed, were threatened by the policies of the Crown. But like his fellow conspirator, he had personal reasons for disliking the new regime. Rumors of the forthcoming suppression of the Superior Council by the Spanish, in which his position as attorney general would be abolished, had circulated widely throughout the colony. That he used his office to advance his own interests was probably true. According to [Antonio de] Ulloa [first Spanish governor of Louisiana], the attorney general was especially embittered over the disapproval by the Crown of a contract that he had proposed to import Negro slaves on exceedingly profitable terms for those involved.[6] His influence with the mass of the people and with the mercantile and landed groups made him a natural leader of the opposition.

It is believed that the initial scene of the conspiracy was the home of Madame Marie Louise de Pradel, the widow of Chevalier Jean de Pradel. The day was sometime during the summer of 1768. The garden of her mansion, near the city and adjoining the property of La Frénière, was ideally located for the secret meetings of the plotters. Involved in a clandestine affair with Madame Pradel, Foucault was accustomed to spend much time in her home.[7] Here he, La Frénière, and others hostile to Spanish policy hatched their scheme with consummate skill for the expulsion of the Spanish governor.

One of the first moves of the conspirators was to dispatch an undercover mission to Brigadier General [Frederick] Haldimand, who was in command at Pensacola, to seek support from the British in the effort to liberate the province. The British general, however, rejected their proposal for the moment, unwilling to be a party in an uprising against the Spanish and acknowledging insufficient military strength for the purpose.[8]

In retrospect, it is incredible that Ulloa had no inkling of the formation of a conspiracy until it was almost too late to act. In later defending his ignorance, he credited the secrecy to the family ties and connections of La Frénière, who was related by blood and marriage to many of the important families of the colony. Within this intimate circle, secrets could be kept.[9] Nevertheless, the fact that significant aspects of the plot did not get out until the last week before its occurrence points to the circumspection and intense concern of the participants for its success.

The timing of the revolt was the last days of October. It might have occurred earlier during May, when the general tenor of the unpopular decree was known in the city. One is forced at this point to speculate on the reasons for the delay. Apparently, the idea did not really germinate until the mercantile community had ample evidence that Spain intended to merge the economy of Louisiana with that of the imperial system, with insufficient concessions to ensure the prosperity of the merchants, fur traders, and planters. With the growing indebtedness of the regime, there seemed little hope for generous subsidies essential to the well-being of the colony. Moreover, if popular demonstrations in New Orleans were needed to pressure the government, the two most likely groups for this purpose, the Germans and the Acadians, would be more disposed to act when their crops had been harvested. Perhaps one cannot dismiss entirely the debilitating effect of the "long, hot summer." At any rate, postponement past October might be fatal to the execution of the scheme. It was known that Spanish troops were being assembled in Havana to permanently occupy Louisiana. If these soldiers were allowed to reach New Orleans, the chances for success would be remote, if not nil. It was necessary, therefore, to act first.

What had held up the organization and dispatch of an impressive Spanish command to Louisiana? Its presence might well have been the key to Spanish control. At the outset [the marqués de] Grimaldi [first Spanish secretary of state] had counted on the enlistment of the French troops stationed in the colony under [Charles Philippe] Aubry. When this failed, no other recourse remained but to form a battalion of Spanish soldiers to supplement the meager force in the province. In December, 1766, Ulloa had notified the secretary of state of the size of the force that he believed was requisite for the occupation, some seven hundred men with various pieces of artillery.

The organization and transportation of a contingent of troops from Spain to Louisiana remained unfulfilled by the end of October, 1768. At fault was the characteristic procrastination of the Crown, which had failed to react promptly in this emergency, as it had failed similarly in the dispatch of the *situado* [subsidy]. Although Grimaldi should bear some responsibility, the separation of Louisiana from the administration of the rest of the Indies may have further complicated the channels of bureaucratic communication. Despite repeated requests for troops by Ulloa to Grimaldi and [Antonio María] Bucareli [captain-general of Cuba], the enlistment for the province proceeded slowly.[10] By the end of the spring of 1768 some soldiers had arrived in Cuba. In June, Grimaldi notified [Julián de] Arriaga [minister of the Indies] that the remainder of the troops were gathered in Cádiz for embarkation, some of them being ironically of French origin, and were scheduled to sail in mail-carrying vessels to the assembly point in Havana. The desperate economic conditions of the summer prompted Ulloa to appeal again to the secretary of state for haste in the dispatch of troops "because each day new reasons for dissatisfaction and unhappiness arise from this mixed government." At the instigation of Bucareli, Ulloa agreed to await the completion of the cadre in Havana before its transportation to Louisiana.[11] In December, 1768, the ranks of the battalion were still unfilled.[12] Without the additional Spanish troops on the scene, the execution of the conspiracy was far easier.

In the early fall the organizers of the plot laid the groundwork for wider support. To win adherents, La Frénière and Pierre Caresse drew up a memorial containing a list of grievances against Ulloa. Once enough signatures had been procured, it would be presented to the Superior Council for discussion and approval.[13] Toward the end of October, many merchants and ship operators had signed the document, which also called for the expulsion of the Spanish governor.

With startling speed, the conspiracy against the Spanish governor, so long in the making unfolded. On October 21 a colonist, disgruntled over an unfavorable decision of the Superior Council in his business affairs, confided to Ulloa rumors of a plot. Unwilling to give credence to a report from this apparently prejudiced source, the governor took no action until the twenty-fifth, when he learned elsewhere of dissension among the Germans. He immediately dispatched Gilbert Antoine de St. Maxent, a reliable ally of the Spanish, to the Côte des Allemands, or the German Coast, with enough funds to payoff the debts incurred by the regime. Upon his arrival there he was seized by those involved in the conspiracy and imprisoned until its successful outcome.[14]

There was little doubt now that the situation was serious. Upon learning of the treatment of St. Maxent, Governor Ulloa realized for the first time the strength of the opposition to his government. He sent word at once to Aubry of what was happening, conferred with him at length, but obtained no promise of energetic action to suppress the movement. The French governor was apparently unconvinced that events would go beyond a formal protest against Spanish policies. Moreover, the few French troops, only ninety in the city and these mainly old veterans incapable of real combat, militated against adoption of a strong stand. Nor was Ulloa's miniscule force in a position to curb the insurgents, since practically all the soldiers were at posts in the interior and of the sailors only ten or twelve were aboard the *Volante*. Thus the combined French and Spanish forces in the capital totaling only about one hundred men were too small to deal with a large-scale uprising.[15]

Events had now reached a crucial stage for the conspirators. The concentration of rebels in the city was imperative in order to overturn the regime before troops could be sent from Havana or recalled from the frontier posts to create a counterbalance. A sizable popular demonstration in the capital was essential. According to a prearranged plan, two captains of the militia, [Louis] Judice and André[*sic*] Veret, who had been won over by La Frénière, turned to the Acadians for backing. They falsely told the settlers that the Spanish governor had a large amount of money in the treasury, some of which could be used to redeem the paper currency brought by the Acadians from Canada. Although their money had lost all value long before, they were told that it would be honored in Louisiana. Despite the Spanish assistance in their homesteading, they succumbed to the propaganda and believed that their presence in New Orleans would persuade Ulloa to act in their behalf.[16] No doubt some of the recent immigrants still cherished a resentment against their forced settlement near Natchez.

Propaganda was likewise effective among the Germans living on the farms above the city. [Joseph Antoine] Villeré, commandant of the district, convinced the farmers that the Spanish governor had no intention of paying for the fruits and vegetables purchased during the year. To see that all of their bills were met, they should appear as a group in New Orleans and present their demands. Although the debt amounted to a small sum, the credulous colonists felt impelled to act in what they thought was their best interest. Both groups were simply waiting for a signal from their leaders to march to the city.[17]

To Ulloa, the only possibility of coping with the insurrectionists lay with Aubry.[18] On October 27 the French commander, reassured of the loyalty of his force after a conference with his officers and men, confronted Foucault and La Frénière, recognized openly as the ringleaders. They informed him that they intended to force Ulloa to leave the colony "with the least possible disturbance, because things had gone so far that it was impossible to draw back."[19] Other Spanish officials might remain, evidently to ensure the continuance of the partial subsidy that was necessary for the existence of the colony. Aubry protested their decision but did nothing to halt the revolt.

In the development of the movement, the confrontation between Aubry and the conspirators was decisive. In a revolution a turning point is generally reached when an illegal force faces duly constituted authority. In defiance of Aubry's protest, Foucault and La Frénière refused to dissolve their following and abandon their plan to expel the Spanish governor. At the moment the French commander made no move to arrest the traitors. His unwillingness to apply force against the rebels was naturally interpreted as a sign of weakness by the insurgents and ultimately meant the success of the uprising. On the other hand, Aubry's inaction in the crisis might be looked upon by the Spanish government as evidence of disloyalty. Such a compromising position would surely require an explanation in the future. To himself, his justification for a disinclination to act boldly was his tiny command and the belief that his status as a French officer, soon to return to France, required no positive move that might incite bloodshed. Humiliated at being forced to back down, Aubry now endeavored to put the best possible light on events. He maintained thereafter that he had won a partial victory by retaining Spanish sovereignty and avoiding a resort to arms. But he had had no success in disbanding the colonial militia, which had been assembled by the insurrectionists. Five companies, two of which consisted of Germans and Acadians, were in the city under the command of Pierre Marquis, who had been promoted by the Superior Council to the rank of colonel at Foucault's and La Frénière's suggestion.[20]

Although still hopeful of successful negotiations by Aubry, Ulloa made his own preparations against assault by the rebels. He ordered all military personnel to go aboard the *Volante* and invited those of Spanish birth and sympathizers among the French population to join in the defense. The packet was readied for action, with her decks cleared and her cannon loaded with shot and pointed at the city. Actually, the ship's position was advantageous. Because of the fall of the river at this time of year, the heavy batteries in the city could not be brought to bear on the vessel, yet the *Volante's* guns controlled the approaches from the levee to the water's edge. For observation, the militia occupied a two-masted brig, anchored off the bow of the *Volante*. To reinforce his small Spanish contingent, Ulloa asked Aubry's permission to release from the guardhouse twenty Spanish soldiers, who had been imprisoned as deserters, but this was refused on the strange grounds that it might be a provocation to the conspirators.[21] Orders were given by Ulloa for the destruction of important papers and records in case of hostilities. Steps were thus taken to counter any foreseeable acts of violence.

Events now took a more critical turn. On the afternoon of the twenty-eighth, some five hundred Acadians and Germans poured into New Orleans. Urged by the leaders of the conspiracy to make a show of force, they aspired to obtain the consent of the governor to pay the bills and to redeem the worthless Acadian currency. They now reinforced the companies of militia commanded by Marquis. Once in the city, all the insurgents congregated at the home of François Chauvin de Léry, another member of the cabal, who supplied them with wine and muskets. The "good Bordeaux" removed their apprehensiveness and qualms over the consequences of revolutionary acts and stiffened their resolve to back their leaders. For many, the long, tiring march from the farms and the excitement of the occasion prompted overindulgence and intoxication—the ideal moment to bring down the curtain on the performance if only there had been enough Spanish troops at hand, as Ulloa subsequently commented. But this was not to be.

The injection of the popular element was essential for the execution of the plot. At this juncture, to assume more control of the capital, Marquis assumed the authority to patrol the streets with the militia. The cannon at the gates of the city, having been spiked the night before by the insurgents, presented no threat. Aubry, angry and alarmed at the possibility of bloodshed in the streets, hastened to the house of the governor to persuade him to take refuge for the time being aboard the *Volante*. With his wife pregnant and a very small child, Ulloa could hardly be accused of cowardice in avoiding an unequal confrontation with the rebels. As additional precautions, Aubry ordered twenty soldiers to join the Spanish force on the packet, thirty others to guard the central square, and the remainder to be ready to face the Superior Council.[22] In the meantime, he made a final appeal to Foucault and La Frénière to desist from their plans. Whether his remonstrances were as vigorous and outspoken as he subsequently asserted is doubtful, owing to his overly cautious and uninspiring leadership.[23]

On this same day, October 28, at Foucault's request, the Superior Council met to consider the petition signed by a large number of merchants and planters, urging the expulsion of the governor and the restoration of all rights and liberties. In the absence of some councilors it was decided to postpone action on the memorial until the next day. Meanwhile, the council turned over the petition to Huchet de Kernion and Piot de Launay to be studied and reported on at the next meeting. To provide more adequate representation, the leaders recommended the election of six supernumerary members. When this had been complied with, the council adjourned.[24]

The following day the die was cast. At nine o'clock on October 29 the eighteen council members, including the six new representatives, assembled again at Foucault's residence, now the accustomed meeting place, to act on the memorial against the Spanish governor. At Ulloa's insistence, Aubry attended the session in a last-minute effort to convince the assembly of its stupidity and folly in proceeding against the sovereignty of Spain.[25] As part of the scheme of the conspirators, groups of militia and citizenry roamed the streets nearby, shouting defiantly their full support of the council's action. There would be no disruption of the conciliar session by Aubry's soldiers.

As the most significant document of the rebellion, the minutes of the October 29 session of the Superior Council deserve special examination.[26] They contain a full indictment of the Spanish regime, as given in the remonstrance of the merchants and planters, the impassioned harangue by La Frénière in support of the accusations, and the final judgment of the council to remove the executive authority. To the conciliar decree were appended Foucault's reservations and Aubry's protests.

Since the petition of the commercial classes deals with the fundamental question at the heart of the uprising, its recommendations are worthy of note. The arguments to abolish restrictions and restore trade with France and the French islands are difficult to refute.[27] However, to apply the concept of free trade to any part of America might be considered singular in an age dominated by mercantilistic thinking. The petition urges the council to take five important steps to improve the well-being of the colony:

> 1. That the privileges and exemptions which the colony has enjoyed, since the cession made by the Company [of the Indies] to His Most Christian Majesty, be maintained, without any innovations being suffered to interrupt their course and disturb the security of the citizens.
> 2. That passports and permissions be granted from the governor and commissioners of His Most Christian Majesty to such captains of vessels as shall set sail from the colony to any portion of France or American whatever.
> 3. That any ship from any port of France or America whatever, shall have free entrance into the river, whether it sail directly for the colony, or only put in accidentally, according to the custom which has hitherto prevailed.
> 4. That freedom of trade with all nations under the government of His Most Christian Majesty be granted to all the citizens, in conformity to the King's orders to the late M. D'Abbadie, registered in the archives of the city, and likewise in conformity to the letter of His Grace the Duke of Choiseul, addressed to the same M. D'Abbadie, and dated the 9th of February, 1766.
> 5. That M. Ulloa be declared to have in many points infringed and usurped the authority hitherto possessed by the government and council of the colony because all the laws, ordinances, and customs direct, that said authority shall not be exercised by any officer until he shall have complied with all the formalities prescribed, and this condition M. Ulloa has not observed.[28]

In the deliberations and discussion of the council, La Frénière played a major role. With his commanding physical presence, his ringing voice, and his natural eloquence, the attorney general argued convincingly for the expulsion of the Spanish governor. If Foucault was in a roughly general way the Robespierre of the revolution, La Frénière was its Danton. The legal reasoning in his harangue followed two main lines: (1) the competence of the Superior Council as a judicial body, or Parlement, to receive grievances against the governor; and (2) the validity of the complaints of the mercantile elements and other segments of the population. His exposition of these points was comprehensive and emotional. Interspersed with derogatory references to the personality of the governor, it had at times a psychotic quality. His peroration, provided in part below, is to a large extent a reiteration of the demands of the merchants and traders:

> Having maturely weighed all this, I require in behalf of the King:
>
> That the sentences pronounced by the councilors nominated for this purpose, and put in execution against Mess. Cadis and Leblanc, subjects of France, be declared encroachments upon the authority of our Sovereign Lord, the King, and destructive of the respect due to his supreme justice, seated in the Superior Council, in as much as

> they violate the laws, forms, and customs of the colony, confirmed and guaranteed by the solemn act of cession.
>
> That M. Ulloa be declared to have violated our laws, forms and customs, and the orders of His Catholic Majesty, in relation to the act of cession, as it appears by his letter, dated from Havana, on the 10th of July, 1765.
>
> That he be declared usurper of illegal authority, by causing subjects of France to be punished, and oppressed, without having previously complied with the laws, forms, and customs, in having his powers, titles, and provisions registered by the Supreme Council, with the copy of the act of cession.
>
> That M. Ulloa, Commissioner of His Catholic Majesty, be enjoined to leave the colony in the frigate in which he came, without delay, to avoid accidents or new clamors, and to go and give an account of his conduct to his Catholic Majesty; and, with regard to the different posts established by the said Mr. Ulloa, that he be desired to leave in writing such orders as he shall think necessary; that he be declared responsible for all the events which he might have foreseen; and that Mess. Aubry and Foucault be requested, and even summoned, in the name of our Sovereign Lord, the King, to continue to govern and administer the colony as heretofore.[29]

The conciliar resolution for the expulsion of the governor is the third and final section of the recorded proceedings. It repeats, in the main, the accusations and charges of the attorney general and the mercantile group and stipulates the interim restoration of French authority, although granting permission to the lesser Spanish officials, [Esteban] Gayarré, [Juan Joseph de] Loyola, and Martín Navarro, to remain until orders were received from Madrid. As this is a lengthy document, only salient parts are selected:

> The Council . . . has declared and declares that the sentences rendered by the councilors nominated by M. Ulloa and carried into execution against Mess. Cadis and Leblanc, subjects of France, to be encroachments upon the authority of our Sovereign Lord, the King, and destructive of the respect due to his supreme justice vested in his Superior Council; has declared and declares him an usurper of illegal authority in causing subjects of France to be punished and oppressed, without having previously complied with the laws and forms, having neither produced his powers, titles and provisions, nor caused them to be registered, and that, to the prejudice of the privileges insured to them by the said act of cession: and to prevent any violence of the populace, and avoid any dangerous tumult, the Council, with its usual prudence, finds itself obliged to enjoin, as in fact it enjoins, Mr. Ulloa to quit the colony allowing him only the space of three days, either in the frigate of his Catholic Majesty in which he came, or in whatever vessel he shall think proper, and go and give an account of his conduct to his Catholic Majesty. It has likewise ordained and it ordains that, with regard to the posts established by him in the upper part of the river, he shall leave such orders as he judges expedient, making him at the same time responsible for all the events which he might have foreseen. It has requested and requests Mess. Aubry and Foucault, and even summoned them in the name of our Sovereign Lord, the King, to continue to command and govern the colony as they did heretofore. At the same time, it expressly forbids all those who fit out vessels, and all captains, of ships, to despatch any vessel with any other passport than that of Mr. Foucault, who is to do the office of intendant commissary; it has also ordered and

> orders, that the taking possession for his Catholic Majesty can neither be proposed nor attempted by any means, without new orders from his most Christian Majesty; that, in consequence, Mr. Ulloa shall embark in the space of three days in whatever ship he shall think proper.[30]

Despite La Frénière's efforts, the two most prominent members of the council, the French governor and the commissary, dissented from its judgment. Outvoted, almost ignored, Aubry insisted nevertheless on having his protest registered in the formal account of the proceedings: "I protest against the decree of the Council, which dismisses Don Antonio de Ulloa from this colony; their most Christian and Catholic Majesties will be offended at the treatment inflicted on a person of his character; and notwithstanding the small force which I have at my disposal, I would, with all my might, oppose his departure, were I not apprehensive of endangering his life, as well as the lives of all the Spaniards in this country."[31] Having voiced his full opposition to the action of the council, Aubry stalked from the chamber. He had given due warning to the representatives of the impending wrath of the two European monarchs.

On the other hand, Foucault's dissent proposed a modification of the action to be taken against the Spanish governor. Although the Superior Council might suspend Ulloa's authority, it was beyond its power and jurisdiction to force his departure from the colony. From a practical standpoint, Ulloa would be exercising wisdom in sailing for Cuba, as the commissary had already suggested. It is clear that Foucault was aware of the possible adverse repercussion in the courts of Madrid and Versailles. Secretly in full sympathy with the aims of the conspirators, he nevertheless posed as a moderate, an official of the old regime who was acting in accord with his orders from France and with the legal prescriptions and formalities surrounding the assumption of authority in the colony. As the treasurer of the French province, he understood the extreme need for Spanish pesos to maintain the government. So that his position might not be construed in the future as having been fully consonant with that of the rebels, he had his vote incorporated in the record:

> The intention of the King, our master, being that the colony should belong, fully and without reserve, to his Catholic Majesty, by virtue of the treaty of cession, my opinion is, that none of the Spanish officers who have come here by order of their government, can be legally sent away; that, considering the causes of discontent enumerated in the petition of the citizens, and Ulloa's omission to take possession of the colony with the usual formalities, he, the said Ulloa, should be prohibited from exercising the powers of Governor, in anything relating to the French subjects now in Louisiana, or who may come thereto, hereafter, either as colonists or not: and that everything appertaining to the commerce carried on by the French and other nations with the colony, be regulated as it was before his arrival; nevertheless, that all the officers of the Spanish administration should continue their respective functions, in order to provide for the supplies necessary to the town and to the posts, for the payment of all salaries, and for the expenses of the French troops which will continue to serve, and of the works which will be deemed proper; this, until the decision of the

> courts of France and Spain be known, reserving to the delegates of the people the right to address his Catholic Majesty in the most respectful and lawful manner, in order to obtain the privileges they claim.[32]

Of the three sections of the proceedings, La Frénière's oration bears most scrutiny, since his ideas and legal arguments were embodied in the conciliar resolution. His reasoning was intended to provide a legal justification for the removal of the governor. Was the Superior Council competent to judge the constitutionality of the Spanish regime? Although Ulloa had addressed a courteous letter to the council in July, 1765, announcing his proposed arrival in the colony, he never accepted this body as one with important judicial or legislative powers and secretly worked for its abolition. Anyone who has examined the correspondence of the French minister of marine with the colony must conclude that Versailles looked on the governor and the commissary as the real instruments of royal authority. As for the Spanish obligation to preserve the customs, laws, and institutions of the colony, it should be recalled that the cession was unconditional. On the lack of fulfillment of the formalities of possession, a proclamation of authority in the capital and raising the flag of the Spanish Bourbons, La Frénière was right. But in actuality, in the acceptance of Spanish funds and general acknowledgement of orders and decrees, Louisiana was a Spanish dependency. Hence, many of his arguments were without foundation.

One is impressed by the venom and antipathy directed throughout the controversy toward the Spanish governor by his enemies. The terms "tyrant," "oppressor," and "usurper" crop up frequently in the documents and records of the revolt. According to his accusers, he was guilty not only of breaking the laws of the realm and of a pact between two sovereign powers, but also of behaving contrary to the mores and customs of the country. It would be difficult to gather evidence to uphold the condemnation by his critics of his character and behavior. The facts of his pre- and post-Louisiana career repudiate the charges of graft, excessive severity in enforcing decrees, and even moral dereliction implied by his opponents. What idiosyncracy in his conduct or putative expression of superiority was responsible for this unbridled assault on his personal character, one may never know. Popular irrationality of this nature occurs in all times, with variations only in intensity and duration. It was unquestionably an invidious reflection on the political and social conditions in Louisiana in the eighteenth century. Undoubtedly, the successful machinations against [Louis Billouart de] Kerlérec constituted a precedent for the removal of the Spanish official. Unchecked in the past, the leaders of the conspiracy turned to force as a solution to their economic and social ills.

Execution of the expulsion decree represented the last and irrevocable step in the unfolding of the revolt. Would the Spanish governor comply with an order from the Superior Council calling for his withdrawal from the colony within three days? In the minds of the plotters a show of military strength, combined with demonstrations by a hostile populace, would suffice to attain this goal. It is not inconceivable that the determined rebels would have resorted to force to remove Spanish authority. At 2:00

P.M. on October 29, the conciliar scribe delivered a copy of the order to Ulloa aboard the *Volante*. To celebrate the issuance of the decree, Foucault invited the council members to a repast in his apartment.[33] Meanwhile, units of the militia paraded in the streets, and groups of Germans and Acadians, either indulging their thirst anew or recovering from the effects of the heady wine of the night before, roamed unsteadily in various sectors of the city. Shouts of "Vive le roi" and "Vive Louis le bien-aimé" were heard, together with cries of "Vive le bon vin de Bordeaux" and "A bas le poison de Catalogne."[34] Faced with what seemed to be strong popular opposition, the Spanish governor capitulated. Without sufficient Spanish troops at hand, unable to count on the loyalty of the French regulars, and with his family a distinct liability in the event of hostilities, he had perhaps no alternative.[35] The Spanish commissary [Juan José de] Loyola was ordered to end the subsidy to the French officials and soldiers in the city and the outposts and to terminate the delivery of supplies to the Acadians and gifts to the Indians. Only at the solicitation of Aubry was any exception to be made.[36] Ulloa also issued orders for the Spanish troops to evacuate the outposts and return to Havana.

On November 1 Governor Ulloa took his last look at New Orleans. He did not know this, for he must have thought that he would return to the city with the expeditionary force in Havana to reoccupy the province. Accompanied by his family and some close advisers, including the Capuchins, he sailed down the river.[37] But it was on a French frigate, the *César*, which happened to be in New Orleans and was bound for Havana. The *Volante* unfortunately needed repairs and could not have made the trip across the gulf safely. According to Aubry, the commander of the French militia, Marquis, intended to escort Ulloa's ship to the sea and occupy Balize by ousting the Spanish garrison. Only by a dint of threats did Aubry avert this open insult and possible armed clash. It was the first occasion in which his orders had been obeyed by the militia. At Balize the French vessel halted, apparently to secure additional supplies for the voyage and await more favorable weather. News of the delay reached New Orleans and incited fears that the governor was simply stalling for time, until Havana could be notified and Spanish troops, already assembled in Cuba, could be dispatched in large numbers to suppress the movement. Before Marquis' militia could approach Balize, Ulloa and his entourage set sail. On December 3, after a voyage of over three weeks, described by one of the passengers as a "painful navigation," the governor and his party entered the harbor of the Cuban capital.[38]

So far the rebel cause had been victorious. In the expulsion of Governor Ulloa the insurgents had attained their immediate goal. Notwithstanding this success, the future was fraught with uncertainty, with the critical problems of setting up a viable, temporary regime and of reestablishing a permanent relationship with Spain and France.

Notes for "'The Good Wine of Bordeaux': Antonio de Ulloa"

[1]Alexis de Tocqueville, *Democracy in America,* abr., ed., and introd. Andrew Hacker (New York, 1864), 166.

[2]"I found from the first Frenchman to the most inferior of them a Determined & fixed hatred to the Spanish Nation & Government also a Resolution formed by many of them Especially the Merchts, to quit the Country and settle in our Colonies were they sure of meeting with Protection & that desire proceeds as they saw from a Certainty that when Don Ulloa takes possession he means according to the Customs in the Spanish Colonies to make a Monopoly of Whole Commerce and make the rest of the Merchts. trade with them, they say further that Spanish justice to Individuals will not be conducted with that impartiality that they had been used to under the French Government." See Marsh to Haldimand, November 20, 1767, in Clarence W. Alvord and Clarence E. Carter, eds., *Trade and Politics, 1767-1769,* Collections of the Illinois State Historical Library, 16 (Springfield, 1921): 114.

[3]Ulloa emphasized this strongly in his account of the rebellion to Grimaldi: "The inhabitants of that colony live in an independence so general that once a man retires to his home he sees himself as absolute lord without subjection to any authority. From this is born the liberty that reigns among them to do whatever they wish and treat their superior with so little respect that he is governor in name only." See "Noticia de los acaecimientos de la Luisiana," fol. 27.

[4]Crane Brinton, *The Anatomy of Revolution* (revised ed., New York, 1952), 93.

[5]Although discounting the traditional feud between the governor and the commissary, Aubry probably had good reason to complain of his rival's favored status. "I pay dear for the rent of a house," he wrote Choiseul, "while M. Foucault leads a happy, tranquil existence; he has Negroes, cattle, land, coaches and is lodged in a palace that the king has built for him and his employees. God forbid that I am a person of such low character to envy his fate, but I am angry that he wishes to give me only my expenses and that he refuses me the necessary money to maintain with dignity the position that I hold. . . so that I find myself obliged to borrow from and use the rest of my patrimony." See Aubry to Choiseul, April 24, 1765, in C13A45, Colonies, Archives Nationales, Paris, hereinafter cited as AN (transcripts in Library of Congress). An inventory of Foucault's personal papers in 1769 disclosed debts of 60,000 livres. A judgment against Foucault's property was instituted by the *procureur des biens vacans,* or purveyor of unclaimed property, who declared that Foucault had been compelled to turn over approximately 36,000 livres in old billets "to avoid being forced to resign his position." See Aubry to Praslin, October 6, 1769, and September 19, 1769, both in C13A49, Colonies, AN.

[6]"Noticia de los acaecimientos de la Luisiana," fol. 23r.

[7]His relations with her were probably responsible for his refusal to compel the Superior Council to render a judgment in a suit brought by her daughters in France against family property in Louisiana. He ignored letters from Choiseul and Praslin, demanding that action be taken on claims of the Mademoiselles Pradel against their mother. See Choiseul to Foucault, January 5, 1766, and Praslin to Foucault, July 21, 1767, both in Lettres Envoyées, Colonies, B, AN.

[8]Vicente Casado Rodríguez, *Primeros años de dominacíon española en la Luisiana* (Madrid, 1942), 142-43.

[9]Our knowledge of the conspiracy is based to a considerable extent on the facts obtained from a cross-examination of the accused and witnesses and from the confessions of the accused in the trial initiated by O'Reilly in September, 1769. See Proceso incoado contra los sublevados, in Leg. 2543, Audiencia de Sto. Domingo, Archivo General de Indies, hereinafter cited as AGI. A copy of the essential documents is to be found in Leg. 20,854, Consejo de Indias, Archivo Histórico Nacional, Madrid, hereinafter cited as AHN. That the conspiracy in its inception was a kind of family affair seems plausible. La Frénière was married to the granddaughter of Charles Frederick d'Arensburg, a Swedish nobleman and military adventurer, who joined the Company of the Indies in 1721 and migrated to Louisiana. Arensburg's daughters married into the Noyan, Bienville, Masan and Villeré families. Léry, and the captain of a militia company, François Labarre, had married cousins of the attorney general. See Rodríguez, *Primeros años*, 140-41, 147.

[10]See correspondence between Arriaga and various officials of the army and navy; July 23, 1767-April 21, 1768, all in Leg. 2542, Audiencia de Sto. Domingo, AGI.

[11]Grimaldi to Arriaga, June 8, 1768, and Ulloa to Grimaldi, July 20, 1768, both ibid.; Ulloa to Bucareli, July 2, 1768, in Dispatches of the Spanish Governors of Louisiana, W.P.A. Survey of Federal Archives in Louisiana, 11 vols. (Louisiana State University, Baton Rouge): 1.

[12]At the end of the year it consisted of 8 officers, 17 sergeants, 26 corporals, and 363 soldiers. See Rodríguez, *Primeros años*, 270.

[13]Proceso incoado contra los sublevados, in Leg. 2543, Audiencia de Sto. Domingo, AGI.

[14]Rodríguez, *Primeros años*, 144, 155. Some of the money was paid to the Germans, the rest appropriated by Villeré. After enduring some physical hardships, St. Maxent was released on October 30.

[15]"Noticia de los acaecimientos de la Luisiana," fol. 29.

[16]Ibid., fols. 32, 33.

[17]Ibid., fols. 34, 35.

[18]Ulloa's letter of October 26 gave Grimaldi alarming news: "There is no doubt that there is a general conspiracy organized against the sovereignty of His Majesty. The aim is to present a manifesto with charges against me to the Superior Council . . . which will order me to leave with all the Spaniards in the colony remaining thus under the domination of France as before." See Ulloa to Grimaldi, October 26, 1788, in Leg. 2542, Audiencia de Sto. Domingo, AGI. It apparently reached Grimaldi at the same time that he received a full report on the rebellion.

[19]Quoted in Rodríguez, *Primeros años*, 159.

[20]Ibid., 160, 162.

[21]"Noticia de los acaecimientos de la Luisiana," fols. 41, 42; Rodríguez, *Primeros años*, 163.

[22]Rodríguez, *Primeros años*, 166.

[23]In his written account of the rebellion to O'Reilly, dated August 20, 1769, he claimed that he had done everything possible to thwart their plans: "I summoned Monsieur Foucault [on October 27] when I asked what part he intended to play in the crisis, and as he replied in an ambiguous manner, I told him that he would lose his position irrevocably if he did not join me in opposing such a rebellion. . . . On the next day [October 28] I ordered Monsieur La Frénière to my house and told him that I would hold him to blame for the loss of the region. I stated to him that the lives of conspirators had always come to a tragic end." See Aubry to O'Reilly, August 20, 1769, quoted ibid., 398.

[24]These were Pierre Hardi de Boisblanc, Antoine Thomassin, Charles Jean Baptiste Fleuriau, Bobé Descloseaux, Joseph Ducros, and François Labarre, evidently men who would support the ouster of the Spanish governor. See Charles Gayarré, *History of Louisiana*,4 vols. (New Orleans, 1965), 2:192.

[25]Rodríguez, *Primeros años*, 166.

[26]Gayarré, *History of Louisiana*, 2:367-83, includes a translation of the proceedings.

[27]John G. Clark, *New Orleans, 1718-1812: An Economic History* (Baton Rouge, 1970), 168.

[28]Gayarré, *History of Louisiana,* 2:374.

[29]Ibid., 381. Cadis and Leblanc, the two persons singled out in the remonstrance as having been unjustly treated by Ulloa, were French colonists engaged in the slave trade with Martinique. Contrary to decrees of

the Superior Council and to orders from Spain, they imported Negroes of such undesirable and vicious character that Ulloa compelled both traders to send back a number of blacks, much to La Frénière's discomfiture, he being an agent for the two. See "Noticia de los acaecimientos de la Luisiana," fol. 70.

[30]Gayarré, *History of Louisiana*, 2:381-82.

[31]Ibid., 383.

[32]Ibid., 204.

[33]Ibid., 205. I have been unable to locate a copy of the order for the expulsion.

[34]Marc de Villiers du Terrage, *Les dernières années de la Louisiane française* (Paris, 1903), 263.

[35]Aubry, in his explanation of events to the minister of marine, estimated the number of armed men in the town to be nine hundred. See Aubry to Praslin, November 25, 1768, in C13A48, Colonies, AN. In a later version of the incident to O'Reilly, he increased the number to one thousand. See Aubry to O'Reilly, August 20, 1769, in Rodríguez, *Primeros años*, 399.

[36]Ulloa to Loyola, October 30, 1768, in Leg. 3883, Estado, AHN.

[37]Creole tradition had it that some bold rebels at daybreak managed to cut the mooring lines and set the vessel adrift. The discovery several years ago of an ancient anchor in the river immediately revived the old legend.

[38]Aubry to Praslin, November 25, 1768, in C13A48, Colonies, AN; Bucareli to Grimaldi, December 4, 1768, in Leg. 2542, Audiencia de Sto. Domingo, AGI.

ALEJANDRO O'REILLY IN LOUISIANA*

Lawrence Kinnaird

[After the ouster of Governor Antonio de Ulloa by the rebellious French settlers in 1768], the Spanish government still moved slowly but was now determined that the occupation of Louisiana should be undertaken with a great show of force. Lieutenant General Alejandro O'Reilly, one of Spain's most distinguished military men, was selected to command the expedition and given extraordinary power to employ all measures necessary for reestablishment of Spanish authority in the province. In contrast to Ulloa, who could never obtain more than a handful of troops, O'Reilly was given far more than were necessary. Of ships, artillery, and supplies, he also had a surplus. After extensive preparations he sailed from Havana on the *Volante* accompanied by twenty other vessels and more than 2000 first-class troops.[1] Total white population of New Orleans at this time was approximately 1800.[2]

O'Reilly and his squadron arrived in the river before New Orleans August 17, 1769. He disembarked on the afternoon of the 18th and with great ceremony took possession of the province. Three days later he arrested all the leaders of the insurrection. On the 26th he required all the inhabitants to take the oath of allegiance to the king of Spain.[3] Prosecution of the leaders of the revolution was assigned to Félix del Rey, advocate of the royal audiencias of Mexico and Santo Domingo, and the trial was conducted with great legal formality. Five conspirators including Nicolas Chauvin de Lafrénière were sentenced to death, six were given prison terms, and Joseph Villeré, before the end of the trial, met his death in prison under mysterious circumstances. Property of all conspirators was confiscated.[4] Nicolas Foucault alone escaped trial because he was an official of the French government.[5]

Before the trial had ended, O'Reilly turned his attention to the political and economic reorganization of the colony. To prevent an inflation of values, which the great influx of Spanish troops might cause, he issued a proclamation on September 7th fixing prices of foods.[6] Undesirable merchants were expelled and Spanish commercial regulations

*This excerpt is taken from Lawrence Kinnaird, ed., *Spain in the Mississippi Valley, 1765-1794*, 3 vols. (Washington, DC, 1949), 1:21-23.

enforced. However, to give Louisiana an outlet for its products, he proposed free trade for the province with Havana and the ports of Spain. The king gave this recommendation his approval.[7] The Superior Council was abolished, a *cabildo* created, new laws and regulations proclaimed, and governmental expense reduced.[8] By December, O'Reilly was able to send a considerable part of his military force back to Havana.[9] He devised a plan of defense based upon employment of Spanish regular troops and also drew upon the French population to fill many colonial offices. For more effective administration the districts of Natchitoches and upper Louisiana (Spanish Illinois) were placed under lieutenant governors. The first was Athanase de Mézières, a Frenchman of long experience on the Louisiana-Texas frontier.[10] The second was Pedro Piernas who had succeeded to the command of Captain Francisco Ríu in the Missouri country during the latter part of Ulloa's administration. As assistant and special adviser on Indian affairs to Piernas, O'Reilly appointed Louis St. Ange, former French commandant in St. Louis.[11]

The Indian policies of O'Reilly were substantially the same as those of Ulloa with the exception that he ordered abolition of Indian slavery.[12] The French system of controlling the tribes by means of licensed traders and distribution of gifts was continued. Considerable economies were effected, however, by purchasing all goods used for Indian presents through the firm of Ranson and Maxent.[13] Among the tribes of the Louisiana-Texas frontier, hostilities engendered by former French and Spanish rivalry had not entirely subsided and De Mézières was assigned treaties, and supplanted unauthorized traders with those properly licensed.[14] Other lieutenant governors and commandants of frontier posts also devoted a major portion of their efforts to Indian affairs. Louisiana's Indian population far exceeded the white and the maintenance of peace with the tribes was essential to the safety of the settlements. The problem was rendered even more serious by the intrusion of the English traders both from West Florida and British Illinois into the Indian country west of the Mississippi. Furthermore, English merchants along the Mississippi supplied unlicensed French traders with goods and thus diverted much commerce from legitimate Spanish channels. O'Reilly took severe measures to prevent this illegal trade, but as long as the English remained on the Mississippi it never entirely ceased.[15]

O'Reilly investigated the condition of the posts established by Ulloa and decided that none of them was well located either for military or economic purposes. Buildings on Isla Real Católica were demolished and headquarters for river pilots were removed to the old French site of Balize. San Gabriel was turned over to a few German settlers who had established themselves in that district. San Luis de Natchez was entirely abandoned and the Acadians who had been taken there were distributed among the settlements lower down the river.[16] On the Missouri only a few men were retained to guard the mouth of the river and the principal part of the garrison was removed to Ste. Geneviève and St. Louis.[17] By March, 1770, O'Reilly had completed his task of reorganization. As special commissioner of the king, he installed Luis de Unzaga as governor and departed for Havana. Expressing his satisfaction for O'Reilly's work, the king approved all of his acts and recommendations. As a result of O'Reilly's occupation, Louisiana became a dependency of the captaincy-general of Cuba. Thereafter its affairs were placed under the supervision of the Ministry of the Indies in the manner of Spain's other colonies.[18]

Notes for "Alejandro O'Reilly in Louisiana"

[1]Antonio Bucareli y Ursua to Julián de Arriaga, No. 1135, Havana, July 7, 1769, in Lawrence Kinnaird, ed., *Spain in the Mississippi Valley*, 1:86-88, with enclosure.

[2]Charles Gayarré, *History of Louisiana*, 4 vols., 4th ed. (New Orleans, 1903), 2:355.

[3]Alejandro O'Reilly to Juan Gregorio de Muniain, New Orleans, August 312, 1769, in Kinnaird, ed., *Spain in the Mississippi Valley*, 1:90.

[4]Sentence passed by O'Reilly upon leaders of the Louisiana uprising, October 24, 1769, Archivo General de Indias, Papeles procedentes de la isla de Cuba, legajo (hereafter cited as AGI, PC, leg.) 81.

[5]Alcée Fortier, *A History of Louisiana*, 4 vols. (Paris and New York, 1904), 1:221.

[6]"Proclamation Fixing Prices," O'Reilly, New Orleans, September 7, 1769, in Kinnaird, ed., *Spain in the Mississippi*, 1:93-94.

[7]Ibid., O'Reilly to Luis de Unzaga, No. 52, New Orleans, April 3, 1770, in ibid.

[8]O'Reilly to Arriaga, No. 3 and 16, New Orleans, October 17, and December 10, 1769, "Establishment of the New Orleans Cabildo," November 25, 1769, Marqués de Grimaldi to Unzaga, No. 24, March 24, 1770, all in ibid., 97-98, 132-35, 108-25, 163-64.

[9]O'Reilly to Arriaga, No. 23, New Orleans, December 10, 1769, in ibid., 126.

[10]O'Reilly to Grimaldi, No. 21, New Orleans, December 10, 1769, Grimaldi to Unzaga, No. 47, San Lorenzo, October 24, 1770, in ibid., 129, 187; Herbert Eugene Bolton, ed., *Athanase de Mézières and the Louisiana-Texas Frontier, 1768-1780*, 2 vols. (Cleveland, 1914), 1:70-75.

[11]Bernardo de Gálvez to José de Gálvez, No. 24, New Orleans, March 21, 1777, Kinnaird, ed., *Spain in the Mississippi Valley*, 1:236.

[12]"Proclamation by O'Reilly," New Orleans, December 7, 1769, in ibid., 125-26.

[13]O'Reilly to Arriaga, No. 25, New Orleans, December 29, 1769, in ibid., 147.

[14]Bolton, ed., *Athanase de Mézières*, 1:79-110.

[15]Ibid., 1:76-79; Louis Houck, *A History of Missouri*, 3 vols. (Chicago, 1908), 1:77.

[16]O'Reilly to Arriaga, No. 25, New Orleans, December 25, 1769, in Kinnaird, ed., *Spain in the Mississippi Valley*, 1:144-48.

[17]Louis Houck, *Spanish Régime in Missouri*, 2 vols. (Chicago, 1909), 1:78-83.

[18]Royal Cédula, August 17, 1772, Archivo General de Indias, Audiencia de Santo Domingo, leg. 2533.

BERNARDO DE GÁLVEZ: A REEXAMINATION OF HIS GOVERNORSHIP*

Gilbert C. Din

No Spanish governor of Louisiana has received as much admiration and praise as Bernardo de Gálvez.[1] Among other things, he has been singled out as the Spaniard who reconciled Louisiana's French inhabitants to Spanish rule. He did this in part by marrying into the colony's elite, although he was not the first governor to take a French creole bride. Above all, however, Gálvez led forces that defeated the English on the Mississippi and at Mobile and Pensacola during the American Revolutionary War. His military exploits, not to mention the influence of uncle José de Gálvez who was minister of the Indies, earned him promotions that in nine years carried him from the rank of army brevet lieutenant colonel to lieutenant general and from an inconspicuous post at a military school in Spain to viceroy of Mexico, the most prestigious office in the colonies. His meteoric rise was phenomenal. But at age forty and only a year and a half after becoming viceroy, his seemingly brilliant career ended abruptly when he died from an illness.

After publication of John Walton Caughey's 1934 biography, *Bernardo de Gálvez in Louisiana, 1776-1783*,[2] no historian has written a new study of the governor based on archival documentation although there is ample room. Caughey limited his work on Gálvez in Louisiana to his military feats because he gave other topics, including administration of the colony, short shrift. Although new studies on Gálvez have appeared since 1934, they have largely used published materials to heap unabashedly more praise on him. These authors have not ferreted out new information. The Bicentennial celebrations two decades ago repeated the adulation.[3] Only Eric Beerman in a recent Spanish publication, *España y la independencia de Estados Unidos*, has divulged some little known facts about the governor and his uncle.[4]

Needless to say, many of the studies about Gálvez have not revealed a dark side to his character. He was not as experienced an administrator as his biographers assume he was,

*This article is published with the kind permission of the author.

and his uncle's post permitted him to do things that other governors would not have attempted. Because few historians work in Louisiana's Spanish period, little about the interworkings of Gálvez's administration have been disclosed. Too, some historians have been reluctant to criticize a much praised historical figure, and they view any disapproval however accurate as tantamount to heresy.[5]

This study focuses primarily on two areas of Gálvez's administration, both of which involved his father-in-law, Gilbert Antoine de St. Maxent. One area is the governor's position on slavery. For two years St. Maxent, who was a major slaveholder, influenced Gálvez on this subject, and during this time the governor became embroiled with the New Orleans *cabildo* [city council]. The other area is Gálvez's so-called "affair" with Francisco Bouligny that resulted from the governor's nepotic desire to promote St. Maxent's business interests.[6]

Gálvez arrived in Louisiana on December 6, 1776, and took office as governor on January 1, 1777. He was then thirty years old, and this was his first administrative post. Probably because of prodding by his uncle José, General Alejandro O'Reilly, who suppressed the 1768 revolt in Louisiana and was then inspector general of the army, appointed Bernardo colonel of the Fixed Louisiana Infantry Battalion in 1776. José de Gálvez shortly afterwards named his nephew interim governor of Louisiana and he became proprietary governor in 1779.[7]

In New Orleans Gálvez met departing Governor Luis de Unzaga y Amezaga, Unzaga's father-in-law St. Maxent, and the latter's family. Unzaga had married St. Maxent's oldest daughter Elizabeth. All of St. Maxent's children followed their father's pro-Spanish position, the sons working for the government, usually as army officers, and the daughters marrying Spaniards. Gálvez soon began courting Félicité de St. Maxent. By this time, he had already been drawn into her father's web of influence.[8]

On November 2, 1777, Gálvez cemented his ties to the St. Maxent family when he married Félicité without government permission. To accomplish it, he feigned sickness, claiming that he was near death and wanted to keep his promise to marry her before he died. By evading longstanding orders that prohibited top administrators from marrying in the colonies where they served, Gálvez showed that he knew how to manipulate established practices. It was easier for him than for other colonial officials because his uncle was the minister of the Indies. On several occasions, Gálvez used his favored position to achieve his ends. His marriage to Félicité also made him a slaveholder because her father included slaves in her dowry.[9]

On arriving in Louisiana, Gálvez found St. Maxent and other major slaveholders dissatisfied with Spanish slave laws. O'Reilly's establishment of Spanish statutes had distressed many of them. In February, 1770, on the eve of the Irishman's departure from Louisiana, some planters sought permission to punish slaves as had been done in the French era (branding, hamstringing, and execution). Fugitive slaves upset them because flight represented defiance; owners sought absolute control of their blacks. O'Reilly, however, refused to grant the planters' request.[10]

Governor Unzaga, who assumed the full exercise of his office on O'Reilly's departure in early March, 1770, generally agreed with the owners about fugitive slaves. In 1773, when planters in the New Orleans district wanted to create a slave fund to pay for expeditions against runaways and compensate owners for maroons executed or killed while at large, Unzaga acquiesced. He permitted the *cabildo* to call a special meeting to discuss the creation of the fund and petition the Crown for recognition.[11] Because St. Maxent was a major slaveholder owning about two hundred blacks, planter, fur trader, and contractor, and engaged in numerous business activities, he probably tried advising Unzaga. The latter, however, seems not to have listened to him as attentively as Gálvez did when he assumed office in 1777.[12]

The new governor heeded St. Maxent's arguments about slavery because he knew nothing about the institution. St. Maxent lost no time in voicing his position. He stated that owners needed greater discipline of slaves to obtain the labor they owed their masters. The lack of corrective measures injured Louisiana's economic development. Masters needed to punish recalcitrant slaves more severely, restrict their movements, limit the sale of slave goods because it fostered theft, end *coartación* or the right of slaves to purchase their freedom, and stop the emancipation of slaves except by the proper authorities (notaries had the power to write letters of freedom). French planters claimed that Spanish regulations made slaves disobedient.[13]

St. Maxent probably began advising the governor soon after his arrival in Louisiana. On January 28, 1777, Gálvez wrote to his uncle, telling the minister of his recent *bando* in which he permitted a French ship, the *Lastre*, to come up to New Orleans to purchase local products. He urged the Crown to grant Louisiana permission to trade with France and the French introduction of slaves to increase agricultural production. In Spain, the government welcomed the governor's recommendations. On May 10, 1777, Minister Gálvez replied that King Carlos III had approved the entry of French goods and slaves in Louisiana.[14] When they learned of the Crown's decision, Louisiana's large planters celebrated the governor's connections in Spain that had acted quickly and positively in their behalf.

Evidence suggests that only two months after first advising the governor on slaves and trade, St. Maxent again exerted his thinking on Gálvez. On April 2, 1777, the governor received his uncle's November 25, 1776, instructions on the administration of Louisiana. Francisco Bouligny, an officer from the Louisiana Infantry Battalion and planter on leave in Spain, had counseled Minister Gálvez in drawing up the instructions. Several provisions dealt with slaves, but Governor Gálvez refused to proclaim them in Louisiana, probably because of Article 22.[15]

Article 22 troubled the large slaveholders, including St. Maxent. It declared that some masters had been excessively brutal, and it cautioned owners to avoid unreasonable demands and punishment that produced desperation, flight, and uprisings among their slaves. Masters needed to treat Africans well and owed them humanity and justice. The king advised the governor to grant runaways a pardon to induce them to return.[16]

Announced two years later on April 20, 1779, the pardon became the only part of the instructions on slaves that the governor proclaimed. Its belated issuance, however, resulted from a worsening of the fugitive slave problem and not because of his uncle's instructions.[17]

The other portions of Article 22 dealing with slaves remained mute. Governor Gálvez did not issue a *bando* [edict] on blacks that incorporated his instructions nor did he make them public, no doubt because of opposition from St. Maxent and other planters. They represented the provincial elite, and Gálvez curried their favor. With the governor as their champion, the planters must have felt heartened that they might thwart Spanish laws they judged damaging to their interests.

Soon after the November 25 instructions arrived and no doubt advised by St. Maxent, Gálvez in an extraordinary move denied the jurisdiction of a Havana appellate court decision on May 23, 1777. It had ruled in favor of María Juana, a slave who filed a purchase-of-freedom petition the year before. The governor opposed both the Havana court ruling which was by a superior tribunal, and the right of slaves to buy their freedom because first, the royal order cited by the appeals court was directed to Cuba, not Louisiana; and second, the Spanish government had declared when it acquired Louisiana that the colony's usages and customs were not to change without the king's consent.[18]

The second point, often stressed by Frenchmen in the Spanish era, disregards O'Reilly's imposition of Spanish law in 1769, which the king approved.[19] In other words, the earlier decree had been superseded except in the minds of Frenchmen. In his decision on María Juana, Gálvez sided against self-purchase by slaves, which large French planters deplored. The governor used the French argument—which clearly reveals the source of the influence exerted on him—that customs were not to change, a belief that ignored the creole rebellion and O'Reilly's establishment of Spanish law. Gálvez's ruling in María Juana's case helps explain why he never proclaimed the slave regulations contained in the November 25, 1776, instructions. The reason was clearly the governor's tie to his father-in-law and planter friends.[20]

Only after Gálvez wrote in January, 1777, stating his views on slavery did the Crown respond to the 1773 appeal for a fugitive slave fund. For nearly four years, Julián de Arriaga as minister of the Indies had done nothing about it. Now, however, José de Gálvez had succeeded the deceased Arriaga, and he probably advised the king on this matter. It produced the royal *cédula* [decree] of May 14, 1777, in which the king accepted the establishment of a tax on slaves to reward expeditions that pursued runaways and indemnify masters whose blacks were executed or died while being hunted. He, however, prohibited forced contributions; the tax had to be voluntary. But as Louisiana governors later discovered each time they sought to create the fund, planters living outside the New Orleans district largely refused to support it.[21]

But more important here, the king also asked in the May 14, 1777, *cédula* that new regulations be drawn up in Louisiana for the treatment of blacks. There seems little doubt that Governor Gálvez had asked his uncle to permit the colony's residents, who were presumed more knowledgeable, to draft the slave laws. The *cabildo*, which received the charge, moved slowly. In early 1778, the councillors commissioned two of their number, Francisco María de Reggio and Joseph Ducros who were both planters, to prepare the regulations for the conduct of blacks. They intended to restore to slaveholders the rights that Spanish law had taken from them.[22]

Reggio and Ducros labored many months on their project. When they finished, the council printed the regulations in French which it named the *Code Noir ou Loi Municipale* (Black Code or Municipal Law). Reggio and Ducros modeled the *Loi Municipale* on the 1724 French *Code Noir*, and it diminished the rights of Afro-Louisianians, both free and slave. It did away with Spanish regulations on slavery. Among the new rules manumissions had to be approved judicially, notaries could not write letters of freedom, and self-purchase was no longer valid. Other provisions forbade interracial marriages and concubinage, prevented slaves from marrying persons belonging to other plantations, and prohibited marriages between free blacks and slaves. Slaves could not complain of abuse by their masters. The *Loi Municpale* included the police measures found in the 1724 *Code Noir* and the 1751 police regulation of French governor Vaudreuil. Reggio and Ducros presented the *Loi Municipale* to the *cabildo* on October 16, 1778, and the city council distributed copies throughout lower Louisiana for the notable citizens to discuss. They could then submit their impressions to post commandants or send them directly to the *cabildo*.[23]

On February 19 and 26, 1779, the councillors debated the planters' observations. When they finished, they invited the notable and distinguished citizens (primarily slaveholders) of the New Orleans vicinity to attend an extraordinary town meeting on March 1, to give their opinions. At that meeting, the *cabildo* would adopt the most convenient measures proposed.[24] The junta attracted about twenty-five planters, including St. Maxent, who listened to the reading of the ordinances on the discipline of blacks. Upon completion, they asked that a code be made of their measures, which did not contravene the laws of the kingdom or those in use in the province. Of special importance was their request that the *laws of the province be respected.* By this means, the planters sought royal recognition of their treatment of slaves. They asked the *cabildo* and the governor to petition the king to approve the articles and implement them in Louisiana. Thirty-three persons signed the minutes of the March 1 meeting, which indicated their approval of the minutes. They included Governor Gálvez, St. Maxent, the *cabildo* members, and other planters.[25] Unfortunately, no copy of their finished document was preserved. Only the printed draft of the *Code Noir ou Loi Municipale* has survived.

The *cabildo*'s victory in drafting new slave regulations was short-lived because the council had already alienated Governor Gálvez. He, however, had concealed his feelings. In October, 1778, about the same time the *cabildo* sent the *Loi Municipale* to the districts of lower Louisiana for the notables to examine, it perhaps sensed that it could increase its power in the colony. It tried to gain rights in an area that had long rankled the sensibilities of some Frenchmen, especially Reggio's; it was direction of Charity

Hospital. What they attempted to do, however, struck at the power of the governor because taking charge of Charity Hospital would infringe on his authority. Leaders in the *cabildo* must have believed that they could dictate to the governor. Instead, Gálvez flinched at their brazen attempt to increase their authority at his expense. Vicar General Cirilo de Barcelona, the nominal head of Charity Hospital, warned Gálvez about the *cabildo*'s intention in December, 1778. But he only rebuked it. He withheld further action until he showed the *cabildo* his ability to crush the *Loi Municipale*.[26]

On March 2, 1779, the day after Governor Gálvez approved the slave regulations and the *cabildo* minutes, he wrote to his uncle. He accused the city councillors of subversion, hostility to Spain, unappreciativeness of the many benefits the king had bestowed on them, and some of them of having participated in the 1768 rebellion. The governor was purposely ambiguous in his accusations, and he portrayed the councillors' attack on his power as an attack on Spain. Although he told his uncle that he would substantiate his charges, he never did. Perhaps Gálvez finally realized that the *Loi Municipale* was contrary to Spanish law and violated his uncle's 1776 instructions. That would explain why he did not openly oppose the *Loi Municipale*, preferring instead to sweep everything under the rug. The arrival of a new government *asesor* (legal adviser) well versed in Spanish law in June, 1779, possibly helped him abandon the *Loi Municipale*. Neither Gálvez nor the chastised *cabildo* ever discussed it again.[27] The war against Great Britain which soon started drew the governor away from slave problems, and he never again concerned himself with them.

While Gálvez was promoting the interests of St. Maxent and the planter class from 1777 to 1779, relations with Lieutenant Governor Francisco Bouligny steadily worsened. Gálvez charged him with wrongdoing in his March 2, 1779, letter to the minister of the Indies that also criticized the *cabildo*. Bouligny had returned to New Orleans on April 2, 1777, bringing Minister Gálvez's November 25, 1776, instructions to the governor. These orders had named Bouligny lieutenant governor with charge of settlements, commerce, and Indian affairs. Over the next two years, however, the governor allowed him to exercise little power in these areas. Minister Gálvez in Spain had appointed Bouligny because of his knowledge of Louisiana and the advice he had provided. But Governor Gálvez had not been involved in the appointment, and he purposely prevented Bouligny from assuming the duties assigned to his office, probably because they would diminish the governor's authority. He was jealous of his position in Louisiana; he wanted to be *jefe máximo* (supreme chief). His desire to maintain ultimate control had led him to abandon support for the slave owners and *cabildo*. By 1778 or possibly sooner, St. Maxent recognized that Bouligny's post as lieutenant governor could allow him to increase his fortune. The business man had been in the Indian trade, and he knew that considerable money could be made in it. But Bouligny stood in the way, and he had to be removed to enable the Frenchman to assume this potentially lucrative post.[28]

In 1778 Gálvez's dislike for Bouligny was well developed. The latter had advised José de Gálvez in Spain about Louisiana affairs, and the governor wanted to be the

Crown's sole adviser in the colony. Gálvez had aligned himself with the French planters, and Bouligny did not share all their beliefs. He had informed the minister that some planters abused their slaves, and he was responsible for Articles 22 and 23 in the governor's instructions that called for gentler treatment of slaves. Another important reason for disliking Bouligny involved his duties. When this official arrived in Louisiana, Governor Gálvez sent out notices to the post commandants on April 2 and 11, informing them of Bouligny's post as lieutenant governor and Gálvez's immediate subaltern. In the April 11 announcements, Gálvez called him the second military chief in the colony. Appointing Bouligny second military chief exceeded Minister Gálvez's orders. Possibly a scribe was responsible for the error, but more likely it was the governor himself. Gálvez knew that he had named Bouligny second military chief, although he later denied it.[29]

The first signs of discord between Bouligny and Gálvez surfaced in April, 1778, following the arrival in New Orleans of the American rebel James Willing, whose expedition had plundered British settlements upriver in West Florida. When a British warship soon arrived in New Orleans demanding the surrender of the rebels and restoration of their seized spoils, the governor protected Willing and his men. Gálvez then consulted Bouligny about Spanish military preparations because he was second in command of military affairs (This is proof that Gálvez knew of Bouligny's appointment to this post). The lieutenant governor, however, acted cautiously, more so than Gálvez liked. Bouligny worried that the governor was willing to risk a fight with the British and believed that it was possible to resist them in the countryside if New Orleans fell. Bouligny disagreed because lower Louisiana's many rivers, bayous, and dense forests would make fighting difficult if not impossible. The lieutenant governor questioned Gálvez's judgment; he considered it safer to deploy all their defenses in advance and request assistance from Havana. Bouligny also wanted his duties as the governor's immediate subaltern delineated, a position he claimed was equivalent to the "king's lieutenant." Bouligny tried to couch his letter in words that did not offend the sensitive governor. He declared that he possessed only friendship and veneration for Gálvez, and his defeat of the British would shroud him with "immortal glory."[30]

By now, however, Gálvez was determined to remove Bouligny as second in military command and lieutenant governor. Bouligny was not as intrepid as the governor, and he had contradicted him on the course of action to pursue. Gálvez preferred a free hand in running the colony, and he wanted to favor his father-in-law, who recognized the commercial possibilities of Bouligny's office.

By May 1778, after the British danger had subsided, Gálvez found the excuse to remove Bouligny as second in military command when higher ranking army officers arrived from Havana with reinforcements. The governor revised the chain of command to include two officers who outranked Bouligny; he was only a brevet lieutenant colonel. Gálvez's insertion of temporarily assigned officers in Louisiana's chain of command was the only time that it occurred. In June he called a council of officers that upheld the principle of seniority and pointed out that Bouligny had authority only as lieutenant governor in charge of settlements, commerce, and Indian affairs; he was not the colony's second military chief. When Gálvez learned that his friend Esteban Miró was arriving to be the Louisiana Battalion's sergeant major, or second ranking officer after Gálvez, it further downgraded Bouligny because now four army officers, including Lieutenant Colonel Pedro Piernas of the Louisiana Battalion, were ahead of him. Bouligny pleaded with the governor to keep him as the king's lieutenant, and he wrote to Minister Gálvez, arguing his point of view. Bouligny entrusted his letter to the governor to send to Spain for a court decision, but Gálvez did not do so.[31]

After removing Bouligny as second military chief, the governor continued to undermine him. On October 21, Gálvez secretly instructed post commandants to return to him quietly the April, 1777, announcements that proclaimed Bouligny lieutenant governor and second military chief as well as any other correspondence he had sent them. Many of the letters they returned disappeared. The reason why Gálvez did this is clear: He had sent the announcements of Bouligny's appointment, and now he tried to shift responsibility. He claimed that the lieutenant governor had proclaimed himself second in military command. Perhaps, too, Gálvez concluded, it might facilitate Bouligny's removal as lieutenant governor. The problem quickly came up because Bouligny was becoming aware of the governor's intentions.[32]

When the first immigrants from the Canary Islands arrived in New Orleans on November 1, 1778, Bouligny sensed power slipping from his grasp. Gálvez had arrogated to himself authority on new settlements despite the fact that jurisdiction in these matters properly belonged to the lieutenant governor. Soon Gálvez announced a journey up the Mississippi to inspect settlement sites and entrusted interim command of New Orleans to Colonel Manuel González. Bouligny then insisted on a new council of officers to re-examine the post of second in military command. He stubbornly clung to the belief that the Crown had given him this position. At the meeting, the officers not surprisingly again asserted the opinion that Minister Gálvez had appointed Bouligny only lieutenant governor. Bouligny then demanded to know why Gálvez had proclaimed him second military chief. Rather than admit error, Gálvez accused him of sending the announcements. The unfounded charge caused the proud Bouligny to lose his temper, and he lashed out disrespectfully that Gálvez had impugned his honor. The governor abruptly terminated the meeting. But the next day as he left to inspect settlement sites, Gálvez permitted Bouligny to establish the immigrants who had come from Málaga in Ouachita.[33]

When Gálvez returned to the city in December, he refused to have Bouligny proclaimed lieutenant governor in the *cabildo* as the latter now wanted. It produced Bouligny's despondent December 10 resignation as lieutenant governor; he gave poor health as the reason. But it was not believable, and the resignation forced Gálvez to reconsider his treatment of Bouligny. Gálvez had to tread carefully because he had not yet explained to his uncle his dealings with the lieutenant governor or concocted an explanation of why he had stripped him of authority. It seemed preferable to allow Bouligny to settle the immigrants from Málaga on Bayou Teche, not Ouachita, while he devised an excuse for the lieutenant governor's removal.[34]

When Gálvez announced his proposal, Bouligny withdrew his resignation and agreed to establish the Malagueños in the Attakapas District west of New Orleans. Gálvez gave him command of the district as lieutenant governor, with authority to settle the Spaniards and decide cases on appeal from the local commandant. His commission as lieutenant governor charged with settlements, commerce, and Indian affairs was slashed to this modest extent. But Gálvez still hesitated rescinding completely his uncle's appointment of Bouligny.[35]

Nevertheless, he was working towards Bouligny's removal. He notified his uncle about Bouligny's alleged misconduct in the same vitriolic letter of March 2, 1779, in which he accused the *cabildo* of wrongdoing. Gálvez charged that Bouligny was filled with "erronious ideas," and he promised to send the minister documents to prove the official's illegal conduct. Ironically, he complained that Bouligny thought only of his own self-interest. Nowhere in the letter did Gálvez provide specific information about the claimed malfeasance of Bouligny.[36]

To get proof for his case against the lieutenant governor, on March 26, 1779, Gálvez sent interrogatories to the officials who had attended the juntas held in June and November, 1778, that examined Bouligny's appointment. The interrogatories asked if Bouligny had demanded to be regarded as the king's lieutenant and second in military command; if Gálvez had behaved well while Bouligny had not; if Bouligny had insisted on a second junta, where he importuned the officers and acted disrespectfully; and if he had obstinately persisted on Ouachita as a settlement site. The cautious officials obligingly supplied the answers Gálvez wanted. But the governor must have realized that the interrogatories were a sham; he did not send them to Spain. He needed new charges of misconduct against the lieutenant governor before he could write to his uncle again.[37]

In Spain, Minister Gálvez waited anxiously for a full accounting of the charges the governor lodged in his March 2 letter. When several months elapsed without further explanation, the minister wrote again and ordered Bernardo to substantiate his charges. If he had valid reasons, he could suspend Bouligny as lieutenant governor.[38] Gálvez received the letter in New Orleans late in 1779, and he interpreted it as giving him the authority to remove Bouligny.

While the governor worked against him, Bouligny spent the first eight months of 1779 at New Iberia settling the Malagueños. The war against Great Britain began while he was there. Gálvez notified post commandants in August about hostilities and instructed them to ready their forces to join him on the Mississippi for an attack on the British posts upriver. But he did not inform Bouligny who learned about the war from Commandant Alexandre DeClouet of the Attakapas-Opelousas District. Bouligny immediately gathered his men to add to DeClouet's troops going to meet Gálvez. When Bouligny arrived on the Mississippi, the governor rebuked him for abandoning New

Iberia. Gálvez's puzzling behavior raises the possibility that after the campaign he had intended to reprimand Bouligny for failing to join him and shirking combat. The governor's conduct toward Bouligny did not improve throughout the war. Bouligny served with distinction on all three campaigns of the Louisiana regiment in West Florida without receiving a promotion. In contrast, Gálvez freely promoted other officers who participated in only one campaign.[39]

With Louisiana at war against neighboring British West Florida, Bouligny's duty as an army officer took precedence. He still had the title of lieutenant governor but that did not last long. After the Mississippi River campaign, Gálvez returned to New Orleans in October, 1779. There, among other things, he examined Bouligny's settlement accounts at New Iberia. Problems were present because large sums of money had been spent and not all of the settlers had houses. Bouligny supplied a lengthy explanation of the many obstacles that he had encountered; they included floods, the lack of lands on high ground, and shortages of building materials. He offered to return to New Iberia to complete the work. Gálvez, however, only allowed him to return temporarily. In November the governor appointed *cabildo regidor* Nicolás Forstall to assume command at New Iberia. In January, 1780, before he sailed to attack Mobile, Gálvez ordered the New Orleans accounting house to suspend Bouligny's salary as lieutenant governor and to prohibit him from further involvement in settlements and commercial and Indian affairs. It terminated the appointment that Bouligny had received in Spain. But Gálvez still had not explained to the king that officer's alleged irregular conduct.[40]

Five months later, after the conquest of Mobile, Gálvez passed through New Orleans. On June 5, he wrote to his uncle explaining Bouligny's removal. Gálvez no longer focused on the lieutenant governor's alleged misconduct in 1777 and 1778 because he had a new reason. He described Bouligny's accounts at New Iberia, as "the most solid proof of his irregular management and disorderly proceedings." This was the reason for his removal as lieutenant governor. Gálvez promised to send the evidence after the war. But for now, he accused Bouligny of poor record keeping, about which the governor was uninformed when, on March 2, 1779, he first complained about him to the minister. Absent, too, were the charges made in the interrogatories of March 26, 1779, and against the *cabildo*. After the war, Juan Ventura Morales scrutinized Bouligny's expenditures at New Iberia and found several irregularities. The government dismissed most of them as unimportant but insisted that unauthorized exploration expenses be paid because they had nothing to do with settlement. By 1786 Bouligny had returned 364 *pesos* to the royal treasury. That was the extent of his "irregular management and disorderly proceedings."[41] A close examination of Gálvez's complaints against Bouligny in 1779 reveals that they were spurious. He used them to strip the lieutenant governor of his post and replace him with St. Maxent.

While Gálvez tarnished Bouligny's reputation, he worked to create a better image of his father-in-law. In 1779 the governor praised him in a dispatch about the conquest of Manchac. He wrote that St. Maxent was the first man to penetrate the British fort, entering the bastion through a porthole. But it stretches the imagination to believe that the older Captain St. Maxent actually led younger and more vigorous soldiers in charging and penetrating the enemy fort, especially when the writer was the nepotic Bernardo de Gálvez. Not long afterwards, St. Maxent became the colonel of the New Orleans militia. He also had government contracts to provide the colonists from Málaga and the Canary Islands with materials and foodstuffs for their settlement.[42]

As a self-made man who built his own fortune in Louisiana, St. Maxent sought opportunities. He wanted the province to resume trade with France. That nation bought Louisiana's furs and hides while Spain did not. After the conquest of Pensacola, St. Maxent journeyed to Spain with the governor's blessing. In Madrid he provided the government with information about Louisiana. In October he petitioned the king for the right to commerce with France and manage the trade with the natives. Advised by the minister of the Indies, the king consented and appointed St. Maxent lieutenant governor in charge of the Indian trade. He received permission to send goods worth 380,000 *pesos* for the Native American trade in Louisiana and West Florida, 200,000 *pesos* of which were for his personal commerce. Arthur Preston Whitaker has described the blatant favoritism St. Maxent received as having the "smell of nepotism." It was so notorious that it quickly forced the Spanish government in its 1782 *cédula* on free trade to allow all Louisianians to commerce with France. St. Maxent found goods for the Indian trade in France and Spain, but on his voyage home the British seized his two ships and took them to Jamaica. He bought back his ships and part of his goods and returned to Cuba, where customs officials accused him of smuggling because he illegally paid British merchants with specie. Soon St. Maxent was suspended from office. He spent years in Louisiana under house arrest and under a cloud of suspicion. Gálvez's effort to promote the Frenchman's fortune had ended in failure.[43]

Before Bernardo de Gálvez took final leave of Louisiana in 1781, his temper became known during the siege of Pensacola. Naval officers, particularly Admiral José Calvo de Irazábal, had set it off by their reluctance to risk their ships crossing the shallow sand bar at the entrance to Pensacola Bay. Gálvez then broke the impasse with the navy and entered the bay with four Louisiana ships which were directly under his command. Later he adopted the motto "Yo Solo," by which he ignored the officers and sailors, including a brother-in-law, who had accompanied him. Moreover, at a dinner filled with army and navy officers after the fleet entered Pensacola Bay, Gálvez lashed out in a blistering tirade against the navy, bitterly condemning the sluggards. The next day more sensible subordinates engaged in damage control to prevent the incident from becoming public knowledge and, indeed, events of that night were largely quashed. But so angry was Gálvez during the siege that for a time he refused to permit naval ships with formidable artillery to bombard British Fort George. He seemed to want to deprive the navy of any credit for the conquest of Pensacola. His behavior, however, might have prolonged the siege.[44]

Bernardo de Gálvez's quest for victories persisted after he left Louisiana and West Florida. Because of his uncle's influence, older and more experienced officers were bypassed when the king appointed Bernardo commander of the Franco-Spanish expedition to conquer British Jamaica, the next major objective in the allies' war plans. When he sailed from Havana to Guarico (Cap Français, Saint-Domingue) to take charge of the force that was to assemble there, he took all the Spanish war vessels with him. He left Juan Manuel de Cagigal as captain general of Cuba with instructions to conquer the Bahamas but provided no warships. Cagigal had to scrounge them from Americans to get protection for Spanish troop transports. The unexpected arrival of Cagigal and his expedition at Nassau, Providence, surprised the British, and he seized the islands without firing a shot or losing a man. Gálvez, meanwhile, had become stuck in Guarico because of money shortages, rebellions in South America, and British naval superiority in the Caribbean after the defeat of the French fleet under the comte de Grasse. When Gálvez learned of Cagigal's victory and the praise he received in the press, the general's unrestrained envy became well known to subordinates.[45]

That was not all, however. Many of the officers around Bernardo, including capable and high-ranking officials, felt the sting of persecution by the Gálvez clan. Among them were Cagigal, Irazábal, José Bautista Bonet, Victorio de Navia, Pedro González de Castejón, José Solano, Miguel Alderete, and Francisco de Miranda, all of whom exercised important roles in Spain's war effort in the Caribbean and Gulf of Mexico. The general kept his uncle informed about officers whose conduct displeased him, and the Crown issued orders for their arrest on the basis of questionable evidence. Because the accused were essential to the war effort, even Gálvez did not implement the orders, at least not until after the war. Miranda and Cagigal were among those accused of smuggling. Miranda eluded arrest but not Cagigal, who was seized and spent years in prison. In 1785, Miranda wrote to King Carlos III from the safety of London, accusing the minister of the Indies, his nephew Bernardo, and the bishop of Havana for his legal difficulties. He charged that the minister detested Americans (Miranda was a Venezuelan creole), Bernardo had a love affair with his image in the press, and the bishop delighted in noisey intrigues. Miranda and Cagigal received pardons only after the death of both Bernardo and José de Gálvez. Miranda in time became the precursor of Spanish American independence while Cagigal left in manuscript an unflattering account of the Gálvez family and its thirst for victories, honors, and public adoration.[46]

It was no accident that less than three years after the demise of José de Gálvez and with a new king (Carlos IV) on the Spanish throne that the ministry of the Indies was abolished in 1790. The power that Minister Gálvez had exercised with the approval of Carlos III was now divided among five ministries. The new administrative system also deprived the king of direct authority over the colonies.[47] Perhaps prescience led Caughey many years ago to avoid delving into Bernardo de Gálvez's administration of Louisiana and his role in the war effort after leaving the colony. While it is true that some governors used their offices to promote their interests, what distinguished Gálvez from the others was that he had an uncle in a powerful office in Spain to protect him. Contrary to the flattering studies about the youthful governor, an impartial examination of his conduct in Louisiana reveals that he committed serious errors. He tried to ingratiate himself to the large French planters by restoring their ability to deal freely with slaves, even to the point of subverting Spanish law. To cover his error in naming Bouligny second military chief and remove him as lieutenant governor, Gálvez made false accusations. He engaged in nepotism by flagrantly promoting the interests of St. Maxent. Instead of confronting problems openly and honestly, he resorted to guile and deceit to achieve selfish ends that turned out badly for everyone except himself. All of this shows that Gálvez was not an experienced administrator when he arrived in Louisiana.

Notes for "Bernardo de Gálvez: A Reexamination of His Governorship"

[1]Works that praise Bernardo de Gálvez include José Rodulfo Boeta, *Bernardo de Gálvez* (Madrid, 1976); Buchanon Parker Thomson, *Spain: Forgotten Ally of the American Revolution* (North Quincy, MS, 1976); C. de Reparaz, *"Yo Solo," Bernardo de Gálvez y la toma de Pensacola en 1781* (Barcelona, 1986); Lorenzo G. LaFarelle, *Bernardo de Gálvez: Hero of the American Revolution* (Austin, 1992); and two by Jack D. L. Holmes, *The 1779 "Marcha de Gálvez": Louisiana's Giant Step Forward in the American Revolution* (Baton Rouge, 1974), and "Bernardo de Gálvez, Colonial Governor, 1777-1785," in Joseph G. Dawson III, ed., *The Governors of Louisiana, From Iberville to Edwards* (Baton Rouge, 1990): 56-60.

[2]John W. Caughey, *Bernardo de Gálvez in Louisiana, 1776-1783* (1934; reprint ed., Gretna, LA, 1972).

[3]Among other works, see Jack D. L. Holmes, "Bernardo de Gálvez: Spain's 'Man of the Hour' During the American Revolution," in *Cardinales de dos independencias (Noreste de México—Sureste de los Estados Unidos*, ed. Beatriz Ruiz Caytán et al. (Mexico City, 1978): 161-74; Ralph Lee Woodward, Jr., ed., *Tribute to Don Bernardo de Gálvez* (Baton Rouge, 1979); and Thomas Fleming, "Bernardo de Gálvez: The Forgotten Revolutionary Conquistador Who Saved Louisiana," *American Heritage*, 33 (1982): 31-39.

[4]Eric Beerman, *España y la independencia de Estados Unidos* (Madrid, 1992). Beerman confines himself to discussing Gálvez's military role in the war.

[5]Jack D. L. Holmes in a conversation with the author, New Orleans, March 1980.

[6]J. Horace Nunemaker borrowed the term "Bouligny affair," from Roscoe R. Hill, *Descriptive Catalogue of the Documents Relating to the History of the United States in the Papeles Procedentes de Cuba Deposited in the Archivo General de Indias at Seville* (Washington, DC, 1916), 505. See Nunemaker's article, "The Bouligny Affair in Louisiana," *Hispanic American Historical Review*, 25 (1945): 339-63. Originally, the last name of Gálvez's father-in-law was only Maxent, but he added Saint or St. to make it more distinguished. Information provided by Eric Beerman.

[7]Alejandro O'Reilly to [José de Gálvez], Puerto de Santa María, May 7, 1776, Archivo General de Indias, Papeles procedentes de Cuba, legajo (hereafter abbreviated as AGI, PC, leg.) 2586; Bernardo de Gálvez patent of promotion, Aranjuez, May 22, 1776, AGI, Audiencia de Santo Domingo (hereafter abbreviated as SD), leg. 2654; royal order to the governor of Louisiana, Madrid, July 19, 1776, AGI, PC, leg. 174B. O'Reilly in 1776 was trying to overcome his debacle of the year before in the invasion of Algiers, which resulted in the loss of many Spanish soldiers. Perhaps he also sought the favor of the minister of the Indies.

[8]On St. Maxent, see Ramón Ezquerra, "Un patricio colonial: Gilbert de Saint-Maxent, teniente gobernador de Luisiana," *Revista de Indias*, 11 (1950): 97-170; and James Julian Coleman, Jr., *Gilbert Antoine de St. Maxent: The Spanish-Frenchman of New Orleans* (New Orleans, 1968). Both are sympathetic studies of St. Maxent. See also Eric Beerman, "The French Ancestors of Félicité de St. Maxent," *New Orleans Genesis*, 17 (1978): 403-6.

[9]María del Carmen Galbis Díez, "Bernardo de Gálvez (1785-1786)," in *Los virreyes de Nueva España en el reinado de Carlos III,* ed. José Antonio Calderón Quijano, 2 vols. (Seville, 1972), 1:329-30; C. H. Haring, *The Spanish Empire in America* (New York, 1963), 126; Hans W. Baade, "The Law of Slavery in Spanish Luisiana, 1769-1803," in Edward F. Haas, ed., *Louisiana's Legal Heritage* (Pensacola, 1983), 64. On November 26, 1781, in Havana Gálvez and Félicité were married again, this time in church. See Guillermo Porras Muñoz, "Acta de matrimonio de Bernardo de Gálvez y Felicitas St. Maxent," *Boletín del Archivo General de la Nación* (Mexico City), 16 (1945): 277-83.

[10]Petition of the *cabildo síndico procurador general* (public advocate) and the leading citizens to the governor, New Orleans, February 27, 1770, Alejandro O'Reilly regulations, New Orleans, February 28, 1770, both in AGI, PC, leg. 110; Juan José Andreu Ocariz, *Movimientos rebeldes de los esclavos negros durante el dominio español en Luisiana* (Zaragoza, Spain, 1977), 41-43; Bibiano Torres Ramírez, *Alejandro O'Reilly en Indias* (Seville, 1968), 145-46. Through Governor Gálvez's benevolence, St. Maxent became the colonel of the New Orleans militia battalion. A glimpse of St. Maxent's anti-black bias can be seen in his refusal to dine with black militia officers or have them sit with white officers of the same unit. The incident occurred at Fort San Felipe de Placaminas near the mouth of the Mississippi River. Kimberly S. Hanger, "A Privilege and Honor to Serve: The Free Black Militia of Spanish New Orleans," *Military History of the Southwest,* 31 (1991): 83.

[11]Actas del Cabildo, Libro 1:67-68, August 6, 1773, WPA transcriptions of the New Orleans Cabildo minutes in Spanish (cited hereafter as Actas del Cabildo, Libro in Roman numerals, Volume if appropriate in arabic numbers in parentheses, page numbers, and date); 1:113-14, August 27, 1773.

[12]Unzaga's age and experience probably prevented him from being influenced by St. Maxent as easily as the impressionable younger Gálvez. This is a point that Gálvez biographers have overlooked or ignored. Unzaga became governor of New Orleans on December 1, 1769. O'Reilly to Julián de Arriaga, No. 16, New Orleans, December 10, 1769, in Lawrence Kinnaird, ed., *Spain in the Mississippi Valley, 1765-94*, 3 vols. (Washington, DC, 1946), 1:132-35. On St. Maxent's fur-trading, see John Francis McDermott, "The Exclusive Trade Privilege of Maxent, Laclède and Company," *Missouri Historical Review*, 29 (1935): 272-78.

[13]The thinking of St. Maxent and other large slaveholders is derived from the document they drew up to control slaves. It is the *Code Noir ou Loi Municipale*, which was written in 1778. It is in the Library of Congress; Parsons Collection, Humanities Research Library, University of Texas, Austin; and elsewhere. The *Code Noir ou Loi Municipale* was not royal legislation as Jack D. L. Holmes, in "The Abortive Pointe Coupée Conspiracy," *Louisiana History*, 11 (1970): 343, and Thomas N. Ingersoll, in "Free Blacks in a Slave Society: New Orleans, 1718-1812," *William and Mary Quarterly*, 3d ser., 48 (1991): 180, believe. See Baade, "Law of Slavery," 64-67.

[14]José de Gálvez to Bernardo de Gálvez, No. 75, May 10, 1777, AGI, PC, leg. 569. In January, 1777, Governor Gálvez must have told his uncle that planters in Louisiana needed new regulations to control slaves. He probably did so in a private letter that has not survived.

[15]Royal instructions to the governor of Louisiana, San Lorenzo, November 25, 1776, AGI, PC, leg. 174B. Minister Gálvez drew up the instructions for the king. Gilbert C. Din, ed., *Louisiana in 1776: A Memoria of Francisco Bouligny* (New Orleans, 1977), 14-17. The formal appointment of Bouligny as lieutenant governor, dated in San Lorenzo, November 25, 1776, is in AGI, PC, leg. 566. His appointment is also mentioned in the instructions to the governor. Despite his name, Bouligny, born in Alicante, was a Spaniard and not a Frenchman.

[16]Royal instructions to the governor of Louisiana, San Lorenzo, November 25, 1776, AGI, PC, leg. 174B; Gilbert C. Din, *Francisco Bouligny: A Bourbon Soldier in Spanish Louisiana* (Baton Rouge, 1993), 76-77. Article 22 of the instructions also called for punishing severely persons who sold blacks liquor, guns, and gunpowder and received payment in stolen goods. Article 23 prohibited nocturnal black dances and assemblies, and required masters to use prudence and gentleness to insure that black Catholics married in the Church. Article 24 warned of the great harm and scandal caused by many free female mulattoes who lived "dishonestly." Minister Gálvez instructed the governor to consult with the vicar general so that the women might have the choice of mending their lives and living honestly. Otherwise, they faced deportation to Haiti.

The prohibition of black assemblies and dances reflected large planter thinking that was paranoidal and showed no understanding that Africans benefited from these activities. But all efforts at prohibition in New Orleans ultimately failed, and they probably mostly misfired even in the countryside where records are almost nonexistent. Masters did not want Catholic marriages for their slaves because they preferred to sell family members individually. A copy of the November 25, 1776, instructions to the governor of Louisiana that probably belonged to Bouligny is in the Rosemond E. and Emile Kuntz Collection, Special Collections, Howard-Tilton Library, Tulane University.

[17]Actas del Cabildo, 1:273-74, April 9, 1779; Andreu Ocariz, *Movimientos rebeldes*, 44. A copy of Gálvez's pardon of April 20, 1779, to fugitive slaves in the Historic New Orleans Collection. Spanish archival records do not have a copy because the governor neither sent one to Spain nor filed one with local records which the Spaniards later removed to Havana and Seville.

[18]Baade, "Law of Slavery," 62-67; Laura L. Porteous, ed. and trans., "Index to the Spanish Judicial Records of Louisiana," *Louisiana Historical Quarterly*, 11 (1928): 338-52. María Juana's suit, in the Louisiana Historical Center, New Orleans, is 620 pages long.

[19]Marqués de Grimaldi to Luis de Unzaga, El Pardo, March 24, 1770, in Kinnaird, ed., *Spain in the Mississippi Valley*, 1:163-64. Before the 1768 rebellion, the Spanish government already intended to replace French law and institutions in the areas where they remained. Governor Antonio de Ulloa had started this process although he moved slowly. John Preston Moore, *Revolt in Louisiana: The Spanish Occupation, 1766-1770* (Baton Rouge, 1976), 52-54.

[20]In discussing planter resistance to Spanish slave laws in 1777 to 1779, Baade, in "Law of Slavery," 62, calls it a "slaveholders' *Fronde*," by which he invokes the aristocrats' uprising against absolutism in seventeenth-century France. The absolutists in Louisiana's case, however, were the masters.

[21]Actas del Cabildo, 1:232, October 10, 1777. In 1779, 1784, 1792, and 1795, governors tried to revive the fugitive slave fund, and they failed each time. Large numbers of slaveholders beyond the New Orleans district refused to contribute to it. A major reason for their refusal was that disbursements from the fund favored the large slaveholders of the New Orleans District who suffered more from runaways.

[22]Ibid., 1:184-85, May 16, 1775; 1:197-198, November 24, 1775; 1:243, February 13, 1778; 1:249, May 22, 1778; 1:273-74, April 9, 1779.

[23]Ibid., 1:255, October 16, 1778. For a discussion of the *Code Noir ou Loi Municipale*, see Thomas N. Ingersoll, "Slave Codes and Judicial Practice in New Orleans, 1718-1807," *Law and History Review*, 23 (1995): 47-54. Ingersoll states that at least twenty of the seventy-two articles restricted free blacks or slaves who tried to buy their freedom. It allowed free blacks to be sold into slavery and limited slave access to guns and horses.

[24]Actas del Cabildo, 1:266-67, February 19 and 26, 1779; Baade, "Law of Slavery," 64-66.

[25]Baade, "Law of Slavery," 62-63, Actas del Cabildo, 1:267-68, March 1, 1779; Ingersoll, "Slave Codes," 47-54. Ingersoll, who is unaware of the conflict between Gálvez and the *cabildo*, suggests that the *Loi Municipale* was enforced locally.

[26]Stella O'Conner, "The Charity Hospital of Louisiana at New Orleans: An Administrative and Financial History, 1736-1946," *Louisiana Historical Quarterly*, 31 (1948): 18-19. Led by Reggio, the *cabildo* tried for several years to gain power over Charity Hospital from Governors Gálvez and Esteban Miró and later from Andrés Almonester y Roxas, who became the patron of the institution after rebuilding it and endowing it with funding. See Gilbert C. Din and John E. Harkins, *The New Orleans Cabildo: Colonial Louisiana's First City Government, 1769-1803* (Baton Rouge, 1996), 219-22.

According to Holmes, in "Bernardo de Gálvez," 57-58, Gálvez in 1782 removed Pedro Piernas as interim military governor of Louisiana because he exceeded the instructions that Gálvez had given him and had cooperated with the *cabildo*. Gálvez's action again shows his displeasure with a subordinate who overshot his orders and with the *cabildo* councillors.

[27]Bernardo de Gálvez to José de Gálvez, No. 255, New Orleans, March 2, 1779, AGI, SD, leg. 2662; Baade, "Law of Slavery," 66-67. On June 11, 1784, *Síndico Procurador General* Leonardo Mazange mentioned that the exemplary penalties authorities wanted to impose on recently apprehended fugitive slaves were not available because the black code (*Loi Municipale*) prepared in 1778-79 had not been submitted to the Crown for approval. The *cabildo* thereupon charged *Alcalde Ordinario* Reggio to proceed against the culprits according to the Laws of the Indies. Ibid., 66.

[28]Bernardo de Gálvez to José de Gálvez, No. 255 reserved, New Orleans, March 2, 1779, AGI, SD, leg. 2662. The formal appointment of Bouligny as lieutenant governor, dated in San Lorenzo, November 25, 1776, is in AGI, PC, leg. 566. Proof that Bouligny carried the 1776 instructions for the governor is in José de Gálvez to the governor of Louisiana, No. 54, Madrid, December 13, 1776, which reads, "Instructions of His Majesty which are sent to you with the captain of battalion of that Province Dn. Francisco Bouligny," in AGI, PC, leg. 174B. See also Din, *Francisco Bouligny*, 79-95.

[29]Gálvez to post commandants, New Orleans, April 11, 1777, AGI, PC, leg. 1. Gálvez's April 2, 1777, announcements about Bouligny to post commandants have disappeared. See the copy Bouligny reproduced in his June 3, 1779, letter to Gálvez in AGI, PC, leg. 2358.

[30]Bouligny to Bernardo de Gálvez, New Orleans, April 13 and 14, 1778, both in AGI, PC, leg. 2358. On Willing, see John Walton Caughey, "Willing's Expedition Down the Mississippi, 1778," *Louisiana Historical Quarterly,* 15 (1932): 5-36; on Gálvez favoring his father-in-law, see Thomas D. Watson, "A Scheme Gone Awry: Bernardo de Gálvez, Gilberto Antonio de San Maxent, and the Southern Indian Trade," *Louisiana History*, 17 (1976): 5-17; and Arthur Preston Whitaker, ed. and trans., *Documents Relating to the Commercial Policy of Spain in the Floridas, with Incidental Reference to Louisiana* (Deland, FL, 1931), xviii-xxix.

[31]Two letters of Bouligny to Bernardo de Gálvez, New Orleans, June 3, 1778, Bouligny to José de Gálvez, New Orleans, June 3, 1778, all in AGI, PC, leg. 2358; Nunemaker, ed., "Bouligny Affair," 342, with the depositions of officials, 349-63.

[32]Gálvez to post commandants, New Orleans, October 21, 1778, AGI, PC, leg. 1; Nunemaker, ed., "Bouligny Affair," 340-41, 345-46.

[33][Gálvez] to Bouligny, New Orleans, November 12, 1778, and Bouligny to Gálvez, New Orleans, December 3, 1778, both in AGI, PC, leg. 2358. See also the depositions of officials in Nunemaker, ed., "Bouligny Affair," 349-63. On the Canary Island immigrants and Bouligny's preference for Ouachita, see Gilbert C. Din, *The Canary Islanders of Louisiana* (Baton Rouge, 1988), and "Francisco Bouligny's 1778 Plans for Settlement in Louisiana," *Southern Studies*, 16 (1977): 211-24. Gálvez selected four settlement sites for the Canary Islanders, two of which, Barataria and Galveztown, were disastrous choices.

[34]Bouligny to the king, New Orleans, December 10, 1778, [Gálvez to Bouligny], New Orleans, December 11 and 23, 1778, all in AGI, PC, leg. 2358.

[35]Bouligny to Gálvez, New Orleans, January 8, 1779, ibid. On Bouligny in New Iberia, see Gilbert C. Din, "Lieutenant Colonel Francisco Bouligny and the Malagueño Settlement at New Iberia, 1779," *Louisiana History*, 17 (1976): 187-202; Mathé Allain, "Bouligny's Account of the Founding of New Iberia," *Attakapas Gazette*, 14 (1979): 79-84, 124-31; Glenn R. Conrad, "Some Observations on the Founding of New Iberia," *Attakapas Gazette*, 22 (1987): 41-46. Several Spanish documents on New Iberia's founding have been published in Maurine Bergerie, *They Tasted Bayou Water. A Brief History of Iberia Parish* (New Orleans, 1962). Bouligny devoted much energy to making New Iberia a successful settlement as his many letters attest.

[36]Bernardo de Gálvez to José de Gálvez, No. 255 reserved, New Orleans, March 2, 1779, AGI, SD, leg. 2662.

[37]Nunemaker, ed., "Bouligny Affair," 347-63, reproduces Gálvez's interrogatories and the replies he received.

[38]José de Gálvez to the governor of Louisiana, No. 282 reserved and No. 310, Aranjuez and San Ildefonso, June 25 and August 30, 1779, respectively, both in AGI, PC, leg. 174A.

[39]Bouligny to Gálvez, New Iberia, August 25, 1779, and Casa de Champaña, September 3, 1779, with attached "List of the People who left New Iberia and have arrived here with the Detachment of Monr. DeClouet," Bouligny, Casa de Champaña, September 3, 1779, [Gálvez] to Bouligny, [n.p., n.d.], all in AGI, PC, leg. 600; and Bouligny's last service sheet, made on the day he died, New Orleans, November 25, 1800, Bouligny-Baldwin Collection, Historic New Orleans Collection. See also Bouligny to Luis de Las Casas, New Orleans, January 4, 1794, AGI, PC, leg. 1396, which shows Bouligny's bitterness at the injustice Gálvez had inflicted on him.

[40]Gálvez to Bouligny, New Orleans, October 11, 1779, AGI, PC, leg. 2358; Gálvez to Bouligny, New Orleans, October 11 and 26, 1779, Bouligny to Gálvez, New Orleans, October 12 and 28, 1779, all in AGI, PC, leg. 600; [Gálvez] to Bouligny, New Orleans, November 2, 6, 10, and 23, 1779, Biblioteca Nacional (Madrid), Sección de Manuscritos, "Colección de documentos sobre Luisiana, 1767 a 1792" (hereafter cited as BN, CDL) 3 vols.; Bouligny to Gálvez, New Orleans, November 3, 1779, BN, CDL, Gálvez instructions to Nicolás Forstall, New Orleans, November 15, 1779, AGI, PC, leg. 192; "Instructions that Dn. Martín Navarro . . . Principal Accountant of the Army and Royal Treasury . . . should observe," Gálvez, New Orleans, January 8, 1780, AGI, PC, leg. 82; [Gálvez] to Juan Ventura Morales, New Orleans, January 12, 1780, AGI, PC, leg. 83.

[41]Bernardo de Gálvez to José de Gálvez, No. 388, New Orleans, June 5, 1780, Confidential Despatches of Don Bernardo de Gálvez, WPA Translation, 2:162; Din, *Francisco Bouligny*, 117, 124-26.

[42]Beerman, *España y la independencia de Estados Unidos*, 49. For evidence that St. Maxent supplied goods to settlements, see O'Reilly to Julián de Arriaga, No. 25, New Orleans, December 29, 1769, in Kinnaird, ed., *Spain in the Mississippi Valley*, 1:147; [Bernardo de Gálvez], "Ynstrucción que deberá observar el Subteniente Dn. Antonio Maxent, Comandante de la Nueva Población de Valenzuela," New Orleans, May 18, 1779, AGI, PC, leg. 192; and various documents in AGI, PC, leg. 2358.

[43]Whitaker, tran. and ed., *Documents Relating to the Commercial Policy of Spain*, xxviii-xxix; Watson, "A Scheme Gone Awry," 5-17. Esquerra, "Un patricio colonial," 119-24, 125-28, 132-34, 137-53. Prosecution of the law suit against St. Maxent did not end until 1799, if then, which was five years after his death. In 1799 a court in Spain found St. Maxent guilty of illegally exporting specie and ordered him to pay the amounts shipped out, 37,190 *pesos*, and court costs of 3,559 *reales*. The duque de Castro Terreño, son-in-law of the late José de Gálvez and legal counsel for the children of the deceased Bernardo de Gálvez, protested stating that he did not have documents on this matter. He sent to Louisiana for them, but the records in the case end at this point.

[44]Beerman, *España y la independencia de Estados Unidos*, 136-42, 148-49, 160; Eric Beerman, "'Yo Solo' no solo: Juan Antonio Riaño at Pensacola in 1781," *Florida Historical Quarterly*, 58 (1979): 174-84.

[45]Beerman, *España y la independencia de Estados Unidos*, 187-235; for an uncritical look at Gálvez in Guarico, see Guillermo Porras Muñoz, "El Fracaso de Guarico," *Anuario de Estudios Americanos*, 26 (1969): 569-609. On the conquest of the Bahamas, see Eric Beerman, "La última batalla de la guerra de la independencia norteamericana no fue Yorktown: La expedición hispano-americana a las Bahamas en 1782," *Revista de Historia Naval*, 2 (1984): 89-102; James A. Lewis, *The Final Campaign of the American Revolution: Rise and Fall of the Spanish Bahamas* (Columbia, SC, 1990). On the French Navy during the war, see Jonathan R. Dull, *The French Navy and American Independence: A Study of Arms and Diplomacy, 1774-1787* (Princeton, 1975).

[46]Beerman, *España y la independencia de Estados Unidos*, 191-235 passim; on Miranda, see José María Pérez Cabrera, *Miranda en Cuba (1780-1783)* (Havana, 1950).

[47]Haring, *The Spanish Empire in America*, 107. Charles Edward Chapman, in *Colonial Hispanic America: A History* (New York, 1933), 202, recognizes the great power that José de Gálvez wielded but attributes the changes that took place after his death to graft and corruption.

THE PROVINCIAL GOVERNOR-GENERAL: MANUEL GAYOSO DE LEMOS*

Jack D. L. Holmes

The newly appointed governor-general of Louisiana and West Florida left his former command at Natchez on July 29, 1797, and traveled to New Orleans. Stopping at the home of his friend, Étienne Boré, Louisiana's first successful sugar producer, Manuel Gayoso de Lemos wrote to the municipal council of New Orleans. He advised the *cabildo* members that he would soon arrive to take his oath of office. On August 5 he appeared in the chambers of that massive cabildo building, delivered his appointment and instructions to the Baron de Carondelet, and then took his oath to protect the Roman Catholic Church, to defend all royal edicts, and to promote justice and wise government in accordance with Spanish laws and customs.[1]

In many ways the new post was not altogether strange to Gayoso. Having advised governors-general Esteban Miró and Carondelet and participated in their defensive plans for the province during his eight years at Natchez, Gayoso was familiar with most of the features of Louisiana provincial administration. The multiplicity of duties pressed upon him, the host of new officials, both religious and secular, military and civilian, and the pressing problems of defense against potential enemies in the United States, England, and France, offered renewed challenges to a man skilled at solving the tangled puzzles of Louisiana politics. True, the people of Lower Louisiana were of French extraction, with different customs and language from those Anglo-Americans in Natchez. But Gayoso was as fluent in French as he was in English. His pleasing personality, coupled with a profound sense of the royal dignity incumbent upon the king's messengers, prepared him for another opportunity to serve his master's interests.

For almost two years Gayoso combined the functions of magistrate, municipal council chairman, vice-patron of the church, commander in chief of the regular and militia forces, guardian of the purse strings, and social leader of a growing metropolitan area at

*Reprinted by permission of Louisiana State University Press from *Gayoso: The Life of a Spanish Governor in the Mississippi Valley, 1789-1799*, by Jack D. L. Holmes. Copyright © 1965 by Louisiana State University Press.

the heart of a vitally important province. Although his hands were tied more than at Natchez by the Spanish colonial system of conflicting jurisdiction, Gayoso brought his virtues—as well as his vices—to the office. In comparing the greatest governors-general of the Spanish Dominion of Louisiana, historians usually place Bernardo de Gálvez, Alejandro O'Reilly, or the Baron de Carondelet at the apex of success. Gayoso was given but two years to demonstrate that he belonged in the first rank.

His first duties were naturally confused with the final actions of his predecessor, Carondelet, who had been appointed to the presidency of Quito.[2] The outgoing governor-general spent many hours signing certificates of merit for the military, religious, and political members of his administration, most of whom remained to assist the new governor-general. There was considerable packing, and his wife and two children were ill. Finally, there was the matter of Carondelet's *residencia*. Unless otherwise exempted, royal governors, governors-general, viceroys, and other major officials underwent an examination of their years in power. In some cases the hearings were conducted secretly by judges appointed for that purpose, as in the case of Governor-General Esteban Miró.[3] In other cases, as in the example of Carondelet, the governor-general succeeding to that office conducted the examination of his predecessor's conduct in office.[4]

On August 7, Gayoso ordered his proclamation posted at convenient public gathering places throughout New Orleans. Citizens read that anyone having a complaint against Carondelet would have thirty days to appear at Government House. At the end of that time three men and/or their families had filed their protests for being expelled from Louisiana during the 1793 French Jacobin scare, and Nicolás Forstall protested being relieved from command of the post of Opelousas. Inasmuch as these complaints were not directed against the $3,000 Carondelet had deposited in his *residencia* account, but represented general complaints on which the king had already acted negatively, Gayoso ruled that the *residencia* was completed. The *cabildo* listed the merits of Carondelet's term as governor-general and wished him bon voyage as he left for Balize in September.[5]

As Carondelet sailed to his new post, Gayoso turned his full attention to the problems of Louisiana. Social festivities followed his inauguration. There were fancy banquets and numerous toasts given by members of the *cabildo*, New Orleans merchants, and individuals anxious to make the acquaintance of their new governor-general. When the society matrons proposed a fancy ball, Gayoso suggested they wait until the arrival of Sra. Gayoso. He wrote her, "The ladies here are very anxious to have you in Town."[6]

From the time of Alejandro O'Reilly, it had been customary for governors-general to issue a *bando de buen gobierno*, which was a proclamation of general laws governing the policing and regulation of public morals in New Orleans.[7] In January, 1798, Gayoso followed the custom and issued a *bando* published by the *Moniteur de la Louisiane* printer. The regulation consisted of eleven pages and twenty-three articles in French and Spanish. Although Gayarré said, "It contained nothing worthy of any special notice,"[8] Gayoso's *bando* was one of the most interesting pieces of local legislation in Spanish Louisiana. A cursory examination of its provisions gives one a glimpse of Spanish social and economic practices. Because they believed in keeping the Sabbath, for example, the *bando* provided penalties for working or running carts on that day. The authorities disapproved of such games as monté, roulette, craps, and lansquenet. Firearms, knives of certain types, and bayonets were also forbidden. Persons without jobs or visible means of support were to be sentenced to the public works. All visitors to the city were required to be registered with the ward commissioners or magistrates within twenty-four hours. Billiard parlors and taverns were to keep set hours of opening and closing; but the latter might, according to the regulation, keep their doors slightly open to deliver necessary beverages to "sick persons" at unseasonable hours.

Other local regulations attempted to protect the New Orleanians against fires. The city had been almost totally destroyed in 1788 and again in 1794. When disastrous fires of this nature showed the need for engines, pumps, buckets, and axes to fight fires, they were purchased and placed at convenient locations in the various wards. When another fire broke out on May 26, 1795, two additional policemen were added to the New Orleans force to guard against arson.[9]

Laissez-faire was virtually unknown in Spanish New Orleans. Most economic activities were regulated by the government. Prices of meat, bread, and rice were rigidly set on a weekly basis; and all sales of merchandise were equally supervised. As in O'Reilly's time, taverns were licensed and regulated. No liquor could be sold to Indians or Negro slaves.[10] The *cabildo* appointed a commissioner to make monthly inspections of the meat and fish markets near the river to determine the quality, condition, and quantity of cattle butchered, to inspect weights, and to fix prices. Merchants led by Fernando Alzar & Co., protested against allowing Negroes to sell goods on the streets and levees as peddlers, and Gayoso replied by requiring all proper merchants and slaves to be duly licensed by the governor-general.[11]

Because many New Orleanians complained about the pressure from Charity Hospital to buy their caskets there, the *cabildo* ruled that the public was free to purchase these terminal resting places from whomever they pleased.[12] In order to prevent crime in the dark shadows of New Orleans' streets, the *cabildo* created a force of night watchmen (*serenos*) and constructed the now famous Bourbon Street-style lamps on the principal corners. From special funds in the Lighting Department wicks, sulphur, flint, and broken panes of glass were replaced.[13]

To pay for fire fighting equipment, Gayoso followed the *cabildo*'s 1795 decree and ordered the residents of New Orleans taxed on the number of chimneys they owned in their houses or properties. Thus, the philanthropist Andrés Almonester y Roxas paid an annual tax of $9.38 for his twenty-five chimneys, and the annual revenue from this source from the four wards often exceeded $4,000. Master bricklayers were paid two dollars each per day spent inspecting the chimneys. Funds from this source also went into the Lighting Department.[14]

When the inhabitants protested against this tax because it hit the lower classes as well as those most able to pay, Gayoso was persuaded to change the form of taxation in

1799. Because the poor presumably ate little bread, their diet consisting primarily of rice and corn, Gayoso persuaded the *cabildo* to pass a tax of fifty cents a barrel on flour consumed by bakers in the manufacture of bread, less 5 percent for loss occasioned by rats. The new source of revenue, which was destined to the Lighting Department, amounted to $275 for January and February, 1799; and in March, $222.[15]

In other ways the New Orleans *Cabildo* was successful in obtaining revenues for specific purposes. Taxes on sugar cane rum, or tafia, produced almost $3,000 annually. Rental of the government houses constructed by Bernardo de Gálvez produced enough money to construct a storehouse for rice amounting to almost $5,000. Thirty-six tavern keepers paid an annual license fee of forty dollars each. A tax on each head of beef slaughtered at the market and wharfage duties made up additional sources of revenue.[16]

Gayoso discovered that the low-lying city was constantly inundated during times of the river's rise. Carondelet had asked for $6,000 in 1792 to pave the sidewalks; and Gayoso ordered all inhabitants to keep their sidewalks clean, swept, and sprinkled at lease once a day in the summer and as often as possible in the winter. By 1803, however, a visiting physician was able to write, "The means to be employed in rendering New Orleans healthful, are: 1st, to raise its streets, and to give them a sufficient incline for the drainage of the waters. . . ."[17] Sanitary conditions at the end of the eighteenth century were still in such a deplorable condition that disease, particularly yellow fever, raged in epidemic proportions.[18]

Zoning regulations existed in New Orleans as they did in Natchez, and shortly after Gayoso arrived, the *auditor de guerra* and lieutenant-governor, Nicolás María Vidal, petitioned the new governor-general to disallow construction of buildings on the wharves and levees of the town.[19] Gayoso ordered vehicles, coaches, and horses to stay off the levees.[20]

Other decrees relative to the public safety and health were included in Gayoso's all-inclusive *bando*. He warned the owners of dogs to keep them confined, for within three days of the publication of the decree, all animals wandering in the streets would be killed. No person was allowed to keep gunpowder in excess of twenty-five pounds in his store or warehouse. Dead animals were to be buried, and no one could keep swine within the confines of the town. No one could wash his clothes below the point where vessels were careened, and stiff penalties were meted out to litterbugs.[21]

Gayoso found that in questions relating to civic order, finances, and public health, he was forced to cooperate with the New Orleans *Cabildo*. Formed by O'Reilly in 1769 in keeping with Spanish traditions of municipal government, the *cabildo* was a focal point of local self-government in New Orleans. The jurisdiction of this body extended to the far corners of Louisiana, but generally the councillors confined their attention to local matters. Carondelet recommended the addition of six members, and on December 23, 1796, the king approved the request. In keeping with the Spanish tradition of selling posts in the *cabildo* to the highest bidders, Gayoso, as head of the council conducted the elections. The price of the office was $1500, and the deductions from the annual salary of

$100 did not leave much for the trouble and hard work of those who had bid successfully for the position. Yet, the jobs were sought by many who hoped to serve the king, their own interests, or those of their friends.

Gayoso announced that the successful purchasers in 1797 were Darby Danycan, Jaime Jordá, Gilberto Andry, José LeBlanc, Juan de Castañedo, and Francisco Riaño.[22]

The *cabildo* considered a host of problems facing the city and, as presiding officer, Gayoso was forced to spend much of his official time examining complaints and recommending action. Poor Claudio Francisco Girod denied adulterating his vinegar, and one of the *cabildo* members, Nicolás Forstall, had trouble paying the money he owed to the San Lázaro lepers' hospital. Was Almonester doing the proper job at the Ursuline Convent's building program? Couldn't the city raise the salary of the hangman to fifteen dollars monthly? Had Bartolomé Lafond repaired all the gutters around the city as agreed?[23]

One of Gayoso's concerns was education in New Orleans. Between 1770 and 1774, royal decrees concerning the establishment of proper educational facilities for New Orleans had been granted, but the Spanish schools were not supported by the French population, who preferred to send their children to private schools managed by secular Frenchmen. The classes in the Spanish school hardly exceeded thirty pupils, and in 1788 the schoolhouse was destroyed in the famous fire. Six Franciscans came to Louisiana in 1787, some for the purpose of teaching in the school. By 1791 Father Ubaldo Delgado conducted primary classes. In 1796 a royal order reminded the governor-general that the earlier decrees regarding education should be implemented and that teachers be appointed to instruct the people of Louisiana in the Spanish language. It was Gayoso's first official duty to announce this reemphasis on education to the *cabildo*.[24]

Girls from good families and orphans alike attended the overcrowded classrooms of the Ursuline Convent, which was the most important school for females in the colony. Young Irene Folch, daughter of Vicente Folch y Juan, commandant at Pensacola, arrived in New Orleans in 1796 from Havana for the purpose of attending the Ursuline school.[25]

In addition to government-supported charitable institutions, Gayoso also supported philanthropy when he found it in individual citizens. Francisco Dunegan Beaurosier, a founder of San Fernando de Florisante in Missouri, had taken in as many orphans as he could, educating them and caring for them in his own home with no subsidy or support from the government. In recognition of his services in this instance, and because of his service to the Crown in repelling Indian attacks while an officer in the militia, Gayoso recommended him for an annual salary of $100 beginning on January 1, 1794.[26]

With a population of almost 10,000 at the end of the eighteenth century, New Orleans was an urban center.[27] In addition to being the political capital and economic *entrepôt* of the province, "La Ville" was the cultural and social heart of Spanish Louisiana. Travelers never ceased to marvel at the beauty of the crescent-shaped Mississippi as it formed one flank of the blocklike French Quarter. During Gayoso's term as governor-general, New Orleans society was already formed of the first families who could trace their forebears back to the early eighteenth-century French founders. It was a gay city, ready and eager at the first excuse to attend masked balls and operas. Theater seats were usually reserved for the first families, and even then they were difficult to obtain.[28] Following the disaster at Cap Français and the plight of the royalist emigrés from Paris, theater companies did a thriving business in New Orleans.[29] As in the case of economic matters, the theater was regulated by the governor-general, from the censorship of objectionable plays or the use of indecent language, to the manner in which tickets would be distributed among the public. Traffic outside the theater was also regulated during performances to prevent disturbing the actors and spectators. All shows began at precisely 5:30 in the evening. Spectators were forbidden to stand, wear their hats, or smoke during the performances.[30]

Carnival, Mardi Gras, and Fasching are universal explosions of hilarity, intoxication, and last-fling gaiety before the austere period of Lent in most Catholic countries. New Orleans was no exception, and its season during the Spanish domination was hardly less exciting than in modern days. As in the case of the opera and theater, all balls were strictly regulated as to the time and place, masks, guard duty, musicians, singing, whistling, and the kind of attire permitted or forbidden on certain occasions.[31]

Gayoso stepped into Carondelet's vacated position as the social leader of New Orleans. Convivial and bon vivant, Gayoso thoroughly enjoyed a good time and wanted to share the festive celebrations of New Orleans with his friends. He invited Mrs. Stephen Minor to attend the Carnival celebrations, even though he confided to Minor himself, "A million of attentions occupies me just now, the gay time of the Season gives me more trouble than to Command ten thousand men."[32]

But Carnival was a mild season by comparison to the wild rejoicing, celebrating, and cheering which took place on the arrival of the duc d'Orléans in February, 1798. Accompanied by the dukes of Montpensier and Beaujolay, and the marquis de Montjoye, the duc d'Orléans remained in New Orleans for almost five weeks, during which time they were lodged with Gayoso at the Government House. No stranger to courtly procedure, Gayoso utilized his training as O'Reilly's adjutant at Cádiz when the comte d'Artois and duc de Bourbon had been there during the joint Franco-Spanish operations directed against Gibraltar in 1780.[33]

Gayoso wrote to Godoy describing the royal visitors and complaining about the infinite expense their visit had cost him, in spite of the many banquets, balls, and dinners thrown by the leading inhabitants. Drawing from his own payroll funds, Gayoso spent $3,000 in addition to the $1,100 drawn from other funds. New Orleanians themselves had never opened their hearts and homes in more generous fashion. But for Gayoso the visit presented many problems in addition to the financial ones. He had to arrange the group's transportation to Havana and back to Europe and somehow keep it from being captured by roving corsairs of England or the United States. The princes, who had traveled down the Mississippi incognito, were forced by circumstances to continue the masquerade as far as Havana to avoid detection and possible embarrassing capture.[34] Moreover, the princes's too frequent contact with the Negro slaves of Louisiana did not bode well for the Spanish policy of careful isolation of their slaves from the infectious strain of *revolutionitis* which had attacked those in Santo Domingo. Louisiana planters were still mindful of the conspiracy of Negro slaves on the Poydras plantation at Punta Cortada [Pointe Coupée] in 1795 and the rumbling tremors of lesser movements. The French visitors cheerfully suggested liberation for all Negroes they encountered, and Gayoso had a very ticklish problem on his hands.[35]

By the end of March, however, the royal visitors had embarked for Havana, and Gayoso was able to turn his attention to the growing economic issues which faced his desperate colony. The annual subsidy which Mexico supplied to Louisiana via Havana had grown in the face of mounting defense costs and boundary commission expenses from $500,000 to $800,000 in 1797.[36] Resourceful and not always meticulous in keeping records, Gayoso was able to keep the ship of state from floundering during 1798 when cruising English men-of-war hoped to intercept the rich shipment from Veracruz. Long delayed, the subsidy more often than not was retained in Havana for the captain-general's "extraordinary expenses." So obnoxious had this practice become to Gayoso that he suggested Louisiana be placed under the direct supervision of the viceroy of New Spain, especially since Louisiana's security was the key to Mexico's future.[37]

By the end of 1798 Gayoso was in desperate straits. He borrowed from the merchants, appropriated $7,000 belonging to the Ursulines, and wrote pleading letters to the captain-general, viceroy, and numerous Spanish officials. Gayoso's pleas were finally heard and on December 12, the corvette *Ardilla* and the merchant ship *Fidela* left Veracruz bound for New Orleans with a cargo of gunpowder and $100,000. By April, 1799, another convoy had brought an additional $484,239; and the pressure on Gayoso's finances eased somewhat.[38] To his friend, Stephen Minor, he wrote gleefully, "Never such a sum came into this Town at one time since its foundation. Everything is in the greatest plenty therefore at present we do not feel the scourge of War."[39]

Gayoso's somewhat unorthodox handling of government finances at Natchez had involved him with the army accountant and the intendant on numerous occasions. Unfortunately, he did not mend his ways when he advanced to the governor-generalship of the province. He was not the meticulous accountant who jealously watched every cent and rendered complete and unassailable accounts to his sovereign. On the other hand, Gayoso had a broadness of vision that took in the entire spheres of business, politics, and trade with one quick glance. Not content to permit the status quo comfort to dim his vision of the future of New Orleans, Gayoso attempted to intercede with the king on behalf of reducing the duties on western exports to 6 percent. Gayoso's contacts along the Mississippi knew of and appreciated his efforts. James Garrard of Frankfort praised the governor-general for his forward-looking policy "by which the city of New Orleans must become one of the greatest markets in the world."[40]

Gayoso also devoted a good deal of attention to the problem of flooding during times of the river's greatest rise in the spring. His first inspection of the province, undertaken shortly after he took the oath of office, was concerned with the condition of the dikes, levees, and bridges which protected the low-lying Louisiana bottom land. On the basis of this reconnaissance, Gayoso issued a circular on March 6, 1798, requiring the various commandants of the province to call together their magistrates, syndics, and major landowners to discuss the question of placing all public levees and other internal improvements in a state of good repair.[41]

Most inhabitants answered the call to duty by offering a self-imposed tax on the basis of their landholdings for the governor-general to use to hire the necessary workers or to pay the soldiers employed on the works.[42] Sometimes a resident would refuse to serve in the work crews or pay for the repair of essential levees. Because the complete success of the programs depended on the entire cooperation of the people, Gayoso allowed no one to escape his obligations. Jean Baptiste Pechoux of the La Fourche de Chetimachas District refused and was incarcerated until he quickly changed his mind.[43] Gayoso might have been embarrassed when a syndic reported that the governor's own father-in-law, Stephen Watts, had failed to send slaves to repair breaks in his dikes, so Gayoso issued the necessary instructions for the work to be done.[44]

Gayoso's relations with the commercial trading firm of William Panton, John Leslie, and Thomas Forbes, operating out of Pensacola and furnishing trade goods to the Indian nations under Spain's protection, continued to be cordial although the intendant ad interim, Juan Ventura Morales, attempted to stop the lucrative trade. Panton, whose original temporary license had been extended since 1790 as a result of the warm support of Carondelet and Gayoso, had considered quitting the Louisiana and West Florida trade in the face of growing competition from the United States, especially after the Treaty of San Lorenzo. Gayoso attempted to placate Panton and intercede with the king on his behalf, but Morales' constant interference in any matter which remotely involved finances undid much of Gayoso's work.[45]

The dispute between Gayoso and Morales extended to virtually every aspect of government. The basic cause lay in the nature of the Spanish colonial system of overlapping jurisdiction, which was supposed to maintain centralization and improve the quality of government. The intendant system was a French import, first established by Philip V for Spain in 1718 for the purpose of ironing out the numerous wrinkles of Spanish financial and judicial administration. Temporarily suspended, it was reestablished in 1749, and on December 4, 1786, the king promulgated a lengthy, 306-article regulation governing the conduct of intendants in New Spain. Charles III hoped that this system would replace the inefficiency of American colonial government, and he made the intendant subordinate to no viceroy or governor. Ostensibly, jurisdiction over all matters involving smuggling, trade, collection of revenue, municipal finance, military expenses, agriculture, industry, land grants, and every conceivable aspect of administration belonged solely to this treasury official.[46]

Martín Navarro, first intendant of Louisiana during the Spanish régime, worked closely with Governor-General Miró and the rare disputes which arose between the two were usually settled amicably. From 1788 to 1794 the intendancy was united to the office of governor-general, but when Carondelet complained about the multiplicity of duties, the two were separated once again. Francisco Rendón, former Spanish minister to the United States, became intendant on August 26, 1794, but less than two years later he assumed the functions of intendant and *corregidor* at Zacatecas in New Spain.[47]

Juan Ventura Morales the army accountant and legal advisor (*contador*), was appointed intendant ad interim in 1796. His pioneer studies of more efficient accounting methods in the Department of Immigration and Indian Affairs caught the attention of superiors who considered him an ideal watchdog over the expenditures of governors who were perhaps, overextravagant in their management of Louisiana affairs. By 1799 he had become the principal accountant of the army and royal treasury for Louisiana and West Florida, with virtually dictatorial powers over expenses and lands. Long a foe of the political and military governors and commandants of the province, he made enemies in all places and was on one occasion kicked and struck by a schoolmaster for larceny and was implicated in an unsavory adulterous affair in which the wronged husband was poisoned.[48]

When Gayoso assumed the governor-generalship of the province, Morales wrote the understatement of his long career: "I predict that things will be stormy for the Intendancy."[49] Gayoso had already had a run-in concerning the respective powers of a subdelegate of the treasury, Vicente Folch y Juan, when the latter was commandant at San Fernando de las Barrancas. On that occasion Gayoso denied that the treasury department had jurisdiction over military matters.[50]

A serious dispute centered on the question of who had authority to grant lands in the provinces. On September 9, 1797, with the sad experience at Natchez fresh in his mind, Gayoso issued a proclamation regarding the admission of new settlers into Louisiana. Its general purpose was to attract actual farmers and artisans by forbidding unmarried immigrants without slaves to receive land. He also reiterated the exclusion of public worship by the Protestants and clarified the religious provisions of private worship as extending only to the first generation of immigrants.[51]

On October 22, 1798, the king revived Article 81 of the instructions for the intendants of New Spain and applied it to Louisiana. This gave the intendant the exclusive jurisdiction over granting and distribution of lands in Louisiana. Morales accordingly drew up his own ordinance, but Gayoso refused to publish it as the intendant demanded. Splenetic correspondence between the two shattered the shaky truce between intendant and governor-general; and Morales, who was supported by influential ministers in Spain, won the case. Morales' ordinance, which was posted at the usual public places in New Orleans in March, 1799, was clearly anti-American. Anyone living in Louisiana less than two years who could not produce legal title to his land was required to give it up. Those who had more than two years' residence were obligated to pay for their lands at a price set by Morales or the royal treasury. Inasmuch as a vast majority of immigrants who had held lands in Louisiana since 1789 had come from the United States, the intent of Morales' regulations proved he was "a headstrong individual with antipathy toward things American."[52] Gayoso recognized that the soft, easy-going policy, which had won so many Americans to Spain for ten years, was now completely upset by Morales; but there was little he could do under the circumstances. He reluctantly accepted Morales' power over land grants, but continued to urge the Spanish ministers to change an obnoxious situation which threatened the very existence of Spanish power in Louisiana.[53]

By 1799, Morales had made Gayoso's life and his official duties completely miserable. The governor-general's hands were virtually tied by the backbiting Morales, who seemed to delight in obstructing every aspect of government from defense to Indian affairs to business matters. Morales blocked the payment of funds to the Spanish boundary commission. He objected to the repair and construction of new cannon emplacements for the galleys. The intendant interfered with the duties of the pilots and guides at Balize and with the powers of the captain of the port, José de Hevia.[54]

When Morales insisted on written requests for funds involving military activities, such as improving fortifications and the disposition of galleys in the fleet, Gayoso complained that if the request were complied with, it would mean the enemy would learn of the Spaniards' defensive plans and render them useless. Moreover, the maintenance of secret agents in the "conspiracy" of Kentucky and other western American settlements would be out of the question, inasmuch as the success of their activities depended on absolute secrecy.[55]

Gayoso pleaded with Godoy to unite once more the intendancy and governor-general, or at least to replace the ad interim intendant with someone like Rendón, whose cooperative attitude would allow the activities of government to proceed in an orderly manner. Although the Prince of the Peace, Gayoso's main contact at court, was in favor of his suggestion, popular resentment toward Godoy as the Queen's favorite resulted in his removal on March 28, 1798. He was replaced with Francisco de Saavedra, described as a "man of firm character, well-organized head, considerable knowledge, great disinterestedness, and incorruptible honesty." Unfortunately, he was in sympathy with the intendant, and he refused to change the separation, which he felt would result in economy in government.[56]

The temporary release afforded by the simple pleasures could not take Gayoso's mind from the constant pressures of his office. His health suffered from the strain of his many obligations, and he often complained of sore, red eyes.[57] In addition to the above mentioned duties, Gayoso also exercised a judicial role in Louisiana government. On several occasions the duties involved were merely perfunctory, such as approving an inventory of the papers of deceased individuals.[58] In several cases, however, Gayoso was expected to use Solomon-like wisdom in rendering justice. Particularly ticklish were cases involving the manumission of slaves belonging to deceased owners. Renato Trahan had willed freedom for his Negro mistress and her mulatto children. When the heirs disputed the will, Gayoso ruled that the fifth part of the estate of the deceased went to the slave because she was the mother of Trahan's children. He added that the purchase price of her freedom would be subtracted from that sum.[59] On another occasion, a Negress,

Margarita Josepha, pleaded with Gayoso for her manumission on the grounds that she was half white and her children were sired by a white man. In this instance, Gayoso decreed her freedom.[60]

As vice-patron of the Church, Gayoso fell heir to that interesting arrangement between church and state so typical in colonial Latin America. Spanish kings from the time of the Reconquest had won the right to appoint bishops and other hierarchy posts as well as the privilege of supporting the church financially. After the conquest of America in the fifteenth and sixteenth centuries, this *patronato real* power was extended by the monarchs to their viceroys, captains-general, and governors. From the time of O'Reilly, in 1769, Spanish governors in Louisiana showed a keen interest in the work of the church. In 1770 O'Reilly followed the suggestions of the Capuchin Father Dagobert in recommending the formation of eleven parishes supplied with eighteen priests.[61] Father Cirilo de Barcelona, who served as chaplain with the Gálvez expeditions of 1780-81, acted the role of auxiliary bishop of Cuba until 1787 when the Provinces of Louisiana and the Floridas were placed under the jurisdiction of the newly created Diocese of St. Christopher of Havana. In 1787 the pastor of St. Louis Parish Church in New Orleans, Fray Antonio de Sedella, was appointed commissioner of the Holy Inquisition for Louisiana, but the violent opposition of Governor-General Miró resulted in his temporary expulsion and the end of all attempts to establish that institution so opposed by the people of Louisiana.[62]

The little New Orleans church burned to the ground during the 1788 fire, and Andrés Almonester y Roxas offered to loan the *cabildo* sufficient money to build a new one. It was finished, despite continual bickering and acrimonious charges against Almonester in December, 1794, and the following year it was made a cathedral. In 1791 the king divided the Havana diocese; and on April 25, 1793, Pope Pius VI decreed the establishment of an independent diocese for Louisiana, the second one in what is today the United States.[63]

When the bishop, Luis Ignacio María de Peñalver y Cárdenas, arrived in New Orleans in July, 1795, he found the moral climate of Louisiana completely depraved. Prostitution, adultery, miscegenation, bastardy, and riotous living were common. Of 11,000 persons in the New Orleans parish, less than 400 ever attended services. In the space of two years, only thirty officers and men from the Louisiana Regiment attended Mass. Published attacks on church and state led to anarchical conditions. Impudent and sacrilegious songs were sung at the dinner table. Fathers proudly recognized their natural children, and mothers were not properly educated to raise their sons and daughters in the ways of righteousness.[64]

The bishop inspected the province and reported a necessity for appointing additional priests and creating new parishes. As vice-patron, Gayoso was responsible for all such appointments. He usually followed the custom of allowing the bishop to recommend the creation of a parish or the appointment of a certain priest to a post. Then the governor-general gave his approval and drew up an official appointment, a copy of which was forwarded to the intendant, where a pay sheet was drawn up for the new priest or funds allotted for a new church or parish. Gayoso was able to expand the money granted for churches' expenses from $694 to $834 annually, exclusive of the salaries of the priests and other religious functionaries.[65] On the recommendation of Bishop Luis, he also appointed chaplains for the various military corps under his jurisdiction.[66] When the bishop and the mother superior of the Ursuline Convent requested additional funds from the government for enlarging classrooms, it was Gayoso who granted the request.[67] Gayoso was also responsible for firing priests or sacristans who were derelict in their duties.[68] Finally, on several occasions Gayoso met with the bishop and the troubled partners of a marriage which was threatened, thus forming a type of marriage council to persuade the couple to adjust their differences.[69] When any inhabitant complained about excessive fees for marrying, baptizing, or burying by the priests, the governor-general was expected to warn the church to charge no more than set by law.[70]

As administrator of the provinces, Gayoso had charge of all the posts from St. Marks, Florida, to Natchitoches in northwestern Louisiana. The governor-general of Louisiana and West Florida was subordinate to the captain-general of Cuba, but in the closing months of Carondelet's term of office, the governor-general acted independently of Cuba. Gayoso was, however, subordinate to the conde de Santa-Clara, captain-general of Cuba. In 1801 there was a suggestion that Louisiana and West Florida be combined in a separate government, but the retrocession of the province to France ended all hopes of an independent government.[71]

Gayoso continued to supervise the immigration of the French emigrés which began under Carondelet's governor-generalship. One ambitious program, initiated by Philippe Enrique Neri, baron de Bastrop, centered around the Ouachita Valley in 1795. Carondelet supported Bastrop's ambitious plans for a colony of French and Flemish nobility and set aside almost 900,000 acres on the eastern side of the valley in 1796. Gayoso suspected Bastrop of wanting to settle Protestants in Louisiana against his orders and, for once in agreement with Morales, the governor-general suspended Bastrop's contract until the king might decide.[72]

Gayoso also opposed any aid extended to the settlement planned by the marquis de Maison Rouge, a friend of Bastrop, who envisioned an agricultural paradise also in the Ouachita area, which he described in a glowing flyer intended to attract farmers and artisans to the "promised land." He had been authorized to settle three hundred families from Holland to the Ouachita Valley.[73]

On the other hand, Gayoso favored the establishment of loyal Spanish subjects at the frontier posts along the Mississippi and Missouri rivers. James White had demonstrated his loyalty toward Gayoso during the Natchez revolt of 1797, and the governor-general rewarded him with the command of the newly created Spanish post of New Feliciana. A number of Americans chose to live under Spanish rule, rather than United States jurisdiction, and they followed White. These people were so successful that a number of others made plans to join them the next year.[74] Another group settled across the Mississippi from Natchez at a post its commandant, Joseph Vidal, named "Concordia" in honor of the friendly relations between Americans and Spaniards on both sides of the river.[75] Still other Americans settled at Bayou Boeuf.[76] In all these instances Gayoso used extreme caution and allowed no one whose loyalty to Spain had not already been demonstrated to immigrate to Spanish Louisiana.

James Mackay, a Scot in the service first of the Canadian fur traders and later an explorer for the Missouri Company, founded a settlement at St. Andrew (Bonhomme, Missouri) in 1798. He complained to Gayoso that the exclusion order given against introducing Protestants to Upper Louisiana had caused a mortal blow to the nascent community. Lack of sufficient Catholic settlers and the failure of the government to send a priest to the area left it open to incursions of the Indians. Gayoso was interested in populating Louisiana, but only with solid pro-Spanish settlers; therefore, he had decreed that no Americans were to be permitted to settle there.[77]

Gayoso supported the nascent community of Hopefield, née Campo de la Esperanza, which was located opposite the former site of San Fernando de las Barrancas on the Arkansas shore of the Mississippi. He wrote the commandant there, Benjamin Fooy, that as soon as peace was declared he would devote his full attention to making Hopefield a flourishing settlement. As in the case of St. Andrew, however, Gayoso decreed that no Americans be permitted to colonize across the Mississippi.[78]

As complex as his political duties were, no matter how involved he might become with economic and social difficulties in New Orleans and in the province, notwithstanding his numerous arguments with the intendant, and over and above his duties as vice-patron, Gayoso never lost sight of the primary function for which he had been designated governor-general. He was supposed to protect the frontiers of Louisiana and West Florida. He was charged with maintaining the friendship of the Indians and of the Americans on his borders.

Notes for "The Provincial Governor-General: Manuel Gayoso de Lemos"

[1]Gayoso to *cabildo* of New Orleans, House of Mons. Boré, August 4, 1797, Parsons Collection, University of Texas; minutes of New Orleans *Cabildo*, August 5, 1797, 4:20-24. Gayoso advised the Crown he had taken official charge of his office as required by law. Gayoso to Pedro Varela y Ulloa, New Orleans, August 9, 1797, and Varela y Ulloa to Gayoso, Madrid, December 19, 1797, Archivo General de Indias (Seville), Audiencia de Santo Domingo (hereafter cited as AGI, SD, leg.), 2546.

[2]Juan Manuel Alvarez to Prince of the Peace, San Ildefonso, August 14, 1797, Archivo Histórico Nacional (Madrid), (hereafter cited as AHN), *estado*, leg. 3900; Carondelet to Favrot, No. 34, New Orleans, March 12, 1797, in Favrot Papers, 5; Bernard Marigny, *Thoughts upon Foreign Policy of the United States* (New Orleans, 1854), 20, thinks the position to which Carondelet was appointed, was "beneath his talents and the rewards that he deserved." Carondelet did not so express himself.

[3]Two *expedientes* dealing with Miró's *residencia* and complaint session (*pesquiza*), done between 1793-1805, are in AHN, Consejo de Indias, Escribanía de Cámara, leg. 21055, No. 5; and 20927, No. 5. See Jack D. L. Holmes, ed., *Documentos inéditos para la historia de la Luisiana, 1792-1810* (Madrid, 1963), 8. The only other governor-general besides Miró and Carondelet to have a *residencia* was Luis de Unzaga y Amezaga, taken by Miró as judge from 1785-1791, ibid., leg. 20900. A discussion of the *residencia* is in Charles H. Cunningham, "The Residencia in the Spanish Colonies," *Southwestern Historical Quarterly*, 21 (1918): 253-78.

[4]Carondelet's *residencia* is in AHN, Consejo de Indias, Escribanía de Cámara, leg. 20925, No. 3.

[5]Ibid.

[6]Gayoso to Peggy, New Orleans, September 1, 1797, in the papers owned by Mrs. C. Grenes Cole of New Orleans (hereafter cited as Cole Papers), New Orleans.

[7]O'Reilly's regulations are sketched in Holmes, "Some Irish Officers in Spanish Louisiana," 236-39. A discussion of Miró's *bando*, June 1, 1786, is in Caroline Meade Burson, *The Stewardship of Don Esteban Miró, 1782-1792* (New Orleans, 1940), 108-109, 205. Carondelet's police ordinance of June 1, 1795, can be found in the Louisiana file, Miscellaneous manuscripts, Library of Congress; and has been published in *Appendix to an Account of Louisiana* (1804), lxvii-lxxxiii; and edited by Padgett in "A Decree for Louisiana, issued by the Baron de Carondelet," 590-605. Another copy is in Biblioteca Nacional (Madrid), (hereafter cited as BN), tomo 19,509, fol. 1.

[8]Charles Gayarré, *History of Louisiana*, 4 vols. (New York, 1854), 3:386; a copy of the *bando* is in the Bancroft Library, University of California, from which the New York Public Library's copy was made. Another copy is in the Missouri Historical Society, Gayoso de Lemos Papers. It has been translated in Frederic L. Billon, comp., *Annals of St. Louis in its Early Days under the French and Spanish Dominations* (St. Louis, 1886), 275-83. Newspaper accounts were written by W. D. Hays, Jr., "Tulane Acquires Tome Unseen by Most Historians," and Perry Young, "Crap-shooting, Blasphemy, Liquor, were Banned by Blue Laws of de Lemos," for the *New Orleans Times-Picayune*, undated clippings in Cole Papers.

[9]Document No. 39, May 31, 1795, Miscellaneous Spanish Records, New Orleans Public Library, 1:15-16; Carondelet to Gayoso, New Orleans, December 11, 14, 1794, AGI, Papeles de Cuba (hereafter cited as PC), leg. 30. Interesting accounts of fire-protection are in Henry P. Dart, ed., "Fire Protection in New Orleans in Unzaga's Time," *Louisiana Historical Quarterly*, 4 (1921): 201-4, hereafter cited *LHQ*; John Bunyan Clark, "Fire Protection in the Old South" (Ph.D. dissertation, University of Kentucky, 1957).

[10]Jack D. L. Holmes, "Spanish Regulations of Taverns and the Liquor Trade in Colonial Louisiana," unpublished paper read at the Louisiana Academy of Sciences, Lafayette, Louisiana, April 15, 1961.

[11]Minutes of the New Orleans *Cabildo*, September 30, 1797, 4:82-84; October 6, 1797, 4:85-86.

[12]Ibid., September 7, 1797, 4:77.

[13]Documents, 1795-1797, in Miscellaneous Spanish Documents, New Orleans Public Library, 1:13-17, 71-76, 90-91; Arthur P. Whitaker, *Mississippi Question, 1795 1803. A Study in Trade, Politics, and Diplomacy* (New York, 1934), 39.

[14]Statement of Juan de Castañedo, January 30, 1795, and revenues, January 1-December 31, 1797; inspection by Francisco Bernucho and Antonio Dubois, September 23, 30, 1797, in Miscellaneous Spanish Documents, New Orleans Public Library, 1:17-26, 70; Minutes of the New Orleans *Cabildo*, September 30, 1797, 4:82-84.

[15]Minutes of the New Orleans *Cabildo*, April 19, 1799, 4:14-16, 25; Whitaker, *Mississippi Question*, 277, n32.

[16]Report by Juan de Castañedo, New Orleans, December 31, 1797, Miscellaneous Spanish Documents, 1:41-51; Minutes of the New Orleans *Cabildo*, July 13, 1797, 4; Jack D. L. Holmes, "Some Economic Problems of Spanish Governors in Louisiana," *Hispanic American Historical Review*, 42 (1962): 541.

[17]Gayoso's *bando de buen gobierno*, 1798; Carondelet to Aranda, No. 1, New Orleans, November 6, 1792, AHN, estado, leg. 3898; Reflections of Paul Alliot to Jefferson, New York, April 13, 1804, in James A. Robertson, ed., *Louisiana Under the Rule of Spain, France, and the United States, 1785-1807*, 2 vols. (Cleveland, 1911), 1:39; Whitaker, *Mississippi Question*, 41.

[18]Laura L. Porteous (trans.), "Sanitary Conditions in New Orleans under the Spanish Régime, 1799-1800," *LHQ*, 15 (1932): 610-17. This letter from P. D. Barran, public magistrate of the *cabildo*, to the membership of that body, January 24, 1800, shows how bad sanitation in New Orleans was at the turn of the century. Governor W. C. C. Claiborne to James Madison, near government house, New Orleans, December 17, 1809, in Clarence E. Carter, ed., *Territorial Papers of the Untied States, The Territory of Orleans 1803-1812*, 18 vols. (Washington, 1940), 9:859-60, shows that the conditions had changed little during the decade following.

[19]Petition of Vidal, New Orleans, 1797, and Gayoso's comments, New Orleans, September 25, 1797, AGI, PC, leg. 221-a.

[20]Gayoso's *bando de buen gobierno*, 1798.

[21]Ibid.

[22]Minutes of New Orleans *Cabildo*, September 22, 1797, 4:47-57; Henry E. Chambers, *History of Louisiana*, 3 vols. (Chicago, 1925), 1:378, state that Louis Darby d'Amicaut was appointed instead of LeBlanc. De la Ronde's commission is signed by Gayoso, New Orleans, June 6, 1798, Parsons Collection, University of Texas; Danican resigned his post in 1799 and was replaced by Gabriel Tonbergne, who bought the regidor's post for $500 on April 30. Document No. 379, Box 80, New Orleans *Cabildo* Museum Records (in the safe of the Cabildo). The salaries of the various *cabildo* members are in AGI, PC, leg. 538-b. Salaries for 1802 are in A. P. Nasatir, ed., "Government Employees and Salaries in Spanish Louisiana," *LHQ*, 29 (1946): 984-86.

[23]Minutes of the New Orleans *Cabildo*, 1797, 4:passim.

[24]Ibid., August 5, 1797, 4:73. The educational history of New Orleans during the Spanish period may be gleaned from Roger Baudier, *The Catholic Church in Louisiana* (New Orleans, 1939), 217; Claiborne to Jefferson, near Natchez, August 24, 1803, and Daniel Clark to Secretary of State (Madison), New Orleans, September 8, 1803, with enclosures, in Carter, ed., *Territorial Papers of the United States, Orleans*, 9:22, 38; David K. Bjork, trans. & ed., "Documents Relating to the Establishment of Schools in Louisiana, 1771," *Mississippi Valley Historical Review*, 11 (1925): 561-69; Council of The Indies to King, February 27, 1772, translated in Louisiana Documents, National Archives, Record Group 59; Berquin-Duvallon, *Vue de la colonie, espagnole du Mississippi, ou des provinces de Louisiane et Floride Occidentale* (Paris, 1803), 293-95.

[25]Pontalba to (Jeanne Françoise LeBretton des Charmeaux) his wife, New Orleans, March-July, 1796 (W.P.A. translation of copies made by J.W. Cruzat of Pontalba's journal, Louisiana State University Archives, hereafter cited as *Pontalba's Journal*), 41, 116, 144, 159. An interesting account of the Ursulines is Heloise Hulse Cruzat, "The Ursulines of Louisiana," *LHQ*, 2 (1919): 5-23. On February 23, 1770, O'Reilly set $120 annually as the pay for each of the nuns, plus $30 for each of the twelve orphans. By an order of September 14, 1787, the amount was increased to $216 and $50 respectively. The Spanish nuns left for Havana after the retrocession of Louisiana to the French. Pay sheets of Ursulines, AGI, PC, leg. 538-b.

[26]Gayoso to Santa Clara, No. 126, New Orleans, April 26, 1798, AGI, PC, leg. 1501-b.

[27]Population of New Orleans in 1785 was 4,980; in 1788, 5,338; in 1803, almost 9,000. Census accounts in François-Xavier Martin, *History of Louisiana, from the Earliest Period* (New Orleans, 1882), 239-40, 251; *Appendix to an Account of Louisiana*, lxxxv-lxxxvii. The 1803 census shows 3,948 white persons; 1,335 free people of color, and 2,773 Negro slaves. It does not include the free people of color in the second ward of the St. Charles District, which might swell the total to almost 9,000.

[28]Pontalba to his wife, March 19, 20, 1796, and passim.; *Pontalba's Journal*, 37, 51, *passim*, refers to meetings of the local theater's stockholders' organization for the purpose of distributing boxes.

[29]Berquin-Duvallon, *Vue de la colonie*, 29-31, discusses the comedy, "La Mort de César," See also, Minter Wood, "Life in New Orleans in the Spanish Period," *LHQ*, 22 (1939): 692. An article dealing with opera in New Orleans after the Spanish period is Nellie Warner Price, "Le Spectacle de la Rue St. Pierre," *LHQ*, 1 (1918): 215-23.

[30]Regulation of Carondelet, New Orleans, October 1, 1792, AGI, PC, leg. 30.

[31]Carondelet's regulation, New Orleans, November 1, 1792, AGI, PC, leg. 206; Berquin-Duvallon, *Vue de la colonie*, 31-39; Wood, "Life in New Orleans in the Spanish Period," 688-91. The Council of New Orleans followed the Spanish pattern of governing balls and the use of masks and disguises during the Mardi Gras season. *Moniteur de la Louisiane*, February 4, 1806.

[32]Gayoso to Minor, New Orleans, February 14, 1798, Gayoso Papers, Louisiana State University; Minor to Gayoso, Natchez, December 25, 1798, AGI, PC, leg. 215-a. Gayoso was also interested in the comedy and expressed pleasure at a script sent him by Jean Baptiste Berret, Premiér Cotte Alemande, June 14, 1798, AGI, PC, leg. 215-a.

[33]Gayoso to Prince of The Peace, No. 18, confidential, New Orleans, April 18, 1798, AHN, *estado*, leg. 3900, draft in AGI, PC, leg. 178-b; Geoffrey T. Garratt, *Gibraltar and the Mediterranean* (New York, 1939), 76-100.

[34]Correspondence concerning the Duke of Orleans and his American tour is in Carlos Martínez de Irujo to Prince of The Peace, No. 12, Philadelphia, November 10, 1796; No. 83, December 5, 1797, AHN, *estado*, leg. 3896 bis; Irujo to Prince of The Peace, No. 90, Philadelphia, January 19; No. 102, may 4, 1798, ibid., leg. 3897; Gayoso to Prince of The Peace, No. 15, New Orleans, February 24, 1798; No. 16, March 1, 1798; No. 18, Confidential, April 18, 1798, ibid., leg. 3900; Morales to Hormazas, No. 214, New Orleans, March 3,

1798, ibid., leg. 3902; Gayoso to Santa Clara, No. 103, New Orleans, February 24, 1798, AGI, PC, leg. 1501-a; No. 108, March 20, 1798; draft, Santa Clara to Gayoso, Havana, March 28, 1798; Gayoso to Santa Clara, San Phelipe de Placaminas, March 21, 1798, ibid.; Minor to Ellicott, New Orleans, March 19, 1798, and Ellicott to Pickering, Natchez, February 20, 1798, Southern Boundary MSS., II. Published accounts include Jane Marsh Parker, "Louis Philippe in the United States," *Century Magazine*, 62 (1901): 746-57; "Louis Philippe in the United States," *American Pioneer*, 1 (1842): 414; Gayarré, *History of Louisiana*, 3:389-90.

[35]Stephen Minor told Gayoso about the dangerous pro-Negro talk of the duc d'Orleans and his party. Minor to Gayoso, Natchez, February 15, 1798, AGI, PC, leg. 215-a. On the Negro uprising, see Carondelet to Las Casas, No. 140, Confidential, New Orleans, July 30, 1795, AGI, PC, leg. 1441; Guillaume Duparc and Joseph Vázquez Vahamonde, List of the Criminals at Pointe Coupée, May 29, 1795, and supporting documents on the case, AGI, PC, leg. 31; Carondelet to Las Casas, Very Confidential, New Orleans, May 3, 1795, AHN, *estado*, leg. 3899.

[36]Morales to Marqués de Branciforte, New Orleans, June 28, 1798, copy in Archivo General de la Nación (Mexico), Historia, (hereafter cited as AGN), tome 334. See Jack D. L. Holmes, "Some Economic Problems, 522, 540; expenses for the province of Louisiana in 1785 were $537,285. Those of North Carolina with almost ten times the population, were $56,930. Martin, *Louisiana*, 240-44. Defense costs were the difference. By 1800 the total subsidy had risen to more than $866,739. With other revenues the total income for the province was in excess of $1,198,828; the expenses, which included salaries for militia, regular troops, public officials, pensions, Indian expenses, fortifications, hospitals, intrigue, religious affairs, boundary commission, evacuation of the posts, construction of houses, ship repairs, rental of houses, the manufacture of bread, repayment of loans to the treasury, etc., amounted to something more than $1,050,645. Account of Gilbert Leonard, New Orleans, February 4, 1800, AGI, SD, leg. 2638. This covers the year 1799.

[37]Gayoso to Azanza, New Orleans, August 2, 1798, AGN, Historia, tomo 334, folios 30-38, and edited by Jack D. L. Holmes, "La última barrera: la Luisiana y la Nueva España," *Historia Mexicana*, 10 (1961): 637-49.

[38]Gayoso to Santa Clara, No. 154 1/2, New Orleans, June 7, 1798, AGI, PC, leg. 1501-b; Gayoso to Santa Clara, No. 204, New Orleans, February 15, 1799, ibid., leg. 1502-a; Gayoso to Branciforte, Very Confidential, New Orleans, July 9, 1798, AGI, PC, leg. 2365; Gayoso to Saavedra, No. 1, Confidential, New Orleans, February 24, 1799, AHN, estado, leg. 3901; Gayoso to Saavedra, No. 5, New Orleans, April 21, 1799, AGI, SD, leg. 2638; Azanza to Saavedra, No. 190, Mexico, December 7, 1798, ibid.; No. 230, January 5, 1799, ibid., Gayoso to Saavedra, No. 6, New Orleans, April 21, 1799, ibid.; Morales to Soler, No. 23, Confidential, New Orleans, March 31, 1799, AGI, SD, leg. 2615.

[39]Gayoso to Minor, New Orleans, April 25, 1799, Gayoso Papers, Louisiana State University.

[40]James Garrard to Gayoso, Frankfort, Kentucky, April 23, 1799, AGI, PC, leg. 2371.

[41]Gayoso to Santa Clara, No. 8, New Orleans, December 18, 1797, AGI, PC, leg. 1502-b; Gayoso to the Bishop, October 28, 1797, cited in bishop to Gayoso, New Orleans, October 30, 1797, AGI, PC, leg. 102; Gayoso to J. Armand, New Orleans, August 28, 1797, Remy Papers, Louisiana State University; Minutes of the New Orleans *Cabildo*, August 11, 1797, 4:26-27; Gayoso's proclamation of March 6, 1798, AGI, PC, leg. 215-b.

[42]Evan Jones to Gayoso, La Fourche, June 14, 1798, AGI, PC, leg. 215-b.

[43]Evan Jones to Gayoso, La Fourche, June 14, 1798; Pechoux to Gayoso, New Orleans, June 19, 1798; and Gayoso to Jones, New Orleans, June 20, 1798, AGI, PC, leg. 215-b.

[44]Gayoso to Carondelet, No. 700, Natchez, October 28, 1796, AGI, PC, leg. 34; Lorenzo Sigur to Gayoso, Iberville, November 28, 1797, AGI, PC, leg. 215-a; Gayoso to Minor, 1797-1798, various letters, Gayoso Papers, Louisiana State University. Dam repairs were also a major concern of Gayoso's successor, the marquis de Casa-Calvo, who was forced to use royal funds and soldier labor to protect royal lands below New Orleans. Ramón de López y Angulo to Eugenio Llaguno y Amirola, No. 16, New Orleans, April 30, 1800, AGI, SD, leg. 2638. A typical bridge over these levees and dikes is shown in Ponset's petition, March 2, 1796, in AGI, Planos, Luisiana y Floridas, No. 181.

[45]Carondelet to Panton, New Orleans, August 15, 1797; Folch to Panton, Pensacola, January 9, 1798; John Savage to Panton, Leslie, & Co., Madrid, February 25, 1797; Panton to John Forbes, Pensacola, August 15, 1797; Morales to Panton, New Orleans, February 1, 1797; Gayoso to Panton, New Orleans, March 10, 1798; Panton to Robert Leslie, Pensacola, July 18, November 8, 1796, all in Panton-Forbes Papers, Mobile Public

Library; Gayoso to Saavedra, New Orleans, May 1, 1799, AGI, PC, leg. 179-a; Morales to Saavedra, No. 282, 283, New Orleans, March 31, 1799, Spanish MSS., Mississippi Valley, New Orleans Museum, 4:329-30.

[46]Lillian Estelle Fisher, *The Intendant System in Spanish America* (Berkeley, 1939); and Lillian Estelle Fisher, "The Intendant System in Spanish America," *Hispanic American Historical Review*, 8 (1928): 8-13; Luis Navarro Garciá, *Intendencias en Indias* (Seville, 1959).

[47]Las Casas to Gardoqui, No. 13, Havana, February 24, 1794, and Carondelet to the King, New Orleans, March 11, 1794, AGI, SD, leg. 2546; decree of October 7, 1794, cited in Carondelet to Gayoso, New Orleans, April 23, 1795, AGI, PC, leg. 22; Burson, *The Stewardship of Miró*, 57-59; Gayarré, *History of Louisiana*, 3:334.

[48]Biographical data on Morales is in his service record, AGI, PC, leg. 565; his decree of July 17, 1799, AGI, PC, leg. 2366; and paysheet, AGI, PC, leg. 538-b. The charges against his character were made by Casa-Calvo to Someruelos, No. 29, New Orleans, September 30, 1805, AGI, PC, leg. 142-a; on the intendancy in Louisiana, see the critical remarks of Berquin-Duvallon, *Vue de la colonie*, 168-71.

[49]Petition of Morales, Cádiz, September 2, 1788, AGI, Contratación, leg. 5532; Valdés to Intendant of Louisiana, San Ildefonso, September 13, 1787, AGI, PC, leg. 2317-b; Gutiérrez de Arroyo to Gayoso, New Orleans, September 30, 1794, AGI, PC, leg. 47; Morales to Azanza, No. 1, New Orleans, May 2, 1796, AGI, SD, leg. 2565; Morales to Prince of the Peace, No. 1, May 2, 1796, AHN, *estado*, leg. 3902; Morales to Pedro Varela y Ulloa, New Orleans, August 18, 1797, AGI, SD, leg. 2546.

[50]Folch to Gayoso, San Fernando de las Barrancas, December 16, 1795, AGI, PC, leg. 52.

[51]Gayoso's instructions to commandants for admission of new settlers, New Orleans, September 8, 1797, AGI, PC, leg. 2354; a similar ordinance was issued on January 1, 1798, ibid., and leg. 2365; a certified copy dated March 5, 1799, New Orleans, is in the Territorial Papers, Louisiana, National Archives, Record Group 59, with a printed copy in "Documents," in ibid. Translations are also in Gayarré, *History of Louisiana*, 3:386-88; Martin, *History of Louisiana*, 276-77; and a summary in Chambers, *History of Louisiana*, 1:388.

[52]A copy of Morales' ordinance dated–de Julio de 1799, is in the Florida Papers, National Archives, Record Groups 59. Correspondence on the subject is in Morales to Pedro Varela y Ulloa, No. 174, New Orleans, October 16, 1797, ibid., and includes the correspondence between Morales and Gayoso from February through July, 1799. A brief discussion of the ordinance is in Francis B. Burns, "The Spanish Land Laws of Louisiana," *LHQ*, 11 (1928): 557-81.

[53]Gayoso to Guillermo Duparc, New Orleans, March 12, 1798, AGI, PC, leg. 215-a. Gayoso's correspondence on the dispute with Morales is almost as voluminous as that of Morales. An early statement of his opposition to Morales' methods and procedures is Gayoso to Prince of the Peace, No. 2, New Orleans, September 5, 1797, AHN, *estado*, leg. 3900. The best single source for Gayoso's complaints on the entire dispute with Morales is Gayoso to Saavedra, No. 17, New Orleans, May 1, 1799, AGI, PC, leg. 179-a.

[54]Gayoso wrote, "The intendant places more obstacles in my way than the enemy . . . His unmitigated ambition forces him to intervene in military and political matters which tie my hands, his selfish ambition and indifference to the true interests of the king, are the causes which he claims in order to pester me and cover his own selfish desires." Gayoso to Santa Clara, No. 22, Confidential, New Orleans, February 17, 1799, AGI, PC, leg. 1502-b.

[55]Gayoso to Santa Clara, New Orleans, August 31, 1797, ibid.; Gayoso to Saavedra, No. 17, May 1, 1799; Gayoso to Prince of the Peace, New Orleans, August 17, September 4, 5, 1797, AHN, *estado*, leg. 3900.

[56]Ibid.; Prince of Peace to Saavedra, San Lorenzo, December 29, 1797, AGI, SD, leg. 2546; Cayetano Soler to Mariano Luis de Urquijo, Aranjuez, May 25, 1799, AHN, *estado*, leg. 3901. A short sketch of Saavedra is in David Humphreys to Pickering, No. 133, Madrid, March 30, 1798, Letters of David Humphreys, National Archives, Record Group 59. Morales' subsequent action in closing New Orleans to the Americans without replacing it with another port as required by the Treaty of San Lorenzo, earned him the enmity of President Adams; Morales was soon replaced by López y Angulo, who called Morales' various activities reprehensible. López y Angulo to Cayetano Soler, New Orleans, August 8, 1801, Spanish MSS., Mississippi Valley, New Orleans, 4:345; Gayarré, *History of Louisiana*, 3:398-99. Ultimately, Morales was again returned to the intendancy of Louisiana and West Florida where he plagued civil governors and commandants.

[57]Gayoso to Minor, New Orleans, September 22, October 23, 1797, Gayoso Papers, Louisiana State University; Gayoso to Peggy, two dozen letters, August-November, 1797, Cole Papers. The author is

presently editing the Gayoso-Minor-Peggy correspondence. Gayoso's house in New Orleans, located at 616 St. Peter Street, is known today as the "Le Petit Théâtre du Vieux Carré." A portrait of Gayoso, painted by one of his descendants, Pedro de Lemos, used to hang in the gallery.

58*Judge* Manuel de Gayoso conducted an official inventory of the papers of Beltrán Gravier, New Orleans, October 6, 1798, New Orleans Cabildo Museum (safe), file 82.

59Gayoso to Luis deBlanc, New Orleans, November 1, 1797, and February 13, 1798, Gayoso Papers, Louisiana State University.

60Margarita Josepha to Gayoso, Santa Genoveva, June 20, 1798, and Gayoso's reply, July 7, 1798, AGI, PC, leg. 215-a.

61O'Reilly's statement, New Orleans, February 14, 1770, AGI, PC, leg. 2357, and also in Lawrence Kinnaird, ed., *Spain in the Mississippi Valley, 1765-1794*, 3 vols. (Washington, DC, 1949), 1:159-60; Baudier, *Catholic Church in Louisiana*, 179-82. *Recopilación de leyes de los reinos de las Indias*, 4 vols, 5th ed. (Madrid, 1841), 1:54, shows the duties and obligations of the church and the governors.

62Baudier, *Catholic Church in Louisiana*, 200-212; Burson, *The Stewardship of Miró*, 210-32; Royal order of September 14, 1781, cited in Luis Mariano Pérez, *Guide to the Materials for American History in Cuban Archives* (Washington, 1907), 434.

63Luis Marino Pérez, *Guide to the Materials for American History in Cuban Archives* (Washington, DC, 1907), 448. The royal decree was November 23, 1793; the papal decree is cited in Baudier, *Catholic Church in Louisiana*, 215-30.

64Luis Peñalver y Cárdenas' report of November 1, 1795, to the Minister of Grace and Justice, Eugenio Llaguno, is in BN, vol. 19,509, folios 24-27; a summary is in Baudier, *Catholic Church in Louisiana*, 229-31. Other complaints on religious laxity and moral depravity in Louisiana and Florida are in Luis to Carondelet, New Orleans, June 17, 1796, AGI, PC, leg. 102; Carondelet to Luis, New Orleans, January 16, March 9, 1796, AGI, PC, leg. 102; and Joseph Antonio Caballero to Antonio Coruel, San Lorenzo, November 13, 1799, in Robertson, ed., *Louisiana*, 1:355-58.

65List of church expenses and suggestions for additions, New Orleans, September 27, 1797, AGI, PC, leg. 538-b; list of chapel expenses, ibid.; Morales' statement of church expenses, New Orleans, March 11, 1801, following his recommendation of September 26, 1799 (which is the same as Gayoso's of 1797), AGI, SD, leg. 2638. Following his 1796-1797 inspection of Louisiana, Bishop Luis recommended the expansion of funds for rebuilding the St. Louis church. Luis to Gayoso, New Orleans, February 14, 16, 1798, AGI, PC, leg. 2365. On Gayoso's appointments of clerical officers, see Gregorio White to Gayoso, La Fourche, June 5, 1798, AGI, PC, leg. 215-b; Luis to Gayoso, New Orleans, April 1, 1799, AGI, PC, leg. 102.

66Gayoso to Santa Clara, No. 112, New Orleans, April 17, 1798, AGI, PC, leg. 1501-a; Bishop Luis to Gayoso, New Orleans, December 20, 1797, October 23, 1798, March 30, 1799, AGI, PC, leg. 102.

67Bishop to Gayoso, New Orleans, April 19, 1799, AGI, PC, leg. 102, and cited in Samuel Wilson, Jr., "An Architectural History of the Royal Hospital and the Ursuline Convent of New Orleans," *LHQ*, 29 (1946): 618.

68Luis to Gayoso, New Orleans, March 27, 1799, AGI, PC, leg. 102.

69Gayoso to Bishop, New Orleans, May 9, 1799, ibid., asking the bishop to meet with him Luis de Macarty and the latter's wife, Juana l'Erable, for the purpose of arranging a reconciliation.

70Guillermo Duparc to Gayoso, Pointe Coupée, February 6, 1798, AGI, PC, leg. 215-a.

71Enrique White to William Panton, St. Augustine, January 2, 1797, Panton-Forbes Papers, Mobile Public Library; Duvon Clough Corbitt, "The Administrative System of the Floridas, 1781-1821," *Tequesta*, 1 (1942): 41-62.

72Bastrop's memorial, New Orleans, March 14, 1795, enclosed in Carondelet to Rendón, New Orleans, March 16, 1795, AGI, PC, leg. 2364; expediente on the Ouachita, 1796-1800, National Archives of Cuba (Havana), Floridas, 595, leg. 11; Casa-Calvo to Carlos Villemont, New Orleans, March 20, 1801, AGI, PC, leg. 70-b; Charles A. Bacarisse, "Baron de Bastrop," *Southwestern Historical Quarterly*, 58 (1921): 188, 191. Joseph Piernas, a retired sub-lieutenant, also had dreams of a substantial settlement in western Lake Charles. His project and description of the area are in Holmes, ed., *Documentos de la Luisiana*, 131-69, and the somewhat inaccurate earlier translation by Jack D. L. Holmes, "Joseph Piernas and a Proposed Settlement on the Calcasieu River, 1795," *McNeese Review*, 13 (1962): 59-80.

[73]Maison Rouge's memorial, enclosed in Carondelet to Rendón, New Orleans, March 9, 1795, AGI, PC, leg. 2364; Maison-Rouge's description of the Ouachita, March 17, 1795, printed flier, ibid., leg. 2354; Gayoso to Minor, New Orleans, September 22, 1797, Gayoso Papers, Louisiana State University; Minor to Gayoso, Natchez, October 6, 7, 1797, AGI, PC, leg. 2371. These colonization movements are discussed in Gilbert C. Din, "Colonización en la Luisiana española: proyectos de emigración en la Luisiana del siglo xviii" (Ph.D. dissertation, Historia de América, Facultad de Filosofía y Letras, Universidad de Madrid, 1960).

[74]This James White may be the same who represented North Carolina in the Continental Congress and was involved in the "Spanish Conspiracy" with Gayoso in 1789, traveling to New Orleans under the name Jacques Dubois. He later served as judge of the Attakapas District in 1807, and was the grandfather of Chief Justice E. D. White. Thomas Perkins Abernethy, *The South in the New Nation, 1789-1819*, 4 vols. (Baton Rouge, 1961), 1:159 Carter, ed., *Territorial Papers of the United States: Mississippi*, 5:100-101n; James White to Gayoso, Natchez, October 4, 1798, AGI, PC, leg 142-a; Gayoso to Minor, New Orleans, November 29, 1798, Gayoso Papers, Louisiana State University; Narsworthy Hunter to the editor of the *Philadelphia Impartial Observer*, February 4, 1800, and Daniel Clark, Sr., to Claiborne, Clarksville, June 18, 1800, in *Papers in Relation to the Official Conduct of Governour Sargent* (Boston, 1801), 5-7, 25. Petitions of inhabitants from New Feliciana asking land include that of Richard Tickell to Gayoso, New Feliciana, September 2, 1797, and Gayoso's approval for 300 arpents, September 23, 1797, in Kuntz Collection, Tulane University. A petition asking for a regulation to prevent stock running wild from a number of settlers (1798) is in AGI, PC, leg. 2354. Regulations, June 26, 1798, by commandant Josef Deville Degoutin are in ibid. New Feliciana included the old Bayou Sara section of the Natchez District. Gayoso to Santa Clara, No. 99, New Orleans, January 23, 1798, AGI, PC, leg 1501-a; Gayoso to Isaac Johnson, New Orleans, November 30, 1798, AGI, PC, leg 215-1, in which the governor asked Johnson to draw up regulations similar to those which governed at Natchez. See also, Minor to Gayoso, Bayou Sara, July 9, 1798, AGI, PC, leg 215-b.

[75]Concordia was commanded first by Vidal and later by Minor. Minor delivered the post to the French on January 12, 1804, AGI, PC, leg. 70-a. On the early history of the post, see Robert Dabney Calhoun, "A History of Concordia Parish, Louisiana," *LHQ*, 15 (1932): 44-67, 214-33, 428-52, 618-45.

[76]Petition of John Tear and Patrick Gurnet, Bayou Boeuf, September 13, 1798, AGI, PC, leg. 215-b. Other Americans asked for lands under Spanish jurisdiction near the Escambia and Pensacola rivers. Memorial to Gayoso, Tensaw, November 8, 1798, and approval, November 20, 1798, AGI, PC, leg. 206.

[77]Mackay to Gayoso, New Orleans, Jun 8, 1798, AGI, PC, leg. 2365; Louis Houck, ed., *Spanish Régime in Missouri*, 2 vols. (New York, 1971), 2:71; part of Mackay's diary is in Carondelet to Prince of The Peace, No. 78, Confidential, New Orleans, June 3, 1796, AHN, *estado*, leg. 3900; Carlos deHault deLassus to Stoddard, March 6, 1804, in Billon, ed., *St. Louis*, 367; Santiago Mackay to Gayoso, St. Andrew du Missouri, November 28, 1798, AGI, PC, leg. 215-b; Gayoso to Saavedra, New Orleans, November 22, 1798, AGI, PC, leg. 2365; Carondelet to Prince of The Peace, No. 8, Confidential, New Orleans, June 3, 1796, and appointment, May 121, 1796, AGI, PC, leg. 2364; A. P. Nasatir, "John Evans, Explorer and Surveyor," *Missouri Historical Review*, 25 (1931): 224-38.

[78]Gayoso to Fooy, New Orleans, July 18, August 14, 1798, March 2, 1799; Gayoso to deHault deLassus, New Orleans, July 18, 1798, certified copies, Hope-field, July 13, 1808, in Missouri Historical Society, St. Louis. Fooy's land holdings are shown in the plats of the Crittenden County (Arkansas) County Clerk's Office, Township Plats, Vol. 1. His political activities in Arkansas territorial government are briefly cited in Carter, ed., *Territorial Papers of the United States*, 13-15, 19: *Louisiana-Missouri, Arkansas*, passim.

PART III

ADMINISTRATION AND LAW

THE ADMINISTRATIVE SYSTEM IN THE FLORIDAS, 1781-1821*

Duvon Clough Corbitt

Upon superficial examination of the administrative system used in the Floridas during the second Spanish period, it would appear to have been simplicity itself. On closer investigation, however, it proves to have been about as complicated as Spanish genius could make it with the material at hand. The traditional check and balance system was there in all its glory, not only in the provinces of East and West Florida themselves, but also in the relations of their officers with the higher authorities. Loosely joined together under a common chief (who was also either captain general of Cuba or viceroy of New Spain), and placed in a precarious position with respect to the Indians and other neighbors, the Floridas presented special problems, the study of which reveals at the same time the strength and the weakness of Spanish institutions. And finally, the attempts to apply the Spanish Constitution of 1812 to the provinces (1812-1814 and 1820-1821) produced results of a nature not to be found elsewhere in the Spanish dominions. The purpose of the present study is to outline the regular administration in the Florida provinces.

THE CAPTAINCY GENERAL OF LOUISIANA AND THE FLORIDAS

When in 1779 Spain decided to take part in the American Revolution, her province of Louisiana was attached to the captaincy general of Cuba. The governor of the province was responsible to the captain general in Havana, but he enjoyed and exercised the right of corresponding directly with the young and energetic Bernardo de Gálvez, who upon hearing of the declaration of war, seized the initiative and attacked the British posts along the Mississippi. By March of 1780 Manchac, Baton Rouge, Natchez, and Mobile were in his hands, and preparations were under way for an attack on Pensacola. He was rewarded for his activity by an appointment to govern Louisiana and the newly conquered territory

*This article was first published in *Tequesta*, 1 (1942): 41-54. Reprinted here with the kind permission of the author and the Historical Association of Southern Florida.

with complete independence from the captain general of Cuba, and since Pensacola was expected to be in possession of the Spaniards soon, its district was added to the new jurisdiction. The appointment, dated February 13, 1781, reads:

> The King, having considered the great extent acquired by the Province of Louisiana through the conquests that you have made of the English Forts and Settlements on the Mississippi and at Mobile, and having in mind the decorum with which you should be treated as Commander-in-Chief of the Army of Operations at Havana; has been pleased to decree that, for the present, and while you govern Mobile and Louisiana, their administration shall be independent of the Captaincy General of the Island of Cuba, and that Pensacola and its district shall be added to your jurisdiction as soon as they are occupied by the forces of the King, who fully authorizes you to govern and defend them through Substitutes during your absence.[1]

Gálvez's first step in his new capacity was to inform Colonel Pedro Piernas, his subordinate in New Orleans, of the change. Although nothing was said about the creation of a captaincy general, colonial officials assumed that such was the intention,[2] and later events proved that they had judged correctly. The term was officially adopted a few years later (in 1784) when East Florida was added to the new jurisdiction.

East Florida, however, seems to have been first organized as a separate administrative unit, from the tenor of the royal order appointing Vicente Manuel de Zéspedes to take over its government from the British authorities. The order conferred on Zéspedes "the Government and captaincy general of the City of St. Augustine and the *Provincias de Florida*, with an Annual Salary of four thousand *pesos* (for the present) payable from the Royal Treasury, and Rank of Brigadier in the Royal Armies."[3]

Although in the copy of the order in the Archivo Nacional de Cuba the word *Provincias* appears in the plural, it seems likely that only East Florida was intended. This is indicated by the fact that Zéspedes never tried to assume jurisdiction over anything farther west than the St. Marks region. What was intended by the term "captaincy general" is uncertain. It is possible that the home authorities planned to set up a government in East Florida equal in rank to that in Louisiana and West Florida, but it is more likely that the term was used to indicate that Zéspedes was the commander of all troops in the territory. Later governors were occasionally referred to by that title. On the other hand, the term "captaincy general" may have been used carelessly by the persons who drafted the order. Numerous examples of such carelessness might be cited from Spanish colonial documents.[4]

If a new captaincy general was intended, a change of heart was soon wrought in the Peninsular authorities, for Bernardo de Gálvez was given jurisdiction over a captaincy general consisting of Louisiana and both Floridas.[5] At the time he was also made captain general of Cuba and given the promise of the viceroyalty of New Spain when it should become vacant. According to the historian Pezuela, this promise was given because Bernardo's father, Matías de Gálvez, then viceroy was in very bad health. When the ship bearing Bernardo to Cuba touched at Puerto Rico, the young captain general learned of his father's death. The three months that he spent in Cuba, beginning February 4, 1785, was only a period of preparation for the transfer to New Spain, much to the disappointment of the Cubans who had been looking forward to his administration of their island.[6]

Louisiana and the Floridas seem to have been considered in Spain as a monopoly of Bernardo de Gálvez, for, although another captain general was appointed in Cuba, they continued under his command until his death on November 30, 1786. The personal factor is clearly indicated by the disposition of those provinces after his decease, when a royal *cédula* [decree] transferred the captaincy general of Louisiana and the Floridas from the viceroy of New Spain to José de Ezpeleta who was then governing Cuba. The *cédula* enumerated the following reasons for the change: (1) the "particular merit, services, activities, and military ability" of Ezpeleta; (2) his "zeal and love" for the royal service; (3) the fact that he was "the only Executive Officer who could give the assistance, and speedy succor needed by Louisiana and the Floridas."[7] A fourth reason might have been given: the difficulty of communication between those provinces and Spain by way of Mexico City.

In order to prevent exasperating delays, Gálvez had found it necessary to authorize his subordinates in New Orleans, Pensacola, and St. Augustine to communicate directly with Spain, simply sending him duplicates of their correspondence. This privilege allowed to his subordinates was not new in Spanish administration: It had been more or less an unwritten law of the Spanish government to learn about colonial affairs from more than one source. There was not an officer of importance in the colonies but had an associate or a subordinate who exercised the privilege of writing directly to the home government. Gálvez himself, while governor of Louisiana, had been very active in the enjoyment of this right. Between 1777 and 1781 he had sent 462 letters to the Minster of the Indies and only 304 to his immediate superior, the captain general of Cuba. Those to the captain general were often duplicates or summaries of those sent to Spain, but a careful perusal of the correspondence shows that much was written home which the captain general did not hear about. Even if Gálvez had forbidden his subordinates in Louisiana and the Floridas this right, it is very likely that the Spanish government would have overruled his orders.[8]

The experience of Ezpeleta amounts to almost positive proof of this assertion. His appointment as captain general of Louisiana and the Floridas removed any necessity for direct communication between those provinces and Spain, since mail between them had necessarily to pass through Havana. Realizing this fact, and desiring naturally to increase his control of the new jurisdiction, Ezpeleta ordered the practice stopped on the ground that it was no longer necessary.[9] His attitude was logical, but the home government wanted as many checks on its colonial officers as possible and his order was countermanded.

The wisdom of combining the government of Louisiana and the Floridas with that of Cuba was questioned by Governor Esteban Miró of Louisiana in a letter to the ministry of January 11, 1787. He believed that he himself should have been given the office of captain general, but the ministry thought otherwise. The decision was made for administrative reasons and not because of any lack of confidence in Miró's ability, as is demonstrated by the fact that upon the retirement of Intendant Martín Navarro of Louisiana early the next year the duties of the latter were given to the governor along with the corresponding increase in salary.[10]

A few years later Miró's successor, the baron de Carondelet, developed a similar ambition to be captain general. In this he had the support of his brother-in-law, Captain General Luís de las Casas of Cuba, and that of Diego de Gardoqui, then secretary of treasury. In 1795 the king authorized his minster Godoy to erect Louisiana and the Floridas into a *comandancia* whenever he saw fit to do so and the next year Las Casas authorized Carondelet to act as *comandante general interino*. He filled this position from December, 1796, to August, 1797, when the continental provinces were returned to their former status. In 1801 Captain General Someruelos of Cuba recommended a separate government for them, but the cession of Louisiana to France was then pending and nothing was done about the suggestion.[11]

What appears to have been the last attempt to separate the Floridas from dependence on the captain general in Havana was made in 1807. Governor Vicente Folch of West Florida suggested the appointment of such an officer in the Florida provinces and went so far as to nominate himself for the position, alleging his long experience on that frontier. The home authorities, however, had other opinions on the subject and Folch's proposal was passed up.[12]

The loss of Louisiana to Spain reduced the captaincy general to East and West Florida, but Spain managed to keep a hold on the territory as far west as the Mississippi until the revolution of 1811 in West Florida, at which time the Perdido River became the *de facto* boundary, though the Spaniards in the province continued to claim the Mississippi boundary for some time to come.[13]

The captaincy general of the Floridas was temporarily destroyed by the application of the Spanish Constitution of 1812. By that famous document all chiefs of provinces were transformed into *jefes superiores políticos*, and an attempt was made to separate political from military functions. If the Florida provinces had contained sixty thousand inhabitants each they would have been entitled to a *jefe superior político* in each of their capitals, but together they could muster scarcely a sixth of that number. Therefore, East and West Florida were attached to the province of Havana as mere districts (*partidos*) and their respective governors became simple *jefes políticos*, a term used to designate subordinate officers representing the *jefes superiores* in important cities. This was in 1812. The next year, when the Diputación Provincial of Havana[14] met to decide on the permanent status of the Floridas, it was voted to further reduce them to mere parishes of the partido attached to the city of Havana because they did not have the five thousand persons necessary to be rated as districts. This change was to take effect in 1815, but the Floridas escaped this additional humiliation because Ferdinand VII returned to the throne of Spain and abolished the Constitution, with whose abrogation they rose again to the status of provinces, and together made up the captaincy general of the Floridas. The *jefe superior político* in Havana became captain general and the *jefes políticos* in Pensacola and St. Augustine resumed their governorships. It should be mentioned, however, that custom was strong, and the constitutional period so short, that the time-honored titles were used even in many official documents even when the Constitution was in effect. Such combinations as "*capitán general jefe superior político*" and "*gobernador militar y jefe político*," were in frequent use at the time and indicate the confusion that reigned.

The restored regime lasted until the 1820 revolution in Spain reinstated the Constitution. This automatically abolished the captaincy general and reduced the Florida provinces once more to districts, or *partidos* of the Cuban province of Havana. The question of further reducing them to parishes because of insufficient population was again suggested, but before it was acted upon orders came to hand over the Floridas to the United States.[15]

Complications in the business of administering the captaincy general of the Floridas were due to a number of circumstances. In the first place it was not self-supporting and depended upon a *situado*, or subsidy from New Spain to make up the annual deficit. Since Cuba depended on a similar subsidy, the captain general in Havana could not supply the deficiency in the Floridas from his island jurisdiction. Any naval forces used, except a few galleys and gunboats built for river and coastwise service, were under the command of the *comandante general del apostadero* of Havana, who was the commander of the Spanish West Indies Fleet. Some of the naval commanders were very jealous of their positions, and consequently were often at cross purposes with the captains general.[16]

The right of the governors to correspond directly with the home government has been mentioned. In judicial matters there was always the possibility of an appeal to the *audiencia* in Puerto Príncipe (now Camagüey), Cuba. Still more troublesome were the handling of Indian affairs and the relation of the Florida officials with the intendant in Havana, topics that have been reserved for separate treatment.

THE INTENDANCY OF LOUISIANA AND WEST FLORIDA

The disasters of the Seven Years' War led Spain to make a number of changes in her colonial system including the introduction of intendancies into America. The creation of the Cuban intendancy in 1764 led the way. Louisiana followed in 1780 with the appointment of Martín Navarro as intendant on February 24. As Spanish dominion was extended over West Florida, Navarro's jurisdiction extended until all the province came under his financial supervision by 1781.

In Cuba the intendant was an officer equal in rank to the captain general, and independent of him. In New Spain, on the other hand, the viceroy with the title of superintendent was in charge of the financial administration. The Louisiana plan was a kind of compromise between those of Cuba and New Spain. The governor there controlled land grants until 1798. He was also responsible for Indian affairs,[17] but was obliged to consult the intendant in cases involving finance, such as duties on the fur trade, permits for commerce with foreign countries to secure Indian goods, and licenses for the use of foreign ships to haul these goods as well as the furs. It was necessary to spend thousands of dollars each year to keep the friendship of the Indians, and this called for the joint action of the governor and the intendant also.[18]

Upon the promulgation of the *Ordenanza de intendentes* for New Spain in 1786, the Louisiana intendant was instructed to follow it in so far as was practicable, with the reservation, however, that of the four causes mentioned therein—*justicia, policía, hacienda y guerra*—only two, *hacienda y guerra*, were to come under his jurisdiction, justice and police being especially charged to the care of the governor.[19] There were many matters calling for the joint action of the two officers; yet, they seem to have coöperated without much friction. For example, the comment by Miró on his relations with Navarro on the question of a change of Indian policy: "It is my plan, to which the intendant, with whom I always proceed in accord in Indian affairs, agrees. . . ."[20] Professor Whitaker's careful study revealed the same kind of coöperation during the administration of Francisco Rendón (1794-1796).[21] Not until the appointment of a man with a contentious turn did the harmonious relations between governor and intendant cease, i.e., Juan Ventura Morales, of whom more later.

Such cordial relation may have resulted from the instructions sent to the first intendant, Martín Navarro, putting him in subordination to the governor.[22] It is remarkable, however, that this was done because a few days previous to the signing of the instruction an order to the captain general of Cuba concerning his relations with the intendant in Havana stated that the king desired to have

> treated with decorum an officer like the *intendente de ejército y real hacienda*, who is so important to His Majesty that in him is vested the collection, preservation, and disbursement of all branches of the revenue, with complete independence of you; and . . . who is a *jefe principal*, without other superior than the *Superintendente General de Real Hacienda de Indias*.[23]

Navarro retired from the Louisiana intendancy in 1788, at which time Governor Miró was invested with the powers of the office.[24] The inclusion of the phrase, "for the present," in Miró's commission as intendant suggests that the union of the offices was looked on as temporary; nevertheless, it was continued until well into the term of Miró's successor, the baron de Carondelet. In 1793 there was appointed another intendant, Francisco Rendón, who reached his post early the next year.[25] According to Professor Whitaker this move was made in order to insure the operation of the new commercial system promulgated the year before.[26] No further combination of the offices of governor and intendant occurred until long after Louisiana had passed from Spanish control.

The last occupant of the intendancy in New Orleans was Juan Ventura Morales, who achieved lasting fame by his action in closing the American deposit at New Orleans; in fact, he might be called the last of the Louisiana-Florida intendants for, with the exception of an occasional suspension from office after he went to Pensacola, he held the position until its abolition in 1817. Morales became acting intendant of Louisiana and West Florida in 1796 on the retirement of Rendón. Ramón López de Angulo, a full-fledged intendant, succeeded him in 1800, but was summarily removed the next year upon his violation of the laws by marrying a New Orleans girl named Marie Delphine Macarty.[27] Morales again became provisional intendant and held office until the Spanish colors were struck in 1803. As a matter of fact, he remained in Louisiana three years longer, refusing to leave until expelled by the American authorities.

For some time after the lowering of the flag Morales and the other Spanish officials in New Orleans were at a loss what to do because no definite orders were sent to govern their conduct. But Morales stayed long after such orders came. He may have hoped for another diplomatic shake-up which would return Louisiana to Spain. Doubtless, he did not relish the idea of living at the frontier post of Pensacola after his taste of more attractive life in New Orleans. Furthermore, in Pensacola he would drop to the level of Governor Vicente Folch y Juan who, as *subdelegado* of the intendancy, had long been his subordinate. Moreover, these two officers had developed an antipathy for each other that approximated hatred, and matters did not mend after the Americans took over Louisiana. Morales continued to give orders from New Orleans as though Folch were still his subordinate, to the confusion of the commandant at Mobile and others. Contradictory orders were issued about trade through that port with the American territory up the river.[28] The climax to the situation was reached in January, 1806, when Governor William C. C. Claiborne peremptorily ordered Morales to leave Louisiana, and Folch flatly refused to allow him to land at Pensacola, forcing him to leave the port with his goods and papers, and to disembark at Mobile.[29] Naturally Morales protested to Spain and he was ordered to proceed at once to Pensacola and assume the authority of intendant of the province. Both he and Folch were admonished to "try to preserve the best of harmony, and to avoid disputes and contentions."[30]

But Morales willed it otherwise. Even before this admonition reached him he was accusing Folch of making innovation in the financial administration of West Florida and proceeded to take matters into his own hands as far as the western part of the province was concerned, issuing orders to the officers commanding the troops on the Pascagoula River. The officers appealed to Folch, who informed the intendant that only the commandant at Mobile had such right. Mutual recrimination followed until the latter appealed to Spain. The king commanded all documents concerning the quarrel to be forwarded to him for examination,[31] and in the meantime Morales was off on another tack with Folch.

Before Morales' arrival in Pensacola the finances of West Florida had been administered by the traditional *oficiales reales* in the form of an accountant and a treasurer, supervised by the governor as *subdelegado* of the intendancy in New Orleans. In addition to the *oficiales* there were clerks, warehousemen, porters, etc., many of whom were also officers or soldiers of the garrison.[32] With the transfer of the seat of the intendancy to Pensacola in 1806, the number of clerks and minor employees in the financial department increased, and there was added an *asesor*, or legal adviser.

This appointment is interesting because the first *asesor* was José Francisco Heredia, the father of the famous Cuban poet, José María Heredia. Thus it came about that the poet lived in Pensacola between the ages of three and seven, his favorite sister, Ignacia, being born there in 1808. Of more importance to the present study is the fact that José Francisco received his appointment from the intendant of Cuba, who, upon reporting the move to Spain for royal approval, was curtly informed that he had exceeded his authority; Morales' assistant should have been appointed by the captain general.[33] Heredia remained in Pensacola as *asesor* to the intendant, however, until 1810, at the salary of one thousand *pesos* assigned him by the Cuban intendant.[34] Thereafter the *auditor de guerra*, or legal adviser to the governor, acted as *asesor* to the intendant of West Florida.[35]

The appointment of Heredia illustrates the confusion as to the supervision of the intendancy in Pensacola. Both the Cuban intendant and Morales contended that the right should belong to the former instead of to the captain general in Havana. The reprimand that followed failed to settle the matter, and before long the two Havana authorities were at swords points about Florida finances as well as their respective position in Cuba itself.[36] The situation became acute during the administration of Captain General Juan Ruíz de Apodaca (1812-1816), who claimed absolute control over West Florida finances under an instruction of January 26, 1782, to Bernardo de Gálvez as captain general, in which the latter was referred to as the *superintendente de real hacienda de la Luisiana y de la Florida Occidental*. A bitter dispute lasted until the arrival in Cuba of two more pacific personalities—Captain General José Cienfuegos and Intendant Alejandro Ramírez. On August 9, 1816—exactly forty days later—the argument that had promoted hard feelings for a generation was settled.

Cienfuegos and Ramírez adopted the simple expedient of giving honor to whom honor was due, and in so doing each obtained the full coöperation of the other. The question of finances in the Floridas was settled by Cienfuegos's turning the whole matter over to Ramírez until the king's will on the point should be ascertained—a logical move since both Cuba and the Floridas were dependent on a subsidy from New Spain which was usually sent to Havana for distribution. Royal approval of the Cienfuegos-Ramírez agreement was given on September 3, 1817, Ramírez being made *superintendente* of the Floridas as well as of Cuba.[37]

The foregoing imbroglio over the *superintendencia* was scarcely terminated when the intendancy of West Florida was abolished. Morales, who in 1810 achieved his heart's desire by becoming a full-fledged intendant (hitherto he had been only provisional), was promoted to the intendancy of Puerto Rico, Morales was relieved in 1819 and dropped out of the colonial administration.

The last years of Morales in Pensacola deserve a parting comment. Rare were the epochs when he was not the center of a storm. On one occasion he was suspended from office on account of his failure to report properly the results of a hurricane on October 11 and a fire on October 24, 1810, which destroyed many records.[38] Perhaps the dispute in 1812 over who should be his substitute can be laid to contagion. The a*uditor de guerra,* as the intendant's legal adviser, and the accountant, as second in the financial administration, each claimed the law on his side. Nevertheless, an order of the regency passed over both claimants and conferred the provisional intendancy on the governor of Pensacola.[39] Another and more serious difficulty arose in 1817, though the exact nature of the trouble is not very clear. Finally, however, the king announced that "he was pleased to proclaim the innocence of the Intendant of Pensacola, Don Juan Ventura Morales," without mentioning any specific accusation.[40] At this juncture Morales was transferred to Puerto Rico,[41] and with his departure the West Florida intendancy came to an end. Finances there had long since ceased to justify the payment of four thousand *pesos* for their administration;[42] in fact, it is doubtful whether any reason could be produced for ever having had an intendancy in Pensacola other than that of providing employment for a man released by the loss of Louisiana. During the closing years of Spanish rule in West Florida the governor supervised the treasury administration as *subdelegado* of the *superintendente de real hacienda in Havana,*[43] Alejandro Ramírez. It should be remembered, that during much of 1818 the province was occupied and administered by American armed forces.

With the abolition of the intendancy in Pensacola the financial systems of East and West Florida were harmonized for the first time. It is true that on at least two occasions the governors of the former had requested the creation of an intendancy in St. Augustine, but always with the view to the office for themselves. The first was made as soon as it was known that Miró had been entrusted with the office left vacant by Navarro in New Orleans. The petition was laid before the captain general of Cuba early in 1790 and was forwarded to Spain on March 26. There was a prompt negative reply on July 9.[44]

A second suggestion for the creation of an intendancy in East Florida was made by the governor of the province in 1799, with the ostensible purpose of removing certain evils attendant on the existing system. He would even have been satisfied with the establishment of a *subdelegación* of the Havana intendancy, but the authorities in Spain merely instructed the governor to report any irregularities that might occur in the finance administration to them.[45] Except for the two constitutional periods (1812-1814 and 1820-1821), when municipal finance was temporarily in the hands of the city government of St. Augustine, the accountant and the treasurer, supervised by the governor as the representative of the captain general in Havana, were responsible for the financial part of the East Florida government until 1816. At that time the governor automatically became *subdelegado* of the Cuban *superintendente* by the relinquishment by Cienfuegos of control of Florida finances.

During the constitutional periods the municipality of St. Augustine was responsible to the Diputación Provincial in Havana for all of its activities. This affected East Florida during both periods; West Florida only during the first, since Pensacola had insufficient population in 1820 to warrant municipal government. There was an *alcalde* in Pensacola for a time who disputed with the governor the control of many phases of the administration, but this will be better treated in another connection.

Notes for "The Administrative System in the Floridas, 1781-1821"

[1]Archivo Nacional de Cuba (hereinafter cited as ANC), Floridas, legajo 2, no. 1. The copy here is one sent to Pedro Piernas on August 18, 1781.

[2]Miró to Gálvez, April 9, 1782, ibid., legajo 3, no. 7.

[3]A copy of the order, dated October 31, 1783, is in ibid., legajo 10, no. 6.

[4]The results of a recent study of the use of the term "*capitania general*" in connection with Cuba have not been entirely satisfactory. See Duvon C. Corbitt, *The Colonial Government of Cuba* (Manuscript Ph. D. thesis in the library of the University of North Carolina).

[5]Jacobo de la Pezuela, *Historia de la Isla de Cuba*, 4 vols. (Madrid, 1869-1878), 3:199.

[6]Ibid., 3:199-200. Jacobo de la Pezuela, *Diccionario de la Isla de Cuba*, 4 vols. (Madrid, 1863), 2:382-83.

[7]ANC, Floridas, legajo 10, no. 9. The *cédula* is dated March 3, 1787.

[8]See the letterbooks of Bernardo de Gálvez, ibid., legajo 15, nos. 77 and 79.

[9]Ezpeleta to Valdés, December 6, 1787, AGI, Papeles de Cuba, 86-6-16 (transcript in the McClung Collection. Lawson McGhee Library, Knoxville, Tennessee). A translation appears in the East Tennessee Historical Society's *Publications*, 12 (1940): 116-17. See also ANC, Floridas, legajo 3, no. 7 and legajo 10, no. 6.

[10]Ibid., Reales Ordenes, 8:523-24.

[11]Arthur P. Whitaker, *The Mississippi Question, 1795-1803* (New York, 1934), 29. See also chapter 2, note 3.

[12]I. J. Cox, *The West Florida Controversy, 1798-1813* (Baltimore, 1918), 214-15. Folch's letter to Godoy on the subject was dated August 8, 1807, ibid., 215, note 41.

[13]ANC, Floridas, legajo 13, no. 8.

[14]Each province had an advisory and legislative body called a *diputación provincial*. It is proposed to treat this body in more detail in the study of the effects of the Constitution of Floridas.

[15]ANC, Gobierno Superior Civil, legajo 861, no. 29160. *Diario del Gobierno Constitucional de la Habana*, December 6, 1820.

[16]Pezuela, *Historia de la Isla de Cuba*, 3:115-19. José María Zamora, *Biblioteca de la legislación española* (Madrid, 1844-1849), 3:334-45. See Corbitt, *The Colonial Government of Cuba*, chapter 2. From 1812 to 1816 the captain general was also the naval commander. This was probably due to the fact that the incumbent, Juan Ruíz de Apodaca, had been a naval officer.

[17]Whitaker, *The Mississippi Question*, 30 and chapter 2, note 6.

[18]See the correspondence of Miró, Navarro, McGillivray and Panton in *Georgia Historical Quarterly*, 21 (1937): 72-83. For similar documents see Duvon C. and Roberta Corbitt, eds., "Papers Relating to Tennessee and the Old Southwest, 1783-1800," East Tennessee Historical Society's *Publications* for the years 1937 to 1941.

[19]Instructions of June 7, 1799, to Ramón López de Angulo, ANC, Floridas, legajo 16, no. 126. The *Ordenanza de intendentes* appears in Zamora, *Biblioteca de legislación ultramarina*, 3:371-88.

[20]Miró to Sonora, June 1, 1787, East Tennessee Historical Society's *Publications*, 11 (1939): 77-78.

[21]Whitaker, *The Mississippi Question*, 31.

[22]Ibid., chapter 2, note 6.

[23]W. W. Pierson, "Establishment and Early Functioning of the Intendencia of Cuba," *James Sprunt Historical Studies*, 19:93. Carlos de Sedano y Cruzat, *Cuba desde 1850 á 1873* (Madrid, 1873), 60.

[24]A copy of Miró's commission is in ANC, Reales Ordenes, 8:523-24.

[25]Gardoqui to the intendant of Cuba (Pablo Valiente), October 30, 1793, ibid., Floridas, legajo 14, no. 48. Whitaker, *The Mississippi Question*, chapter 2, note 7.

[26]Ibid., note 7. Professor Whitaker cited a memorandum by Gardoqui dated May 25, 1793.

[27]Whitaker, *The Mississippi Question*, 161, gives an account of the López y Angulo affair. A copy of the order removing him from office is in ANC, Reales Ordenes, 15:59.

[28]Cox, *The West Florida Controversy*, 148-82.

[29]ANC, Floridas, legajo 18, no. 48.

[30]Ibid., legajo 14, no. 48. The orders from Spain were dated March 31, 1806.

[31]Ibid., legajo 2, no. 24.

[32]Ibid., legajo 17, no. 242 and legajo 18, no. 87.

[33]Two copies of the order, dated May 7, 1806, are in ibid., legajo 18, no. 50.

[34]For data on the residence of the poet and his father in Pensacola see José María Heredia, *Poesías completas* (Havana, 1940-1942), 1:19.

[35]ANC, Floridas, legajo 18, no. 149.

[36]The argument was not definitely settled until 1854 when the two positions were united. Joaquín Rodríguez San Pedro, *Legislación ultramarina*, 16 vols. (Madrid, 1865-1869), 1:75. See Duvon C. Corbitt, *The Colonial Government of Cuba*, chapter 2 for an account of the attempts to settle the trouble.

[37]Duvon C. Corbitt, "The Contention over the Superintendencia of the Floridas," *Florida Historical Quarterly*, 15 (1936): 113-17.

[38]ANC, Floridas, legajo 18, no. 144.

[39]Ibid., legajo 18, no. 149.

[40]Ibid., legajo 19, no. 34. The royal order in question was signed on February 19, 1817.

[41]Morales was relieved of the intendancy of Puerto Rico December 30, 1819, at his own request. Ibid., Reales Ordenes, 23:579-81. He had been in the administrative service since 1777 at which time he was appointed clerk in the *secretaria de gobierno* of Louisiana. Bernardo de Gálvez to José de Gálvez, December 30, 1777, ANC, Floridas, legajo 15, no. 79.

[42]This salary was assigned to Morales by an order of March 21, 1810, which made him full intendant, ibid., Reales Ordenes, 18:267.

[43]The intendancy of Cuba was raised to a *superintendencia* in 1812, at which time Cuba was divided into three provincial intendancies.

[44]A copy of the king's reply if found in ANC, Floridas, legajo 14, no. 79. Another copy is in ibid., Reales Ordenes, 4:483-84. The reply stated that there was absolutely no need for such an intendancy, but rather for a punctual observance of the Laws of the Indies.

[45]Ibid., Floridas, legajo 16, no. 130. The reply was dated June 18, 1799.

GOVERNMENT, LAW, AND POLITICS*

Morris S. Arnold

By a secret covenant of November 3, 1762, France ceded the western part of Louisiana to Spain, but plans for transferring possession of the colony were held in abeyance for a considerable time. It was not until about two years had elapsed that word of the agreement even reached Louisiana. Two more years passed before Antonio de Ulloa, the first Spanish governor, arrived on March 5, 1766.

Not surprisingly, the treaty by which France transferred the sovereignty over Louisiana to Spain made no mention of what legal system was to be in effect under the new regime. The royal letter of April 21, 1764, by which Louis XV notified the Louisiana governor of the cession, did, however, express the hope that the king of Spain would order "the judges ordinary and the Superior Council [to] continue to render justice according to the laws, forms, and usages of the colony."[1] In fact, it seems to have been the original Spanish plan not to replace French law with Spanish, at least not immediately,[2] but in the event that was done.

Ulloa ran into considerable difficulty when he attempted to establish his authority in the province and was expelled from it late in 1768.[3] It was nine months before General Alejandro O'Reilly resumed Spanish control. When he did, he did so swiftly, firmly, and (some say) cruelly. Within two months of his arrival he had held treason trials resulting in the execution of five of the principal participants in the bloodless revolution against Ulloa. Significantly, the judgment in the case recited that the Spanish court had proceeded "*segun nuestras leyes*" ("according to our laws").[4] It was a portent of things to come.

On November 25, 1769, O'Reilly abolished the Superior Council and issued two documents known today as O'Reilly's Laws. One of these documents consisted of ordinances creating the *Ayuntamiento* or secular *cabildo* of New Orleans as a replacement for the Superior Council; these ordinances also regulated the *cabildo*'s judicial functions.[5] The other document was a set of *Instructions* containing rules of civil and criminal

*This article is a condensed version of chapter 6 of Morris S. Arnold, *Colonial Arkansas* (Fayetteville, AR: University of Arkansas Press, 1992), 125-70. Reprinted here with the kind permission of the author and The University of Arkansas.

procedure, the substantive law of crimes, and provisions for testate and intestate succession.[6] These two instruments left no doubt as to the sources employed to produce them, for annotations to two Spanish digests, the *Recopilación de las Indias* and the *Nueva Recopilación de Castilla*, were provided by the draftsmen. The first of these works is a digest of Spanish ultramarine law before 1680 that deals mainly with public-law matters; the second is a digest of Castilian law and concerns itself with private law.[7] Professional lawyers were at work: The preamble to these *Instructions* stated that they were digested and arranged "by the Doctor Don Manuel Joseph de Urrustia and the counsellor Don Félix del Rey."

Because the *Instructions* did not cover every substantive legal area, and because their preamble contained a somewhat tentative declaration that they were to serve "until a more extensive information upon those laws [i.e., Spanish law in general] may be acquired," it used to be a question much mooted whether Spanish law ever completely superseded French law in Louisiana. It is now established beyond doubt that O'Reilly deliberately annihilated French law, that he introduced Spanish law wholesale, and that he had had royal authority to do so in advance and royal approbation afterwards.[8]

Confusion about what country's law was in effect, and ignorance of its substance, caused problems at Arkansas Post. While, as we have seen, O'Reilly formally replaced French law with Spanish in 1769, he seems not to have relayed that message to the posts, at least not to the Arkansas. In one matter, the nature of which is unclear, the commandant was ambiguously instructed in August of 1770 that "the Ordinances of the kings of France and Spain must be adhered to."[9]

By the autumn of 1770, however, some order was beginning to emerge from the confusion. A letter from Arkansas dated October 4 mentions the "penal code,"[10] an evident reference to the substantive criminal provisions of O'Reilly's *Instructions* of November 25, 1769. The next month, someone, probably the governor, wrote from New Orleans to Lieutenant Joseph Orieta (who had taken over at the Arkansas) and commended him for asking for "a printed copy of the penal code."[11] Interestingly, it appears from this letter that the remote post of *Los Arcos*, as the Spaniards called the Arkansas settlement, had not been sent a copy of these laws when they were sent to the other forest posts; and it had taken a letter to New Orleans to correct the bureaucracy's forgetfulness.

Probably at the same time that he finally sent his penal code to Arkansas, O'Reilly also sent along another printed document dated February 12, 1770, and styled "Instruction to which *lieutenants particuliers* [*i.e.*, civil commandants] ought to conform . . . in all that belong to the police and the administration of justice, civil as well as criminal."[12] These instructions gave commandants jurisdiction to judge "verbally" demands that did not exceed twenty *piastres*; cases exceeding this sum were reserved to the court of the governor general in New Orleans.[13] Commandants were also given jurisdiction over successions: In the case of a testate succession, the goods of the deceased were to be delivered for administration to his widow or, if none, to his heirs; if there were no widow or heirs, the administration was to be entrusted to some other suitable person.[14] If the value of the estate was less than one hundred *piastres*, the commandant could immediately liquidate it; having assembled the interested parties in his house, he was then to make distribution of the proceeds to the widow and heirs. "having regard to the widow's right to nuptial gains." If there were minor heirs, the commandant was to appoint a guardian for them. Larger estates required a formal inventory, appraisal, and public auction before distribution.[15] The *Instructions* set fees that the commandant could charge for supervising successions.[16] An appeal lay to the governor's court in New Orleans in succession cases, though not in other civil causes.

In criminal matters the commandant had a vague and inconsequential authority. He could proceed to judgment only "if the criminal cause was quite light."[17] No precise jurisdictional boundary was defined, and perhaps in the nature of things that was not possible. The draftsman of the *Instructions* resorted instead to examples: "A quarrel, or injurious words of little consequence," were the kinds of criminal cases within the commandant's judicial competence. Even then he was not allowed to punish anyone; he was supposed to call the parties before him, reprimand the offender, and try to establish peace between them.[18] Obviously, no appeal could lie from such a "judgment." In serious criminal matters (again only examples are given: killing, wounding, theft) the commandant was to take the depositions of witnesses and send a report (*information*) to the governor, keeping the prisoner under guard until the governor decided what to do.[19] In this procedure, as in others, the commandant acted both as interrogating officer and as surrogate notary; in this latter capacity he was assisted by two witnesses who were to be present throughout the entire proceeding.[20]

In French Louisiana there had been a number of provincial notaries in some of the remote outposts. The Spanish, however, very severely limited the number of notaries and none were allowed outside New Orleans.[21] Therefore, the post commandants were given notarial powers in places beyond the city. "Since there are no longer any notaries [écrivains] established. . . who can draft and authenticate the acts and contracts of the *habitants*," the *Instructions* noted, the commandants were authorized to make *procurations*, and to sign all other necessary acts, with the assistance of two witnesses. Any instrument that created a mortgage, as, typically, a marriage contract did, was supposed to be reported to the government notary at the Cabildo in New Orleans; the date and all the particulars should be sent so that the notary could make a public record of them.[22]

The commandant's police duties also found a place in this document. A commandant was to allow no one to settle in his bailiwick who did not have the written permission of the governor.[23] Only two "cabarets" (bars) were to be allowed in each jurisdiction, and only habitants of good repute and conduct should be licensed. The commandant was to instruct licensees expressly not to sell any strong drink to slaves unless they had with them the written permission of a master whose signature was known. A violation of this provision would bring a fine of ten *piastres* (to be given to the church) and permanent revocation of the seller's license.[24] There was a bounty on deserters for which the commandant was eligible,[25] and he was to make sure that no one without a passport journeyed into his jurisdiction.[26] As though all this were not enough, he was to keep his *habitants* [settlers] from trafficking with the English on the boats that traveled the Mississippi and in the English posts established on that river's left bank.[27] It also fell to him to oversee the building and repair of roads and enclosures (levees); they were to be built and maintained at the expense of the *habitants*.[28]

A very interesting duty of the commandant of a judicial or administrative sort deserves separate mention. In the event a runaway slave was captured and it was determined that his master was a local resident, the slave was to be interrogated to discover his reason for fleeing. If he had run away because he had not proper food or shelter, the commandant was to proceed against the master, collect costs, and impose a fine of ten *piastres* to be given to the church.[29]

Another important document of relevance, dated January 26, 1770, contained instructions that O'Reilly sent to his lieutenant governors at Natchitoches and St. Louis defining their police duties and judicial jurisdiction.[30] Their authority in civil matters extended to cases in which the demand did not exceed one hundred *piastres*.[31] In larger civil cases, the lieutenant governors were authorized to proceed up to the judgment stage, at which point they were to send the file to the governor for his determination.[32] In all civil cases the rules of civil procedure formulated in 1769 were to be adhered to. In serious criminal matters, the lieutenant governors were empowered to proceed up to the judgment stage, following the rules of criminal procedure promulgated in 1769, and they were then to pass the matter to the governor for decision.[33]

If the Arkansas commandant had followed his instructions, his jurisdiction would have been rather restricted. His criminal judicial jurisdiction was clearly trivial, although his police investigative duties were quite considerable. Civil cases in which the demand did not exceed twenty *piastres*—that is, twenty dollars—could not have been of much importance. It follows that the people of the Arkansas who were of a mind to resort to a technically competent governmental authority for the settlement of their disputes would often have had to go elsewhere.

Even if it had occurred to some eighteenth-century Arkansan to apply to the lieutenant governor at Natchitoches for relief, that avenue was specifically closed by the *Instructions* to post commandants. Section One of those instructions provided that "as to cases which exceed [twenty *piastres*], they shall be judged by the Governor General, to which tribunal the parties shall repair either in person or by someone charged with their powers. . . ."[34] Incredibly, then, in nontrivial civil matters persons who followed these rules were expected, either personally or through an attorney, to make the trek to New Orleans for an adjudication of their difficulties. According to Jean Baptiste Bénard de La Harpe, it was twelve or fifteen days by river from the mouth of the Arkansas to New Orleans, and the return trip consumed forty to fifty days.[35] Even though the use of attorneys was specifically authorized, resort to regular governmental tribunals for sorting out disputes would have been very difficult at the least. At times, and for some Arkansans most of the time, it would have been next to impossible.

The meager record evidence that survives, however, reveals a process of practical adaptation that made the system more tolerable. As noted above, post commandants were given authority to adjudicate "verbally" the civil matters within their competence. This evidently meant that there was no need for written pleadings, the taking of depositions, or even (until sometime later) a written judgment. The rules of civil procedure of 1769 did sometimes require written pleadings and depositions, but they applied only in the governor's court and the courts of the lieutenant governors. In the nature of things, then, the cases in which commandants had the power to proceed to judgment would leave no trace on the records. These cases were no doubt handled as part of the administrative routine of the post, and with respect to them the commandant was the final arbiter. Since there was no appeal from the commandant's judgment, and no trace in the Spanish judicial records of anything like a writ of prohibition, there is reason to believe that a commandant who wished to do so could exceed his jurisdiction without much fear of interference from the central authority. Even in the absence of record evidence, it would be a reasonable guess that this often happened at Arkansas Post.

Indeed, occasional glimpses of litigation at the Arkansas positively show that the Spanish government winked at, indeed encouraged, the exercise of unauthorized judicial power by the commandant and that the hardship which strict adherence to the rules would have produced was thus obviated in actual practice. For example, in 1770 a merchant named Tounoir took a great deal of bear oil from the boat of a hunter named Francoeur to satisfy a debt. Lambert, an *engagé* of Francoeur, petitioned the commandant in writing to order Tounoir to replace the oil; Francoeur owed him wages, he said, and he claimed preference to Tounoir because his claim was "due for hard work." Captain François Demasellière, the commandant, thereupon ordered Tounoir to return the oil. When Tounoir refused, the commandant was obliged to send his sergeant to execute his order. At this point, Francoeur asked to have set off a debt of 944 *pesos* that Tounoir owed him; the note evidencing this debt, unfortunately, was in New Orleans in the hands of De Clouet, the former commandant. Demasellière wrote to the governor to ask that he order this note paid since Francoeur had nothing but his gun. The commandant then ordered Tounoir to pay court costs—that is, the sergeant's fee for taking the oil back; when Tounoir refused, Demasellière had him jailed. A short time thereafter the commandant ordered Tounoir to leave the post, but before doing so, Tounoir got Francoeur to sign some sort of "certificate," probably a release of Tounoir's note; and, to insult the commandant and literally as a parting shot, as he was leaving at high noon, Tounoir and his company fired off a volley of thirty rounds. Francoeur thereafter signed an affidavit that he executed the release to Tounoir when he "was drunk and thus it is of no value."[36]

This case, involving a great deal more than twenty *piastres*, if we assume that it was considered a civil case, obviously did not fall within the commandant's jurisdictional limits. Yet it seems reasonably clear that Demasellière found it impossible to do nothing, so he did his best to resolve the dispute. In fact, the governor was of the view that the commandant, far from having exceeded his jurisdiction, had been too timid. When the governor received the commandant's request to collect the note from Tounoir to Francoeur, he wrote him that he should have handled the matter himself: The proper procedure, the governor scolded, was to "hear both sides, taking the testimony of reputable witnesses on both sides, and then give me the arguments on both sides."[37]

In fairness to Demasellière, there was no way that he could have known from the *Instructions* (assuming that they had arrived by then, which as we saw is doubtful) that this was the proper procedure. The whole conflict was beyond his cognizance. What O'Reilly suggested that the commandant should have done corresponds more with the *Instrucción* to the lieutenant governors than with the *Instructions* to the commandants. But O'Reilly's orders in this case were in fact the only practicable way to govern a remote and mobile population like that at the Arkansas. Besides, it would have made no sense whatsoever to compel the commencement of the suit in New Orleans when the first act of the court here would probably have been to order the Arkansas commandant to take the depositions of witnesses at or in the environs of his post. The New Orleans court not infrequently asked the Arkansas commandant to act as a master to gather facts for the settlement of disputes involving Arkansas facts.

No judgment was rendered in this case. For our immediate purposes, however, the lesson is plain enough. Despite what the *Instructions* had said, when the Arkansas commandant was faced with a case that was beyond his power to adjudicate, he was expected to act as a master, gather facts, and send the file to New Orleans for decision. The procedure involved was more a matter of common administrative sense than of adherence to formal rules and was at least partly shaped by practical difficulties created by geography.

Toward the end of the Spanish period, at the time that Arkansas Post was becoming a truly stable settlement, an extremely interesting criminal proceeding took place there.[38] In 1791, Anselmo Billet *dit* Lajeunesse wounded Francisco Lecler with a hatchet. On his way to New Orleans to seek medical attention, Lecler stopped at the Royal Hospital at Natchez where he expressed a desire to initiate criminal charges against Billet. Manuel Gayoso de Lemos, the governor at Natchez, took Lecler's sworn deposition, and a physician provided him with a certificate describing his wounds. He continued his journey to New Orleans where he pressed his case before the *cabildo.* Governor [Esteban] Miró then ordered Capt. Juan Ignacio Delinó de Chalmette, the Arkansas commandant, to take the sworn depositions of relevant witnesses and send them along with his recommendations on the case to New Orleans for final decision.

Delinó first deposed four witnesses: Pedro Jardela, Luis Jardela, Cayetano Bougine (Vaugine), and Pierre Lefevre. None of the men had actually seen the incident; but they all testified that they had found Lecler sitting on the floor in François Ménard's house, wounded in the knee and in a great deal of pain. Lecler said at that time that Billet had struck him, but he had expressed no view on whether he had done it maliciously. The captain then deposed Billet who maintained steadfastly that he had been working at Ménard's house with a hatchet and that he had wounded Lecler accidentally.

After weighing the testimony, Delinó rendered a kind of interlocutory decision. He said that "according to the said depositions [*declaraciones*] it does not seem that the said wound given by the accused Anselmo Lachenesis [Lajeunesse] was effected with bad intentions." He therefore released Billet from the jail of the fort, but cautioned him to be available for the governor's questioning, should he request it. The depositions and the commandant's view of the case were sent to the governor in New Orleans: It was still pending in 1792 when the record ends.

This is the best example of a complete legal proceeding at the Arkansas in the entire eighteenth century. Delinó did an excellent job of questioning the witnesses, and the transcript of their testimony, covering about twenty pages, was nicely prepared. Second Sgt. Manuel Reyes acted as *escribano* (notary). The depositions were written in Spanish, but the interrogation was done in French; and when the testimony was read back to the deponents for their signatures, Cayetano Vaugine translated it into French for them. It can hardly be coincidental that this professional piece of legal and administrative work occurred just as Arkansas Post was beginning to achieve some respectability.

Residents of Arkansas who were temporarily in New Orleans or who had removed there could, of course, take advantage of the general, province-wide jurisdiction of the governor's court to sue an Arkansas resident. On April 8, 1771, for instance, Santiago Jacquelin and his wife, María Montcharvaux, sued François Ménard, who was then in Arkansas, for an accounting.[39] The claim was that Ménard had agreed to act as agent for Madame Montcharvaux, and a list of notes and personal belongings of hers was attached to the complaint. With the advice of his assessor, a law-trained advisor, the governor sent a dispatch to Fernando de Leyba, commandant at Arkansas, directing him to summon Ménard and to take his deposition in order to learn what he had done with Madame Montcharvaux's effects. Having received the order, Leyba first summoned his sergeant and swore him to act as *escribano pro tempore* (*ad hoc* notary). He then summoned Ménard, had him sworn, and questioned him as to the affairs entrusted him by the plaintiff. Ménard admitted that he was supposed to collect Doña María's notes and personal effects and account for them. He accounted for the notes, but in some of the personal effects he claimed property by virtue of a gift. All of this Leyba transmitted to New Orleans for "His Lordship to determine what he may find suitable."

The case shows that the local Arkansas commandant acted as an examining magistrate or master for cases in which post residents were sued in New Orleans. The flexibility made possible by the civilian habit of relying on depositions taken outside the presence of the parties is exposed to view here. Had viva voce testimony in open court in front of the parties been required, as it usually was in common-law courts, the province-wide jurisdiction of the governor's court would not have been nearly so useful. It would not very often have been reasonable to expect witnesses and parties to travel from the forest settlements to attend hearings and give testimony. The centralized authority of the governor's court in New Orleans made it possible to collect evidence from the remotest posts and bring it together in a central point for evaluation and eventually for rendering judgment.

Once judgment was rendered against an Arkansas resident in a suit initiated in New Orleans, the Arkansas commandant was expected to execute it. For instance, in 1787 François Ménard sued Anselmo Billet, a resident of the post who had acted as surety on a note that De Villiers had executed for the purchase of a slave. De Villiers had died in 1782, and his estate was insolvent; thus a cause of action had accrued against Billet. Ménard prayed judgment on the strength of the note and asked that a writ of execution against Billet issue to the commandant of *Los Arcos*. The court complied with the request.[40] In 1791 Santiago Gaignard sued a resident of Arkansas Post, Juan Bautista Saussié, for contribution. Gaignard claimed that he had paid a note owed by both him and the defendant that had been endorsed by the original payee to De Villier's widow; and he presented her receipt as evidence of the payment. He asked for summary judgment, as a common lawyer would say, and for a writ of execution to the commandant of Arkansas Post.[41]

Another class of case which bears on Arkansas legal history is the sort that involves occurrences at the Arkansas but does not involve Arkansas residents. These might he expected to have arisen fairly frequently in an *entrepôt* like the post. An extremely interesting example is the case of *Pourée v. Chouteau*.[42]

In March of 1782, Eugène Pourée outfitted a *bateau* in New Orleans in which he received freight "subject to the ordinary conditions of carriage by water." One of his shippers was Auguste Chouteau, a well-known St. Louis merchant. On reaching the Yazoo River, a party of Englishmen attacked Pourée's *bateau* and compelled him to descend to Natchez. After joining a convoy there for safety, the boat resumed its voyage. On reaching the St. Francis River, Pourée encountered a *bateau* belonging to a Mr. Labaddie; its crew having informed him that English brigands had attacked and pillaged them near what is now Memphis, Pourée decided to retreat to Arkansas Post until conditions improved. After a stay of some length there, he learned that the Englishmen had retired inland and he set off again, arriving safely at St. Louis after a considerable delay. Pourée wanted to recover from his shippers the extra expenses occasioned by the delays. These included payments to Choctaw Indians for reconnoitering for the preservation of the *bateau*; payments to Quapaw Indians who accompanied Pourée to the St. Francis River; rent for a house at Arkansas Post in which the cargo was stored; payment for 150 trips of cart for loading and unloading the *bateau* at Arkansas Post; wages of a crew sent down from St. Louis to man the vessel when it resumed its trip; payment of men at Arkansas Post for outfitting the *bateau*; payment for seventeen hundred pounds of biscuit bought at the Arkansas and eight hundred pounds of bacon; and the cost of powder and balls.

When Chouteau refused Pourée's demand, Pourée sued him in the court of the lieutenant governor in St. Louis. He recited the facts and closed his petition by noting his surprise that M. Chouteau would not pay his proportionate share of the increased expenses and by making known his view of the substantive law applicable to the case. He claimed that had he not completed the voyage at all due to *force majeure*, the shipper would not have been entitled under the law to a refund; likewise, "if the master makes a second equipment, the shippers are obliged to pay expenses." Pourée's complaint, in other words, doubled as a "brief" for his view of the relevant legal principles.[43] M. Chouteau answered simply that he had paid in advance, and he added his own view of the applicable rule: ". . . it would be a great wrong to shippers to have to pay a second time the freight upon a venture embarked in a *bateau*, upon which the freight had already been paid before it left port."[44]

The lieutenant governor, rather than decide the case himself, referred it to arbitration. Each party named one arbitrator, and these arbitrators elected a third. The record noted that "this tribunal shall finally decide and determine this cause according to the rights of each party." The arbitrators were all well-known and well-respected merchants of St. Louis. Though the record does not say so, the parties presumably agreed to this mode of settling their differences. The arbitrators decided that Chouteau was obligated to pay for some of the extra expenses occasioned by the layover at Arkansas Post, but not nearly as much as Pourée was claiming.

The manner of proceeding in civil cases in the lieutenant governor's court in St. Louis, as at the Arkansas, was a model of simplicity. Some cases were heard on oral plaint. If written pleadings were used, an informal petition initiated the action. The petition told the plaintiff's story simply, reciting the facts in a straightforward, though sometimes discursive way. No particular form was prescribed; as in common-law bill procedure, all the plaintiff had to do was to set out the salient features of his case.[45] The defendant replied with an answer containing a counterclaim to which the plaintiff answers; but only rarely will the plaintiff otherwise file a responsive pleading.

In 1782, however, the commandant reported only fifteen *habitant* families at the Arkansas; and five of these abandoned the river later that year.[46] The smallness of the population is almost certainly attributable to the cataclysmic events that occurred at the post in the 1780s. Only a few months after the post was moved, Spain sided with the American colonists and declared war on Great Britain.[47] Arkansas Post was the most vulnerable of all the Spanish forts in the Mississippi Valley because of its isolation and the small number of troops stationed there. Until it was reinforced by twelve soldiers in 1781, the garrison at full strength boasted only a captain and twenty soldiers. The possibility of a British attack on the post was therefore very much on the minds of its soldiers and *habitants*. In this tense atmosphere, two German soldiers (members of the Spanish detachment) and several American settlers at the post were accused early in 1782 of plotting to betray it. They had planned to open the gates of the fort to British sympathizers who would then butcher the garrison. De Villiers took depositions from various people, including those accused, and sent the record and the defendants to New

Orleans where a special tribunal sentenced two of the Americans and the two German soldiers to death.[48]

Most unfortunately, the records of the De Villiers's proceedings cannot be located. But when Governor Miró wrote to the captain general in Havana for confirmation of the sentence, though his letter was short, he revealed a great deal in it.[49] He described Arkansas Post as being very vulnerable since it was 250 leagues [*sic*] from its nearest northern neighbor. Arkansas was an immense country, he said, inhabited by innumerable Indians among whom lived many wandering Englishmen, the one group influencing the other; the British were "as hard to get rid of as a hydra-headed monster." The governor then went on sheepishly to admit that the record he was sending would reveal an error: The accused had not been confronted by the two witnesses against them. But since it would take too long to get the witnesses to New Orleans, Miró asked that the captain general overlook *esta pequeña falta* ("this small error"). Time was of the essence, and Miró closed by saying that allowing such acts as these to go unpunished leads to occurrences like the Natchez rebellion of the previous year—"fatal consequences" Miró termed them. The short reply from Cuba followed three and a half weeks later: The captain general let the convictions stand, and the sentence was carried out.[50] This case provides another example of legal norms yielding to political exigency and reveals again the highly subjective character of the process of adjudication in eighteenth-century Arkansas.

Arkansas Post long remained a place where it was well, whatever your nationality or status, to keep your political opinions to yourself. In 1788 François Ménard, by now surely the richest man at the post, confided to the Abenaki medal chief that it would not be long until the Americans took over Louisiana; and he allowed that the tribe had better look to taking the right side in the event of a struggle. So at least Joseph Tessié, in his deposition, accused Ménard of saying; no one else had heard it, but three sergeants of the garrison swore that they were in the room when the words were alleged to have been spoken. Tessié had turned to them and repeated what he claimed Ménard had said. Captain Josef Vallière sent the depositions and Ménard to New Orleans. He apologized for not sending a pre-trial examination of the defendant, but the post had no jail, a defect that he was hoping soon to remedy.[51]

The procedure for obtaining and perfecting a land grant from the Spanish government of Louisiana can be reconstructed with remarkable ease from printed sources. That is partly because the number of unadjudicated claims based on Spanish land grants remained large well into the nineteenth century.[52] Since ultimate resolution of these claims depended on their validity under Spanish law, many people were drawn to ransacking the old books for ordinances and regulations dealing with grants for the Spanish royal domain; and many of these laws found their way into print at various times after the American takeover.[53]

As soon as O'Reilly had established himself in authority in New Orleans, he made an extensive trip into the interior of what is now the state of Louisiana to make inspections, hear complaints, and generally inform himself on the state of governmental affairs in some of the more remote posts in lower Louisiana. Of course, he did not journey as far north as the Arkansas. Upon his return, he issued a set of regulations bearing on the concession of land. Under them, each newly arrived family was entitled to a plot of six or eight arpents in front by forty in depth. The grantees as *quid pro quo* were expected to build levees and ditches during the first three years of their possession and were obligated to keep the roads in repair. Within the same three-year period, moreover, they were "bound . . . to clear the whole front of their land to the depth of two arpents." If grantees did not fulfill these conditions, the regulations provided, "their land shall revert to the king's domain and be granted anew." During the initial three years of possession, which had the aura of a probationary period, written permission from the governor to make an alienation was required; and he was not to give it unless, "on strict inquiry, it shall be found that the conditions above explained have been duly executed."[54] There was also a requirement that the entire front of each concession be enclosed during the three-year period, but it was not made an express condition of the grant.[55] All grants were to be made by the governor, and the government surveyor was to fix the bounds in the presence of the local commandant and two settlers. These last four were to sign a *procés-verbal* reciting the events, and three copies of it were to be made: One for the archives of the *cabildo*, one for the governor, and one for the proprietor "to be annexed to the titles of his grant." Though these regulations were clearly generated by local conditions encountered by O'Reilly on his visits, and while they specifically mention Opelousas, Attakapas, and Natchitoches more than once, it seems that the general intended these rules to be observed everywhere in Louisiana: They close with his injunction to the "governor, judges, *cabildo*, and all the inhabitants of this province, to perform punctually to all that is required by this regulation."[56]

Not until 1797 was further regulation of land concessions made. In that year Governor Gayoso laid down some rules on who was qualified to receive grants. A stranger who was not a farmer or artisan, and who was unmarried and propertyless, was ineligible for a concession until he had been a resident for four years. Unmarried artisans, on the other hand, were privileged, and could qualify after having exercised their art or profession for three years. Married persons could immediately receive two hundred arpents plus fifty arpents for each child. The regulations specifically stated that a new settler would "lose [his lands] without recover, if, in the term of one year, he shall not begin to establish himself upon them or if in the third year he shall not have put under labor ten arpents in every hundred." Grants were, moreover, to be made contiguously, as to do otherwise "would offer a greater exposure to the attacks of the Indians, and render more difficult the administration of justice, and the regulation of the police. . . ."[57]

When in 1798 the power to regulate land concessions passed to the intendancy, Juan Ventura Morales issued an extensive set of regulations on the subject. No grant was to exceed eight hundred arpents. Grantees "on the river" were under the duty to build levees and canals, make and maintain roads, and construct necessary bridges. All settlers were to clear and put in cultivation within three years the whole front of their concessions to a depth of at least two arpents; if they did not, the rules provided, "the land granted [will be] remitted to the domain. . . ." O'Reilly's restraint on alienations during the "probationary" period was repeated, as was Gayoso's instruction on the necessity for contiguous grants.[58]

An interesting feature of Morales's rules was that, for the first time, they fixed the point at which title passed to the grantee. O'Reilly's regulations had not directly spoken to that point. Morales's regulations noted that some people had thought that title passed when their petition for a grant was filed, others when the order of survey was given, and still others when the survey was made. None of these people was right according to Morales: "Real titles" were required before the grant was perfected. These were to be issued when the surveyor's *procés-verbal* and a certified copy of it were sent to the intendant. At that point, the intendant, with the consent of the king's attorney, would deliver "the necessary title paper." Those occupying lands without such titles, unless they perfected their titles within six months, were "to be driven therefrom as from property belonging to the Crown," except that those who had been in possession ten years or longer would be allowed to stay after paying "a just and moderate retribution."

There is no evidence whatever that any of this vast array of regulation had the slightest impact in Arkansas. Only 29 claims totaling just over eight thousand acres were confirmed in the entire state of Arkansas by the first American land board which reported in 1812. (By contrast, 1,311 claims in Missouri were confirmed.)[59] Among the Arkansas claims, 14 were confirmed on the basis of settlement rights, 7 on the ground of ten years' possession, and only 8 on the strength of a "concession." Even these last were not complete titles under Spanish law. Four were "concessions" from commandants—1 from Vallière and 3 from De Vilemont. Even under the most liberal construction of O'Reilly's laws, as we have seen, a local commandant had no power to grant lands from the royal domain. The other 4 concessions were from governors, 3 from Miró and 1 from Gayoso; but none of these was supported by a real title and thus would have failed under Morales's regulations. There was not a single regular Spanish land title ever made out in the entire state of Arkansas. Captain Amos Stoddard estimated that 95 percent of the land claims in upper Louisiana were incomplete,[60] but this estimate turned out to be low since only 13 complete titles were ever proved up in the whole Missouri Territory.[61] The lack of anxiety among Arkansas residents about complying with the land law was, according to Lafon, a New Orleans engineer, easily explained. "Land situated so remote from population and commerce," he said, speaking of Arkansas Post, "was held in very little estimation, scarcely worth paying the fees of office for the file papers."[62]

The conveying practices of commandants and settlers at the Arkansas are illustrated by an instructive pair of documents available in the Archives of the Secretary of State of Missouri in Jefferson City. The first is Joseph Bougy's petition (in French) requesting permission to settle at Arkansas Post: "To Monsieur de Valliere, captain of infantry, civil and military commandant of the Post of Arkansas: Joseph Bougy, *habitant* of the Post of Kaskaskia, saying that he would like to come settle in this place of Arkansas with his family, humbly prays that it would please you to grant him eight arpents on the ordinary depth on the bank of this river. The applicant will pray for the saving of your days *etc.* Arkansas, 24 September, 1787. Mark X of Joseph Bougy." The only other document in this chain of title was the following (in Spanish): "I certify the said land [as] belonging to the royal domain. Arkansas, 25 September 1787. Josef Valliere."

This last document was the only semblance of a grant that Bougy had. It was actually only a statement by the commandant that the land was vacant. Beginning in the 1790s, the commandant who endorsed a petition for a land grant almost always prefaced his certificate of vacancy with a statement such as, "I consider the petitioner worthy of the favor that he asks." But during the Spanish period the commandants at the Arkansas never actually purported in writing to make grants form the royal domain. A new formula introduced at the Post just before the American takeover, however, adopts a tone that stops just short of purporting to make a grant. [Francisco] Caso y Luengo, the last Spanish commandant at the Arkansas, seems responsible for the new language. A good example of it comes from February 26, 1803, when Pierre Lefevre petitioned for an addition to one of his tracts so that he could cut enough trees to build a sawmill. He asked that Caso y Luengo "deign to accord [*acordar*] him an extension of the depth of his land, which he believes, far from prejudicing anyone, would be much to the advantage of the settlement." The commandant replied that since the "proposal would redound much to the benefit of this settlement, I find no objection to me granting him what he asks. . . ." This artful reply comes about as close to using words of grant as one can without actually doing so. Caso y Luengo used these and similar words in many of his endorsements.

It is abundantly clear, however, despite the law, that the settlers at the Arkansas regarded their land as having been granted to them as soon as the commandant endorsed their petitions. For instance, on May 7, 1799, Charles Drouot, *habitant* of the post, petitioned Captain Carlos de Vilemont for 240 arpents of land. De Vilemont endorsed the request by replying: "I consider the petitioner worthy of the favor that he requests and it appears to me that the land he wants is vacant and belongs to the royal domain." The next instrument in this chain of title is one signed by Drouot which states: "I certify that I have ceded the above-mentioned concession to Monsieur Pierre Lefevre, in faith of which I have subscribed [this instrument] at the Arkansas. . . ." Clearly, though erroneously, Drouot believed that the commandant's endorsement was a concession that he had given him an alienable interest in realty. Indeed, petitioners for land in Arkansas often revealed a belief that commandants had the power to give *une concession* or *conseder la . . . tierra*—to grant a concession or concede land. After the American takeover Arkansas commandants were actually bold enough to claim that they had possessed a power that in fact the land regulations had clearly denied them. For instance, when in October of 1804 Henry Cassidy became anxious about the title to land that he claimed on the St. Francis, he obtained an affidavit from Caso y Luengo stating that, when he was commandant, he "had conceded him a portion of land in the place called the little prairie."

The commandants and *habitants* of the Arkansas thus very clearly ignored the extensive set of land regulations promulgated by various eighteenth-century governors and others. It was simply too costly and too complicated to comply, especially when the benefits of conforming seemed in any case not very great. An interesting contrast to this insouciance, on the other hand, is provided by the few eighteenth-century wills executed at the Arkansas that have survived. The stakes were higher in the case of wills than in the case of land grants since very often a great deal of personalty, especially receivables and slaves, would purport to pass under them. For instance, in 1791 François Ménard executed a will and codicil at the post shortly before he died, leaving to his wife his fourteen slaves (three of whom were runaways), his desk (bureau) full on notes and bonds, and his liquor and other merchandise, subject to a trust in favor of his illegitimate daughter Constance.[63] Ménard also declared his ownership of a house in New Orleans situated in the Rue de la Madame Boisclare.

Captain Juan Ignacio Delinó de Chalmette, called to Ménard's bedside at four o'clock one morning, did quite a serviceable job of drafting this will and codicil. He caused them to be executed, moreover, in accordance with the formal requirements prevailing in Louisiana. O'Reilly's *Instructions* of 1770 to the post commandants had indicated that wills sought to be signed by the testator, surrogate notary, and five witnesses—two to aid the commandant's attestation and three others.[64] But O'Reilly's Laws of 1769 specifically said that "if there be no notary [attesting], there must be present five witnesses, residents of the place in which the will shall be made; if, however, it be impossible to procure the last mentioned number, three may suffice." The *Nueva Recopilación de Castilla* was cited in support of this proposition.[65] Delinó had only three witnesses to the will and codicil, but this, as just demonstrated, was evidently authorized by O'Reilly's Laws. It is likely that this was in any event the custom at the Arkansas since only other complete specimen of a will executed there in the eighteenth century is executed precisely the same way—indeed, with the same witnesses.[66]

The Spanish archives of Arkansas Post had grown quite large when, on March 23, 1804, they were delivered to Lt. James B. Many of the United States Army. There were over two hundred items, dating at least to 1780, listed in the inventory that Many signed by way of receipt for their delivery by Captain Francisco Caso y Luengo.[67] The archives themselves have, unfortunately, been lost, but the inventory reveals a good deal of instructive data.

The commandant's notarial duties consumed a significant portion of his time. There were recorded in the archives eight wills, seven marriage contracts, five other contracts (*acuerdos* and *convenios*), a large number of bonds and receipts, numerous deeds (of land, houses, slaves, and livestock), and three deeds of emancipation. The commandant's judicial duties were also considerable. There were almost thirty successions, and this kind of case presumably accounted for a great deal of the commandant's judicial work. It could be rather remunerative as well, especially if the estate was large and thus required some time to inventory and settle. For instance, on May 27, 1778, De Villiers had to travel two leagues downriver from the post to inventory the goods of Pierre de Laclède Liguest, the founder of St. Louis, who had died in his trading boat near the mouth of the Arkansas.[68] It took three days and fifteen pages to list all his goods. De Villiers also acted as coroner in this instance, for he noted that, having inspected the body, Laclède's "death had occurred naturally."

Adversarial litigation at the Arkansas may have been rare, but the condition of the evidence is such that statements on this subject are exceedingly hazardous. The inventory of the Post archives records the presence of five petitions (*instancias*), probably written complaints whose function was the initiation of litigation. The existence of six *procesos* is also mentioned, and these are probably case files that had been advanced at least to the deposition stage. This seems a rather small number of cases, but probably both the *instancias* and *procesos* have to do with litigation that would eventually be decided in New Orleans. It is well to recall that matters within the commandant's power to decide could be initiated and determined "verbally" according to O'Reilly's Instructions of 1770, so the number of suits adjudicated by the commandant may have been rather larger than the archives at first seem to indicate. In 1792 commandants were ordered to begin keeping a written book of judgments,[69] and the mention in the inventory of a "book which contains various *determinaciones*" may be evidence that the Arkansas commandants conformed to that requirement. But without such a book it is impossible to tell what the litigation rate in eighteenth-century Arkansas was.

Still, some interesting conclusions can be drawn from even so meager a record as this. For instance, four of the five *instancias* and three of the six *procesos* involved merchants on one side or the other; François Ménard alone was a party to five of these eleven cases. Marriage contracts seem to have been employed by relatively few people: Seven within a space of twenty-five years is not a very large number. The social status of the parties to them, moreover, tended clearly toward the *bourgeoisie*: Luis Dianna, Joseph Lambert, Juan Larquier, Luisa Jardela, and Joseph Bartolomé, parties to marriage contracts, were all probably of this class. Likewise, those who executed wills were either propertied or of old French families. François Ménard, Andrés López, Jean Baptiste Duchassin, and René Soumand were all merchants; Luis Lefevre, though hardly well off, was a member of an important post family. Not much is known of the social and economic status of Pedro Burel, but it is a reasonable guess that he was among the more well-to-do residents of Arkansas.

As was the case in the French period, therefore, it appears that the social and economic class of those persons who adhered to European legal traditions and resorted to regular modes of dispute settlement was quite narrow and their number very small: They were, for the most part, the merchants and *habitants* of the post. The hunters, the *coureurs des bois*, the bulk of the Arkansas population of roughly 450 at the end of the Spanish period, simply regulated their lives by whatever light nature could provide. Many claimed to owe obeisance to no state and steadfastly refused to take part in the ordered, agrarian community that De Villiers and others had so desperately wished to create. They preferred instead to pass their lives in silent beauty and danger.

Notes for "Government, Law, and Politics"

[1]Royal Letter of April 21, 1764, quoted in Hans W. Baade, "Marriage Contracts in French and Spanish Louisiana: A Study in 'Notarial' Jurisprudence," in *Tulane Law Review*, 53 (1978): 31, n.159.

[2]For the details, see ibid, 31-33.

[3]Ibid, 33.

[4]Ibid, 36.

[5]Translations are available in *Louisiana Law Journal*, 1 (1841): 1; Lawrence Kinnaird, *Spain in the Mississippi Valley, 1765-1794*, 3 vols. (Washington, 1949), 1:108; *American State Papers, Misc.* 1 (Washington, DC, 1834): 350.

[6]There is a translation in *Louisiana Law Journal*, 1 (1841): 27.

[7]See Baade, "Marriage Contracts in French and Spanish Louisiana," 40.

[8]Ibid., 35-36, 43, 89; Batiza, "The Unity of Private Law in Louisiana under Spanish Rule," *Inter-American Law Review*, 4 (1962): 139.

[9](?) to Demasellière, August 10, 1770, Archivo General de Indias, Seville, Papeles Procedentes de Cuba *legajo* (hereafter cited AGI, PC, leg.), 107.

[10]De Virzaga to Governor, October 4, 1770, AGI, PC, *leg.* 107.

[11]Governor Unzaga to Orieta, November 7, 1770, AGI, PC, *leg.* 107.

[12]For the posts to which these *Instructions* were first sent, see Baade, "Marriage Contracts in French and Spanish Louisiana," 37-38. Arkansas Post was not among them. Professor Baade very kindly supplied me with a copy of this document, which he found in AGI, PC, *leg.* 188A. There is another copy in the Missouri Historical Society at St. Louis, which I have also consulted. This document will be cited hereafter as *Instructions*.

[13]*Instructions*, § 1.

[14]Ibid., § 2.

[15]Ibid., § 4.

[16]Ibid., § 2.

[17]Ibid., § 8.

[18]Ibid.

[19]Ibid., § 6.

[20]Ibid., § 7.

[21]Baade, "Marriage Contracts in French and Spanish Louisiana," 39.

[22]*Instructions*, § 10.

[23]Ibid., § 14

[24]Ibid., § 15.

[25]Ibid., § 17.

[26]Ibid.

[27]Ibid., § 19.

[28]Ibid., § 20.

[29]Ibid., § 18.

[30]*Instrucción a que se arreglarian los Tenientes de Governador* . . . New Orleans, January 26, 1770 (cited hereafter as *Instrucción*). Unlike the *Instructions* to the civil commandants, this document was not printed. Professor Baade very kindly provided me a copy from AGI, PC, *leg*. 2357. I also made use of a copy of this document at the Archivo General de Indias in Seville.

[31]*Instrucción*, § 1.

[32]Ibid., § 2.

[33]Ibid., § 3.

[34]*Instructions*, § 1.

[35]Bénard de La Harpe to the duc de Choiseul, Minister of the Marine, August 8, 1763 (Transcript in Little Rock Public Library).

[36]Lambert to Demasellière, June 1, 1770, AGI, PC, leg. 107; Francoeur to Demasellière, June 16, 1770, AGI, PC, leg. 107; Demasellière to O'Reilly, June 28, 1770, AGI, PC, leg. 107; Demasellière to O'Reilly, July 15, 1770, AGI, PC, leg. 107; Demasellière to ?, July 15, 1770, AGI, PC, leg. 107.

[37]Governor (?) to Demasellière, July 20, 1770, AGI, PC, leg. 107.

[38]What follows is taken from *Declaraciones tomadas sobre el herido qe vajo de Arkanzas nombrado Francisco le Cler*, August 19, 1791, Judicial Records of Spanish Louisiana, Louisiana History Center, Louisiana State Museum, New Orleans.

[39]What follows is taken from "Index to the Spanish Judicial Records," *Louisiana Historical Quarterly*, 8 (1925): 314-16, hereafter cited *LHQ*. I have also examined the original papers in Montcharvaux vs. Francisco Ménar(d), April 18, 1771, Judicial Records of Spanish Louisiana, Louisiana History Center, Louisiana State Museum, New Orleans.

[40]Francisco Ménard vs. Anselme Billet, August 29, 1787, Judicial Records of Spanish Louisiana, Louisiana History Center, Louisiana State Museum, New Orleans.

[41]Santiago Gaignard vs. Juan Batista Saussié, January 25, 1791, Judicial Records of Spanish Louisiana, Louisiana Historical Center, Louisiana State Museum, New Orleans.

[42]There is a transcription and translation of the record of this case in "The Case of Pourée against Chouteau," in the Missouri Historical Society's *Publications*, 2 (1900): 68.

[43]Pourée's petition appears in ibid., 69-71.

[44]Chouteau's answer appears in ibid., 72.

[45]For examples of petitions in St. Louis civil litigation, see Frederic Louis Billon, *Annals of St. Louis in Its Early Days under the French and Spanish Dominations* (St. Louis, 1886), 131, 136, 151, 155, 162, 174, 179. In Douglas, "The Spanish Domination of Upper Louisiana," *Proceedings of the Wisconsin Historical Society*, 74 (1914): 83, the author says of the lieutenant governor's court: "The proceedings were summary. The injured party addressed a petition to the governor setting forth the particulars of his complaint written in the French language."

[46]Stanley Faye, "The Arkansas Post of Louisiana: Spanish Domination," *LHQ*, 27 (1944): 639.

[47]What follows is based on Gilbert C. Din, "Arkansas Post in the American Revolution, *Arkansas Historical Quarterly*, 40 (1980): 4 *et seq.*

[48]Ibid, 13, n.28; Faye, "The Arkansas Post of Louisiana," 639.

[49]For the following, see Miró to Cagigla, May 5, 1782, AGI, PC, *leg.* 1305.

[50]Din, "Arkansas Post in the American Revolution," 4 *et seq.*

[51]Vallière to Miró, May 16, 1788, AGI, PC, *leg.* 140.

[52]In Joseph White, *A New Collection of Laws, Charters, and Local Ordinances of the Governments of Great Britain, France, and Spain, Relating to the Concession of Land in Their Respective Colonies*, 2 vols. (Philadelphia, 1837), 2:10-11; an 1829 letter from White to Henry Clay appears in which White estimates that unsettled claims "in Louisiana, Alabama, Missouri, Arkansas, and Florida yet cover ten or twelve million acres.

[53]The most complete compendium is the work by J. White, *A New Collection.*

[54]White, *A New Collection*, 2:220.

[55]Ibid., 230.

[56]Ibid., 231.

[57]Ibid., 231-233,

[58]Ibid., 234-40.

[59]*See generally*, on the subject of Spanish land claims in Missouri, Violette, "Spanish Land Claims in Missouri," *Washington University Studies*, 3 (1921), 167. Also useful are Louis Houck, *A History of Missouri* , 3 vols. (Chicago, 1908), 1:34 *et seq.*, and John Thomas Scharf, *History of St. Louis*, 2 vols. (Philadelphia, 1883).

[60]Amos Stoddard, *Sketches of Louisiana* (Philadelphia, 1812), 245.

[61]Scharf, *History of St. Louis*, 1:32.

[62]*American State Papers, Public Lands,* 3 (1834): 294.

[63]The will, executed July 27, 1791, is included in the papers in a case brought in 1793 by Ménard's widow. See Spanish Judicial Records, Louisiana History Center, Louisiana State Museum, February 14, 1793.

[64]*Instructions*, § 11.

[65]See *Instructions, Louisiana Law Journal*, 1 (1841): 49.

[66]The will of Louis Lefevre, executed October 13, 1793, has survived in a number of copies. I have made use primarily of the one in *Probate Record Book AA*, 14-15, at the Probate Clerk's Office, De Witt, Arkansas. Deputy Circuit Clerk Tommy Sue Keffer brought this instrument to my attention. The witness to both the Ménard and Lefevre wills were Jean-Baptiste Duchassin, François Vaugine, and Manuel Reyes. The only other will executed at Arkansas Post in the eighteenth century that I have discovered was that of Captain Balthazar De Villiers. It is in AGI, PC, *leg.* 107. But this is a Spanish translation of a French original and the attestation seems not to have been copied; only a signature is indicated at the end. This will was executed on April 14, 1782, and a codicil to it followed in May.

[67]The inventory is in AGI, PC, *leg.* 140 and covers four pages.

[68]AGI, PC, *leg.* 191.

[69]Jack D. L. Holmes, *Gayoso: The Life of a Spanish Governor in the Mississippi Valley, 1789-1799* (Gloucester, MA, 1968), 67.

THE OFFICES AND FUNCTIONS OF THE NEW ORLEANS *CABILDO**

Gilbert C. Din

The municipal government of Spanish New Orleans is one of the most neglected and misunderstood institutions of colonial Louisiana.[1] Although state histories, for example, invariably mention the *cabildo*,[2] the Spanish-style city government Gov. Alejandro O'Reilly established on December 1, 1769, their discussions are generally faulty. At least part of the blame for the continuing misconceptions about the *cabildo* lies in the lack of in-depth studies of the institution. This is much at variance with Spain and Spanish America, where *cabildo* studies have produced a plethora of books and articles.[3] Perhaps if more studies of the Crescent City's Spanish government were present, the word "cabildo" would have a meaning in New Orleans beyond the modern-day museum building.[4]

Governor O'Reilly intended to establish a *cabildo* in New Orleans from the moment of his arrival. The *cabildo* minutes begin on August 18, 1769, the day O'Reilly and the Spaniards assumed power in the city and the province, although the institution did not then exist. In October, after the trials of the leaders of the 1768 Creole rebellion ended, two Spanish jurists, Félix del Rey and Manuel José de Urrutia, began two compilations summarizing Spanish laws. Their compilations, known collectively as the Code O'Reilly, were published in Spanish and French on November 25, 1769. One of the documents contains the regulations for the governance of the New Orleans *Cabildo*.

That body met initially on December 1, when the first officials, the *regidores perpetuos*, took office. On that day, O'Reilly installed Col. Luis de Unzaga y Amezaga as governor of New Orleans and its immediate district and as the president of the *cabildo*, a post all governors subsequently exercised. Unzaga assumed the governorship of all of Louisiana when O'Reilly left the province in March, 1770.[5]

The nucleus of the *cabildo* rested in its six *regidores perpetuos* (permanent councilmen) and two *alcaldes ordinarios* (annually elected judges).[6] These eight officials (*capitulares*) made up the voting body of the city council. O'Reilly personally selected

*This article was first published in *Louisiana History*, 37 (1996): 5-30. Reprinted with the kind permission of the author and the Louisiana Historical Association.

five of the *regidores* from the French planter class[7] because he and later governors believed that persons of property would govern in the best interest of society, a concept then widely accepted across Western culture. The post of *regidor* was permanent, inheritable, and venal (there was no fixed term of service, officeholders could leave the post to their sons or anyone else, or the office could be sold). The first *regidores* did not pay for their posts, but all subsequent holders did.[8]

Because the New Orleans *Cabildo* lasted only thirty-four years, it did not foster the family dynasties often found in Spanish America where families retained the office of *regidor* for generations. Although several fathers in New Orleans left their office to sons, with one exception two individuals rather than families held the office the longest, Francisco de La Barre for twenty-six years and Nicolas Forstall for thirty-one years. However, Joseph Ducros and his son Rudolfo J. Ducros held their seat for the full thirty-four years of the *cabildo*'s life in Louisiana.[9]

The first five *regidores* in seniority held collateral offices, where they individually exercised additional *cabildo* duties. In order of seniority and prominence the collateral posts were *alférez real* or royal standard bearer, *alcalde mayor provincial* or provincial judge, *alguacil mayor* or chief constable, *depositario general* or custodian of properties and funds, and *receptor de penas de cámara* or receiver of court fines. The sixth councilman was a *regidor sencillo* (simple councilman), who held no collateral office. In 1797, when six additional *regidores* were added to the *cabildo*, they were all *regidores sencillos*.[10]

The *regidores* also performed additional duties in two other capacities, as annual commissioner (*comisario anual*) and as monthly commissioner (*comisario mensual*). Two annual commissioners were elected in the first regular meeting (*ayuntamiento*) in January. Their duties consisted of seeing that contracts made with the *cabildo* were carried out and communicating with other officials about *cabildo* business. The annual commissioners also audited the accounts of Charity Hospital, the parish church, and the city treasury. The office of monthly commissioner rotated according to rank and seniority. This official had responsibility for enforcing municipal ordinances and regulations, particularly food prices and market conditions. He collected market rents and fees and held auctions for city contracts. Because of their judicial duties, the *alcaldes ordinarios* did not hold collateral posts or serve as annual or monthly commissioners.[11]

In addition to the two *alcaldes ordinarios*, councilors elected two non-voting officeholders every January 1. One was the *síndico procurador general*, frequently and erroniously called attorney general; his office, however, was more analogous to that of the tribune of ancient Rome. He was neither the chief law enforcement officer nor a prosecutor. His duty was to protect the public welfare, guard against abuses and dangers, and insure that *cabildo* officers and contractors carried out their obligations. He often first brought problems to the attention of the council and proposed solutions. If a councilman made a suggestion on how to remedy a problem, the *síndico procurado general* investigated to determine if it was practical and legal. He also listened to public opinion and gauged reaction to issues.[12]

The other non-voting council official was the *mayordomo de propios*, or city treasurer. He administered municipal funds, receiving and disbursing them, and kept records of transactions. He was important in carrying out city business, particularly contracts, and he worked closely with the annual and monthly commissioners. He was involved in nearly everything concerning city finance and his responsibilities grew as the council assumed new obligations in running the city. Of special importance was supervising the lighting department and the night watchmen (*serenos*), duties his office assumed in the mid-1790s.[13]

Also fundamental to the operation of the *cabildo* was the *escribano* or scribe. Although an employee, his post was both prestigious and rewarding. He was a notary public and the terms *escribano* and *notario publico* were interchangeable. To serve in the post, candidates had to know both Spanish and French, pass a demanding examination, and pay the required fees. Similar to the *regidores*, the *escribano* needed a royal appointment and the office was permanent, inheritable, and venal. The *escribano's* principal duty was to record and preserve the minutes of the *cabildo* meetings as well as many other municipal documents. He kept several logs in which he made entries, and ran the *cabildo* archives in the *casa capitular* (city hall). Documents could not leave the archives, but the *escribano* made copies for interested parties. O'Reilly appointed Juan Bautista Garic, former clerk of the French Superior Council, as the first *escribano*. His familiarity with Louisiana's laws and customs eased the transition from French to Spanish rule.[14]

The post of *cabildo escribano* was remunerative. Its value, greater than that of *regidor,* rose steadily throughout the Spanish period. Although not salaried, the *escribano* received fees for his services and, more importantly, tips and perhaps bribes. The only control the *cabildo* had over this royally appointed official was to fine him for infractions, but it rarely did so because most *escribanos* were conscientious in fulfilling their duties.[15]

In addition to these essential *cabildo* officials, the city added numerous employees to its work force. They were porters, an inspector of weights and measures, a public printer, a town crier, and caretakers of the Bayou St. John drawbridge and Carondelet Canal. Other employees included court bailiffs, prison officials, a hangman, interpreters, appraisers, and surveyors, some of whom worked only part-time. Beginning in 1779, the *cabildo* elected two *alcaldes de barrio* or ward commissioners for New Orleans. In 1792 they grew to four and later to seven as the city and its suburbs grew. Also in the 1790s, the council elected *síndicos de distrito* or district syndics (deputies of post commandants), who served along the Mississippi River beyond the city but still within the New Orleans district. Both the *alcaldes de barrio* and the *síndicos de distrito* were roughly equivalent to justices of the peace. When a night watch began in New Orleans in the 1790s, the *serenos* (watchmen), who became city employees, had police and firefighting duties and responsibility for keeping the street lamps lit.[16]

The officials of the New Orleans *Cabildo* served two primary functions: 1) to provide judicial services, and 2) to administer the city.[17] The council's judicial functions will be described first.

On January 1 of each year, the *cabildo capitulares* elected two *alcaldes ordinarios* (judges who tried cases in which the principals had no *fuero* or legal privilege, which entitled them to trial by special military or ecclesiastical tribunals). The *alcaldes ordinarios* could be reelected for an additional year of service if the vote was unanimous. They then had to wait two years to become eligible for reelection. In authority and prestige, the *alcaldes ordinarios* outranked the *regidores* who elected them. Knowledge of the law was helpful but not essential. The *alcaldes* usually sat with a trained legal adviser, either the government *auditor de guerra* (judge advocate) or the intendancy *asesor* (assessor). Occasionally, the same royally-appointed person held the two offices of *auditor de guerra* and *asesor*, which required him to advise both *alcaldes ordinarios*, in addition to his other obligations. It sometimes meant that the *alcaldes* heard cases without the presence of a legal adviser.[18]

The *alcaldes ordinarios* sat individually on their own courts and heard both criminal and civil cases. Criminal cases ranged widely from libel, contempt of court, and perjury to runaway slaves, assault and battery, treason, and murder. Civil cases concerned debt, probate succession, disputed property, and slave emancipation, and sometimes involved large sums of money. Cases came from throughout Louisiana, not just New Orleans and its immediate district. *Alcaldes ordinarios* heard only civil appeals, with the magistrate who decided the case sitting with two *regidores* elected by the council; a vote of two decided the matter. The losing party could still appeal the decision to a higher court, but because it required posting a large sum of money as bond it rarely happened. The courts of the *alcaldes ordinarios* held concurrent (equal) jurisdiction with the court of the governor.[19]

In addition to the *alcaldes ordinarios*, other *cabildo* officials held courts or performed legal duties. The second-ranking *regidor*, the *alcalde mayor provincial* (provincial magistrate), exercised judicial authority for crimes committed in rural areas. He was expected to render justice speedily and his sentences could not be appealed. In 1798 a *Santa Hermandad* (Holy Brotherhood of rural police) began operating under his supervision to pursue fugitive slaves and apprehend military deserters. White volunteers who served without pay made up the *cuadrilleros* (patrolmen). The post of *alcalde mayor provincial* was vacant between 1779 and 1783, and again between 1792 and 1798, on the deaths of its officeholders, Santiago Beauregard and Luis Toutant Beauregard. In 1798 Pedro de La Roche purchased the office from the Beauregard family.[20]

The third *regidor* in rank exercised the collateral post of *alguacil mayor* (chief constable). His most important legal duties included maintaining public order in the city, supervising the royal jail, and appointing prison personnel. He was to search out illegal activities in the city, such as gaming, and insure that public establishments, such as taverns and billiard halls, closed at the appointed hour.[21]

The fourth *regidor* performed the functions of *depositario general* (custodian of properties and funds seized by the *alguacil mayor* for the courts). He supervised the disposition of property at the appropriate time and paid creditors. He also cared for intestate properties.[22]

The final collateral office was that of *receptor de penas de cámara*. This official's primary duty was to record and safekeep fines. He was accountable for the funds, and could disburse them only by order of a judge. The post fell vacant in 1789, when the officeholder died, and a replacement was never made. Because of this, the *regidores* thereafter numbered only five until 1797, and eleven from that time forward.[23]

The Spanish legal system in New Orleans differed in several respects from the French system. The Spaniards introduced more courts and judges than the single court of the French Superior Council. Spanish legal codes were based on Roman law while French law was founded on the *Coutume de Paris*. Roman law, however, was the common source for both the French and Spanish criminal codes.[24] Moreover, the *alcaldes ordinarios*, the *alcaldes de barrio*, and the district syndics were usually French. For example, of the sixty-eight *alcaldes ordinarios* in New Orleans in the Spanish period, forty-four were French and twenty-four were Spaniards.[25]

Besides involvement in the legal system, the *cabildo*'s other principal responsibility was municipal administration, which it generally sought to discharge efficiently. But in drawing up regulations for the *cabildo*, Governor O'Reilly either did not want it to perform many functions or was short-sighted in reckoning the city's needs. On December 10, 1769, he wrote to Minister of the Indies Julián de Arriaga, discussing the establishment of the *cabildo*, its officials, costs, and income. He told Arriaga that the municipality's yearly income would be about two thousand pesos *fuertes*. He added, "With this sum, the *cabildo* will be able to pay for the city fiestas, royal obsequies, salaries of porters, and various other unavoidable expenses which it will have."[26] He did not calculate that in time some of the "other unavoidable expenses," such as levee repair, drainage, police, lighting, and insuring an adequate food supply, would be enormous. Because of O'Reilly's limited vision, the *cabildo* began the task of administering New Orleans slowly because it had only the small budget and narrow authority he had imposed. Moreover, the French Superior Council had provided a poor model because it had largely ignored the city's needs. Urban government in Louisiana properly began with the Spaniards.[27]

As the Spanish period progressed, the *cabildo* exceeded the limitations that O'Reilly had decreed. It assumed rights in taxing that Spanish law prohibited, and it engaged in activities for the public welfare which he had forbidden. It did so deliberately to make the city a better place in which to live.

A major area where the *cabildo* had no responsibilities in Spanish law was public works.[28] It nevertheless became involved in the construction and care of levees, streets, gutters, roads, and bridges. When it learned that it could not force owners to keep up levees, streets, and gutters that fronted on their property, the *cabildo* assumed responsibility. O'Reilly had entrusted upkeep of the segments of the levee that bordered the city on the property owners living nearest to them. But landowners were often negligent or slow in repairing the levee. Consequently, as early as 1772 the city began using public funds for repairs.[29] The *cabildo* gradually expanded its maintenance program, eventually to include levees upriver, where if flooding occurred, the city would suffer damage. Gov. Esteban Miró asked for *cabildo* intervention in 1789, when planters upriver could not afford to mend their levees and some of them abandoned their lands.[30] In 1790s, the council arranged loans to needy planters for levee repairs. Governor Carondelet issued an ordinance in 1792, calling on syndics (and creating these officials where they did not already exist) to compel owners to fix their levees. In 1796 Carondelet had six gates constructed above the city to divert floodwaters if the levee at Tchoupitoulous, a problem area, ruptured. Thereafter, the city's expenditures for levee repairs decreased substantially. Through the years, the *cabildo* spent large sums of money to keep the city dry of flood waters.[31]

New Orleans' unpaved streets presented several problems. In dry weather, they released clouds of dust, and in the rainy season, they became quagmires that inconvenienced horse-drawn vehicles and pedestrians. The streets needed efficient drainage to remove water introduced by floods, storms, and seepage from the river. The *cabildo* accepted responsi-bility for the streets, but it initially worked to force property owners to keep street gutters (small and wood-lined covered ditches that ran parallel to the sidewalks) in good repair. The lot owners, however, often evaded compliance. The city gradually assumed the obligation, building gutters and ditches to improve drainage. Because these facilities easily fell into disrepair, the task as well as the expense seemed never ending.[32]

Regulation of the marketplace was imperative to insure an ample and comestible food supply at a reasonable price to both producers and consumers. The Spanish system of paternalistic municipal government called for setting prices, inspecting for quality, and insuring accurate weights and measures. It sought to protect buyers and guarantee honesty in business transactions.[33] Although Governors O'Reilly and Bernardo de Gálvez issued tariffs setting food prices in 1769 and 1777 respectively, which were almost identical,[34] it was up to the *cabildo* to see that other foods, especially bread and beef, were available to the public. Both commodities fluctuated in price, flour (the basic ingredient in bread) more so than beef. Because lower Louisiana did not produce flour, it was imported, and the price varied with availability. Because of a shortage of small coins in New Oreans, the price of a loaf of bread remained constant (a *real* or about 12 1/2 cents), but the size of the loaf changed, ranging from forty-eight ounces (three pounds) to a mere thirty ounces. On occasions when flour was in short supply, rice flour was mixed with it. When shortages caused the price of flour to soar, the monthly commissioner frequently decreed new prices (actually loaf sizes) for bread.[35]

In procuring beef for the New Orleans marketplace, the *cabildo* initially agreed to monopolistic contracts if the vendor's price was the lowest, the taxes paid the highest, and the quality of the meat acceptable.[36] When the monopolistic system proved inadequate to meet the city's needs, the *cabildo* allowed open competition in furnishing cattle, and this method worked much better. The quality of the meat improved and the amount of revenue the city collected increased. The change from monopoly to free competition in supplying meat showed that the *cabildo* could be flexible if the public benefited.[37]

By the late 1790s, the sale of bread and beef generated thousands of *pesos* for the city and the revenue helped to finance other operations.[38] Besides watching the bakers and the butchers to insure that they did not defraud the public, the *cabildo* monitored many other vendors.

O'Reilly neglected to create the office of *fiel ejecutor*, or inspector of weights and measures, which was a collateral office and found in many *cabildos* throughout Spanish America. For several years, the New Orleans *Cabildo* ignored this oversight until abuses galvanized it into action in 1773. The *cabildo* gradually compelled vendors who used weights and measures to have them inspected. Nevertheless, until the end of the Spanish era, dishonest merchants and peddlers sought to defraud their customers and city officials needed to remain vigilant against their nefarious ways.[39]

In 1780 the *cabildo* built the first public food market in New Orleans, and it continued to build and rebuild markets throughout the Spanish era. Fire destroyed one market in 1788, and the city's population growth necessitated larger and improved facilities. The first market was mainly for the sale of beef and mutton.[40] In 1799 the *cabildo* added a fish market. The city charged vendors fees for using the stalls and tables. These fees helped to defray construction and maintenance costs. The markets enjoyed public approval from the start because they provided cleaner food and allowed inspectors to insure honest weights and measures. Still there were many vendors who did not utilize the markets. Among them were the vegetable, game, and firewood peddlers, as well as slaves sent by planters to sell farm produce in the city. In addition, the *cabildo* made no effort to regulate the market for Africans in Congo Square in the rear of the city, and it failed in its effort to tax vendors who sold their wares on the levee.[41]

In 1772 the *cabildo* became involved in helping to license physicians, surgeons, and druggists in the city. O'Reilly issued a decree on the medical community before he left the province, but he gave the council no authority to regulate it.[42] When no one else accepted responsibility for medical oversight, the *cabildo* moved to fill the void. Initially, would-be physicians and surgeons had only to present their credentials to be licensed. As time passed, however, the *cabildo* required more proof of a candidate's ability, and finally it established examinations administered by physicians and surgeons already practicing in the city. Only after candidates passed their examinations and the *cabildo* approved them did the governor grant them a license to practice their profession. In 1800, upon the advice of the judge advocate, the *cabildo* removed its *regidores* from the examining board, ending its involvement in the licensing of physicians and surgeons.[43]

Shortly after the *cabildo* was established, it approved a pharmaceutical code drawn by Dr. François Le Beau and began licensing pharmacists. The *cabildo* occasionally had to act against unlicensed vendors of medications. Licensed pharmacists also complained about medical practitioners who skirted the law and sold drugs. The council generally supported the pharmacists and eventually prohibited physicians and surgeons from selling medications. The licensing of pharmacists passed out of *cabildo* hands before the end of the Spanish period. In 1803 the governor's office issued licenses for pharmacists, and the *cabildo*'s sole duty in this area was to help schedule examinations.[44]

The *cabildo* was also involved with administration of several New Orleans hospitals. Charity Hospital consumed the most attention and energy. The French Superior Council, a forerunner of sorts of the Spanish *cabildo*, had had several of its members on the board of Charity Hospital, which the vicar general headed. When the Spaniards took possession of Louisiana, the governor supervised the hospital while the vicar general remained the nominal head of the hospital board. The change irritated persons in the French community, but they did not act for years. In 1778-79 and in the 1780s, several French *regidores* on the *cabildo*, led by François Marie de Reggio, attempted to assert Gallic control over the institution. As such a change would have diminished the authority of both Louisiana's governor and vicar general, Gálvez and Miró rejected the proposed change.[45]

Smarting from this rebuff, French *cabildo* members soon channeled their ire into an attack on Andrés Almonester y Roxas, a Spaniard who had amassed a tidy fortune in real estate before developing an interest in civic philanthropy. In 1782 Governor Miró gave him permission to rebuild Charity Hospital, which had been severely damaged in the 1779 and 1780 hurricanes. The *cabildo regidores*, who had ignored the hospital's ruined condition, protested vehemently but futilely. Almonester also received a patent from the Crown, making him the hospital's patron and director. Even after he purchased the most prestigious post on the *cabildo*, that of *regidor-alférez real* from the son of his deceased rival Reggio in 1790, other *regidores* on the *cabildo* still sought to humiliate him. They succeeded temporarily when a poorly informed Governor Carondelet removed Almonester as the hospital's patron. It took a royal order to reinstate him. Not even his death in 1798 prevented some *regidores* from attacking the patron's appointed physician to Charity Hospital several years later. The hostility that some of the *regidores* had for Almonester reveals a division among the *cabildo*'s *capitulares* that was usually not visible on the surface.[46]

Two newer hospitals—the San Lazaro Hospital for lepers and the smallpox hospital—run by the *cabildo* did not consume nearly as much energy. Both began under the Spaniards and were not permanent, operating only when circumstance warranted. The first leper facility was established in 1785 and was only a small building, housing a few afflicted persons. In 1797, the *cabildo* sold the "hospital," but the next year a need for it developed again. On this occasion, the council gave the attending physician a house in the city for the patients. Although the leper hospital operated beyond the Spanish era, there is doubt if any genuine cases of leprosy occurred during the colonial period. John Duffy believes the disease was misdiagnosed and was really African yaws.[47]

But there was no mistaking smallpox. In 1779, when the disease struck the colony, the first smallpox hospital—actually an isolation or detention center—was erected across the Mississippi River from New Orleans. Isolation to prevent the afflicted from spreading the highly contagious sickness was then the only known way to fight smallpox. The hospital, which had no regular staff, was used only as needed. In 1787 it briefly reopened when the disease reappeared. More serious to New Orleans, however, was the 1802 smallpox epidemic. Inoculation[48] to prevent serious smallpox cases was used on a voluntary basis in 1787. Inoculated persons were as contagious as those who contracted the disease naturally, and they, too, had to be isolated. Motivated by either religious scruples or superstition, Gov. Manuel Juan de Salcedo in 1802 hesitated permitting inoculation. Although some persons in the city had heard of a new method, vaccination with cowpox, to fight the contagion, no one knew how to administer it and, in any case, the cowpox virus was unavailable. Salcedo's opposition to inoculation delayed its use and might have contributed to increasing the death toll that numbered between six and twelve hundred persons, many of them slaves.[49]

In dealing with these diseases, the *cabildo* did the best job it could given the times and circumstances. In coping with these medical emergencies, it proved itself to be more enlightened than Louisiana's last colonial governor.

The *cabildo* attempted to exercise authority beyond New Orleans in the area of slave regulation. In 1773 it created a slave fund to pay for the apprehension of runaway slaves and compensate owners whose bondsmen were killed while fugitives. The fund, generated by taxes on slaveholders, required royal approval. In 1777 the Crown responded that contributions to the fund had to be voluntary, but the fund, which had started on a provisional basis in 1773, was already in trouble. Many slaveholders outside the New Orleans district refused to contribute to it. Overall, the fund represented the interests of large slave owners, who seem to have had more difficulty controlling their bondsmen than the small slaveowners. In 1778-79 the *cabildo*, which was dominated by large planters, also tried to draw up stringent rules to regulate the conduct of both slaves and free blacks. Initially supported by Bernardo de Gálvez, the plan failed when the *regidores* lost the governor's support and their regulations were never sent to Spain. The slave fund, which operated by fits and starts, ceased functioning in the 1780s because planters refused to make voluntary contributions.[50]

In 1790 the *cabildo* voiced its disapproval of the moderate slave code issued by the Crown the year before, the *Real cédula de su Magestad sobre la educación, trato y ocupaciones de los esclavos*. Although Governor Miró generally did not enforce it, his successor, the barón de Carondelet, tried to implement the code, thereby earning the enmity of many planters. Meanwhile, the 1789 French Revolution and the Haitian slave uprising two years later contributed to unrest among Louisiana's bondsmen. After the 1795 Pointe Coupée slave conspiracy was suppressed, planters on the *cabildo* who did not support the governor believed that a slave or African insurrection was still possible. They attempted to create a board to identify and deport unruly blacks, both slaves and free men of color. Carondelet, however, refused either to permit *cabildo* encroachment on his prerogatives or accept the measures it favored, and he successfully squashed the *regidores*' anti-African initiatives.[51]

The *cabildo*'s effort to deport unruly blacks probably would have failed in any case because many planters objected to being taxed and to losing slaves. The money the *regidores* proposed to raise through a tax was to be used as partial compensation to owners whose slaves were deported. As it was, in 1795 many slave owners resisted Carondelet's levy of six *reales* per slave to recompense the Pointe Coupée owners who lost fifty-four slaves through execution and imprisonment. The recalcitrant planters did not believe that they should compensate the Pointe Coupée masters who had failed to control their slaves. A few months later, they also foiled Carondelet's plan to revive the slave fund.[52]

Although they failed in their effort to regulate blacks, the councilors obtained the governor's consent to halt all slave imports in February, 1796, while conditions within the colony remained unsettled. But within a few years cotton and sugarcane emerged as important cash crops, and many planters, eager to make money, ultimately favored rescinding the ban to provide new slaves for increased agricultural production.[53]

When these planters began airing their feelings in 1800, the *cabildo síndico procurado general* tried to retain the ban on slave imports. He outwardly believed that resuming the introduction of slaves would jeopardize colonial security. But his real motive may have been to get the governor to crack down on what the *síndico* called a lenient attitude toward slaves. This effort failed, and although the governor and intendant decided to renew the external slave trade, slave importions did not begin until the American era.[54]

The *cabildo*'s effort to draw up province-wide slave regulations generally miscarried. Members of the city council who wanted harsh regulations were the large slaveholding planter-*regidores*. But the planters of the New Orleans district, the bailiwick of the *cabildo regidores*, faced stiff opposition from slaveholders outside the district, who refused to contribute financially to the slave fund.[55]

Besides the many areas of *cabildo* activity already examined, the council also served as a link between the city's inhabitants and the Crown. The council performed this role in various ways. It arranged for celebrations and pageantry when royal children were born, and on the death of a monarch (Carlos III) and the crowning of his successor (Carlos IV). It organized celebrations for victory in war and when the government decreed new trade regulations that benefited the city and province.[56]

The *cabildo* participated in religious pageantry as well, sitting on chairs in the front section of the city's St. Louis Church (Cathedral after 1795) with other colonial officials and marching in the many municipal religious processions. These functions set an example for the New Orleans inhabitants and represented a tie to the colony's distant European rulers. The *cabildo* also petitioned the Crown for assistance when calamities, such as hurricanes and fires, occurred, and the city council supported the governor and intendant when trade laws were suspended because New Orleans was in dire straits. Following the destructive fires of 1788 and 1794, the *cabildo* decreed new building regulations to prevent more conflagrations. But many of the city's property owners, particularly the poor who made up the vast majority of New Orleans' inhabitants, failed to comply with the costly building regulations.[57]

The New Orleans municipal council assumed these and other obligations in attempting to administer the city. It succeeded in numerous areas and failed in some. A lack of sufficient public and private finances and lack of support from the governor sometimes stymied the city government in its efforts.[58] Nevertheless, when all of its activities are examined, one can readily see that the New Orleans *Cabildo* performed a variety of useful and needed functions that helped enormously in governing the city. Although the governor was the superior royal official in the colony and president of the *cabildo*, the most active members in city administration were usually the *regidores* and the *sindico procurado general*. Carondelet stands out among the governors because he often led the city fathers into new areas of administration that served to improve the quality of life in New Orleans.[59]

City government in New Orleans differed substantially from the norm in the rest of Spanish America, especially in the Borderlands that today make up the southern fringe of the United States. The municipalities of San Antonio, Laredo, Santa Fé, Los Angeles, and San José, for example, had smaller populations, weaker economies, and suffered more from isolation than New Orleans. By the late eighteenth century, the Spanish military had seized control of city government in most areas of the Southwestern Borderlands, and only San Antonio's was still functioning independently. Moreover, New Orleans differed from most Spanish American cities in several other respects: The Crescent City's population boasted a higher per capita income, and the municipality's *cabildo* engaged in more activities that helped local residents and spent less on ceremonial functions that entertained but diverted scarce resources from essential services.[60] Nevertheless, New Orleans could still have used more income because its subtropical climate, location next to a dangerous river, and periodic torrential rains and hurricanes exposed it to hazards that many cities did not experience.

A greater potential hazard to the *cabildo* was the governor who could—and sometimes did—veto any council action. On the whole, however, from 1769 to 1799 Louisiana's governors cooperated with the *cabildo* in providing sound administration for the city. That spirit of cooperation and harmony collapsed in 1799 after the death of Gov. Manuel Gayoso de Lemos.

During its last four years, the *cabildo* declined in power when the corrupt and mean-spirited Judge Advocate Nicolás María Vidal became the acting civil governor (1799-1801). For twenty years prior to going to Louisiana, he had served in his home colony of New Granada (today Colombia), where he observed royal officials dominating *cabildos*. On arriving in New Orleans, Vidal deliberately set out to increase his political power, and he succeeded after Gayoso's death, when he became the acting civil governor. Gayoso was succeeded by the incompetent Governor General Salcedo (1801-1803), whom Vidal seems to have controlled, and Vidal's policy of confrontation with the *cabildo* continued. Spain provided no redress because *cabildo* appeals to the Crown often failed to reach the royal ear. After 1795 the Spanish government all but abandoned Louisiana because the first secretary Manuel de Godoy looked for an opportunity to rid Spain of the colony.[61]

It was also in the late Spanish period in Louisiana when Vidal and Salcedo held sway that a number of visitors to New Orleans described the *cabildo* in unflattering ways. But their depictions of the city government in its final years are not an accurate measure in determining the *cabildo*'s effectiveness during its thirty-four year lifespan.[62] The city government must be judged more fairly than by the superficial descriptions of poorly informed and often biased travelers inasmuch as the *cabildo* carried out a variety of useful activities that contributed significantly to improved living conditions in New Orleans.

It is ironic that in the twentieth century the building (the *casa capitular*) that housed the Spanish city government and its archives has received more attention in New Orleans than the institution for which it was constructed. Indeed, the building has even acquired the *cabildo*'s name! This is unfortunate because this naming convention puts the cart before the horse. It is time that this order was reversed. As I have written elsewhere, and say here from an historian's perspective, the "real significance" of the *casa capitular* "is as a monument of the *cabildo*'s existence."[63] Perhaps in time this will be recognized.

Notes for "The Offices and Functions of the New Orleans *Cabildo*"

[1]Two Ph.D. dissertations have focused on the New Orleans *Cabildo*: Ronald R. Morazán, "Letters, Petitions, and Decrees of the *Cabildo* of New Orleans, 1800-1803" (Ph.D. dissertation, Louisiana State University, 1972); and John E. Harkins, "The Neglected Phase of Louisiana's Colonial History: The New Orleans *Cabildo*, 1769-1803" (Ph.D. dissertation, Memphis State University, 1976). The first work consists of translated documents for a four-year period but with notes that provide wider-ranging information. The second study relies heavily on WPA translations that are sometimes inaccurate, and does not utilize additional documentation from the Spanish archives that would have provided more information on the *cabildo*, its officials, and other Spanish administrators who dealt with the institution.

Published sources that deal exclusively with the *cabildo* are few. See John G. Clark, "The Role of the City Government in the Economic Development of New Orleans and City Council, 1783-1812," in *The Spanish in the Mississippi Valley, 1762-1804*, edited by John Francis McDermott (Urbana, IL, 1974), 133-48; and Ronald R. Morazán, "The *Cabildo* of Spanish New Orleans, 1769-1803: The Collapse of Local Government," *Louisiana Studies*, 12 (1973): 591-605. Neither study examines the *cabildo*'s offices and functions.

[2]The word "*cabildo*" will be capitalized when referring to the phrase New Orleans *Cabildo*. In other references to the institution or to other *cabildos*, the word will not be capitalized.

[3]The exception is, of course, Harkins' "Neglected Phase." Many of the older state histories, those by Francis-Xavier Martin, Charles Gayarré, Alcée Fortier, and Henry E. Chambers among others, have inadequate and often inaccurate descriptions of the Spanish-style city government. Even Edwin Adams Davis, *Louisiana, A Narrative History*, 3rd. ed. (Baton Rouge, 1971), has errors in his analysis of the *cabildo*.

On Spanish American *cabildo* studies published in Spain, see, for example, Pilar Ponce Leiva, "Publicaciones españolas sobre *cabildos* americanos (1939-1989)," *Revista de Indias*, 50, núm. 188 (1990): 77-81. She found 150 works published in Spain between 1939 and 1989 on Spanish American *cabildos*. She calls the "classic works" on *cabildos* (those cited most frequently) to be Constantino Bayle, *Los cabildos seculares en la América española* (Madrid, 1952), and Guillermo Lohmann Villena, *Los regidores perpetuos del Cabildo de Lima (1535-1821). Crónica y estudio de un grupo de gestión* (Seville, 1983). In this country, John Preston Moore's two-volume study, *The Cabildo in Peru Under the Hapsburgs: A Study in the Origins and Powers of the Town Council of Peru, 1530-1700* (Durham, NC, 1954), and *The Cabildo in Peru Under the*

Bourbons: A Study in the Decline and Resurgence of Local Government in the Audiencia of Lima, 1700-1824 (Durham, NC, 1966), appears to be the work cited most often.

[4]The word "*cabildo*" properly refers only to the institution and not to the building, which was the *casa capitular*. The minutes of the New Orleans *Cabildo never* used the word to mean the building. In Spanish America, however, *cabildo* was sometimes used for the building, too.

[5]Actas del Cabildo, Libro I, New Orleans, August 18, 1769, WPA typescript in Spanish on microfilm (subsequent citations will be by *libro* in roman numbers, followed by *tomo* in parentheses if appropriate, page number, and date); David Knuth Bjork, "The Establishment of Spanish Rule in the Province of Louisiana, 1762-1770" (Ph.D. dissertation, University of California, Berkeley, 1923), 151; David Ker Texada, "The Administration of Alejandro O'Reilly as Governor of Louisiana, 1769-1770" (Ph.D. dissertation, Louisiana State University, 1969), 130-31. The regulations governing the New Orleans *Cabildo* can be found in several places; they are in English in "Establishment of the New Orleans Cabildo," Alejandro O'Reilly, New Orleans, November 25, 1769, in Lawrence Kinnaird, ed., *Spain in the Mississippi Valley, 1765-94*, 3 parts (Washington, DC, 1949), 1:108-25 (hereafter cited as *SMV*); and in Spanish in Bibiano Torres Ramírez, *Alejandro O'Reilly en las Indias* (Seville, 1969), 187-202. The second part of the Code O'Reilly is the "Reglamento para juzgar las causas civiles y criminales en la Luisiana," in ibid., 203-25. Del Rey and Urrutia based both parts of the Code O'Reilly on the *Recopilación de leyes de los reynos de las Indias*.

O'Reilly imposed Spanish law on Louisiana in all areas during his administration. The second part of the Code O'Reilly was a digest to acquaint the inhabitants with Spanish law, particularly the *Recopilación*. As the introduction noted, the Code O'Reilly was to serve as a model until the Spanish language became known and more extensive information about Spanish law acquired.

[6]The Spanish term *regidor* will be used for this official because the English words of alderman, magistrate, and commissioner are not the equivalent. Hereafter the term "councilors" shall be used only when meaning both the *regidores* and the *alcaldes ordinarios*. Spanish city government in New Orleans differed substantially from local government in this country. For example, the governor was the head of the city government and had to approve everything; *regidores* bought their offices and served for life, or until they relinquished the office; and only the *regidores* and *alcaldes ordinarios* elected officials who worked for the *cabildo*.

[7]The six *regidores* O'Reilly appointed were Francisco María de Reggio, Pedro Francisco Olivier Duvezin, Carlos Juan Bautista Fleuriau, Antonio Bienvenu, Joseph Ducros, and Denis Braud. All were planters except Braud, who was a printer. The planters and Luis de La Chaise, who became an *alcalde ordinario* for 1770, had earlier been selected by Antonio de Ulloa to serve on a tribunal he established before his expulsion in 1768.

Perhaps the legal experts Del Rey and Urrutia erred in the salary they assigned to five of the *regidores*. According to the *Recopilación de leyes de los reynos de las Indias*, 3 vols. (facsimile rpr. of 1791 ed.; Madrid, 1942), *Lib*. 2, *Tit*. 10, *Ley* iiii (*sic*), only the *regidor-alférez real* should have received one hundred *pesos* yearly and the other *regidores* fifty *pesos* per year. The pay records of the *regidores*, however, show that they all received one hundred *pesos* yearly, paid quarterly (Archivo General de Indias, Papeles procedentes de Cuba, legajos [hereafter cited as AGI, PC, leg.] 538B and 566).

Denis (Dionisio) Braud served as *regidor* only until 1773, when he returned to France without government permission. His office was sold at auction and purchased by Daniel Fagot. See Henry P. Dart, "The Adventures of Denis Braud, The First Printer of Louisiana, 1764-1773," *Louisiana Historical Quarterly*, 14 (1931): 349-60, hereafter cited *LHQ*; and Florence M. Jumonville, "Frenchmen at Heart: New Orleans Printers and Their Imprints, 1764-1946," *Louisiana History*, 32 (1991): 282-98 passim.

[8]Actas del Cabildo, I, 2, December 1, 1769; Torres Ramírez, *O'Reilly*, 1991. The sum paid to the government when an office was purchased was based on its appraised value, not its purchase price. In the first sale of the office, the government received half of its appraised value and one-third in all subsequent sales. In addition, the government charged the purchaser the *media anata* (half of the yearly salary, or fifty *pesos* in this case), and 18 percent of the two above sums (the half or third of the appraised value and the *media anata*) to ship the money to Spain.

[9]See Table 4 in Harkins, "Neglected Phase," 62-63; and Clarence H. Haring's discussion of "The Cabildo," in *The Spanish Empire in America* (New York, 1947), 147-65.

[10]Actas del Cabildo, I, 4, December 1, 1769; IV, (2), 38, September 22, 1797. O'Reilly, or his legal experts del Rey and Urrutia, selected the collateral offices for New Orleans arbitrarily. The city could have had additional or fewer collateral posts (see Bayle, *Los cabildos seculares*, for the many offices contained in Spanish American *cabildos*).

The six persons who bought their seats as *regidores* in 1797 were Francisco Riaño, Luis Darby Danycan, Jaime Jordá, Gilberto Andry, Joseph Leblanc, and Juan de Castañedo. Only one was a planter (Danycan), two were army officers (Andry and Leblanc whose father was a planter), two were merchants (Riaño and Jordá), and one was a former government employee who was possibly in business (Castañedo). In the last years of the *cabildo*, four of the eleven *regidores* were Spaniards. Andrés Almonester y Roxas, who became a *regidor* in 1790, died in 1798 and left his office to his French Creole brother-in-law. In 1801 Andry sold his office to Domingo Bouligny, an army officer, who was born in New Orleans. Because of Bouligny's Spanish father, a dedicated career army officer, he can be regarded as more Spaniard than French Creole, which his mother was.

[11]Morazán, "Letters," 1:xxxiv, 2:80; Actas del Cabildo, III, (3), 6, June 11, 1792; IV, (3), 159, March 21, 1800; IV, (4), 200, April 23, 1802. Only one monthly commissioner was elected until 1801. Because the duties of this official had increased, Gov. Manuel Juan de Salcedo suggested electing two each month, and it was done (ibid., IV, (4): 18-19, July 25, 1801).

[12]Torres Ramírez, *O'Reilly*, 188, 199-200. The text in ibid, refers to the *síndico procurador general* only as *procurador general*. But *síndico* is part of the title and it is used in the New Orleans *Cabildo* minutes. Bayle, in *Los cabildos seculares*, 225-51, has a lengthy discussion of this official in Spanish America.

[13]Ibid., 200; Actas del Cabildo, III, (3), 49, February 1, 1793; Morazán, "Letters," xxxii-xxxiii.

[14]Torres Ramírez, *O'Reilly*, 191, 200-201; O'Reilly to Arriaga, Nos. 19 and 16, New Orleans, both December 10, 1769, *SMV*, 1:127-28 and 133 respectively; Hans Baade, "Marriage Contracts in French and Spanish Louisiana: A Study in 'Notarial Jurisprudence,'" *Tulane Law Review*, 53 (1979): 13.

[15]Laura L. Porteous, ed. and trans., "Index to the Spanish Judicial Records of Louisiana," *LHQ*, 20 (1937): 875-79; Actas del Cabildo, II, 167, April 11, 1783; III, (2), 10, March 14, 1788; III, (2), 110-12, August 20, 1790; III, (3), 172, October 24, 1794. A "Table of Fees, demandable by Judges, Lawyers, Escribanos, Attorneys, and the other Officers of Justice," is in Benjamin Franklin French, ed., *Historical Memoirs of Louisiana from the First Settlement of the Colony to the Departure of Governor O'Reilly in 1770: With Historical and Biographical Notes*, 5 vols. (New York, 1853), 5:285-88. See also Sally Kittredge Reeves, "Spanish Colonial Records of the New Orleans Notarial Archives," *Louisiana Library Association Bulletin*, 55 (1992): 7-12, for the records left behind by the Spanish-era notaries.

[16]The Actas del Cabildo contain numerous references to the institution's employees. See, for example, ibid., 1, 275-76, April 30, 1779; III, (1), February 17, 1786; III, (2), 167, January 14, 1792; IV, (1), 193-94, January 13, 1797.

[17]The *cabildo*'s duty to administer to the whole province can be almost totally dismissed. It rarely attempted to do so. Two examples will illustrate the institution's inaction and failure when it tried. In 1787, in drawing up instructions for the commandant of Natchitoches, Gov. Esteban Miró told him that medical practitioners in that community had to be licensed in New Orleans, presumably by the *cabildo* which was then examining would-be physicians and surgeons. However, the Actas del Cabildo show no doctor who was ever licensed for Natchitoches following the issuance of the order ("Ynstrucción a que deberá arreglarse en el mando político y militar del puesto de Natchitoches . . . Dn. Joséf López del la Peña," (Miró), New Orleans, April 1, 1787, AGI, PC, leg. 118). Moreover, when the *cabildo* sought to establish a slave fund that embraced lower Louisiana, the outlying districts first protested being taxed and then refused to contribute voluntarily (see text below).

[18]Torres Ramírez, *O'Reilly*, 192-94. If an *alcalde ordinario* fell sick, the *alférez real* could fill in for him, but not the other councilmen holding collateral offices. The sixth councilman, the *regidor sencillo*, could be elected *alcalde ordinario*, and after 1797 so could the additional new *regidores*. The officeholders had to be at least twenty-six years old, and respected members of the community. Nicolas Forstall, a *regidor sencillo*, was elected *alcalde ordinario* on six occasions. See also Louis G. Kahle, "The Spanish Colonial Judiciary," *Southwestern Social Science Quarterly*, 32 (1951): 26-37.

[19]Kate Wallach, *Research in Louisiana Law* (Baton Rouge, 1958), 210-11; Texada, "Administration," 135, 151-52; Henry E. Chambers, *A History of Louisiana—Wilderness, Colony, Province, Territory, State, People*, 3 vols. (Chicago, 1925), 1:300, 303; Fortier, *A History of Louisiana*, 2:5, 391-92; Gálvez to Miró, Havana, April 15, 1785, AGI, PC, leg. 11. For an idea of how Spanish law and courts functioned in Louisiana, see Porteous, ed. and tran., "Index to the Spanish Judicial Records," *LHQ*, 5-28 (1922-1945). The governor had courts which heard *fuero* and non-*fuero* cases. Because he was the senior ranking army officer in the province, he was often involved in courts-martial, too. For a view of the Spanish legal system in operation in an outpost, see Morris S. Arnold, *Colonial Arkansas, 1664-1804: A Social and Cultural History* (Fayetteville, AR, 1991), which updates his earlier discussion in *Unequal Laws Unto a Savage Race: European Legal Traditions in Arkansas, 1686-1836* (Fayetteville, AR, 1985), 43-112.

[20]Torres Ramírez, *O'Reilly*, 195-96; Morazán, "Letters," 1:134; Actas del Cabildo, III, (2), 21, April 18, 1788. See also Juan José Andreu Ocariz, *Movimientos rebeldes de los esclavos negros durante el dominio español en Luisiana* (Zaragoza, Spain, 1977).

[21]Torres Ramírez, *O'Reilly*, 196-97, 201-2.

[22]Ibid., 197-98.

[23]Ibid., 198-99. In the 1780s and 1790s, vacant *regidor* seats and absences arose from death, illness, work on plantations, and other causes. For example, in 1779 Governor Gálvez appointed *regidor sencillo* Nicolas Forstall commandant of New Iberia, and later he became commandant at Opelousas. He frequently missed *cabildo* meetings and a replacement, whom the Crown authorized Forstall to select in 1787, took office only in 1790. Forstall reclaimed his seat in 1795. In the *cabildo*'s last years, the *regidores* often paralyzed municipal affairs by staying away from meetings to protest the actions of Acting Civil Governor Vidal and Governor Salcedo (see Morazán, "The Cabildo of Spanish New Orleans," 591-605, and text below).

[24]For two studies on the French legal system in Louisiana, see Jerry A. Micelle, "From Law Court to Local Government: Metamorphosis of the Superior Council of French Louisiana," *Louisiana History*, 9 (1968): 85-107; and James D. Hardy, Jr., "The Superior Council in Colonial Louisiana," in *Frenchmen and French Ways in the Mississippi Valley*, edited by John Francis McDermott (Urbana, IL, 1969), 87-101.

[25]Harkins, "Neglected Phase," 107, 128, 130.

[26]O'Reilly to Julián de Arriaga, No. 16, New Orleans, December 10, 1769, *SMV*, 1:132-35.

[27]Clark, in "The Role of the City Government," 137-38, shares this assessment.

[28]O'Reilly's prohibition against *cabildo* involvement in public works is in his land ordinance of 1770, which is published in French, ed., *Historical Memoirs*, 5:289-91, and in *LHQ*, 11 (1928): 237-40.

[29]Actas del Cabildo, I, 79, May 15, 1772.

[30]Caroline Maude Burson, *The Stewardship of Don Esteban Miró* (New Orleans, 1940), 267.

[31]Baron de Carondelet, "Governor Carondelet's Levee Ordinance of 1792," translated by Laura L. Porteous, *LHQ*, 10 (1927): 513-16; Actas del Cabildo, III, (3), 161, September 12, 1794; III, (3), 186, December 19, 1794; III, (3), 202, February 6, 1795; IV, (1), 53, August 29, 1795; IV, (1), 75, November 27, 1795; IV, (1), 106, April 1, 1796; IV, (1), 127, June 3, 1796.

[32]Morazán, "Letters," 1:67, 70n; Torres Ramírez, *O'Reilly*, 266. On the city accepting responsibility for gutters, see Actas del Cabildo, I, 165-66, August 6, 1774; I, 185, June 2, 1775; I, 193, October 20, 1775; I, 272-74, March 24, 1779; I, 285, June 19, 1779; IV, (1), 106, April 1, 1796; IV, (1), 126-27, June 3, 1798; IV, (2), 126-27, June 3, 1798; IV, (3), 8-10, January 30, 1799; IV, (4), 10-13, October 24, 1800. The *cabildo* minutes usually refer to the gutters as *puentes*, which has confused some historians.

[33]Moore, *The Cabildo in Peru Under the Hapsburgs*, 169, in which he quotes the *Recopilación de leyes de los reynos de las Indias, Lib.* IV, *Tit.* IX, *Ley* XXII.

[34]Both tariffs, dated September 7, 1769, and July 15, 1777, are published in *SMV*, 1:93-94 and 239-41 respectively. The price of bread depended on the cost of flour, and therefore could rise or fall. Vegetables, too, which were relatively expensive, were unregulated in price.

[35]Actas del Cabildo, III, (3), 82, August 9, 1793, contains a schedule for changing the price (size) of bread depending on what a barrel of flour cost.

[36]Torres Ramírez, *O'Reilly*, 257; Porteous, ed. and trans., "Index," *LHQ*, 6 (1923): 525.

[37]Actas del Cabildo, II, 66-67, August 3, 1781; II, 70-71, August 31, 1781; IV, (1), 108, April 8, 1796; IV, (1), 131-35, June 17, 1796. Under monopoly contracts, city officials purchased meat for themselves at a lower price than the public. But the real problem with this system was that suppliers failed to provide sufficient quantities of meat and in good condition.

[38]To raise revenue for the city, O'Reilly initially placed taxes on the city's inns, taverns, billiards halls, butchers, imported brandy, and city lots on two sides of the Plaza de Armas (Jackson Square). He estimated that the taxes would yield about two thousand *pesos* (*SMV*, 1:134, O'Reilly to Arriaga, New Orleans, December 10, 1769). As the city's population grew, taxes on meat, bread, liquor, businesses, anchorage, and various other items produced increased revenue. As 1801 began, the city had a surplus in funds of 13,839 *pesos*, 4 1/2 *reales*. That year it spent 15,243 *pesos* and collected in revenue 12,587 *pesos*, 3 1/2 *reales*. Expenses were high because the *cabildo* paid 5,000 *pesos* to the widow of Andrés Almonester as partial payment for the construction of the *casa capitular*; 2,275 *pesos*, 4 *reales* for repairs to the jail; and 3,514 *pesos*, 1/2 *real* for drainage (Ramón Ezquerra Abadía, "Un presupuesto americano: El del cabildo de Nueva Orleans al terminar la soberania española," *Anuario de estudios americanos*, 5 (1948): 686-901.

[39]Actas del Cabildo, I, 103-4, March 5, 1773; I, 207, July 5, 1776; III, (3), 62-64, April 19, 1793; Morazán, "Letters," I, xxvii.

[40]Actas del Cabildo, I, 277-78, May 21, 1779; II, 28, June 2, 1780.

[41]Ibid., IV, (2), 61, October 20, 1797; IV, (2), 67-68, October 27, 1797; IV, (2), 125, May 11, 1798; IV, (2), 130-31, June 1, 1798; IV, (2), 132, June 8, 1798; IV, (2), 166, November 23, 1798; IV, (2), 132, June 8, 1798; IV, (2), 166, November 23, 1798; IV, (2): 176, December 15, 1798; IV, (3), 40-41, June 14, 1799; IV, (3), 73, September 20, 1799; IV, (3), 114, November 29, 1799; IV, (3), 171, April 25, 1800. See also Robert A. Sauder, "The Origin and Spread of the Public Market System in New Orleans," *Louisiana History*, 22 (1981): 281-97.

[42]O'Reilly had his medical decree published in French, "Le premier soin d'un Gouvernement sage, etant de fixer a chacun les bornés de ses propriétés & de veiller a la conservation de Citoyens, j'ai cru devoir établir comme dans tous le États polices, les Règlements suivants, concernant l'exercise de la Médicine & la chirurgie," February 12, 1770, AGI, PC, leg. 188A. See also Douglas Crawford McMurtrie, ed., "A Louisiana Decree of 1770 Relative to the Practice of Medicine and Surgery," *New Orleans Medical and Surgical Journal*, 86 (1933): 7-11. Earlier, the French had issued similar regulations; see Heloïse H. Cruzat, trans., "Cabildo Archives: Ordinance of the Superior Council Regulating the Practice of Medicine, Surgery and Obstetrics," *LHQ*, 3 (1920): 86-88.

[43]Actas del Cabildo, 1:77-78, May 8, 1772; IV, (3), 127-28, January 17, 1800; IV, (3): 129, January 24, 1800. The *cabildo* examined only civilian medical practitioners, and not those who worked for the army or government.

[44]Ibid., 1:17, January 12, 1770; IV, (2), 147-48, July 27, 1798; IV, (3), 78, September 27, 1799; IV, (3), 111-12, November 22, 1799; IV, (3), 116-17, December 6, 1799; IV, (5), 77, June 17, 1803; IV, (5), 80, July 15, 1803; John Duffy, ed., *The Rudolph Matas History of Medicine in Louisiana*, 2 vols. (Binghamton, NY, 1958-62), 1:185-86. Possibly surgeons were selling drugs again at the end of the Spanish period. See Berquin-Duvallon in James Alexander Robertson, ed., *Louisiana Under the Rule of Spain, France, and the United States, 1785-1807*, 2 vols. (Cleveland, 1911), 1:201-2.

[45]Stella O'Connor, "The Charity Hospital of Louisiana at New Orleans: An Administrative and Financial History, 1736-1946," *LHQ*, 31 (1948): 18-20; Burson, *The Stewardship*, 217-18. See also John Salvaggio, *New Orleans's Charity Hospital: A Story of Physicians, Politics, and Poverty* (Baton Rouge, 1992): 14.

[46]O'Connor, "The Charity Hospital," 22-27; Actas del Cabildo, III, (3), 93-94, October 18, 1793. On Almonester, see Jack D. L. Holmes, "Andrés Almonester y Roxas: Saint or Scoundrel?," *Louisiana Studies*, 7 (1968): 47-64; and Samuel Wilson, Jr., "Almonester: Philanthropist and Builder in New Orleans," in *The Spanish in the Mississippi Valley, 1762-1804*, edited by John Francis McDermott (Urbana, IL, 1974), 183-247. Almonester did not hesitate to butt heads with other council members. Some of them, however, got along well with him. His civic philanthropy included rebuilding at his own expense the St. Louis Cathedral and other buildings in New Orleans. Almonester also agreed in the early 1790s to rebuild the *casa capitular*, which was destroyed in the 1788 fire, with the *cabildo* repaying him when it could afford to do so (Samuel Wilson, Jr., and Leonard V. Huber, *The Cabildo on Jackson Square* [New Orleans, 1970], 28-35).

[47]Actas del Cabildo, III, (1), 66, November 18, 1785; IV, (2), 87-88, December 22, 1797; Duffy, ed., *The Matas History*, 1:259-60; Morazán, "Letters," 1:191-92n.

[48]Inoculation consisted of exposing persons to what was usually a mild case of smallpox. These individuals then developed an immunity to the often fatal disease. On Governor Miró's actions with the settlement of Valenzuela in the 1787 smallpox scare, see (Miró) to Nicolás Verret, New Orleans, June 6 and October 24, 1787, both in AGI, PC, leg. 200; and (Miró) to Verret, New Orleans, June 5, 1788, AGI, PC, leg. 201.

[49]Actas del Cabildo, I, 264-65, February 8, 1779; III, (1), 150-51, June 8, 1787; III, (1), 163, October 5, 1787; IV, (4), 169-70, February 12, 1802; IV, (4), 171-73, February 19, 1802; IV, (4), 190-92, March 22, 1802; Morazán, "Letters," 1:li-liii, 36n, 2:82n, 83-84, 95; Duffy, ed., *The Matas History*, 1:199, 216; John Duffy, *Epidemics in Colonial America* (Baton Rouge, 1953), 38; Burson, *The Stewardship*, 119.

[50]Actas del Cabildo, I, 109-110; I, 232, October 10, 1777; I, 243, February 13, 1778; I, 249, May 22, 1778; I, 266, February 19, 1779; I, 267, February 26, 1779; I, 268, March 1, 1779; Bernardo de Gálvez to José de Gálvez, New Orleans, March 2, 1779, Archivo General de Indias, Santo Domingo (hereafter cited as AGI, SD), leg. 2662; Hans W. Baade, "The Law of Slavery in Spanish Louisiana, 1769-1803," in *Louisiana's Legal Heritage*, edited by Edward F. Haas (Pensacola, 1983), 62-63.

In 1784 the *cabildo* exerted pressure on Acting Governor Francisco Bouligny to apprehend runaway slaves who were then numerous in lower Louisiana. Among them was the Jean St. Malo (Juan San Malo) gang, which had killed a number of whites and Africans. Using a combination of army and militia personnel, both white and black, Bouligny was able to arrest many runaways and most of the St. Malo gang (see Gilbert C. Din, "*Cimarrones* and the San Malo Band in Spanish Louisiana," *Louisiana History*, 21 (1980): 237-62). In examining this episode, Gwendolyn Midlo Hall, in *Africans in Colonial Louisiana: The Development of Afro-Creole Culture in the Eighteenth Century* (Baton Rouge, 1992), 231-35, expresses much sympathy for the fugitives but, in the opinion of this writer, does not describe accurately the Spanish legal system or many of the events.

[51]Actas del Cabildo, 3:(2), 90-91, February 25, 1790; III, (2): 107, July 23, 1790; IV, (1), 2-5, April 25, 1795; IV, (2): 10-12, 13-19, May 2, 1795; Jack D. L. Holmes, "The Abortive Slave Revolt at Pointe Coupée, Louisiana, 1795," *Louisiana History*, 11 (1970): 341-62. Javier Malagón Barceló, in *Código Negro Carolino (1784)* (Santo Domingo, 1974), traces the development of a black code for Santo Domingo in 1784 to the 1789 *Real Cédula*, which called for improved treatment for slaves and gave cabildos a major role in enforcing the provisions. Carondelet issued his own regulations on slave control in 1795 (James A. Padgett, ed., "A Decree for Louisiana, Issued by the Baron de Caroldelet, June 1, 1795," *LHQ*, 20 (1937): 590-605.

[52]Francisco Rivas to Carondelet, No. 14, Galveztown, (1795); and (Carondelet) to (post commandants), New Orleans, June 4, 1795, both in AGI, PC, leg. 211A; Nicolas de Verbois to Carondelet, Iberville, August 15, 1795, AGI, PC, leg. 31; and Andreu Ocariz, *Movimientos rebeldes*, 179-212.

[53]Copies of the Cabildo's resolution of February 19, 1796, to prohibit the introduction of blacks and mulattoes and Carondelet's decree on slave imports are in Archivo Histórico Nacional, Estado (hereafter cited as AHN, Est.), leg. 3900, February 19, 1796; See also John G. Clark, *New Orleans, 1718-1812: An Economic History* (Baton Rouge, 1970): 192, 203, 217-19.

For some years, the *cabildo* had sought to prevent the introduction of Creole slaves from the Caribbean because of discipline problems. Masters habitually sold blacks who misbehaved and they often ended up in

Louisiana. In 1792 the *cabildo* voted to stop the entry of slaves from the Caribbean, which the Crown approved on January 1, 1793. Slave owners in Louisiana preferred *bozales*, unassimilated slaves from Africa, and the government issued licenses to a number of Louisiana shipowners to bring them (Actas del Cabildo, III, (2), 179, February 10, 1792; Charles Gayarré, *History of Louisiana*, 4 vols. (1885; reprint ed., New York, [1972]), 3:214; Andreu Ocariz, *Movimientos rebeldes*, 103-6).

[54]Morazán, "Letters," 1:168-86; Paul F. Lachance, "The Politics of Fear: French Louisianians and the Slave Trade, 1786-1809," *Plantation Society in the Americas*, 1 (1979): 175-77.

[55]Actas del Cabildo, IV, (3), 206-7, August 8, 1800; IV, (3), 208-22, August 16, 1800; Morazán, "Letters," I, viii, 168-86, 197. If Carondelet's 1795 police regulation was as "Draconian" as some writers suggest, there would not have been a need for new measures in 1800. Judge Advocate Vidal attributed the planters' problem with their slaves to mistreatment. Morazán, "Letters," 2:195-203, especially 201-3.

[56]Sources on these subjects are extensive. See, for example, Actas del Cabildo, I, 22, 25-26, June 30, 1771; I, 58-59, October 4, 1771; II, (2), 40-41, December 15, 1780; II, 202-3, January 30, 1784; III, (2), 54-56, April 17, 1789; III, (2), 56-59, April 24, 1789; III, (2), 59-51, May 8, 1789; III, (3), 29-31, October 31, 1792; III, (3), 32, November 16, 1792; AHN, Est., leg. 3892*bis*, Exped. 1, "Expediente sobre ampliaciones de reglas para el gobierno de la Luisiana por medio de neutrales"; Burson, *The Stewardship*, 258. Peter Marzahl, in "Creoles and Government: The Cabildo of Popayán," *Hispanic American Historical Review*, 54 (1974): 636-56, discusses the link the cabildo of Popayán, Ecuador, served between the community and the Crown.

[57]The documentation is abundant. See for example: Martin Navarro to José de Gálvez, No. 1, New Orleans, September 30, 1779, AGI, PC, leg. 633; Navarro de José de Gálvez, No. 22, New Orleans, August 29, 1780, AGI, SD, leg. 2586; Carondelet to Luis de Las Casas, New Orleans, August 31, 1793, AGI, PC, leg. 1442; Actas del Cabildo, III, (2), 12-13, March 26, 1788; III, (2), 16-19, April 4, 1788; III, (3), 187-89, December 19, 1794; IV, (1), 46-47, July 17, 1795; IV, (1), 146-47, July 29, 1796; Brian E. Coutts, "Martín Navarro: Treasurer, Contador, Intendant, 1766-1788: Politics and Trade in Spanish Louisiana," 2 vols. (Ph.D. dissertation, Louisiana State University, 1981), 1:197-98.

[58]The upper classes in Spanish American cities controlled local government, including *cabildos*. They decreed low taxes, few services, and many fiestas, which consumed much of the municipal revenue. The numerous lower classes paid the bulk of the taxes rather than the wealthy. The wealth of the upper classes or even a high volume of commercial activity in a city was no indication that the municipal government had ample revenue or engaged in worthwhile civic projects (see Ezquerra Abadía, "Un presupuesto," 685-701. He calculates that on a per capita basis New Orleans' income was nearly twice as high as Havana's, five times as high as Mexico City's, twelve times as high as Santiago de Chile's, and twenty times as high as Buenos Aires'. Ibid., 695-701). Despite the appearance that New Orleans had ample revenue, at times it also had many expenses.

Spaniards and to a lesser degree Spanish Americans, however, often had a deep sense of civic philanthropy and engaged in projects that helped the cities they lived in. Among favored projects were construction of churches or local government buildings, parks, fountains, and statues. Sometimes public-spirited individuals contributed to helping the masses. Andrés Almonester is an excellent example of Spanish civic philanthropy in New Orleans.

[59]Carondelet's efforts to improve the city are more visible in the *cabildo* minutes than in the published literature, where he is usually described as a controversial governor. See Thomas M. Fiehrer, "The Baron de Carondelet as Agent of Bourbon Reform: A Study of Spanish Colonial Administration in the Years of the French Revolution" (Ph.D. dissertation, Tulane University, 1977); James Thomas McGowan, "Creation of a Slave Society: Louisiana Plantations in the Eighteenth Century" (Ph.D. dissertation, University of Rochester, 1976); Ernest R. Liljegren, "Jacobinism in Spanish Louisiana," *LHQ*, 21 (1938): 47-97; and Carl A. Brasseaux, "François-Louis Hector, Baron de Carondelet et Noyelles," in *The Louisiana Governors: From Iberville to Edwards*, edited by Joseph G. Dawson III (Baton Rouge, 1990), 64-69. Writers have often criticized Carondelet for overreacting in crises or have misunderstood his slave policies. Brasseaux discusses the controversy surrounding Carondelet while taking a position that is generally against him. The governor's shortcomings, however, should not diminish his many constructive accomplishments that benefited the New Orleans residents. Among them were lighting, police, flood control, and construction of Carondelet Canal. The *cabildo*, including the slaveholders on it, appreciated his efforts and set up a plaque in public to commemorate his work. It was written in Spanish, French, and English, the languages then current in the city;

another plaque placed in the *casa capitular* was written only in Spanish (Actas del Cabildo, IV, (1), 150-51, August 19, 1796).

[60]David J. Weber, *The Spanish Frontier in North America* (New Haven, 1992), 324-26; Ezquerra Abadía, "Un presupuesto americano," 675-701. *Cabildos* have been studied to a limited degree in other areas of the southern fringe of the United States (the Spanish Borderlands). See Florian F. Guest, "Municipal Institutions in Spanish California, 1769-1821" (Ph.D. dissertation, University of California, Los Angeles, 1961); Mattie Austin Hatcher, "The Municipal Government of San Fernando de Bexar, 1730-1800," *Southwestern Historical Quarterly*, 8 (1905): 227-352; Marc Simmons, *Spanish Government in New Mexico* (Albuquerque, 1968); and Gilbert R. Cruz, *Let There Be Towns: Spanish Municipal Origins in the American Southwest, 1610-1810* (College Station, TX, 1988). Cruz entitles the final chapter of his study "Spanish Municipalities in North American History," but he ignores New Orleans because he appears unaware that it had a *cabildo*.

[61]Morazán, "The Cabildo of Spanish New Orleans," 591-605; Gilbert C. Din, *Francisco Bouligny: A Bourbon Soldier in Spanish Louisiana* (Baton Rouge, 1993): 1, 188-91, 199-200. Vidal has managed to escape serious scrutiny by historians of Spanish Louisiana. Jack D. L. Holmes, who wrote more about him than anyone else, was uncritical and failed to expose the real man. See his "*Dramatis Personae* in Spanish Louisiana," *Louisiana Studies*, 6 (1967): 152-55; and "Vidal and Zoning in Spanish Louisiana," *Louisiana History*, 14 (1973): 271-82.

[62]Among the works are Berquin-Duvallon, *Travels in Louisiana and the Floridas in the year 1802*, translated by John Davis (New York, 1806); François Marie Perrin du Lac, *Travels Through the Two Louisianas, and Among the Savage Nations of the Missouri; Also in the United States, Along the Ohio and Adjacent Provinces, in 1801, 1802, & 1803* . . . (London, 1807); Paul Alliot, "Historical and Political Reflections on Louisiana," in *Louisiana Under the Rule of Spain, France, and the United States, 1785-1807*, edited by James Alexander Robertson, 2 vols. (1910-1911; repr. Freeport, NY, 1969), 1:32-143; Claude César Robin, *Voyage to Louisiana by C. C. Robin, 1803-1805*, translated by Stuart O. Landry, Jr. (New Orleans, 1966); John Pintard, "New Orleans 1801: An Account by Pintard," edited by David Lee Sterling, *LHQ*, 34 (1951): 217-33; and John Sibley, "The Journal of Dr. John Sibley, July-October, 1802," *LHQ*, 10 (1927): 474-97.

[63]Gilbert C. Din and John E. Harkins, "The New Orleans Cabildo: Colonial Louisiana's First City Government, 1769-1803" (Baton Rouge, 1996). The book-length manuscript has been accepted for publication by Louisiana State University Press. The late Samuel Wilson, Jr., of New Orleans helped greatly to make the city's inhabitants and others aware of the building through his numerous writings. See his essay about the building, "The Colonial Period, 1723-1803," in Wilson and Huber, *The Cabildo on Jackson Square*.

DO IT! DON'T DO IT!: SPANISH LAWS ON SEX AND MARRIAGE*

Jack D. L. Holmes

Sexual morality as regulated by the government has always posed a problem, since one man's morality did not extend to his neighbor. Ernest Hemingway suggested a light-hearted approach to the dilemma: ". . . what is moral is what you feel good after and what is immoral is what you feel bad after."[1] Contrary to popular negative opinion as to the quality of Spanish laws—another example of the *Leyenda Negra*—the body of laws relating to marriage and the rights of women was, perhaps, the most involved and protective of any nation in the world.[2] Yet, in the studies of Spanish legal history, there has been but disappointing use of these basic sources, as pointed out in two revealing studies by Professor Hans W. Baade of the University of Texas.[3]

Since there is invariably a gap between the laws and the actual practices, it is necessary to examine individual cases to determine whether the laws were being obeyed or ignored. Still, as a point of departure, it is useful to see what the law *said,* and in the case of Spanish Louisiana and, after 1783, West Florida, which Spanish laws attempted to regulate sex and marriage.

On November 25, 1769, Gen. Alejandro O'Reilly applied a series of Spanish laws to Louisiana. They were based on the *Recopilación de Castilla,* the 1680 *Recopilación de leyes de los reynos de las Indias,* and, *Mathieu de criminali contraversia.*[4]

Rape was treated in the first decree: "He who shall ravish a girl, a married woman, or a widow of reputable character, shall suffer death, and his property shall be confiscated to the use of the person injured, but if the said person be not of reputable character, the judge shall inflict such punishment as he may think suitable to the case."[5]

O'Reilly's Code also addressed the problem of adultery,[6] that crime "which a man commits knowingly (*á sabiendas*) by having intercourse with a married woman, or one

*First published in Edward F. Haas, ed., *Louisiana's Legal Heritage* (Pensacola, FL: Published for the Louisiana State Museum by the Perdido Bay Press, 1983), 19-42. Reprinted with the kind permission of the publisher.

betrothed (*desposado*) to another man."[7] As for the punishment for such offense, O'Reilly declared, "The married woman, convicted of adultery, and he who may have committed the same with her, shall be delivered up to the will of the husband; with the reservation, however, that he may not put the one to death without inflicting the same punishment on the other."[8] Apparently, O'Reilly was unaware of the liberalization of Spanish laws regarding punishment for this offense. "The woman who commits [adultery] ought to be banished, for the punishment of death imposed by Ley 15, Título 17, p. 7, has been mitigated. At present, the laws which permitted relations to kill the adulterer are obsolete."[9] As a matter of fact, this is the *only* section of O'Reilly's Code which was negated by the Council of the Indies because it was "objectionable."[10]

Pimps and panderers "who entrap women, inducing them by cunning arts, or procuring them to prostitute their bodies," were, by Spanish law, divided into five types.[11] Punishment for the first offense was set at a hundred lashes and ten years hard labor in the royal galleys. A second conviction brought the same whipping plus "perpetual condemnation" to the galleys, "although they may be under twenty years of age." How a pimp condemned to a life of hard labor in the galleys could exercise a third offense is not explained, but the penalty was set at death.[12]

O'Reilly condemned husbands who consented that their wives live in concubinage with another man "or who shall have induced her to commit the crime of adultery." For the first offense he decreed ten years at hard labor in "some fortress," and for the second conviction, a hundred lashes and imprisonment for life.[13] The same punishment was meted to "those who carry on the infamous trade of enticing women to prostitution, by procuring them the means of accomplishing the same."[14]

Spanish law provided that those guilty of incest would be punished the same as adulterers plus "the confiscation of half his property."[15] O'Reilly's Code provided that "he shall be guilty of fornicating with a relation in the fourth degree shall forfeit half his property to the profit of the public treasury, and shall, moreover, be punished corporally, or banished, or in some other manner, according to the rank of the person and degree of the kindred. If the said crime be committee between parents and their offspring, or with a professed nun, the same shall be punished with death."[16]

Spanish law also frowned on that "detestable crime" (*pecado nefando*) or sodomy. Such "sodomites who commit an abominable sin, having connection with one other contrary to nature or natural custom,"[17] were, if convicted, to be burned and their property confiscated.[18] The *Novísima recopilación* (Ley 1, Título 30, Libro 12) stated, "it is not necessary that the perfection or consummation of the crime should be proved, but the proof of acts approaching to, or very near its conclusion, will be sufficient to produce the punishment mentioned in the text."[19] O'Reilly's code stated, "He who shall commit the detestable crime against nature shall suffer death and his body shall afterwards be burned, and his property shall be confiscated to the profit of the public and royal treasuries."[20]

O'Reilly also forbade illicit sexual liaisons between members of the clergy and female members of the flock: "The woman who shall be publicly the concubine of an ecclesiastic shall be sentenced for the first time to a fine of a mark of silver, and to banishment for one year from the city or from the place where the offense may have been committed. The second time she shall be fined another mark of silver, and banished for two years, and in case of a relapse, she shall be punished by one hundred lashes, in addition to the penalties aforesaid."[21]

Finally, O'Reilly considered what should be done to boys and girls who persisted in illicit sex. He warned, "If fornication be committed between bachelors and girls, they shall be admonished by the judge to discontinue every kind of intercourse with each other, under the penalty of banishment of the man, and confinement of the girl, for such time as may be necessary to operate a reformation. If this menace have not the desired effect, the judge shall put the same into execution, unless the rank offense shall be submitted to the consideration of the judges, collectively, to apply the remedy which their prudence and zeal for the repression of such disorders may suggest. They shall punish all other libidinous offenses in proportion to their extent, and to the injury occasioned thereby."[22]

Of course, theory and practice are not always identical in law, as *Blackstone's Commentaries on the English Law* and Solórzano Pereira's critique of the *Recopilación de leyes de los reinos de las Indias* in *Política Indiana* suggest.[23] The relative permissiveness during the French dominion during the first half of the eighteenth century continued under the Spanish domination from 1766 until final expulsion of the Spanish officials in 1806. Moreover, there was little change in evidence following American occupation after 1803.

French attitudes toward sex were conditioned by the frontier situation, and French marital laws were little changed following Spanish occupation.[24] When Bishop Luis Peñalver y Cárdenas arrived in New Orleans in 1795, he wrote reports concerning the prevalence of prostitution, adultery, miscegenation, bastardy, and other results of lascivious conduct among the populace.[25]

While there is a danger in making sweeping generalizations based on a relatively small number of incidents, two decades of research in the primary sources have led me to conclude that the people in charge of colonial Louisiana favored sexual permissiveness. Governor Carondelet tried to explain the character of the Louisiana population to Bishop Luis. He described the great liberty and "total independence" of the young men. By the time they reached the age of ten they had learned to hunt, fish, ride and ramble. Between the ages of 15 and 20 they were usually married.[26]

Toward the end of Spanish rule, French Préfect Pierre Clément de Laussat met a "pretty, slender young lady riding a horse," whom he compared to a wood nymph with youth, elegance, and beauty. He was astonished to learn she was barely fourteen years old and had already been married for six months. Laussat explained that she was a creole and that among these folks and the Acadians, early marriages and large families were quite common: "eighteen to twenty [children] astonished no one."[27]

Although marriage *was* the socially approved channel through which sexual passion might be expended, the age-old alternatives kept pace in Spanish Louisiana, notwithstanding O'Reilly's admonition to the judges to keep a watchful eye upon fornication. Gossip, then as now, commonly centered on the promiscuous activities of the famous and not-so-famous.[28]

The regular non-married sexual alliances or *concubinato* were common during the colonial period, and for several generations thereafter. Spanish law provided that "the married man who lives in concubinage with a single woman" was obliged to give her a dowry equal to a fifth of his property, but if she were married, he lost one-half of his property.[29] Certainly, this was preferable to an early law of the *Recopilación de leyes de Indias* which specified the punishment of a branding, double in the Indies to that inflicted in Spain.[30]

Unfortunately, the laws against the practice were not administered uniformly. Mons. Labussière of Opelousas, who maintained a mistress named Chenet, was arrested and sent to New Orleans.[31] During a heated debate in the New Orleans *Cabildo* on May 2, 1788, prosecutors urged the application of royal decrees against the practice, all of which urged prosecution of those guilty of concubinage.[32]

In 1766 Father Clemente de Saldaña wrote that keeping a mistress in Louisiana was such a common practice that no one bothered to comment on it: it was *not* a source of scandal![33] Auxiliary Bishop Cirilo de Barcelona claimed in 1772 that Louisiana women were generally more honest than the women in Spain, but they still suffered from "small sins in morals which might be remedied in time."[34] Governor Esteban Miró in 1786 condemned the practice, particularly among the free black, mulatto, and quadroon women who felt no compulsion to work as long as they were supported by their "*maris*." Miró even condemned bizarre and garish dress by these women as evidence of their "misconduct."[35]

Inter-racial alliances had existed from the earliest European occupation of Louisiana, and the products of miscegenation were a common sight in French and Spanish Louisiana.[36] An early careful observer of Louisiana customs, the Pennsylvania historian, John Fanning Watson, described the "beautiful yellow women" who had no more ambition "than to become the concubine of a white gentleman." Watson felt they were "a good race of women; they are faithful ones who never desert their *maris* (or supporters) in any case of adversity," but he also noted they never married, and their children "however rich . . . must do as their predecessors—the daughters can at most *settle* as their mothers before them. . . . I do not know of a single case of a white gentleman marrying any one of the concubines, but I know those who deplored their position."[37]

Watson may not have known anyone who married his black or colored mistress, but there are cases when it happened. Moreover, in one case a high-ranking white official, who kept a mulatto mistress, left his entire estate to his natural, mixed-blood daughters. Dr. Nicolás María Vidal was *auditor de guerra*, or legal counselor to the governor, whose advice was sought on various points of law.[38] As a young man in Cartagena de Indias (present-day Colombia), Vidal had lived with a *mulata* and a negress, by each of whom he had natural daughters. Upon his arrival in New Orleans in 1791, he took as his mistress Eufrosina Hisnard, a free mulattress, by whom he sired two quadroon daughters. María de las Mercedes (Merced in some records) caused an international incident in Pensacola when she appealed to Andrew Jackson as territorial governor to intercede with Spanish officials to recover documents regarding her late father's estate. When Spanish Governor José María Callava demurred, Jackson jailed the outraged official and obtained the documents himself. Merced Vidal did not live up to Watson's dire predictions for women of her class. She was married to another mixed-blood creole and had two children and was accepted in her social circles in Pensacola and New Orleans.[39]

Dr. Vidal's experience was hardly an exceptional one. A glimpse at the Spanish census for 1820 in Pensacola revealed a large number of unmarried mothers—Negro and mulatto "seamstresses" for the most part—who lived openly with their white *maris*. At least thirty-nine mothers of illegitimate children in such a small population indicates that such liaisons at the military garrison-town were common.[40]

And so it was in the Spanish Mobile District, wrestled from the British in 1780. During 1788 an Irish priest named Father Michael Lamport spent a good portion of his parish duties for Nuestra Señora de la Purísima Concepción in marrying such interesting couples as Richard Bailey, a white English Protestant, and an unidentified Indian "heretic woman," while at the same time baptizing their two children, María and Martha.[41] Dr. John Chastang, the patriarch of a large mixed-blood family in the Mobile District—"Master of Harigay Hall"—married his black mistress, who had formerly been his slave but whom he subsequently freed. Their many children became prominent land and cattle barons in early Alabama. Apparently, Dr. Chastang's sexual and racial choices did not damage the family's reputation in the St. Stephens area where they all lived.[42]

Racism was rare, but it did not exist, particularly where such interracial couples were concerned. Lieutenant Domingo Bouligny, an important Spanish military officer and son of one-time acting governor-general Francisco Bouligny, condemned the Chevalier d'Anemours when he presented his mulatto mistress to the Ouachita Post settlers and expected them to shower her with honors. "The commandant here," Bouligny wrote, "so forgetful of his duty, received this whore publicly as his house guest and included her among the invitations to parties and dances which were given by the most prominent people in town." When the girl died, her grieving *mari* held an elaborate funeral to which the leading officials and military officers were requested to attend with their wives. Such intermingling, opined Bouligny, would surely lead to widespread revolts among the black slaves.[43]

It was a rare officer in the Spanish line regiment, the Louisiana Infantry Regiment, who did not maintain a "*casa chica*" or kept a mistress. Bishop Luis noted the practice in a 1799 report: "They do not blush at carrying the illegitimate issue they have by them to be recorded in the parochial registries as their natural children."[44] Certain it is, that a large number of names appear in the records which show that this practice was, indeed, prevalent.

Of course, the sexual connections between black and white were responsible for the mulatto population of the Gulf Coast. Problems which arose during the American dominion seem not to have affected the colonial settlers. Thus, Garret E. Pendagrast [Pendergast?}, a white settler from the Tensaw River section near Mobile, joined his free mulattress mistress Isabel in having their free quadroon daughter Sophia baptized at Harigay Hall on November 8, 1801.[45] Such events were a common occurrence, particularly in the Spanish Mobile District and Pensacola.

Notwithstanding the prevalence of unmarried couples living together, the church attempted to convince "by friendly persuasion" those living in sin to have their relationship sanctified by marriage. Thus, when Jacobo Herman, a Lutheran who had been living with a Catholic widow named Waible, asked for government permission to marry her, Governor-general Carondelet recommended to Bishop Luis that the ceremony be performed either in Natchez or Opelousas.[46]

On the other hand, the government sometimes disapproved to the point where love matches were deliberately broken up. Antonio Panis, son of a prominent Sainte Geneviève settler, faced government opposition to his continued illicit relationship with María Luisa, a mulattress slave belonging to Vidal Beauvais. Although Panis and his paramour were the parents of two children, María Luisa's master broke up the union by sending the girl to his son-in-law who lived some thirty leagues away and across the river at San Carlos. Stubborn Antonio then fled to the American side of the river, borrowed money to purchase his mistress's freedom, and unsuccessfully pleaded with the Spanish government to intercede on his behalf. Not only had the couple lived together "without legal or moral sanction," but Antonio's presence in American territory was an additional impediment.[47]

Miscegenation also occurred between white men and Indian women, as it had since the initial contacts of the races in the fifteenth century. French trappers and British traders often took pride in their mixed offspring, and the names Colbert and McGillivray suggest such *mestizo* children played an important historical role in the southeast.[48] During the Spanish dominion, the practice continued. Samuel Martin deserted his white family and took up with an Indian mistress in the Chickasaw Nation because, as he claimed, "my debts drove me to it."[49]

Benjamin Payatt, one of the more notorious mean frontier ruffians, took an Indian girl as his mistress and, when her father objected, he killed him and fled from Alabama to the Natchez District, now a fugitive for murder as well as counterfeiting. Apprehended by a constable in the Natchez District, Payatt slipped his bonds, killed the law officer and escaped once more.[50] Lieutenant-governor Athanase de Mézières reported that white deserters from Spanish regiments frequently found refuge among the Arkansas villages where they purchased captive Indian women. They paid them no wages, other than "the promise of quieting their lascivious passions."[51]

As unfortunate as such behavior was in Louisiana and West Florida, it was an improvement over New Mexico, where Father Pedro Serrano wrote in 1761 that the Comanches publicly deflowered young slave girls at the Taos Fairs. Afterwards they turned their unfortunate victims over to the new owners with the leering phrase, "Now you can take her; now she is good."[52] American agent among the Creeks, Benjamin Hawkins, claimed all Indian women were sensuous and showed "the temper of the mule, except when they are amorous, and then they exhibit all the amiable and gentle qualities of the cat."[53]

When the records cite "mixed marriages," they are not referring to a racial mixture, but rather to the union where one of the partners was a Roman Catholic, and the other was not. During the 1790s in Natchez, for example, Father Francis Lennan maintained separate records in the Parish of Our Savior of the World concerning such "mixed marriages."[54]

Although the *Recopilación de Leyes de los Reinos de las Indias* contains a number of regulations governing marriages in general,[55] they were only loosely followed along the Spanish-American frontier. There seems to be but little difference in the modifications forced on metropolis institutions by the frontier whether we discuss the Spaniards, the French, or the English. What English common law called informal marriages without benefit of documents, licenses, blood tests, or other trappings of the metropolis, the Spaniards considered "clandestine marriages," and in 1791, Captain-general Luis de Las Casas warned against permitting them in Spanish Louisiana and West Florida.[56]

A royal order in 1792 banned the *More Anglicano* which sanctioned such loose marriages: "Protestants of whatever sect they may profess," were still free to marry each other, or even Catholics, but the ceremony was to be performed by a Catholic priest before two witnesses and with the approval of the local commandant. Such a formula had been established at the Council of Trent. Such marriages as the alleged one between Andrew Jackson and Rachel Donelson Robards, said to have been performed by a justice of-the-peace in Bayou Pierre, were declared null and void.[57] Those Protestant ministers still in Spanish Louisiana and West Florida were warned against performing marriage ceremonies, even for members of their own flock. Adam Cloud, an Episcopalian minister in the Natchez District, reported that several couples had applied to him to marry them, but Cloud asked government permission to do so.[58]

Cloud's subsequent violation of the law resulted in his expulsion from the district, and continued complaints from the Irish priests in Natchez indicated that the Protestants were flaunting the government ban on such marriages.[59] Still, a number of Protestants did abjure "their errors" of faith and joined the Catholic church, which was the designed purpose of the easy pressure adopted in West Florida. In the Mobile District, Father Michael Lamport married Protestants and "heretics" and baptized their children as well.[60]

Even more controversial were the laws concerning marriage among black slaves. On the one hand their planter-owners urged them to cohabit for the purpose of increasing their wealth with the resulting children. According to C. C. Robin, some planters even forced their female slaves to spend their "free time" in paid prostitution.[61] Yet, official government attitudes as expressed in the laws, whether referring to the *Code Noir* of 1724 or subsequent Spanish codes, were opposed to the sexual exploitation of black slaves.[62] One official report noted that between 1777 and mid-August 1791, there had been only 54 marriages of black or mulatto slaves, yet the baptism of their children reached 205. The custom followed by these blacks was described as "*maries en face pieux*," or "*a la faz de las Estacas, ó por de la Iglesia*." That is, they merely announced before their friends at the fort gate and, with an English-style "common-law marriage," proceeded to live together as man and wife.[63]

Double standards of justice seemed to prevail regarding whites and blacks, if the Natchitoches experience is any indication. Lieutenant-governor Athanase de Mézières in 1770 ordered that any *black* woman "whose profligacy shall become scandalous," should be "exposed on a wooden horse and subsequently flogged." As for *white* women guilty of prostitution, they would be punished "to the full extent of the royal ordinances pertaining to the matter." Since O'Reilly's 1769 ordinance made distinctions based on the *class* standing of the guilty culprits, it may be assumed that few white women were exposed on the wooden horse![64]

A Spanish royal decree of May 31, 1789, called upon slaveowners to foment the marriage of their own slaves within the plantation compound so as to avoid the difficulty inherent when slaves of one master sought to marry those of another. Should the distance between plantations be such that married slaves belonging to different owners could not get together with their mates, then the wife was to follow the husband. To compensate the owner of the wife, *peritos,* or expert appraisers, would establish a monetary value for her, which the owner of the husband's slave should then pay to the wife's master. Should the husband's master decline to buy the new wife, the Spanish decree allowed the wife's owner to buy the slave husband, again at the price set by the appraisers.[65]

Spanish laws protecting the rights of the couple, as well as the state, were elaborate and eminently fair by modern standards. Permission from the parents, or if they were deceased, from other responsible family members, was a prevailing requirement seldom waived.[66] For government employees, especially military personnel, express permission from the Ministry of War was also required, and the dossiers used to petition for such approval are a valuable genealogical source. Lieutenant-colonel Enrique de Ocerin, a military engineer and knight in the Royal Corps of Hijosdalgo de la Nobleza de Madrid, furnishes a guide to these *expedientes matrimoniales*, along with a valuable analysis of Spanish legal theory concerning marriages.[67]

Ocerin cites Juan Martínez de la Vega's study of military marriages to prove that Spain was probably the first European nation to regulate military marriages and set the pattern which other countries followed.[68] In 1632, for example, Philip IV addressed the problem concerning the failure of Spanish troops marrying in Italy to obtain a dowry.[69] The Crown modified military marriages in 1701, 1716 and 1760 before setting up the pension fund known as the *Montepío Militar* on April 20, 1761. This set forth the basic requirements for brides-to-be: daughters of noble fathers, or at least of "good citizens" whose *limpieza de sangre* showed no tainted ancestors (meaning blacks, Moors or Jews); girls with a dowry of at least 20,000 *reales de vellón* (roughly $2,500 in eighteenth century funds or property) for daughters of noble fathers, or *50,000 reales de vellón* from less "distinguished" girls; and permission from the parents or legal guardians/relatives. The law stated that any officer marrying without first securing such military permission under the *Monte Pío* could be dismissed from the service and, if he died first, his widow would receive no pension.[70]

These requirements remained in effect until the Army Organic Code of June 9, 1821.[71] At various times, the rules were amended to fit certain needs, as with the March 23, 1776, decree, which required permission from parents or guardians of *both* bride and groom prior to receiving the war ministry's approval.[72] When some officers attempted to speed up the procedure by claiming they had given their "word of honor" to their fiancées, and had promptly set up housekeeping with them, Carlos III declared that henceforth any such miscreants would be promptly separated from the service.[73]

If an *expediente matrimonial* or marriage dossier lacked certain documents, a widow might be excluded from benefits unless these requisite papers were supplied. Lieutenant Juan Mier y Terán received approval from the *Consejo de Guerra* on October 6, 1804, to marry María Gertrudis Armand de Courville, but with the proviso she not be entitled to draw her pension because the dossier lacked a key document, unless her husband died in action. Five days later when the document was supplied, the Minister of War, Josef Casvallero, granted her full rights under the *Monte Pío*.[74]

In 1773 the Crown approved the application of Alexandro Cousot, a captain of grenadiers in the Louisiana Infantry Regiment, to marry Doña Francisca Paget, but without her *Monte Pío* protection unless she produced a dowry of 50,000 *reales de vellón* and justified her nobility, "as required in Article 5, Chapter 6" of the pension regulation.[75]

How generous were such military pensions to army widows? In the case of Doña Genoveva Damarrón, the widow of Captain Juan Trudeau of the Louisiana Batallion (predecessor of the Louisiana Infantry Regiment), his salary while on duty was $62 per month. Following his death in June 10, 1772, her pension began the next day at the rate of 3,000 *reales de vellón* per year. Converting the currency, she got about $250 per year as opposed to his salary of about $750 per year.[76]

Although dower rights were carefully guarded under Spanish law, a wife was able to sell property and renounce her rights. Thus, Celeste Lasausale, wife of Henry Caller in the Mobile District, sold his lot on Conception Street in 1799, and in the sale agreed to renounce "the laws which protect the dowry, *senatus consultus,* New Constitutions, the Laws of Foro, the [*Siete*] *Partidas,* and of Madrid."[77]

As in so many laws, Louisiana and West Florida did not follow exactly the Spanish laws covering the other provinces in America. This is particularly true when we consider the law forbidding government employees and high-ranking officials from marrying women from their districts in America.[78] Cecilio Odouardo, chief military counselor and tax assessor for Louisiana, was given permission to marry Louisiana native Doña María Boucher de Grand-Pré in 1773.[79] It was a usual practice in Spanish Louisiana for unmarried governors to choose for their wives the creole (Louisiana-born) ladies whose family connections facilitated wide acceptance of Spanish rule. Two examples show how this was done.

When Bernardo de Gálvez (interim-governor from January 1, 1777; governor "*en propiedad*" from 1779) lay on what he thought was his "death bed in 1777," he was married to Doña Felicité de St. Maxent, widow of Juan Bautista Honorato d'Estrehan. In his capacity as vicar general and priest of St. Louis Parish in New Orleans, Fray Cirilo de Barcelona blessed the secret marriage because the governor-general had *not* obtained the required permission from the Ministry of War. Four years later, after the 1781 campaign against Pensacola, Havana's bishop blessed the marriage once more in a public ceremony.[80]

Governor-general Manuel Gayoso de Lemos apparently ignored the prior-permission requirement when he married Elizabeth Watts on April 23, 1782, but she died within three months, and official records are silent on this marriage. On January 14, 1796, however, Gayoso signed a marriage contract with his deceased wife's sister, Margaret Cirilo Watts, promising "to celebrate their nuptials according to the rites of the church as soon as the marriage licenses or publication of banns are obtained." The couple then began housekeeping together, and their son Fernando was born July 14, 1797. When Gayoso took over as governor-general in New Orleans, he arranged for Bishop Luis to baptize young Fernando and to marry the parents the same day—December 10, 1797. War Ministry permission had finally arrived. Such irregularity in the procedures did not prevent the widow Margaret from drawing her *Monte Pío* pension following the death of Gayoso in 1799.[81]

With successive changes from French to Spanish in Louisiana, and from English to Spanish in West Florida, the *meum et tuum* of private law continued to govern such relationships as marriage. Thus, when Étienne Ferland died at Natchez n 1794, he left a young widow with nursing infant twins. She bore his name, "but as she said, only under contract of marriage." The Spanish government accepted the legality of her marriage.[82]

During his pastoral visit to West Florida in 1791, Auxiliary Bishop Cirilo de Barcelona baptized a number of children and wed their parents at the same time.[83] It was not that the rural folks deliberately flouted the institutional procedures of metropolis marriages, but rather, that the expediency dictated by frontier conditions obviated such things as marriage licenses, publication of the banns, or tuxedo rentals! There was little difference whether they were Protestant, Catholic or non-professing; whether they were French, English, or Spanish. They all did it at times.

Martínez de la Vega argued that man by nature was a social being whose heart was formed by affection, and that marriage was "the basic cell in society for the foundation of its sustenance."[84] Joseph Villars Dubreüil, a prominent Louisiana creole, wrote moralistic essays on the conduct among married persons and urged the Louisiana legislature to regulate marriage and inheritance rights.[85]

If the marriage did not work out, the Spanish church provided for a type of permanent separation called divorce in the records. American Louisiana discussed the desirability of divorce in 1806,[86] but as Professor Baade noted, under Spanish dominion, there was a provision for divorce under the jurisdiction of an ecclesiastical tribunal.[87] As with many aspects of church law, however, the government also played an important role. Henrique Henréquez wrote from Havana on November 29, 1791, regarding "divorce cases (*causas de divorcio*) the couple should proceed with strict compliance to what His Majesty has disposed in his *Royal Pragmática*."[88] A Texas case involving the divorce of Josefa Castañeda and the Marqués de Casacastillo defined the power of ecclesiastical judges in divorce cases.[89]

The divorce of Juan José Dorquigny resulted in his being jailed and an appeal as far as the Consejo de Indias. On July 23, 1786, the *Consejo* ordered him released, but to appear in Havana within five months to rejoin his estranged wife or to follow divorce proceedings as decreed. In either case, he was forbidden to return to Louisiana under any pretext.[90]

The Natchez District, which had been under English control from 1763 to 1779, had a long experience with Protestant divorces. In 1786, a longtime resident of Natchez, Anthony Hutchins, explained to the court what relationship a divorce had to a subsequent marriage.[91] A type of divorce existed in the case of James Smith and his wife, Sarah. "For divers causes and mutual consent, we, from this time forward, are to remain and live apart and separate each from the other, having no dependence on each other for livelihood or things of this world." Apparently Sarah had reason to regret her signing, which she claimed she only did to satisfy her husband, and she petitioned for justice from Governor Gayoso in 1792.

Gayoso ordered a local sheriff to examine the situation and act according to justice. On June 19, 1794, James Smith testified as to the rectitude of his position. He claimed she was an orphan on whom he bestowed money, "a suit of clothes," paid her debts, and lavished affection upon her. For three years all went well, but, according to James, "my wife grew sullen and abusive and on the most trifling occasions called me dirty names." James discovered the source of this change in disposition: "she had engaged in a intrigue with a neighbor who had seduced her and to whom I believe she prostituted herself." Finally, James said, they divided up their property and he left her. Sarah Smith then had her chance to testify.

They were "only tolerably happy" for three years, she declared: "their tempers did not suit." She claimed she did not separate from him willingly although "they lived in great dispute." She lived dependent on her brother-in-law, William Joyner, with her two children. Joseph Miller then testified he heard Sarah boast that she would leave her husband and follow William Collins (the "other man") "over the world." Upon hearing the testimony of the couple and the witness, Gayoso decreed on July 1, 1794, that they were to be permanently separated with an equal division of the community property.[92]

Another divorce was rendered at the Baton Rouge post by Captain Josef Vázquez Vahamonde, the commandant, in the presence of parish priest Carlos Burke and Miguel Mahier. Leonora Mullen had petitioned for justice at Pointe Coupée or *Punta Cortada* on

August 9, 1794, complaining James Mullen, her husband, abused her badly and tore her clothes off her back, sold her property and deserted her, leaving her penniless. Anselme Blanchard reported to Vázquez Vahamonde from New Feliciana that the wife had always behaved herself and gave her husband nothing of which to complain. James Mullen then testified and showed an April 22, 1792, agreement signed by "Nelly Mullen" and him which stated, "James Mullen has delivered to Nelley Mullen all her property, debts, dues and demands from the beginning of the World to this day, and they have both agrede [sic.] never to have aney demands or clames against each other." Based on the proper settlement of finances, James Mullen gave Leonora his note-on-demand for $58 and the post commandant signed the divorce agreement on September 26, 1794, as witnessed by Father Carlos Burke and others.[93]

Not even prominent government employees were free from marital break-ups. *Guarda-almacén* (royal quartermaster and supply officer) Miguel Eslava at Mobile had been married to Hypolite Alexandre since July 10, 1794, and they had several children.[94] On November 24, 1803, however, Hypolite petitioned Mobile Commandant Cayetano Pérez for separate maintenance for herself and children while the Ecclesiastical Tribunal considered the evidence, took testimony from witnesses, and rendered a decision in her divorce request. It seems that her husband had abused her and thrown her out of the house.[95] Eslava refused to give his wife any financial aid whatever because, he maintained, he was a treasury official and outside the jurisdiction of the Mobile commandant.[96]

The entire question was submitted to Dr. Nicolás María Vidal, the *auditor de guerra*, or military and legal advisor for Louisiana and West Florida, for his opinion, which he gave on December 14, 1803. Since the acting-commandant of Mobile (Pérez) took over the treasury functions as well as the political and military ones, whatever Pérez had decided in the Eslava-Alexandre matter should prevail. As for Hypolite's request for financial assistance during the pending divorce, Vidal felt the $20 per month decreed by Pérez sounded reasonable, providing Eslava had that much money, but if not, he should still be required to give his wife as much as he could afford. In this divorce case, Fathers Juan Francisco Vaugeois of Mobile and James Coleman of Pensacola intervened when Eslava attempted to sell three of his slaves in 1807 before the divorce was final.[97] What these various divorce cases illustrate is that the rights of the contracting parties in marriage dissolution were protected by a benevolent government, acting in concert with the church.

If marriage was the accepted channel for releasing sexual energy, and divorce was the approved solution of non-functional marriages, we must not ignore the pre-marital and extra-marital sexual liaisons which seemed to flourish. Seduction of the "helpless" female by the "predatory" male is a tale often told in the archival records. In the Mobile District, for example, Juana (Jane, nicknamed Jabota) Chastang yielded to the promises of Dr. Thomas Blair, became pregnant, and then suffered the indignity of seeing her lover flee the district before he could be sued for breach of promise.[98]

As Juana (Jabota) saw her slender figure swell, her sister, Goton, came up with a possible solution to her "problem." She had been approached by Agustín Rochon, scion of another noted Mobile family, who was trying to seduce her. With a ploy as old as the hills, Agustín suggested that his friend Benjamin Dubroca, son of another "in-family" of the district, might be persuaded to marry the pregnant Juana if Goton yielded to his pleas. Goton did, but Benjamin and Agustín did not. They had fled before the wrath of an outraged Chastang father, who promptly appealed to the parish priest for justice and won a $2,000 judgment against the Rochon family for breach-of-promise and seduction.[99]

A husband whose wife was seduced by another man might also appeal for justice from the government. John Barcley, the successful pioneer builder of a cotton gin in Natchez in 1795,[100] had entrusted his wife and child to his "good friend and neighbor," James Todd, while he journeyed to the United States. When he returned to Natchez with the blueprints for Whitney's gin in his mind, he discovered his family had increased by one, although he had been absent for more than a year. He discovered that his friend Todd had taken his stewardship too seriously, and in the lawsuit filed against him, Barcley won an award of $300 in damages.[101]

Another Natchez scandal affected Elizabeth Denham and her father, Reuben. Benjamin Kimball seduced Elizabeth who was soon with child. When Kimball aided in performing a frontier-style abortion, the rogue added insult to injury by spreading a rumor that the girl's own father had impregnated her and then had aborted the resulting "problem." Reuben promptly filed suit against Kimball for "making false statements and debauching Elizabeth." The errant Kimball was subsequently ordered out of the Natchez District.[102]

No one, it seems, was immune to having his wife or fiancée seduced. Mobile's commandant, Vicente Folch y Juan, offered the hospitality of his home and board to Ensign Lorenzo de Rigolene, not aware that the visitor would begin an affair to Folch's wife. After all, Rigolene had letters from Folch's friends in Spain, and he was a noted officer in the Flanders Walloon Guards. The young ensign sat at Folch's table, borrowed money at no interest, and took too seriously the old Spanish welcome, "*mi casa es su casa.*" While Folch was on duty inspecting the district, Rigolene spent his evenings in bed with Folch's wife, María de la Merced Bernardina Rodríguez Junco. Folch learned of the affair from a loyal slave and became determined to catch the pair *in flagrante delicto.*

With several officers and witnesses, his alleged trip to the far points of his command was cut short as the group sneaked back into the fort and exposed the naked couple with lights before an outraged husband. "I left my musket and retired to my room to feel the pain of my disgrace," Folch wrote Governor-general Esteban Miró, his uncle. "This is the way an ungrateful officer, whom I had received in my home as a brother, has repaid me!"[103]

Folch quizzed his tearful wife about the incident, only to learn she had been forced to submit—several times it seems. In consideration of his sons and daughters, Folch said he would not take vengeance, but until the truth of the matter might be resolved, he would keep her and her lover in jail "until it appears for sure that she did not give in willingly." In concluding his complaint, Folch said that in Spain a man's wife would be protected by kin, but on the frontier of Louisiana and West Florida, "the vile seducers who always direct their attacks against the most vulnerable women," were not checked by such *dueñas*.[104]

On the other hand, there was reason for wives to complain about their husbands who left them in Spain and went to America, where they became sexually promiscuous. Spain's official policy was to frown on behavior and to threaten dishonorable discharge to military personnel who took mistresses in America while legally married to wives in Spain. A rotation plan sought to bring husbands back to their spouses after a reasonable tour of duty.[105] Husbands who were found guilty of living with strange women in the Indies while their wives remained in Spain, were to be punished and returned to the homeland.[106] The clergy was urged to investigate such incidents and try to persuade such errant husbands to eschew their evil ways and return to their wives in Spain and "resume their husbandly duties with their legitimate wives."[107]

Tomás and Ventura Villaró were two brothers who came afoul of this proscription in 1796. Both had mistresses in Louisiana while their legitimate wives were still living in Cataluña, Spain. Bishop Luis condemned such profligate behavior and warned that such men set a bad example for the moral Christian climate in Louisiana. Two days later, Governor-general Carondelet gave order for sending the Villaró brothers back to Spain.[108]

Doctor-patient relationships often led to fornication. Dr. Blair seduced Juana Chastang, as noted above. In Opelousas, Dr. Carnotte prescribed sexual therapy to one settler's wife when her outraged husband broke in and caught them in bed. M. Despau promptly filed suit against the doctor in what must be one of the earliest examples of "malpractice" in Louisiana, but the "sensuous doctor" had fled the district before he was brought to trial.[109]

In Pensacola, two physicians came to blows over the attention paid by Dr. Juan Ruby to the wife of Dr. Eugenio Antonio Sierra. Dr. Ruby felt that Sra. Sierra would be cared for better if she moved to his home so that he might minister to her needs around the clock. Dr. Sierra labeled Ruby a "lascivious, old-man," and hit him with a stick. Dr. Ruby promptly filed suit for assault and battery.[110]

Bigamy was a double-edged problem for the government and church. According to a royal decree of February 18, 1754, and subsequent *real cédula* of March 19, 1754, the "crime" of bigamy was a "*mixto fuero*," that is, it belonged both to the Inquisition and Royal Justice. The Royal Council discussed the problem during 1757 and 1766 and agreed to leave the "said crime" to the Inquisition.[111] In 1770, however, bigamy and polygamy were crimes under the jurisdiction of the civil authorities, and the Inquisition no longer was involved.[112] Those persons who were married at one time to two women were in the seventh rank of those who "caused public scandal," according to White, who noted the punishment for this crime was 200 lashes and ten years in the galleys.[113]

Buenaventura Collell should have been relaxed. His father, Francisco Collell, was commandant of Galveztown, which included an *isleño* settlement, during the American Revolutionary War. Unfortunately, not even a prominent father could save a son from such errant behavior as bigamy. The younger Collell married Francisca Esteves in Barcelona before going to Louisiana. He had married in 1788 Constance Condé while at St. Louis, but when the bigamy was discovered, Governor-general Carondelet ordered the young Collell jailed and his property confiscated.[114]

Rumor was not sufficient to condemn a person for bigamy, however, and Dr. Juan José Dorquigny, the French surgeon sited above, was charged by his first father-in-law, Antonio Marmillón, with bigamy and attempted murder. The investigation revealed that d'Orquiny had actually divorced his first wife in Philadelphia, and he was subsequently cleared of all charges.[115] Various cases in the Natchez District illustrate that the practice of bigamy was widespread along the Spanish-American frontier, and indeed, in established areas as well.[116]

Spain's protection of its vassals in and out of marriage certainly puts a dent in the old hackneyed "*leyenda negra*." Here was a sovereign anxious to provide his subjects with channels of expression not inconsistent with the aims of society. As White quotes from the Spanish laws, "Marriage being so advantageous to the welfare of the state, our laws favor it in various ways."[117]

Naturally, frontier conditions worked their modification on marital institutions just as the frontier changed all manner of metropolis conditions. That sex and marriage continued to defy the accepted norms of approved behavior should not be construed as unique on the Spanish-American frontier in Louisiana and West Florida. After all, Alfonse Kerr properly observed, "the more things change, the more they remain the same."

Notes for "Do It! Don't Do It!: Spanish Laws on Sex and Marriage"

[1]Ernest Hemingway, *Death in the Afternoon* (New York, 1932), Chapter 1.

[2]See, for example, Joseph M. White, *A New Collection of Laws* . . ., 2 vols. (Philadelphia, 1839); and Gustavus Schmidt, *The Civil Law of Spain and Mexico* (New Orleans, 1851).

[3]Hans W. Baade, "The Form of Marriage in Spanish North America," *Cornell Law Review*, 61 (1975): 1-89; "Marriage Contracts in French and Spanish Louisiana: A Study in 'Notarial' Jurisprudence," *Tulane Law Review*, 53 (1979): 1-92.

[4]A copy of O'Reilly's regulations is in the Parsons Collection, Humanities Research Center, University of Texas at Austin. It has been translated in Lawrence Kinnaird, *Spain in the Mississippi Valley*, 3 vols. (Washington, 1946), 1:114 et seg. It is also in "Digest of the Laws of Louisiana," in *Annals of Congress*, 8th Congress, 2nd Session, 1804-1805 (Washington, 1852), 1550-1551. Referred to hereafter as Code O'Reilly.

[5]Code O'Reilly, Section V, Par. 5. Should a victim's relations not accuse a rapist, "any of the people' might do so: White, *New Collection of Laws*, 1:116.

[6]Code O'Reilly, Section 5, Par. 6, citing *Recopilación de Castilla, Libro* VIII, *Título 20, Ley 1.*

[7]White, *New Collection of Laws*, 1:228.

[8]Code O'Reilly, Section 5, Par. 6.

[9]White, *New Collection of Laws*, 1:240-41.

[10]Marqués de Grimaldi to Luis de Unzaga, No. 24, El Pardo, March 24, 1770, *Archivo General de Indias (Sevilla), Papeles procedentes de la Isla de Cuba* (hereafter cited as AGI, PC), *legajo* 174.

[11]White, *New Collection of Laws*, 1:225. The Spanish word for pimp is *alcahuete.*

[12]Ibid., 1:241-42.

[13]Code O'Reilly, Section 5, Par. 7, citing *Recopilación de Castilla, Libro* VIII, *Título* 21, *Ley* 5.

[14]Code O'Reilly, Section 5, Par. 8, citing *Recopilación de Castilla, Libro* VIII, *Título* 21, *Ley* 5.

[15]White, *New Collection of Laws*, 1:249.

[16]Code O'Reilly, Section 5, Par. 9, citing *Recopilación de Castilla, Libro* VII, *Título 18, Libro 3; and Ley VIII, Título* 10, *Ley* 7.

[17]White, *New Collection of Laws*, 1:225.

[18]Ibid., 1:252.

[19]Ibid.

[20]Code O'Reilly, Section 5, Par. 10, citing *Recopilación de Castilla, Libro* VIII, *Título* 21, *Ley* 1.

[21]Code O'Reilly, Section 5, Par. 11, citing *Recopilación de Castilla, Libro* VIII, *Título* 19, *Ley* 1.

[22]Code O'Reilly, Section 5, Par. 12, citing *Mathieu de re criminali contraversia*, 59.

[23]Juan de Solórzano Pereira, *Política Indiana* (Madrid, 1648).

[24]Rodolfo Batiza, "*La unidad del derecho privado en Luisiana durante el régimen español,*" *Interamerican Law Review* (*Revista Jurídica Interamericana*), 4 (1962): 121-37 (Spanish) and 139-56 (English). A popular "study" of sexual mores in colonial Louisiana is Herbert Asbury, *The French Quarter, an Informal History of the New Orleans Underworld* (New York, 1936), 11-13, 47-50.

[25]Luis Peñalver y Cárdenas (Bishop of Louisiana) to Eugenio Llaguno y Amirola (Minister of Grace and Justice), New Orleans, November 1, 1795, *Biblioteca Nacional* (Madrid), Ms vol. 19,509, folios 24-27, cited in Jack D. L. Holmes, *Gayoso: The Life of a Spanish Governor in the Mississippi Valley, 1789-1799* (Baton Rouge, 1965), 224-25.

[26]Baron de Carondelet (Governor-general of Louisiana and West Florida) to Bishop Luis, New Orleans, June 9, 1796, AGI, PC, *leg.* 2354.

[27]Pierre Clément de Laussat, *Memoirs of My Life . . .*translated by Sister Agnes-Josephine Pastwa; Robert D. Bush, ed. (Baton Rouge, 1978), 63-65.

[28]For example, Anthony Hutchins of Natchez, spread the rumor that American boundary commissioner Andrew Ellicott and his son were sharing the sexual favors of their housekeeper, although the story was probably false: Stephen Minor to Manuel Gayoso de Lemos, Natchez, October 21, 1797, AGI, PC, *leg.* 2371.

[29]White, *New Collection of Laws,* 1:242.

[30]*Recopilación de leyes de los reinos de Indias, Libro* VII, *Título* 8, *Ley* V.

[31]Carondelet to Luis Andry, New Orleans, October 20, 1795, AGI, PC, *leg.* 22.

[32]Minutes of the New Orleans *Cabildo,* May 2, 1788, manuscript originals in the New Orleans Public Library Archives. Cited were laws of November 19, 1771, February 20, 1777, and December 21, 1787.

[33]Father Clements de Saldaña to Joseph Antonio de Armona, New Orleans, March 30, 1766, *Biblioteca Nacional* (Madrid), Ms vol. 18-745-29, quoted in Vicente Rodríquez Casado "*Costumbres de los habitantes de Nueva Orleáns en el comienzo de la dominación española,*" *Miscelánea, Revista de Indias* (Madrid), 2 (1941): 174, 177.

[34]Charles E. A. Gayarré, *History of Louisiana, The Spanish Dominion* (New York, 1854), 57.

[35]Ibid., 179. The original is in the Minutes of the New Orleans *Cabildo* for the 1786 sessions.

[36]H. E. Sterkx, *The Free Negro in Ante-Bellum Louisiana* (Rutherford, NJ, 1972), 60, 66.

[37]John F. Watson, "Notitia of Incidents at New Orleans in 1804 and 1805," *American Pioneer,* 2 (1843): 233-36.

[38]Jack D. L. Holmes, "*Dramatis Personae* in Spanish Louisiana," *Louisiana Studies,* 6 (1967): 152-55.

[39]Vidal's will, New Orleans, April 25, 1798, New Orleans Notarial Archives, Notary Pedro Pedesclaux, fol. 288-292, cited in Jack D. L. Holmes, "Merced Vidal: A Remarkable Black Woman in Spanish West Florida," unpublished paper read to the Florida Historical Society, (Orlando, 1980).

[40]Duvon C. Corbitt, "The Last Spanish Census of Pensacola, 1820," *Florida Historical Quarterly,* 24 (1945): 30-38. For a complete study of the census, see William S. Coker and G. Douglas Inglis, *Spanish Censuses of Pensacola, 1784-1820: A Genealogical Guide to Spanish Pensacola* (Pensacola, 1980).

[41]Baptismal books, Parish of *Nuestra Señora de la Purísma Concepción,* Mobile Chancellor's Office, I, fol. 22.

[42]Marriage records in ibid., I, fol. 72. See Jack D. L. Holmes, "The Role of Blacks in Spanish Alabama: The Mobile District, 1780-1813," *Alabama Historical Quarterly,* 37 (1975), 5-18.

[43]Domingo Bouligny to Marqués de Casa-Calvo, Ouachitá, April 7, 1800, AGI, PC, *leg. 70-B.*

[44]Louis Houck, ed., *The Spanish Régime in Missouri,* 2 vols. (Chicago, 1909), 2:221.

[45]Baptismal book, Parish of *Nuestra Señora de la Purísima Concepción,* Mobile Chancellor's Office, I.

[46]Bishop Luis to Carondelet, New Orleans, January 2, 1797, AGI, PC, *leg.* 102.

[47]Carondelet to Zenón Trudeau, New Orleans, January 16, 1796, AGI, PC, *leg.* 23.

[48]John W. Caughey, ed., *McGillivray of the Creeks* (Norman, OK, 1938).

[49]Manuel Gayoso de Lemos to Esteban Miró, No. 126, Natchez, June 10, 1791, AGI, PC, *leg.* 41.

[50]Gayoso to Carondelet, Natchez, July 9, 1792, in ibid.

[51]Athanase de Mézières to Luis de Unzaga y Amézaga, Natchitoches, May 20, 1770, in *Athanase de Mézières and the Louisiana-Texas Frontier, 1768-1780*, Herbert E. Bolton, ed., 2 vols. (Cleveland, 1914), 1:166. My thanks to Professor Russell Magnaghi of Northern Michigan University for sharing this and the subsequent reference with me in 1974.

[52]Fray Pedro Serrano to Viceroy Marqués de Cruillas, 1761, cited in Charles W. Hackett, ed., *Historical Documents Relating to New Mexico, Nueva Vizcaya and Approaches Thereto, to 1773,* 3 vols. (Washington, 1923-1927), 3:486.

[53]Benjamin Hawkins to Mrs. Eliza Trist, Cusseta in the Creek Nation, November 25, 1797, in *Letters of Benjamin Hawkins, 1796-1806*, vol. 9, *Collections of the Georgia Historical Society* (Savannah, 1916), 256.

[54]Many of Father Lennan's entries for such "mixed" marriages are in the archives of St. Joseph's Cathedral, Baton Rouge. A brief guide is Elizabeth Becker Gianelloni, "Miscellaneous Records of St. Joseph Cathedral, Baton Rouge," *Louisiana Genealogical Register*, 16 (1969): 121-25. For an example in the Mobile District, see permission given by Commandant Cayetano Pérez, on July 26, 1810, to a Protestant, Elias Morben [Morgan?] to marry a Catholic girl, Anna Parna, in Parish of *Nuestra Señora de la Purísma Concepción* of Mobile Marriage Records, Vol. I, fol. 37.

[55]See *Libro* VII, *Título* II, *Leyes* I-ix.

[56]Luis de las Casas to Juan Nepomuceno de Quesdada [Governor of East Florida], Havana, October 29, 1791, cited in Quesdada to Marqués de Bajamar, No. 8, *San Agustín de la Florida*, April 20, 1792, AGI, *Audiencia de Santo Domingo, legajo* 2588.

[57]Ibid., being an "*expediente sobre el modo de contraher válidamente sus matrimonios los anglo-americanos y demás Protestants domiciliados en la Luisiana y Floridas y instrucción sobre el particular*" (dossier concerning the method by which Anglo-Americans and other Protestants living in Louisiana and the two Floridas may contract matrimony together with instructions and orders concerning the same). A copy is also in the archives of the Parish of *Nuestra Señora de la Purísima Concepción*, Mobile, Marriages, miscellaneous documents.

[58]Holmes, *Gayoso*, 81-83. Stephen Minor to Gayoso, Natches, October 29, 1791, AGI, PC, *leg*. 46.

[59]Ibid.; Jack D. L. Holmes, "Spanish Religious Policy in West Florida: Enlightened or Expedient?" *Journal of Church and State*, 15 (1973): 259-60.

[60]Marriage and baptismal records, Parish of *Nuestra Señora de la Purísma Concepción*, Mobile Chancellor's Office, *passim*.

[61]C.C. Robin, *Voyage to Louisiana . . .*, translated by Stuart Landry (New Orleans, 1966), 246-47.

[62]Carl A. Brasseaux, "The Administration of Slave Regulations in French Louisiana, 1724-1766," *Louisiana History*, 21 (1980): 141.

[63]Auto, New Orleans, August 16, 1792, repeating Theodoro Thyrzo. Henrique Henríquez, Havana, November 29, 1791, Artículo 30, in Parish of *la Purísima Concepción,* Mobile, Marriage, I.
[64]Athanese de Mézières, Proclamation, Natchitoches, January 21, 1770, translated in Carl A. Brasseaux, "Official Correspondence of Spanish Louisiana (1770-1803)," *Revue de Louisiane/Louisiana Review,* 7 (1978): 177.

[65]"*Real cédula de su magestad sobre la educación, trato y ocupaciones de los esclavos en todos sus dominios de Indias, é Islas Filipinas, baxo las reglas que se expresan,*" Aranjuez, May 31, 1789, and printed at Madrid, 1789. Chapter 7 concerns "*matrimoinio de esclavos.*" A copy is in the *Archivo General de la Nación* (México), *Reales Cédulas,* 144, fol. 34. See also, *Recopilación de leyes de los reinos de Indias, Libro* VII, *Tomo* 5, *Ley* 5; and White, *New Collection of Laws*, 1:23.

[66]*Pragmática* of March 23, 1776, in Santos Sánchez, *Cédulas de Carlos III* (Madrid, 1792), 1:424-38, *Leyes* 1-19.

[67]Enrique de Ocerin, *Induce de los expedientes matrimoniales de mililtares y marinos que se conservan en el Archivo General Militar (de Segovia) (1761-1865)* (Madrid, 1959), 1:lv.

[68]Ibid., 1:lvii, citing Juan Martínez de la Vega, *Matrimonios militares.*

[69]Ocerin, *Induce de los expedientes matrimoniales,* lvii-lix.

[70]Ibid., lix-lx. The April 20, 1761 decree is in ibid., *Apéndice* No. 1, 662-69.

[71]Ibid., lx.

[72]Cited in *Expediente matrimonial* of Juan Barnó y Ferrusola, in *Archivo General Militar de Segovia.*

[73]Julián de Arriaga to Governor of Louisiana [Unzaga], No. 171, San Lorenzo, October 15, 1774, AGI, PC, *leg.* 174-A.

[74]*Expediente matrimonial* of Juan Mier y Terán, October 6, 1804, *Archivo General Militar de Segovia.*

[75]Julián de Arriaga to Governor of Louisiana [Unzaga], Madrid, July 15, 1773, AGI, PC, *leg.* 174-A.

[76]Royal Order, El Pardo, March 20, 1773, sent in Arriaga to Unzaga, same date, No. 116, in ibid.

[77]Translated Spanish Records, Mobile Probate Court, I, 246-247.

[78]*Recopilación de leyes de los reinos de las Indias, Libro* V, *Título* 2, *Ley* 44; Richard Konetzke, "*La Prohibición de casarse los oidores o sus hijos é hijas con natuarles del distrito de la Audiencis,*" in *Homenaje a Don José María de la Peña y Cámara* (Madrid, 1969), 105-20.

[79]Julián de Arriaga to Governor of Louisiana [Unzaga], Aranjuez, May 26, 1773, AGI, PC, *leg.* 174-A.

[80]María del Carmen Galbis Díez, "Bernardo de Gálvez," in *Los virreyes de Nueva Espaã en el reinado de Carlos III,* edited by José Antonio Calderón Quijano, 2 vols. (Sevilla, 1967-1968), 2:329-30; Eric Beerman, "The French Ancestors of Felicité de St. Maxent," *Revue de Louisiane/Louisiana Review,* 6 (1977): 69-75.

[81]Holmes, *Gayoso,* 122-24.

[82]May Wilson McBee, trans. and comp., *Natchez Court Records, 1767-1805, Abstracts of Early Records* (1953; reprint ed., Baltimore, 1979), 154.

[83]Confirmation records, baptismal, and marriage registers for the Parish of Nuestra Señora de la Purísma Concepción, Mobile Chancellor's Office. An *expediente* on the pastoral visit is in AGI, *Audiencia de Santo Domingo, legajo* 2531.

[84]Martínez de la Vega, *Matrimonios militares,* quoted in Ocerin, *Induce de los expedientes matrimoniales*, lvi.

[85]"Princips de conduit pour les personnes maries. . . ." undated essay; and translation of a bill drawn up by Joseph Villaré Dubreüil, no date [1806?], William R. Perkins Library, Duke University, Flowers Collection.

[86]Samuel S. Mahon, "A Discourse on Divorce: Orleans Territorial Legislature, 1806," *Louisiana History,* 22 (1981): 434-37.

[87]Hans. W. Baade, "The Form of Marriage," 45, n205.

[88]Auto, New Orleans, August 16, 1792, quoting from Theodoro Thyrzo, Henrique Henríquez, Havana, November 29, 1791, Parish of Nuestra Señora de la Purísma Concepción, Mobile Chancellor's Office, Misc. Marriages.

[89]*Castañeda v. Marqués de Casacastillo,* March 12, 1787, Bexar Archives, University of Texas at Austin, No. 0092.

[90]*Catálogo de los fondos cubanos del Archivo General de Indias, Tomo* I, Vol. 2: *Consultas y decretos, 1784-1820* (Madrid, 1930), 49.

[91]Statement of Anthony Hutchins and Isaac Johnson, Natchez, April 3, 1786, in McBee, *Natchez Court Records*, 178.

[92]*Sarah Smith v. James Smith,* in ibid., 194-96.

[93]*Expediente* (dossier), 1792-1794, Mullen v. Mullen, AGI, PC, *leg.* 30.

[94]Marriage record in Parish of Nuestra Señora de la Purísma Concepción, Mobile Chancellor's Office, Marriages, fol. 11; Baptismal records for Miguel [Jr.], May 1, 1798 [born May 20, 1797] and Getrudis Francisca, May 19 [born May 6, 1795], in Baptismal records, ibid., fols. 49, 61.

[95]Her petition, November 24, 1803, AGI, PC, *leg.* 587.

[96]Cayetano Pérez to Juan Ventura Morales, Mobile, December 1, 1803, AGI, PC, *leg.* 587.

[97]Vidal's opinion, sent to Morales, New Orleans, December 14, 1803, in ibid.; Father Juan Francisco Vaugeois to Francisco Maximilliano de San Maxent, Mobile, April 8, June 16, 1807, AGI, PC, *leg.* 75.

[98]Carondelet to Manuel de Lanzós, New Orleans, March 25, 1795, AGI, PC, *leg.* 22.

[99]The case is in the first volume of marriage records for the Parish of Nuestra Señora de la Purísma Concepción, Mobile Chancellor's Office. It is summarized in Jack D. L. Holmes, "Alabama's Forgotten Settlers," Notes on the Spanish Mobile District, 1780-1813," *Alabama Historical Quarterly*, 33 (1971): 97. Apparently, Dr. Blair did marry Juana, for his son, Tomás Bler [Blair?] was born in New Orleans, although

no mention is made of his legitimacy! See marriage record of Tomás Bler to Eufracia Lami, Mobile, June 21, 1815, Mobile Parish Records, fol. 45.

[100]Jack D. L. Holmes, "Cotton Gins in the Spanish Natchez District, 1795-1800," *Journal of Mississippi History,* 31 (1969): 161-66.

[101]*Barcley v. Todd,* June, 1796, in McBee, *Natchez Court Records,* 281.

[102]Holmes, *Gayoso,* 64-65.

[103]Folch to Miró, Mobile, July 7, 1788, AGI, PC, *leg.* 52. On Folch, see Jack D. L. Holmes, "Three Early Memphis Commandants: Beauregard, DeVille DeGoutin, and Folch," *Papers of the West Tennessee Historical Society,* 18 (1964): 14-26.

[104]Folch to Miró, July 7, 1788. According to his petition, Madrid, January 24, 1787, AGI, *Audiencia de Santo Domingo, legajo* 2657, Rigolene served seven years in the Royal Flemis Guard before transferring to the Louisiana Infantry Regiment at lower pay!

[105]*Recopilación de leyes de los reinos de Indias, Libro* VII, *Título* 3, *Ley* 1.

[106]Ibid., *Ley* 3.

[107]Ibid., *Libro* I, *Título* VII, *Ley* xiv.

[108]Bishop Luis to Carondelet, New Orleans, March 9, 1796; and Carondelet to Bishop Luis, New Orleans, March 11, 1796 (draft), both in AGI, PC, *leg.* 102.

[109]*Despau v. Carrière,* June 26, 1799, Opelousas [St. Laundry Parish Archives], now in Louisiana State Archives, Baton Rouge.

[110]The suit is in AGI, PC, *leg.* 268. Dr. Sierra was also involved in another suit caused by a different wife! See the *sumaria* and *petición, San Marcos de Apalache*, January 8, 1800, AGI, PC, *leg.* 134-A.

[111]Royal Decree, San Ildefonso, September 8, 1766, copy in AGN, *México, Reales Cédulas,* Vol. 89, fols. 96-97.

[112]*Real Cédula,* February 5, 1770, in Santos Sánchez, *Cédulas de Carlos* III, 1:159-60.

[113]White, *New Collection of Laws,* 1:226, 242.

[114]Collell to Carondelet, St. Louis, October 20, 1794, Louisiana Collection, Bancroft Library, Berkeley, CA.; Carondelet to Zenón Trudeau, New Orleans, January 27, 1795, AGI, PC, *leg.* 22; *Crown v. Buenaventura Collell,* AGI, PC, *leg.* 172-B; Carondelet to Bishop Luis, New Orleans, January 16, 1796, AGI, PC, *leg.* 102; Carondelet to Zenón Trudeau, New Orleans, January 20, 1796, ibid., *leg.* 23.

[115]*Expediente* on d'Orquiny, July 24, 1796, AGI, *Audiencia de Santo Domingo, legajo* 2588; see also note 90.

[116]MacBee, *Natchez Court Records,* 216, 320-21, and *passim.*

[117]White, *New Collection of Laws,* 1:47.

PART IV
SPANISH LOUISIANA IN THE AMERICAN REVOLUTION

OBSERVERS AND SPANISH INVOLVEMENT, 1778*

Light Townsend Cummins

All the supplies sent to Louisiana for the Americans had arrived by the summer of 1777, and they languished in Santiago Beauregard's warehouse at New Orleans. Governor [Bernardo de] Gálvez envisaged the sequence of events connected with their delivery: an American expedition would come down the Mississippi, receive the supplies, conquer West Florida, and then offer the province to Spain. The governor believed his part in this would be twofold. First, he would secretly give the supplies to the Americans, and second, he would ensure Spanish neutrality between the warring sides once the rebels attacked West Florida. "In case the colonies take the English posts along the river," José de Gálvez [minister of the Indies] had written his nephew, "and they wish to deliver them to His Majesty, you may receive them in deposit, always taking care to see this will not cause violence with the British." The minister of the Indies recommended that young Gálvez establish a Spanish protectorate in West Florida since the British would probably find that preferable to having the rebels control the conquered territory.[1] Providing military supplies to the Americans would be a cheap price to pay in laying the groundwork for such a turn of events.

As time passed, however, no American expedition presented itself on the river, though rumors of an invasion circulated in West Florida.[2] During the summer, Governor Gálvez wrote his uncle, "According to reports from Pensacola and the repeated rumors given by the English on this river, it looks as though the Americans are disposed to come down the river this summer, numbering four to six thousand men, with the intention of dislodging them from their posts and take Pensacola."[3] Once the reports of an impending American expedition on the Mississippi reached Spain, they passed from José de Gálvez to [Conde de] Floridablanca. When the minister of state asked [Conde de] Aranda to query the congressional envoys in Paris about American intentions, the American

*Reprinted by permission of Louisiana State University Press from *Spanish Observers and the American Revolution*, by Light Townsend Cummins.

representatives gave the Spanish ambassador strong assurances that there was indeed the intention to send a force to conquer Pensacola in return for Spain's promise to hold the area in trust.[4]

Nevertheless, the year 1777 wore on, and still there was no glimpse of the Americans on the river. The Continental Congress had on several occasions discussed such an expedition but for a variety of reasons had decided not to approve it. "It was vain," Henry Laurens remarked, "to hope for Secrecy of an enterprise which had been often talked of in different states & long suspected by the enemy." Furthermore, the troops needed for the campaign could not be spared. Others who opposed the venture worried that Spain would not cooperate fully.[5] Governor Gálvez, however, was unaware of Congress' decision. His worry was that no Americans had come to collect the supplies and that some of them might spoil in Louisiana's subtropical climate. He and the observer Eduardo also wondered if rebel commanders on the Atlantic Coast might be unaware that the shipments of the cloth, gunpowder, rifles, and medicine they had requested had arrived at New Orleans. Deciding to write the Continental Congress and inform them about the supplies, the governor carefully composed an oblique letter that would not implicate Spain if it fell into British hands. With measured circumspection, he informed the Congress that the articles mentioned in its earlier communication to his predecessor had arrived at New Orleans and that these effects would be delivered to representatives who carried appropriate accreditation. He added that until then, concerned parties in New Orleans had arranged for the goods' safe storage. The governor dispatched his letter to Philadelphia in the hands of a "citizen of confidence" who sailed to the Atlantic Coast under the cover of buying a cargo of flour for the Louisiana garrison.[6]

Congress did not need to be reminded about the supplies by Governor Gálvez. Some of its members had already received word of the shipments from two other sources. In early June, 1777, Oliver Pollock wrote the Commerce Committee of the Congress and told them about supplies arriving at New Orleans from Spain. Pollock probably knew about them because of his many merchant contacts in the city.[7] Congress had also received word of the shipments from Arthur Lee, who informed the Commerce Committee that a person of consequence in Spain had assured him that "supplies of Blankets, & clothing as well as Military Stores would be ordered out to Havanah and New Orleans, there to be lodged for our use & to remain until we should send for them."[8] The Commerce Committee of the Congress had taken action to secure these supplies at New Orleans before it received the letter from Governor Gálvez. It appointed Oliver Pollock congressional agent at New Orleans and organized an expedition to claim the goods. By its action, it legitimized Pollock as its official representative in Louisiana, agreeing to guarantee any debts he might contract in New Orleans in support of the American cause. The committee wrote Governor Gálvez:

> We have employed Mr. Oliver Pollock who resides at New Orleans for our Agent; and have Instructed him to charter or buy suitable Vessels to Transport these stores Coastwise until they can get into some of our Ports or Inlets to land them. He is

> instructed to consult your Excellency in this business, and we pray your favourable attention to this business—that you will advise in all things needful—and Protect the Ships, Cargoes & Mr. Pollock if occasion shall so require. . . .We are compelled to go farther in our requests and beg that you will also supply him with money if it becomes necessary to defray the charges and Expenses that will accrue on the transshipping of the Stores. He must grant receipts for what you supply and we will repay the amount by our Agent at the court of Spain.[9]

A former West Florida planter, James Willing, became the commander of the troops organized in the United States to convey the letter and take delivery of the supplies. A brother of the powerful Philadelphia merchant Thomas Willing, who was one of Robert Morris' partners, he seemed a natural choice to lead the expedition. He had lived near Natchez during the early 1770s and had had business dealings with Pollock at New Orleans. Young Willing met with the Commerce Committee to discuss plans for the mission.[10] The committee furnished him an introduction to Bernardo de Gálvez and Oliver Pollock's letter of appointment as commercial agent.[11] Beyond those communications to Gálvez and Pollock, record of the committee's specific instructions to James Willing has been lost. It appears, however, that Congress did not authorize an attack on West Florida as part of the expedition's assignment.

After meetings with the Commerce Committee, Willing, armed with a Continental captain's commission, left for Fort Pitt, on the Pennsylvania frontier, with permission from Congress to recruit his men.[12] He gathered thirty or so volunteers, secured the flatboat *Rattletrap*, and began his journey down the Ohio River on January 10, 1778. News of the expedition preceded it, alarming British commanders all along the Mississippi. Gálvez heard about Willing's progress, as well, and assumed that the expedition was to secure the supplies and attack West Florida, since Willing's men began plundering as soon as they reached British settlements on the Mississippi. On February 16, an advance guard arrived at the plantation of Anthony Hutchins, took the planter prisoner, and seized some of his property.[13] As Willing and his men continued down the river, they engaged in similar raids against individual British residents.[14] Willing also took the small English settlement of Concord, near the Arkansas River on the British side of the Mississippi. Upon their arrival at Natchez, the Americans forced a bloodless surrender from the local British commander. Willing coerced the inhabitants at Natchez into oaths of fidelity to the Continental Congress, which many swore with reluctance.[15]

Willing's expedition created chaos for the British along the Mississippi River. Governor Gálvez received numerous reports of the expedition's advance as it approached New Orleans. These confirmed his opinion that Willing's force intended to take West Florida, although it puzzled Gálvez that the attack had apparently begun before the supplies had been delivered. Nonetheless, he knew his duty and began to discharge it. Gálvez' instructions bid him cooperate with any rebel force sent to receive the supplies and conquer the neighboring English province. In early March, he therefore initiated actions designed to facilitate the Americans' arrival in New Orleans while protecting Spanish neutrality.

Governor Gálvez issued a formal proclamation of neutrality and publicly instructed his upriver commanders to provide refuge for British citizens escaping from the American expedition. The governor also secretly wrote his subordinate commander at Spanish Manchac, Juan de la Villebeuvre, and told him that if the Americans asked to turn over to Spain the territory they were conquering, Villebeuvre could accept it as a Spanish protectorate. "As it might happen that the American who is found in command there," the governor wrote Villebeuvre, "might wish to cede to His Majesty those territories they have conquered from the English along the river, I ought to inform you that you should accept the cession."[16] Gálvez wrote his uncle José that the American expedition that planned to attack West Florida had apparently arrived on the Mississippi. He promised to follow his instructions regarding the transfer of the supplies and accept control of West Florida when the rebels offered it.[17]

Gálvez also permitted Oliver Pollock to prepare for Willing's arrival at New Orleans. Pollock had learned from several American partisans coming down the river that Willing carried his formal appointment as the congressional agent in Spanish Louisiana. That emboldened him, and he made ready for the American captain's arrival at New Orleans. Pollock later recalled, "In February, 1778, I receiv'd intelligence of Capt. Willing's approach, & immediately I waited on his Excellency the Governor & took ev'ry necessary arrangement with him. I was therefore extremely solicitous to comply with the Orders I had received from the Honorable Mr. Laurens, Mr. Morris, & Mr. Smith a secret Committee of Congress to Charter Vessels & Transport a large quantity of Merchandise by Sea & also to send as much as possible up the River, for the use of the United States."[18] Gálvez most likely welcomed Pollock's sponsorship of Willing and his men, since that removed the Spanish governor from direct contact with the Americans. Such might soften the anticipated British charges of favoritism that Governor Peter Chester [governor of West Florida] would probably level at Gálvez.

While arrangements went forward at New Orleans, the American expedition continued to move south, ravaging British settlements along the way. Near Manchac, Willing's advance party captured the British frigate *Rebecca*, a sixteen-gun vessel, which the Americans quickly appropriated for their own use. They also raided British plantations along the Mississippi and Amite rivers, although they spared those belonging to rebel sympathizers.[19] Excess and wanton destruction marked many of the seizures. Gálvez received reports "that the Americans shot hogs, killed cattle, broke bottled wine, burned dwellings and in other ways laid waste" to many individual plantations.[20] Thrown into turmoil, many British citizens along the river took advantage of Gálvez' invitation of sanctuary. They fled by the hundreds, and Spanish posts all along the west bank of the Mississippi overflowed with refugees.

Once at New Orleans, Willing met with Governor Gálvez, with Pollock as translator. To the governor's surprise, the American captain did not offer Spain any of the territories conquered by his expedition nor did he express an interest in attacking Mobile or Pensacola. What is more, he seemed unaware of any such plan on the part of the Congress. To Gálvez, Willing's chief motivation appeared revenge against particular British residents along the river, owing to personal differences that arose from his residence in West Florida before the Revolution. The American commander had apparently acted on his own initiative in ordering his men's attacks, and had no instructions to conquer West Florida. Willing wanted two things from the governor: the supplies sent from Spain and official permission to sell his plunder at New Orleans. Pollock echoed Willing in these petitions. Armed with the letter appointing him congressional agent, Pollock agreed in wanting to move ahead promptly with liquidating the spoils of the expedition in the name of the Congress.[21] Gálvez carefully considered the developments in view of his orders from Spain specifically requesting him to cooperate with any Americans sent to receive the supplies. A review of his instructions convinced him that the conquering of West Florida might have been a secondary American objective. Since his instructions did not cover the selling of prizes, he gave liberal interpretation to the standing directive from the court on such matters and decided to allow the Americans to sell what they had seized. In addition, he permitted Pollock use of port facilities to outfit the captured British frigate *Rebecca* as a privateer.

Pollock's appointment as congressional agent brought a change to the governor's plan to deliver the supplies to the Americans. He had intended for Santiago Toutant Beauregard to deal directly with the American troops. Such matters could be handled directly and personally by Pollock. Beauregard therefore "sold" the supplies to Pollock soon after the American expedition's arrival at New Orleans. These transactions took place without problems. In late March, Gálvez wrote his uncle, "Having arrived in this city a Captain Willing, commissioned to receive here the effects that were sent to me from the mother country with destination to the English colonies, I ought to inform Your Excellency that the major part of these effects have already left the city, and as soon as all of them have been delivered, I will inform Your Excellency."[22] Pollock chartered several vessels to transport the supplies to the Atlantic Coast. His sloop *Virgo* quickly left New Orleans, followed several weeks later by other vessels, "with more Goods for the United States." Throughout the fall, Pollock dispatched additional ships and bateaux to the colonies.[23] While Willing and his men enjoyed the freedom of the city, Pollock organized a public auction of articles and slaves captured by the expedition. The sale attracted a large crowd of New Orleanians, and spirited bidding brought considerable profit to the American cause. It also prompted a strident protest from Governor Chester, of West Florida, who sent a British warship to New Orleans with a formal letter of complaint. Chester expressed shock and indignation at the hospitality afforded Willing and the American troops at New Orleans, arguing the this could only be interpreted as a violation of Spanish neutrality. The British governor warned Gálvez that he would attack Louisiana if Spain departed further from its proclaimed neutrality. "I have judged it proper to inform your Excellency," he wrote, "that I sent a Detachment of Troops to

Manchac in order to establish a base for the protection of that area." Chester also began to augment British troop strength elsewhere along the Mississippi.[24]

Gálvez politely refused to be intimidated by three additional British warships calling separately at New Orleans during the several months following. Their captains demanded a full restoration of captured British property and an immediate end to the refuge provided the Americans.[25] In the end, the governor compromised and did return some of the seized English goods not yet sold by Pollock, although he allowed the Americans to remain. He explained to the British that he had extended exactly the same privileges to loyal British subjects when they wanted to sell prizes at New Orleans. Nonetheless, the behavior of the Willing expedition gravely concerned Governor Gálvez because he recognized the critical circumstance the raid had created, namely, bad relations with the British in West Florida. In this regard, he promised his uncle José that he would "take whatever measures and precautions necessary," to defend Louisiana "against any invasion the English might attempt."[26] But though the British reacted vocally to Willing's raid, they did nothing more than complain.

The residents of Louisiana hailed Governor Gálvez for the stern manner and calm strength he exhibited in standing up to the British in the crisis. What they did not know, however, was that he had never been very worried about a British attack during the tense months after Willing's arrival at New Orleans, since he had had an observer at Pensacola during the time the American was conducting his raids in West Florida and the information he got from the agent convinced him that the British would not deliver on their threats. The observer mission had been arranged in early 1778, before news of Willing's expedition reached New Orleans. The observer, Captain Jacinto Panis, of the Louisiana Regiment, had left for West Florida in February, 1778, on a seeming routine voyage. The ostensible purpose of his visit to Pensacola was to discuss with Governor Chester the problem of runaway slaves from the colonies who took refuge in neighboring territory. In reality, Panis had instructions to gather as much information as possible about the British army and navy in West Florida.[27]

Captain Panis traveled to both Mobile and Pensacola, remaining in the British colony for several months. He carried a letter of recommendation to Chester from Bernardo de Gálvez, along with a "box of white sugar and a cask of wine" as gifts to the Englishman. Panis was well received by the inhabitants of the British province during his travels, although news of the raid by Willing placed him in the unexpected position of having to vouch continually for Spanish neutrality. Nonetheless, at the very time Chester wrote his strongly worded complaint to Gálvez regarding the American raid, the British governor also played host to Panis at Pensacola. Even with the strained relations, Chester afforded Panis every courtesy as his guest. Panis responded with an eloquent profession of Spanish neutrality. "I cannot entertain the least doubt of the Sincerity of his last assurances which I have received from him," Chester wrote the Louisiana governor, "but I flatter myself, that His Excellency will continue the Same friendly disposition whenever occasions offer." The series of discussions Chester and Panis held about the problems facing the two colonies resulted in an agreement for the return of runaway slaves.

While away from New Orleans, Panis compiled a report on the status of English military defenses in West Florida. He also talked with numerous residents about the revolt, gaining a fuller understanding of British intentions regarding both the Spanish in Louisiana and the American rebels. He drafted a proposed plan of attack on Pensacola should Spain enter the war. He submitted a valuable description of the British post at Mobile:

> The fortifications are, as you know, in very bad condition; they consist of a regular square, built of brick, and flanked with breastworks, trench, and glacis, as before, situated very near the barracks and at the shore of the bay for defense by sea, as on land by Indians. Its walls are going to ruin. Almost all of the artillery is dismounted, and the trenches in some places are choked up. The barracks are in equally bad repair; in the front and side sections are housed the small garrison of forty-five soldiers, commanded by a captain, lieutenant, and sergeant; the other side, the northeast, is uninhabitable, for nothing but its walls remain, the rest having been consumed by fire.[28]

Panis provided similar descriptions of the English military works at Pensacola, even in greater detail. Panis reported that passage of the American expedition down the Mississippi had caused a full-scale mobilization of British troops in the province and a commitment from Governor Chester to remedy the weaknesses of all his garrisons in order to bring them to fighting readiness. That suggested to Governor Gálvez that Chester would be unable to make good on his threats to deal harshly with Louisiana. In addition, once war between Spain and Great Britain came in 1779, Panis' reports became the blueprint for a Spanish attack on West Florida.

The Willing expedition marked a turning point for Louisiana in the American Revolution. It exacted an immediate price for Spain: the end of all possibility of good relations between British West Florida and Spanish Louisiana. Many West Florida residents, along with the entire British government at Pensacola, thereafter viewed the Spanish in Louisiana as the enemy in an immediate sense. A gap existed in the lower Mississippi Valley between Spain's rhetoric as a neutral and the reality of its role in the revolt. In particular, Governor Chester reacted to the Willing raid by redoubling his military defenses in the western part of his province, especially at garrisons on the Mississippi River.

The period between the American raid in the early spring of 1778 and Spain's entry into the war during 1779 became a time of constant tension as both Bernardo de Gálvez and Peter Chester increased their defenses, prepared for conflict, and carefully watched each other's activities. The pressures greatly decreased Louisiana's ability to participate in the captain general's observation network based at Havana. Instead, Bernardo de Gálvez focused his attention on West Florida and worried about British military affairs in the region that had a direct, local impact on Spanish Louisiana. After late 1778, emphasis on collecting general information about the American Revolution moved away from New Orleans and became the concern almost exclusively of the captain general at Havana.

Notes for "Observers and Spanish Involvement, 1778"

[1]J. de Gálvez to B. de Gálvez, August 15, 1777, royal order, Archivo General de Indias, Seville (hereafter cited as AGI), Cuba 191.

[2]These rumors even came to the attention of the British cabinet. See Lord Sandwich to German, January 28, 1777, Public Records Office, London, Colonial Office, 5, 162:170.

[3]B. de Gálvez to J. de Gálvez, June 2, 1777, no. 57, in "Confidential Dispatches of Don Bernardo de Gálvez to his Uncle José de Gálvez" (Typescript in Correspondence of the Governors of Louisiana, Special Collections Division, Howard-Tilton Memorial Library, Tulane University, New Orleans).

[4]"Carta de Franklin a Aranda," April 7, 1777, Yela Utrilla, Juan Fernando, *España ante la independencia de los Estados Unidos*, 2 vols. 2nd ed. (Lerida, 1925), 2:94-95.

[5]Henry Laurens to John Rutledge, August 12, 1777, Paul Smith, ed. *Letters of Delegates to Congress*, 1774-1789, 22 vols. to date (Washington, DC, 1976-1995), 7:466-68.

[6]B. de Gálvez to J. de Gálvez, August, 9, 1777, no. 76, AGI, Santo Domingo 2547.

[7]Commerce Committee of the Congress to the governor of Louisiana, June 12,1777, AGI, Cuba 112.

[8]Ibid.

[9]Ibid.

[10]Regarding the Willing family and its part in the American Revolution, see Thomas Willing Balch, ed., *Willing Letters and Papers, Edited with a Biographical Essay of Thomas Willing of Philadelphia, 1731-1821* (Philadelphia, 1922), and Burton Alva Konkle, *Thomas Willing and the First Financial System* (Philadelphia, 1937).

[11]Commerce Committee of the Congress to the governor of New Orleans, November 7, 1777, AGI, Cuba 112.

[12]At Fort Pitt, George Morgan supplied Willing with enough provisions to last thirty men approximately 180 days. See George Morgan to James Willing, January 17, 1788, in General Edward Hand Papers, Historical Society of Pennsylvania, Philadelphia.

[13]For studies of Willing's raid, see John W. Caughey, "Willing's Raid down the Mississippi, 1778," *Louisiana Historical Quarterly*, 15 (1932): 5-36; Robert V. Haynes, *The Natchez District and the American Revolution* (Jackson, 1976), 51-75; José Rodulfo Boeta, *Bernardo de Gálvez* (Madrid, 1976), 65-69; and J. Barton Starr, *Tories, Dons, and Rebels: The American Revolution in British West Florida* (Gainesville, 1976), 78-121.

[14]Willing in fact apparently issued written passes to some rebel sympathizers which offered them protection from the marauding of his men. See Pass Signed by James Willing, March 3, 1778 (Gratz Collection, Historical Society of Pennsylvania).

[15]"Capitulación de Natchez," February 21, 1778, AGI, Santo Domingo 2547.

[16]B. de Gálvez to Juan de la Villebeuvre, March 20, 1778, no. 133, ibid. For information on Villebeuvre's career as a post commander, see Jack D. L. Holmes, "Juan de la Villebeuvre and Spanish Indian Policy in West Florida, 1784-1797," *Florida Historical Quarterly*, 58 (1980): 387-99.

[17]B. de Gálvez to J. de Gálvez, March 24, 1778, no. 133, AGI, Santo Domingo 2547.

[18]Oliver Pollock, "Events in the Public Career of Oliver Pollock, 1776-1782, as Related by Himself," September 18, 1782, in James A. James's *Oliver Pollock: The Life and Times of an Unknown Patriot* (1937; reprint ed., Freeport, 1970), 348-49.

[19]John Caughey, *Bernardo de Gálvez in Louisiana, 1776-1783* (Berkeley, 1934), 122.

[20]Ibid., 121.

[21]"Disposition of Pollock," in James Wilkinson's *Memoirs of My Own Time,* 3 vols. (Philadelphia, 1816), 3:Appendix A.

[22]B. de Gálvez to J. de Gálvez, March 24, 1778, no. 136, AGI, Santo Domingo, 2547.

[23]Pollock, "Events in the Public Career of Oliver Pollock," in James's *Oliver Pollock,* 350-51.

[24]Chester to B. de Gálvez, May 28, 1778, AGI, Santo Domingo, 2547.

[25]Caughey, *Bernardo de Gálvez,* 123.

[26]B. de Gálvez to J. de Gálvez, June 9, 1778, no. 166, AGI, Santo Domingo 2547.

[27]John W. Caughey, "The Panis Mission to Pensacola," *Hispanic American Review,* 10 (1930): 480-89.

[28]Ibid., 486-87.

VICTORY ON THE MISSISSIPPI, 1779*

Eric Beerman

translated and edited by Gilbert C. Din

DECLARATION OF WAR

After recovering from wounds suffered in the invasion of Algiers in 1775, and through the influence of his uncle José de Gálvez, minister of the Indies, Bernardo de Gálvez was appointed colonel of the Fixed Louisiana Infantry Battalion and acting governor of Louisiana. Before leaving Madrid because of the possibility of his death in war, he entrusted Diego Paniagua with notarial power of July 6, 1776. Gálvez arrived in New Orleans before the end of the year.[1]

When Captain General Diego José Navarro of Cuba received the royal order of May 18, 1779, on Spain's decision to declare war on Great Britain, he sent a copy to Bernardo de Gálvez with instructions to expel the English from the Mississippi River, Mobile, and Pensacola. The Spanish court sent the war announcement to all high officials in America; and Minister of the Indies Gálvez personally wrote to his nephew Bernardo on May 18, about the coming conflict. The war became official on June 21. The formal declaration of hostilities was published in Havana on July 22, and another proclamation announced the expulsion of the English from Cuba and the treatment of North Americans as friends.[2]

Bernardo de Gálvez received the declaration of war in August, weeks after its promulgation in Madrid. But he had begun preparations for the conflict upon his arrival in Louisiana. Even before receiving the recent orders, he had directed the commandant of Pointe Coupée, Captain Carlos de Grand-Pré, to construct a post on the Mississippi to observe English Colonel Alexander Dickson, who was building Fort New Richmond in

*This excerpt is taken from Eric Beerman, *España y la independencia de Estados Unidos* (Madrid, Spain: Fundación Mapfre América, 1992), 43-59. Reprinted here with the kind permission of the author, translator, and publisher.

Baton Rouge.[3] Dickson had informed the commandant of Spanish Manchac, Raimundo Dubreuil, about England's intention to seize New Orleans as soon as war was declared.[4]

In answer to Gálvez's appeal for reinforcements for Louisiana, Captain General Navarro prepared the second battalion of the España Regiment with 671 men.[5] But following the orders of the naval commandant general of Cuba, Juan Bautista Bonet, that expedition did not weigh anchor because the English navy was blockading Havana. It was the first of many delays that occurred during the war.[6] The battalion arrived in Louisiana only after the Mississippi River campaign had ended.

On August 16, Gálvez notified the military post commandants about the declaration of war. He ordered them to keep it secret and prepare to attack the English posts at Fort Bute in Manchac and New Richmond in Baton Rouge. They were to defend themselves if the English struck first. A week later, Commandant Dubreuil of Spanish Manchac informed the governor that English intentions at Fort Bute across the bayou from him appeared to be more defensive than offensive.[7]

In an important order to Captain General Navarro, Minister José de Gálvez explained the strategy to follow in the war in America. The plan would influence the career of his nephew, whom he named chief of the Mississippi expedition. The minister's order also revealed a joint Spanish-American plan to attack the English in Savannah, St. Augustine, and in the upper Mississippi River valley. His instructions read in part, "The King has decided that the principal objective of his arms in America . . . is to eject the English from the Gulf of Mexico and the Mississippi." The king wanted an expedition composed of land and naval forces to assault Mobile and Pensacola immediately. He called those posts "the key to the Gulf of Mexico," and the Mississippi River "a mural of the vast empire of New Spain [the viceroyalty of Mexico]." The king appointed Bernardo de Gálvez to command the expedition despite the fact that there were more experienced officers available. He also named Bernardo proprietary governor of Louisiana. At the same time the British were being attacked in West Florida, "up to three thousand troops from the United States were to besiege St. Augustine in Florida, and perhaps make another diversion along the banks of the Mississippi."[8]

Meanwhile the Americans continued their fight against the English. The American diplomat John Jay in Madrid tried to obtain the free navigation of the Mississippi from the Spaniards. The diligent Spanish agent in Philadelphia, Juan de Miralles, however, informed the American Continental Congress that the Spanish court would not accede to it, although he recommended that it was advantageous to the royal treasury to permit Americans on the Ohio River to send their products down the Mississippi to sell in New Orleans.[9]

THE SEIZURE OF FORT BUTE OF MANCHAC

Besides the Spaniards, the English also knew about the possibility of war. They were preparing to launch an offensive against Louisiana, and they were then reinforcing

Fort Bute at the confluence of the Mississippi River and Bayou Manchac with four hundred German mercenaries of the Waldeck Regiment. Publicly, the English alleged that they were only reinforcing their defenses against an attack by Bernardo de Gálvez from New Orleans. Gálvez, nevertheless, believed that the English were preparing to assault New Orleans as soon as they received news of the declaration of war. He further believed that the best defense was a good offense. That was the reason he had devoted the last three years to preparations, and he was ready to execute the royal order to expel the English from the Mississippi.[10]

Gálvez's concern about an English attack on New Orleans was justified. The Spaniards intercepted a letter written by Colonel Elias Durnford, commandant at Fort Charlotte in Mobile, that informed the English officials in Natchez about the projected attack on the city. Gálvez believed that two enemy expeditions would assail it: one composed of fifteen hundred men who would descend the Mississippi from Canada and join the English detachments at Natchez, Baton Rouge, and Manchac; and a second expedition would come by sea from Pensacola with the same number of troops.[11]

While he waited for the English attack, Gálvez convoked a council of war composed of his closest advisers on July 13. He informed them about Louisiana's critical situation. Intuitively, he felt the presence of eight hundred English soldiers, not counting their Indian allies, in the forts and posts on the Mississippi. He also informed the council that New Orleans faced the probability of attack from different fronts: from Fort Bute by land; from the nearby lakes (Lakes Pontchartrain, Borgne, and Maurepas); and from the German Coast, upriver from New Orleans. Gálvez declared that he had only 600 men, 450 of them recruits, to defend Louisiana. He asked the officers to present a plan to defend the city if it was attacked.[12]

With one exception, all the officers in the council agreed that New Orleans' defense demanded priority and the need to concentrate their forces in the city. Captain Manuel de Nava recommended that the commandants of the isolated posts "surrender with the best terms possible if they are attacked." Only the Catalan Esteban Miró opted for a more aggressive plan: the construction of four forts on the Mississippi, below the English at Fort Bute. If war was declared, the soldiers at these posts would seize Fort Bute or, if New Orleans were attacked, they would descend the river to assist the capital. When Gálvez gave his opinion, he called the officers' plans too cautious, and he declared that the best defense for the city was to attack the English posts on the Mississippi.[13]

The governor followed through with preparations of his secret "defensive" plan for the capital. He charged War Commissary Juan Antonio Gayarré with the confidential arrangements for the operation against the English posts on the river. When Gálvez learned in August that war had been declared, he informed only a select few, among them Gayarré and the post commandants on the Mississippi. He told them that he had been appointed proprietary governor of Louisiana. By mid-August, Gálvez and Gayarré had the plans for the attack on Manchac ready, and they tentatively chose August 23 as the day to leave New Orleans. But five days before the date selected, one of the most destructive hurricanes of that epoch interrupted their plans. In three hours the storm sank all the boats readied for the expedition, except the frigate *Volante*. It devastated many of the city's residences and warehouses, the latter stocked with foodstuffs for the expedition. The hurricane ruined the harvest, killed some of the livestock, and caused great consternation among the populace. Nevertheless, the governor urged the inhabitants to continue the enterprise before the English, who had not suffered as much damage, attacked.[14]

Supported by the inhabitants, Gálvez proceeded with his defensive plans for the capital and stationed his troops along the most obvious invasion routes to prevent an attack from Manchac or Pensacola. To replace some of the sunken vessels, boats arrived from neighboring areas to transport the expedition. Gálvez also recovered four ships from the Mississippi. He loaded the boats with ten cannons and munitions. He placed Julián Alvarez in charge of the flotilla while he retained command of the land forces. Only a week after the hurricane Gálvez had the expedition ready. He gave Lieutenant Colonel Pedro Piernas interim military command of New Orleans and Martín Navarro, the army accountant and his friend, civil authority.[15]

Gálvez wanted to surprise the English in their posts before they knew about the state of war. Thus, on the morning of August 27, he gathered everyone he could enlist on the German and Acadian coasts. On the same afternoon, his small army of 667 men, including Oliver Pollock, agent for the American congress, and 7 of his compatriots, began their march. These troops moved bravely through thick forests and seemingly impassable routes, without tents or other indispensable equipment for a long journey. With the same enthusiasm men of all colors and castes followed him, including 160 Indians whom Gálvez recruited in Opelousas, Attakapas, and Pointe Coupée and on the Acadian Coast. He ably demonstrated his gift to command a diverse group of men.

The troops marched in a lively fashion but maintained their order. The regular soldiers formed a column, whose left flank was protected by the Mississippi and the armed boats that transported the artillery. Their right flank was a thick forest. To prevent a surprise attack, black soldiers and Indians formed a vanguard, a quarter league in front of the main body. The militia and the German settlers made up the rearguard. With the Spanish expedition underway, the English commandant at Fort Bute, Colonel Dickson, was still ignorant about the declaration of war, but he learned that Gálvez and his troops were approaching.[16]

On September 6, Manchac, situated fifty miles above New Orleans, was reached. Illnesses and fatigue had reduced the expedition by a third. When he neared the enemy fort, Gálvez informed his soldiers about the declaration of war and his orders to attack. The next morning at dawn, the militia assaulted Fort Bute by surprise, while the regular soldiers guarded a strategic position upriver to stop a possible attack by four hundred English troops. Two days before, they had been observed leaving the fort for Baton Rouge with artillery and foodstuffs. Gálvez's father-in-law, Gilberto Antonio de Saint-Maxent, captain for the white militia, entered Fort Bute first, through a gunport, followed by his men. The Spaniards forced the fort's surrender without losing a man. The captured garrison consisted of a captain, a lieutenant, a sublieutenant, and about twenty soldiers. Before the war, Saint-Maxent had been sent to Manchac, where he remained forty-two days, posing as "a Frenchman angry at Spain." He made a plan of the fort and discovered its weaknesses, which were the gunports. Gálvez appointed Antonio de Saint-Maxent, son of the captain, the new commandant of Fort Bute.[17]

THE SPANISH VICTORY ON THE LAKES

While preparing plans for the attack on the English forts on the Mississippi, Gálvez perceived the danger the English reinforcements from Mobile and Pensacola might cause. They would not come up the mouth of the Mississippi, which was well-guarded, but would cross Lakes Borgne, Pontchartrain, and Maurepas, and reach the Mississippi between New Orleans and Baton Rouge. To stop their reinforcements from reaching the river, he ordered his army and navy commandants to prevent any English attack.[18]

The Spaniards won their most important naval battle during the Louisiana campaign on the lakes. It was the work of a New Orleans creole, Vicente Rieux, who was not an army or navy officer. Gálvez had given him command of an armed brigantine to guard the lakes against English ships transporting troops to Forts Bute, New Richmond, and Panmure, which were sent by General John Campbell at Pensacola or Colonel Elias Durnford at Mobile. In early September, Rieux guarded the passage that connected Lakes Pontchartrain and Maurepas. Knowing that any English vessel coming from Pensacola would have to go through it, he ordered his men to disembark and set up their swivel guns. He fell trees to form a barricade and hid waiting for English ships. Soon, on September 7, one approached. When it was a half-shot away, Rieux opened fire and ordered his men to run about and shout loudly to make the enemy believe that they were five hundred. Frightened, the English sought shelter below deck. At that point Rieux leaped on board the vessel with his men and, after hand-to-hand combat with the few soldiers remaining on deck, took them prisoner. The English were greatly surprised that a mere fourteen men, all Louisiana creoles, had captured them. The prisoners included Captain Alberti, a lieutenant, sublieutenant, 54 grenadiers of the German Waldeck regiment, and a dozen sailors. Waldeck Lieutenant Nolde died in the combat. For his service, Rieux was promoted to the rank of militia lieutenant.[19]

Carlos de Grand-Pré heard about the action while he was posted at Roche-à-Davion, a strategic point on the Mississippi. He had a detachment of regular soldiers and militia to stop English communication on the river. Once he cut their passage to Natchez, he seized the nearby English posts on the Amite River and Thompson Creek (New Feliciana). As a reward, he received command of the Pointe Coupée district with a detachment of soldiers at each captured post.[20]

Meanwhile, Sublieutenant Francisco Collell, commandant of the nearby post of Gálveztown, ordered Sergeant Juan Bautista Mentzinger with eight men to guard the Amite River. They seized two boats returning to Pensacola after taking food and munitions to Fort Bute and loaded with two companies of Waldeck troops. José Pauly and his Spanish forces from Gálveztown captured Fort Graham, a nearby post on the Amite. Pauly's work earned him promotion to militia captain.[21]

While these operations on or near the Mississippi were occurring, on nearby Lake Pontchartrain Captain William Pickles, in the service of the American navy and on board the frigate *Morris* (formerly the *Rebecca*), searched for the English brigantine *West Florida*. It dominated the lakes, seizing Spanish and American boats. Gálvez financed the *Morris* because he wanted the *West Florida* destroyed.[22] In one of the few naval battles on the lakes during the war, on September 10, Captain Pickles spied the *West Florida* and demanded its surrender. English Lieutenant John Payne refused, and Pickles boarded the *West Florida* with his men. They killed four, including Payne, and took the others prisoners. It was an impressive battle because the *West Florida* had 2 cannons of six pounds, 2 of four pounds, 1 of one and one-half pounds, and a crew of thirty. The *Morris* had only 4 cannons of two and one-half pounds. The only American loss in the battle was, in the words of Captain Pickles, "Brown, a traitor to our cause, who jumped in the water and swam to shore."[23]

The Spaniards changed the name of the *West Florida* to *Gálveztown*, and it became the model for the famous brigantine on the insignia of Bernardo de Gálvez. Pickles later captured three schooners and a brigantine returning to Pensacola, two sloops coming from there loaded with foodstuffs, and another schooner with a similar cargo on the Mississippi. Pickles continued to serve the Spaniards on Lake Pontchartrain. On September 26, he took 122 Indians to New Orleans, and days later he captured a ship on the Mobile coast, with 13 slaves worth $2,665.[24]

THE CONQUEST OF BATON ROUGE AND NATCHEZ

Gálvez let his men rest five days in the newly conquered post of Manchac before beginning the fifteen-mile march to Baton Rouge. With the victories on the Amite River, Thompson Creek, and on the lakes, the Spaniards had cut any English hope of reinforcing Baton Rouge. Gálvez took five prisoners on his way to Baton Rouge and reached the outskirts with only two hundred men of the Louisiana Battalion. After the conquest of Manchac, Gálvez sent some officers to reconnoiter the fort at Baton Rouge. They confirmed that it would be difficult to assault because of its excellent fortifications. These consisted of a moat nine feet deep and eighteen feet across, a tall and steep stockade, thirteen heavy cannons, and a defensive force of more than four hundred regular soldiers, many of them Waldeckers and one hundred armed settlers. The governor knew that most of his troops were Louisiana natives, many of them married with families, whose deaths in battle would fill the province with mourning. He consequently ordered the entrenchment of the artillery to minimize casualties, despite the clamor of his men who wanted to assault the fort.

The site Gálvez seemingly selected to place the artillery was on the edge of a forest near the fort. It looked good for deception, and he used it to distract attention from the actual site where the Spaniards established themselves. He sent to the first location an Indian detachment and the white and black Louisiana militias. On the night of September 20, protected by a tree parapet, they made noise and feigned an attack. The English were diverted, the Spaniards who were hidden beyond a field set up their batteries within range of the fort. Only after the Spaniards were protected from gunfire did the English learn about the deception.

At dawn on the 21st, the Spanish shelling began, accurately directed by artillery officer Julián Alvarez. In three and a half hours, the bombardment dismantled the fort. The English had no choice but to send two officers to surrender, which Gálvez rejected unless the garrison was taken prisoner. He also demanded the surrender of Fort Panmure in Natchez. The English accepted the terms within twenty-four hours. After burying their dead, the garrison departed the fort with military honors to a distance of 500 steps. At that point, the 375 English soldiers surrendered their arms and flags and became prisoners of war.[25]

One of the Americans who accompanied Gálvez on the Mississippi campaign was Oliver Pollock. In a letter dated September 23 and written to the Americans in Natchez, he encouraged them to support the Spaniards because they were helping the American cause. He wrote: "I am happy to inform you that his most Catholic Majesty the King of Spain has declared the Independency of the United States of America, and war against our tyrannical enemy Great Britain . . . Col. Dickson has capitulated to Governor Gálvez, and surrendered his garrison as prisoners of war. He has obliged himself to withdraw the British forces from your quarters, and deliver up the Fort [Panmure in Natchez] to the Spanish officer who goes there for that purpose."[26]

After the surrender ceremony in Baton Rouge, Gálvez sent Captain Juan de la Villebeuvre with fifty soldiers to take Fort Panmure in Natchez. He went with English Captain Barber, who carried a letter from Colonel Dickson for Captain Anthony Forster, commandant of Fort Panmure. The English formally surrendered the fort on October 5. Besides Captain Forster, two lieutenants, three sergeants, two drummers, fifty-four soldiers, and thirteen women and children also gave up.[27]

A couple of days later, the Natchez garrison and loyalists were surprised by the news from Pensacola that war had been declared between Spain and Great Britain. General John Campbell in Pensacola was no doubt astonished to learn that Natchez had surrendered and its garrison was *hors de combat*, without having been able to begin the hoped for attack on New Orleans. The Spanish military had acted first and won the contest. The two English posts seized had more than five hundred men who were militia or free blacks, whom Gálvez freed because it was too difficult to guard them.[28]

In all, the Spaniards achieved great victories in their campaign on the Mississippi. They had seized three forts: Bute in Manchac by assault, New Richmond in Baton Rouge by bombardment, and Panmure by treaty. The Spaniards captured 550 regular soldiers, not counting sailors, armed inhabitants, Indians, and blacks, plus 21 officers, including Colonel Dickson, commander of the English establishments on the Mississippi. In these actions, the Spaniards suffered only two wounded men: Juan Hébert of the 2nd Company of the Iberville militia, whose widow continued to receive his pension when he died in 1798, and Maturino Landry of the Lafourche militia. According to British sources, English losses in the battles were 36 dead, 10 wounded, and 485 taken prisoner. These figures agree with Dickson's account in the *London Gazette*, which varied slightly from the Spanish version. This campaign was the first Spanish victory in the war, and it helped to clear the English from the Mississippi. They had sought to prevent Spanish assistance from reaching the Americans via the river.[29]

In his account to the court of the campaigns on the lower Mississippi in 1779, Gálvez demonstrated great pleasure in the zeal displayed by the Louisiana militia in all their engagements. He singled out the Acadian companies, in whom burned the memory of English cruelty in the Seven Years' War, which forced them to abandon their homes in Canada. He praised the companies of free blacks and mulattoes, who were always in the forefront showing their valor. He complimented the Indians who exhibited their humanity by their noble example of not harming the English settlers although they surrendered with arms. The behavior of the natives was due in large measure to the excellent manner in which Santiago Tarascón and lieutenant of the Opelousas company José Sorrel led them. Both men understood Indian languages and customs.[30]

Shortly after the victories on the Mississippi and despite releasing the captured blacks and armed settlers, the Spaniards still had more than five hundred prisoners in New Orleans and only fifty soldiers to guard them. In mid-October, the English garrison taken prisoner at Fort Panmure arrived in the city. But they came at the same time that the reinforcements sent by the Cuban captain general reached New Orleans. Gálvez gave the prisoners the freedom of the city. In return the English did not violate their liberty. Similarly, the Indian prisoners did not cause the slightest problem. All the English captives, including Colonel Dickson, commented on the good treatment they received in New Orleans.

Dickson admitted to Gálvez that the English had planned to attack New Orleans from Canada and Pensacola once war was declared. Because Captain General Navarro had been critical of the Louisiana governor's bold offensive plan, Gálvez happily informed him of the English plan to attack New Orleans from both the north and east.[31] Bonet, the commander of the Navy Department in Havana, congratulated the Louisiana governor for his victories and offered to help him conquer Mobile and Pensacola as quickly as possible. The English were having trouble sending assistance to those forts from Georgia because of the presence of the French naval squadron under Count Estaing in Savannah and Charleston. Nevertheless, according to Juan de Miralles, the Spanish agent in Philadelphia, the English in New York were dispatching reinforcements to Pensacola and St. Augustine. Miralles had instructions to encourage an American attack on St.

Augustine to distract English attention and facilitate the Spanish conquest of Mobile and Pensacola.[32]

For his victories above New Orleans, Brigadier Bernardo de Gálvez was promoted to the rank of field marshal by King Carlos III.[33] From his headquarters at Morristown, General George Washington congratulated Miralles for the Spanish conquests on the Mississippi.[34] The king of France, Louis XVI, also complimented Carlos III for his success and informed him that soon Count Estaing would arrive in Madrid to discuss future operations with the minister of the Indies.[35]

Bernardo de Gálvez must be recognized not only for his undeniable brillance in directing the campaign on the lower Mississippi but even more for his vision in carrying it out, despite the timidity of his advisers and uncooperative weather. The black and mulatto militia served with distinction and received silver medals as rewards. Above all, Gálvez inspired his soldiers, the white and black militias, and the armed inhabitants to strike first instead of waiting in New Orleans to be attacked.[36]

The consequence of the Mississippi campaign not only prevented an English attack on New Orleans, but assured Spanish retention of this region of the lower Mississippi. It relieved English pressure from Canada on Spanish establishments in Missouri such as St. Louis in the Upper Mississippi Valley and allowed help to be sent to the Americans. After the victories on the river and lakes, the governor began preparations for an expedition against Mobile. But he found time to write to Uncle José informing him of the success of the Mississippi campaign. He attached to his letter the diary he kept during the expedition to present to the king. Gálvez entrusted the diary and letter to his brother-in-law, militia lieutenant Maximiliano de Saint-Maxent. On the voyage to Spain, the English seized Saint-Maxent's ship. He threw overboard the valuable documents in his care before he became a prisoner. However, there was a copy of the diary and letter.[37]

Gálvez sent the copies to the court with José Vallière, who sailed from Havana on November 15, 1779, on board the mail frigate *Cortés.* He also took several flags captured at the English forts on the Mississippi. The frigate arrived at El Ferrol on December 21. Vallière quickly journeyed to Madrid. On arriving at court, Gálvez's diary was published in abbreviated form in the *Gaceta de Madrid* on December 31, but it contained some errors. The corrected diary with the governor's letter to his uncle of October 14, were published in the *Gaceta de Madrid*, on Friday, January 14, 1780. They informed the Spanish people of the great victory achieved in Louisiana by the new army field marshal.[38]

Notes for "Victory on the Mississippi, 1779"

[1]Bernardo de Gálvez to Diego Paniagua, Madrid, July 6, 1776, Archivo Histórico de Protocolos de Madrid, protocol 17640. [Editor's Note: Gálvez probably left a will in his care should he die.]

[2]John Walton Caughey, *Bernardo de Gálvez in Louisiana, 1776-1783* (Berkeley, 1934), 149, in which he cited José de Gálvez to Bernardo de Gálvez, Aranjuez, May 18, 1779, Archivo General de Indias, Papeles procedentes de Cuba, legajo (cited hereafter as AGI, PC), leg. 569; royal order, Aranjuez, May 18, 1799, AGI, Audiencia de Santo Domingo (cited hereafter as SD), leg. 2082; Navarro to Bernardo de Gálvez, Havana, July 28, 1779, AGI, PC, leg. 112.

[3]Bernardo de Gálvez to Carlos de Grand-Pré, New Orleans, June 14, 1779, AGI, PC, leg. 1.

[4]Raimundo Dubreuil to Bernardo de Gálvez, Manchac, July 5, 1779, AGI, PC, leg. 112. [Editor's Note: The Spaniards had a small fort across Bayou Manchac. Its chief purpose was to watch the English. Governor Antonio de Ulloa had established it.]

[5]Navarro to Bernardo de Gálvez, Havana, August 11, 1779, AGI, SD, leg. 1229.

[6]Bonet to José de Gálvez, Havana, August 12, 1779, AGI, SD, leg. 2081.

[7]Bernardo de Gálvez to Grand-Pré, New Orleans, August 16, 1779, Dubreuil to Bernardo de Gálvez, Manchac, August 22, 1779, both in AGI, PC, leg. 112.

[8]Reparaz, *"Yo Solo," Bernardo de Gálvez y la toma de Pensacola en 1781* (Barcelona, 1986), 35-36; José de Gálvez to Navarro, San Ildefonso, August 29, 1779, AGI, PC, leg. 1290.

[9]Juan de Miralles to José de Gálvez, Philadelphia, September 24, 1779, AGI, SD, leg. 2598; Samuel Huntington, Philadelphia, September 28, 1779, Archivo General de Simancas, Estado (cited hereafter as AGS, Est.), leg. 172; "Congressional Credential to John Jay as minister plenipotentiary in Spain," Philadelphia, September 29, 1779, Archivo Histórico Nacional (cited hereafter as AHN), Est., leg. 3885.

[10]Bernardo de Gálvez to José de Gálvez, New Orleans, July 3, 1779, AGI, SD, leg. 2543.

[11]Elias Durnford to William Horn, Mobile, July 3, 1779, AGI, SD, leg. 2082; Bernardo de Gálvez to Navarro, New Orleans, October 16, 1779, AGI, PC, leg. 2351, cited in Caughey, *Gálvez*, 149-50.

[12]Eric Beerman, intro., *"Yo Solo": The Battle Journal of Bernardo de Gálvez during the American Revolution*, trans. E. A. Montemayor (New Orleans, 1978), xiii.

[13]Council of war, New Orleans, July 13, 1779, AGI, PC, leg. 112.

[14]Bernardo de Gálvez to Grand-Pré, New Orleans, August 21, 1779, AGI, PC, leg. 1; *Gaceta de Madrid*, December 31, 1779; "Campaña de Luisiana. . . Bernardo de Gálvez," Servicio Histórico Militar, Sección de Conde de Clonard, 31; "Noticia . . . Luisiana D. Bernardo de Gálvez," Biblioteca Nacional, Sección de Manuscritos, ms. 19249.

[15]C. Fernández-Shaw, *Presencia española en los Estados Unidos* (Madrid, 1972), 332-33.

[16]Dickson to Bernardo de Gálvez, Manchac, August 30, 1780, AGI, PC, leg. 2358.

[17]"Campaña de Luisiana"; Real Cédula de Indios to Gilberto Antonio de St. Maxent, San Lorenzo, October 30, 1781, AHN, Est., leg. 2858; "Inventario. . . del fuerte Bute," Manchac, September 8, 1779, AGI, SD, leg. 2572; service sheet of Antonio St. Maxent, AGS, Secretaría de Guerra (cited hereafter as SG), leg. 7291; Margaret Fisher Dalrymple, ed., *The Merchant of Manchac: The Letterbooks of John Fitzpatrick, 1768-90* (Baton Rouge, 1978), 355.

[18]"Relación que doy yo d. Basilio Jiménez," Baton Rouge, September 22, 1779, AHN, Est., leg. 3901.

[19]*Gaceta de Madrid*, January 14, 1780; Francisco Collell to Bernardo de Gálvez, Galveztown, September 7, 1779, AGI, PC, leg. 192; M. Eelking, *German Mercenaries in Pensacola during the American Revolution, 1779-1781*, trans. L. Krupp, 14-15; José de Gálvez to Rieux, El Pardo, January 12, 1780, AGS, SG, leg. 6912.

[20]Bernardo de Gálvez to José de Gálvez, New Orleans, October 16, 1779, AGS, SG, leg. 6912; *Gaceta de Madrid*, December 31, 1779.

[21]*Gaceta de Madrid*, December 31, 1779; Collell to Bernardo de Gálvez, Galveztown, September 3, 7, and 10, 1779, AGI, PC, leg. 192; service sheets of Collell and Pauly, both in AGI, PC, leg. 161A; Jack D. L. Holmes, *The 1779 "Marcha de Gálvez": Louisiana's Giant Step Forward in the American Revolution* (Baton Rouge, 1974), 16.

[22]Oliver Pollock to José de Gálvez, New Orleans, June 16, 1778, AGI, SD, leg. 2596; José de Gálvez to Bernardo de Gálvez, San Ildefonso, October 3, 1779, AGS, SG, leg. 6912. The *Rebecca* was seized by the American adventurer James Willing at Manchac in 1778. Pollock signed two receipts in New Orleans for 15,948 pesos in the name of Bernardo de Gálvez to refit the frigate. Pollock receipts of August 5 and September 12, 1778, AGI, SD, leg. 2598.

[23]*Gaceta de Madrid*, December 31, 1779; Pickles to Pedro Piernas, Lake Pontchartrain, September 12, 1779, AGI, PC, leg. 192.

[24]Bernardo de Gálvez to José de Gálvez, New Orleans, October 16, 1779, AGS, SG, leg. 6912; Pickles, "Seizure made by the Corsair *Morris*, October 8, 1779," AGI, PC, leg. 701.

[25]"Artículos de capitulación entre Bernardo de Gálvez, Alejandro Dickson, sobre el Misisipí," Baton Rouge, September 21, 1779, AGI, PC, leg. 83; Eric Beerman, "Bernardo de Gálvez and the 1779 Battle of Baton Rouge," *Sons of the American Revolution*, 75 (1980): 32-33.

[26]Caughey, *Gálvez*, 157-58; Pollock to the Natchez inhabitants, September 23, 1779, AGI, PC, leg. 192.

[27]Dickson to Forster, Baton Rouge, September 21, 1779, and "Artículos de capitulación del fuerte Nueva Richmond de Baton Rouge," September 21, 1779, both in AGI, PC, leg. 2351; Edward Byrne, Natchez, October 6, 1779, AGI, PC, leg. 192.

[28]Campbell to Forster, Pensacola, October 9, 1779, AGI, PC, leg. 192.

[29]*Gaceta de Madrid*, January 14, 1780; Bernardo de Gálvez to José de Gálvez, New Orleans, October 16, 1779, AGS, SG, leg. 6912; *London Gazette*, March 28-April 1, 1780.

[30]Gaceta de Madrid, January 14, 1780; José de Gálvez to [the king], El Pardo, January 12, 1780, AGS, SG, leg. 6912.

[31]Bernardo de Gálvez to Navarro, New Orleans, October 16, 1779, AGI, PC, leg. 2351.

[32]Bonet to Bernardo de Gálvez, Havana, November 12, 1779, AGI, SD, leg. 2543; Bonet to José de Gálvez, Havana, November 15, 1779, AGI, SD, leg. 2081; Juan Miralles to José de Gálvez, Philadelphia, November 13 and 24, 1779, AGI, SD, leg. 2598.

[33]José de Gálvez to Bernardo de Gálvez, El Pardo, January 10, 1780, AGS, SG, leg. 6912.

[34]Washington to Miralles, Morristown, February 28, 1780, AGI, SD, leg. 2598.

[35]Louis XVI to Carlos III, Versalles, July 6, 1780, AGS, Est., Libro 168.

[36]Royal file, El Pardo, February 6, 1780, AGS, SG, leg. 6912.

[37]Royal file, Aranjuez, April 30, 1780, ibid.

[38]*Gaceta de Madrid*, January 14, 1780; Holmes, Marcha de Gálvez, 19. José Vallière was born in France. His service sheet is in AGS, SG, leg. 7292, X, 20.

THE SPANISH CONQUEST OF BRITISH WEST FLORIDA, 1779-1781*

Albert W. Haarmann[1]

The news of the fall of British posts on the Mississippi reached Mobile in October. This intelligence was passed on to Pensacola, but the commander there, General John Campbell, did not believe the report and considered it a Spanish ruse to draw him out in the open. Later the same month, another report reached Pensacola, but once again the general refused to believe the report. After issuing several conflicting orders, he decided to strengthen his position at Pensacola while it was further decided that Mobile would have to make do with what it had.[2] With his base now secure, Bernardo de Gálvez was free to direct his attention towards Mobile and Pensacola.

Gálvez encountered considerable opposition from the authorities in Havana on the method of conducting the forthcoming campaign. The captain general of Cuba wanted a primarily naval campaign against Pensacola, whereas Gálvez favored the taking of Mobile first, both to deny Pensacola a source of supply and to control the Indians in that district. Gálvez was confronted with other problems too; he needed more troops, artillery, supplies, and ships. Havana refused to give him what he wanted.[3] Despite the lack of support, Gálvez decided to proceed with an attack upon Mobile.

Mobile was situated at the head of a large bay, approximately thirty miles long and six miles wide. The spacious harbor was considered a very good anchorage, although the Royal Navy never did take advantage of it. The town was located on the west bank of the Mobile River, extending nearly a half mile back on a plain above the river and almost a mile along its bank. Fort Charlotte stood near the bay at the lower end of town.[4]

The fort was a square, solid masonry structure with four bastions and embrasures for thirty-eight guns. From bastion to bastion it measured 300 feet. Within the fort were barracks, a powder magazine, a bakery, and several wells. The fort had been built by the French about 1717 of locally made brick and oyster-shell lime and was known as Fort

*First published in the *Florida Historical Quarterly*, 39 (1960): 114-34. Reprinted here with the kind permission of the publisher.

Louis de la Mobile. When their troops took over the post in 1763 upon the completion of the Seven Years' War, the British renamed it Fort Charlotte in honor of the queen of the young king of England. It had fallen into disrepair by 1779 but necessary repairs were ordered when hostilities became apparent.[5]

The garrison at Mobile numbered more than 300 men. It was a mixed force drawn from the 4th Battalion of the 60th Regiment, the Royal Artillery, engineers, small detachments from the Pennsylvania and Maryland Loyalists, volunteers from amongst the local inhabitants, and artificers. A number of African Americans were employed as servants and in other tasks.[6]

Captain Elias Durnford, a British army engineer and a veteran of the Seven Years' War, was in command at Mobile. He had distinguished himself during the siege of Havana. In 1763 he had been appointed commanding engineer and surveyor general for the newly created province of West Florida. For a time he had served as lieutenant governor of the province.[7]

The expedition against Mobile did not begin auspiciously. Gálvez sailed on January 28, 1780, with a force of 745 men, regulars from the Regiments of the Prince, Havana, and Louisiana, the Royal Artillery Corps, and militiamen, whites, free blacks, and mulattoes.[8] While at sea the eleven-ship squadron was struck by a storm that separated the ships. By February 10 the expeditionary force had reassembled and lay off the entrance to Mobile Bay. Strong winds and a heavy sea made Gálvez determined to enter the bay at once. Six vessels ran aground during the attempt but three were soon afloat. The continuing bad weather hindered the landing of troops and supplies and their efforts to refloat the other three vessels. Men and supplies were unloaded from the grounded vessels and two smaller craft were floated again. The remaining ship, a frigate, was hard aground and was later abandoned. The ravages of the sea took a toll of supplies and ammunition; they had been lost or ruined during the storm, the grounding of the vessels, and the transfer of the cargo ashore.

Everything ashore was in a state of confusion. The landings were made in such disorder that Gálvez considered abandoning his artillery and baggage and retreating overland; however, he soon learned that he was not expected so he decided to press the siege of Mobile.

An emissary previously sent to Havana meanwhile had convinced the authorities in that quarter that Gálvez needed reinforcements. They finally relented and sent 567 men of the Regiment of Navarra. This force set out in several transports on the tenth of February and reached Mobile on the 20th, where they entered the bay and landed their troops without incident.

The appearance of the Spanish expeditionary force created considerable confusion in Mobile, and Gálvez was able to assemble and reorganize his forces without interference from the British. Despite the losses suffered on account of the weather, Gálvez was able to report excellent morale amongst his troops.

The last days of February were spent in final preparations for the siege and ferrying troops to a point closer to Mobile. On the 28th the troops crossed the Dog River and established a camp. The Spanish had their first encounter with the English on the 29th when a scouting party of four companies was fired upon from the fort.[9]

On the following day the Spanish general, aware of his superior forces, summoned Durnford to surrender. The British commander declined, stating that his forces were larger than Gálvez imagined, and that his love of king and country and of his own honor directed him to refuse any offer of surrender until he was convinced that resistance was futile. Gifts were exchanged and proper concern was expressed for prisoners in Spanish hands. With this observance of the amenities of formal eighteenth-century warfare, the adversaries got down to the business at hand.[10]

Durnford sent a dispatch to his superior in Pensacola on March 2, giving a full report of his situation. He related that as soon as the Spanish flag left the fort, he drew his troops up in the square and read Gálvez's summons to them. The men were told if any were afraid to stand by him, that he would open the gates and let that man pass from the fort. "This had the desired effect, and not a man moved. I then read to them my answer to the summons, in which they all joined in three cheers and then went to our necessary work like good men."[11]

On the fifth and sixth there were further exchanges of letters. This time the topic was the burning of the town. Many houses had been set afire by the English to deny shelter to their besiegers. Gálvez in turn had offered not to set up his batteries behind any house if Durnford would stay his incendiarism. The English commander declined, stating that he must do everything in his power to defend his post, and if it included burning houses, he would do so. That ended the affair.[12]

Meanwhile Durnford had received word from Campbell concerning a relief column from Pensacola. He welcomed the news and promised to defend the fort to the last.[13]

While the exchange of letters had been going on between Gálvez and Durnford, the Spanish were making further preparations for the siege, and the troops worked with a will. They hauled cannon and prepared fascines and other material for the attack. By March 9 they were ready to open their trench.

The trench was opened on the night of the ninth by a work party of 300 men protected by 200 armed men. Gálvez made a speech to raise their morale and the work went well all night. At dawn English fire forced the Spanish to stop their work after they had suffered six killed and five wounded. Bad weather interrupted the work for a day, but by the morning of the 12th the Spanish had a battery of eight 18-pounders and one of 24 in position.[14]

Scouting parties returned to the Spanish camp on the 11th and reported sighting two English camps near Tensa.[15] This was the relief column that Campbell had promised Durnford.

On March 5 the 60th Foot from the Pensacola garrison set out on the 72-mile march to Mobile. The next day the remainder of the Waldeckers marched out. Campbell himself followed with the Pennsylvania Loyalists and artillery. All told, the column numbered 522 men. The relief column marched through a wilderness devoid of a single human dwelling. Campbell's force reached Tensa, a point about thirty miles above Mobile on the eastern channel of the Mobile River, on the tenth, but lost valuable time building rafts to transport the men and their equipment downstream.[16]

As soon as the Spanish finished their battery, they opened fire upon Fort Charlotte. The English replied, and a vigorous exchange ensued. Spanish guns were played upon the walls of the fort and managed to make breeches in two places. Whenever one of the fort's guns was dismounted, another soon took its place; true to the tradition of their corps, the Royal Artillerymen served their pieces until all shot was expended. At sundown the English raised the white flag and asked for terms.[17]

Fort Charlotte was surrendered on March 14. Captain Durnford capitulated on much the same terms that Gálvez granted Dickson at Baton Rouge. The small garrison marched out with colors flying and drums beating. Once outside the fort, the men grounded their arms but the officers were permitted to retain their swords.[18]

Accounts differ, but one, perhaps final, Spanish report listed 13 officers, 113 soldiers, 56 sailors, 70 militiamen, and 55 armed Negroes in the surrendered garrison.[19] The booty included 35 cannon and 8 mortars.[20] During the siege the garrison had only one man killed outright and eleven wounded, two of whom subsequently died. The bombardment of the fort was decisive, but hunger and the lack of reinforcements from Pensacola were important factors.

Gálvez kept the relief column at Tensa under observation. On the 17th Spanish scouting parties brought news that Campbell was returning to Pensacola. Waldecker accounts of the return journey describe it as a trying march. It rained continuously and the route of march was a quagmire. Swollen streams could only be crossed single file by using fallen trees, and men who fell into the water were lost. The bedraggled column reached Pensacola on the 19th.[21]

With the surrender of the fort and the return to Pensacola of the unsuccessful relief column, active campaigning for 1780 came to a close.

Now that Mobile was captured, Gálvez turned his attention to the operations against Pensacola. His force included almost as many troops as Campbell had in his regular garrison, although the British commander had numerous Indian allies. Gálvez had hoped for further reinforcements from Havana but wavering officials there ruined any hopes for immediate action. A fruitless exchange of correspondence ensued and Gálvez failed to wring any further assistance from Havana. Finally a garrison was left at Mobile under the command of Colonel Josef de Ezpeleta while the greater part of the troops returned to either New Orleans or Havana. Gálvez went to Havana to plead for men and supplies.

In recognition for his services to the Crown, Gálvez was made field marshal in command of Spanish operations in America and granted the augmented title of Governor of Louisiana and Mobile. These were well deserved honors. In the face of all sorts of odds—lack of support from Cuba, the elements, the near-disastrous landings, and the threat of a British relief column from Pensacola—he did well. Once established ashore, he managed the operation with alacrity and chivalry. Gálvez maintained the morale of his troops and conducted the siege in a commendable manner.

In January, 1781, General Campbell decided to attack Mobile. On the third he sent Colonel Von Hanxleden of the Waldeck Regiment with 60 men of his own corps, 100 men of the 60th Regiment, provincials of the Pennsylvania and Maryland Loyalists, a few militia calvarymen, and about 300 Indians to conduct the attack.

The German colonel was ordered to take an outpost on the east shore of Mobile Bay known as the Village or Frenchtown. He was to delay the attack until the seventh when a pair of frigates would be on station in the bay to cooperate with him and cut communications with Mobile. This outpost was held by 150 men commanded by Lieutenant Ramón del Castro of the Regiment of the Prince.

A bayonet attack at dawn had actually penetrated the Spanish works before they recovered and repulsed the attackers in some bitter hand to hand fighting. When their commander fell, the assaulting party gave up the attack and subsequently returned to Pensacola. Besides their commander, the attackers had 2 officers and 13 men killed and 3 officers and 19 men wounded. The gallant defenders suffered almost equal losses, 14 were killed and 23 wounded.

The failure to carry the post has been variously placed on the Waldeckers and the Indians. In view of their known casualties and comparatively small numbers, the onus for the failure probably cannot be placed upon the Germans. The Indians, with their decisive strength and known lack of propensity for attacking fixed fortifications, undoubtedly must be considered the responsible party.[22]

In August, 1780, Gálvez went to Havana to see to the arrangements for the campaign against Pensacola. When he sailed on October 16, he headed an expedition that included 4,000 troops and a fleet of 64 warships and transports. Once again nature intervened. While at sea, the fleet was struck and dispersed by a hurricane. Gálvez was forced to return to Havana, arriving there on November 17, where he learned that the ships had been scattered to ports about the Gulf of Mexico and at least one vessel had been lost at sea.[23]

Undaunted by this reverse, Gálvez made preparations for another expedition. Once again he encountered delays as the officials in Havana dragged their feet. Meanwhile, at his insistence, 500 men were sent to reinforce Mobile on December 6. The commander of the small convoy transporting these troops later reported that his ships could not negotiate the channel at Mobile, so he sailed to Balize on the Mississippi, where the troops were landed. He then returned to Havana. However, just a few days after the unsuccessful attempt upon the channel at Mobile, two English frigates penetrated the bay and played their part in the unsuccessful attack of January 7.[24]

As preparations were being pushed for the forthcoming expedition, other commanders received instructions. Word was sent to Louisiana for the troops there to embark and join Gálvez' squadron. The troops at Mobile were ordered to march by an overland route.[25]

About 1,300 troops were embarked aboard the ships and the squadron set sail again on February 28, 1781. At sea Gálvez informed his commanders that once they arrived off Pensacola he planned to land on Santa Rosa Island and secure the east side of the passage into the bay in order that the fleet could enter the harbor without the risk of a crossfire. Once in the harbor, he planned to await reinforcements from Louisiana and Mobile.[26]

The Bay of Pensacola angled to the northeast and was shielded by Santa Rosa Island, a sandspit of an island on a east-west axis. About nine miles up the bay, on the north shore, lay the town proper. At this time Pensacola was a town of about 200 frame houses. The town occupied about a mile of bay shore and was approximately a quarter of a mile in depth. Its east and west boundaries were set by curving arroyos. In the center of the town was a large plaza, largely occupied by a stockade with several batteries on the waterfront. About 1,200 yards north of the plaza rose Gage Hill. The hill was 300 yards in width and extended to the northwest. On the southeast end of the hill the British had erected Fort George with its outworks in a position that dominated the town. The hill continued to slope upward, about 22 feet in 900 yards. This point was too far away to protect the town but it did overlook the work of the fort. To protect the fort, the British erected two redoubts. The most advanced, known as the Queen's, was a circular battery with wings, built on the high ground some 900 yards from Fort George. About 300 yards below this work was the second redoubt, known as the Prince of Wales'. This redoubt was oblate in shape and served principally to protect communications between the fort and the advanced redoubt.

At the entrance to the bay, opposite Santa Rosa Island, on the heights overlooking the passage into the harbor, was the Red Cliffs Fort, also known as Barrancas Coloradas by the Spanish. This fort mounted eleven guns, five of which were 32-pounders, and was garrisoned by approximately 140 officers and men. About a mile to the east and near the water level, was a blockhouse at a place known as Tartar Point, which the Spanish called Aguero. Opposite these works lay Point Sigüenza, the western tip of Santa Rosa Island. This point had been fortified at one time but when the Spanish arrived, all they found were a few dismounted guns and a burnt stockade.[27]

A British army return of March 15, 1781, gave the strength of their forces in West Florida as 750 fit for duty with a total of 1,193 effectives.[28] This force was almost exclusively in the garrison at Pensacola. The troops were from the 16th and 60th Regiments, the Maryland Loyalists and the Pennsylvania Loyalists, both Provincial units, and the Waldeck Regiment. Despite the mixed background of the defenders, they were fairly well trained and experienced soldiers. To these must be added the sailors from Royal Navy vessels in the harbor and Indians who later joined the besieged garrison.[29]

On March 9, 1781, the fleet arrived off Santa Rosa and made immediate preparations to land. A force of grenadiers and light infantry under the command of Colonel Francisco Longoria was put ashore that evening. Soon after they landed, the troops started marching to the west to secure the works at Point Sigüenza. Marching all that night, they reached their destination early the next morning. Instead of encountering the defended works they expected, all they found was a demolished work and three dismounted cannon. Shortly after their arrival the light infantry captured some men from the British frigate *Port Royal* who had come ashore to take off some cattle. The Spanish were soon sighted and the fort at Red Cliffs and two English frigates opened fire upon them but with little effect. To protect his squadron and make the English ships keep their distance, Gálvez selected a site and ordered the construction of a battery. During the afternoon an English schooner entered the harbor, bearing booty, including Gálvez' dinner service, taken from a Spanish vessel. The captured foodstuffs provided some welcome supplies for the Pensacola garrison.[30]

The Spanish started to work on their battery early on the 11th and in the afternoon they were able to open fire upon the frigates *Mentor* and *Port Royal*, forcing them to change station. Meanwhile the entrance to the harbor had been sounded and the squadron attempted to enter the port. When the largest Spanish ship touched bottom, the whole squadron came about and returned to their former anchorage. During the evening the weather turned.[31]

On the following day the weather was still bad and Gálvez became concerned for the safety of the ships and the ultimate success of the operation. As he did not have command of the Spanish naval vessels, he tried to convince the naval commander that if the ship of the line *San Ramon*, a 64, could not enter the bay, at least the smaller ships should try to enter the port where they would be protected in the event of another storm. The naval commander complained about the lack of information on the depth of the water, the channel, and the lack of pilots. He was also worried about the possibility of cannon fire from the Red Cliffs raking his ships. Realizing that the naval commander was reluctant to act, and being without any authority over the naval forces, Gálvez finally decided to act on his own. On the 14th he ordered one of his vessels from Louisiana, the brig *Gálveztown*, to sound the passage into the harbor that night.[32]

A sloop from Mobile joined the squadron on the morning of the 16th and informed them that Colonel Ezpeleta would march to the shores of the Perdido River with 900 men. A request was made for boats to make the crossing. The squadron commander ordered the provisioning of small boats and sent a small armed vessel to cover the crossing.[33]

Tired of waiting and armed with information from the sounding of the passage into the harbor, Gálvez decided to enter the bay with the *Gálveztown* and three row galleys, vessels that were under his control. He still entertained fears that a storm might disperse or wreck the fleet. He hoisted a broad pennant on his flagship and led the four-ship flotilla into the harbor under heavy fire from the guns atop Barrancas Coloradas. The vessels suffered some damage to their rigging but no personnel casualties. Men aboard the remaining ships in the squadron cheered his successful entrance into the harbor.[34]

On the following day, the 19th, fired by Gálvez' example, the rest of the fleet was determined to enter the harbor that day. Early that afternoon the ships set sail and within an hour they were safely over the bar and inside the harbor. Despite another heavy cannonade from the guns of the Red Cliffs Fort, the ships suffered only superficial damage and no personnel losses. During the squadron's entrance into the bay, Gálvez sailed about in a gig, offering assistance, and incidentally setting a fine example, to any vessel that might require it.[35]

With his fleet in a protected anchorage, Gálvez could now act with more certainty. He entered into an exchange of correspondence with General Campbell concerning the destruction of property and the lines along which the siege would be fought. Although the garrison commander rejected Gálvez' proposals, he was willing to negotiate for the safety of the town and the noncombatants. During this exchange the blockhouse at Tartar Point and some buildings at the Cliffs were set afire by troops as they withdrew to the Red Cliffs Fort. This, plus reports of ill-treatment of Spanish prisoners by the English, angered Gálvez and he broke off negotiations with Campbell's envoy.

At mid-morning of the 22nd, the force that had marched overland from Mobile was sighted along the opposite shore inside the harbor. Gálvez immediately crossed the bay with 500 men to reinforce Ezpeleta's column and permit them to rest. Meanwhile, other troops prepared for a crossing of the bay.[36]

On the 23rd a convoy of 16 ships arrived from New Orleans.[37] The ships had sailed on February 28 and had on board 1,400 troops, including contingents of regulars from the Regiments of Navarra, the King, Soria, Louisiana, and other regiments of the line, over 100 dragoons, and militia, both white and black, plus cannon, ammunition, and other supplies.[38] Within the town of Pensacola, where the reinforcements had been sighted, orders were given to men of the 16th and 60th Regiments to take up stations in the redoubts above Fort George.[39] The Spanish, meanwhile, were making a reconnaissance of the harbor area to select a suitable campsite close to town.

The Spanish commander realized that a direct assault upon Pensacola's defenses would only result in prohibitive casualties. A siege, therefore, was his only recourse. First he had to select a suitable campsite, then open trenches and approaches, and finally emplace his artillery in positions to batter the British works and bring about the reduction of the fortifications.

With the exception of 200 men left in garrison on Santa Rosa, all Spanish troops were ferried across the bay on the 24th and moved into the first of several camps. Although the new sites provided the Spanish with a better base for their operations, they were immediately exposed to attacks, especially those harassing raids that favored Indian open order tactics. During the last week in March and throughout April, the Indians carried the attack to the Spanish, keeping them on a constant alert and hindering their preparations for the siege. Spanish outposts and stragglers were attacked both day and night. These were usually small scale hit-and-run raids, although on several occasions the Indians were out in strength and were supported by a few fieldpieces and a company or two from the garrison. Many of the Spanish casualties during this period were due to these Indian raids. In his journal, Major Farmar makes frequent references to Indians returning from a foray with their grisly trophies.[40]

The Indians were from the southeastern tribes; Choctaws, Creeks, and Chickasaws, usually led by white men or half-breeds.[41] Perhaps the most noted of the Indian chieftains was the Creek, Alexander McGillivray. He had tremendous influence among the Creeks and was a staunch friend of the English. Later he was wooed by Spain, successfully, and by the United States, rather unsuccessfully.[42]

It was during this period of skirmishing that the Spanish commander himself was wounded. On the tenth the Quartermaster had been sent out to select a new campsite in the hills northwest of Pensacola. Two days later the Spanish moved to the new site and started to entrench their camp. Guns were set up covering avenues of approach and work on a redoubt was started to cover the ground about the camp. At first the English did nothing, but late in the day parties of Indians and a small number of the garrison came out to skirmish with the Spanish. Light infantry was sent out to oppose these parties, but they had orders not to enter the woods where the Indian had the advantage. While the Spanish stood their ground and fired their volleys, it was with little effect. Realizing that nothing could be accomplished with this manner of fighting, Gálvez ordered his light infantry to retire to the protection of the nearest battery. Gunners were given orders to fire grape at any party of the enemy that approached too closely to the Spanish works. Not long after he gave this order, the Spanish commander was advised that several parties of the enemy with two small cannon were advancing from different points. He went out to one of the advanced batteries to survey the situation. While at the battery, he was struck by a bullet in the left hand which went on to furrow his abdomen. Although he was obliged to retire to his quarters and undergo treatment, he was at the active head of his army within ten days. During his recuperation, Ezpeleta commanded the troops.[43]

At the end of March two events occurred that soon galvanized the Havana authorities into action. First, the *San Ramon*, the most powerful ship on the Pensacola expedition, returned to Havana on the 29th, and her captain was under a cloud for his failure to enter Pensacola Bay and return there. Then, on April 7, it was reported that a strong nine-ship English squadron had been sighted on March 31. This latest bit of information caused the captain general to call a council of war. It was decided to send all available warships under the orders of Chief of Squadron Josef Solano and reinforcement of 1,600 troops commanded by Field Marshal Juan Manuel de Cagigal. With surprising haste the troops were embarked and the artillery, munitions, and other stores were loaded aboard more than a score of vessels.[44]

Although it had been decided at the council of war that a French squadron then at Havana would not accompany the Pensacola relief expedition, a later conference of the French captains decided in favor of joining their Spanish allies. The French squadron was commanded by M. de Montelle and included four ships of the line and four frigates. On board were 800 troops of the Agenois Regiment.[45]

The ships sailed from Havana on April 9[46] and arrived off Pensacola on the 19th.[47] While at sea the Spanish crews were canvassed to find out how many men from the fleet could be used ashore. The Spanish admiral was most cooperative. It was found that at least 1,400 men could be withdrawn from the vessels to assist in the operations ashore.[48]

The squadron from Havana was cautious in its approach to Pensacola until it was learned that Gálvez controlled the port. Representatives from the newly arrived squadron met with him and offered to serve under his command. Arrangements were soon made to put the men ashore.

Perhaps the words of a member of the expedition can best sum up the reaction of Gálvez' command:

> General Gálvez received us with many expressions of pleasure and friendship toward our General Cagigal. All the army welcomed us with infinite joy, for not only were they fatigued with the endless and not well-combined marches they had made in the 42 days since they had disembarked at the island of Santa Rosa, but by the various camps which they occupied, the entrenchments and so forth (seven counting this one), the construction or revetments, fascines, and other defenses. Besides this they considered all their work useless, and were in despair of the enterprise. The army numbered, including militia and Negroes, 3,701 men. Of these 500 were out of action, and so they were able to count on only 2,000 regulars for the attack. The garrison numbered 800 regular troops, 200 seamen, and 1,000 savage Indians for the woods. Thus their conjecture was not unfounded. With the consolidation of our detachment, 1,504 troops of our navy, and 725 French, the army amounted to 7,803 effectives.[49]

The reinforced Spanish army, and their French allies, set themselves to two tasks, reconnaissance and reorganization. Gálvez and his staff reconnoitred the high ground about the Queen's Redoubt and the other defenses of Pensacola. The besieging army was reorganized into four brigades, to be commanded by Brigadier Gerónimo Girón, Colonel Manuel Pineda, Colonel Francisco Longoria, and Captain of Ship Felipe López Carrizosa, respectively. Captain of Ship M. de Boiderout commanded the French contingent.[50]

The last week in April saw the beginning of the more formal aspects of the siege. Engineers and artillerists selected sites for the trenches and batteries. Quite often these parties were fired upon by the cannon of the fort or harassed by parties of Indians and troops from the garrison. After several attempts to open the trenches had been frustrated, they were finally started on the night of the 28th.

Once the work began, it went forward with a will. Working parties numbered over 600 men and were supported by 800 men at arms. It was necessary to relieve these details under the cover of darkness as they were exposed to a heavy cannonade from the British artillery during the hours of daylight. As the work progressed, small batteries of four and eight pounders were set up to protect the working parties. Until the Spanish could mount heavier artillery, they had to endure the fire from the well-served artillery of the garrison.[51]

Despite the heavy English fire, the Spanish were able to emplace a battery of six 24-pounders and a few mortars on the night of May first.[52] Early the next morning the

British resumed their bombardment of the lines. At nine o'clock the Spanish unfurled flags over their batteries and began to reply to the enemy fire.[53] The exchange of fire continued throughout the day and only slackened towards nightfall. Despite the day-long exchange, casualties were light on both sides. The Pensacola garrison lost one man killed and five wounded. Spanish casualties were eight wounded. There was no material damage to the British works and during the night they strengthened the exposed side of the Queen's Redoubt. Spanish working parties continued to extend the trenches towards the advanced redoubt.

May third was a repetition of the previous day. British artillery commenced to fire upon the large Spanish working parties and soon brought down counter-battery fire upon themselves. Once again both sides suffered slight casualties. In his journals, Farmar records that the besiegers lost one man killed and two wounded.[54] Certainly a small casualty rate for that expenditure of shot and shell.

Combat on the fourth began as on previous days; British guns opened fire early in the morning. They kept it up until ten o'clock that morning. Meanwhile parties of troops had been observed coming out of the town and infiltrating towards the Spanish lines. This movement was reported to the commander of the trenches, Pablo Figuerola, who ignored the information. The British had collected about 200 troops on the low lying ground before the redoubt on the Spanish left. Ninety-four Provincials, commanded by Major McDonald, were formed to make a direct attack upon the Spanish works. Over a hundred Waldeckers under their commander, Lieutenant Colonel Albrecht von Horn, would support the attack.

At 12:30 the British mortars, howitzers, and cannon opened fire again. The rapidity and accuracy of the barrage forced those in the trenches to seek cover. Despite the cannonade and the unusual signals that were observed between the garrison and its field force, the Spanish in the trenches sat down to their noon meal. Only a pair of sentries were exposed to the fire to observe enemy movements in the direction of the fort. When they had completed the barrage, the garrison artillery signaled that the following salvos would be without shot. At that, the Provincials went over to the attack.

The Spanish in the trenches, grenadiers from the Irish and Mallorca Regiments and three companies of marines, were completely surprised. When their commander sat down to lunch, they relaxed their vigilance and stacked their arms. Only the guard observed the fort, but he was so inexperienced that the British signals were ignored. The attackers did their deadly work with bayonets. The grenadiers felt the first blows of the attack and took flight, screaming, "We are lost! We are bayoneted!"[55] They spread disorder to the nearby companies of marines. Many of the grenadier officers and non-commissioned officers had stood their ground and fell in the attack and were later buried with honors for their bravery. The Provincials, having driven off the Spanish, spiked several guns, set fire to all combustibles, and returned to their lines. Gálvez reported 19 killed and a like amount wounded. One Provincial was killed and a trooper wounded. A Spanish relief column arrived too late to interfere with the withdrawing attackers.[56]

Although the garrison achieved a minor tactical success in the only hand to hand fighting of the siege, it did not affect the outcome nor did it seriously delay the plans of the Spanish. The commander of the trench was later arrested and put on trial for his part in the trenches that day.[57]

Following the sally, the Spanish resumed their siege operations. The work was hindered by a heavy rainfall and the trenches were flooded. The continued exchange of artillery fire inflicted some casualties on both sides.

On the night of the sixth preparations were made for an attack upon the Queen's Redoubt by 700 grenadiers and light infantry. The columns were underway shortly after midnight, but some troops arrived at their positions too late, and with a bright moon above, it was decided to cancel the attack and return to the lines. The Spanish later learned that the English were particularly vigilant that night and any attacks would have probably ended in a costly repulse.[58]

Early on the morning of May 8 the British resumed their bombardment of the Spanish works. The Spanish replied with a howitzer set up in one of the redoubts. Farmar reported:

> About 9 o'clock, A.M., a shell from the enemy's front battery was thrown in at the door of the magazine, at the advanced redoubt, as the men were receiving powder, which blew it up and killed forty seamen belonging to H.M. ships the Mentor and Port Royal; and forty-five men of the Pennsylvania Loyalists were killed by the same explosion; there were a number of men wounded, besides. Capt. Byrd, with seventy men of the 60th Regiment, immediately went up to the advanced redoubt and brought off 2 field-pieces and one howitzer, and a number of the wounded men; but was obliged to retire, as a great quantity of shell was lying about the field.[59]

The explosion at first alarmed the Spanish camp, but once it was learned that the Queen's Redoubt has been blasted and that the works were on fire, Brigadier Girón was ordered to take over the damaged redoubt. The Spanish troops moved forward under the cover of the burning redoubt and soon poured a heavy blaze of small arms fire down upon the Prince of Wales' Redoubt. This musketry was supported by the Spanish artillery. Within the middle redoubt, an officer and thirty soldiers and sailors were soon wounded by the fusillade from the Spanish-occupied advance redoubt.[60]

The loss of the advanced redoubt made Fort George untenable. Early that afternoon a flag of truce was raised over the fort and the British offered to surrender. The commanders and their staffs met and soon agreed to the articles of capitulation and arrangements for the surrender.

Pensacola was occupied by two companies of grenadiers on the ninth. The surrender of Fort George took place the following day. General Campbell led his troops out of the fort with drums beating and colors flying; in keeping with the capitulation, the garrison was accorded the honors of war. The defeated garrison marched to a point some 500 yards from the fort where they surrendered their flags and laid down their arms, the officers being permitted to retain their swords. Two companies of Spanish grenadiers were detailed to garrison the fort, and the French light infantry occupied the middle redoubt. The surrender of the Red Cliffs Fort, which was included in the capitulation, took place on the 11th.

With the siege over, the Spanish sang a *Te Deum* for their victory and many of the troops began to re-embark for an immediate return to Havana.[61]

In a return of prisoners a few days after the surrender, Gálvez reported, 1,113 men as captives. This figure did not include African Americans or the 56 deserters that went over to the Spanish during the siege. Besides the prisoners, there were 224 women and children dependent upon the garrison. The Indians who had helped in the defense of Pensacola made off during the negotiations for the surrender.[62]

During the siege, the garrison had suffered casualties of more than a hundred killed plus scores of wounded. Most were inflicted by the explosion in the advance redoubt. Spanish army losses were 75 killed and 198 wounded, while the navy had 21 killed and 4 wounded.[63]

Considerable booty was captured at Pensacola. In a letter of May 26, 1781, Gálvez reported the taking of 143 cannon, 6 howitzers, 4 mortars, and 40 swivel guns. Over 2,000 muskets and numerous other weapons and tons of military supplies fell into Spanish hands.[64]

The British garrison embarked on board Spanish transports on June first and sailed for Havana a few days later. This was the first step in the repatriation of these troops. One of the articles of capitulation provided for the prompt return of the garrison to a British port and an exchange of prisoners. The only restriction was that these troops could not serve against Spain or her allies until exchanged, which in accordance with the Treaty of Aranjuez, did not include the Americans. This later caused some bad feelings among the Americans towards Spain. However, once the Pensacola garrison was landed at New York, although British command opinion was divided on this issue, General Sir Henry Clinton ruled against their employment until exchanged.[65]

With the surrender of Pensacola, the whole province of West Florida was in Spanish hands. England later confirmed the Spanish victory at the peace table; not only did she give up West Florida, but she ceded East Florida as well.

In recognition for his services to the Crown, Gálvez was promoted to lieutenant general, raised to the nobility, being titled the Conde de Gálvez, and granted a coat of arms that bore the outline of the brig *Gálveztown* and the motto, "Yo Solo," for his forcing of the entrance to Pensacola Bay. There were other emoluments for his victory. He was appointed in 1784, Viceroy of New Spain, the highest post in Spanish America.

Notes for "The Spanish Conquest of British West Florida, 1779-1781"

[1]An excellent source and guide in the preparation of this paper has been John Walton Caughey's *Bernardo de Gálvez in Louisiana, 1776-1783* (Berkley, 1934).

[2]Peter J. Hamilton, *Colonial Mobile* (Boston, 1910), 312.

[3]Lawrence Kinnaird, ed., *Spain in the Mississippi Valley, 1765-1783,* 3 vols. (Washington, 1946), 2:364-73, cites several letters relative to the forthcoming campaign.

[4]Hamilton, *Colonial Mobile*, 223, 298.

[5]The description of the fort is based on several bits of information contained in the Hamilton book.

[6]Hamilton, *Colonial Mobile*, 312-13.

[7]Ibid., 534-35.

[8]Caughey, *Bernardo de Gálvez*, 174.

[9]Ibid., 176-77.

[10]Hamilton, *Colonial Mobile*, 313-14.

[11]Ibid., 315.

[12]Ibid., 313.

[13]Ibid., 315.

[14]Caughey, *Bernardo de Gálvez*, 180-81.

[15]Ibid.

[16]Hamilton, *Colonial Mobile*, 315.

[17]Caughey, *Bernardo de Gálvez*, 181.

[18]Hamilton, *Colonial Mobile*, 315.

[19]Caughey, *Bernardo de Gálvez*, 182 and footnote 33.

[20]Ibid., 183.

[21]Hamilton, *Colonial Mobile*, 315. For a Waldeck account, see Max von Eelking, *The German Allied Troops in the North American War of Independence,* translated from the German & abridged by J. D. Rosengarten (Albany, 1893), 218-25.

[22]Information on this raid is based upon Caughey, *Bernardo de Gálvez*, 194-95; Eelking, *German Allied Troops*, 223; Hamilton, *Colonial Mobile*, 316-17; and Buckingham Smith, ed., "Robert Farmar's Journal of the Siege of Pensacola, 1781," *Historical Magazine and Notes and Queries* (1860), 171.

[23]Bernardo de Gálvez, "Diary of the Operations Against Pensacola," *Louisiana Historical Quarterly,* 1 (1917): 44.

[24]Ibid., 44-47.

[25]Ibid., 47-48.

[26]Ibid.

[27]For an excellent article on Pensacola's defenses, see Stanley Faye, "British and Spanish Fortifications of Pensacola, 1781-1821," *Florida Historical Quarterly*, 20 (1942): 277-92. Also extant are two contemporary maps by Captain-Lieutenant Henry Heldring of the Waldeck Regiment and Acting Engineer at Pensacola in 1781. These maps are in the General Clinton Papers at the William L. Clements Library of Americana, the University of Michigan.

[28]*Diary of Frederick Mackenzie* (Cambridge, 1930), 2:412.

[29]The composition of the Pensacola garrison is based on entries in Farmar's Journal.

[30]Gálvez, "Diary of the Operations," 48-49; Smith, ed., "Farmar's Journal," 166.

[31]Gálvez, "Diary of the Operations," 49.

[32]Ibid., 49-50.

[33]Ibid., 51. Although it is stated in Farmar's Journal, 166, that Indians prevented this river crossing, Ezpeleta's column did join up with Gálvez on the 22nd.

[34]Gálvez, "Diary of the Operations," 52.

[35]Ibid. All ships entered the bay except the *San Ramon*, which returned to Havana on March 29th.

[36]Gálvez, "Diary of the Operations," 53-56.

[37]Ibid., 58.

[38]Kinnaird, ed., *Spain in the Mississippi Valley*, 2:421-423.

[39]Smith, ed., "Farmar's Journal," 167.

[40]Ibid., 167-70; Gálvez, "Diary of the Operations," 58-71.

[41]There are entries throughout Farmar's Journal relative to the arrival of parties of Indians.

[42]"McGillivray, Alexander," *Encyclopaedia Brittannica*, 14:573.

[43]Gálvez, "Diary of the Operations," 64-65.

[44]Francisco de Miranda, "Miranda's Diary of the Siege of Pensacola, 1781," translated from the Spanish by Donald E. Worcester, *Florida Historical Quarterly*, 29 (1951): 164-65.

[45]Ibid., 166.

[46]Ibid.

[47]Ibid., 173.

[48]Ibid., 172.

[49]Ibid., 176.

[50]Gálvez, "Diary of the Operations," 67.

[51]Ibid., 70.

[52]Ibid., 71.

[53]Smith, ed., "Farmar's Journal," 170.

[54]Ibid.

[55]Miranda, "Miranda's Diary," 187.

[56]Accounts of this sally are in ibid., 185-188; Gálvez, "Diary of the Operations," 72-73.

[57]Miranda, "Miranda's Diary," 188.

[58]Ibid., 189-90; Gálvez, "Diary of the Operations," 73-74.

[59]Smith, ed., "Farmar's Journal," 171.

[60]Ibid.; Miranda, "Miranda's Diary," 191-92; Gálvez, "Diary of the Operations," 74.

[61]Gálvez, "Diary of the Operations," 75; Miranda, "Miranda's Diary," 192.

[62]Gálvez, "Diary of the Operations," 75.

[63]Ibid.

[64]Ibid, 84.

[65]Smith, ed., "Farmar's Journal," 171; *Mackenzie*, 560-64, 566-67, 574, 578.

PART V

ECONOMICS

THE COMMERCE OF LOUISIANA AND THE FLORIDAS AT THE END OF THE EIGHTEENTH CENTURY*

Arthur P. Whitaker

I might take as a sub-title for this paper "Economic factors in the decline of the Spanish Empire in America," for it is an inquiry into the commerce of Louisiana and the Floridas in the latter part of the eighteenth century in relation to that subject.

A well known passage in Leroy Beaulieu's *Colonisation chez les peuples modernes* will serve as the starting-point for this inquiry. After a brief discussion of the Bourbon reforms in colonial government and an enumeration of the commercial concessions to the colonies, beginning in 1765 with the West Indies, he concludes: "The more important a colony was, the longer it (the Spanish government) delayed to open the colony to commerce."

He then adds the interesting conjecture that the Spanish government "seems to have wished to make an *experimentum in anima vili* by sacrificing first Cuba and Puerto Rico, . . . then Louisiana . . ." before extending its liberal innovations to such precious colonies as Mexico and Peru.[1] By *experimentum in anima vili* he means of course "trying it on the dog." This is a stimulating conjecture, and the succession of dates makes it seem very plausible. But were the Spanish concessions to Louisiana and later the Floridas in fact such an experiment? In order to answer this question we shall have to examine the successive commercial regulations and the reasons for their adoption. After showing what Spain was trying to do in these border provinces, we shall try to explain why it failed and to point out the significance of the failure.

Spanish commercial concessions in Louisiana began with the royal decree of 1768.[2] This decree applied to Louisiana alone, as the Floridas were then in English possession. It permitted Spanish subjects, including those of both the Peninsula and Louisiana, more extensive privileges than were then accorded the bulk of the Spanish colonies. Trade

*First published in the *Hispanic American Historical Review*, 8 (1928): 190-203.

could be carried on through nine habilitated ports of Spain; and, while it was hoped that Spanish goods would be used in the traffic, permission was given for trade to be carried on with other European countries provided the goods and returns passed through one of the habilitated ports and paid a duty on importation and re-exportation. In 1778 the *reglamento de comercio libre* made some modifications in this system;[3] but the results of both measures were far from satisfactory. British smugglers, enjoying the free navigation of the Mississippi River, virtually monopolised the commerce of Louisiana.[4]

The war of the American Revolution gave Spain an opportunity to re-orient its policy in Louisiana. One of its chief war aims, as expressed by [the conde de] Floridablanca, was "to expel from the Gulf of Mexico some people who are causing us infinite vexation,"[5]—that is, British smugglers, especially those on the Mississippi. The same policy that led to the conquest of British West Florida and to its logical consequence, the closing of the Mississippi to all foreigners by the proclamation of 1784,[6] was also responsible for a revision of the laws regulating the commerce of Louisiana.

This revision took the form of the *cédula* [decree] of 1782,[7] whereby trade between France and Louisiana-West Florida was permitted to Spanish subjects—a necessary consequence of the expulsion of British smugglers, for Spanish merchants and manufacturers had proved unable to supply the colony. Direct trade with France was legalised in order to compensate the colonist for the suppression of contraband trade and to remove all pretext or reason for its revival. It might also be said in passing that this *cédula* was not dictated solely by considerations of state. The governor of Louisiana, Bernardo de Gálvez, was the son-in-law of an influential French creole; and Bernardo's uncle, José de Gálvez, the colonial secretary, was the champion of French interests at the Spanish court.[8]

Even this concession to foreign trade was not enough. In the course of the 1780s many others were made and still others demanded.[9] Frequent "special permissions" enabled American ships to do a profitable if irregular business at St. Augustine[10] and New Orleans.[11] British merchants, with the consent of the Spanish government, took over the extensive Indian trade of the Floridas, and carried it on with British goods in British ships directly to London and back, without so much as a curtsey at a Spanish port. In 1788, the sacred Mississippi itself was thrown open to the Kentuckians as far south as New Orleans, and a thriving commerce soon developed.[12] Without the consent of the court, but under cover of the *cédula* of 1782, a considerable traffic with Philadelphia was built up by way of French Santo Domingo.[13]

These and other amplifications and abuses of the *cédula* enraged the die-hards in Spain, and in 1788 they were able to obtain from the king an order directing a reconsideration of the whole subject. The *consulados* of the habilitated ports were called on for their advice, and all of them condemned the court's liberal measures.[14] One of their reports takes us back to the medieval problem of the mouse that ate the consecrated wafer, for it suggested that English contraband flour was endangering the souls of the colonists, not because it was contraband, but because it was made of an uncanonical mixture of peas and beans with wheat and was therefore unfit for use in the celebration of the mass.[15] Most of the reports, however, took the less exalted ground that the *cédula* was ruining Spanish merchants by facilitating an immense contraband trade in the gulf.

The matter was discussed for several years with Spanish thoroughness and deliberation. Martín Navarro, just returned from the intendancy of Louisiana, was consulted, and advised a further extension of privileges to Louisiana and the Floridas.[16] In 1790, the office of director of colonial commerce was created,[17] and Diego de Gardoqui, former envoy to the United States, was appointed director. In 1790, and again in 1791, he submitted recommendations,[18] urging in the latter case that the three provinces be thrown open to the commerce of all nations with which Spain had a commercial treaty—*i.e.*, to England as well as France, but not to the United States. His arguments were powerfully reinforced by the outbreak of war (May, 1793) between Spain and France. The commerce of the border colonies was dislocated, and consequently, in July, 1793, the substance of Gardoqui's proposals was incorporated in a new *reglamento de comercio*.[19] Though a provisional, war-time measure, this *reglamento* remained in effect until 1802, on the eve of the return of Louisiana to France.[20]

What was the court seeking to accomplish by these various measures? Special considerations of course operated in each case, as we have already suggested; but beneath the surface drift of opportunism ran an undercurrent of persistent policy. We may begin our definition of this policy by stating what it was not; and this brings us back to Leroy Beaulieu's conjecture. With the possible exception of the decree of 1768, as amended in 1778, none of these commercial regulations was ever designed as an *experimentum in anima vili*, to be extended if successful to the rest of the Spanish empire. On the contrary, the concessions to Louisiana and the Floridas were of limited duration and of a provisional nature, and they were intended to effect the ultimate assimilation of these border provinces to the conventional type of Spanish colony.[21] At the same time, it was recognised that no abrupt change must be made, and above all that the peculiar circumstances of these colonies required special treatment. Louisiana and the Floridas were frontier provinces, and their function was to serve as barrier against the economic and territorial aggression of the Anglo-Americans to the northward and eastward. Since their thousand-mile frontier made military defense impossible, it was essential that a numerous and thriving population should be built up in them. Here was a problem that was largely economic. Laborers must be induced to settle in the provinces, capital must be obtained for exploitation, and commerce must be so ordered as to stimulate the immigration and increase of both capital and labor. The court, however, was not working in the void. It was bound by tradition and by opinion in Spain. The policy adopted under these circumstances was to promote the prosperity of the border colonies, and at the same time to assure their loyalty to the Crown and make them as profitable as possible to Spanish industry and commerce, effecting a gradual substitution of Spanish for foreign goods, merchants, and ships in their commerce.[22]

It may be mentioned in passing that in 1788 the court gave further encouragement of the development of Louisiana by liberalising the immigration laws. Generous land grants were made, the importation of slaves was permitted, and Protestantism was tolerated, in order to induce the American frontiersmen and other foreigners to settle in Louisiana and West Florida as subjects of his Catholic Majesty.[23] With the history of this interesting effort we are not concerned, and it is mentioned only because it was a companion-piece to the commercial concessions and is another evidence of Spain's eagerness to foment the growth of these barrier provinces.

We may now inquire into the reasons for the failure of the Spanish commercial policy in Louisiana and the Floridas; for of course it was an utter failure. In 1795, by the Treaty of San Lorenzo, Spain surrendered Louisiana itself. It was not that these provinces failed to increase in numbers and prosperity. On the contrary, Louisiana flourished under Spain as it never had under France.[24] Nevertheless the Spanish policy was a failure, for its object was not only to make the province large and prosperous, but also to render it profitable to Spain, to prevent contraband trade, and to cultivate in the growing population an increasing loyalty to the Spanish Crown. Instead of this, Spaniards had a steadily diminishing opportunity to share in the mounting prosperity of the provinces, Spanish trade with other portions of the empire suffered from contraband trade through Louisiana,[25] and economic dependence on the outside world fostered among the colonists a feeling of indifference or hostility to his Catholic Majesty.

To Spanish statesmen one of the most alarming aspects of the failure was the leakage of gold and silver through Louisiana to the outside world.[26] In 1788 the imports into that province were valued at 1,200,000 *pesos*, its exports at 660,000 *pesos*. The balance of some 500,000 *pesos* was paid in various ways; in part by the illicit exportation of specie. In 1794, a single ship, the *Noah's Ark*, left New Orleans with 46,000 *pesos* in gold and silver; and although this ship was overtaken and searched and the 46,000 *pesos* confiscated,[27] its misfortune was unique. The governors and intendants of Louisiana repeatedly warned the court that it was impossible to put a stop to this specie-running, and undesirable if possible, since it was the colony's only means of balancing exports and imports. This specie, however, was provided by the Spanish government itself, which, by way of *situado* or subvention and for the purchase of tobacco, was sending about 740,000 *pesos* a year to New Orleans.[28] This sum passed into commercial circulation and most of it soon passed out of the province and into the hands of foreigners. Quite naturally the government objected to a system whereby it paid over half a million *pesos* a year for the violation of its own laws and the enrichment of foreigners; but it never succeeded in putting a stop to the practice as long as it possessed Louisiana.

The radical defect was the inability of Spanish merchants and manufacturers to compete with foreigners. I believe that this factor was decisive in Louisiana and the Floridas, and that, with due allowance for local circumstances, the Spanish commercial system failed in the rest of America for the same reason that it did in these frontier provinces. The reasons will have to be indicated very briefly.

First of all, let us make due allowance for local circumstances. The most important of these was that in both Louisiana and the Floridas the bulk of the population consisted of aliens, who preferred the commodities of their native country to those of Spain. As an instance of the difficulties Spanish merchants encountered in overcoming such prejudices, we may mention the case of one who brought several casks of Rioja wine to New Orleans. In order to break down the sales-resistance of the colonists, he gave away samples of his wine; but an observer testified that when the creole connoisseurs tasted it, they made as wry a face as if they had taken an emetic. Not a single cask of the Rioja was sold.[29]

Such predilections made it more difficult for the Spanish merchant to establish himself in the province; but they were certainly not an insuperable obstacle. It is hardly necessary to multiply instances of the British conquest of foreign markets in the face of such prejudices. These same Louisiana creoles had welcomed British contraband in the 1760s and 1770s; but they had welcomed it because of the low price of British goods, and this was precisely the bait that Spanish merchants were unable to offer. As Martín Navarro said in discussing this problem, the colonist could not be expected to pay eight *pesos* for a Spanish blanket when he could buy a British blanket for four.

The fault was partly the manufacturer's, partly the merchant's, and partly the merchant marine's. It had been suggested that the Spanish manufacturer was handicapped by the wealth of the Indies, for Spain's abnormally large gold supply raised the level of prices in the Peninsula, with the result that it was flooded with cheap foreign goods and the Spanish manufacturer was ruined.[30] At any rate, by the middle of the eighteenth century the volume of production was small, the quality of the goods low, and the enterprise of the manufacturers almost nil. For instance, when the Creek Indians were at war with the Georgians in 1786, they were given some shotguns of Spanish make; and Alexander McGillivray reported in disgust that the worthless guns burst at the second or third shot. As for enterprise, the Spanish manufacturer could not even follow where his government pointed the way. In 1789 Martín Navarro was sent by the king to England and France to gather samples and information that would enable Spaniards to duplicate the goods consumed in Louisiana and the Floridas. Navarro did his part admirably but the manufacturers did theirs miserably. Nothing ever came of the attempt.[31]

The merchants and seamen of Spain must also bear some of the responsibility. Diego de Gardoqui, who sailed from Cadiz to New York by way of Havana in 1784-1785, has left us a vivid account of the indolence, ignorance and corruption of Spanish seamen, and of the incompetence of the petty Spanish merchants at Havana, who, he said, almost made him ashamed that he was a Spaniard.[32]

The same utter inadequacy of Spanish industry and commerce to the needs of the colonies is apparent throughout Spanish America. It has been estimated that 25 percent of the commerce of these colonies was in the hands of foreigners.[33] That even 75 percent of it was in Spanish hands was due to the remoteness of most of the colonies, to the monopolistic laws, and to the scarcity of good ports, which facilitated the suppression of contraband. As soon as the Spanish domination was ended by the wars of independence, Spanish merchants began to lose their hold on the colonial market and ultimately disappeared almost entirely. This elementary fact is in striking contrast with the experience of the thirteen colonies of British North America before and after their revolution.

The inadequacy of Spain's economic system to the needs of its colonies was more evident in Louisiana and the Floridas, but it can be traced in every case. Just how inadequate it was is apparent from Humboldt's and Peuchet's analyses of the trade of Spain's colonies from 1760 to the end of the century. These analyses show that Spain's commerce with her colonies amounted substantially to an exchange of goods for the output of its American mines, and for a very few other colonial products.[34] The Spanish economic system did not permit any general development of the resources of the colonies. I say the economic, not the political system. Spain has been reproached for neglecting Argentina, and there is some justice in the reproach; but in the Mississippi Valley, where the situation resembled somewhat that in Argentina, the Spanish government made every effort, through modification of its commercial system and immigration laws, to stimulate settlement and agriculture; but to no avail.

The trouble was not with the colonial system which had its good points; nor was it antiquated conservatism, for Louisiana and the Floridas enjoyed a freedom of trade unparalleled in the British colonies of that day; nor altogether a faulty commercial organisation, for the flourishing Virginia tobacco trade was a model of inefficiency; nor yet the corruption and incompetence of colonial officials, for the Spanish governors were no worse than the British in this respect. It was the very resemblances that were Spain's undoing. Spain tried to accomplish with its empire what the French ad British were doing with theirs, namely to derive economic benefit from it; but since it lacked the indispensable economic organization its efforts resulted merely in a succession of irritations to the colonists, of disappointments to the Spaniards, and of affronts to foreigners. An immense contraband trade was but one symptom of the disorder, other symptoms were backstairs intrigues in Spain, revolutionary plots in the colonies, and international crises.

The latter half of the eighteenth century saw the beginning of that vast increase in production and in the volume of international trade that is still going on today, and Spain, with an inadequate coal supply and other deficiencies, was unable to keep pace. Its inability to provide its colonies with goods and other capital for their development arrayed against Spain both the colonists, who thought a golden prosperity was in store for them if they could but shake off the Spanish yoke, and foreign investors, who were ready to supply the needed capital.[35]

The process was accelerated in Louisiana and the Floridas by the pressure of American skippers and frontiersmen, but ultimately it spread to the rest of the Spanish empire.[36] It will be remembered that the revolution in South America proceeded from two bases, Caracas and Argentina, and these were the two regions where foreign economic penetration had made the greatest progress. It has been said that in three centuries the United States rushed through a development that required 1500 years in Europe. With more justice it might be said that the commercial history of Louisiana from 1768 to 1800, evolving from monopoly through contraband to partial freedom, then greater freedom, and finally to separation from Spain, is a rapid epitome of the decline of the Spanish empire. By the end of the eighteenth century a different kind of El Dorado lured on another generation of gold-diggers, and the commercial conquistadores of the new era rifled the pockets of prostrate Spain with as much skill and as little compunction as a Cortés or a Pizarro plundering Aztecs and Incas in the sixteenth century.

The Floridas and Louisiana were not a laboratory in which the Spanish government conducted experiments in colonial policy, and for that very reason their history gives us a clearer insight into the reasons for the decline of the Spanish empire in America. The empire fell not so much because of decay within as because of pressure from without, and it was precisely in these provinces that the pressure was strongest in the eighteenth century. The efforts of the government at adaptation merely demonstrated the inadequacy of Spain's national economy. Her merchants and manufacturers could not compete with foreigners; and yet the total exclusion of foreigners was made impossible by the proximity of Americans and Englishmen. And so Spain found itself paying for the maintenance of law and order, while outsiders reaped the rewards, and the colonists were weaned away by commercial intercourse with aliens. World-wide economic development decreed the exploitation of successive areas of the Spanish Empire, and as Spain was unable to conduct or direct their exploitation it had to yield to its superiors in the modern world.

Notes for "The Commerce of Louisiana and the Floridas at the End of the Eighteenth Century"

[1]Leroy Beaulieu, *Colonisation chez les peuples modernes,* 4th ed. (Paris, 1891), 32-33.

[2]Charles Gayarré, *History of Louisiana*, 4 vols. (New Orleans, 1903), 3:44; a printed copy of this decree, dated March 23, 1768, is in the Archivo General de Indias (Seville), leg. 2665. Hereafter referred to as AGI.

[3]Gayarré, *History of Louisiana,* 3:116. Gayarré does not give the date. See also H. van der Linden, *L'Expansion coloniale de l'Espagne,* 403.

[4]J. A. James, "Spanish Influence in the West during the American Revolution," in *Mississippi Valley Historical Review,* 4 (1917-1918): 194; Gayarré, *History of Louisiana,* 3:45-46; AGI, leg. 2667, *extracto* of an *informe* by the governor of Louisiana (Bernardo de Gálvez) of October 24, 1779.

[5]Juan F. Yela Utrilla, *España ante la independencia de los Estados Unidos,* 2 vols. (Lerida, 1922), 2:187.

[6]Arthur P. Whitaker, *The Spanish-American Frontier, 1783-1795* (1927; reprint ed., Gloucester, 1962), 33-36.

[7]AGI, SD, leg. 2665, Real Cédula, dated El Pardo, January 22, 1782, signed "Yo El Rey", with rubric, and countersigned "Jph de Galvez." The greater part of the cédula is printed in M. Serrano y Sanz, *España y los Indios Cherokis y Chactas en la segunda mitad del siglo xviii* (Seville, 1916), 15-18.

[8]The reasons for the adoption of the *cédula* are discussed in a memorandum, unsigned and undated, in AGI, SD, leg. 2665. The memorandum is enclosed in a cover endorsed "Pa. el Sor. Lerena, la Luisiana," and begins "Exmo. Sor. Queriendo el Rey favorecer a los habitantes de la Luisiana. . . ." See also *resumen,* dated January 9, 1779, of a representation by Manuel de las Heras, Spanish consul at Bordeaux, ibid., SD, leg. 2667; and Martin Navarro's *memoria* on the *estado actual* of Louisiana, enclosed in his despatch No. 23 to José de Gálvez, dated New Orleans, September 24, 1780. An English translation of this memorial is printed in James A. Robertson, *Louisiana Under the Rule of Spain, France and the United States,* 2 vols. (Cleveland, 1911), 1:235 *et. seq.*, where the editor assigns the conjectural date *Ca.* 1785 to the document.

[9]Some of these modifications are mentioned in the memorandum cited at the beginning of the preceding note. Not all the modifications, however, were in the greater freedom (cf., Gayarré, *History of Louisiana,* 3:187-88).

[10]AGI, Papeles de Cuba, leg. 2352, Gardoqui to Conde de Gálvez, New York, September 20, 1786, No. 21; Archivo Histórico Nacional (Madrid), Sección de Estado, leg. 3893, Gardoqui to Floridablanca, March 13, 1786, No. 8. *reservada.* These archives will hereafter be referred to as AHN, and the Sección de Estado as Est.

[11]AGI, SD, leg. 2544, Miró and Navarro to Valdés, New Orleans, April 1, 1788, No. 56; AHN, Est., leg. 3893 bis, Gardoqui to Floridablanca, New York, December 6, 1787, No. 221.

[12]On the Indian trade, see Whitaker, *Spanish-American Frontier*, 36-46; and on the Mississippi, see ibid., 101-2.

[13]In a letter to Floridablanca of June 3, 1787, Gardoqui complained that this illicit commerce was interfering with his negotiation with Jay (AHN, Est., leg, 3893 bis, despatch No. 192). Many other letters in this series relate to contraband.

[14]A draft of the order to the *consulado* of San Sebastian, dated Aranjuez, April 21, 1788, is in AGI, SD, leg. 2665. The replies of the *consulados* of La Coruña, Santander, Barcelona, San Sebastian, and Bilbao are also in this legajo. The most interesting is the reply of Barcelona, which is dated June 19, 1788.

[15]Ibid., *informe* of the *consulado* of Coruña, dated May 10, 1788.

[16]AGI, SD, leg. 2665, (Valdés) to Navarro, October 28, 1788, draft; ibid., Navarro to Valdés, January 15, 1789, No. 2, copy, certified by Navarro.

[17]The office of *director del comercio de Indias* was created by a royal decree of April 25, 1790. At the same time the colonial system was reorganised by the suppression of the two colonial secretariats created in 1787, and by the distribution of their functions among the appropriate departments of Spain itself. The director of colonial commerce was subordinated to the ministro de hacienda. This decision is recorded in AHN, Est., "Actas de la Suprema Junta de Estado," April 26, 1790.

[18]Gardoqui's first *dictamen* (autograph, signed) is undated, but the approximate date is fixed by an autograph note appended by Valdés, which is in the same legajo with the first, is signed, and dated San Lorenzo, October 12, 1791.

[19]AGI, PC, leg. 2353, Gardoqui to the Captain General of Cuba, Aranjuez, June 9, 1793, copy.

[20]The *reglamento* of 1793 remained in effect until October 1802, and its termination coincided with Intendant Morales's well known order suppressing the right of deposit at New Orleans that the citizens of the United States had enjoyed under the Treaty of San Lorenzo (Dunbar Rowland, ed., *Official Letter Books of W. C.C. Claiborne, 1801-1816*, 6 vols. (Jackson, 1917), 1:207.

[21]This is made clear by Gardoqui's second *dictamen* cited in note 18 above.

[22]AGI, SD, leg. 2665, minute of the Junta Suprema de Estado, May 25, 1789, signed "Eugo. de Llaguno."

[23]Whitaker, *Spanish-American Frontier,* 101-7.

[24]This statement is based on the following statistics of population, shipping and value of exports of Louisiana: (1) *Population*—After more than sixty years of French rule, the population of Louisiana numbered only 12,000; in less than forty years of Spanish rule, the number had increased to 50,000 (Villiers du Terrage, *Les derniéres années de la Louisiane française* [Paris, 1904], 368). (2) *Shipping*—In the whole French period (1699-1763), the largest number of entries in any one year was seventeen (in 1722 and again in 1725). In the period 1732-1756, the number of entries fluctuated between twelve (1739) and two (1754 and 1755); the average being about six entries (and as many sailings) per year (N. M. M. Surrey, *The Commerce of Louisiana during the French Régime, 1699-1763* [New York, 1916], 77). The most striking fact of all is that there was no increase in the number of entries and sailings, which merely fluctuated about a very low mean. Under the Spanish rule, the situation was totally different. In 1788, 25 ships were constantly engaged in the commerce of Louisiana (AGI, SD, leg. 2665, Navarro to Valdés, January 15, 1789, No. 2, copy). In 1790, the number of sailings from New Orleans was 91, the number of entries 42 (AGI, Papeles de Cuba, leg. 2319, "Libro General de Asiento"). The discrepancy between entries and sailings in this year is no doubt to be explained by the Nootka crisis. In 1794, the governor reported that a hundred ships were not sufficient for the commerce of Louisiana. This was after the outbreak of the general European war, which gave a great impulse to the commerce of Louisiana. It received a further impulse from the Treaty of San Lorenzo, as will appear from the statistics given in Edward Channing, *A History of the United States,* 6 vols. (New York, 1905), 4:311 and notes. (3) *Value of exports*—Under France, the average annual value of exports from Louisiana in a typical period (1750-1754) was less than 500,000 *livres*, including bills of exchange (Surrey, *Commerce of Louisiana,* 217). In 1788, under Spain, the value of exports, not including bills of exchange, was about 2,640,000 *livres* (*i.e.*, 660,000 *pesos*: Navarro's letter to Valdes, *cit. supra*); in 1800 it was about 7,8000,000 *livres* (*i.e.*, 1,958,000 dollars: Gayarré, *History of Louisiana,* 3:443, quoting Pontalba. See also Channing, *History of the United States.*) The foregoing statistics are of course only approximate, but they represent with substantial accuracy the great increase in prosperity that took place in New Orleans under the Spanish régime, before 1793 as well as after the outbreak of the European war and the conclusion of the Treaty of San Lorenzo.

[25]The volume of this contraband trade through Louisiana is impossible to determine and difficult to estimate. Navarro said in 1789 that it was too insignificant to matter. Gardoqui said in 1791 that it was notorious and extensive. Pontalba in 1800 estimated its annual value at $500,000, or one-fourth of the total value of Louisiana's export trade (Gayarré, *History of Louisiana,* 3:443).

[26]In 1787, Phineas Bond declared that contraband trade with the Spanish colonies had brought "at least 500,000 dollars . . . into this port [Philadelphia] last year." ("Letters of Phineas Bond," in American Historical Association, *Report,* 1 (1896): 542). The abuse was discussed by Miró in his despatch No. 1 to Lerena, dated September 26, 1790 (AGI, SD, leg. 2665). This despatch indicates that about 400,000 *pesos* a year in specie (*plata*) was sent annually from Louisiana to French Santo Domingo in violation of the law.

[27]AE, 87-3-22, Rendón to Gardoqui, New Orleans, Nov. 5, 1794, No. 2 *reservada*. This case has a long and complicated history. The merchants got their money back, but the case was not settled until 1802 (AE, 87-3-22, Morales to Soler, May 31, 1802, No. 95).

[28]Ibid., SD, leg. 2665, Navarro to Valdés, January 15, 1789, No. 2 copy.

[29]*Resumen* of representation by Manuel de las Heras, cited in note 8. This instance is all the more striking because, according to Gardoqui, of all the Spanish wines, those of Rioja "se semejan mas al [*i.e.*, "a él"] de Burdeos en suavidad, colór, y ligereza." (Gardoqui's dictamen of October 12, 1791, cited above in note 18).

[30]Leroy Beaulieu, *Colonisation,* 38.

[31]There are numerous documents in AGI, SD, leg. 2665, relating to this mission.

[32]AHN, Est., leg. 3893, Gardoqui to Floridablanca, Havana, January 13, 1785, *reservada,* not numbered. In 1789 Gardoqui was still suffering from the recollection of the Havana merchants' ineptitude. Writing about them to Floridablanca on March 4, 1789, he said: ". . . *No son mas que unos tenderos de una clase comun, sin mas instruccion de su profecion que de un miserable mecanismo de menudear las mercancias que las fian.*" AHN, Est., leg. 3893, No. 24 *confidencial.*) In view of Gardoqui's own commercial experience, it is to be presumed that he knew what he was talking about.

[33]Jacques Peuchet, *Etat des colonies et du commerce des Europeéans dans les deux Indes, depuis 1783 jusque en 1821,* 2 vols. (Paris, 1821), 1:346-47.

[34]Ibid., 345-46, quoting Humboldt.

[35]Gayarré, *History of Louisiana,* 3:172, quoting Miró's complaint of the lack of capital in Louisiana.

[36]An excellent account of the economic penetration of Louisiana by the United States before the purchase in 1803 is given by Louis Pelzer, "Economic Factors in the Acquisition of Louisiana," Mississippi Valley Historical Association, *Proceedings,* 6 (1912): 109 *et seq.* The writer did not have access to the Spanish archives, and consequently was unable to make his survey complete or to show how Spanish policy was influenced by the American penetration. Some information on this subject, for the period 1783-1795, is given in my recent book *The Spanish-American Frontier, 1783-1795*, 216-22. See also Channing, *History of the United States.*

BOOM AND BUST: THE RISE AND FALL OF THE TOBACCO INDUSTRY IN SPANISH LOUISIANA, 1770-1790*

Brian E. Coutts

French royal officials, speculators such as John Law, and the French Crown itself had placed great hopes in the development of the tobacco industry in French Louisiana. Some officials even anticipated that Louisiana tobacco might someday be grown in sufficient quantities to supply all the needs of the French Tobacco Monopoly. These lofty expectations were never realized, although tobacco production did reach 400,000 pounds in 1740.

By the time of the transfer of the colony to Spain in 1763 the perils of war and erratic shipping had almost killed the industry. Most planters had switched to the more profitable production of indigo. Historian Jacob Price claims that the failure of the French government's efforts to develop the tobacco trade resulted from a misunderstanding about costs. In Louisiana, he writes, labor was expensive and freight dear, yet French authorities expected Louisiana tobacco to be competitive in price in the French market with Virginia tobacco, grown in an established market, with abundant labor, and much closer to Europe. Fortunately, the Spanish officials had no such illusions.[1]

The project to encourage the development of tobacco cultivation in Louisiana under the Spanish began very inauspiciously in late 1770. Governor Luis de Unzaga, in September of that year, received instructions from the viceroy of New Spain to collect all available tobacco in the colony for shipment to Veracruz for use in the newly formed Renta de Tabaco, a royal monopoly operating various factories in Puebla, Mexico City and other locations. Unzaga consented to the idea because of the obvious advantages it offered to the royal treasury. He advised the people of the district of New Orleans to bring forth within fifteen days all the tobacco they might have and gave more distant posts a month to ship theirs. Two inspectors were hired to inspect and grade the tobacco. In all,

*This article first appeared in *The Americas*, 42 (1986): 289-309. It is reprinted here with the kind permission of the author and publisher.

some 98,000 pounds of tobacco were collected, principally from Natchitoches, and shipped to Veracruz on board the royal brig *El Santo Cristo de San Romas*. The tobacco was paid for with a special *situado* of 10,000 *pesos* granted by the viceroy.[2]

On May 20, 1771, the Crown approved Unzaga's actions and stated that it was his majesty's wish that in the future, he supply the viceroy of New Spain with all the allotment of tobacco that he might request and which the crops of that colony might provide. Unfortunately, nothing more was heard from the Mexican authorities for five years, by which time interest in New Spain as a potential market for Louisiana tobacco had been all but forgotten.[3]

A revival of interest in Louisiana tobacco by Mexican authorities took place in 1776. A royal order of May 21 of that year requested the governor of Louisiana to develop and encourage, where possible, the cultivation of tobacco, with the aim of supplying the Renta (Royal Tobacco Monopoly) of New Spain. To this end, the governor was to make contracts with the growers of his province and to provide assistance where necessary to encourage the planting of tobacco.[4]

The renewed interest in Louisiana tobacco had two distinct sources. First, the tobacco shipped from Louisiana in 1770 had been judged to be of excellent quality—ideally suited to be mixed with local supplies for Mexican consumers. Second, the principal growing regions of Orizaba and Córdoba in New Spain could not supply the increasing needs of the monopoly. The total consumption of legitimate tobacco in New Spain in the form of *puros* and *cigarros* was 2,700,000 pounds in 1775. Officials of the monopoly hoped to obtain at least one-fifth of this, or 500,000 to 600,000 pounds from Louisiana to mix with the tobacco produced in that kingdom.[5]

A major obstacle to the expansion of this trade between Louisiana and New Spain was the difficulty of shipping the tobacco, first by sea to Veracruz, and then overland by mule to the warehouses of the various factories. Mexican authorities recommended that Louisiana tobacco be shipped in *tercios* protected by mats and cords of palm, or in barrels to retain quality and to protect against shrinkage and putrefaction. The weight of each *tercio* or barrel was to be limited to seven *arrobas* (1 *arroba* = 25 pounds) to facilitate transportation overland from Veracruz.[6]

Despite Crown encouragement, favorable prices, and a guaranteed market, tobacco production in Louisiana's principal growing regions of Natchitoches, Opelousas, Pointe Coupée, and Attakapas grew extremely slowly during the last years of the 1770s. Only 138,808 pounds were shipped from New Orleans to Veracruz in 1779. Governor Bernardo de Gálvez, heavily involved in prosecuting the war against the English settlements along the Mississippi, had scant time to devote to encouraging tobacco production. Because of this, in early 1780, Gálvez assigned the task of directing the project to Intendant Martín Navarro. A year later on June 5, 1781, the Crown assigned Navarro the special commission of encouraging the cultivation of tobacco in Louisiana.[7]

Navarro thus added responsibility for tobacco to his many other tasks of supervising the economic development of the colony, settling immigrants, supplying war material, auditing the accounts, and acting as an administrator in the absence of the governor. Despite this pressing workload, Navarro began the commission with his usual zeal. On April, 12, 1780, he wrote the minister of the Indies, José de Gálvez, that the newly conquered region of the Natchez possessed fertile soils ideally suited for the cultivation of tobacco and that tobacco currently grown there was of excellent quality and regularly enjoyed a good market in London. To demonstrate its excellent qualities, Navarro shipped a barrel to Spain to be examined by the Minister of the Indies. Navarro added that 400,000 pounds were currently produced in the Natchez region and that it was absolutely necessary to find a market for it if the local planters were to be reconciled to Spanish rule.[8]

An experimental shipment of seventy-six barrels, purchased from Natchez growers at nine *sueldos* a pound was shipped to Veracruz in large casks and barrels on board the bilander *Santa Rosa* in April of 1780. The remainder of Natchez tobacco purchased by Governor Bernardo de Gálvez was shipped in July of that year in the five ships conveying English prisoners to Veracruz.[9]

Despite initial efforts to encourage the cultivation of tobacco, the industry grew slowly in the first years of Navarro's commission. Only 189,396 pounds were shipped to Veracruz in 1780. The viceroy of New Spain wrote Navarro on April 19, 1781, to complain that the quantities of tobacco were very short that year and in order to avert serious danger to the Renta asked him to make the most dedicated efforts to remit all available tobacco supplies in 1781.[10] Navarro wrote First Minister Gálvez that tobacco was in short supply that year because of the turbulence of war. He added that he had taken every possible step to accommodate the anticipated shortage in New Spain. The sale of Louisiana tobacco to the French colonies had been prohibited and the inhabitants were encouraged to expand production. In September Navarro wrote to each of the commandants in the principal growing regions to enlist their aid in encouraging the growth of the industry. To the commandant of Pointe Coupée he wrote: "I advise you on your part to make public the royal will in your jurisdiction and to assure those inhabitants that all that is grown we will buy and pay for in whatever quantity that conditions dictate."[11] The anticipated boost in production from the Natchez region failed to materialize in 1781 when some of the English planters rose in rebellion and destroyed most of the tobacco crop.[12]

By 1782 Navarro had become convinced that tobacco offered perhaps the greatest hope for the future development of the colony. He wrote to Gálvez: "for my part I continue to encourage cultivation where possible not only in order to satisfy the advices of your excellency but as well because I know that it is the principal object of those which will make this colony flourish."[13] Navarro complained that without the calamities of war, hurricanes, drought, floods of the Mississippi, and the shortage of silver, much more advance would have been made in tobacco production. He added that some of the planters were a bit timid and reluctant to begin cultivating a crop almost foreign to them, and one exposed to the vagaries of weather. They were also uncertain about accepting paper money in return for their products. These were not the only difficulties. Each district had its particular problems that could be alleviated only by time and the protection of the sovereign.[14]

Navarro then began a lengthy analysis of each of the principal growing regions. The soils of Opelousas and Attakapas were excellent for tobacco, but transportation costs to New Orleans would absorb most of the potential profits. In order to encourage these planters to abandon indigo in favor of tobacco, Navarro felt it would be necessary to purchase tobacco on location and to ship it at the expense of the Crown to New Orleans. He thought it might be necessary to find a port along that coast suitable for sending boats to receive tobacco. If this proved impossible, it would be indispensable to establish storehouses in order to receive it in New Iberia and transport it to New Orleans at the cost of the treasury. If this were done, he felt that the price paid to producers might be lowered to reduce the additional costs to the Crown.

Navarro described the post of Natchitoches as one established by poor farmers, who through industry had continued to battle against the irregularity of the seasons and now produced a small quantity of tobacco of excellent quality. Navarro cited a shortage of laborers as the major obstacle to expanding production in this district. The best means of rectifying this shortfall and encouraging increased production, he felt, would be to provide them with a sufficient number of slaves, perhaps 400, at the expense of the Crown, to be repaid inside two years with tobacco plus a small handling fee. This would compel them to devote all of their energies to tobacco and would lead to the rapid development of the district in the shortest possible time.

The district of Natchez, wrote Navarro, was much admired both for its high elevation and fertile soil. He felt that it was deserving of attention, since tobacco from this region was of excellent quality. Additionally, Navarro related that lying at the upper part of the river it was in a position to dominate the province. Thus he argued that it would be best to develop and solidly fortify it. So far, the district had contributed little to the province's production of tobacco save for a small quantity produced in 1779.

Furthermore, Navarro added that the district of Natchez was composed of two classes of people: the comfortable and the very poor. The former, with sufficient slave labor converted their tobacco to *andullos* (rolls) while the poor, the majority of whom were vagrants, pressed their tobacco into *toneles* (hogsheads)—the easiest method—and sold it without subjecting it to conversion to *andullos*, a process requiring more time and application. This latter problem, Navarro thought, could be remedied by sending some experienced workers from Havana to teach them to press the leaf in a mode similar to that used in Cuba for shipment to Spain's European factories. The end product would be ideally suited for the making of *cigarros* in New Spain.

The remaining portions of the province, extending from Iberville to the Balize, were not suitable for the cultivation of tobacco because of the irregularity of the seasons and heavy rains. Despite this, Navarro reassured the Crown that rapid development of the province in terms of increased production would be assured once peace had been established.[15]

The Crown responded to Navarro's *informe* on April 11, 1783. It requested him to work in conjunction with the interim Governor Esteban Miró and to observe the advice of the new viceroy of New Spain, Matías de Gálvez. As for his proposals, the Crown responded favorably to only one of his initiatives, that of providing slave laborers through Crown-backed loans. Several months later, a second royal order authorized the construction at New Orleans of two warehouses for storing tobacco. Navarro, however, decided not to go ahead with the projected storage facilities. The present facilities, he informed Gálvez, including one warehouse 300 feet by 30 feet wide, one of the best in America, were more than adequate.[16]

The most pressing problem to emerge during the early 1780s with regard to the Louisiana tobacco trade was the question of quality control and shipping techniques. Early in 1781, the viceroy of New Spain began complaining that the methods being used to ship tobacco to Veracruz were unsatisfactory. The viceroy enclosed a letter from the director of the Renta, Felipe de Hierro. Hierro complained that some of the tobacco from Natchez was green and without proper seasoning. He strongly objected to sending the tobacco *a granel* (loose) and reminded Navarro that the preferred technique for shipping was *enterciado* (bundled). The latter process involved bundling the *tercios* using mats and cords of palm and was the technique used by growers in the towns of Orizaba and Córdoba in New Spain for shipping tobacco to the factories.[17]

Since 1778 Louisiana tobacco had been shipped to Veracruz using a number of techniques. Some was rolled into the *andullos* and packed loose in the holds of ships; and some was pressed and shipped in barrels. The customary way of packing tobacco at Natchez for shipment to London during the English domination had been in the form of *toneles* (large hogsheads) weighing up to a thousand pounds. The directors of the Renta had regularly clamored against such harmful packing techniques and on one occasion shipped 2,000 blankets from Ixmiguilpan, 8,000 mats and 113 *arrobas* of twine from Campeche in order to make *tercios*. There is no record of these supplies ever arriving. Of the two techniques used by Louisiana shippers—in barrels or loose in *andullos*—the latter was least injurious, claimed the Mexican authorities, though the technique worked only when shipping rolled tobacco. Unfortunately, the rolled tobacco was really best suited for making snuff and the Renta had abolished their *Fábrica de Rapé*. The rolls arrived so compact, claimed Hierro, that it was difficult to separate the leaves, rendering the mixture useless for making *puros* (cigars). The only other possible use for it then was to convert it to *cernido* (powder) for making *cigarros* (cigarettes), a process which required drying it in the sun and then mixing it with tobacco from the towns of Orizaba and Córdoba. Not only was the process time-consuming but considerable shrinkage took place. To alleviate all these inconveniences, the director repeated his demands for shipping tobacco in leaves, in *manojos* (small bunches), and *enterciado*.[18]

The major obstacle to fulfilling the desires of the Renta was the lack of subjects trained in making *tercios*. The director of the Renta proposed two plans to alleviate this problem. First, he suggested sending two *tercios* from Orizaba or Córdoba on each of two separate ships leaving Veracruz for New Orleans, hoping that after examination New Orleans authorities would see the simplicity of the technique and instruct the growers of its obvious benefits. The other idea was to send from two to four men from the villas of Orizaba and Córdoba, knowledgeable in the technique of *enmanojar* and *enterciar*, in order to instruct the growers of Louisiana.[19]

Navarro favored the second of these two proposals and in March of 1783, four instructors—Manuel Hernández, José Antonio Castillo, José Arzava and Ysidro Guzman, natives of Córdoba and Orizaba—arrived in New Orleans at the expense of the Renta to begin teaching the local growers in the preferred techniques of shipping tobacco. Navarro decided to split the four up, sending one each to Natchez, Natchitoches, Pointe Coupée and Opelousas and Attakapas, with the aim of putting the new method into practice. To further encourage a shift to this new technique, Navarro offered bonuses for all tobacco shipped to New Orleans in the new mode.[20]

His orders and instructions to José Antonio Castillo, designated instructor for the Natchitoches District, demonstrate his careful attention to detail and wide knowledge of the terrain. Navarro instructed Castillo to go directly to the homes of the tobacco planters when he arrived in Natchitoches and patiently instruct them in the mode of preparing tobacco in the Mexican style. He was to take two *manojos* (weighing about two pounds) from New Orleans as examples, and once there search for trees useful for making *tonotes* (wood for packing). Navarro felt that the Louisiana oak tree, which grew in abundance there, might be useful for making these staves.[21]

Since it was impossible to bring tobacco from Natchitoches *enterciado* (*tercios* of 150 to 200 pounds), because of transportation problems, Navarro urged Castillo to demonstrate carefully the method of preparing and shipping the *manojos* so that they would arrive in New Orleans well bound and properly conditioned, ready for immediate shipment to New Spain. As well, Castillo was to make recommendations regarding planting, cutting, and curing of tobacco best suited for producing *manojos*. When this task was completed, Castillo was to return to New Orleans with the first shipment of tobacco in order to give instructions for the manufacture of *tercios*.[22]

Meanwhile, Navarro's initial optimism about the new method was soon altered by reports coming in from the growing regions. The growers of Natchitoches, Avoyelles and Pointe Coupée wrote to Navarro that it was impossible to introduce the new technique that year because they lacked the buildings and storehouses necessary for converting the tobacco to *manojos*. They added that it would be extremely costly to ship tobacco using the new method since the volume would be increased while the actual weight was diminished.

Growers in Natchez protested that a major obstacle to employing the new technique was the fact that their fields were located a great distance from their dwelling and storage facilities. It was the opinion of the instructor sent to that district that the most suitable method there would be to *cernerlo* (reduce it to a powder) and place it in barrels or to fold it into *andullos* for use in making snuff. Only in the region of Opelousas was the new method greeted with much enthusiasm.[23]

In July of 1784 Navarro wrote to the viceroy of New Spain that none of the growers who put their tobacco in the mode of *manojos* were too enamoured with the technique because of its numerous inconveniences. What the directors of the Renta failed to realize, claimed Navarro, was the undeveloped frontier nature of the colony. There were virtually no open roads for wagons or carriages. Many of the posts were established at great distances from New Orleans. The introduction of this new mode would make necessary a storehouse in each district in order to receive and bundle the tobacco into *tercios*. This would require the hiring of additional employees to receive it and add the risks of shipping it to the capital to be borne by the Crown. Navarro concluded that the only suitable and cost efficient method of shipping large quantities of tobacco from Louisiana was in the form of *andullos* which could be shipped loose or wrapped into the bundles, the former being the cheaper method of shipment. The four instructors now in New Orleans, claimed Navarro, had concluded that to bundle the *andullos* into *tercios* would be of little benefit to the Renta.[24]

Upon receipt of Navarro's correspondence, the authorities in New Spain reluctantly agreed and on April 15, 1785, informed the intendant that they had concluded that Louisiana tobacco could be shipped in *andullos* (rolls) and *a granel* (loose) to be bundled into *tercios* in Veracruz. They asked him to seek passage on the first available ship for the four instructors from Orizaba and Córdoba. Navarro was instructed to sell the mats, blankets, and cords used in making *manojos*. Henceforth, all tobacco was to be shipped in *andullos* and *a granel* except for those of Natchez which could be put into *toneles* of a size and weight suitable for transportation from Veracruz to the factories. The Audiencia Gobernadora, acting in the name of the deceased viceroy, Matías de Gálvez, reminded Navarro to warn the Natchez growers that the hogsheads must be small enough to fit into the baskets (two per mule) and must never come in large barrels.[25]

With the question of the mode of shipping tobacco settled for the moment, Navarro was forced to turn his attentions to other problems, most notably the problem of supply.[26] The cultivation of tobacco, which began very slowly in the 1770s and whose growth was interrupted by the wartime conditions prevailing between 1779 and 1783, expanded rapidly after 1783. Despite the labor-intensive nature of the industry, favorable prices and a guaranteed market prompted planters of indigo to shift to the more profitable cultivation of tobacco. Many new planters entered the industry in the mid-1780s and sizeable numbers of American immigrants were attracted to the Natchez and Pointe Coupée Districts, bringing with them large numbers of slaves.

By late 1784, Mexican authorities, who had repeatedly demanded larger and larger shipments of Louisiana tobacco, for the first time began to be alarmed that the supplies from Louisiana might exceed the amount needed. Felipe de Hierro, Director General of the Monopoly, in a long *informe* repeated statements made earlier by the monopoly. First, he claimed that the consumers of New Spain preferred Mexican tobacco to all others, despite the fact that other tobaccos might be of excellent quality. He noted that a large part of the consumers in Mexico were women, who "by their natural delicacy" preferred the milder Mexican tobaccos to the stronger, more aromatic tobaccos of other regions. Because of this, the Renta could not afford to displease them without disastrous results to the Monopoly.[27]

Hierro added that shipments of 600,000 to 700,000 pounds of Louisiana tobacco would exceed demand. Not only that, but they would upset consumers and lead to a loss of revenue for the Monopoly. He noted that the taste of Mexican consumers dictated a mixture of one-fifth part Louisiana tobacco with four-fifths parts from the towns of Córdoba and Orizaba. Since the total consumption of New Spain in cigars and cigarettes had remained constant at about 2,600,000 pounds, it followed that shipments of tobacco from Louisiana ought not exceed 520,000 pounds.[28]

Once set in motion, however, the expansion of tobacco cultivation in Louisiana was impossible to stop. The industry entered a veritable boom after 1785. Navarro advised his old friend Bernardo de Gálvez, the new viceroy, in December of 1785, that the crop of 1785 would surely exceed one million pounds. Gálvez replied that he would accept the one million pounds for 1786 but that future shipments ought to be limited to the amounts requested by the directors of the Monopoly. Navarro took the precaution of informing the respective commandants of the number and weight of *andullos* assigned to each district. Only in Natchez was more tobacco being shipped than requested. Navarro informed Gálvez that in case of excessive supplies he would give preference to the ancient Spanish posts of Natchitoches, Opelousas, and Pointe Coupée in preference to Natchez. This decision was approved by the viceroy on March 30,1786.[29]

Navarro's obvious frustration with the authorities in New Spain over tobacco production became apparent in late 1785. For five years Navarro had been bombarded with a series of instructions, orders, and letters requesting him to use all means possible to stimulate the expansion of tobacco cultivation in the colony. And now, having seen the industry expand beyond all expectations, he was being pressured to reduce cultivation. Navarro wrote a long letter to Gálvez, barely disguising his obvious frustrations. Navarro wrote: "after having propagated the cultivation of tobacco in this province to more than the one million pounds that is needed by the Royal Monopoly of New Spain, and since the king will not purchase it, these inhabitants would be severely prejudiced, if by my part I do not find them a means of disposing it."[30] Navarro requested that he be authorized to allow tobacco to be shipped to any of the ports in France permitted for trade. Gálvez agreed in January of 1786.[31]

The fears of overproduction were greatly reduced by the decision of the Spanish Crown to establish the first *rapé* (snuff) factory in Seville, Spain. Since 1684 the Crown at its royal factory in Seville had produced tobacco *en polvo*, a special kind of powdered snuff, golden in color, perfumed with water *de azahar* (orange flower water). However in the eighteenth century, the custom of using snuff, thicker, darker and stronger than *polvo* had been introduced from France. Its use was prohibited in Spain by a royal *cédula* of November 15, 1735. However, increasing contraband and a growing preference for this kind of snuff manufactured at the newly created royal factory in Seville after July 25, 1786.[32]

Unlike the manufacture of *polvo* and cigars, the production of this new snuff was a highly mechanized operation. The original personnel for the new factory in Seville, five operators and three children were brought from France with the expressed purpose of instructing local workers in the fine art of making *rapé*.[33]

Shortly before the promulgation of the royal *cédula* establishing the new factory, Navarro was advised by a royal order of June 17, 1786, to gather all the best tobacco from Natchitoches and other locations to be shipped to Seville for the making of snuff, with the costs to be paid for by the viceroy of New Spain. Navarro wrote to José de Gálvez, on November 25, 1786, that he had decided to divide the tobacco cultivated in Louisiana into two equal parts, sending a quantity in barrels to the president of the Casa de Contratación, in Cádiz, and the remainder to Veracruz. Additionally, he advised Gálvez that tobacco was generally received in New Orleans in late December and stored in the royal storehouses until mid-February, when it was loaded and shipped to Veracruz, since that was the most favorable season for shipping in the gulf. For shipment to Spain, he felt it would be better to wait somewhat longer, perhaps until late March.[34] A royal order of December 20, 1786, enclosed instructions from the commissioner of the Royal Renta for Tobaccos of Europe, Sebastián Arrieta, and asked Navarro to send all available tobacco suitable for making snuff. Another royal order dated August 18, 1787, mentioned the figure of one million pounds which should be shipped to Spain without prejudice to the one million pounds shipped to New Spain, all costs of both to be paid for by the viceroy of New Spain.[35]

On November 25, 1786, Navarro wrote a long *informe* to the minister of the Indies, José de Gálvez, describing the nature of the tobacco industry in Louisiana and discussing the potential for future expansion of cultivation. First, he noted that production in the previous year (1785) was approximately 1,150,000 pounds of tobacco, with 150,000 pounds being consumed locally and the remainder purchased by the Crown.[36] He added that he did not believe it would be difficult to extend the cultivation. Tobacco in Louisiana, he wrote, was traditionally prepared in *andullos* of four to five pounds, several examples of which he had forwarded to the Crown for inspection. These rolls were often imperfectly made, causing the tobacco to decompose and putrefy. It was supposed, claimed Navarro, that the tobacco of this colony exceeds that of Virginia in quality, but the variety in which it is cultivated made him doubt whether its quality allowed it to be sent to Spain. Two means of shipment were possible: in *andullos* or pressed into hogsheads. The first involved putting the leaves in rolls about four inches thick. In this procedure, the tobacco was first shaped to its desired form, then wrapped in its own leaves covered with a cloth and tightly pressed by a laborer who wrapped a cord around the bundle. After the roll was laid out to dry, its shape was fixed and the cord and cloth were removed to be replaced by strips of bark.[37]

The main problem in making rolls, claimed Navarro, was that the growers did not compress them sufficiently, which led to excessive fermentation when they were exposed to heat. In addition, the poor situation of some of the growers obliged them to put tobacco into rolls before it had been properly cured and allowed to sweat. Finally, growers here, wrote Navarro, used excessively thick cords to compress it, and in their haste to produce rolls for the market often produced improperly cured, unsweated, and improperly compressed *andullos*, which meant that they did not conserve well from one year to another. An added inconvenience to this technique was the need for drying sheds to protect it before shipment. Tobacco in *andullos* was paid for by the Crown at the rate of ten *sueldos* or two *reales de vellón* for each French pound (a French pound was six and two-thirds percent larger than the Spanish).

The second means of shipment mentioned by Navarro was in *toneles* or hogsheads as used in Virginia. Navarro felt this procedure might be more suitable for the long ocean voyages to Europe. It also offered certain advantages to both the growers and the Crown. First, Navarro claimed that twenty slaves could pack all the tobacco that one hundred slaves could not reduce to rolls. Additionally, the tobacco was packed so tightly that air could not be introduced thereby preventing destruction and putrefaction. For the Crown, this procedure also offered benefits. The cost of packing would be assumed by the growers. The price paid was three *sueldos* less per pound. Most importantly though, the tremendous losses experienced in shipping *andullos* would in all likelihood be greatly reduced. Navarro agreed to follow the dictates of the Crown as to the preferred method of shipment, asking only that prompt orders be sent along with a sufficient quantity of silver to make the necessary purchases.[38]

While waiting to hear from the Crown, Navarro wrote José de Gálvez that he hoped that the growers would increase their acreages and that within a year would find themselves instructed in the preferred method of shipping. He shipped 900 barrels of tobacco in *andullos* and 6 barrels *en rama* (raw, unprepared) to Seville. The latter, wrote Navarro, containing some 1,443 pounds, were designed for experiments, to see if they retained good quality during the voyage. Navarro requested that these be examined in the royal factory to check for quality preparation and comparison with the *andullos*.[39]

In Spain, various experiments were carried out with the Louisiana tobacco. Some eighty-four bottles of snuff were prepared from the large and small *andullos* from Natchitoches and from the *andullos* pressed in Natchez. The superintendent of the factory in Seville concluded that the tobacco from Natchitoches in large rolls was superior to that with which he had been working. The tobacco in small rolls from the same location, though the quality of the leaves was good, had largely decomposed in shipping. As for the tobacco from Natchez, the superintendent concluded that though the leaves might have been good, they had entirely decomposed in shipping and were useless for making snuff.[40]

Following these experiments, the director of the factory in Seville issued the following instructions for shipping tobacco from Louisiana. First, only the best leaves should be used, dried in the sun, soaked in vinegar, to aid fermentation. After two months in this condition, the tobacco should be mixed with molasses and pressed into hogsheads of about 1,000 pounds. The director reemphasized the key aspects of preparation: vinegar, molasses, and proper curing in the sun. Without these, he claimed, the leaf could not last long without spoiling for lack of fermentation. Using the methods suggested by Navarro in *andullos* or *toneles*, he felt, would mean that the tobacco would not be able to arrive in Europe with it natural juices and strength. Molasses, he stated, was an important requisite to making good snuff.[41]

Navarro received a copy of the instructions from the director of the factory along with a royal order of May 12, 1787, asking that he ship one million pounds to Spain. Navarro replied to Gálvez, that from the instructions he had deduced that the preferred mode for shipping tobacco was pressed into hogsheads of 1,000 to 1,100 pounds, which he had noted in several letters, was the standard practice in Virginia, the only difference being the use of molasses and vinegar. He added that he had immediately forwarded a copy of the instructions to Natchez, but it would probably arrive too late to alter that year's crop. Upon receiving the instructions, the planters in Natchez wrote Navarro that the tobacco produced there was in every way similar to that of Virginia, adding that they had never heard of using vinegar or molasses in the preparation of tobacco.[42]

Despite receiving the instructions, the Natchez planters continued in their old pattern of putting the tobacco in *andullos*. Having already shifted from making hogsheads in the early 1780s, to satisfy the Renta of New Spain, they were reluctant to shift a second time back to their original mode of packing. Navarro wrote the new minister of the Indies, Antonio Valdés, in March of 1787, that the Natchez growers continued to send their crops to the capital in *andullos*. When he inquired why, they responded that it was not humanly possible to convert them to *toneles* at the current price of six *sueldos, 6 dineros*. If this was unsatisfactory, they threatened to return to the cultivation of indigo. Navarro told Valdés that it was not possible to treat these individuals in the same way as if they had been born in and accustomed to the laws of Spain. Rather it was necessary to win them over with persuasion and kind words. With this in mind, he reported, he had called a meeting of the principal planters to hear their complaints.

With Colonel Thomas Hutchins as their spokesman, the Natchez planters presented their case. The Virginians, he said, sold tobacco cheaper than they did, but this was because they were able to obtain supplies at much cheaper prices than Louisiana planters. Second, he claimed that to carry out the new procedures would necessitate the building of a considerable number of new buildings to dry the tobacco in the shade.

The result would be that tobacco in *toneles* would be far less profitable than tobacco in *andullos*. Having heard all complaints, Navarro wrote, he had agreed to raise the price of tobacco shipped it *toneles* to twenty-five *maravedís* per pound, the same as for *andullos*. This high price seemed to content the growers and, Navarro added, would undoubtedly attract thousands of new growers to the industry. Navarro's actions were approved by a royal order on September 27, 1788.[43]

In Spain, Pedro Llerena, the new secretary of state for Finance, advised Valdés August 14, 1787, that the majority of tobacco coming from Louisiana in *andullos* had lost its strength and had decomposed due to inadequate preparation for shipping. He asked Valdés to give the appropriate orders to Navarro to insist that all future shipments (not just from Natchez) come in the form requested by the director of the factory in Seville. A royal order to this effect was issued, August 18, 1787. However, it was impossible to obtain compliance since tobacco shipped to New Spain was supposed to go in *andullos* and one could hardly expect the planters to employ two different techniques for shipping tobacco.[44]

The failure to attend to the instruction of the director of the factory in Seville proved to be the ruination of the industry. Meanwhile, tobacco cultivation in the last years of the decade of the 1780s experienced a veritable boom. In 1787 tobacco shipped from Louisiana to Spain and New Spain exceeded one and a half million Spanish pounds for the first time, and in 1788 production surpassed two million pounds.

The greatest expansion of cultivation took place in the Natchez district where by 1789 more than 1.4 million pounds of tobacco were being produced. Even in Pointe Coupée, tobacco production more than doubled from the mid-1780s to 74,960 pounds in 1789. Tobacco planters began borrowing money from New Orleans merchants against revenues from future crops to purchase more slaves and thus expand cultivation.

In Spain, however, the tremendous expansion of shipments of Louisiana tobacco began to prove difficult to market. More than 2.5 million pounds were shipped to Seville in 1789, creating a huge surplus at the factory. A royal order of July 25, 1790, instructed Governor Esteban Miró to limit future shipments to two million pounds. The growing surplus of Louisiana tobacco in Spain was the subject of earnest discussions at several meetings of the newly created Junta del Estado. A surplus of more than 3,709,764 pounds already existed in Seville storehouses by December of 1790. At a special meeting of the Junta convoked on December 21, 1790, some five key decisions were taken which were to drastically affect the future prosperity of the colony of Louisiana. First, the Junta approved Governor Miró's disposition about the admission of 2.5 million pounds to Spain from the crop of 1789. Second, the Junta advised Miró to admit only two million pounds from the crop of 1790. Third, and most important, the Junta concluded that it would accept only 40,000 pounds from the crop of 1791, since the tobacco was suitable only for *rapé* and attempts to use it in making cigars and cigarettes had met with disapproval from Spanish consumers. Fourth, for the large quantity of tobacco produced in Louisiana in excess of 40,000 pounds, a special *Reglamento de Comercio* would be formed to provide a suitable outlet. Finally, an attempt would be made to sell in Holland the current glut of almost four million pounds of Louisiana tobacco.[45]

In New Spain, a similar problem of oversupply finally led to the curtailment of future shipments of tobacco from Louisiana. By 1788, a surplus of more than 1,260,154 pounds of Louisiana tobacco was in storage in Mexican warehouses. On October 27, 1789, after consulting with the directors of the Monopoly, viceroy Conde de Revillagigedo, on the advice of the fiscal of the Real Audiencia y Real Hacienda, Ramón de Posada y Soto, advised the governor of Louisiana of the serious problems and prejudices caused to the tobacco monopoly by Louisiana tobacco. He advised the governor that he had decided to prohibit any future shipments after 1789.[46]

The impact of these two decision of 1789 and 1790 had disastrous effects on the Louisiana economy. Most of the planters, who had speculated heavily in the purchase of new slaves to open new acreages of cultivation, were bankrupted. A large number of prominent New Orleans merchants suffered severe financial problems because they were unable to obtain repayment of large loans made to the planters, most of whom were bankrupted by the collapse of the boom. The district of Natchitoches and the adjacent Red River District, with no market for their tobacco, went into a long period of decline. Immigrants in search of riches from tobacco stopped moving to Natchez. The entire population could justly feel that it had been led down the proverbial garden path by the Spanish authorities.

Politically, the impact was also felt. Though the Crown later raised the quota to 120,000 pounds in 1794 and to 200,000 pounds in 1796, the effects of the decrees of 1789 and 1790 were extremely demoralizing to the entire population, including the royal officials. The collapse of the tobacco industry, writes on observer: "led to a shortage of merchandise, the Indians were restless, and any form of organized trade was unprofitable."[47] Many settlers, finding it impossible to continue in their accustomed lifestyle, resorted to illegal trading with the Indians or entirely abandoned their land. When news of the French Revolution reached Louisiana, some former planters eagerly supported the Jacobin cause and called for a restoration of French rule in Louisiana.[48]

So rapid and complete was the collapse of the tobacco industry, that in 1795 when the Crown decided to raise the Louisiana quota to 200,000 pounds, only 148,823 pounds could be found, and all of this from Natchitoches. Intendant Francisco Rendón wrote Diego Gardoqui that the cultivation of tobacco had been entirely abandoned in all the posts save Natchitoches. A year later, in December of 1796, acting Intendant Juan Ventura Morales, in response to a plea that he send tobacco for the snuff factory in Seville, could only reply that he was shipping 43 hogsheads from Kentucky, the only quantity available in the province. By 1800 most planters had shifted to cotton production.[49]

The success of the tobacco industry was the result of diligence on the part of Martín Navarro, extremely favorable prices, a guaranteed market, and the attraction of an old industry with which at least some of the planters had had long experience. The collapse of the industry was brought on by overproduction, a lack of attention to careful packing and shipment, and the displeasure of Mexican and Spanish consumers. Above all, it was the result of misguided decisions by both Spanish and Mexican authorities. Having clamored for Louisiana tobacco for more than a decade, they abandoned it in an instant and brought on the economic ruination of a large sector of the colony's merchants and planters, as well as discrediting all future projects of the Spanish Crown in Louisiana. Intendant Martín Navarro fortunately escaped the collapse of the industry he had nurtured along for ten years. He left New Orleans on the frigate *San Miguel* bound for Cádiz with a cargo of tobacco, June 15, 1788.[50]

Notes for "Boom and Bust: The Rise and Fall of the Tobacco Industry in Spanish Louisiana, 1770-1790"

[1]Jacob Price, *France and the Chesapeake: A History of the French Tobacco Monopoly, 1674-1791, and of its Relationship to the British and American Trades* (Ann Arbor, 1973), 1:357.

[2]Testimonio del Expediente Sobre Siembra y Cultivo de Tabaco en Luisiana, 1782, Archivo General de Indias, Sección 11, Papeles Procedentes de Cuba, legajo 610 (Hereinafter cited AGI, PC followed by the legajo number). The *Renta de Tabaco* has recently been the subject of an excellent study by David Lorne McWatters, "The Royal Tobacco Monopoly in Bourbon Mexico" (Ph.D. Dissertation, University of Florida, 1979).

[3]Julian de Arriaga to Luis de Unzaga, May 20, 1771, Lawrence Kinnaird, ed., *Spain in the Mississippi Valley, 1765-1794*. 3 vols. Annual Report of the American Historical Association for 1945 (Washington, DC, 1946), 2:193.

[4]Real Orden to Governor of Louisiana, Aranjuez, May 21, 1776, Archivo General de Indias, Sección 5: Gobierno, Audiencia de Mexico, legajo 1622 (Hereinafter cited as AGI, Mexico followed by the legajo number).

[5]Testimonio de expediente a consequencia de real orden sobre fabrica de cigarros con oja de maiz y traer tabacos de la Luisiana, AGI, Mexico 1622. The word *puro* was a short form for *cigarro puro*. The addition of the word is attributed to a French priest Labat who wrote about the advantages of the cigar in 1700. The word *cigarros* probably referred to a primitive form of cigarette, which was introduced to New Spain from Guatemala in 1776, the tobacco being wrapped in maize leaves instead of paper. These *cigarros* were popular in many parts of Spanish America and were later introduced in Europe. A good discussion of Spanish tobacco customs is: José Pérez Vidal, *España en la história del tabaco* (Madrid, 1959).

[6]Advice of Felipe de Hierro and José de la Riva, Directores de la Renta, Mexico, October 10, 1776. In: Testimonio de expediente a consequencia. . ., AGI, Mexico 1622. McWatters, "The Royal Tobacco Monopoly," describes a *tercio* as being made up of 80 to 100 smaller bundles of tobacco known as manojos. These *tercios*, in turn were bundled using mats of cord and palm, 60.

[7]Martín Navarro to José de Gálvez, No. 7, New Orleans, April 11, 1780, AGI, PC 633; Real Orden, José de Gálvez to Sr. Intendente, June 5, 1781, AGI, PC 569.

[8]Navarro to José de Gálvez, No. 8, April 12, 1780, AGI, PC 633.

[9]Navarro to José de Gálvez, April 12, 1780, and marginal notation, Archivo General de Indias, Sección 5: Gobierno, Audiencia de Santo Domingo, legajo 2633, No. 190 (Hereinafter cited as AGI, SD followed by the legajo number and document number if given).

[10]Navarro to José de Gálvez, No 52, June 25, 1781, AGI, SD 2633, No. 201.

[11]Navarro to Nicolas Delassize (de la Chaise), September 18, 1781, AGI, PC 83.

[12]Navarro to José de Gálvez, No 100, September 10, 1781, AGI, SD 2633, No. 207.

[13]Navarro to José de Gálvez, No 111, April 30, 1781, AGI, SD 2533, No. 214.

[14]Ibid.

[15]*Informe*, Martín Navarro to José de Gálvez, No 127, September 12, 1782, AGI, SD 2633, Nos. 219-22.

[16]Navarro prepared the design for the warehouses in the absence of a trained engineer in the colony. One of them was built in 1789. A copy of Navarro's plans exists in AGI, Mapos y Planos, Luisiana y Florida, Nos. 96 and 97; Real Orden a Navarro, November 22, 1783, AGI, PC 569.

[17]Martín de Mayorga to Navarro, April 26, 1781, AGI, PC 610; Felipe de Hierro to Mayorga, March 1, 1781, AGI, PC 610.

[18]Expediente sobre la Siembra y cultivo tabaco en la provincia de Luisiana, Dirección General de la Real Renta de Tabaco, 1782, AGI, PC 610.

[19]Felipe de Hierro to Mayorga, Mexico, July 22, 1781, in Ibid. A marginal notation read, "advise Sr. Navarro of these providences."

[20]Navarro to Martín Mayorga, March 24, 1783, AGI, SD 2633, No. 254.

[21]Instrucción de lo que deve observar José Antonio de Castillo, Martín Navarro, March 20, 1783, AGI, SD 2633, No. 258.

[22]Ibid.

[23]Navarro to Mayorga, March 245, 1783, AGI, Sd 2633, No. 254.

[24]Navarro to Matías de Gálvez, July 27, 1784, AGI, SD 2633, No. 303.

[25]Audiencia/Gobernadora de Mexico to Navarro, April 19, 1785, AGI, PC 610. The four instructors left New Orleans on the brig *San José*, each receiving a gratification of 25 *pesos*. Navarro to Audiencia/Gobernadora de Mexico, July 30, 1785, AGI, PC 610.

[26]The tobacco was first sown in a seedbed. When it had sprouted four leaves it was transplanted and placed in prepared holes a foot broad and three feet apart. The leaves had to be watered and protected from encroaching weed and insects. This required careful and continuous weeding. When a desired number of leaves had grown (usually 12 in Louisiana) the top of the plant was pinched off to prevent seeds developing. Suckers growing out at the base were also pinched off. At the harvest the leaves were stripped from the stalk and strung on long poles to air. When dry, they were then piled in heaps to sweat. Finally, at the proper stage of dryness they were ready for manufacture into *andullos*.

[27]Testimonio del Expediente sobre la siembra y cultivo tabaco en la provincia de la Luisiana, Dirección General de la Real Renta de Tabaco, 1782, AGI, PC 610.

[28]*Informe*, Felipe de Hierro to Riva, October 20, 1784, AGI, PC 610.

[29]Navarro to Conde de Gálvez (Bernardo), December 12, 1785; Conde de Gálvez to Navarro, March 30, 1786, AGI, PC 610.

[30]Navarro to Conde de Gálvez, No. 22 December 14, 1785, AGI, PC 610.

[31]Ibid., Conde de Gálvez to Navarro, January 26, 1786, AGI, PC 610.

[32]José Pérez Vidal, *España en la historia del tabaco,* 76-83.

[33]Ibid.

[34]Real cédula en la que se previene se fabrique nueva labor de tabaco rapé, July 22, 1786, AGI, SD 2633, No. 562; Navarro to Sonora (José de Gálvez), No. 426, November 25, 1786, AGI, SD 2633, No. 350.

[35]Real Orden, Marqués de Sonora to Navarro, December 20, 1786, AGI, PC 560; Real Orden to Navarro, San Ildefónso, August 18, 1787, AGI, SD 2633, No. 350.

[36]Local consumption involved the manufacture into pipe tobacco, cigars, and to supply a small snuff factory in New Orleans. Regarding the latter see: Alexo Lardin sobre el reconocimiento de una cajas de quinta exencia (essencia), November 20, 1786, Louisiana State Museum, Judicial Records of the Spanish Cabildo, No. 178611201. Tobacco was also used in the Indian Trade.

[37]A more exact description of making *andullos* is in Joseph C. Robert, *The Story of Tobacco in America* (Chapel Hill, 1949), 50-51.

[38]*Informe*, Navarro to José de Gálvez, No. 427, November 25, 1786, AGI, SD 2633, No. 355.

[39]Navarro to José de Gálvez, Nos. 484 and 485, April 20, 1785, AGI, SD 2633, Nos. 373 and 374.

[40]Pedro de Lerena to Marqués de Sonora, El Pardo, January 28, 1787, AGI, SD 2633, No. 581.

[41]León de Torres, Director de la Fábrica de Rapé en Sevilla, y Arana, to Señores Administradores Generales, March 7, 1787, AGI, SD 2633, No. 589.

[42]Navarro to Marqués de Sonora, No. 542, August 28, 1787; Statement of Natchez Growers, August 20, 1787, AGI, SD 2633, Nos. 382 and 385.

[43]Navarro to Antonio Valdés, No. 64, March 7, 1788, AGI, SD 2533, No. 297, with enclosure, "Representation made by the Inhabitants of Natchez," undated; Real Orden a Navarro, San Ildefónso, September 27, 1788, AGI, SD 2633, No. 404.

[44]Pedro de Lerena, First Minister of the Treasury, to Antonio Valdes, First Minister of the Indies, San Ildefónso, August 14, 1787; Real Orden to Navarro, San Ildefónso, August 18, 1787, AGI, SD 2633, Nos. 611 and 615.

[45]Minutes of the Junta de Dirección de Indias, December 21, 1790, AGI, SD 2633, Nos. 692-727.

[46]Conde de Revillagigedo, Viceroy of New Spain, to Señores Directores de Tabaco, October 27, 1787, in Expediente sobre tabaco, Testimonio No. 3, 1804, AGI, Mexico 1622.

[47]Ernest R. Liljegren, "Jacobinism in Spanish Louisiana, 1792-1797," *Louisiana Historical Quarterly*, 22 (1939): 22.

[48]Ibid.

[49]Francisco Rendón to Diego Gardoqui, No. 89, November 30, 1795, and No. 124, April 18, 1796, AGI, SD 2613; Juan Ventura Morales to Diego Gardoqui, No. 62, December 1, 1796, AGI, SD 2613; Ramón de López y Angulo to Cayetano Soler, No. 36, January 20, 1801, AGI, SD 2617.

[50]Navarro retired from the Intendency, May 10, 1788, turning his papers over to Esteban Miró, in whom the king had decided to invest the additional responsibilities of intendant. On June 15 he boarded the frigate *San Miguel* bound for Cádiz, which he reached on September 4, 1788. Miró to Antonio Valdés, June 15, 1788; Real Orden to Esteban Miró, San Ildefonso, September 4, 1788, AGI, SD 2633, Nos. 46 and 49.

REED AND FORDE MERCHANT ADVENTURERS OF PHILADELPHIA: THEIR TRADE WITH SPANISH NEW ORLEANS*

Arthur P. Whitaker

In the long chapter of revolutionary history extending from the establishment of our own independence through the French Revolution, the Napoleonic Era, and the emancipation of Spanish and Portuguese America, one of the least spectacular but most significant changes was the dislocation of Spanish American commerce.[1] As Peuchet pointed out in 1821 in his continuation of Raynal, this dislocation was a matter of great consequence not only because of the volume of Spanish American commerce, but also because of its special character: Spanish America was then the world's chief source of supply of gold and silver.[2]

Peuchet also pointed out that Raynal, whose book was first published in 1770, was unable to foresee the great changes that were soon to take place in America. We may add that, even at the close of the American Revolution, no one could have been expected to foresee the great changes that were soon to take place in the commerce of Spanish America. Practically all of it was monopolized by Spain and most of it was concentrated in the single port of Cadiz. Though smuggling was still widespread, Spain was then at the height of its "Bourbon renaissance" and the court seemed to be making considerable progress in its efforts to adjust its regulations to the needs of colonial commerce, stamp out smuggling, and prepare Spanish industry and shipping to meet the needs of the colonies. At no time for more than a century past had Spain's prospects of rendering effective its ostensible monopoly appeared more flattering than in 1783. Yet within a quarter of a century these prospects had been utterly destroyed and the commerce of Spanish America had fallen into the hands of foreigners—the English, the French, the Dutch, and the Americans. The loss of Spain's commercial control over her colonies was soon followed by loss of political control as well. By 1825 all of continental Spanish

*This article first appeared in the *Pennsylvania Magazine of History and Biography*, 61 (1937): 237-62. It is reprinted with the kind permission of the publisher.

America had achieved its independence. It is interesting to compare the commercial sequel of independence in the former Spanish colonies with that in the former English colonies; for while the bulk of the commerce of the United States reverted to England very shortly after the close of the American Revolution, Spain never regained in independent Spanish America the commercial preponderance that she had enjoyed during the colonial period.

In the United States, Philadelphia was one of the main centers of interest in Spanish America throughout this revolutionary era. Many books and pamphlets about Spain and Spanish America were published and many Spanish American revolutionary agents and sympathizers lived or visited in Philadelphia; and its merchants and sailors took a leading part in opening up the forbidden trade with Spanish America and thus in initiating the commercial revolution that preceded and contributed to the political emancipation of that region.

Conspicuous among these Philadelphia merchants were John Reed and Standish Forde of the firm of Reed and Forde. To be sure, their trade with Spanish America was confined for the most part to a single port, New Orleans, during a comparatively brief period (about 1787-1803), and New Orleans is not often thought of as a Spanish American port, since it, together with the rest of Louisiana, was annexed to the United States as long ago as 1803. But from the American Revolution to the Louisiana Purchase, New Orleans was a Spanish port; it possessed more importance for the United States than almost any other port in Spanish America, and our annexation of Louisiana was due at least in part to the trade which American merchants built up with New Orleans while it was still under the dominion of Spain. The following pages contain an account of the part that Reed and Forde of Philadelphia played in opening up trade with one corner of Spanish America and in promoting the territorial as well as the commercial expansion of the United States in the first generation after independence.

There was nothing petty or parochial or humdrum about Reed and Forde's business. Their far-flung correspondence, though yellowed by time, still conveys the yeasty flavor of the age of innovation and expansion in which they lived; and it shows how profoundly economic activities were influenced by the political upheavals and the wars of the period. Their correspondence extended from Boston to Savannah, from New Orleans to Malabar and from Cap Français and Jamaica to Marseilles, Lisbon, Bordeaux, and London. It contains a host of names familiar in the history of American business, politics, and diplomacy: George Washington, Edmund Randolph, Alexander Hamilton, Andrew Jackson, Clement Biddle, Robert Morris, and Diego de Gardoqui: Governors Mifflin of Pennsylvania, and his brother Daniel; Moses Austin, lead miner of Virginia and Missouri, and later colonizer of Texas; Daniel Clark, Jr., merchant and consular agent of the United States at New Orleans; and the adventurer Philip Nolan and his more notorious associate, James Wilkinson, soldier, merchant, politician and arch-conspirator.

Reed and Forde not only engaged in foreign commerce both on their own account and on commission, and owned and operated their own ships, captained by members of their own families, but also engaged in many kinds of financial operations and bought and sold western lands, for which they procured settlers and on which they operated flour mills. They lent money to Edmund Randolph and Robert Morris, and sold bank stock to George Washington.[3] In 1787 they complained that Alexander Hamilton was neglecting the interests of one of their clients in New York, and they were reluctant to excuse Hamilton even on the ground that he was preoccupied with his work in the Federal Convention.[4] When the new federal government was established, they were among the merchants—excoriated by the Anti-Federalists—who sought to turn an honest penny by buying up depreciated paper currency of the old Congress and the several states, in the hope that the Hamiltonian financial system would be adopted and this currency redeemed at par.[5] In the course of these various enterprises, they were constantly taking risks that appalled their more conservative creditors—for, though they lent money, they themselves were deep in debt throughout most of this period, and that fact doubtless goes far to explain their conduct. It is characteristic of them that, in writing about a projected venture of theirs in the Mississippi trade, they said that this "speculation" would "not be hazardous."[6] In their energy, in the multiplicity of their interest, and in their readiness to try their fortune in new fields, Reed and Forde seemed to be animated by the spirit of those merchant adventurers who had extended English trade to the White Sea, the Levant, and the East Indies in the 16th and 17th centuries—and also by the spirit of the American frontier. Thus they were fitted by temperament for the undertaking that engaged most of their time and attention between the end of the American Revolution and the Louisiana Purchase, namely, the development of trade with the Ohio Valley. To this even their trade with New Orleans was subsidiary at the outset, though ultimately it became independent.

Even before the close of the American Revolution, Philadelphia merchants were developing an interest in the trade through the Ohio Valley with New Orleans. According to the report of a Spanish agent at Philadelphia who wrote in February, 1783, the Atlantic coast was then infested with so many British warships that these merchants were unwilling to risk maritime shipments and sought compensation by sending their goods across the mountains to the Fort Pitt (Pittsburgh) region and the Illinois country, exchanging them for flour and furs and shipping the flour in flat boats down to the New Orleans market where it commanded an even higher price than usual because the war between Spain and England had made it difficult to obtain supplies from the normal source, Vera Cruz.[7] Thus in this war, as in so many others during the eighteenth century, the war-time embarrassments of Spain and its colonies promoted the economic penetration of Spanish America by foreigners; for during war-time the Spanish commercial monopoly had to be relaxed, and when peace was restored, neither foreigners nor colonists were willing to surrender the mutually advantageous trade that the war had opened up.

With the end of the American Revolution, the reopening of trade with England, and the flush times that followed, the attention of these Philadelphia merchants was diverted from the Ohio Valley and New Orleans—but only for a brief period. It soon developed that in their optimism they had imported far more English goods than could be sold in the

East; and so some of them sought to dispose of the surplus in the rapidly growing settlements of the Ohio Valley. Reed and Forde doubtless shared this interest; and they also owned thousands of acres of land in the Ohio Valley which they wished to enhance in value by promoting the settlement of the West.[8] Unless, however, the western people could find an outlet for their produce, they would be unable to purchase eastern goods, and western lands would be likely to rise in value. The only practicable outlet for western produce was by way of the Mississippi River, and both banks of that river in its lower course were in the possession of Spain. At that time the Spanish court forbade the Americans and all other foreigners to trade with New Orleans or even to navigate the Mississippi.[9] It was, therefore, to the interest of our Philadelphia merchants as well as the western people to find some means of breaking Spain's monopoly of the Mississippi.

The general business depression that followed close on the heels of the American Revolution[10] had a decisive influence in determining Reed and Forde to try to open up the Mississippi trade. The widespread political discontent which resulted from that depression made it possible for them—and other like-minded persons—to succeed in doing so. Reed and Forde were hard hit by the depression; their debts were large and their creditors, Cruger, Ledyard and Mullett, of New York and London, were clamoring for payment.[11] So they were ready to try any expedient, no matter how novel or hazardous it might be, if only it promised to bring in some ready cash. Their existing interest in western trade and land speculation pointed clearly to the Mississippi trade. Here the political discontent of the period came to their aid. This discontent was particularly keen in the West, where, by a happy coincidence, it produced the "Spanish conspiracy" just when such a development was most needed by Reed and Forde. The Spanish conspiracy was an intrigue in which James Wilkinson and other frontiersmen concerted with the Spanish officials of Louisiana a plan ostensibly designed to separate the trans-Allegheny West from the United States. Whether or not the western conspirators really intended to promote the secession of the West, they certainly intended to promote its trade by inducing Spain to open the Mississippi River to them.[12]

In the latter effort they met with a considerable measure of success. The first important move in the conspiracy was James Wilkinson's descent down the Ohio and the Mississippi to New Orleans in 1787. He contrived somehow to get past the intervening river ports to the creole capital.[13] Then, by playing alternately on the Spaniard's fear that the West might attack Louisiana, and their hope that it might secede from the Union, he induced first the local officials and then the court itself to permit the westerners to export their produce down the Mississippi to New Orleans.[14] This privilege, formally granted by a royal order of 1788, continued in force until 1795, when by the Treaty of San Lorenzo, Spain granted the citizens of the United States the free navigation of the Mississippi throughout its course and the privilege of transshipping their cargoes at New Orleans.[15]

Wilkinson's descent to New Orleans in 1787 thus opened one side of the great circular trade that was soon to link Philadelphia with the Ohio Valley and New Orleans. The other side of it—which required access to New Orleans by way of the Gulf of Mexico and the lower Mississippi—was never formally opened by the Spanish court; but even before Wilkinson's first arrival at New Orleans, means had been found of evading Spanish prohibitions and selling Philadelphia merchandise in New Orleans. This was made possible by the permission to trade with French St. Domingue which the Spanish court had granted Louisiana in 1782; for the Americans too had the privilege of trading with St. Domingue and their cargoes were transshipped there and sent to New Orleans thinly but adequately disguised as French property. Even in their despatches to the court, the Spanish officials of Louisiana admitted that the volume of imports received from Philadelphia by this route was considerable.[16] New Orleans—and other Spanish America ports as well—paid for American goods partly in specie. To the Americans, that was one of the chief attractions of the trade; for, as we have already noted, Spanish American was then the world's chief source of supply of gold and silver, commodities that were scarce and in great demand in the United States. Though the exportation of specie from the Spanish colonies was prohibited under severe penalties, it was relatively easy to smuggle it out. Phineas Bond, the British consul at Philadelphia, reported to his government that in 1787 five hundred thousand dollars worth of specie was brought from Spanish America to that port alone.[17] Some of this—just how much we cannot say—came from New Orleans; for hundreds of thousands of dollars worth of specie was smuggled out of the province every year, most of it going to St. Domingue.[18] Some of this, we may safely assume, went from St. Domingue to Philadelphia. Thus the merchants of Philadelphia had still another reason for sharing with Wilkinson and his fellow westerners their desire to promote trade between the United States and New Orleans.

Indeed, it is possible that some Philadelphia merchant or merchants had a hand in Wilkinson's first expedition to New Orleans and so in the beginning of this important phase of the Spanish conspiracy, for it was a trading venture with Philadelphia backing that took him to Kentucky at the end of the Revolution;[19] but it will require further research to substantiate this conjecture. At any rate, if any Philadelphia merchants were responsible for his going to New Orleans, it was almost certainly not Reed and Forde. This is rather surprising, since he and they had similar interests and were connected with each other in a roundabout way. Wilkinson's wife was Ann Biddle, a sister of Clement Biddle who backed Wilkinson's Kentucky venture in 1784; and we know that when Clement Biddle failed in 1785, Reed and Forde were among his creditors.[20] So one might be ready to believe that Wilkinson and his schemes were one of the more or less doubtful Biddle assets acquired by Reed and Forde in 1785, and that they were thus involved in Wilkinson's New Orleans venture two years later. This problem is all the more curious because we know that Reed and Forde did send an agent of their own to New Orleans in 1787 and that he returned to the United States about the same time as Wilkinson and with news equally encouraging to American merchants.[21] Nevertheless, it is virtually certain that this unidentified agent was not Wilkinson, and that the latter's connection with them was first formed early in 1788 after his return from New Orleans, and that the connection was formed through John Lewis, of Fredericksburg, Virginia. Lewis kept a store at

Fredericksburg, which was supplied by Reed and Forde, and when Wilkinson approached Lewis early in 1788 about a credit for a venture to the Ohio and New Orleans, the latter naturally sought to interest them in the venture.[22] Thus it appears that Reed and Forde had developed an interest in the Mississippi venture simultaneously with Wilkinson but independently of him, and that the two were brought together by their common association with Lewis.

In 1788 and again in 1789 Reed and Forde were concerned with Lewis and Wilkinson in expeditions from the Ohio Valley to New Orleans.[23] Both of these expeditions turned out badly, and Reed and Forde had little to show for their pains but a sheaf of Wilkinson's notes amounting to the tidy sum of £2300 Pennsylvania currency—about $7,000.[24] They had made their preparations carefully, had obtained passports from the Spanish envoy in the United States, Diego de Gardoqui, and Standish Forde himself had accompanied the expedition of 1789 to New Orleans; but one important element of success they still lacked: a permit from the Spanish officials at New Orleans.[25]

This they obtained from a Philadelphia capitalist, Joseph Ball. Ball in turn had obtained it from Oliver Pollock,[26] whose services at New Orleans during the American Revolution had given him some influence there. Reed and Forde now formed with Ball an association that is important in the history of the New Orleans trade, for a large part of that trade was carried on under it during the next five years, and it soon involved two other men, Daniel Clark, Jr., and Daniel W. Coxe, who were destined to expand the trade greatly and give it political significance. Ball, as well as Reed and Forde, had already made a venture in the Mississippi trade and had burnt his fingers in it; but though both parties had failed separately they believed that they would succeed by joining forces. This they now did. Ball provided not only the New Orleans permit, but also the capital,[27] while Reed and Forde contributed their first-hand knowledge of trade on the Ohio and the Mississippi and their mercantile establishment and general experience. Wilkinson was excluded from direct participation in the enterprise, but he was still expected to furnish letters of introduction to the Spanish officials of Louisiana.[28]

The financial backing that Reed and Forde received from Ball was a godsend to them. Cruger, Ledyard, and Mullett were angrily demanding payment and charged that Reed and Forde were responsible for "the distress of those to whom we are in debt through your default of payment—some languishing in jail and others on the brink of ruin." Reed and Forde protested that they were indeed sensible to the distresses of others; they only wanted their creditors, in their own interest, to "wait the issue of an adventure for a much larger sum" than those already made. "The speculation we propose," they wrote with irrepressible optimism, "will not be hazardous." Cruger, Ledyard, and Mullett waited—and not for the last time.[29]

The speculation that was not hazardous was, of course, another venture down the Ohio and Mississippi to New Orleans, with Reed in charge this time. In the autumn of 1789 preparations for his journey were pressed actively. With a due regard for the amenities, and to make smooth Reed's path in New Orleans, Forde despatched in a ship to that port various tokens of his esteem for the Spanish officials whom he had met on his own recent visit there: to the governor's secretary, Andrés López de Armesto, three barrels of "our Pippin apples," one for Governor Miró and the other two for López de Armesto himself; also a beaver hat for Armesto (an important personage, the governor's secretary); and another beaver hat for Gilberto Leonard, the intendant's secretary. Forde also sent López de Armesto, for himself, a "box of segars," since he was "fond of smoaking," and, for his wife, a canister of Hyson tea and six loaves of sugar[30]—several years were still to elapse before Etienne Boré succeeded in making sugar from Louisiana cane.

Lest these polite attentions should make López de Armesto forget that business is business, Forde followed up his oblation of the Hyson tea and beaver hats and loaves of sugar with a quick reminder of their recent conversations about trade, and then wrote, "If you will be so good as to procure and send forward by the first conveyance a register for sloop or schooner that will enable me to send a vessel to your port it will be much to my interest, and I shall take care to record it among the many civility [*sic*], I received from you and other friends in New Orleans."[31] "Civility" was certainly not too strong a word for a service that involved a flagrant violation of Spanish law. Nor is it to be assumed that such civilities on the part of the Spanish officials at New Orleans were rewarded only with literal loaves of sugar. Though the discreet correspondence of Reed and Forde does not speak openly of such matters, the uninhibited Wilkinson soon afterwards wrote to an agent who was about to take a cargo of tobacco down to New Orleans that of course the Spanish officials would expect to get their cut; and he authorized his agent to offer Gilberto Leonard four thousand dollars to get the tobacco accepted for the king's stores.[32]

Forde's experience on his own recent trip to New Orleans was useful on this occasion. He gave Reed a letter of introduction to "Mr. Noland," the well-known Philip Nolan, and told him to apply to Wilkinson, who was then in Kentucky, for other letters, especially to the Spanish governor of Natchez (Manuel Gayoso de Lemos). Wilkinson was to be asked to pay his debt in flour and tobacco, which could be sold on the way down the river, that is, at such Spanish posts as Natchez and Baton Rouge, as well as at New Orleans. Reed was also advised to take all the tin he could obtain, which could be sold to the hunters at "Lancela Grass" (L'Anse à la Graisse) and at Natchez. Furs and skins should be taken in exchange, for they were in great demand at Philadelphia. Forde announced with pleasure that Governor Miró had not, as rumored, been removed from the governorship of Louisiana, so that "everything [remains] as we could wish." Finally, he urged Reed to let him have a description of his boats and cargo, so that insurance might be taken on them at Philadelphia.[33]

Reed made the trip to New Orleans in 1790, and the results were favorable enough to confirm him and his partner in their determination to pursue the trade.[34] It was apparently at this time that they established one of their principal agencies in the West, a store at Natchez, where they sold the neighboring planters flour from the Ohio Valley and general merchandise from Philadelphia and received indigo, tobacco, and peltry in payment.[35] These were sent down to New Orleans where they were sold or else, together with the returns for shipments made by sea to New Orleans, exported to Philadelphia by way of French St. Domingue.

For the next three years the trade continued on this footing, with results that were more satisfactory to Reed and Forde than to their principal creditors, Cruger, Ledyard, and Mullett. The latter alternately threatened and plead with their elusive debtors, who protested that any considerable payment on the debt would deprive them of the capital necessary for the continuance of their Mississippi trade, which, they asserted in 1792, was their "main resource."[36] Mullett, on the other hand, declared that this trade had been "the source of three successive years of disappointment," and declared that he and his partners would "apply to the Federal Court" unless they received a considerable payment at once. By authorizing Henry Cruger to draw on them for $2000 at sixty days and promising another payment to the same amount within four months—the time it would require their ship, the *Gayoso* to make the trip to New Orleans and return—Reed and Forde succeeded in averting the threatened suit.[37]

The custom-house records of Philadelphia[38] show how important a part they played in the growing trade with New Orleans and also how important that trade was to them. According to the list of entries at Philadelphia for 1791 (which may be taken as typical of the period 1789-1793), nine ships arrived there from New Orleans in that year. Of these nine, five brought cargoes that were consigned wholly or in large part to Reed and Forde. Moreover, a ship arrived from Cap Français (St. Domingue) with a cargo of tobacco consigned to John O'Bannon, who was Reed and Forde's principal agent in the Ohio Valley; and since this tobacco was admitted duty free as produce of the United States, we may assume that it was Kentucky tobacco which had been shipped through New Orleans and that Reed and Forde were interested in it. One of these nine arrivals was their own ship, the *Gayoso*, which was regularly engaged in the New Orleans trade and which they had tactfully named for Manuel Gayoso de Lemos, at this time governor of Natchez and later of all Louisiana and West Florida.

The cargoes consigned to Reed and Forde from New Orleans consisted for the most part of tobacco and peltry, which came sometimes from Louisiana and sometimes from Kentucky or some other part of the Ohio Valley. Twice there were consignments of logwood, which had probably been brought to New Orleans from Campeche and twice Reed and Forde received a box of "segars"—possibly a retort courteous from Secretary López de Armesto. It is interesting to note that in these same ships came consignments for John Vaughan, who had introduced Reed and Forde to the Spanish envoy, Gardoqui, in 1788, and for William E. Hulings, who later moved to New Orleans and at one time, towards the close of the Spanish régime, acted as United States consul there.

The Philadelphia port records also indicate that in 1791 Reed and Forde were confining their attention almost exclusively to New Orleans; at any rate, they very seldom received a consignment from any other port. The reason may have been that the safer and more profitable commerce with Europe and the West Indies was in the hands of such merchant princes as Stephen Girard, Thomas Fitzsimmons, and Willing, Morris, and

Swanwick, whose names are prominent in the port records for this year and with whom Reed and Forde, still suffering from their losses in the depression of 1785-1787, did not have the resources to compete.

In 1793, first Great Britain and then Spain went to war with France. This conflict brought about some important changes in Reed and Forde's New Orleans trade. At first they expected it to be highly beneficial to them, since their ships would have a great advantage over ships under the flags of the belligerents[39] and it was likely that their Ohio Valley flour would command fancy prices in New Orleans and the West Indies. More than this, they counted upon gaining admission to even richer markets in other parts of Spanish America, from which foreigners were normally excluded but which would probably be opened in the stress and confusion of war-time. It was partly this latter consideration and partly the wish to put an end to an expensive competition that led two of their New Orleans agents, Daniel Clark, Jr., and Daniel W. Coxe, who had hitherto done business independently of each other, to form a partnership as soon as they received news that the war had begun. Informing Reed and Forde of the formation of their partnership, they said that they were confident the war would stimulate trade between the United States and New Orleans, and added: "The secret avenues also by which considerable quantities of goods are introduced from this place into the other Spanish dominions, are additional reasons for supposing that this trade must daily become of more importance, and as the articles generally imported are of a necessary nature, Government will doubtless continue to wink at the mode in which the business was carried."[40]

During the next few years, government had to spend most of its time winking, for the outbreak of war between Spain and France had, by putting an end to trade between New Orleans and French St. Domingue, destroyed the only device that had ever given even a semblance of legality to the forbidden but active trade between New Orleans and the United States. Henceforth, American ships had to carry two sets of papers, posing as Spanish while they were in the Mississippi and promptly throwing off the mask as soon as they sailed out of the mouth of the river, so that they might enjoy the rights and immunities of neutrals. Moreover, if these ships sought to break the long voyage from Philadelphia to New Orleans by stopping—as they had usually done in peace-time—at one of the West Indies, whether British, French, or Spanish, they laid themselves open to capture by the privateers that infested that focal point of American commerce. The war increased the hazards as well as the profits by the New Orleans trade.[41]

Far from being daunted by these hazards, Reed and Forde showed more enthusiasm than ever for the trade. In June, Forde wrote his partner who had already gone to Kentucky, "You will do well to ship all the Flour Beef Pork Butter and lard that you can possably purchase and casks of Whisky for [if] ever it answered to sen down the Ohio it must be this and the ensuing season."[42] For a time all went well. Operations were facilitated by a passport from the Spanish chargé permitting a ship of theirs to go to Havana and New Orleans;[43] and the latter port was temporarily thrown open to American trade without disguise because of a fire that had destroyed half the city.[44] The *Gayoso* was captured off the Delaware capes by the *Little Democrat*, one of Genêt's privateers; but when brought into port as a prize it was promptly released.[45]

Luck seemed to be on the side of Reed and Forde. Together with their original backer in the New Orleans enterprise, Joseph Ball, and their newer associate, Daniel W. Coxe, they decided to expand their operations and import goods from France for sale to the French creoles of Louisiana. The latter province was still under the dominion of Spain, and Spain and France were still at war with each other; but goods brought from Bordeaux could be made United States property by breaking the voyage at Philadelphia. So no agreement was made whereby Coxe was to take the ship *Tristram* to Bordeaux, sell its cargo and 100 shares of stock in the Delaware and Schuylkill Canal, and either sell or mortgage 50,000 acres of Reed and Forde's lands in western Virginia. With the proceeds, he was to buy French goods, such as brandy, wine, laces, silk hose, and black ostrich feathers, and ship them to Philadelphia in the *Tristram* or some other ship or ships. The reason for sending the ship to Bordeaux rather then Marseilles, with which Reed and Forde sometimes did business, was probably the increasing activity of the Barbary corsairs. "No captains or sailors," wrote Reed and Forde in 1793, "will venture to the Mediterranean in the summer season in American Bottoms unless security is given for their Ransom in case of capture by the Algerines."[46]

Coxe sold the *Tristram's* cargo in Bordeaux at good prices, established a credit of 320,000 *livres* with the house of Corbeaux Père et Fils of that port, and despatched three ships to Philadelphia with cargoes worth 304,000 *livres*. Coxe himself sailed in one of these vessels, the barque *John* which carried a cargo worth 124,000 *livres*. The ship had an easy crossing until it came within sight of the Delaware capes; but there it was captured by the British privateer *Experiment*, taken to St. Georges, Bermuda, and condemned as a lawful prize. "Thus has a voyage been frustrated," wailed Coxe, "that would have netted us at least 40,000 dollars."[47]

Though the *Tristram* arrived safe, sales in Philadelphia itself were dull, contrary to all expectations, and by this time Reed and Forde had suspended shipments to New Orleans owing to the confusion caused by George Rogers Clark's projected invasion of Louisiana under the aegis of Citizen Genêt.[48] Then the Whiskey Rebellion in the western counties of Pennsylvania unhinged the trade not only in the Ohio Valley, but also in Philadelphia; for besides reducing sharply the exportations of western produce, it also prevented Reed and Forde from making a shipment of Philadelphia shoes to New Orleans. "The shoemakers with whom we have contracted," they wrote Daniel Clark, Jr., "have all been on the campaign against the Western Insurgents. We inclose their apologies for not complying with the Contract."[49] They also lost another of their ships, the *Betsy*, which, like the *John*, was captured by the privateer *Experiment* within sight of land, taken to Bermuda, and condemned. A third ship, the *Betsy and Hannah*, was seized by the British in the West Indies and also suffered condemnation, partly because its captain was bribed by the British to betray Reed and Forde's interests—or so they charged—and a fourth ship, the *Molly*, was caught by embargo when it touched at New York on its way from New Orleans to London.[50]

As if all this were not misfortune enough, in November, 1794, they suffered what they described as one of the worst disappointments of their commercial career when the brig *Swallow* from New Orleans brought them, instead of the rich returns in produce and specie that they had expected, a letter from Daniel Clark, Jr., informing them that he had practically nothing to send them. They held Clark responsible for their disappointment and wrote him reproachfully: "When we recollect that in consequence of advice from Mr. Coxe we wrote you that he would go from this to New Orleans with a property of at least 30,000 Dollars we are surprised to find that you have made no exertions to aid both him and us."[51]

Throughout the following year, they continued their complaints until at last in February, 1796, Clark let himself go in a letter in which he countered charge with charge. They had paid no attention to his advice, he complained, and had sent goods that, even when they arrived in proper condition, were unsalable, such as port, sherry, and sheepskin shoes, for which there was no demand in New Orleans; or if they sent the right articles, they delayed doing so until the market was glutted. Moreover, they had had the effrontery to divert to their own uses a shipment that Clark had intended for a London creditor. It was quite evident, however, that the main cause of Clark's irritation was the fact that he had been excluded from the Bordeaux venture in the *Tristram*, had not even been adequately informed about it, and yet had been expected to look after the important New Orleans end of it—for the benefit of Ball, Coxe, and Reed and Forde. He was not ready to break with them, however, for he said that he expected to visit Philadelphia soon and hoped to "settle all matters between us on such a footing as to leave no room for future difficulties." He wrote in conclusion: "I must beg leave to remark that I think the present difficulties might have been avoided had you been more communicative and less sanguine in your expectations from me. . . ."[52]

Despite this plain speaking, Reed and Forde continued to be sanguine in their expectations of the New Orleans trade, which they counted upon to extricate them from their increasingly trying situation; but it continued to disappoint them. In December, 1796, they confessed to one of their correspondents: "We have been in expectation for a large sum of money from New Orleans which would have enabled us without inconvenience to have discharged the amount obtained [by us] from the Bank of Columbia, but the season is so far advanced that we cannot now expect it."[53] Indeed, the general depression of 1796-97 dealt them such a severe blow that it is a wonder that in their already weakened condition they were able to survive it. They were deeply involved in the affairs of John Nicholson and Robert Morris, who failed at this time and whose failure nearly ruined them too.[54] Their embarrassments were further increased by the threat of war between the United States and Spain, which caused a rise of 10 percent in insurance rates to New Orleans,[55] and by the stagnation of the market for western lands, of which Reed and Forde seem to have accumulated some 400,000 acres.[56]

In order to tide themselves over the crisis, they sold seventy shares of Columbia Bank stock to George Washington, who later complained that they had charged him too much;[57] bought some of bankrupt Robert Morris's property at a sheriff's sale;[58] and urged Clark and their other agents "to use the greatest exertion in collecting" the debts due them.[59] Moreover, since one of the causes of their difficulties was the refusal of the Bank of Columbia to extend their credit, they began a campaign for proxies for the next election of directors of the Bank of the United States.[60]

What with one resource and another, they succeeded in staving off disaster during this crisis. Through appeals to the British Court of Admiralty and representations to the joint commission established under Jay's Treaty, they obtained compensation for the seizure of the *John* and other losses of the same kind.[61] In other cases they collected insurance on their losses, for they had been among the earliest clients of the recently established Insurance Company of North America.[62] Already in the summer of 1796 they had made a conditional sale of most of their western lands, although at a much lower price than they had counted on.[63] Despite the general stagnation of trade they were able occasionally to make a modest sale. Early in 1797, when the United States government was preparing to take possession of Natchez, in conformity with the treaty of 1795 with Spain, the Treasury Department bought from Reed and Forde, through their New Orleans agent, Robert Cochran, some $2,200 worth of goods for the new post.[64]

The near-disaster of 1797 forced Reed and Forde to curtail their operations, particularly in the West; and henceforth the Mississippi trade was less important to them and they played a less prominent part in it than at any other time since they first entered it some ten years earlier. They had already ordered the closing of their store at Natchez[65] and now they sent out an agent to liquidate their business in the Ohio Valley.[66] They even cooled towards the New Orleans trade, which, while it had not yielded the profits they expected, had at any rate been their "main resource" for a considerable time and had provided the most frequent employment for their ships ever since 1789. In a letter to a New Orleans correspondent they said, "There has been no vessels from this for New Orleans for several months. Every person here has got tired out with the trade."[67] As a matter of fact, Philadelphia, which, through the activities of Reed and Forde and other merchants, had taken the lead in opening up trade with New Orleans, did fall behind New York in the development of that trade during the next few years.[68] Reed and Forde did not, however, abandon it completely. Until the end of the Spanish régime, they continued to send their ships and cargoes to the creole capital, consigning them to various firms, such as Cochran and Rhea, and Chew and Relf. They also continued to do business with Daniel W. Coxe and with Daniel Clark, Jr. And despite the resolution they had made in 1797 to liquidate their affairs in the Ohio Valley, they still owned more than 20,000 acres of land there as late as 1802. It was not easy to sever the connections and break the habits of a decade.[69]

The foregoing account of the activities of Reed and Forde, does not pretend to be either complete or well-rounded, for they were in business both before 1783 and after

1803 and in that period they had many other interests besides the Mississippi trade. Nevertheless, it focuses attention on the aspect of their business that was, on the whole, the most important to them and that seems to possess the greatest historical interest. Their activities in the Mississippi trade are significant because they provide another illustration of the influence of eastern capital on the development of frontier settlements and show how deeply, even in those times, the welfare of the people in the Mississippi Valley was affected by events in the eastern United States and Western Europe. Their greatest significance however, lies in the contribution that Reed and Forde made to the opening up of trade with Latin America and to the territorial expansion of the United States.

Reed and Forde were pioneers in the development of trade between the United States and Spanish America. They were not the very first to enter this field but they were in the vanguard; and the importance of their achievement is not diminished by the fact that New Orleans was soon annexed to the United States. When they began to trade with it, it was a Spanish port, and like all the other Spanish ports in America it was closed by law to the commerce of the United States. The pattern of their behavior was the same as that of their fellow-countrymen who both then and subsequently invaded the wider Latin American field: in both cases, it was bribery, chicanery, the low prices of their goods and the war-time necessities of Spain that enabled them to penetrate the barrier and break the monopoly set up by Spain; and in both cases the lures were the same—to find employment for ships and markets for goods, and to obtain Spanish gold and silver and products not obtainable in the United States or Europe. Quite appropriately, John Reed's son, Midshipman Reed, first saw real service in warships sent to protect United States commerce with Latin American during the Spanish American wars of independence—once with the *Congress* in the Caribbean in 1817, and again with the *Macedonian* off the coast of Chile in 1819.[70]

Reed and Forde contributed to the territorial expansion of the United States through the acquisition of Louisiana, for they and their associates paved the way for this acquisition by promoting the commerce of the United States on the Mississippi. Even when their own direct interest in it declined, as it did after 1797, their associates and other Americans carried on, and, with the aid of the rights of navigation and deposit conceded by Spain in the treaty of 1795, gave the trade a greater extension than it had ever had before. Foremost among these Americans was Daniel Clark, Jr.,[71] who, but for the business that Reed and Forde threw his way, would probably not have been able to survive the reverses that he suffered in the early 1790s and remain in business at New Orleans.

Historians have often overlooked or misunderstood the influence of the Mississippi trade upon the acquisition of Louisiana. For instance, Charles A. Beard recently published a book in which he says that in our history there have been two types of territorial expansion—the agrarian, which seeks land for farmers, and the capitalist, which seeks commercial advantages, markets for manufactured goods, and fields for the investment of surplus capital; and Beard says that Louisiana belongs to the agrarian type of acquisition.[72] The facts do not support this classification, for Jefferson's main purpose in the negotiation that led to the Louisiana Purchase was not to obtain land for farmers, but to protect and foster American commerce on the Mississippi trade was solely, or at least preponderantly, a western concern. What has been said above shows that this commerce was of interest to eastern merchants and shipowners as well as to western farmers; that the former were more directly interested in the trade than were the latter; and that prominent among the eastern capitalist—commercial groups responsible for the development of the Mississippi trade, and consequently for our acquisition of Louisiana, were those adventurous merchants, Reed and Forde of Philadelphia.

Notes for "Reed and Forde: Merchant Adventurers of Philadephia: Their Trade with Spanish New Orleans"

[1]With some slight alterations, this paper is printed as it was read at a meeting of The Historical Society of Pennsylvania on March 8, 1937. It is based mainly upon that Society's manuscript collection, "Reed and Forde, Business Correspondence, 1763-1823." In the following notes, documents in this collection will be cited merely by the title of the volume or box in which they are to be found, such as "Correspondence, 1800-1803," "Letter Book, 1787." As stated in the text, this article does not pretend to give a comprehensive account of the business activities of Reed and Forde; and even for the particular subject treated here, their voluminous papers doubtless contain pertinent documents that I have not examined. Though its scope is limited, I hope that it may possess some significance in itself and that it may also suggest certain possibilities of research to which historical students have so far given little attention, namely, the study of the beginnings of United States commerce with Latin America as revealed in the business correspondence of the period. In Philadelphia alone there are several important manuscript collections of this kind that have hardly been touched—at any rate, for this purpose. Data obtained from such sources should of course be checked and supplemented by data obtained from Spanish and Spanish American sources, as I have tried to do in this paper. In this way, important contributions could be made to the diplomatic and political as well as the economic history of the period.

[2]Jacques Peuchet, *État des colonies et du commerce des Européens dans les deux Indes, depuis 1783 jusque en 1821,* 2 vols. (Paris, 1821), 1:8, 272.

[3]Randolph: Correspondence, 1800-1803, 1. Heron to Reed and Forde, August 25, 1801, enclosing Randolph's bill in payment of the loan. Morris: Letter Book, 1796-1788, Reed and Forde to Robert Morris, June 6, 1797; same to same, August, 3, 1797. The Reed and Forde Papers contain many other letters about their business dealings with Morris and John Nicholson. Washington: ibid., Reed and Forde to Walter Smith, March 24, 1797; to George Washington, June 5, 1797. Reed and Forde were prominent enough in their day to achieve mention in Abraham Ritter's Philadelphia and her Merchants (Philadelphia, 1860), 57, 169; but Ritter did not regard them as important enough to merit extended discussion—or perhaps he did not have access to their papers. On page 57 he mentions them, with other merchants, as "giving life to the plot [a plot on Water St.] sixty years ago"; on page 169 he gives their business address as No. 91, Front Street. According to *The New Trade Directory for Philadelphia, Anno 1800* (Philadelphia, 1799), Reed and Forde's place of business was then at 61 Water Street (116); Standish Forde's residence was at 27 Vine Street (105) and John Reed's at 143 Chestnut Street (115). In the *Directory*, Reed is spelled "Read," and in Ritter, Forde appears as "Ford." In this paper I have followed the spelling that Reed and Forde themselves used.

[4]Letter Book, 1787 Reed and Forde to Peter Anspach, September 15, 1787.

[5]This is mentioned in several of Reed and Forde's letters of 1789; among others, in Standish Forde's letter to John Reed (then on his way to New Orleans), January 7, 1790 (erroneously dated 1789): Letter Book, 1789-90.

[6]Letter Book, 1788-90, Reed and Forde to Thomas Mullett, October 13, 1789.

[7]Archivo General de Indias, Seville, Audiencia de Santo Domingo, 146-3-11, Francisco Rendón to José de Gálvez, Philadelphia, February 28, 1783, No. 72 duplicate. I am unable to say how extensive an interest Reed and Forde had in this trade in 1783; but that they did have an interest in it then is shown by the fact that on

September 2, 1783, they sold one James Elliot some goods which were sent to Pittsburgh (Shipping and Miscellaneous Accounts, 1783-1794, undated and unsigned memorandum of this transaction).

[8]In a letter of November 20, 1787, Reed and Forde explained their difficulties partly by "the purchase of real property" that they had made; but they defended the purchase on the ground that it had enabled them to dispose of "some [otherwise] unsaleable goods" (Letter Book, 1787, Reed and Forde to Messrs. Cruger and Mullett, November 20, 1787). One tract of their western lands (34,180 acres on the little Kanawha river in western Virginia) was obtained under patents from Governor Patrick Henry of Virginia dated August 4, 1785, and was part of a 300,000 acre tract surveyed by George Tudor and John Vanderen on the joint account of Josiah Willard, William Gibbs, and Reed and Forde, and another unidentified person (Letter Book, 1788-1790, 242, copy of quit claim). According to their own statement, they owned at least 90,000 acres of western lands in 1787, 40,000 in (Monongalia and Harrison counties) the present West Virginia and 50,000 in Kentucky (Letter Book, 1787, Reed and Forde to Jno. Cleves Sims [*sic*], August 24, 1787). Many other documents bearing on this subject are contained in a box, labeled "Western Lands."

[9]Arthur P. Whitaker, *The Spanish American Frontier, 1783-1795* (Boston, 1927), 28-30, 68, and *The Mississippi Question, 1795-1803* (New York, 1934), 80. For detailed information regarding commercial regulations in Spanish Louisiana, see the same writer's *Documents Relating to the Commercial Policy of Spain in the Floridas. . . [and] Louisiana* (Deland, 1931), especially the Historical Introduction and Docs. 4, 23, 25; and for a more general discussion, see his article, "The Commerce of Louisiana and the Floridas at the End of the Eighteenth century," *Hispanic American Historical Review,* 8 (1928): 190.

[10]Edward Channing, *A History of the United States*, 6 vols. (New York, 1905), 3:408-27.

[11]Correspondence, 1786-1790, Cruger, Ledyard and Mullett to Reed and Forde, February 1, 1786, and same to same, July 5, 1787; Letter Book, 1787, Reed and Forde to Cruger and Mullett, November 20, 1787.

[12]Whitaker, *Spanish American Frontier*, 96-97; Temple Bodley, *Littell's Political Transactions* (Louisville, 1926), xl, xli (somewhat inaccurate, but shrewd).

[13]Arthur P. Whitaker, "James Wilkinson's First Descent to New Orleans in 1787," *Hispanic American Historical Review*, 8 (1928): 82-97.

[14]William R. Shepherd, "Wilkinson and the Beginnings of the Spanish Conspiracy," *American Historical Review*, 9 (1903-1904): 490.

[15]Samuel Flagg Bemis, *Pinckney's Treaty* (Baltimore, 1926), chapter 8, and Whitaker, *Spanish American Frontier*, chapter 14.

[16]Whitaker, *Mississippi Question*, 82, notes 2 and 3. Additional information is contained in Archivo General de Indias, Seville, Audiencia, de Santo Domingo, leg. 2544; Miró and Navarro to Valdés, April 1, 1788, No. 56. This despatch states that the New Orleans officials decided to return 63,300 *pesos* held in royal treasury in connection with the trial of several leading merchants of New Orleans for trading with Philadelphia; the reason for this act of grace being the fire that had recently destroyed a large part of New Orleans and the necessity of animating the merchants to supply the city and build it up again. In 1794 another very destructive fire at New Orleans again furnished the local officials with an excuse for openly permitting the trade with the United States that, as is shown in this article, was all the while prosecuted clandestinely but actively.

[17]"Letters of Phineas Bond," in American Historical Association, *Report*, 1896, 1:542.

[18]Whitaker, *Mississippi Question*, 82, 133-34. Martín Navarro, former intendant of Louisiana, said in 1789 that French St. Domingue was the main channel by which specie from Spanish America passed into the hands of foreigners, and that for this reason the French boasted that St. Domingue was worth more to them than the whole of Mexico (Archivo General de Indias, Audiencia de Santo Domingo, leg. 2665, Navarro to Valdés, January 15, 1789, No. 2, copy). Of course, France as well as other European countries obtained a great deal of Spanish American gold and silver through trade with Spain itself. Peuchet, *État des Colonies*, 208 (apparently speaking of the period about 1780-90) says that France obtained about 50,000,000 francs worth of gold and silver a year in this way.

[19]Thomas Robson Hay, "Some Letters of Mrs. Ann Biddle Wilkinson from Kentucky, 1788-1789," *Pennsylvania Magazine of History and Biography*, 56:34-35, 53-55, discusses this question.

[20]Correspondence, April 1782-1785, Timothy Pickering to John Lawrance, Philadelphia, February 28, 1785. After introducing Reed and Forde and mentioning another Philadelphia firm, Lamb and Checkly, Pickering

wrote: "Colo. Clement Biddle has this day shut up. The gentlemen above named [i.e., Reed and Forde, and Lamb and Checkly] are his creditors, merely by indorsing his bills or notes. They have therefore the best claims to securities for their dues. Colo. Biddle has a farm or tract of land, at Katskill, and other lands elsewhere, which they wish to attach." Pickering then requested Lawrance to do all he could for them, assured him that they would honorably pay any expenses he might incur, and added, "as they are strangers to you, I pledge myself for such payment."

[21]Letter Book, 1788-1790, Standish Forde to John Lewis, March 10, 1788: "The gentleman is now in town [Philadelphia] that I informed you had been to New Orleans on our business. I shall detain him a few days longer till I hear your determination as I think he will be very necessary for your plan." This letter refers to an earlier letter (February 6) to Lewis on this same subject; but the latter does not identify the "gentleman." together with other letters that passed between Lewis and Forde during this year, it shows that the "plan" was a venture down the Ohio and Mississippi. The "gentleman" who was in Philadelphia on March 10 could not have been Wilkinson himself, since he had already returned to Lexington, Ky., arriving there on February 24. (Thomas Robson Hay, *General James Wilkinson: The Last Phase* (New Orleans, 1936), 122.

[22]Hay, *Wilkinson*, 121-22.

[23]The Reed and Forde Papers contain documents too numerous to cite relating to these two ventures. They are contained in Letter Book, 1788-1790, and correspondence, 1786-1790.

[24]Letter Book, 1788-1790, 323, itemized list. Wilkinson was jointly indebted with Samuel Blackburn for the greater part of this sum. Blackburn had been associated with him in an adventure in 1789. In 1803 Reed and Forde were still trying vainly to collect this debt from Wilkinson (Correspondence, 1800-1803, James Graisbury to Reed and Forde, January 3, 1803).

[25]Letter Book, 1788-1790, Reed and Forde to Thomas Mullett, Philadelphia, September 27, 1789. Speaking of the Ohio-New Orleans expedition from which Forde had just returned, they wrote that it had "turn'd out profitable altho we were subject to many disadvantages from the want of permits."

[26]Hollingsworth Papers (Historical Society of Pennsylvania), Levi Hollingsworth to John Cannon, November 21, 1788. Hollingsworth had expected that he and Cannon would be asked by Pollock to do business for him under this permit; but, he said, Ball had been empowered by Pollock to do it, and would probably be associated with "Hair" (Andrew Hare, of Kentucky) in the enterprise (I am indebted for this note to Mr. Victor L. Johnson, a graduate student at the University of Pennsylvania.) The New Orleans fire of 1788 furnished the local officials with a pretext for issuing this permit. Early in 1789, Governor Miró forwarded to the court with his endorsement Pollock's petition for permission to import a large quantity of flour from Philadelphia and flour and tobacco from Kentucky, with the privilege of exporting duty-free the specie received in payment. The main argument with which Miró supported this extraordinary proposal was that it would enable Pollock to pay his debts at New Orleans, where he owed 74,087 *pesos* to the government, and 59,442 *pesos* to private persons. (Archivo General de Indias, Seville, Audiencia de Santo Doming, leg. 2553, Miró to Valdés, February 12, 1789, no. 164, duplicate.) I am unable to say whether the court granted the petition, but think it did not, since that would have been contrary to policy. Permits of the kind mentioned by Hollingsworth were granted by the local officials on the pretext that an emergency of some kind or other existed. For information about Oliver Pollock, see the sketch by James Alton James in the *Dictionary of American Biography* 21 vols. (New York, 1935), 15:50-51, and Roy F. Nichols, "Trade Relations and the Establishment of the United States Consulates in Spanish America, 1799-1809," in *Hispanic American Historical Review*, 13 (1928): 290-91.

[27]Letter Book, 1788-1790, John Reed to Standish Forde, June 11 and July 6, 1789 (two letters), stating that (Joseph) Ball was determined not to accept any more of Andrew Hare's drafts, and was disposed to enter into the business proposed by Forde (who was then in New Orleans). Ibid., Joseph Ball to Oliver Pollock, April 9, 1789 (copy), introducing Standish Forde. Correspondence, 1791-1794, Reed and Forde to Henry Cruger, March 3 (1793), draft stating that the payments they had recently made him (£450 on June 30, $2,000 on November 5, and the $1,229.10 "paid to Mr. Frazier") had represented profits on operations which they had been enabled to undertake by the establishment of a certain credit. This credit was probably established for them by Ball, and the operations were certainly their Ohio Valley-New Orleans ventures. These letters do not speak explicitly of the agreement between Ball and Reed and Forde, and I have not found the articles of agreement in the correspondence of the latter; but the tenor of their correspondence for the period seems to show clearly that the facts were as stated in the text.

[28]Letter Book, 1788-1790, Standish Forde to John Reed, undated letter (*c.* November 16, 1789); same to James Wilkinson, November 3, 1789.

[29]Ibid., Reed and Forde to Thomas Mullett, September 23, September 27, and October 7, 1789. Correspondence, 1786-1790, Thomas Mullett to Reed and Forde, September 18, 24, and 28, 1789.

[30]Letter Book, 1788-1790, Reed and Forde to David Hodge, undated (*c.* October 9, 1789), same to "Don Senior Andre," October 9, 1789, Standish Forde to "Don Senior Andre," undated (*c.* November 25, 1789), and to "Gilberto Esquire," about same date.

[31]Letter of Reed and Forde to "Don Senior Andre" of October 9, 1789, cited in preceding note.

[32]Whitaker, *Mississippi Question*, 142; Mary Verhoeff, *The Kentucky River Navigation* (Louisville, 1917), 226-28.

[33]Letter Book, 1788-1790, Standish Forde to John Reed, undated (*c.* November 16, 1789), and November 25, 1789.

[34]John Lewis was not so well pleased. He confessed himself disappointed with the results of Reed's trip, and said he had hoped to get at least the amount of Wilkinson's bill on (Philip) Nolan: Correspondence, 1786-1790, Lewis to Reed and Forde, August 24, 1790. See below, note 56.

[35]Correspondence, 1786-1790, David Ferguson to John Reed, Natchez, June 10, 1790; same to Reed and Forde, July 4, 1790; same to same, November 20, 1790. In this last letter, Ferguson said there was about $13,000 due Reed and Forde for goods sold at Natchez, and that he had sold some goods to Kentuckians to be paid for in tobacco delivered at New Orleans the following spring. Letter Book, 1788-1790, Standish Forde to David Hodge (New Orleans merchant), November 25, 1789.

[36]Correspondence, 1791-1794, Reed and Forde to Henry Cruger, August 28, 1792 (draft): "At present our main resource is from the Missisipe[;] by the last advise we had monys in our agents hands but there is no chance of recovering it until our Brig Gayoso returns which will be some time in October."

[37]Ibid., Thomas Mullett to Reed and Forde, No. 31, Dowgate Hill, London, July 8, 1792; Henry Cruger to Reed and Forde, New York, November 2, 1792; John Cruger to Reed and Forde, New York, November 8, 1792; Henry Cruger to Reed and Forde, February 27, 1793; Reed and Forde to Henry Cruger, March 3 (1793), draft.

[38]Port of Philadelphia, Arrivals of Ships, 1791 (bound vol., MS., Custom House, Philadelphia). John Leamy was the only other Philadelphia merchant who received a number of consignments from New Orleans comparable with that received by Reed and Forde.

[39]Letter Book, 1793-1794, Reed and Forde to Daniel Clark, Jr., April 10, 1793.

[40]Correspondence, 1791-1794, Daniel W. Coxe and Daniel Clark, Jr., to Reed and Forde, New Orleans, March 6, 1793; Daniel Clark, Jr., to Reed and Forde, March 16, 1793. Coxe and Clark's statement is especially interesting in view of the fact that a heated debate had raged in Spain over the relation of New Orleans to contraband trade with other parts of Spanish America and the influence of this contraband trade on the decline of legitimate Spanish trade with America. For this subject, see Whitaker, *Documents Relating to Commercial;* Historical Introduction, xli-xliii and Doc. No. 9; and "Spanish Commercial Policy in Louisiana and Florida at the End of the Eighteenth Century," *Hispanic American Historical Review*, 8 (1928): 190-203.

[41]Letter Book, 1791-1794, Reed and Forde to Coxe and Clark, May 26, 1793; same to Captain Thomas Morgan, December 16, 1794. See also the letter cited in note 39, above. For a general description of the commerce of Louisiana from 1793 to 1803, see Whitaker, *Mississippi Question*, chapters 5 and 8.

[42]Letter Book, 1793-1794, Forde to Reed, June 19, 1793.

[43]Ibid., Reed and Forde to Dr. Joseph de Jáudenes, "Minister for His Catholic Majesty," September 5, 1793. Actually Jáudenes was not a minister but only a chargé d'affaires (*encargado de negocios*).

[44]Ibid., Standish Forde to John Reed, June 19, 1793. Reed had again gone to the Ohio Valley on business.

[45]Letter Book, 1793-1794, Reed and Forde to Daniel Clark, Jr., August 23, 1793; same to "Mr. Genet, Minister for the French Republic," undated (*c.* end of December, 1793); same to Edmund Randolph, Secretary of State, February 28, 1794.

[46]Letter Book, 1793-1794, Joseph Ball and Reed and Forde to Daniel W. Coxe, January 4, 1794; Reed and Forde to Coxe, December 28, 1793 and January 6, 1794; Reed and Forde to Testart and Gerin, undated, *c.* May 14-26, 1793 (Algerines).

[47]Correspondence, 1791-1794, Daniel W. Coxe to Reed and Forde, St. Georges, Bermuda, August 27, 1794; Letter Book, 1793-1794, Reed and Forde to Edmund Randolph, Secretary of State, September 23, 1794.

[48]Letter Book, 1793-1794, Reed and Forde to Peter Davis, March 4, 1794 (Clark); Correspondence, 1791-1794, same to H. Cruger, Esq., August 28, 1794, draft (*Tristram*).

[49]Ibid., Reed and Forde to Daniel Clark, Jr., October 5 and December 16, 1794.

[50](1) *Betsy*: Letter Book, 1793-1794, Reed and Forde to James and William Perot, August 18, 1794; same to Bridger Goodrich, December 12, 1794. (2) *Betsy and Hannah*: ibid., same to Johnston McClenachan defended himself in an updated letter which will be found in a box labeled "Correspondence, 1806-1829. Undated Letters." (3) *Molly*: ibid., same to Alexander Hamilton, Esq., April 15, 1794; same to Captain Thomas Morgan, April 20, 1794; same to Leffingwell and Pierpoint (of New York), April 22, 1794; same to Messrs. Morgan and Strother (of London) April 30, 1794. Reed and Forde also complained that General Montbrun had seized the cargo of the *Betsy* at "Jacomell" and had paid for it in second quality flour worth only one-third the value of the cargo seized: ibid., Reed and Forde to "Mr. Fauchett" (the French Minister), December 6, 1794; same to Edmund Randolph, Esq., December 6 1794, with text of letter drawn up by Reed and Forde for Randolph's signature.

[51]Letter Book, 1793-1794, Reed and Forde to Daniel Clark, Jr., November 10, 1794.

[52]Correspondence, 1796, Daniel Clark, Jr., to Reed and Forde, February 12, 1796.

[53]Letter Book, 1796-1798, Reed and Forde to James M. Lingan, December 7, 1796.

[54]Ibid., formal note in the third person from Standish Forde to John Nicholson, June 6, 1796, requesting an interview to arrange for the payment of $10,000, part of Reed and Forde's claim against him; a similar note of the same date to Robert Morris (amount not mentioned); Reed and Forde to Robert Morris, August 2, 1797, asking for the immediate payment of $5,000 in cash on Morris's account. In this last letter, they said that Morris's notes were to expire on August 11, that they could not renew them even at 2 1/2 percent per month, and that "Our distresses for funds, independent of the engagements for you are more than we can get thro." They also spoke with evident bitterness of "the few friends we have left" and reproached Morris with deeming "the sacrifice of R. and F. of little consequence."

[55]Letter Book, 1796-1798, Reed and Forde to Robert Cochran (of New Orleans), November 26, 1796: "They now demand ten per cent for the insurance owing to the expected Spanish war." Reed and Forde evidently meant insurance rates for American property in American ships between Philadelphia and New Orleans. In August, 1793, they stated that the insurance rate for such shipments was 3 1/2 per cent: whereas it was then under 20 per cent for Spanish property in American ships and not less than 25 to 30 per cent for Spanish property in Spanish ships (Letter Book, 1793-1794, Reed and Forde to Daniel Clark, Jr., August 9, 1793). As early as October 1, 1796, Reed and Forde had said in a letter to Daniel Clark, Jr., "There appears to be a general apprehension of a War with Spain" (Letter Book, 1796-1798). This fact is interesting because Spain's failure to execute the treaty of 1795, which was later advanced as a pretext for war by the Federalist war-hawks, was not yet an issue.

[56]Ibid., Reed and Forde to Heber Chase, August 22, 1796, stating that they owned 340,000 acres of land in Monongalia, Harrison, and Randolph counties, and 57,236 acres in Ohio county. Besides this, they seem to have owned many thousands of acres of land in Kentucky. In a letter of October 24-28, 1796, to John Lewis (ibid.), Forde asked Lewis to pay his debt to Reed and Forde, and observed, "lands are so unsaleable that they would answer us no good purpose."

[57]Ibid., Reed and Forde to Walter Smith, March 24, 1797; same to George Washington, June 5, 1797, countering with the assertion that they themselves would lose by the transaction since the notes they had received in payment for Washington's 70 shares, as well as for 300 additional shares, had become of very doubtful value.

[58]There are several allusions to this transaction in both their correspondence and letter books for 1797 and 1798.

[59]Letter Book, 1796-1798, Reed and Forde to John Davis, January 30, 1797; same to Daniel Clark, Jr., February 24, 1797; same to David Ferguson, May 4, 1797.

[60]Letter Book, 1797-1798, Reed and Forde to James M. Lingan, November 25, 1796. Accompanying this letter is a list of shareholders of the Bank of the United States in the Southern States, with the number of shares owned by each. Ibid., Reed and Forde to James M. Lingan, December 14, 1796.

[61]Ibid., Reed and Forde to Samuel Bayard (London), December 5, 1797, stating that in consequence of his letter of July 24 they had drawn upon him for £1300 sterling and were impatiently awaiting advice of further sums recovered on their account.

[62]Letter Book, 1793-1794, Reed and Forde to the "President and Directors of the Insurance Co. [of] N[orth] A[merica]," December 14, 1794, asking for $8,000 down payment on the full amount ($10,000) of their insurance on half the cargo of the barque *John*. The Reed and Forde Papers contain many other documents relating to insurance taken out by them on their ships; and they tried—whether successfully I cannot say—to insure the flatboats that they sent down the Mississippi.

[63]Letter Book, 1796-1798, Reed and Forde to Heber Chase, August 22, 1796.

[64]Ibid., Standish Forde to Robert Cochran, October 8, 1797.

[65]Letter Book, 1793-1794, Reed and Forde to David Ferguson, June 2, 1794. Their decision to close the Natchez store was probably due to the moratorium on debts in that district proclaimed by the Spanish governor Gayoso in favor of the planters. For several years after 1794 Reed and Forde were engaged in correspondence with Ferguson and others about the collection of debts contracted at their store. See for example Correspondence, 1800-1803, James Graisbury to Reed and Forde, July 18, 1802, and Lyman Harding to Reed and Forde, October 6, 1803. Harding, who wrote from Natchez, said that not $100 had been collected from the whole mass of their claims, but that this was not surprising since the claims were so old that the doctors who had not left the country or gone bankrupt had almost forgotten their existence.

[66]Letter Book, 1796-1798, Reed and Forde to George Wilson, November 24, 1797; same to Col. Richard C. Anderson, same date. John O'Bannon was their agent in this affair.

[67]Ibid., Reed and Forde to Robert Cochran, February 24, 1797.

[68]Whitaker, *Mississippi Question*, 136-37. As the table on page 137 shows, trade between Philadelphia and New Orleans picked up again in the years 1800-1802. The statement on page 136 that in 1787 no ship cleared from New Orleans for the United States does not mean that no ships sailed between those ports. As stated in the present article, prior to 1793 the trade was carried on by way of French St. Domingue.

[69](1) Western lands: Correspondence, 1800-1803, W. Croghan to Reed and Forde, September 13, 1802. (2) New Orleans: ibid., Chew and Relf to Reed and Forde, May 20, July 12, August 8, 1802, and January 21, February 21 and June 10, 1803; James Graisbury to Reed and Forde, July 18, 1802, and January 3, 1803. These letters relate to transactions that were typical of Reed and Forde's New Orleans business at this period. Early in 1802, their ship, the *Fame*, Captain Graisbury, arrived at New Orleans with a cargo consisting mainly of cordage. This was sold for them by Chew and Relf. With part of the proceeds, Graisbury bought provisions which he took in the *Fame* to Capt. François (St. Domingue—Haiti), returning thence to New Orleans. With the rest of the proceeds, Chew and Relf arrived in poor condition, but Chew and Relf refused to admit that they were responsible since it was in good condition when they shipped it, and they had given Reed and Forde advance notice so that the cotton might be insured. (3) Clark: In their letter of May 20, 1802, cited above, Chew and Relf spoke of "Mr. [Daniel] Clark" as being in Philadelphia at that time and in touch with Reed and Forde. In their letter of June 10, 1803, Chew and Relf mentioned "Mr. Coxe" (presumably Daniel W. Coxe) but not as associated with Reed and Forde in that venture. Three of the above letters were written from New Orleans during the closure of the American deposit, but not one of them mentions it. Graisbury's letter of January 3, 1803, merely said that business at New Orleans was dull, probably because of the "sudden changes."

[70]Correspondence, 1806-1829, John Reed, Jr, to his father, U.S. Frigate *Congress*, Lynhaven Bay, September 24, 1817; same to same, U.S.S. *Macedonian*, "Valparaso" (i.e., Valparaiso, Chile), October 15, 1819; same to same, U.S.S. *Macedonian*, Boston Harbour, June 21, 1821. These letter, together with other documents in the same box, show that John Reed, Jr., was born in Philadelphia October 8, 1794, and that his warrant as midshipman in the United States Navy was dated November 30, 1814; that his cruise in the *Congress* took him to the mouth of the Mississippi (December 1816-May 1817), thence to Haiti to visit President Pétion and "His Black Majesty Christophe," thence *via* the island of Margarita to Cumaná and La Guaira (Venezuela), and

thence back to the United States (September, 1817); that his second trip to South America, in the *Macedonian*, took him to Valparaiso, where the ship had arrived by mid-October, 1819; and that the *Macedonian* left Valparaiso on March 18, 1821, returning *via* Rio de Janeiro and arriving at Boston on June 20, 1821. Though Midshipman Reed was a man of action, not of words, his letters contain some information about the martial activities of Morillo and Bolívar in Venezuela and Lord Cochrane on the coast of Chile, and also about the wretched condition of the people in both countries. The correspondence in this box also shows how the personal influence of the elder Reed with the Navy Department procured preferential treatment for Midshipman Reed.

[71]For further information about Clark's activities at New Orleans prior to the Louisiana Purchase, see the sketch by I. J. Cox in the *Dictionary of American Biography*, and Whitaker, *Mississippi Question*, 93-95, 243-51, and notes.

[72]Charles A. Beard, *The Idea of National Interest* (New York, 1934), chapter 3.

ECONOMIC LIFE BEFORE THE LOUISIANA PURCHASE*

John G. Clark

When Will and Sam Johnson arrived at New Orleans in April, 1801, with a boatload of flour from Pittsburgh, they found a host of opportunities for dealing profitably. Their flour was sold advantageously just prior to the arrival of large quantities from Baltimore and Philadelphia and on large numbers of flats riding the spring flood to New Orleans from the Upper Valley. Flour prices dropped rapidly, making it possible for the Johnsons to purchase at a much cheaper price than they sold, with the aim of taking it to Havana. An agreement was struck for the freighting of the flour aboard the ship *Ocean*, but when the time came to load, the ship was nearly full and a portion of the Johnson's flour remained on shore. The arrival of seven vessels on May 1, seeking cargoes of flour, stimulated a rise in flour prices, and the Johnsons bartered their remaining supply for cotton, securing space aboard the *Neptune* bound for New York. Will traveled with the latter vessel while his brother went to Havana where he sold the flour and purchased sugar for New York—where the two men were reunited.

This business venture reflects not only flexibility, ingenuity, and risk taking by the Johnsons but reveals also the notably augmented choices available to entrepreneurs operating out of New Orleans. For the most part, the days were over when vessels arrived at New Orleans and departed in ballast or when produce rotted on the levees for want of shipping to overseas markets. An established port of call for the vessels of a number of nations, particularly the United States, France, and Great Britain, the city was hardly less prepared to provide the necessary services for planter, merchant, and shipowner than were older ports such as New York or Philadelphia. The agglomeration of people in the place called New Orleans became residents of a genuine city sometime during the Spanish period. A municipal government was established which assumed responsibilities and provided services hitherto within the purview of the provincial government, adding new

*Reprinted by permission of Louisiana State University Press from *New Orleans, 1718-1812: An Economic History*, by John G. Clark. Copyright © 1970 by Louisiana State University Press.

functions as necessity demanded. In this process, the city gained an identity of self—absent during the French period—which was manifested in the *cabildo*'s persistent efforts to improve the economic position of the municipality as well as to raise its own standing vis-a-vis the colonial government of Louisiana.

During the last years of Spanish rule, New Orleans was hardly the backwater village it had been even as recently as Kerlérec's administration. The *cabildo*, growing increasingly sensitive to any incidents that remotely slighted or diminished its institutional dignity and prerogatives, engaged in 1802 in a stout defense of its right to a larger box in the Casa de Comedias. Charging that the *cabildo* box was suddenly and arbitrarily divided so that the space was inadequate, the councilmen demanded that Governor Salcedo rectify this insult. The governor told the *cabildo* to stop wasting its time on such trivia, whereupon the indignant council hired a lawyer to protect its prerogatives and criticized the governor for flouting its rights. Calling upon precedent, the group pointed out that in Havana the *cabildo* occupied a spacious box in the very center of the theater. Salcedo, unimpressed with the facts of history, suspended and arrested four *cabildo* members for pursuing this unseemly argument. And in the best tradition, the shows went on in spite of the discomfort of the offended city fathers. Even before this dramatic confrontation, the theater had become as inseparable a part of the cultural landscape as the *cabildo*, with both institutions providing the community with a degree of autonomy normally associated with cities.

By 1803 the population of New Orleans stood at some 8,000, although some estimates go as high as 11,000. Another 3,000 people were located below the city. These figures reflect some growth since the census of 1777 placed the population of the city and surrounding areas at 3,000. Most of the increase resulted from immigration, although the Creoles of Louisiana reported that drinking water of the Mississippi stimulated the propagation of the race. It may have been true that Louisiana women became pregnant more easily than others, but it was also true that the general unhealthiness of New Orleans contributed to an appalling infant mortality rate. A smallpox epidemic in 1802 snuffed out the lives of 1,500 children; yellow fever took others, and measles and other childhood diseases still more. More than prolific parents were needed to build a thriving city.

Like most cities, New Orleans offered a variety of the innocent and not-so-innocent of life's diversions. Indeed, to certain ascetic visitors to the city, New Orleans represented almost the epitome of human vice. Visitors of the Protestant persuasion were especially shocked at the looseness in manners and morals displayed in New Orleans. The moral fibre of the strict Presbyterian might well feel assaulted when witnessing gay, colorful throngs disporting in the streets with religious relics and statuary. Others might inveigh against the abundance of tippling houses located at every cross street, crowded and riotous places of intoxication whose taps were eternally going. The apparent spread of luxury and ostentation supplied another source of inspiration for the moralist. High living was the rule among the smart set, the well-to-do who distinguished themselves by the expensiveness of their apparel, vehicles, home furnishings, and other visible symbols of wealth. One perceptive visitor, however, penetrating the facade of luxury, warned travelers not to be fooled by the beautiful houses along the Mississippi into thinking that New Orleans enjoyed a well-distributed affluence. After walking the streets of the city, Paul Alliot observed homes "whose construction and roofs show a depth of poverty which is surprising."[1]

There were rich and poor in New Orleans as in any other city in the world. Also, as one might expect in a city still in a frontier stage, the streets were in wretched condition, unlighted during most of the period and filled with mud or chuckholes depending upon the season. When floodwaters topped or penetrated the levees in front of the town, the waters spilled into the streets. When they receded, tons of fish were left to decay along with other garbage, providing a proper environment for the microscopic and macroscopic carriers of contagion that abound in a city, as well as contributing a variety of smells to offend the sensitive nostrils of visitors. The *cabildo* devoted considerable energy and substantial portions of a limited budget to dealing with such problems with but qualified success. The same was true with fire prevention, crime, and other hazards of urban dwelling.

For all the natural and man-made calamities that disrupted and occasionally destroyed life in New Orleans, life went on as usual within the confines of the stockade and five gates that separated town from country. For one down from Pittsburgh on a flatboat in 1801, the fact that New Orleans could not boast a college or public library did not diminish the image of a large and beautiful town with some houses of elegant construction. By this time the town had been almost totally rebuilt following the major fires in 1788 and 1794. As in the French period, the town formed a square, now somewhat larger, extending from the crescent of the river north toward Lake Pontchartrain and containing in 1800 some 1,600 houses, mostly of brick or stone covered with tile and plaster. The suburbs were already forming around the city, one in particular, St. Mary, noted by Alliot at the time of the transfer as the residence of many wealthy planters and merchants and also as a center of considerable illicit trade. The extensive plantations of Boré, Livaudais, and others delighted the view of visitors who approached the city from the sea and may well havc ill-prepared the seaborne travelers for the great stench that emanated from New Orleans.

As for the residents of the town, there was probably enough going on to take their minds off the local odors and other inconveniences of eighteenth century urban living. Many of the more common diversions were open to the people of all classes and of all races seven days a week, with Sunday being no less a day than any other for business as well as fun and games. Gambling, although illegal and the object of much legislation and occasional raids, was indulged in openly by all ranks and colors with cash in their hands. Dancing was legal and easily the most popular recreation in the city. By 1805, there were some fifteen public ballrooms, with an ordinary ball attracting some five hundred people. Sunday was a big day for dancing, the theater, and opera—the latter introduced during the 1790s.

Of concern to the authorities was the availability of most of these pleasures to slaves as well as whites. Frequent efforts were made to eliminate such activities among the slaves who wandered freely about the city. The regulations were repeated and strengthened frequently enough to indicate their general ineffectiveness. Slaves were forbidden to sell or purchase liquor, to assemble at night, to gamble, to dance the tango before evening services, to possess firearms, to duel, or to be in town without the written permission of their masters. The reputation of the quadroon women was notorious enough by 1786 to prompt Governor Miró to attack the hair styles of these unfortunates, ordering them to comb it flat or provide a cover if combed high. Slave revolts in the 1790s in St. Domingue caused great uneasiness in Louisiana, where there were abortive slave uprisings which resulted in even more stringent slave laws in New Orleans.

The population of New Orleans consisted mostly of Europeans, Americans, and African Americans. There were but few Indians remaining in the area by 1800, so not too much should be made of the reputation of New Orleans as America's first melting pot. As a seaport, it naturally attracted a variety of peoples but no more so than New York and probably much less so than a cosmopolitan center such as Marseilles. Basically, the French Creole, the Anglo-Saxon, and the African American jostled for living space, with the Anglo-Saxons and the blacks numerically preponderant after the Louisiana Purchase. In its class structure New Orleans was not much different than any other established American city. High society began with the governor and intendant, both Spanish and transient, and included an indigenous aristocracy composed of members of the *cabildo*, officers in the occupation force and the local militia, wealthy planters, and successful merchants, many of whom served in official capacities.

Francisco Bouligny, who accompanied O'Reilly to Louisiana in 1769, served in the military, pursued commerce, was lieutenant governor in 1777, and senior official in the colony when Governor Gayoso died in 1799. Nicholas Forstall, one of the *cabildo* members arrested in 1802, served earlier as commandant at Attakapas and was an important merchant in New Orleans. Denis de la Ronde, also arrested in 1802, served in the militia and was a businessman. Evan Jones, a militia officer and Spanish subject, was almost arrested when appointed vice-consul for the United States at New Orleans in 1801. B. Gravier and Étienne Boré were successful planters. These men in official capacities and other influential and wealthy individuals such as Gilbert Antoine de St. Maxent, Daniel Clark, Jr., Michel Fortier, Oliver Pollock, and Pierre Philippe de Marigny de Mandeville were among the aristocracy of the city.

For the most part such individuals arrived at their exalted social status through success in business or planting. Many individuals pursued both occupations concurrently, although the tendency was to advance from the counting house to the plantation veranda. The class system was not entirely closed to newcomers, as there was apparently considerable opportunity for upward social mobility based upon prior economic success.

Nor were conditions during the last decades of Spanish rule favorable to the establishment of a caste system. Hurricanes and floods wiped out planters; fires burned out merchants in 1788 and 1794; and epidemics carried off people of all classes. Opportunities and risks assured the existence of an upper crust but also guaranteed changes in personnel.[2] Manners and morals among the elite were, however, fairly stable, being the creation of the French Creole, who attempted with some success to maintain a cultural enclave in the face of an increasing influx of Anglo-Saxons.

In 1779 Governor Bernardo de Gálvez explained to his uncle that "persons of distinction" resisted service in the militia where they were compelled to stand in rank next to their shoemakers and barbers. Gálvez, sympathizing with the plight of the elite, created a cavalry troop for this class. The *caribiniers* would now ride while the common sort walked. Urban growth called for a large number of petty tradesmen to service the needs of each other and other citizens. Including tailors, carpenters, butchers, bakers, and candlestick makers, and a variety of other occupations and skills, the class of petit bourgeois probably accounted for the vast majority of the town's white population. This group, including a number of free men of color who could own property and pursue a trade, ran the gamut from the wealthy if socially unacceptable bartender or cabaret owner to the peddler wandering about the town or set up in temporary headquarters upon the levees. This class of trader tailed off into the marginal economic groups, primarily city slaves engaged in selling the surplus of their gardens and loot from nocturnal activities, or Indians peddling vegetables, fish blankets, and trinkets. With the expansion of the port and market at New Orleans, transients such as sailors and upriver boatmen composed an increasing number of the more lively if temporary inhabitants of the town.

In this diverse community, the *cabildo* functioned as the institution responsible for the maintenance of law and order. The difficulties experienced by this reasonably efficient organ of government were frequently monumental. Wars and their consequences periodically stymied progress in the city, cut off food supplies, and threatened the populace with economic and nutritional starvation. Floodwaters at intervals devastated farm lands and inundated New Orleans. Three great hurricanes swept through the colony in August, September, and October, 1794, ruining crops and destroying buildings and shipping. Immense destruction, estimated in excess of $3 million, was caused by the fire of 1788 which reduced to ashes more than eight hundred houses and buildings. Coming, as Governor Miró mourned, just after the colony had recovered from two hurricanes, the fire wiped out the stock of every merchant in town as well as the residences of the most aristocratic families. Rebuilding began, much of it destined for burning in the lesser fire of December 8, 1794, which destroyed most of the structures remaining from the French period, as well as the city's flour reserve.

New Orleans always mended rapidly after these shocks, partially through the exertions of the *cabildo* and the willingness of the Spanish government to provide necessary relief, and because of the inherent powers of recovery found in a growing town. Established by Governor O'Reilly conformably to the Spanish tradition of local self-government, the *cabildo* exercised a direct and increasing influence upon the daily economic life of the town. Provided with a permanent revenue based on a tax base which the *cabildo* constantly sought to widen, the governing body exercised responsibility in a variety of areas that expanded as the city grew. Repair and construction of roads, bridges, and levees; regulation of the port; establishment of city lighting, sanitation, police and fire prevention services; regulation of the local food market—all of these and other matters—were properly within the cognizance of the *cabildo*. Of these duties, none was more difficult or more pressing than the regulation of the market place.

The root of the problem in this area was to guarantee an adequate and edible food supply at a price equitable to producer, manufacturer, and consumer. Acting fully within the tradition of paternalistic municipal government, the *cabildo* intervened directly to set prices, inspect for quality, assure the use of standard weights and measures, and prevent recurrent food shortages from benefiting monopolists and forestallers at the expense of the public welfare. Private interest, on the other hand, employed various tactics to circumvent the regulatory authority of the public agency. Conflict between the public welfare and private interest continued into the American period, fought out with much the same results as in other parts of the United States. Deterioration in effective regulation by the municipal government and ultimate weakening of its power to intervene came about as the *cabildo* voluntarily surrendered some unenforceable authority or had some of its authority stripped away by the action of a more powerful sovereign body.

In Louisiana, the tradition of regulation in the public welfare endured longer than in many parts of the United States, and during the Spanish period regulatory powers were persistently utilized by the city with some success. Simultaneously, the *cabildo* came to view the city as possessing interests separate from both the colony and the Spanish empire.

The local government did not solve the problem of food supply, which was eventually taken care of by the movement of farmers into the Upper Mississippi Valley. Time and again, as in the French period, the city suffered serious food shortages. In 1772, 1779, and 1781, the *cabildo* used city funds to purchase foodstuffs from a variety of sources. Both Governor Miró and the *cabildo* acted quickly to alleviate pressures on the food supply following the great conflagration in 1788. Miró cooperated with Oliver Pollock to obtain flour, medicines, and other items form Philadelphia. In 1794 the war, fire, and hurricanes brought new misery to the colony, prompting the *cabildo* to authorize agents to purchase foodstuffs. In 1796 the *cabildo* contracted with Daniel Clark, Jr., to supply rice which the city then sold. The *cabildo* also requisitioned flour from merchants who had any stock, distributed it to the city's bakers, and then administered the sale of bread to the populace.

Conditions were so serious in 1796 that the *cabildo* requested supplies from Havana and Vera Cruz, chartering a boat from John McDonogh to carry them; invited merchants in the United States to forward flour to New Orleans; contracted with Clark and others for corn; and purchased rice as a hedge against further scarcity. In an effort to stretch existing supplies of flour and rice *cabildo* members almost donned the baker's caps and aprons in supervising experiments in which various mixtures of rice and flour were baked into bread to achieve an edible combination. In both 1800 and 1803 the *cabildo*, fearing further shortages, formally and successfully requested that the intendant prevent rice exports.

The *cabildo* needed to guarantee the availability of about six hundred barrels of flour monthly which would provide each citizen of the city with something under a pound of bread daily. City authorities tried to ascertain the precise quantity of flour baked into bread for the bakers paid a tax on each barrel. This revenue, along with a tax on the butchers, supported the street lighting system. At the same time, the *cabildo* regulated the price, weight, and quality of the bread offered to the public at retail, just as it regulated through similar measures the vending of meat in the city. In both instances, the regulations sought to protect the public as well as to provide an annual revenue to the city for the support of necessary public services. There was an obvious need for such regulation.

Before John Fitzpatrick was thrown out of New Orleans by O'Reilly, he confided with obvious satisfaction to some associates that he had managed by a strategem to conceal some "excessively rotten" flour from the *cabildo* which was searching for spoiled flour and throwing it into the river. Frequently, hereafter, the *cabildo* complained that in spite of regulations and inspection, bakers obtained rancid flour which they mixed with good flour, selling the product as fresh bread. Moreover, retailers of bread were repeatedly accused of using fraudulent weights. In times of shortage, the problem was especially critical because merchants met flour-laden vessels on the river, purchased the stock, and held it for high prices. Bread prices were fixed in 1793 by the use of a sliding scale hitched to the price of flour, and the *cabildo* posted official prices each week throughout the Spanish period and into the American. Regulations were passed protecting the right of the public to buy in small lots ahead of the retailers by prohibiting retailers from purchasing provisions and supplies in large units in order to resell. In 1773 a gauger was appointed to protect against abuses in the weighing and measuring of foodstuffs and liquors. In 1793 he became the inspector of weights and measures and, armed with official weights, confiscated large numbers of inexact weights.

Periodically, subcommittees of the *cabildo* stormed through the warehouses seeking out and destroying spoiled flour or, if pressures on the food supply existed, as in 1779 when many new families arrived, authorizing the expenditures of city funds for the purchase of food to be stored for distribution when required. The *cabildo* was also active in its efforts to secure a regular meat supply for the city.

When Louisiana was ceded to Spain, the meat supply of the city was obtained largely by hunting parties operating in the wilderness to the northeast and northwest of Natchez and through imports of salt beef from stocks in the French West Indies which originated in the English colonies, Ireland, and other places. To regularize the supply and stimulate the development of domestic herds, the *cabildo* in 1770 or 1771 granted a monopoly of the meat market to an individual after competitive bidding. Those interested in obtaining the contract bid a particular sum and suggested the details of the agreement, such as quantities, prices, and the location of the slaughter sheds. The primary contractor, acting as lessee of the butcher shops located in the central meat market, let subcontracts to other individuals who were the actual suppliers of meat.

This system did not solve the problem of supply as only an increase in population and thus in the demand for meat would induce individuals to enter the livestock industry. By the 1780s, however, significant beginnings had been made in the Attakapas and Opelousas districts as well as at Pointe Coupée and the German Coast. In 1781 the *cabildo* amended the system of contracting by drawing up its own requirements with which the highest bidder must comply. Contractors, nevertheless, experienced difficulties in meeting their obligations, some stemming from disagreement with the subcontractors and others from the severe inflation existing during the 1780s when large sums of paper money circulated at a great discount in the colony. In 1789 the *cabildo* decided to end the contract system and establish a free meat market by allowing livestock raisers to transport and sell their herds on their own terms to the butchers of the city. At the same time, the *cabildo* retained a tax of three *reales* per head of cattle sold in the city and fixed the retail price of meat.[3]

Within those limits the meat market remained free, as was the wish of interested parties in New Orleans, Attakapas, and Opelousas. The *cabildo* set the retail price of beef and pork, responding to shortages in supply by authorizing price increases; supervised and policed the operation of the central meat market in which the butchers rented stalls form the city; and tried to keep the pens and slaughter sheds outside of the city limits. In general, these activities seem to have assured the city an adequate supply of meat at moderate prices as well as guaranteeing it a revenue of more than 4,000 *piastres* annually, which increased in 1799 when the butchers' tax was raised. The *cabildo* acted shrewdly in this particular matter for it was seeking a revenue to support the street lights and the residents of the city had refused to pay a chimney tax for such purposes. Nor were the butchers happy about the new tax rates. But at that moment an association in Attakapas proposed to pay for the street lights if they were granted the monopoly of New Orleans. Informed of this, the butchers willingly agreed to an increase in the tax without a price hike with the understanding that no monopoly would be granted.

Responsive to public needs in the critical area of food supply, the *cabildo* exercised its authority with discretion. Although composed of prominent merchants and planters, the public body acted energetically to prevent forestalling and price fixing, to maintain quality control, and otherwise protect the consumer without damaging the wholesaler and retailer. In 1798 the *cabildo* listened sympathetically to vegetable retailers protesting the imposition of a weekly tax on their stands. The council frequently acted against itinerant peddlers who sold spoiled foods of unknown derivation and who littered the levees with their refuse. Municipal authority was exercised in other areas as well. Apothecaries were regulated by a price tariff. And in 1801 the *cabildo* granted the monopoly of the firewood supply to a single contractor in order to thwart the efforts of wood retailers to make excessive profits during the winter season.

No brief is presented for the total success of such measures. When the Americans took over, bakers were still mixing bad flour with good to sell at the established prices; peddlers moved their shops from spot to spot on the levee, prompting fifty New Orleans merchants to petition the *cabildo* for the removal of these competitors; and tavern owners were in collusion to fix the price of wines purchased at public sales. Nonetheless, the city government recognized the existence of such practices and sought to eliminate or control them through the application of methods derived from the medieval city. Such concepts as fair price, reasonable profit, consumer access to the market place, purity in products, accuracy and standardization of weights and measures, and prohibitions against engrossment and forestalling were all applied in the name of the public welfare. Climaxing during the Spanish period, the role of the city government in these matters then declined in the face of contradictory concepts of the market place introduced by Americans and current in other cities throughout the United States. The city government, in any event, had quite enough to do in providing other less controversial but basic services for the growing population.[4]

The maintenance, improvement, and construction of public works were among the pressing responsibilities of the *cabildo*, which, unlike the regulation of the market, involved the outlay of considerable sums of public monies. As in most cities, budgetary considerations compelled the city government to formulate projects on a somewhat smaller scale and perhaps less rapidly than the legitimate needs of the city demanded. Inadequate revenues plagued New Orleans no less than other urban areas around the world making it likely that a performance gap would always exist between the quality and variety of services offered to and the services demanded by the public. Thus, visitors and residents alike complained about the disrepair of the streets and levees, the lack of street lights, inefficient drainage and sanitation systems, inadequate police and fire protection, and other similar deficiencies.

O'Reilly's political settlement assured the city government an annual revenue of about $2,000 by allocating the revenue of specific taxes to the *cabildo*. An anchorage tax on vessels, initiated by the French, was retained for the upkeep of levees and harbor. Similarly earmarked was a tax of one *piastre*, later raised to two, on each barrel of tafia imported at New Orleans. Taxes were also levied on taverns, billiard halls, rooming houses, butchers, and bakers. At intervals thereafter, licenses were required for the operation of dancehalls, vegetable and fish stands, and for auctioneers, river pilots, and other professions. The public gauger, port warden, and other officers charged fees, the bulk of which went for the salaries of the civil servants. By 1776 the revenue from cabaret owners alone surpassed the total city budget of 1770. No wonder, since there were three times more cabaret owners paying taxes, to say nothing of the enterprising individuals selling unlicensed hooch from mobile shops.

Spain was reasonably liberal in committing funds from its own sources to finance public improvements in New Orleans, while Spanish colonial officials were permissive in allowing the city to broaden its tax base. In 1772 the Crown sanctioned the leasing of royal lands by the city to prospective storeowners, with the revenue accruing to the *cabildo*, and in 1801 the Crown donated land for sale to help the city defray the expenses of the lighting system. Spain was also willing to lend funds to the city on a six year repayment plan. Still, in 1790 the *cabildo*, faced with the danger of a break in the levee along some abandoned lands, was constrained to increase the debt of the treasury. Moreover, since the public spirit of the citizenry disintegrated when confronted by the tax collector, the city lost unknown sums when the bakers reported the use of less flour than actually consumed, tafia importers tampered with invoices, or bootleggers and peddlers failed to apply for licenses before vending their goods. The city, constantly in financial trouble, was thus slow rather than lax in paving streets, erecting street lights, and establishing police and fire departments.

The fire of 1788 not only emptied the city treasury, necessitating the raising of funds by voluntary subscriptions to meet the threat of floods which followed the fire, but resulted in the appointment of Oliver Pollock by the *cabildo* to purchase fire fighting equipment in Philadelphia. Mounting violence on city streets and banditry in and around New Orleans after dark motivated the *cabildo* to establish a municipal lighting system in the 1790s. The street lights, eighty-six in number, arrived from Philadelphia in 1794, bids were let for their placement, and means were sought to finance their operation. Rejecting a frontage tax on city lots, the *cabildo* decided upon a chimney tax which the citizens refused to pay, and finally, as noted above, allocated the butcher's tax to support the service. At the same time, the *cabildo* and Governor Carondelet established the night watch or patrol to service the lamps and patrol the streets. The N.O.P.D. was in being. Major disbursements from city funds were made each year to repair levees and gutters, to pave the streets, and to drain and fill low areas in the city.

Governor Gálvez impugned the loyalty of the *cabildo* in 1779, charging that its members "maintain a spirit of rebellion and hatred for the Spanish nation, which they cannot hide. . . ."[5] The *cabildo*, for its part, acclaimed its loyalty, pointing out that it executed royal orders with precision even if harm resulted to the colony. The issue was not one of loyalty—this confused the issue—but of interest and identity. By 1779 the *cabildo* identified with and represented the interests of the municipality. Achieving self-identity, the *cabildo*, as most political bodies, sought to aggrandize its powers at the expense of competing bodies. The dispute between governor and *cabildo* (or executive and, to stretch a point, legislature) that occurred in Louisiana was a faint mirror image of dispute that had occurred in the English colonies of America from their founding.

Although somewhat comic, the controversy between Governor Salcedo and the *cabildo* regarding the theater box symbolized this sense of interest and identity. So, too, did the vigorous criticism directed by the *cabildo* at the commercial regulations of 1793 in which the city fathers defended the interests of the colony vis-a-vis the Spanish empire.

A more positive indication of the *cabildo*'s concern with the interests of the colony occurred in 1797. News that nine English privateers operating in the Gulf of Mexico threatened to intercept the payroll boat due at New Orleans from Havana induced Governor Carondelet to propose that local merchants contribute to the outfitting of an armed vessel to escort the treasure ship into port. The merchants refused. The *cabildo* contributed a thousand *piastres* from a sorely strained treasury. One suspects that the *cabildo*, in tendering this support, thought first of New Orleans, then of Louisiana, and finally, perhaps, vaguely, of the empire.

The budget of the *cabildo* and business in general at New Orleans suffered from serious inflationary pressures during most of the Spanish period. The root of the problem then, as in the French period, lay in the paper money which circulated in Louisiana between 1779 and 1790 and again at the turn of the century. It was somewhat ironic that Louisiana, highly regarded by both French, English, and American business interests as a source of specie, should suffer long years of specie shortages and, for a medium of exchange, rely upon a paper issue which experienced as severe a depreciation as any issued during the French period. The war with England between 1779 and 1783 compelled the first issues of paper not only in Louisiana but in Spain as well. In Spain, the paper depreciated rapidly during the war but then recovered its value and remained stable until the outbreak of the French Revolutionary wars. But in Louisiana the paper enjoyed no such stability.

Governor Gálvez had recourse to the issue of credit certificates in 1779 to alleviate the shortage of specie and finance his campaigns against the English. In 1782 Intendant Navarro authorized the issue of *billetes*, to provide further relief from a shortage of coin presumed to be temporary. Within a year, Navarro suspended all payments in specie, and the colony functioned entirely on a paper system. As in the French period, confidence in the paper eroded rapidly, forcing a slow rise in prices and causing numerous disputes regarding payments. Debtors wished to pay in paper; creditors demanded specie. When a contract stipulated payment in specie, as was the case in James Mather's suit against Francisco Marmillon, the court adhered to the original terms. However, when there was no prior stipulation as to the kind of money to be received, paper was favored. Navarro, for instance, tried in 1783 to shore up the value of the paper by ordering a Bordeaux merchant to accept paper in payment of a bill of exchange.

Rapid depreciation occurred during the postwar period in spite of the tobacco boom and the annual shipment of large sums of money to meet the rising expenses of the colonial establishment. The value of imports surpassed the value of exports, with the gap increasing during the decade and with the Spanish government unable to rectify the situation with specie. The insufficiency of colonial remittances assured a deficit in the trade balance of Louisiana. Unforeseen costs of the war exaggerated the deficit and forced the issue of paper which drove prices up. As Evan and James Jones informed Nicholas Low: "This circumstance has raised the prices of Indigo, Furs & Skins . . . so exorbitantly high that they would in no degree answer as a remittance to any part of the Continent."[6]

The financial situation deteriorated further. J. B. Macarty reported colonial money at a discount of 25 to 30 percent in April, 1784, which was manageable if depreciation had ended there. Confidence in the paper collapsed, however, and by October, the paper was discounted at 50 percent. Thereafter, the discount on colonial paper fluctuated between 60 and 70 percent, depending upon the availability of exports at New Orleans. James Mather explained to a planter correspondent that the current exchange was 160 paper dollars for 100 hard but it was probable that this would decline when the tobacco came down. Both the *cabildo* and Governor Miró were insistent in their demands that the paper be withdrawn and the currency of the colony returned to a specie base. The fire of 1788 dramatized the validity of these demands.

Governor Miró, in 1786, observed that New Orleans contained strong mercantile houses fully capable of handling the commerce of the colony, if unhampered by a lack of capital caused largely by the depreciated paper. He expressed his surprise that so much commercial activity existed in the colony. New Orleans merchants were forced by the absence of specie to purchase the crops of the colony at high prices in paper and sell the produce at prices current in Europe. According to Miró, many merchants sustained large losses in these transactions, with a consequent weakening of the economic foundations of the colony. The situation facing the *cabildo* was no more enviable because its revenues were fixed. It received two *piastres* per barrel of imported tafia, regardless of the price of tafia or the market value of the currency. But the city government paid for goods and services at the inflated prices. Both the governor and the *cabildo* applied to the Crown for a remedy. The fire of 1788 occurred first.

The degree of destruction—involving nearly eight hundred homes and businesses and the city's food supplies—demanded a massive infusion of public funds not only to clear away the debris and begin rebuilding but to alleviate the distress of the homeless and prevent the outbreak of epidemic disease. But the colonial treasury was so strapped for funds that Miró, instead of expanding his welfare program, was compelled to discontinue the daily rations of rice previously issued to two hundred families. In the month after the fire, Miró coupled pleas for increased assistance with appeals for the immediate withdrawal of the paper currency. Instead, however, the Intendant General of Havana decided to retain 100,000 *piastres* budgeted for Louisiana. Before the Crown was able to order the restoration of this sum, Miró and Navarro issued another 100,000 *piastres* of paper to meet urgent needs. The sum of paper outstanding as of August, 1788, totaled 839,000 *piastres*. Only then did the Crown respond to Miró's pleas, authorizing the shipment of specie from Vera Cruz for the retirement of the paper. By 1791 the *cabildo* noted that the colony had returned to a specie base and that the small amount of paper in circulation was received at face value.

Unfortunately, this stability was disrupted by the French Revolutionary wars which threw the monetary system of both mother country and colony into another inflationary spiral. From 1790 to 1795 or 1796, New Orleans conducted its business with an adequate supply of specie money. This was fortunate because the colony received a severe jolt when the Crown ceased purchasing Louisiana tobacco for its Mexican factories. This left Louisiana with one staple product, indigo—the days of which were numbered—and two potential staples, cotton and sugar, both still in the developmental stage. New Orleans, however, received at this time its first substantial imports from the American West, which soon combined with sugar and cotton to more than compensate for the demise of tobacco and indigo as staple crops of the Lower Valley. Political tensions flowing from the French Revolution and republican enthusiasts in the United States, notably the Genêt and Clark plot against Louisiana, induced many a nervous flutter in the stomachs of Louisiana's resident officials. But there is no substantial evidence that rumors of impending invasion blighted business prospects.

Specie scarcity and inflationary pressure caught up with the *cabildo* in 1795. Yielding to necessity, the *cabildo* reversed a hitherto consistent position and rented places on the levee to the small merchants and peddlers that the city normally chased away. War with Great Britain and the destruction of the indigo crops came in 1796. As the *cabildo* sadly noted the following year, British sea power not only reduced the maritime activity of the port, it also reduced the city's revenue. The treasury was penniless and the paper had already depreciated as much as 90 percent. Trade with the Americans provided a source of coin but in adding to the attractions of contraband trade it further reduced revenues. Property values were tumbling, Nicholas Forstall complained when he was forced to sell property in order to pay a debt. There was to be no relief. Paper money was discounted 100 percent in 1801. To advance credit was risky, becoming more so when successive rumors and final confirmation of two cessions swept through the colony. But tight money made credits more necessary than ever. It was either advance credit or forego sales.

It is difficult to ascertain with any assurance the impact of monetary stringency, wars, quasi-war, and threats of war, hurricanes, floods, human and plant diseases, and the rumors and realities of successive cessions upon the economic life of New Orleans and its people. Ninety-nine percent of the people lived inarticulately, in either wealth, comfort, pinchedness, or squalor. The other 1 percent has left some written remembrance of themselves—but unfortunately they were of the elite and better buffered against adversity than most folk. Julien Poydras might complain about hard times but still manage to live in a style sufficient to entertain the duc d'Orleans, future king of France, when he and his two brothers visited New Orleans in 1798. But what of the less affluent? What of Antonio Caperdoni, porter of the *cabildo* in 1795, earning an annual wage of 240 *pesos*, or Juan Percetto, guardian of the prison, salaried at 150 *pesos* yearly? Inflation certainly must have hit hard at such individuals.

Take Juan Percetto, for example. It is not known whether he had a family but his salary is known, as are meat and bread prices. In 1797 the daily consumption of a pound of bread and a pound of meat for a year required 31 percent of his income; in 1798, 40 percent. In addition, there would be clothing, drink, and rent. According to one observer, house rents were so excessively high in New Orleans that they would equal the purchase price in five years. If Percetto had a family, they were on the verge of indigence. The cost of living was more oppressive in 1803 when 50 percent of the daily wage of a laborer or artisan-helper was spent to purchase a loaf of bread and a pound of meat. A master carpenter expended 25 percent. And in all cases, the annual proportion spent on food would be higher if there were periods of unemployment. Wages may well have been high, but prices were higher and it is difficult to accept Laussat's judgment that workers were well to do. Paul Alliot believed that few were able to live in comfort. For many residents, if not most, New Orleans remained a city with an economy of scarcity.

Opportunities for employment in New Orleans for the unskilled or semiskilled free worker were restricted by the lack of an industrial base and by the presence of slavery. The city government and its contractors employed slaves on construction jobs. Slaves were hired out as coachmen, cooks, gardeners, maids, and so on. Stevedores, teamsters and draymen, and garbage collectors frequently were African Americans. Quadroon and darker prostitutes competed with the white professionals, ignoring Governor Miró's order that black women abstain from licentious life. In spite of local ordinances, African Americans hawked a variety of goods from the levee or at street corners. Slaves were also employed by their owners or as hired hands in the few manufacturing establishments located in or near the city.

At the time of the Louisiana Purchase, a number of sawmills and distilleries formed practically the entire industrial plant of the city. At least two cordage factories were operating, one owned by Elisa Winter and the other by Daniel Clark. The latter was located across the end of Royal Street and obstructed the right of way, causing a dispute between Clark and the city government. This plant burned to the ground in 1806 when the tar in storage caught fire. In the suburbs of the city, two cotton mills and a sugar refinery were established, along with a small rice mill. The historian François-Xavier Martin also lists plants manufacturing hair powder, vermicelli, and small shot. Facilities for the construction and repair of ships were available, but the town never progressed far in the construction of either oceangoing or larger river craft.

Vessels were occasionally built in New Orleans. The French commissioner Villars recorded the construction of three vessels all under 300 tons by Beauregard in 1772 and 1773. From 1781 to 1800 none of the fifty-five vessels enrolled and registered at New Orleans were constructed in the city. Firms such as Lieutaud and Company specialized in structural repair and furnished lumber and workers such as ships' carpenters and caulkers. Other firms supplied pitch and tar while the cordage works provided the rigging, and individual blacksmiths or ironmongers hired themselves out to make special repairs.

The economic hub of New Orleans remained the harbor and port facilities. Most employment, from the dock worker to the merchant, concentrated on the single task of moving goods to market and selling goods in the local market. The form of business had not changed much from the days of the Rasteaus, Jung, and Chantalou, even though market possibilities for exports had widened significantly and the quantities involved were many times larger than in the French period. During the Spanish period the products themselves had changed and the points of origin expanded to include many new areas within the Mississippi River Valley. But whether it was indigo from the Farrar plantation, cotton from John Bisland at Natchez, distilled sugar from George Mather above New Orleans, or flour and tobacco from farms in the Ohio River Valley, many essential services were only available in New Orleans. Planter and merchant remained the two principals in the mercantile world.

Uncovering the subjective relationship between these two interests is difficult. One can accept Captain Philip Pittman's evaluation of the French and early Spanish period that planters were treated with great indulgence in economic matters without totally rejecting Paul Alliot's charge, in 1803, that the merchant fixed staple prices and through credits extended to the planter "forces the settler to deliver . . . his products at a price much lower than the current price."[7] The strictures of Berquin-Duvallon and Prefect Laussat, who both condemned the absorption of the townspeople in the material acquisition, represent an accurate observation and an irrelevant value judgment. The observation should also be extended to the planter. Julien Poydras or Étienne Boré were no less acquisitive than Daniel Clark, Jr., or James Mather. The issue is further confused by those who would distinguish between the planter-aristocrat and the bourgeois-merchant. There were wealthy planters to be sure and they attempted to emulate the aristocratic life. But their wealth was gained through the application of bourgeois-capitalist standards, ideals, and methods of operation. This truth became more pronounced following the cession of Louisiana to the United States. The new century, in New Orleans as well New York and Liverpool, was the century of the bourgeoisie.

There is some evidence, however, that planter interest diverged from mercantile interests on certain matters of policy. Following the 1788 fire the merchants, many of whom suffered total losses, requested the privilege of going to any European port to obtain goods for Louisiana. Planters opposed this because they were fearful that such a privilege would allow the most powerful merchants to monopolize commerce and fix crop prices. The planters suggested opening up the trade of New Orleans to all foreign ships. Miró supported their position, recognizing however, that they asked too much. The French Revolutionary wars and Pinckney's treaty forced Spain to concede tacitly most of the planters' demands. It was the planters' object to assure the greatest competition possible among merchants and shippers for the crops of the colony. Established merchants in New Orleans would willingly sacrifice such competition.

Conflicts of interest between merchants and planters became more overt and intense during the American period when new institutions such as banks were established in and controlled by merchants of New Orleans. Then the planters resorted to the territorial and state legislature in an effort to lessen the economic dominance of the city merchants. Conflict was also latent in the increasing number of merchants in New Orleans of overseas purchasers and suppliers.

One individual spoke of the transient nature of merchants who extracted what wealth they could from New Orleans and then left with their fortunes. Others, however, noted the ambition of merchants to amass a fortune for investment in a plantation. Merchants who came and went are less significant than those who remained permanently but whose interests were not identifiable with the community. The appearance of this latter type becomes more marked in the American period as scores of agents of English and American merchants and manufacturers flowed into New Orleans to purchase cotton, sugar, and western produce and sell manufactured wares to the agrarians.

Many individuals about whom something can be learned from extant documents fit all categories so that blanket and inflexible categorizations are untenable. Daniel Clark, Jr., for instance, came to New Orleans as the partner-agent of Daniel Coxe of Philadelphia and was soon one of the first merchants in the city. He served as consular agent, owned a cordage factory, purchased a plantation at Natchez in 1787 and a 208,000-acre tract on the Ouachita River in 1803. He served as a director of at least two banks after 1803 and as territorial delegate to Congress in 1806. A similar pattern was followed by Evan Jones, although he may not have owned any land or worked a plantation. Evan and James Jones were agents of Nicholas Low of New York as well as of William and James Walton and Company of Philadelphia. They purchased crops for the account of these firms and for their own account as well as handling, on commission, the crops of planters. Insofar as they operated on their own account or for Low, it behooved them to purchase at a low price. When acting as commission agents for planters, the object was sale at the highest possible price.

There was room for a conflict of interest in these operations. J. B. Macarty, merchant and owner of a sawmill, purchased American goods on commission for Louisiana planters. In 1783 Macarty instructed Nicholas Low to place an advertisement in the newspapers that "J.B. Macarty, merchant of New Orleans informs the merchts of the United States that he will receive new flour on commission," promising the most careful attention to their interests. But in purchasing flour on commission for the planters, Macarty was obligated to buy at the lowest possible price. Other merchants, Morgan and Mather, Chew and Relf, Joseph McNeil, to name a few, engaged in the same variety of business operations and were undoubtedly faced with the same dilemma. If the planters were resentful about inequities in their relations with the merchants, they remained unexpressed until self-government came to Louisiana and until rural communities discovered identities which they were able to articulate in the legislature and news media.

Specialization in business was rare in New Orleans through the Spanish period and into the early American years. The volume of business in the city was not large enough nor the hazards of trade sufficiently tempered to support the business specialist. Moreover, brokerage, banking, and insurance services among others were unknown in New Orleans until the transfer to the United States. Insurance was obtained elsewhere. Credit was extended from one firm or individual to another as a personal service and on the basis of the borrower's reputation for business integrity, rather than on any objective measurement of his assets. Investment opportunities outside of the traditional sectors of trade and land were almost nonexistent. Times and conditions would change, especially after the War of 1812 and the integration of New Orleans and its hinterland into the American system. But until then, nonspecialists dominated business circles in New Orleans and many of the most successful eventually invested part of their profits in land and slaves.

Beverly Chew and Richard Relf, associated as Chew and Relf at least by 1801, pursued as wide a variety of business activities as possible in New Orleans. They purchased from and sold goods to Reed and Forde of Philadelphia; provisioned, freighted, and leased vessels to St. Domingue, Bordeaux, and London; received English goods on consignment; and bought and sold staples and groceries on their own account. With the American occupation, their interest and occupation proliferated even more. The firm of Morgan and Mather provided many services: collecting debts for and from planters; handling the crops of John Bisland of Natchez; forwarding slop buckets, millinery, and other articles to George Mather's store in St. James Parish; and handling the sales from the sugar factory of George Mather and Company.

The services offered by New Orleans merchants to the plantation economy were so necessary—to say nothing of their convenience and reasonable cost—that it was all but impossible for even the largest planter to bypass them. John Bisland of Cross Creek near Natchez, a store owner and proprietor of a plantation with thirty-six slaves at the turn of the century, grew and purchased staples from others for sale on his own account in the 1780s and later years. Bisland bought from and sold directly to merchants in Scotland whenever possible. In 1802 he accompanied a shipment of 208 bales of cotton, insured for $17,000, aboard the ship *Neptune* for Greenock. Two other New Orleans merchants, James Ewing and James Johnson, accompanied personal consignments of cotton with the full cargo totaling 777 bales. A part of Bisland's cotton was purchased from other planters and some was sold to William Kenner of New Orleans. The expenses of freight, storage, drayage, and loading in New Orleans came to $640, the details of which Kenner handled. Total freight charges came to $2,638, about $12 per bale, the arrangements negotiated by Kenner. Bisland instructed a correspondent in Glasgow to take out insurance. The *Neptune* struck sandbanks off Ireland in September, 1802, and much of Bisland's cotton was ruined, but the insurance claim was settled by the following year.

From start to finish, Bisland and other planters depended upon the services and labor of a number of firms and individuals located in New Orleans. The dependence, of course, was reciprocal, with each party courting the good opinion of the other through the efficient consummation of their business. So long as most merchants in New Orleans acted primarily on their own account and largely as the agents of the planters, the possibility of contention was minimized. When the merchants learned that bread was buttered more thickly by the overseas interest, or when the merchants in association in a banking venture utilized their position to serve only their own welfare, or practices discrimination in the extension of loans, then a form of city-country strife was all but inevitable.

The matter was never quite so clear cut, of course. Ethnic animosities, the organization of political parties, and competing regional interests tended to blur urban and rural divisions—but never to wholly efface them. Besides, it was virtually impossible for planters and farmers in the Mississippi Valley to ship any other way than through New Orleans until the construction of the great canal and railroad systems between the Northeast and the Old Northwest. Merchants in New Orleans became fully aware of their strategic position in the early nineteenth century. The exploitation of all of these advantages by the business community of that city resulted in a perceptible shift in the urban-rural balance of power favorable to the urban interest. While the city might eternally bemoan the existence of a rurally dominated legislature, New Orleans slowly but surely achieved economic ascendance over the country. New steps in this direction were taken in the decade following the Louisiana Purchase.

Notes for "Economic Life Before the Louisiana Purchase"

[1]Paul Alliot, "Historical and Political Reflection on Louisiana," in James A. Robertson, trans. and ed., *Louisiana under the Rule of Spain, France, and the Untied States, 1785-1807: Social, Economic, and Political Conditions of the Territory Represented in the Louisiana Purchase*, 2 vols. (Cleveland, 1911), 1:65-67.

[2]Minter Wood, "Life in New Orleans in the Spanish Period," *Louisiana Historical Quarterly*, 22 (1939): 675, speaks of the prosperity of the later Spanish period as the monopoly of a few merchants, planters, and officials. This exaggerates the intensity of class domination of the economic resources of the city. Some were obviously wealthier than others but many made an adequate living without gaining entrance into the elite. Moreover, there was little stability in the membership of the elite. It may be that class domination was more complete during the first American years than during the Spanish regime.

[3]Hilario Bontet [Hilaire Boutté], the prime contractor in 1781-84, complained that the subcontractors in Attakapas and Opelousas would sell only salted meats rather than drive their herds to New Orleans as the contract called for. Bontet was also caught in the inflationary squeeze. When he made the contract, the paper currency had only lost 15 percent but in 1784 the paper was only worth 40 percent of face value. The cattle owners increased the price of cattle to compensate for depreciation while Bontet could sell to the butchers only at a fixed price. The *cabildo* authorized an increase in the price of meat.

[4]New York City abandoned many similar activities prior to 1803, giving up, for example, the fixing of bread prices in 1802. See Sidney I. Pomerantz, *New York, An American City, 1783-1803: A Study of Urban Life*, Columbia University Studies in History, Economics, and Public Law, 442 (New York, 1938), 170-77. For an excellent discussion of the market-regulating role of colonial American cities, see Carl Bridenbaugh, *Cities in the Wilderness: Urban Life in America, 1625-1742* (New York, 1964) and Bridenbaugh, *Cities in Revolt: Urban Life in America, 1743-1776* (New York, 1964). For the western cities, see Richard C. Wade, *The Urban Frontier: Pioneer Life in Early Pittsburgh, Cincinnati, Lexington, Louisville, and St. Louis* (Chicago, 1964), 81-83, 280-82.

[5]Bernardo de Gálvez to José de Gálvez, March 2, 1779, in *Confidential Dispatches of Gálvez*, 60.

[6]Evan and James Jones to Nicholas Low, April 9, 1784, in Robert Smith and Nicholas Low Papers, Tulane University.

[7]Alliot, "Reflections on Louisiana," 69.

PART VI
NATIVE AMERICANS AND IMMIGRATION

INDIAN POLICY IN SPANISH LOUISIANA: THE NATCHITOCHES DISTRICT, 1763-1803*

F. Todd Smith

Spain's acquisition of Louisiana created difficult Indian problems for the new rulers of the former French colony. First, the natives of Louisiana had forged strong and intimate ties with French traders, and many tribes had been ardent enemies of the Spaniards. Second, the powerful and aggressive British now stood poised just across the Mississippi River from Spanish Louisiana, ready and willing to replace the French by supplying the Indians with an enormous array of trade goods. To gain the allegiance of the province's tribes and keep them from becoming British clients, the Spanish rulers of Louisiana were forced to adopt a radically different Indian policy, one that focused on trade instead of conversion of the natives to Christianity.[1]

The administration of this policy was made more difficult by the great size of the colony. Although New Orleans was the capital of Spanish Louisiana, officials at the frontier outposts of St. Louis, Arkansas Post, and Natchitoches were responsible for the day-to-day relations with the natives of the colony. Each post dealt with different Indian tribes, many of which were at war with those attached to a different post, thus preventing the Louisiana administrators from adhering to a neat, all-encompassing policy for the whole colony. Not only did the governor face bureaucratic problems within the different districts of Louisiana, the Natchitoches district lay on the border with Texas, an entirely different administrative entity. Although Louisiana and Texas were now both Spanish possessions, they were governed separately, and each followed its own Indian policy according to its own needs. Throughout the Spanish period in Louisiana, Natchitoches commandants were forced to manage Indian affairs while being squeezed by the necessities of other jurisdictions. It is a tribute to the abilities of the Spanish officials at Natchitoches that in the face of enormous obstacles they were able to implement a policy that won the allegiance of the Natchitoches district's Indians and maintained relative peace and stability during the four decades that Spain ruled Louisiana.[2]

*This article is published with the kind permission of the author.

Due to events that occurred during the half century before 1762, the Indians of the Natchitoches district were effectively at war with the Spaniards of Texas when Spain acquired Louisiana. The tribes of the Louisiana-Texas frontier had favored the French because they provided the natives with the goods they wanted while the Spaniards refused to do so. The natives desired European metal goods, including guns and ammunition, and were willing to trade horses and animal skins to obtain them. Although the French in Louisiana eagerly entered this commerce, the Spaniards in Texas resisted. Instead, Spanish Indian policy in Texas rested on the backs of Franciscan missionaries whose goal was to convert the natives to Christianity, not acquire their trade. The Crown prohibited the use of force, and priests as well as all other Spaniards were forbidden from distributing firearms to the Indians. Although Spanish methods enjoyed some success among the hunting and gathering Coahuiltecan tribes that grouped around the San Antonio missions, the more powerful tribes rejected Spanish priests and embraced French traders.[3]

No tribe exemplified this trend more than the Caddos. They occupied the key strategic position at the convergence of the Spanish and French empires in North America and comprised the most influential tribe in the Natchitoches district. The Caddos lived in permanent farming villages located along two river systems, the Red and the Neches. In the mid-eighteenth century, four Caddo tribes resided on the Red River: the Kadohadachos, Petit Caddos, Yatasis, and Natchitoches. To the west, along the upper reaches of the Neches River, were the four Caddo tribes that made up the Hasinai confederacy: the Nabedaches, Asinais, Nacogdoches, and Nadacos. Spaniards and Frenchmen entered the Caddo country in the late seventeenth century and established permanent settlements in the early eighteenth century. The Red River Caddos allowed the French to construct trading posts among the Kadohadachos, Yatasis, and Natchitoches. The Spaniards meanwhile founded the capital of Texas at Los Adaes, only a few miles west of the main French trading post at Natchitoches.[4]

The Hasinais tolerated the Spanish presence in their midst because it was minimal—fewer than one hundred soldiers and only several unsuccessful missionaries. Illegal (from the Spanish perspective) French weapons and metal goods flowed freely into Texas from the Red River Caddo villages. Not only did these weapons allow the Caddos to end the threats from their Indian enemies, it also enhanced their position *vis á vis* other tribes in the region. The Red River Caddos became middlemen in the trade with the larger and more warlike tribes that lived farther upstream from the Kadohadachos. They included fellow Caddoan-speaking kinsmen of the Wichita confederacy, namely the Taovayas, Iscanis, Tawakonis, and Kichais, and the newcomers to the region, the Shoshonean Comanches. These tribes and the Caddos, collectively known as the Norteños by the Spaniards, used French weapons to fight their common enemies, the Athapaskan Lipan Apaches and the Siouan Osages.[5]

The Caddos clearly recognized their dependence on their French allies and firearms, and they were willing to fight anyone, including the Spaniards, who threatened to disrupt these intimate ties. The Caddo tribes took a bold and aggressive stance against halfhearted

Spanish attempts to halt the flow of French goods into Texas in 1750 and 1752. Throughout the period, Spanish governors of Texas not only turned a blind eye to the illegal trade, but a few actually engaged in it themselves.[6]

Attacks on the Spaniards did not occur until 1758, when two thousand Norteño warriors assaulted the Franciscan mission for Apaches on the San Saba River in central Texas. The warriors killed eight Spaniards and burned the mission buildings. A Spanish punitive expedition, led by Diego Ortiz Parrilla, attempted to punish the Wichitas in 1759, but met defeat at the Taovaya village on the Red River. The Taovayas were well-armed with French weapons and flew the French flag over their fortified position. During the next few years, the Norteños continued their attacks on the Spanish presidio on the San Saba and the new missions built for the Apaches at El Cañon on the Nueces River.[7]

Thus, the Norteños and the Spaniards of Texas were at war when Spain acquired Louisiana in November, 1762. Spain did not immediately take possession of its new colony. During this time, French traders, namely the son of the founder of Natchitoches, Louis Juchereau de St. Denis, and officials, most importantly Athanase de Mézières, the lieutenant commander of the Natchitoches post, continued relations with the Norteños. The first Spanish governor of Louisiana, Antonio de Ulloa, who arrived in New Orleans in March, 1766, had been instructed to leave the French governmental structure intact. Following a fact-finding trip to Natchitoches in the spring of 1766, Ulloa wisely realized that the French method of dealing with the Indians should remain in place as well. He understood that the Spanish practice of using missionaries as intermediaries with the natives would not work with tribes accustomed to French trade. To eradicate this commerce would only throw the Norteños into the hands of the aggressive British traders. Ulloa kept the Indians satisfied by continuing the flow of goods and using the same French traders who now served the king of Spain. St. Denis *fils* and De Mézières retained their important positions at Natchitoches and serviced the Norteños from there.[8]

For the Wichitas and Caddos, the only immediate consequence of Louisiana's transfer to Spain was increased warfare with the Osages. In the early eighteenth century, the Osages, who resided in two villages located on tributaries of the Missouri River, had diverted their attention toward the French traders in Illinois. Following Spain's acquisition of Louisiana, however, the French traders, who were now Spanish subjects, established themselves illegally on the Arkansas River and supplied the Osages with large numbers of smuggled British guns and munitions. To obtain more of these goods, the Osages began preying on the Red River Caddos and Wichitas to steal horses to trade with the French. According to De Mézières, the Osage onslaught had turned the Red River Valley into a "pitiful theater of outrageous robberies and bloody encounters."[9]

Osage aggression, which would plague Spanish-Indian relations in Louisiana throughout the rest of the century, set off a chain of events. They created a crisis among Spain's administrators and forced Governor Ulloa to take an active role in the formation of Indian policy. To recoup losses to the Osages, the Wichitas, often in conjunction with the Comanches, stepped up attacks on the Spaniards in Texas. The increased Norteño assaults made the interim governor of Texas, Hugo O'Conor, take action that directly affected the Red River tribes. Although both Texas and Louisiana were now Spanish possessions, they were administered separately, a practice that quickly created problems. While Governor Ulloa had no qualms about allowing the French method of trade to continue in Louisiana, Governor O'Conor was determined to stop the illegal commerce that persisted between Indians of his province and traders from Natchitoches. O'Conor, who was charged with investigating the smuggling that Texas governors had earlier permitted with Louisiana, was certain that the rampaging Norteños still received guns and munitions from that province.[10]

Thus, in December, 1767, O'Conor arrested a French trader from Natchitoches en route to trade with the Yatasis, and through them, with the Kadohadachos and Hasinais. The arrest alarmed the Caddo tribes, for, in light of increased Osage attacks, they were desperate that the Texas governor not impede their supply of weapons. In response, the Yatasi chief, Cocay, gathered members of all the Caddo tribes at his village to discuss plans for an attack on the Spanish provincial capital at Los Adaes. St. Denis, whom the Spaniards now employed, met the enraged Caddos. He told them that he opposed their plans, and he urged them to be friendly and peaceful. The Caddos, however, did not return to their villages until they received presents and a promise that their trade would not be interrupted again.[11]

St. Denis brought the incident to the attention of Governor Ulloa. He in turn immediately attempted to dissuade O'Conor from carrying out his plan to disrupt trade with Indian tribes who "have been accustomed to it for a long time past." He warned that the result would have "very evil consequences," such as a violent uprising against the Spaniards, and he expressed concern that the tribes would travel to the "English frontiers to get the things which are withheld from them." Ulloa felt that the best way to maintain peace was to provide the Indians with presents every time they visited "and to assure them that trade will be kept up in the same way as it has been carried on in the past." Although both the Texas and Louisiana governors were soon removed from the scene, their successors ultimately adopted this radical new policy that Ulloa promoted.[12]

The new governors, Alejandro O'Reilly of Louisiana and the Baron de Ripperdá of Texas, realized that peaceful relations with the Indians of their common frontier had to be maintained. Spain was too weak and too poor to afford war with them, especially when they might unite with the British at any time. Also, because hostilities with the Norteños had yet to be resolved, these tribes continued to threaten Texas. With O'Reilly taking the lead, the governors of the two provinces undertook a policy of peace aimed at barring British intrusion and influence and establishing Spanish authority over the Louisiana tribes that had previously acknowledged France.[13]

To put this policy into effect, Governor O'Reilly called upon the man whose knowledge of the Indian inhabitants in Texas and Louisiana was "such as no one else possesses," Athanase de Mézières. De Mézières, who was appointed lieutenant governor of Natchitoches in 1769, informed O'Reilly that he considered the allegiance of the

Kadohadachos to be of the utmost importance to any peace plan because the tribe occupied "the master-key of New Spain." Not only could the Kadohadachos serve as a buffer against British incursions on the northeast flank of Texas, but their influence over the Norteños, especially the Wichitas, might help bring about peace with them as well.[14]

Governor O'Reilly accepted De Mézières' judgment and, in January, 1770, gave him approval to open formal negotiations with the Red River Caddos. To induce their allegiance, De Mézières arranged annual presents for the Natchitoches, Yatasis, Petit Caddos, and Kadohadachos, and he permitted licensed traders to visit the villages of the latter three tribes. After assuring the Red River Caddos of their continuation of their trade goods, De Mézières brought the tribal chiefs to Natchitoches in April, 1770, to establish formal ties with the Spaniards. Tinhioüen of the Kadohadachos and Cocay of the Yatasis received the high distinction of being designated medal chiefs by De Mézières, and both "solemnly promised to show the same love and the same respect" for Spain as they had earlier shown for France. Both chiefs ceded to the king of Spain "all proprietorship in the land which they inhabit, [and] have promised him blind fidelity and obedience."[15]

De Mézières then encouraged the new Spanish allies to take measures to influence the rest of the Norteños to end their attacks. Both Tinhioüen and Cocay sent messengers to inform these tribes that the "most powerful French and Spanish nations are now united by such close ties that to injure one is to offend the other." The two chiefs also promised to abstain from trading with the Norteños in an effort to show the Comanches and Wichitas that only friendly tribes would receive goods. As a result of this pressure, three Wichita chiefs arrived at the Kadohadacho village in August, 1770, desiring to begin negotiations with the Spaniards.[16]

Tinhioüen immediately sent messengers to De Mézières, who set out from Natchitoches accompanied by six soldiers. To demonstrate that the Frenchmen in Louisiana were now subjects of Spain, they added another five Spanish soldiers from Los Adaes to their contingent, in addition to Father Miguel de Santa María y Silva, president of the Franciscan mission. On their way to the Kadohadacho village, the party passed through the Yatasi and Petit Caddo villages where, De Mézières reported, they were sheltered and fed with "visible affection" by the natives. Father Miguel, however, angrily observed that the Indians were very friendly to the French but indifferent to the Spaniards. Obviously, the presence of the French remained the key element in the establishment of peaceful relations between the Norteños and Spain. The Spanish flag, however, was hoisted at each village, and the headmen of each tribe joined the party as it made its way to the Kadohadacho village for the council that Tinhioüen arranged.[17]

At the meeting, De Mézières informed the Wichita leaders that their trade from Natchitoches had been suspended because of their attack upon the mission on the San Saba River and their subsequent battle with Parrilla. He made it clear that all Frenchmen in Louisiana were now subjects of the Spanish king. De Mézières insisted that the tribes "should profit by the good example and inviolable fidelity of the friendly" Kadohadachos and also ally themselves with the Spaniards. Both Tinhioüen and Cocay at once seconded the speech with effective arguments "so worthy of their well-known loyalty."[18]

The Wichita spokesman replied that their discord with the Spaniards had resulted from the latter's alliance with the Apaches and the establishment of missions for them at San Saba and El Cañon. He told De Mézières that their former allies, the Comanches, had turned on them because the Wichitas were now seeking peace with the Spaniards. But fearful of a Spanish attack, the Wichitas still refused to go to either San Antonio or Los Adaes to conclude a peace treaty with Texas. Although De Mézières was disappointed with their decision, he optimistically arranged to meet the Wichitas again in the spring to continue negotiations.[19]

Unfortunately for De Mézières, the Spaniards in his party reported to the new governor of Louisiana, Luis de Unzaga y Amezaga, that the meeting had failed miserably and would lead to further hostilities. Unlike his predecessor O'Reilly, Governor Unzaga was suspicious of De Mézières' loyalty to Spain and forbade him to meet the Wichitas in the spring of 1771. Nonetheless, peace was achieved the following September, when the Hainai chief, Bigotes, escorted the Kichai, Iscani, and Tawakoni headmen to Natchitoches to sign a treaty with the Spaniards. The next month, Tinhioüen completed negotiations with the Wichitas by persuading the Taovaya chiefs to meet De Mézières in Natchitoches and agree to peace. Within two years of setting the peace process in motion, De Mézières had succeeded in getting the Wichitas and the Caddos to pledge their allegiance to the Spanish rulers of Louisiana.[20]

De Mézières realized, however, that lasting peace with the Wichitas, and ultimately a treaty with the Comanches, rested upon Spain's ability to supply them with trade goods, including arms and munitions. The Frenchman persuaded hesitant Governor Unzaga to allow him to travel up the Red River and meet the Wichitas and Comanches in the spring of 1772 to make these arrangements. His expedition was successful, and the headmen of each tribe accompanied De Mézières to San Antonio to conclude peace with Governor Ripperdá of Texas. Upon his return to Natchitoches in July, 1772, De Mézières reestablished trade with the Wichitas and sent licensed traders to their villages.[21]

Unfortunately, Spanish Louisiana's method of dealing with the Indians through trade continued to meet resistance from Spanish Texas and the Viceroyalty of New Spain. Despite pledging peace in San Antonio, the Comanches and Wichitas kept raiding horse herds in Texas to obtain animals to sell in Louisiana. Throughout the early 1770s, Viceroy Antonio María de Bucareli, whose adviser was ex-Governor O'Conor of Texas, continually turned down Governor Ripperdá's requests to trade with the Norteños from Texas instead of Louisiana. However, with the reorganization of New Spain's far northern frontier and the creation of the Provincias Internas in 1776, jurisdiction over the Wichitas and Comanches was transferred to Texas and trade with them was conducted from the new post of Nacogdoches. The peace process that Frenchmen from Natchitoches had initiated finally bore fruit in 1786, when the Spaniards of Texas and New Mexico and the westernmost Norteños tribes cemented a firm and lasting alliance.[22]

Back in Louisiana, Spanish administrators faced the problems of keeping their Caddo allies protected from the rampaging Osages and beyond the reach of scheming British traders. While De Mézières employed the Caddos to help tie the Norteños to Spain, he hoped to use all these tribes in a war of annihilation against the Osages. He first suggested the plan to Unzaga in February, 1772, but the Louisiana governor decided instead on negotiations. Continued Osage attacks, however, forced Unzaga to change his mind by the end of the year, and he authorized the Indians of the Natchitoches district to make war upon the Osages, "even to the point of destroying them." He went even further on March 19, 1773, by approving De Mézières' plan which called for a joint Spanish-Indian campaign against the Osages. Four weeks later, however, Governor Unzaga countermanded his order in the hope of gaining peace with the Osages through the less expensive measure of diplomacy.[23]

Unzaga's methods gained partial success. By the end of 1773, both the Little and Big Osages made peace treaties with the Spaniards in St. Louis. By May, 1775, it was apparent that the Osages did not believe that these treaties applied to either the Arkansas or Natchitoches districts. They resumed their attacks on the Wichitas and Caddos as well as the Quapaws on the Arkansas River; these tribes then requested De Mézières' assistance and participation in an assault upon the Big Osage village. But Governor Unzaga refused because he did not want to disrupt the profitable trade that had developed between the Osages and the St. Louis merchants. He realized that if he ordered the lieutenant governor in Missouri to punish the Osages by cutting off trade with them, English traders from the Mississippi's east bank would easily fill the void. Louisiana's Spanish administrators were never able to solve this vexing dilemma.[24]

The Indian situation in Louisiana had not changed significantly by early 1777, when Bernardo de Gálvez replaced Unzaga as governor. The Osages had made peace with the Quapaws and the Spaniards in the Arkansas district. It greatly lessened the possibility that the Osages would join the British, whose presence on the Mississippi had increased because of the rebellion in their North American colonies. Therefore, Governor Gálvez ignored De Mézières' repeated calls for an offensive war against the Osages, who continued to plunder the Natchitoches district. The Caddos, who bore the brunt of these attacks, were left especially vulnerable because of a "cruel epidemic" (small pox) which struck them in 1777-78 and killed nearly a third of the tribe.[25]

As warfare with the Osages continued to weaken the Caddos, a faction emerged among the Kadohadachos that favored abandoning their village on the Red River and joining the Petit Caddos downstream. In the spring of 1779, Tinhioüen announced to De Mézières that he wished to travel to New Orleans to discuss the situation with Governor Gálvez. De Mézières quickly informed the governor that he felt that the Kadohadachos occupied "one of the most important keys to the western country," and must be implored to remain in their village because it provided a barrier against the Osages and illegal British traders. Gálvez heeded De Mézières' advice and greeted Tinhioüen in May, 1779, with "dignity [and] spectacle," decorating him with a large medal and showering him with presents "of considerable importance." Through this warm reception, Gálvez successfully convinced Tinhioüen to keep the Kadohadachos at their traditional village.[26]

Following this meeting, however, conditions changed dramatically in Louisiana. First, the man who had almost single-handedly orchestrated the conversion from French to Spanish rule in the Red River Valley, Athanase De Mézières, died in November, 1779. Although his successor as Natchitoches commandant, Étienne de Vaugine, was an able man, De Mézières' ability to win the confidence and trust of the Indians of the district was irreplaceable. Second, by the time De Mézières died, Spain had declared war on Great Britain, and Governor Gálvez concentrated almost all his attention on military affairs and ignored Indian problems in Louisiana.[27]

Spain's involvement in the American Revolution produced a shortage of Indian trade goods and presents at Natchitoches, which greatly harmed the harried Caddo tribes. Throughout the war which did not end until 1783, the Osages constantly attacked the Caddos, who, because they lacked gunpowder and lead, could neither retaliate nor hunt for fear of Osage marauders. The absence of Spanish trade caused the Caddos to be receptive to British traders who filtered into Louisiana, and they forced Vaugine to send an army party to drive them out in the summer of 1781. By March, 1783, Vaugine was echoing his predecessor De Mézières, by calling for an offensive war against the Osages. However, the new governor of Louisiana, Esteban Miró, followed his own predecessors' lead by turning down the Natchitoches commandant's request.[28]

Governor Miró, like Unzaga, hoped to control the Osages through negotiations and trade rather than through the more expensive alternative of warfare. Therefore, Miró granted the Osages trading rights on the Arkansas River in return for their willingness to make peace with the Caddos. In May, 1785, Governor Miró brought the Kadohadacho and Osage chiefs together in New Orleans and implored them to end their hostilities. Although Kadohadacho chief Tinhioüen hesitated because of the "perfidy and bad faith of his enemies and this made him believe they would not observe it," he ultimately shook the hand of the Osage chief, and both men accepted peace. To cement the agreement, Governor Miró gave them each medals.[29]

Before the year ended, however, Tinhioüen's hesitancy proved correct. In December, 1785, the Osages resumed their attacks on the Kadohadachos and the Wichitan Kichais, who had recently established a village on the Red River between the Kadohadachos and Petit Caddos. In response, Governor Miró suspended the Osage trade and approved the plan of Pierre Rousseau, the new commandant of Natchitoches, which called for the Spaniards to supply the Kadohadachos and Quapaws with enough arms to allow them to make war upon the Osages. Unfortunately, the two tribes did not avail themselves of this opportunity to attack the Osages because, according to Tinhioüen, the number of warriors he had at hand was "very inferior" to that of his opponents.[30]

Instead of attacking the Osages, the Kadohadachos moved their settlement down the Red River nearly halfway between their old village and that of the Petit Caddos. At the same time, the Kichais threatened to leave the area and move toward the Gulf Coast to get away from the Osages. However, Rousseau's successor at Natchitoches, Louis de Blanc, along with help from Tinhioüen, convinced the Kichais in August, 1788, to move their village to a site on the Red River about twenty miles above the Petit Caddo village. The Natchitoches commandant hoped that by having the three villages located near each other, they could better defend themselves against the Osages. But this proved to be inaccurate. In February, 1790, the Kadohadachos moved downstream again and took refuge in the Petit Caddo village because they were "being persecuted incessantly by their enemies," the Osages.[31]

The Spaniards not only failed to protect the Caddos from the Osages, but they also found it difficult to provide them with adequate trade goods. In 1787 Governor Miró unwisely ordered the licensed trader for the Kadohadacho village, Louis Leblanc, to remain in Natchitoches until he paid his debts. It forced the Kadohadachos to turn to the vagabond traders, Louis Lepinet and the Englishman Robert Mignon, who had set up an illegal trading post on the Ouachita River east of their village. Commandant de Blanc, fearful that the Spaniards of Louisiana would lose their influence over the Kadohadachos because of the illegal trade, ordered merchants from Natchitoches to go upstream to the Kadohadacho villages and reopen legal trade. Because of the fall in peltry prices, however, most Natchitoches traders declined to do so. The few who ventured upstream were unable to recapture the Kadohadacho commerce because of the stiff competition from illicit Anglo-American traders who impudently filtered across the Mississippi during the final decade of the eighteenth century.[32]

Although the Caddo tribes received illicit trade goods, they still could not overcome the persistent Osage attacks. New threats to the Natchitoches district emerged in the 1790s as vagrant Choctaws crossed the Mississippi to steal horses and cattle. These were among the many concerns facing the new governor of Louisiana, Francisco Luis Hector, Baron de Carondelet, when he succeeded Miró on December 30, 1791. By the spring of 1792, Governor Carondelet had heard enough unsatisfactory reports about the Osages. He proposed a plan to arm all the allied Indian nations and surround the Osages so as to "finish them once and for all." As with all previous Louisiana governors, however, Carondelet was ultimately convinced by the strength of the Osage tribe and its profitable trade to cancel the war and negotiate a truce instead.[33]

In 1794 Governor Carondelet made peace with the Osages and then turned his attention toward arranging an alliance between them and the natives of the Natchitoches district. He wanted to use these tribes to halt the Choctaws from roaming freely on the Mississippi's west bank. The Kadohadachos, however, recalling the failed treaty of 1785, refused all attempts by de Blanc and his successor at Natchitoches, Félix Trudeau, to meet with the Osages. Carondelet next tried to achieve stability by creating a new lieutenant governorship on the west bank under Carlos de Grand-Pré. He received responsibility for the districts of Natchitoches, Rapide, Avoyelles, and Ouachita (the Red and Ouachita river valleys) in June, 1796. The lieutenant governorship, however, failed because of Caddo intransigence, and the Crown soon named Grand-Pré to the governorship of Natchez, a post he never exercised due to its cession to the United States. Spanish efforts to arrange a truce between the Kadohadachos and both the Osages and the Choctaws failed miserably. The Spaniards were unable to protect the Caddo tribes from being attacked by their enemies. As a result, the Kadohadachos were forced for the third time in twelve years to move their village in 1800. This time they took refuge on Caddo Lake, about thirty-five miles west of the main channel of the Red River. Spain's principal bulwark on the Louisiana-Texas frontier, the Caddos, had finally abandoned their strategic location.[34]

Spain's inability to protect the tribes of the Natchitoches district, mainly the Kadohadachos, and provide them with weapons in the last decades of the eighteenth century, made them receptive to the United States' acquisition of Louisiana in 1803. As Spain had done nearly forty years before, the young republic won the Kadohadachos' allegiance by supplying them with ample trade goods and successfully protecting them from the Osages and Choctaws. In response, the Kadohadachos favored the United States in the tense situation that existed with Spain on the Louisiana-Texas frontier until the end of the War of 1812.[35]

Despite the ultimate shortcomings of Spanish policy in the Natchitoches district, its actual accomplishments were impressive. Spanish administrators not only won the allegiance of the most important tribe of the region, the Red River Caddos, but they used this alliance to forge a lasting peace for Spanish Texas with the previously hostile Comanches and Wichitas. In adopting French policies for the Indians and by employing experienced Frenchmen to carry them out, the Spanish rulers of Louisiana and Natchitoches demonstrated in the face of daunting odds great initiative and adaptability, traits that many earlier historians have found lacking in the Spaniards who ruled the far northern frontier of New Spain in the late eighteenth century.

Notes for "Indian Policy in Spanish Louisiana: The Natchitoches District, 1763-1803"

[1]For Spain's earlier policy in the New World, see Herbert Eugene Bolton, "The Mission as a Frontier Institution in the Spanish American Colonies," *American Historical Review*, 23 (1917): 42-61.

[2]There are no studies which deal solely with Indian policy in Louisiana during the entire Spanish period. However, Elizabeth A. H. John, *Storms Brewed in Other Men's Worlds: The Confrontation of Indians, Spanish, and French in the Southwest, 1540-1795* (Lincoln, 1981), includes Louisiana in a detailed discussion of Indian policy on Spain's far northern frontier. The "Historical Introduction" in Herbert Bolton, ed., *Athanase de Mézières and the Louisiana-Texas Frontier, 1768-1780*, 2 vols. (Cleveland, 1914), contains a masterful summary of the formation of Spanish Indian policy in Lousiana, as well as providing a number of invaluable documents. This work will hereinafter be cited as *ADM*. Two recent overviews contain worthwhile, succinct summaries of the issue. They are David J. Weber, *The Spanish Frontier in North America* (New Haven, 1992); Donald E. Chipman, *Spanish Texas, 1519-1821* (Austin, 1992).

[3]Weber, *The Spanish Frontier*, 186-91.

[4]F. Todd Smith, *The Caddo Indians: Tribes at the Convergence of Empires, 1542-1854* (College Station, 1995).

[5]The best work on the Wichitas during this period is John's three-part study published under Elizabeth Ann Harper, "The Taovayas Indians in Frontier Trade and Diplomacy, 1719-1835," *Chronicles of Oklahoma*, 31 (1953): 268-89, *Southwestern Historical Quarterly*, 57 (1953): 181-201, *Panhandle-Plains Historical Review*, 23 (1953): 1-32. Works about the Comanches include Odie B. Faulk, "The Comanche Invasion of Texas, 1743-1836," *Great Plains Journal*, 9 (1969): 10-50; Catherine Price, "The Comanches [sic] Threat to Texas and New Mexico in the Eighteenth Century and the Development of Spanish Indian Policy," *Journal of the West*, 24 (1985): 34-35; Stanley Noyes, *Los Comanches: The Horse People, 1751-1845* (Albuquerque, 1993). The best work on the Lipan Apaches is Thomas F. Schilz, *Lipan Apaches in Texas* (El Paso, 1987). For the Osages, see Gilbert C. Din and Abraham P. Nasatir, *The Imperial Osages: Spanish-Indian Diplomacy in the Mississippi Valley* (Norman, 1983).

[6]Smith, *The Caddo Indians*, 49-62.

[7]William Edward Dunn, "The Apache Mission on the San Sabá River: Its Founding and Failure, *Southwestern Historical Quarterly*, 17 (1914): 379-414; Robert Weddle, *The San Sabá Mission: Spanish Pivot in Texas* (Austin, 1964); Paul Nathan, trans., and Lesley Byrd Simpson, ed., *The San Sabá Papers* (San Francisco, 1959); Henry Easton Allen, "The Parrilla Expedition to the Red River in 1759," *Southwestern Historical Quarterly*, 43 (1939): 53-71.

[8]For a discussion of Spanish Indian policy in Louisiana immediately follwing the transfer, see John Preston Moore, *Revolt in Louisiana: The Spanish Occupation, 1766-1770* (Baton Rouge, 1976): 84-102.

[9]De Mézières to Luis de Unzaga y Amezaga, May 20, 1770, *ADM*, 1:166-68; De Mézières to Ripperdá, July 4, 1772, *ADM*, 1:304.

[10]John, *Storms Brewed*, 380, 388; David M. Vigness, "Don Hugo O'Conor and New Spain's Northeastern Frontier, 1764-1766," *Journal of the West*, 6 (1966): 27-40.

[11]Ulloa to O'Conor, 1768, *ADM*, 1:128-29.

[12]Ibid.

[13]John, *Storms Brewed*, 383-85.

[14]Ripperdá to the Viceroy, July 6, 1772, *ADM*, 1:327; O'Reilly to De Mézières, September 23, 1769, ibid., 130-31; Report by De Mézières of the Expedition to Cadodachos, October 29, 1770, ibid., 208.

[15]O'Reilly to De Mézières, January 22, 1770, ibid., 132-34; Statement of Payment for Indian Presents, January 9, 1770, Lawrence Kinnaird, ed., *Spain in the Mississippi Valley, 1765-1794*, 3 vols. (Washington, 1946), 1:154-55, hereinafter cited as *SMV*; Contract of Juan Piseros with De Mézières, February 3, 1770, *ADM*, 1:143-46; Instructions for the Traders of the Cadaux, D'Acquioux and Hiatasses Nations, February 4, 1770, ibid., 148-50; Agreement Made with the Indian Nations in Assembly, April 21, 1770, ibid., 157-58.

[16]Ibid., De Mézières to Luis de Unzaga y Amezaga, February 1, 1770, ibid., 140-42; De Mézières to Unzaga, September 27, 1770, ibid., 204-6.

[17]Report by De Mézières of the Expedition to Cadodachos, October 26, 1770, ibid., 206-8. For the Spanish viewpoint see Depositions Relative to the Expedition to Cadodachos, October 30-31, 1770, ibid., 220-30; Fray San Miguel Santa María y Silva to the Viceroy, July 21, 1774, ibid., 2:68-74.

[18]Report by De Mézières of the Expedition to Cadodachos, October 29, 1770, ibid., 1:209-11.

[19]Ibid., 211-13.

[20]Ripperdá to Unzaga, December 31, 1771, ibid., 265; Treaty with the Taovayas, ibid., 256-60.

[21]De Mézières to Unzaga, February 25, 1772, ibid., 283-84; De Mézières to Ripperdá, July 4, 1772, ibid., 284-306; Ripperdá to the Viceroy, July 5, 1772, ibid., 320-22; José de la Peña to Unzaga, September 14, 1772, ibid., 2:22-24.

[22]Weber, *Spanish Frontier*, 222-33.

[23]Din and Nasatir, *Imperial Osages*, 78-84.

[24]Ibid., 90-98.

[25]Ibid., 100-119; De Mézières to Teodoro de Croix, November 15, 1778, *ADM*, 2:231-33; John C. Ewers, "The Influence of Epidemics on Indian Population and Cultures of Texas," *Plains Anthropologist*, 18 (1973): 104-15; Alicia V. Tjarks, "Comparative Demographic Analysis of Texas, 1777-1793," *Southwestern Historical Quarterly*, 77 (1974): 291-338.

[26]De Mézières to Gálvez, May 1779, *ADM*, 2:250-52; Gálvez to De Mézières, June 1, 1779, ibid., 252-54.

[27]Borme to Gálvez, December 29, 1779, ibid., 330.

[28]Din and Nasatir, *Imperial Osages*, 120-45.

[29]Miró to Francisco Cruzat, March 24, 1786, *SMV* 2:171-72; Miró to Gálvez, August 1, 1786, ibid., 182-83.

[30]Rousseau and Louis de Blanc to Miró, March 20, 1787, ibid., 198-99; José de la Peña to Miró, September 22, 1787, ibid., 234.

[31]De Blanc to Miró, August 5, 1788, ibid., 259; de Blanc to Miró, March 27, 1790, ibid., 316-17.

[32]De la Peña to Miró, August 17, 1789, ibid., 232-33; de Blanc to Miró, March 30, 1791, ibid., 407; de Blanc to Baron de Carondelet, February 18, 1792, ibid., 4:9-13.

[33]Carondelet to Ygnacio DeLinó, June 29, 1792, ibid., 56; Carondelet to Zenon Trudeau, December 22, 1792, ibid., 107; Din and Nasatir, *Imperial Osages*, 217-54.

[34]Lawrence Kinnaird and Lucia Kinnaird, "The Red River Valley in 1796," *Louisiana History*, 24 (1983): 189; John Sibley, "Historical Sketches of the Several Indian Tribes in Louisiana, south of the Arkansas, and between the Mississippi and the River Grande," *American State Papers, Class II, Indian Affairs* (Washington, 1832), 721-74; Din and Nasatir, *Imperial Osages*, 278-345.

[35]Smith, "The Kadohadacho Indians and the Louisiana-Texas Frontier, 1803-1815," *Southwestern Historical Quarterly*, 92 (1991): 176-204.

AMERICAN INDIANS IN COLONIAL NEW ORLEANS*

Daniel H. Usner, Jr.

So much of the scholarship on American Indians in colonial North America has concentrated on the populous nations inhabiting the interior that relatively little is understood about those smaller Indians groups situated in the midst of colonial settlements and towns. The praying towns of New England and the mission reserves of Canada are the most familiar of such communities, thanks to recent investigations into the refugees and survivors of seventeenth-century wars.[1] Since so much research is needed on southeastern Indians in general, one is hard pressed to urge emphasis on any particular category of colonial-Indian relations. The large picture of geopolitical, economic, and cultural interaction demands closer attention to the Cherokees, Creeks, Choctaws, Chickasaws, and Caddos before we can afford the luxury of studying smaller, more enclosed Indian communities. Yet to ignore the latter would exclude Indian peoples living within sizable parts of the Southeast—like the tidewater and piedmont Atlantic areas, the Florida panhandle, and the alluvial plain of the Mississippi River—who experienced colonialism differently, but no less importantly, than did the interior tribespeople.[2]

Colonial towns serve as especially informative foci for examining forms of Indian adaptation and persistence different from those that occurred within Indian nations situated in the backcountry of European colonies. In diverse eighteenth-century towns across the Southeast, Indians frequently lived and visited in an array of circumstances. An inestimable number of Indians from many tribes found themselves either being shipped away as slaves from colonial ports or working as slaves in and around them. Charlestown merchants waged slave-raiding expeditions that brought captive Timucuans, Apalaches, Tuscaroras, Yamasees, and Choctaws to households in their town as well as to plantations in Virginia and Carolina. Intimate contact with Europeans and Africans and

*Reprinted from *Powhatan's Mantle: Indians in the Colonial Southeast,* edited by Peter H. Wood, Gregory A. Waselkov, and M. Thomas Hatley, by permission of the University of Nebraska Press.

coercive labor at entirely new tasks undoubtedly changed life for Indian servants and slaves inhabiting colonized areas while channeling Indian influences to the colonial populace. The colonial capitals of Williamsburg, Charlestown, Savannah, and St. Augustine, and eventually such interior centers as Augusta, Fort Toulouse, and Natchez, became important meeting places for Indian diplomats, many of whom traveled long distances to exchange words and gifts with European officials. More regularly these emerging cities were frequented by Indian villagers who lived nearby and, though reduced to tributary or subordinate status by war or flight, participated actively in the social and economic rhythm of town life as boathands, packhorsemen, interpreters, day laborers, and peddlers.[3] All these types of activity were experienced by American Indians in another southern colonial town, named by its French founders "Nouvelle Orléans."

Traveling up the Mississippi River in early March 1699, Pierre Le Moyne d'Iberville was shown by his Bayogoula Indian guide "the place through which the Indians make their portage to this river from the back of the bay where the ships are anchored. They drag their canoes over a rather good road, at which we found several pieces of baggage owned by men that were going there or were returning."[4] Situated between a chain of lakes and the Mississippi, the crescent-shaped bend at what became New Orleans had been mainly used by Indians for transport between waterways and seasonal gathering of food sources. Yet natural conditions that made this site ideal for portage and fishing reduced its potential for permanent occupation.[5] Now a metropolis slowly sinking inside artificial levees and spillways, New Orleans sits on a natural levee, created by sediment deposited during seasonal flooding, that slopes down from a crest of fifteen feet above sea level to almost five feet below sea level. The city's vulnerability to flooding is exacerbated by Lake Pontchartrain to the north and Lake Borgne to the east.[6]

Before European contact Indians used the four-to-eight-mile-wide strip of swampland as a fishing/hunting/gathering station and as a portage between the lakes and the river. The most habitable sites were along Bayou St. John, a few miles long and about twenty feet wide when Iberville traveled it, and on the Metairie ridge, which linked that bayou with Bayou Chapitoulas. From this junction Indians reached the Mississippi by a three-mile portage.[7] Since René-Robert Cavalier de La Salle's voyage down the Mississippi in 1682, this had been a highly volatile area. A Tangipahoa village a few miles above the portage road was destroyed, perhaps by Quinipissas from upriver. By 1699 a group of Acolapissas occupied Metairie ridge, but during the first decade of the eighteenth century some Biloxis and then some Houmas moved in temporarily. English slave raids upriver to the north and French war against the Chitimachas kept the lower Mississippi Delta in turmoil until Jean-Baptiste Le Moyne de Bienville began construction of New Orleans in 1718.[8]

Largely in consequence of this early conflict, enslaved Indians constituted the core of the resident Indian population in French New Orleans, resembling the earlier presence of Native American slaves in such colonial towns as Boston, New York, and Charlestown. French and English colonies in North America allowed and periodically encouraged the enslavement of Indian people from enemy tribes or distant territories. Most captives were transported from one region to another, but many enslaved Indians remained in their locale to be joined by black and Indian slaves imported from abroad. By November 1721 fifty-one Indian slaves lived in the vicinity of New Orleans—twenty-one in town and the rest on farms at Bayou St. John, Gentilly, Chapitoulas, Cannes Bruslée, and Chaouchas. Louisiana's total slave population at the time numbered 161 Indians and 680 Africans.[9]

Indian slaves in the colony belonged to several tribes. "Panis," an epithet for Indians captured above the Arkansas River, were present, but Alibamon, Taensa, and Chitimacha slaves—captives in local wars—also lived in colonial households. Suffering more enslavement than other local tribes, the Chitimachas of Bayou Lafourche became a significant ethnic component in the early slave population of lower Louisiana.

Fear of Indian and black cooperation combined with stable Indian-French relations to reduce the number of Indian slaves in and around the colonial capital, but the economic interests of slaveowners managed to maintain an Indian slave population of 120 persons in Louisiana by 1771. The number of Indian slaves recorded in New Orleans had actually increased to forty-two females and nineteen males of different ages. One also should conjecture that liaisons between Indian and Afro-American slaves produced children who were ascribed by owners to Negro and mulatto identities and that some offspring of Indian woman and white men grew up free. As in other early towns, therefore, a portion of the Indian population was assimilated by the colonial society through slavery.[10]

Only with its transfer to Spain in 1766 did laws prohibiting the enslavement, purchase, or transfer of Indians reach the colony. During the Spanish period the Indian slave populace in the city and the colony at large virtually disappeared. Avenues to emancipation available under Spanish law contributed slightly to this diminution, and undecided petitions by some slaves claiming Indian ancestry were inherited by the Orleans Territory courts of the United States. "It is reported to me," wrote Governor William Claiborne to Secretary of State James Madison in 1808, "that in this Territory, there are now several hundred persons held as slaves, who are descended of Indian families."[11] But by then the inhabitants of New Orleans fell into a rigid tripartite division of racial identity: free whites, enslaved blacks (some actually being mulatto), and free people of color. Nearly 20 percent of the city's 8,500 people were classified as *gens de couleur*, which was synonymous with mixed ancestry. And in the process of making blacks and slaves the same category, the Louisiana Supreme Court ruled in 1810 that "persons of color may be descended from Indians on both sides, from a white parent, or mulatto parents in possession of their freedom."[12] The fascinating legal and social ramifications of this kind of decision aside, continuing absorption into a rapidly growing non-Indian population and a tightening racial structure together caused the apparent disappearance of Indian slaves in New Orleans by the nineteenth century.

Throughout the eighteenth century, the Chitimachas and other *petites nations* sent annual delegations to New Orleans to receive gifts from French and, after 1766, Spanish governors. Other official visits involved providing military assistance to Louisiana, returning runaway slaves, and even requesting pardons for deserting soldiers. Tunicas were the most visible allies among the small tribes in the French war against the Natchez. The Tunicas and other small nations closer to New Orleans fought in later French campaigns against the Chickasaws and in the Spanish seizure of English West Florida posts during the American Revolution.[13]

While deployment of allied Indian warriors against hostile groups helped the colonial government by discouraging unified opposition among Indian nations, paying local Indians to capture runaway slaves promoted hostility between blacks and Indians. Familiarity with the countryside and the promise of rewards made Indians effective bounty hunters.

Diplomatic journeys for the Choctaw nation, most populous and powerful Indian ally of French Louisiana, were annually made to Mobile instead of New Orleans. The proximity of the older colonial port to the Choctaw towns influenced this pattern, but French anxiety over the security of the New Orleans area made it official policy. During the 1750s and 1760s complaints against delayed distributions of gifts provoked more diplomatic missions by Choctaws to the capital, causing repeated consternation among New Orleanians. News of Louisiana's transfer to Spain and of English dominion in West Florida generated further excited journeys of Choctaw chiefs to the city.[14]

New Orleans hosted a series of ceremonial visits in the autumn of 1769, when Alejandro O'Reilly summoned lower Mississippi River tribes after completing the military occupation of Louisiana for Spain. On September 30, chiefs, interpreters, and other persons from the Tunicas, Taensas, Pacanas, Houmas, Bayogoulas, Ofogoulas, Chaouchas, and Ouachas approached the general's house with song and music. Inside he greeted them under a canopy in the company of prominent residents of New Orleans. Each chief placed his weapon at O'Reilly's feet and waved a feather fan over his head. O'Reilly accepted their fans, smoked their pipes, and clasped their hands. Then the Bayogoula leader spoke for the delegation, offering loyalty to the Spanish and requesting that they "grant us the same favors and benefits as did the French." After exhorting the Indians to treat both the English in West Florida and the Spanish in Louisiana peaceably, O'Reilly placed medals hanging from scarlet ribbons around the chiefs' necks and had presents distributed. This procedure was repeated when the Chahtos, Biloxis, Pascagoulas, and Mobilians arrived on October 22, the Chitimachas on October 29, and the Quapaws on November 16.[15]

After the American Revolution, Indian diplomacy in New Orleans entered a new era. Spanish Louisiana contended against the United States for Indian allies, while the Creek, Chickasaw, and Choctaw nations maneuvered to preserve their sovereignty. Indian missions to New Orleans came frequently and in large numbers during the 1790s, including delegations of Cherokees, but the tribes avoided showing signs of exclusive allegiance and therefore refused to make visits to the Spanish governor an obligatory routine. Chiefs often excused themselves from traveling to the city because of bad weather or poor health and, whenever they did complete a junket, complained about inadequate provision and insulting treatment. "They don't say anything in the City," reported Juan de la Villebeuvre from the Choctaw village of Boukfouca, "but in the Nation they murmur very much."[16] At the time Spain ceded Louisiana to the French Republic in 1800, the intensity of intrigue and diplomacy in the city led Pierre-Clément de Laussat, prefect charged with overseeing the transfer, to "count on there descending, after the expression of the country 2 to 3,000 Indians per year to New Orleans: others say 3 to 400 chiefs."[17]

Indians in the New Orleans area provided important goods and services to the colonial town. Indian men frequently visited as packhorsemen accompanying traders or as crewmen paddling or rowing boats. As already seen French and later Spanish governors recruited auxiliaries from neighboring villages for military campaigns and paid bounties to Indians who captured and returned runaway slaves and soldiers.

The continuous presence of Indians in New Orleans—whether as slaves, guides, boatmen, or peddlers—affected how the colonial government regulated interaction among social groups. Like their counterparts in Boston, New York, and Charlestown, New Orleans officials associated both free and enslaved Indians with blacks, free people of color, and lower-class whites in efforts to police behavior on the city's streets and behind its closed doors. In all of these towns Indians were subject during the eighteenth century to the same ordinances that prohibited slaves and free Negroes from carrying firearms, congregating, owning livestock, trading without special permission, and walking the streets after curfew—ordinances intended to reduce insolence and theft aimed at white property owners. In New Orleans much insubordination was attributed to the consumption of alcohol by soldiers as well as by Indians and blacks.

Attrition among the Indian populace around New Orleans was actually reversed in mid-1760s when villagers from the Mobile Bay area and from the Choctaw Nation began resettlement on the north shore of Lake Pontchartrain and along the banks of the Mississippi River. After Great Britain occupied West Florida, the Apalaches, Taensas, Pacanas, Mobilians, Alibamons, Biloxis, Chahtos, and Pascagoulas—many of them Roman Catholic in religion—migrated to the French settlements in lower Louisiana, then discovered that the colony belonged to Spain. Kerlérec realized the benefits to be derived from the approximately eighty Apalache Indians, "being hunters and farmers," and in September 1763 he decided to locate them at the rapids of the Red River. "There," recorded general commissioner Jean-Jacques Blaise d'Abbadie, "they will be useful for aiding vessels ascending the river towards Natchitoches. Moreover, through their hunting, they will be able to supply New Orleans."[18] As they extended authority over the east side of the Mississippi River, above the chain of lakes and bayous that made New Orleans a Spanish island, the English also vied for the services of these immigrant Indians. During the spring of 1768, Montfort Browne met a group of Chahtos and Mobilians building a new village on the Amite River and was welcomed at the palmetto-covered house of Chief Mattaha with a calumet dance. The Indians had already supplied the English at Fort Bute with three boats and, "as I found them a great deal disgusted against the Spaniards' late behavior," Browne persuaded them to settle closer to Baton Rouge after the year's harvest. "As these Savages are a good deal civilized, industrious and excellent Hunters," he wrote, "the acquisition will be the greater."[19]

By the early 1770s at least eight villages were interspersed among colonial settlements between New Orleans and the Red River, totaling more than one thousand Indians. The colonial population within this stretch included about 2,750 Negroes and 2,300 whites (New Orleans itself containing 1,000 Negroes and 1,800 whites), and the plantations below New Orleans included 1,600 Negroes and 450 whites. "The Houma, Chitimacha, and other Indian communities that were dispersed among the plantations," cartographer and naturalist Bernard Romans noted, "serve as hunters, and for some other laborious uses, something similar to subdued tribes of New England."[20] In 1773 the main town of the Houmas, consisting of some forty gunmen, stood on the east bank of the Mississippi sixty miles above New Orleans. Another Houma village was situated across the river. A league below Manchac the Taensas, Pacanas, and Mobilians lived on the west bank in a single town of about thirty gunmen. The Alibamons counted thirty-seven gunmen and lived just above Manchac on the east side. While some Chitimachas were moving down Bayou Plaquemine, about fifteen gunmen and their families remained along the Mississippi. Down the bayou other Chitimachas and some Attakapas and Opelousas totaled another fifty gunmen. The Tunicas still occupied their town, numbering about thirty-five gunmen, on the east bluff above the Pointe Coupée plantations. Above Tunica stood a village of ten to twelve Chahto gunmen and another of fifteen Pascagoula gunmen on the west bank. The Biloxis, numbering nearly one hundred gunmen, had just moved from the west to the east bank a short distance below the Red River.[21] Over the next few decades most of these communities migrated from the Mississippi River either to the Red River habitat of the Apalaches or down Bayous Plaquemine and Lafourche. Also during the 1790s more groups of Choctaws and Coushattas were migrating west of the Mississippi River into Louisiana, though their numbers were overshadowed by the contemporaneous immigration of Anglo-American settlers and Afro-American slaves.[22]

The migration of some Choctaws into the New Orleans area, which began during the 1760s, was more volatile than that of others. Yet in the long run their proximity proved to be the most enduring in New Orleans history. After Great Britain assumed control over West Florida's trade with interior tribes, many Choctaws—especially from the Six Towns district—attempted to maintain ties with the French. They complained of abuses committed by English traders, carried on illicit trade with inhabitants of Louisiana, and committed acts of banditry against settlers in West Florida. General Frederick Haldimand reported in 1768 to General Thomas Gage, "The continual depredations of the Choctaw Indians of the six villages who hunt in and frequent continually the neighborhood of Lakes Pontchartrain and Maurepas where they pillage the inhabitants, kill their animals, and introduce French traders in their country, require that there should be some one of confidence and authority among them who would repress their outbreaks."[23] Groups of

Choctaws were then settling farther down Pearl River, around Pass Christian, and on the north shore of Lake Pontchartrain, where many French settlers also lived resentfully under British rule. As hunting and trading increased in this thickly pine-forested area, colonial residents at Spanish Galveztown and English Baton Rouge exchanged rum, ammunition, and corn for pelts, game, and bear oil produced by traveling Choctaw families. Although it perturbed merchants in Pensacola and Mobile with privileged rights over Choctaw trade and antagonized farmers and planters vulnerable to pilferage, this commerce germinated several new Indian communities across Lake Pontchartrain from New Orleans.[24]

The movement of Choctaws and other groups toward the Crescent City after 1763 discloses how some Indians relied on cities in their adjustment to new political and economic circumstances. By the late eighteenth century, New Orleans had become an important station for the seasonally varied strategies Indians devised to cope with a decline in diplomatic and commercial leverage. Faced with diminishing opportunity in the deerskin trade—manifested by falling prices for pelts and mounting debts to merchants—and with growing numbers of Anglo-American immigrants, Indians in the lower Mississippi Valley resorted to a seasonal cycle of itinerant economic activities.[25] Camps of extended families, formerly the units that spent only winter hunting seasons away from their villages, sojourned more frequently along waterways and roads, trading small quantities of goods with other travelers, farmers, and slaves. While the men hunted to supply local meat markets, women sold leaves and roots, baskets and mats, and even began to pick cotton during the harvest season.[26]

On the outskirts of New Orleans, groups of Houmas, Chitimachas, and Choctaws camped along Bayou St. John and Bayou Road. Hundreds of Indians gathered in late winter to request gifts from officials and to join in the celebration of carnival.[27] On the city's streets and in the marketplace, Indian women peddled baskets, mats, sifters, plants, herbs, and firewood; their men sold venison, wildfowl, and cane blowguns and occasionally earned wages as day laborers and dockworkers. On his way to a Choctaw camp behind the city gates, Fortescue Cuming met on a March afternoon in 1799 "numbers of Indian women with large bundles of wood on their backs, first tied together and then held by a strap carried over their foreheads." A few years later Paul Alliot observed that the Indian men "kill game with great dexterity, and sell it for excellent prices" and that the women "busy themselves in making reed baskets which they sell at good prices."[28]

The impact of Indians upon the culture of New Orleans, through their diversified presence in the colonial city, is not easily measured. Many New Orleanians, identified as white, black, or free colored by the end of the eighteenth century, possessed various degrees of Indian ancestry. Inside urban households and in the marketplace, Indian women influenced cuisine not only through their uses of corn and beans but through a knowledge of the region's wild plants and animals.[29] On the outskirts of town or around its taverns, Indians also shared music, dance, and other cultural expressions with colonists and slaves. Perhaps the most fascinating Indian contribution to New Orleans social life was the ball game called *toli* by the Choctaws and *raquettes* by the French, the city's most popular spectator sport until the arrival of baseball. Before United States acquisition of New Orleans, contests had become Sunday afternoon events behind the city gates. Spectators assembled on the "Communes de la Ville," also called Congo Plains, where players carrying short sticks in both hands tossed the small buckskin ball between two goalposts sometimes placed a half-mile apart. As described by Pierre Clément de Laussat, two prominent black teams in 1803 were the "Bayous," players from the Bayou St. John area, and the "La Villes," those from the city proper. They competed against white teams as well as against each other, and some Indians reportedly belonged to the "Bayous." The particular circumstances in which New Orleanians adopted this ancient Indian ball game are obscure, but its performance over the eighteenth century by Indians in and around the city must have been influential.[30]

For Indians living in the eighteenth-century Southeast, contact with colonists and slaves produced a variety of new settings in which they made decisions and had choices forced upon them.[31] Life in or around colonial settlements was filled with a multitude of challenges, and in an urban setting different kinds of exchange and struggle converged. Colonial towns proved to be destructive intrusions for many Indian groups. The largest tribe in the Mississippi Delta by the early eighteenth century, the Chitimachas, suffered a protracted war as the French tried to establish a permanent base on the river. The beginning of construction at New Orleans in 1718 marked the end of their struggle, but not before many Chitimachas had been captured and enslaved. Colonial towns like New Orleans became hotbeds of anxiety over Indian and slave rebellions.

Many Indian tribes found towns to be places for engaging in diplomacy rather than warfare. Throughout the eighteenth century, Indians traveled to New Orleans from near and far to negotiate agreements that helped them adjust to the European presence. Issues discussed in the government house ranged from the return of runaway slaves and soldiers to the defense of Louisiana against other European colonies and their Indian allies. Indian diplomatic protocol constituted a dramatic form of public interaction in which colonial officials received processions of singers, smoked the calumet, and presented gifts. Theses very formal displays of reciprocal alliance were as much a part of the city's calendar as were Easter, Christmas, and the king's birthday, and even the most ethnocentric of European observers were impressed by the dignity and importance of Indian diplomacy.[32]

At the level of daily life, Indian experiences in New Orleans varied widely. There were some Indian men, women, and children who worked as slaves in households and shops. Employment in long-distance trade and transportation brought Indian men regularly through the city, while the growing urban populace provided a market for foods and other goods produced by neighboring Indian villages. Even in taking advantage of this opportunity, however, Louisiana Indians faced difficulties in the city. Disease and alcohol endangered their health and took the lives of countless individuals. Government efforts to control the behavior of Indians, slaves, and soldiers created mounting vigilance against the activities of Indians inside and outside the city walls. But as the political and economic status of Indian nations continued to decay toward the end of the eighteenth century, New Orleans did not witness a declining Indian presence. Instead, many Indian families turned to the city as a useful way station in a new pattern of adjustment and survival.

Notes for "American Indians in Colonial New Orleans"

[1]For samples of, and bibliographical guidance to the literature on New England and Canadian settlement Indians, see Laura E. Conkey, Ethel Boissevain, and Ives Goddard, "Indians of Southern New England and Long Island: Late Period," and William N. Fenton and Elisabeth Tooker, "Mohawk," both in *Handbook of North American Indians*, vol. 15, *Northeast*, ed. Bruce G. Trigger (Smithsonian Institution Press, 1978): 177-89, 466-80. Documents and scholarship have been combed for the religious dimensions of these northeastern communities in James Axtell, *The Invasion Within: The Contest of Cultures in Colonial North America* (New York, 1985). For socioeconomic and environmental elements, see William Cronon, *Changes in the Land: Indians, Colonists, and the Ecology of New England* (New York, 1983).

[2]An exemplary, and the most comprehensive, study of a South Atlantic coastal tribe is James Merrell, "Natives in a New World: The Catawba Indians of Carolina, 1650-1800" (Ph.D. dissertation, Johns Hopkins University, 1982). Some southeastern coastal communities of Indians are partly covered for the eighteenth century in Christian F. Feest, "Nanticoke and Neighboring Tribes," idem, "Virginia Algonquians," idem, "North Carolina Algonquians," and Douglas W. Boyce, "Iroquoian Tribes of the Virginia-North Carolina Coastal Plain," all in Trigger, *Handbook of North America Indians: Northeast*, 240-89.

[3]These town experiences of southeastern Indians are gleaned from Verner W. Crane, *The Southern Frontier, 1670-1732* (Durham, NC, 1928); Peter H. Wood, *Black Majority: Negroes in Colonial South Carolina from 1670 through the Stono Rebellion* (New York, 1974); Phinizy Spalding, *Oglethorpe in America* (Chicago, 1977); Charles H. Fairbanks, "From Missionary to Mestizo: Changing Culture of Eighteenth-Century St. Augustine," in *Eighteenth-Century Florida and the Caribbean*, ed. Samuel Proctor (Gainesville, 1976), 88-99; J. Leitch Wright, Jr., *The Only Land They Knew: The Tragic Story of the American Indians in the Old South* (New York, 1981); and Kathleen A. Deagan, *Spanish St. Augustine: The Archaeology of a Colonial Creole Community* (New York, 1983).

[4]Richebourg Gaillard McWilliams, trans. and ed., *Iberville's Gulf Journals* (University, AL, 1981), 57.

[5]Marco J. Giardino, "Documentary Evidence for the Location of Historic Indian Villages in the Mississippi Delta," in *Perspectives on Gulf Coast Prehistory*, ed. Dave D. Davis (Gainesville, 1984): 232-57.

[6]Peirce F. Lewis, *New Orleans: The Making of an Urban Landscape* (Cambridge, 1976), 17-30; Rod E. Emmer and Karen Wicker, "Sedimentary Environments, Ecological Systems, and Land Use in Southwestern Louisiana," and Frederick W. Wagner, "Development Problems in the New Orleans Coastal Zone," in *A Field Guidebook for Louisiana*, ed. Richard E. Kesel and Robert A. Sauder (Washington, DC, 1978): 48-53, 124-27.

[7]McWilliams, *Gulf Journals*, 111-12; Richard J. Shenkel and Jon L. Gibson, "Big Oak Island, an Historical Perspective of Changing Site Function," *Louisiana Studies* 13 (1974): 173-86; Richard J. Shenkel, *Oak Island Archaeology: Prehistoric Adaptations in the Mississippi River Delta* (New Orleans, 1980).

[8]Marc de Villiers du Terrage, "A History of the Foundation of New Orleans (1717-1722)," trans. Warrington Dawson, *Louisiana Historical Quarterly* 3 (1920): 157-251, at 161-79; John R. Swanton, *Indian Tribes of the Lower Mississippi Valley and Adjacent Coast of the Gulf of Mexico,* Bureau of American Ethnology Bulletin 43 (Washington, DC, 1911): 274-84, 297-301. Also see Henry C. Bezou, *Metairie: A Tongue of Land to Pasture* (Gretna, LA, 1973), 35-36; and Edna B. Freiberg, *Bayou St. John in Colonial Louisiana 1699-1803* (New Orleans, 1980), 26-27.

[9]Charles R. Maduell, Jr. comp. and ed., *The Census Tables for the French Colony of Louisiana from 1699 through 1732* (Baltimore, 1972), 16-27. Almon Wheeler Lauber, *Indian Slavery in Colonial Times within the Present Limits of the United States* (New York, 1913), is still the most comprehensive treatment of enslaved Indians in North America.

[10]Lawrence Kinnaird, trans. and ed., *Spain in the Mississippi Valley, 1765-1794*, 3 vols. (Washington, DC, 1946), 1:125-26, 196; Wright, *Only Land They Knew*, 126-50, 248-78. For discussions of Indian slavery in the Northeast, see A. Leon Higginbotham, Jr., *In the Matter of Color, Race and the American Legal Process: The Colonial Period* (New York, 1978); and John A. Sainsbury, "Indian Labor in Early Rhode Island," *New England Quarterly*, 48 (1975): 378-93.

[11]Dunbar Rowland, ed., *Official Letter Books of W. C. C. Claiborne, 1801-1816*, 6 vols. (Jackson, 1917), 4:179-81. Hans Baade, "The Law of Slavery in Spanish *Luisiana*, 1769-1803," in Edward F. Haas, ed., *Louisiana's Legal Heritage* (New Orleans, 1983), 43-86, and Stephen Webre, "The Problem of Indian Slavery in Spanish Louisiana, 1769-1803," *Louisiana History*, 25 (1984): 117-35, are important analyses of slavery during the Spanish period.

[12]Charles L. Thompson, ed., *New Orleans in 1805: A Directory and a Census* (New Orleans, 1936); Ira Berlin, *Slaves without Masters: The Free Negro in the Antebellum South* (New York, 1974), 108-32; Virginia R. Dominguez, *White by Definition: Social Classification in Creole Louisiana* (New Brunswick, 1986), 23-26.

[13]Patricia K. Galloway, ed., *Mississippi Provincial Archives: French Dominion*, vols. 4 and 5 (1927-1984; reprint ed., Baton Rouge, 1984), 4:40, 49, cited hereafter as *MPAFD*. Patricia D. Woods, *French-Indian Relations on the Southern Frontier, 1699-1762* (Ann Arbor, 1980), 139; J. Barton Starr, *Tories, Dons, and Rebels: The American Revolution in British West Florida* (Gainesville, 1976), 142-60.

[14]*MPAFD* (1984), 4:46-47, 81-82, 5:38-44, 122, 183, 273-74.

[15]Kinnaird, *Spain in the Mississippi Valley*, 1:101-2, 154-55.

[16]Kinnaird, *Spain in the Mississippi Valley*, 2:185, 258, 3:141-43, 151-52; Miró to Luis de Las Casas, September 10, December 26, 1790, June 28, 1791, Dispatches of the Spanish Governors of Louisiana, WPA typescript in Louisiana Historical Center, New Orleans; Villebeuvre to Carondelet, January 16, February 7, March 30, 1793, *East Tennessee Historical Society Publications*, 29 (1957): 142-43, 152, 30 (1958): 101-2.

[17]Laussat to Minister of Navy, September, 27, 1802, Claude Perrin Victor Papers, the Historic New Orleans Collection, New Orleans; James Wilkinson to William Claiborne, Fort Adams, April 13, 1803, Indian Department Journal, Mississippi Department of History and Archives, Jackson: "I have received the following information from a confidential source in New Orleans, viz: 'Mingo poos Coos has been here, and thro the Interpreter has been invited to bring his people to meet their old friends the French, the Indians are daily comeing in, and the Interpreter has gone over the lake [Pontchartrain] to provide for their accommodation.'"

[18]Carl A. Brasseaux, trans., ed., and annotator, *A Comparative View of French Louisiana, 1699 and 1762; The Journal of Pierre Le Moyne d'Iberville and Jean-Jacques Blaise d'Abbadie* (Lafayette, 1979), 102, 107, 112.

[19]Browne to Hillsborough, Pensacola, July 6, 1768, English Provincial Records, Mississippi Department of Archives and History, Jackson.

[20]Bernard Romans, *A Concise Natural History of East and West Florida* (1775; reprint ed., New Orleans, 1961), 69-71.

[21]List of the Several Tribes of Indians inhabiting the banks of the Mississippi, Between New Orleans and Red River, with their number of gun-men and places of residence, January 1, 1773, William Haldimand Papers, British Museum (microfilm in Louisiana Division, New Orleans Public Library). Other population estimates of these Indian communities for this period can be found in Jacqueline K. Voorhies, trans. and comp., *Some Late Eighteenth-Century Louisianians: Census Records of the Colony, 1758-1796* (Lafayette, 1973), 164-66; Eron Dunbar Rowland, ed., "Peter Chester: Third Governor of the Province of West Florida under the British Dominion, 1770-1781," *Publications of the Mississippi Historical Society: Centenary Series*, 5 (1925): 97; Philip Pittman, *The Present State of the European Settlements on the Mississippi*, ed. Robert Rea, facsimile of 1770 edition (Gainesville, 1973), 24, 35, 36.

[22]The migration of Indians into the Atchafalaya and Red River basins can be traced in Daniel Clark, "An Account of the Indian Tribes in Louisiana, New Orleans, September 29, 1803," in *The Territorial Papers of the United States*, ed. Clarence E. Carter, 26 vols. (Washington, DC, 1934-62), 9:62-64; John Sibley, "Historical sketches of the several Indian Tribes in Louisiana, south of the Arkansas river, and between the Mississippi and river Grand," in *Annals of the Congress of the United States*, 9th Cong., 2d sess. (Washington, DC, 1852), 1076-88; Sibley, *A Report from Natchitoches in 1807*, ed. Annie Heloise Abel (New York: Museum of the American Indian, 1922). For a history of the Choctaws who settled permanently in central

Louisiana, see Hiram F. Gregory, "Jena Band of Louisiana Choctaw," *American Indian Journal,* 3 (1977): 2-16.

[23]Brasseaux, *Comparative View,* 11; Clarence W. Alvord and C.E. Carter, eds., *The Critical Period, 1763-1765* (Springfield, 1915), 200-201, 413-14. Kinnaird, *Spain in the Mississippi Valley,* 2:382-84, 3:53-54; William Panton to Carondelet, Pensacola, April 16, 1792, *Georgia Historical Quarterly,* 22 (1938): 393; John Forbes to Carondelet, October 31, 1792, Panton to Carondelet, November 6, 1792, *East Tennessee Historical Society Publications,* 28 (1956): 131-33; James A. Robertson, ed., *Louisiana under the Rule of Spain, France, and the United States, 1785-1807,* 2 vols. (Cleveland, 1911), 2:103.

[24]Kinnaird, *Spain in the Mississippi Valley,* 2:382-84, 3:53-54; William Panton to Carondelet, Pensacola, April 16, 1792, *Georgia Historical Quarterly,* 22 (1938): 393; John Forbes to Carondelet, October 31, 1792, Panton to Carondelet, November 6, 1792, *East Tennessee Historical Society Publications,* 28 (1956): 131-33; Robertson, ed., *Louisiana under the Rule,* 2:103.

[25]The economic strategies devised by lower Mississippi Valley Indians in the late eighteenth and early nineteenth centuries are discussed in Richard White, *The Roots of Dependency: Subsistence, Environment, and Social Change among the Choctaws, Pawnees, and Navajos* (Lincoln, 1983), 97-110, and Daniel H. Usner, Jr., "American Indians on the Cotton Frontier: Changing Economic Relations with Citizens and Slaves in the Mississippi Territory," *Journal of American History,* 72 (1985): 297-317.

[26]John A. Watkins Manuscript on Choctaw Indians, Howard-Tilton Memorial Library, Tulane University, New Orleans: Fortescue Cuming, *Sketches of a Tour to the Western Country* (1810; reprint ed., Cleveland, 1904), 351-52.

[27]Ibid.

[28]Cuming, *Sketches of a Tour,* 365-66; Robertson, *Louisiana under the Rule of Spain,* France, and the United States, 2:81-83.

[29]Indian influences on Louisiana foodways are explored in Daniel H. Usner, Jr., "Food Marketing and Interethnic Exchange in the Eighteenth-Century Lower Mississippi Valley," *Food and Foodways,* 1 (1986): 279-310.

[30]Pierre Clément de Laussat, *Memoirs of My Life to My Son during the Years 1803 and After,* trans. Sister Agnes-Josephine Pastwa and ed. Robert D. Bush (Baton Rouge, 1978), 53-54; Dominique Rouquette, "The Choctaws" (typescript of a manuscript written in 1850, Louisiana Historical Center, New Orleans), 51-54; George W. Cable, "The Dance in Place Congo," *Century Magazine,* 31 (1886): 518-19.

[31]The broad spectrum of Indian experiences produced by contact with colonial settlers and slaves is skillfully examined in James Merrell, "The Indians' New World: The Catawba Experience," *William and Mary Quarterly,* 3d ser., 41 (1984): 537-65.

[32]Francis Jennings, William N. Fenton, Mary A. Druke, and David R. Miller, eds., *The History and Culture of Iroquois Diplomacy: An Interdisciplinary Guide to the Treaties of the Six Nations and Their League* (Syracuse, 1985), offers a collection of useful approaches to the form as well as the content of Indian-European diplomacy.

A SCHEME GONE AWRY: BERNARDO DE GÁLVEZ, GILBERTO ANTONIO DE MAXENT, AND THE SOUTHERN INDIAN TRADE*

Thomas D. Watson

A Spanish bombardment of May 8, 1781, exploded the powder magazine located within a British redoubt guarding an approach to Fort George, leading to Pensacola's surrender. The victory marked the culmination of a series of campaigns conducted by Bernardo de Gálvez, governor of Spanish Louisiana, in West Florida and broke the sole remaining British foothold along the Gulf of Mexico. Moreover, in achieving this important aim behind Spanish involvement in the American Revolution, Don Bernardo assured for himself heightened prestige, influence, and the generous gratitude of Charles III, his Bourbon master.[1]

Scarcely had the British prisoners been evacuated from Pensacola before Gálvez turned his attention towards consolidating the Spanish position in West Florida. Among other precautions taken, he ordered his commandant-designate of Pensacola, Lieutenant Colonel Arturo O'Neill, to act promptly in establishing amicable relations with the neighboring Indian tribes. Not only had the effective employment of Indian auxiliaries against Spanish troops during the recent fighting greatly impressed the Spanish governor, he also realized that the future security of West Florida depended on winning their friendship and tolerance. Bernardo de Gálvez held strong convictions that successful Indian policy must be based primarily upon trade control. Accordingly, he directed O'Neill to inform the Indians that the Spaniards would provide them with stable trading arrangements as soon as they could be devised.[2]

Apparently Gálvez himself later promised the Southern Indian tribes whose homelands lay within or adjacent to Louisiana and West Florida—the Creek, Choctaw, and Chickasaw nations—treaty congresses at which peaceful relations would be formally

*This article was first published in *Louisiana History,* 17 (1976): 5-17. Reprinted with the kind permission of the author and the Louisiana Historical Association.

established. A generous supply of presents was to be distributed at these gatherings as a means of perpetuating amity between Spaniard and Indian.[3]

The tribal territorial claims of the Creek, Choctaw, and Chickasaw Indians during the era of the American Revolution stretched westward from present-day central Georgia to the Mississippi River and northward from Florida into Tennessee. The Creeks, actually a confederacy containing important enclaves such as the Alabama and Coushatta Indians, were divided into two general groupings, Upper and Lower. The Upper Creek villages lay mostly alongside the Coosa and Tallapoosa rivers around and above the point where they join to form the Alabama. The Lower Creek settlements were situated to the southeastward along the Chattahooche and the Flint. With an overall population of perhaps 20,000, Creek fighting strength ranged somewhere between 3500 to 5000 braves.[4]

The Choctaw villages were located alongside the upper reaches of the Pearl and the lower portions of the Pascagoula and Chickasawhay rivers in present-day southern Mississippi. Numbering around 17,000 in all, factions within the Choctaw Nation included the Small Party, the Large Party, and the Six Towns. Choctaw territorial claims ran northward from the Gulf of Mexico to an east-west line beginning at the confluence of the Yazoo with the Mississippi. They could call on the martial services of between 3,000 and 5,000 warriors.

The lands of the Chickasaw began just to the north of Choctaw territory and extended into the bulge formed by the Mississippi, Ohio, and Tennessee rivers. Never great in numbers, attrition from endemic warfare kept the Chickasaw population small. By the end of the American Revolution the Chickasaw could place perhaps no more than 500 warriors in the field.

The life styles of the Southern Indians bore marked similarities. Theirs was a relatively sedentary existence; they congregated in villages alongside streams, engaged in agriculture, and tended livestock. Extensive hunting during the fall and winter seasons served as an important means of augmenting their subsistence economies. The hunt not only provided a meat supply; it provided peltry, the one resource readily exchangeable for highly coveted European trade goods.

The Southern Indians had been introduced to European trade goods around the turn of the eighteenth century, principally English traders operating out of Charles-Town, and to a lesser extent through their French counterparts located in Mobile and other Louisiana outposts. After the British take-over of the Floridas in 1763, the Southern Indians became extremely dependent on relatively cheap British wares offered by renegade resident traders and annual presents distributed by the Southern Indian Department. Indian artisanship declined almost to the vanishing point. Indeed, British officials consciously encouraged Indian trade dependency and regarded it as a most important means for keeping Indians subservient to British dominion.[5]

Deerskins greatly exceeded in importance all other items of peltry in the Southern Indian trade. In the 1760s the bulk of the peltry flowed through the Atlantic ports of

Charles-Town and Savannah, but in the 1770s the gulf ports of Mobile and Pensacola assumed greater importance. Exports of deerskins from Georgia in the ten-year period beginning with January 1763 averaged over £ 240,000 annually. Afterwards, with the westward flight of game and disturbances preceding open rebellion in the Atlantic seaboard colonies, the center of the trade tended to shift to West Florida. As late as 1779 two cargoes of peltry valued at £ 40,000 were exported from Pensacola. Gross returns in excess of 130 percent seem to have been common.[6]

The profit potential of the Southern Indian trade could scarcely have escaped the attention of Bernardo de Gálvez, whose father-in-law was Gilberto Antonio de Maxent, a veteran Louisiana fur trader. Accordingly, in an age when nepotism and venality were commonplace among colonial administrators, Don Bernardo quickly envisioned means for combining the objectives of securing Indian friendship with increasing the family fortune. In a letter of May 26, 1781, he bared his plan to his influential uncle, José de Gálvez, marqués de Sonora, who as minister of the Indies ranked alongside [the conde de] Floridablanca as a royal favorite.[7]

From the outset of his governorship, Don Bernardo informed his uncle, he (Bernardo) had worked vigorously at befriending the numerous Indian tribes living in and adjacent to Louisiana. His efforts, however, had been handicapped by the scarcity of goods suitable for presents or for conducting the Indian trade. Indian gifts requested in October 1779 had not yet arrived, creating a tense situation. The British in East Florida, with an abundance of presents and trade goods at their disposal, were causing the defection of Indians formerly attached to Spain. In view of the grave threat posed to West Florida and Louisiana by these conditions, the governor informed the minister of the Indies that Maxent was to be dispatched to the Spanish court for direct consultations. His expertise, Bernardo asserted, would prove invaluable in setting aright all matters pertaining to Indian affairs.[8]

Gilbert Antoine de St. Maxent, to use the French form of his name, was a man of remarkable accomplishments. Having arrived in Louisiana from his native Lorraine in his early twenties, he married Isabel La Roche, a young Creole of New Orleans in August, 1749. Maxent subsequently succeeded in parlaying the dowry gained from his marriage into a substantial fortune based largely on profits from the Indian trade.[9]

Maxent in the 1760s had supported the French governor, Chevalier Billouart de Kerlérec, in his acrimonious feud with the intendant, Vincent de Rochemore. In 1763, the grateful Kerlérec rewarded Maxent's loyalty by granting him a monopoly of the Indian trade on the Missouri River. He quickly formed a partnership with Pierre Laclède Liguest that paved the way for the latter's founding in February 1764 of the post of the St. Louis. With Maxent acting as the financier and Laclède as factor at St. Louis for a one-fourth share in the profits, the partnership was extremely lucrative until its dissolution in 1769. The jealous complaints of other New Orleans merchants had led to the revocation of Maxent's monopoly in 1767, causing the arrangement with Laclède to lose its attractiveness. Maxent, however, retained a large interest in the upper Louisiana fur trade as supplier of a number of traders operating in the area.

Unlike many of his fellow Louisianians of the merchant-planter class, Maxent managed to adjust with ease during the colony's transition from French to Spanish control. His wife, Doña Isabel, presented him with daughters in 1766 and 1767 for whose baptisms Martín Navarro, who later became Louisiana's first Spanish intendant, and Gov. Antonio de Ulloa stood respectively as *padrinos*. Maxent also cooperated with Ulloa in the unsuccessful attempt to forestall the October 1768 rebellion which led to Ulloa's ouster from Louisiana. Following the restoration of order in 1769 at the hands of Don Alejandro O'Reilly, Maxent's fidelity received generous recognition. He was commissioned to supervise the transfer of French governmental property to Spanish control; he became a captain of militia; he obtained an appointment as an official purveyor of Indian presents. Maxent afterwards further strengthened his ties to Spanish officialdom by arranging marriages for two daughters, María Isabel and María Felicitas, to O'Reilly's immediate gubernatorial successors—Luis de Unzaga y Amezaga and Bernardo de Gálvez.

Maxent participated energetically in the Gálvez campaigns against the British, being chosen to lead the militia in the surprise attack of September 7, 1779, that overwhelmed the meagerly defended Fort Bute at Manchac. He also took part in the fighting at Baton Rouge, Mobile, and Pensacola, advancing loans of over 76,000 *pesos* to supplement the financing of the latter action.

On October 4, 1781, Maxent addressed a memorial to Charles III requesting direct trade for Louisiana and West Florida with French and "other friendly ports." The principal argument advanced in support of the request stressed the importance of the fur trade to the economic development of the two provinces. Existing commercial regulations, the memorialist observed, required peltry to be shipped only to Spanish ports. Since there was little or no demand for furs in Spain, peltry had to be reexported to northern European market centers. This practice, Maxent maintained, not only increased shipping and handling costs, but it also increased the risks of serious loss through spoilage. Similarly, Spain produced scarcely any items customarily used in the Indian trade, and the necessity of acquiring trade goods through Spanish commercial channels added extra expenses.[10]

Unless timely changes in commercial policy were forthcoming, Maxent argued, the potentially lucrative Louisiana and West Florida fur trade would languish and quite probably be lost by default either to English or Anglo-American merchants. On the other hand, he envisioned quick and dramatic economic growth for the two provinces, increased customs receipts for the royal treasury, and rapid population growth through immigration should his recommendations for trade liberalization be adopted.

The Maxent memorial and recommendations influenced the promulgation of the royal *cédula* of January 22, 1782, which, among other things, opened direct trade for a ten-year period following the establishment of peace between French ports and Louisiana and West Florida subject to 6 percent ad valorem duties. The Spanish Crown, it should be noted, balked at including trade with "other friendly ports" in the provisions of the *cédula* as sought by Maxent. However, its general terms facilitated separate agreements between the court and Maxent designed to place him in firm control of both Indian trade for the two provinces.[11]

Charles III on October 30, 1781, elevated Maxent to the position of "Lieutenant-Governor and Captain-General in all matters relating to the respective Indian nations that inhabit the provinces of Louisiana and West Florida." In addition, Maxent entered into an agreement with the Crown on the purchase and delivery to New Orleans of Indian trade goods valued at 380,000 *pesos*. The terms of the agreement authorized Maxent and a partner, Miguel Fortier of New Orleans, to purchase 200,000 *pesos* in goods for reopening the Indian trade in Louisiana and West Florida. Maxent also was to acquire for the Spanish government presents valued at 80,000 *pesos* for distribution at treaty congresses with the Southern Indians. The remaining 100,000 *pesos* in goods would be stored in royal warehouses in New Orleans as a contingency reserve against wartime disruption to supply. Products of Spanish origin were to be given priority insofar as practical; the balance would be obtained in France. The entire amount of goods was to be assembled and shipped on Maxent's account and risk. Reimbursement for the royal goods would follow their safe delivery in New Orleans.[12]

The agreement also provided for liberal royal assistance in financing the enterprise. Maxent received an advance of 50,000 *pesos* plus drafts on the treasury of New Spain in the amount of 330,000 *pesos* for purchasing the Indian merchandise. In addition, José de Gálvez induced Fernando de Ravago, a Cádiz merchant, to extend Maxent an additional 228,000 *pesos* in credit for his enterprise.[13]

By late 1782 Maxent had assembled trade goods he later valued at 278,000 *pesos* at the ports of Bordeaux and Ostend. A considerable quantity of English items very popular with Indians was included among the goods collected in the Flemish ports. With all preparations complete, the merchandise stowed securely aboard his vessels, *La Margarita* and *La Felicidad*, Maxent departed for New Orleans and home. The ships, however, fell prey to British cruisers and were taken to Kingston, Jamaica, as prizes of war where Maxent and the crewmen of his vessels became British prisoners of war. To extricate himself from this predicament, Maxent availed himself of the services of two local merchant partners, Philip Allwood and Henry Ludlow. Loans in the amount of 66,739 *pesos* from these merchants permitted Maxent to recover through purchase of one vessel, *La Margarita*, to regain around 40,000 *pesos* worth of the condemned merchandise, and to procure sundry provisions. Maxent agreed to repay the loans upon his release and arrival in Havana.[14]

Maxent and the other Spaniards were paroled to Havana before mid-1783. Before departing from Havana for New Orleans, Maxent spent considerable time perfecting plans for the pending Southern Indian treaty congresses and for the general management of Indian affairs. Safely home by August, he assumed his duties as Indian Commissioner in the Louisiana capital.[15]

Developments in Havana in September 1783, however, revealed that Maxent's concerns there by no means had been limited exclusively to Indian affairs. A Spanish dragnet enmeshed a number of individuals implicated in extensive smuggling activity. Notable among those apprehended were a former captain-general of Havana, Juan Manuel de Cagigal; Francisco de Miranda, destined later for historical fame as "*el Precursor*" of Latin American independence; and Phillip Allwood, Maxent's "friend-in-need" of the Kingston sojourn. Evidence gathered in the subsequent investigations indicated that on May 16, 1783, Maxent had placed 27,000 silver *pesos* plus 1,000 *pesos* in bills of exchange in Allwood's hands aboard H.M.S. *Diamond* in the Havana harbor. In addition, Allwood had remained in Havana following Maxent's departure for New Orleans in the expectation of more promised silver on Maxent's account due to arrive from Vera Cruz in August. A royal decree of December 1783 placed Maxent under house arrest, suspended him from active service, and impounded his assets. His influence waned almost overnight.[16]

At this juncture, Bernardo de Gálvez, in Spain following the cessation of hostilities for conferences on postwar policy, instructed Esteban Rodríguez Miró, his governor *ad interim* in New Orleans, to assume Maxent's responsibilities for Indian affairs. Miró accepted the new assignment with many misgivings; Maxent's debacle had placed the plans for absorbing the Southern Indians exclusively within the Spanish orbit in great jeopardy. An Indian parley scheduled for March, 1783, at Galveztown was cancelled in order to buy time for devising solutions to the shortage of presents and trade goods. The 40,000 *pesos* in merchandise that Maxent had salvaged in Jamaica amounted to only one-half the preestablished needs for gifts. Moreover, Indian trade goods were unobtainable in Louisiana at any price. New Orleans merchants, in the light of the Maxent concession, had hesitated to stock merchandise of such dubious resale potential. Since 1782 Miró had been promising compliance in the not-too-distant future to repeated Indian demands at New Orleans, Mobile, and Pensacola for the establishment of trade. Arturo O'Neill's many efforts to obtain trade goods from New Orleans and Havana also had proven fruitless; the inventories of suitable Indian merchandise in Pensacola in 1783 were inadequate to the normal needs of one Creek village. Failure to find a quick remedy for the trade quandary, Miró feared, portended loss of control over the Southern Indians to the newly independent Anglo-Americans.[17]

Miró's fears were well grounded. The fall of Pensacola had reduced the Southern Indian trade to a desperate state. The only remaining outlets were British posts located along the St. John's River in East Florida. Their remoteness from Southern Indian villages rendered them ineffective for carrying on trade at anywhere near normal levels. Nevertheless, in 1782 and 1783, Indians from as far as the Yazoo River were flocking to East Florida to acquire sorely needed supplies and to complain about the deplorable trade conditions.[18]

Despite these inauspicious circumstances, from late May through June, 1784, Miró and Intendant Navarro presided over negotiations in Pensacola with the Creek and in

Mobile with the Alabama, Chickasaw, and Choctaw. The resulting treaties established peace between Spain and the tribes involved, placed them under Spanish protection, and created a set of trading procedures exclusively under Spanish auspices with fixed rates of exchange for deerskins and trade goods. Miró and Navarro later reported that their dealings had met with unqualified success, confidently asserting that Spanish hegemony over the treaty Indians had been elevated to an unassailable position.[19]

The Louisiana officials based their claims of diplomatic triumph largely on having won the friendship and cooperation of Alexander McGillivray, the principal war-chief of the embattled Creek Nation, whose followers by 1784 found their hunting grounds highly coveted by the land-hungry American frontiersmen of Georgia, Wautauga, and the Cumberland District. McGillivray, through whose veins coursed the blood of a Scottish Indian trader father, Lachlan, and of Sehoy, and Indian princess of French-Creek lineage, had been liberally educated in South Carolina and Georgia before the onset of the American Revolution. As Loyalists, father and son earned the wrath of Georgian rebels whose ire led them to confiscate McGillivray property holdings valued at one hundred thousand dollars. Proclaimed an outlaw, Lachlan retired disgustedly to his native Scotland, while Alexander sought haven among his Creek kinsmen at Little Tallassie, the scene of his boyhood years.[20]

McGillivray distinguished himself during the war as a deputy commissary of the British Southern Indian Department by drumming up Creek antipathy toward the American cause. Upon discovery in 1783 of the impending British evacuation of East Florida and its reversion to Spanish control, the disconsolate McGillivray was advised by British authorities to seek a Spanish connection. This, the advice ran, afforded the Creek their best means for thwarting American encroachment.[21]

The Creek chieftain received similar counsel from a Loyalist merchant, William Panton, a principal partner in the St. Augustine-based firm of Panton, Leslie and Company. This trading concern had been formed in January 1783 with official encouragement from British East Florida authorities for the purpose of improving the flow of goods to the Southern Indians. The partners had reacted to the news of the loss of East Florida to Spanish dominion by resolving to remain if possible and, with Spanish consent, to engross the Southern Indian trade.[22]

McGillivray became a key figure in implementing the strategy for attaining these objectives. A one-fifth interest in the firm's profits gave the Creek spokesman added incentive for confirming his natural anti-American inclinations. Under Panton's tutelage, McGillivray opened a lengthy correspondence with Spanish officials requesting Spanish protection for the Creeks from American land-hunger coupled with repeated reminders that Indian loyalty, and hence the security of Louisiana and the Floridas, depended upon the rapid establishment of an adequate trade in the accustomed and preferred English goods.[23]

Governor Miró had been so impressed with McGillivray's ability, influence, and demeanor at the Pensacola congress as to appoint him Spanish agent to the Creek. In this capacity he was charged with promoting Spanish ascendancy among his tribesmen, supervising trade activity, and arresting "illegal" entrants into the Creek domain. With these augmentations to his already extensive powers, McGillivray rendered Panton invaluable assistance in a campaign that eventually succeeded in wringing sweeping concessions from Spanish authorities for Panton, Leslie and Company. A royal decree of March 1789 confirmed the British company in the privilege of conducting the Indian trade directly between the Floridas and London on a duty-exempt basis. This grant was extended only grudgingly after the Spanish court acquiesced in the understanding that no feasible alternative to the trade question existed.[24] The compelling political objective of stemming the American westward advance eventually triumphed over the long-standing Spanish inclination towards a tightly closed commercial policy for its colonies.

In retrospect, the outcome comported well with the economic realities that governed the fur trade in the last quarter of the eighteenth century. With the elimination of France from North America, French production of articles for the Indian trade declined drastically whereas British artisans produced an increasing abundance of relatively low priced goods. Moreover, London at the same time attained complete ascendancy as the entrepôt of the European fur trade.[25]

Even should Maxent somehow have avoided his fall from grace, his ambitious plans for monopolizing the Southern Indian trade probably would have been ineffective without access to British trade channels. Moreover, his frequent illicit dealings with British merchants in West Florida while engaging in the Upper Louisiana Indian trade before the onset of the American Revolution suggest an awareness of this need.[26] This quite likely explains his unsuccessful bid to have trade opened with "other friendly ports" included in the royal *cédula* of January, 1782.

Notes for "A Scheme Gone Awry: Bernardo de Galvez, Gilberto Antonio de Maxent, and the Southern Indian Trade"

[1]James A. Padgett, ed., "Bernardo de Gálvez's Siege of Pensacola in 1781 (as related in Robert Farmar's Journal)," *Louisiana Historical Quarterly,* 26 (1943): 326; Richard Van Alstyne, *Empire and Independence: The International History of the American Revolution* (New York, 1965), 216.

[2]John W. Caughey, *Bernardo de Gálvez in Louisiana, 1776-1783* (Berkeley, 1934), 213; Elizabeth Howard West, "The Indian Policy of Bernardo de Gálvez," Mississippi Valley Historical Association, *Proceedings,* 8 (1916): 100-101.

[3]José de Gálvez to Bernardo de Gálvez, July 1, 1782, Spain, Archivo General de Indias, Papeles Procedentes de Cuba, legajo 1375. This depository will be cited below as AGI, PC. I am indebted to Professor William S. Coker for making available microfilm copies of this and other data from Spanish archives cited in this article.

[4]For background on the Southern Indians see John R. Swanton, *Early History of the Creek Indians and Their Neighbors*, Bureau of American Ethnology Bulletin No. 73 (Washington, 1922); Robert S. Cotterill, *The Southern Indians: The Story of the Civilized Tribes Before Their Removal* (Norman, 1954); and James H. O'Donnell III, *Southern Indians in the American Revolution* (Knoxville, 1973). Precise demographic data on the Southern Indians for the eighteenth century are nonexistent. The figures used are estimates based on information contained in the above-mentioned sources.

[5]John J. TePaske, "French, Spanish, and English Indian Policy on the Gulf Coast, 1513-1763: A Comparison," in *Spain and Her Rivals on the Gulf Coast, Proceedings*, Second Gulf Coast History and Humanities Conference, ed. by Ernest F. Dibble and Earle W. Newton (Pensacola,1971), 21-34.

[6]Paul Chrisler Phillips, *The Fur Trade*, 2 vols. (Norman, 1961), 1:569-73; Walter H. Mohr, *Federal Indian Relations, 1774-1778* (Philadelphia, 1933), 178; Bernard Romans, *A Concise Natural History of East and West Florida*, Floridiana Facsimile and Reprint Series (Gainesville, 1965), 257; John R. Alden, *John Stuart and the Southern Colonial Frontier* (reprint, New York, 1966), 16-17.

[7]Bernardo de Gálvez to José de Gálvez (Photostatic copy), May 26, 1781, John B. Stetson Collection, P.K. Yonge Library of Florida History, University of Florida; Arthur P. Whitaker, ed. and trans., *Documents Relating to the Commercial Policy of Spain in the Floridas, with Incidental Reference to Louisiana*, Florida State Historical Publications, No. 10 (Deland, 1931), xvii-xxix.

[8]Ibid.

[9]Information on Maxent's career appears in James Julian Coleman, Jr., *Gilbert Antoine de St. Maxent: The Spanish Frenchman of New Orleans* (New Orleans, 1968), passim; Lawrence Kinnaird, ed., *Spain in the Mississippi Valley, 1765-1794*, 3 vols. (Washington, 1946), 1:77, 147, 154; John G. Clark, *New Orleans, 1718-1812: An Economic History* (Baton Rouge, 1970), 195-96; and Caughey, *Gálvez in Louisiana*, 14-18, 155. Mrs. H.S. Edrington, a descendant of Maxent's, furnished copies of the wills of Gilberto and Isabel. These provided useful vital statistics on the Maxent family.

[10]Expediente of Maxent (Typescript), October 4, 1782, Elizabeth Howard West Papers, P.K. Yonge Library of Florida History, University of Florida. This source is cited below as "West Papers."

[11]Translations of this *cédula* appear in Whitaker, *Documents*, 31-39, and Kinnaird, *Spain in the Mississippi Valley*, 2:1-4. See also: Clark, *New Orleans*, 223-25; Arthur P. Whitaker, "The Commerce of Louisiana and the Floridas at the End of the Eighteenth Century," *Hispanic American Historical Review*, 8 (1928): 191-92.

[12]Duvon C. Corbitt and Roberta Corbitt, eds., "Papers from the Spanish Archives Relating to Tennessee and the Old Southwest, 1783-1800," East Tennessee Historical Society, *Publications* (1939), 79; Coleman, *Gilbert Antoine de St. Maxent*, 87-88; José de Gálvez to Bernardo de Gálvez, AGI, PC, *legajo* 1375; José de Gálvez to Intendant of Louisiana (Typescript), March 18, 1782, West Papers.

[13]Navarro to Antonio Valdés, October 31, 1787, AGI, PC, *legajo* 633; José de Gálvez to Intendant of Louisiana, March 18, 1782, loc. cit.; Whitaker, *Documents*, 225, n. 16; Coleman, *Gilbert Antoine de St. Maxent*, 104-5.

[14]Coleman, *Gilbert Antoine de St. Maxent*, 88-89, 96-98; Whitaker, *Documents*, 225, n. 16; Invoice of Goods placed on Margarita, Kingston, Jamaica, May 11, 1783, and Monsieur de Maxent, Current Account with P. Allwood, Havana, July 7, 1783, Spain. Archivo Historico Nacional, Consejo de Indias, legajo 21064. This depository will be cited below as AHN, Indias.

[15]Coleman, *Gilbert Antoine de St. Maxent*, 97-98; Maxent, Instructions of July 14, 1783, and Esteban Miró to O'Neill (Typescripts), August, 1, 1783, West Papers.

[16]Whitaker, *Documents*, 225, n. 16; Coleman, *Gilbert Antoine de St. Maxent*, p. 99; Maxent, receipt of May 16, 1783, and Allwood to Ludlow, July 11, 1783, and Allwood to Maxent, July 31, 1783, AHN Indias, legajo 21064.

[17]Miró to Navarro, April 15, 1784, and Miró to Bernardo de Gálvez, April 15, 1784, and Navarro to José de Gálvez, April 16, 1784, and O'Neill to Luis de Unzaga, February 15, 1783, and Alexander McGillivray to O'Neill, March 26, 1784 (Typescripts), West Papers. The McGillivray letter has been published in John W. Caughey, *McGillivray of the Creeks* (Norman, 1938), 72-73.

[18]O'Neill to Unzaga, February 15, 1783, West Papers: Allevin et al. to ?, in Kinnaird, *Spain in the Mississippi Valley*, 2:71-73; J.H. O'Donnell, "Alexander McGillivray: Training for Leadership," *Georgia Historical Quarterly*, 49 (1965): 181-82.

[19]Navarro to José de Gálvez (Typescript) July 27, 1784, West Papers; Jack D. L. Homes, "Spanish Treaties with West Florida Indians," *Florida Historical Quarterly*, 98 (1969): 140-44.

[20]Ibid.; O'Donnell, "Training for Leadership," 182-83; Cotterill, *Southern Indians*, 55-56. For background descriptions of McGillivray see Caughey, *McGillivray of the Creeks*, and Arthur P. Whitaker, "Alexander McGillivray, 1783-1789," *North Carolina Historical Review*, 5 (1928): 181-85.

[21]O'Donnell, "Training for Leadership," 178; David H. Corkran, *The Creek Frontier, 1540-1783* (Norman, 1967), 324.

[22]Joseph Byrne Lockey, *East Florida, 1783-1785, a File of Documents Assembled, and Many of Them Translated by Joseph Byrne Lockey*, ed. by John W. Caughey (Berkeley, 1949), 26-29; Homer E. Wright, "Diplomacy of Trade on the Southern Frontier: A Case Study of William Panton and John Forbes" (Ph.D. dissertation, University of Georgia, 1971), 24-25.

[23]For a concise illustration of McGillivray's role in Panton's Spanish strategy see the edited documents in John W. Caughey, "Alexander McGillivray and the Creek Crisis, 1783-1784," in *New Spain and the Anglo-American West*, ed. by Charles W. Hackett et al., 2 vols. (Los Angeles, 1932), 1:270-85. For Panton's role, see Panton to Lachlan McGillivray, April 10, 1794, in Albert James Pickett, *History of Alabama and Incidentally of Georgia and Mississippi, form the Earliest Times*, 3rd ed. (Sheffield, 1896): 430-31. For McGillivray's interest in the firm, see McGillivray to Charles McLatchy, December 25, 1784, in United States Library of Congress, Division of Manuscripts, East Florida Papers, bundle 116L9; "Debit, Estate William Panton in acct. current with P, L & Co., Concern 'RL' ending 30 September '98," Innerarity-Hulse Papers, John C. Pace Library, University of West Florida; and D.W. *Johnson v. John Forbes & Co.* (1823), Case No. 1999, Louisiana Federal District Court (New Orleans).

[24]Miró to José de Gálvez (Typescript), August, 1, 1784, Joseph B. Lockey Papers, P.K. Young Library of Florida History, University of Florida; Thomas D. Watson, "Merchant Adventurer in the Old Southwest: William Panton, the Spanish Years, 1783-1801" (Ph.D. Dissertation, Texas Tech University, 1972), 71-152.

[25]Phillips, *Fur Trade*, 2:3-4, 7-8, 173, 223; Wayne Edson Stevens, *The Northwest Fur Trade, 1763-1800*, University of Illinois Studies in the Social Sciences, 14 (Urbana, 1926), 147-48.

[26]Clark, *New Orleans*, 195-96.

THE IMMIGRATION POLICY OF GOVERNOR ESTEBAN MIRÓ IN SPANISH LOUISIANA*

Gilbert C. Din

From 1785 to 1791 Spanish immigration policy in Louisiana, in an attempt to accommodate itself to changing conditions, departed from its traditional role of excluding American Protestants. Unable to secure Spanish or European Catholics at little or no expense, with whom to develop and protect the colony, Spain at last turned to the nearest available source for settlers—the United States. Esteban Miró, governor of Louisiana during these crucial years, was extremely important in the formulation of this policy. The influence he exerted, both directly and indirectly, on the Spanish court to modify and determine Louisiana's immigration policy has not been previously recognized.[1]

Spanish immigration laws in Louisiana before Miró's governorship already displayed increasing flexibility. From the time of Spanish acquisition of Louisiana following the Seven Years' War, the value of this border colony as a buffer zone to protect Mexico was recognized, and Spain endeavored, as best a declining empire could, to fill the vastness of Louisiana with a loyal and Catholic population. From the 1760s Spain allowed the entry of Acadians into Louisiana and assisted them in their settlement.[2] In the 1770s the court permitted and encouraged the settlement of Acadians, Frenchmen, Germans, and Irish who were Catholic.[3] At the end of the decade, in order to secure recruits for the fixed regiment in Louisiana, Canary Island families were settled there at royal expense. At the same time and under similar conditions, smaller numbers of families came from Granada and Málaga in Spain to promote the growing of flax and hemp.[4] In 1784 the Crown accepted the proposal of Henry Peyroux to transport to Louisiana the Acadian families then living in France; and this was accomplished in 1785 at an excessive cost.[5]

It was the prohibitive cost of conveying families from across the Atlantic and their failures to become self-sufficient within a short period of time that terminated projects of this kind. Spain lacked the financial resources to underwrite the acquisition of colonists

*This article first appeared in the *Southwestern Historical Quarterly*, 73 (1969): 155-75. Reprinted here with the kind permission of the author and publisher.

in Europe, and to have attempted it en masse would have meant bankruptcy long before the Louisiana "desert" was populated. Colonial officials continued to regard an augmented population as the best defense for the province, but, after the era of trans-Atlantic movements, settlers needed to come from another and less expensive quarter.[6]

Further changes in immigration policy came during the governorship of Esteban Miró. In 1782, in the absence of Governor Bernardo de Gálvez, Miró, senior ranking officer in Louisiana, became the acting military and civil governor. As such, he assumed the task of implementing the provisions of the peace treaty which ended the state of war between Spain and Britain. Under the terms of the Treaty of Paris, British residents in West Florida were given eighteen months in which to terminate their affairs and depart. In 1784 several British ships entered the Mississippi River in order to effect the removal of the British subjects. However, not all chose to leave.[7] After an extension of four months had expired, the remaining residents in West Florida petitioned Governor Miró for permission to remain on their lands under the same terms as they had been living since the Spanish assumed control.[8]

The West Florida residents were British subjects who entered in the years after 1763, when Britain acquired Florida, and Americans who came in mostly during the Revolutionary War. In West Florida they were settled in Mobile, Pensacola, Manchac, and especially in the Natchez District where they were most numerous. Under normal conditions they would not have qualified for residence in the colony because Spanish immigration laws limited entry to Catholics, and most of them were Protestants. Those who remained after the evacuation were destitute, and Governor Miró feared that, if forced out by land, they would merely resettle nearby on the edge of the province, where others would join them, and together threaten the colony's security.[9]

It was at this point in 1785 that Miró unveiled a plan that would reappear elsewhere and be presented by others in the next two years. Concluding that the interests of the colony demanded that the Anglo-American residents remain, the governor proposed a way by which the Protestant settlers might be converted and assimilated through the use of English-speaking Irish missionaries. Already in West Florida since the Spanish conquest, Catholicism was the official religion and the only public worship allowed. In this situation Miró suggested using the Irish missionaries to proselytize among the adults while requiring that their children be baptized and instructed in the Catholic faith. Also public schools would teach the children to become Spaniards, and in time, the governor hoped, they would forget their origins. Those not willing to submit to these conditions would be required to quit the colony, and, if necessary, their transportation expenses would be defrayed by the Crown. Miró sent his suggestions to Bernardo de Gálvez, now viceroy in Mexico, who forwarded them to Spain.[10]

In Spain on March 14, 1786, the Supreme Council accepted the proposal of Governor Miró on how to handle the problem of the Anglo-American families. Those persons wishing to accept the conditions to permit them to remain in West Florida were required to pledge fidelity and obedience to the Spanish government; otherwise they had to leave by sea at their own expense, or at royal cost if impoverished. The Council issued orders to Miró to devise a plan for the establishment of parishes and schools in Natchez and other places which would be staffed with Irish priests. The Council also instructed the bishop of Salamanca to find suitable Irish priests to be sent as missionaries to West Florida. Eventually he located four who agreed to go and who sailed early the next year.[11]

By February 10, 1787, Miró had worked out a scheme for the creation of the parishes. He felt that the Natchez District required two parishes: one to serve both Santa Catalina Creek and Second Creek, and a second for Cole's Creek. Each parish would have a church and residence for a priest, but at Cole's Creek there would also be a residence for a military commander and a barracks for a small detachment of troops to administer justice and prevent contraband and the entry of undesirable persons. The priests would be charged with the teaching of Catholicism together with the teaching of reading and writing in Spanish. Miró considered it imperative to establish these two parishes, but he also suggested a third for Tinzas, fifteen miles above Mobile, where fifty-nine Anglo-American families resided.[12]

The governor soon dispatched his plan to Spain for approval, but the four Irish missionaries reached New Orleans in August, 1787, before a reply came. Since the court had still not authorized expenditures for the creation of the parishes, Miró and Intendant Martín Navarro delayed until two mails had arrived without receiving further instructions before proceeding with the implementation of his plan.[13]

While this activity was taking place in 1786 and 1787, the governor also contemplated means to increase Louisiana's scant population. Quite possibly even before the summer of 1786, Miró considered the feasibility of allowing Americans from the western settlements to enter Louisiana under the same conditions which governed the Anglo-Americans in the Natchez District. By means of additional Irish missionaries, these immigrants from the United States could, like the others, be converted and assimilated, and they would serve to increase the colony's population and bolster its security. It was an ambitious plan fraught with risk, but the retention of Louisiana with only meager resources demanded a bold approach. Miró realized this very well, but his extreme caution prevented him from recommending it to the court until September, 1787, and then he did so indirectly. Before that time, however, he appears to have discussed the plan with visitors in New Orleans, one of whom was Pierre Wouves d'Argès.

In August, 1786, d'Argès passed through New Orleans from Kentucky on his way to France. The middle-aged chevalier of the Order of St. Louis and late captain of grenadiers in the American Revolutionary War had lived for two years in the area of the Falls of the Ohio where he had received lands, but ultimately war between the Americans and the Indians caused his departure. While in New Orleans he spoke with the governor and the intendant about conditions in Louisiana and the American West. The Frenchman later asserted that he presented the Spanish officials with a petition from 1,582 families, most of them German or of German descent and resident in Kentucky, who wished to settle in Louisiana if they were given lands and freedom of religion. Since Spanish policy prohibited the entry of Protestants and denied them freedom of religion, the officials responded that the conditions asked exceeded their instructions, but they urged him to present his petition to the count of Aranda, Spain's ambassador in Paris.[14] Neither Miró nor Navarro in 1786 reported their conversation with d'Argès to Spain, and the governor later denied that the Frenchman presented the petition.[15] Nonetheless, there can be no doubt that d'Argès, whether he had a petition or whether he alone conceived the idea of permitting Americans to settle on Spanish territory, espoused the governor's method by which such immigrants could be admitted. His subsequent proposal to the ambassador in Paris revealed this very clearly.

By February, 1787, the chevalier was in Paris where he informed Aranda of his petition. The ambassador was intrigued by the proposal. Over the next month the Frenchman related news from the Mississippi Valley and enlarged upon details for increasing Louisiana's population and promoting its security. Thus the initial step was taken in the process that revolutionized Spanish immigration policy in Louisiana, and, although it was not done by Miró, he was indirectly responsible through the information and ideas that d'Argès acquired in New Orleans.

The d'Argès proposal reflected Miró's impressions, and it is doubtful if the chevalier added anything original. To the ambassador he stated that American colonists in Louisiana would provide a defensive force and develop the province economically. Spain's expense in their settlement, a consideration of no mean importance, was limited to providing an English-speaking military commander who knew their customs and could organize them into a militia similar to those established down river. D'Argès reasoned that the colonists, assured of their property and free commerce, would adhere to a government that dispensed such advantages. As for religion, and there can be no mistaking Miró's thoughts here, the Frenchman felt that the use of Irish missionaries and a policy of employing only persons of the king's faith in civil and military positions would soon bring about conversions.[16]

In forwarding his correspondence with d'Argès to Spain on April 2, Aranda praised the chevalier and advised that he be heard personally at court. Already a strong advocate of strengthening the province's defenses, the ambassador heartily endorsed the enterprise. He considered that these settlers would be twice as valuable after being relocated in Louisiana and that the province would be made stronger while simultaneously weakening the American West. To Aranda the Natchez defense perimeter required not merely a garrison but also an agricultural population that was disposed to take up arms. He reflected that the prospect of living in peace and the ability to export their produce, conditions which were lacking in the middle Ohio Valley, would soon lure vast numbers of settlers, an opinion that other Spanish officials entertained for several years.[17]

On the thorny religious point Aranda urged that orthodoxy should not be stressed. A worse fate for the empire than lack of religious orthodoxy among its settlers would be the loss of the colony to the same people who might have been settled in the province as vassals committed to its defense. On being established along the Natchez frontier, they would be removed from the principal Catholic settlements downstream. While Catholicism was to continue as the official religion and the only one accorded public worship, the Protestant settlers were to remain unmolested in religious affairs, but without ministers or meetings, conditions that already existed among the Anglo-American residents. Aranda was optimistic about their conversion. Denied government posts, they and their children would be drawn to the official faith in order to gain advancement. Schools staffed with Irish, German, or French priests, who were models of conduct, would teach religious doctrine and the Spanish language. Within a short time these people would forget their origins. The ambassador drew the analogy that in North Africa Spain already utilized Moorish companies in the defense of Ceuta and Oran. In North America Protestants could be employed in a similar capacity.[18]

At the time the d'Argès proposal reached the Spanish court, royal policy regarding the closure of the Mississippi to Americans, as well as Spanish-American relations in general, came under review. After two years of hesitation, the river had been closed in 1784 in the expectation that American settlements in the West would be destroyed by loss of the use of the river as an outlet for their produce. Such was not the result; and the settlements flourished while Louisiana's population grew very slowly. Likewise, Spanish efforts to secure treaty recognition of her fluvial rights were steadfastly rejected by the United States government, and similar efforts to obtain a boundary settlement and commercial treaty equally frustrated the negotiations of Diego de Gardoqui, Spain's envoy to the United States. Beginning in 1786 the Spanish government also became aware of growing disaffection among certain Anglo-American westerners; but, while it wished that the West could be useful in protecting Louisiana, Spain continued to act without much regard to this movement.[19]

By the middle of 1787 the court was prepared to alter its policy of keeping the Mississippi closed. Western sentiment against Spain, as well as against the United States government, was widespread. Seizure of American goods in Natchez in 1786 resulted in the reprisal destruction of Spanish merchandise by George Rogers Clark in upper Louisiana. Increasingly, the closure of the river to Americans appeared to be leading toward an invasion of the province in an effort to open its navigation. Thus the d'Argès proposal seemed to offer an alternate solution on how to cope with the western people: employ them rather than resist them. The chevalier's timely proposal in 1787 coincided with a modification of Spanish policy in Louisiana.[20]

In Aranjuez the count of Floridablanca, the secretary of state, consulted José de Gálvez, the minister of the Indies, about Aranda's suggestion to interview d'Argès. Recent correspondence from North America was reviewed and a search made to determine if the Louisiana officials had mentioned the Frenchman in their dispatches.[21] Since nothing could be learned about the chevalier, Gálvez agreed that it might be useful to hear him, and permission was granted to invite him to Spain. By the end of July, d'Argès was in Madrid.[22]

At the Spanish court d'Argès succeeded beyond his wildest expectation. Floridablanca, now following the counsel of Antonio Valdés, who replaced the recently deceased José de Gálvez, consented to virtually every proposal made by the Frenchman. The chevalier received permission to return to the province and to bring in his 1,582 families, and Americans in general were now authorized to settle in Louisiana and allowed to continue in their religion, but in all other respects were required to obey Spanish law and to swear an oath of allegiance. The wording of Valdés in his memorandum to Floridablanca was ambiguous, and the subsequent royal order based on it seemed to imply that the Spanish government was granting the Americans complete religious freedom.[23] Both Miró in New Orleans and Gardoqui in New York interpreted the royal order of August 23, 1787, in this fashion. If this was the court's intent, it was never stated specifically and, in any event, Miró quickly abridged the order to conform with his program. The establishment of parishes ministered by Irish clerics was again included.

Also, in an effort to quiet the anger of the westerners on the issue of trade, Floridablanca agreed to permit them to send their produce to the Spanish province on payment of a duty of 25 percent. No thought was given at this time in Spain to considering that such a policy might impede the expected immigration. The question of how much land each colonist was to receive was deferred to the judgment of the Louisiana governor. As for an English-speaking commander for the Natchez post, a search was begun that culminated in the appointment of Lieutenant Colonel Manuel Gayoso de Lemos, who arrived in Louisiana in 1789.[24]

Fearful of possible repercussions, the Spanish government chose to disguise the real objective of the d'Argès mission. Officially, d'Argès was to be a commissioner to examine and transmit to the court complaints of the American backwoodsmen against the Spanish government and to reconnoiter western lands prior to the fixation of boundaries. In order to demonstrate the benevolence of the Spanish king pending final determination of boundary settlements, the westerners could send their produce downstream to Natchez and New Orleans paying the 25 percent tariff. However, Floridablanca, lacking faith in the comparatively unknown Frenchman, took steps to circumscribe his behavior because d'Argès' demands for greater authority after receiving his appointment had raised Spanish suspicions. The secretary of state obliged him to act only in concert with Gardoqui or Miró, either of whom could assign an associate to accompany him to the West. When advised of this restriction, the chevalier complained bitterly, protesting that the companion would undo his mission. Unmoved, Floridablanca informed Gardoqui and Miró that care was to be exercised in dealing with both d'Argès and his enterprise lest the settlers be lost. In a note to Gardoqui, the secretary expressed belief that the new commercial policy for the Mississippi might be useful in furthering negotiations with the United States; therefore, the declaration that the river was open, subject to a tariff, was to be delayed until such time as he could obtain a *quid pro quo*.[25]

Late in January, 1788, the royal mail packet *Galveztown*, after a stormy crossing, blew into New York harbor to disembark her passenger, the chevalier of the Order of St.

Louis. No sooner had d'Argès landed than he besieged the Spanish envoy with a barrage of demands. He wanted public recognition for himself as a court-appointed commissioner to hear complaints and to reconnoiter boundaries; and, if denied this, then the alternative would be an immediate declaration that the Mississippi was open, subject to a 25 percent duty. He debated with Gardoqui on virtually every issue: he proposed a change in his route to the West although he had chosen it himself; he insisted that he select his own companion to travel with him to Kentucky; and he haggled about his salary payments. In short, the Frenchman expressed interest in almost everrything except his primary mission—to recruit colonists for Louisiana.[26]

Gardoqui displayed little patience with d'Argès. Having been engaged for some years in efforts to secure a treaty, he was now frustrated that no American government existed with which he could negotiate—particularly at a moment when the Spanish court appeared disposed to concede terms. Furthermore, since 1786 he had been involved in conversations with James White about a separatist movement in the American West that might be useful to Spain, and the envoy perhaps hoped to salvage his diplomatic mission with a positive accomplishment in this area. But with the arrival of d'Argès, he saw in the unbridled Frenchman a threat to his ambitions and was determined to resist him. Gardoqui refused to proclaim the river open because, as he explained, it was Spain's intent to derive some advantage from it. He also argued that many potential emigrants might prefer to pay the import duty rather than move. Moreover, he believed that granting religious toleration was sufficient to attract large numbers of settlers without making further concessions. Gardoqui also hinted to the court that d'Argès was a possible French agent and a speculator in western lands. At length, when the two reached an impasse, the Spaniard proposed that since it was winter d'Agrés should journey to New Orleans by sea and begin his project from that point in the spring. Vanquished, the chevalier reluctantly consented.[27]

In New Orleans in early July, 1787, while Governor Miró still awaited instruction on the establishment of the parishes, Brigadier James Wilkinson floated down the Mississippi River bringing barges loaded with merchandise and initiated the misnamed "Spanish Conspiracy."[28] His notorious plan to detach the American West and gain an alliance with Spain has overshadowed a second proposal concerning immigration that he included in his memorial. Most scholars have tended to regard the second proposal as the brigadier's without giving it much additional attention. However, in this writer's opinion, Governor Miró was solely responsible for this suggestion. Rather than approach the court directly, he chose Wilkinson's opportune visit to advance his plan. A closer examination of Wilkinson's immigration design reveals that it contained many features identical to those propounded by Miró in his suggestions for the conversion and assimilation of the Anglo-American families, as well as the ideas presented by d'Argès in Europe.[29] There can be no doubt that Miró was the common inspiration for all of them.

Wilkinson's immigration scheme was not conditional upon the acceptance of his first proposal and could be acted upon independently. The plan was to admit people from

Kentucky into Louisiana, a process which Wilkinson, or more properly Miró, did not regard as being dangerous because the colony possessed sufficient Spanish troops to prevent any disorders. Those with property were to be preferred since their wealth could be confiscated should they not conduct themselves properly. The Kentucky families were required to take the oath of allegiance to Spain, and in religious matters they were not to be disturbed; however, Catholicism was to remain the only public form of worship. English-speaking Irish priests who were knowledgeable in the prevailing customs would evangelize and educate the younger generation. Wilkinson, in his irrepressible prose, offered assurances that, over a period of time, these immigrants, enjoying their property and without the necessity of paying import duties, would become tied to Spain in both interest and affection. The success of the first immigrants would induce others to join them, and together they would develop the wealth of the province and increase its importance in the Spanish Empire.[30]

In their celebrated dispatch Number 13 of September 25, 1787, supporting the Wilkinson memorial, Miró and Navarro expected the Irish missionaries to be very successful in their work. Any additional expenses entailed in bringing more priests, they explained, could be recouped through increased revenue collected from the expected rise in exports. They advised that the new settlements should be located on both banks of the Mississippi rather than confined only to the eastern levee. Miró and Navarro employed their strongest argument for the admittance of Americans by stating that no force could restrain the settlers if they wished to enter the colony, which in effect cogently summarized the reasons for their settlement on Spanish soil.[31] Unknown to the governor at the moment while he was urging the Crown to permit American Protestants to settle in Louisiana, the court was in the process of forwarding a royal order to this effect and under the same conditions he had expounded, with the exception of those dealing with commerce.

After sending the Wilkinson memorial and their dispatch Number 13, Miró and Navarro began what amounted to a lengthy wait before the court responded. When a royal order arrived bearing news of the d'Argès appointment several months later, it appeared as if all was lost. The governor soon sent a protest to Spain since the appointment probably meant the demise of the Wilkinson project. He argued that if the latter project were used, Wilkinson could also act as an immigration agent, and that it was preferable to have a solitary person engaged in this delicate maneuver. However, because he believed that the chevalier already was in Kentucky and soon would come down the river with his immigrants, he issued instructions to Commandant Carlos de Grand-Pré in Natchez to expect the settlers.[32]

Then developments again took a sudden turn and rescued the Wilkinson enterprise in April, 1788, when d'Argès, having come from New York by sea, unexpectedly disembarked in New Orleans. The Frenchman had not yet commenced his mission, nor would he, as the governor was resolved to detain him until the court acted on Wilkinson's memorial. In May, 1788, with the immigration from Kentucky expected momentarily to get underway, Miró requested a clarification of the duties colonists should pay on entering the province. According to the royal order of July 14, 1787, free entry was authorized for any tools and implements brought by settlers for their private use. Miró, however, questioned if duty should be exacted on goods which the immigrants acquired in exchange for the sale of their lands and other properties. D'Argès brought with him the news that trade was to be allowed and the import duty placed at 25 percent, but Miró wanted it reduced to 6 percent on the surplus goods of the immigrants for fear that it would halt the flow of propertied settlers to Louisiana. Otherwise, the colony might receive only the indigent with no duties to pay.[33] In this manner the governor kept the chevalier cooling his heels in New Orleans while he impatiently awaited instructions concerning Wilkinson.

Court delay on the Wilkinson proposal probably stemmed from the desire to hear Intendant Navarro's opinion in Spain and to await the results of other projects, particularly the d'Argès mission and Gardoqui's private conversations. In May, 1788, months after the brigadier submitted his memorial, the intendant retired from service and departed for Spain. There in November he gave his observations on Wilkinson's plans and essentially reiterated what dispatch Number 13 had previously stated. Navarro, who years earlier had counseled closing the Mississippi in order to destroy the American settlements upstream, now recognized the ineffectiveness of that policy. Instead he said that these people, poor but industrious and self-sacrificing, should be used, and that with their assistance, Louisiana could be developed and made stronger. Navarro rejected the d'Argès mission in order to make way for Wilkinson's better, and more extensive, plan. He added that the d'Argès proposal was one which "could have been for some time effected by Governor Miró and myself if we had known a way, or believed that the court would have set aside the essential point of religion."[34]

On December 1, 1788, the Supreme Council issued orders instructing Miró on how to proceed. This order together with the royal orders sent the previous year on the d'Argès mission constitute the two most important statements of immigration policy issued during Esteban Miró's administration. The government, while setting aside Wilkinson's first proposal until Kentucky became independent, adopted his second proposal on immigration. The conditions for entry of settlers were similar to those stated at the time the chevalier became Spain's immigration official in North America, and thus were now reissued with minor modifications. However, the duty on goods belonging to non-colonists was further reduced from 25 percent to 15 percent, and the governor was authorized to lower it even more for "notables." While the Crown instructed Miró to use d'Argès in some suitable manner, the order confirmed the governor's choice of Wilkinson as his principal immigration agent.[35]

In Louisiana, d'Argès waited uneasily for court instructions and suspected that more was afoot than just the commercial proposal Miró said that Wilkinson had presented on his visit to New Orleans. In June the chevalier sent word to Colonel Richard Anderson that the families could begin their journey down river, and in August he attempted to gain the governor's permission to go himself. Because he was denied permission to travel to Kentucky and had been thwarted in his immigration efforts, d'Argès then decided to employ his free time attending to family matters on the island of Martinique. Delays and lack of transportation postponed his departure from New Orleans until February.[36]

Soon after he left, the long overdue reply to Miró's dispatch Number 13 came on February 25, 1789, and a week later the governor wrote to d'Argès offering him the rank of lieutenant colonel with the salary of 100 *pesos* and the command of the post at l'Ance à la Graisse, near the mouth of the Ohio River. There the governor intended to build a settlement similar to that at Natchez with a church, residences for a priest and a military commander, barracks, and other necessary structures, and he appealed to Wilkinson to send a few families to establish themselves at l'Ance à la Graisse. D'Argès, who was then in Santo Domingo, rejected the offer because of his age, but made the counter proposal that working out of New Orleans and with the rank of colonel, he could visit the families periodically.[37] Thus, with his characteristic demand for further consideration ended the d'Argès mission, and after his return to France in the summer of 1789, his name soon disappeared from Spanish dispatches.

Between 1787 and 1790, a number of persons in New Orleans and New York presented programs on how to increase the movement of people to Louisiana.[38] Spain, of course, readily accepted proposals from those who offered to bring in colonists without special consideration and at no expense to the exchequer. But the Spanish government refused to entertain projects involving expenditure of huge sums of money. It also denied the prospective immigration impresarios the right to sell land for personal profit, to guarantee freedom of religion, and to provide extensive privileges of self-government. Of the various schemes only that of Colonel George Morgan will be discussed here to illustrate the demands made and the reasons why Spanish policy was in opposition to them.[39]

In September, 1788, soon after the United States government rejected his claims to western lands, Morgan sent a memorial to Gardoqui in New York in which he discussed the creation of a settlement on the Mississippi. Because he was very much impressed by the colonel, the Spanish minister, undoubtedly expecting royal acceptance of the project, granted him permission to visit Louisiana to select a site for his colony. By early 1789 Morgan, who was then in upper Louisiana, had selected l'Ance à la Graisse, which he renamed New Madrid, for his projected settlement, circulated word in the American West that the Spanish government had given him an extensive land grant, and began the sale, at forty-eight dollars each, of lots of 320 acres. It was only after he had started his settlement that he wrote about his plans to Governor Miró in New Orleans.[40]

Miró learned of Morgan's unauthorized activities even before the colonel wrote and was aghast at the extent of them. There were many reasons why Miró could not accept Morgan's project. The governor saw no reason to allow the American to enrich himself by selling land the Crown gave away free; Morgan's self-governing settlement was contrary to Miró's principles since it would never engender any inclination on the part of the settlers to abide by Spanish laws and customs, because at the slightest jurisdictional dispute or attempt by the governor to exercise authority over them, they would declare themselves independent; and freedom of religion was against Spanish interests because the new colonists would never become Catholic. When Morgan arrived in New Orleans in May, the governor categorically rejected all of his plans, and he termed the project as equivalent to the creation of a "republic" which in fifty years would be independent. Miró's own plan for admitting Americans was a cautious attempt to develop the province with the only settlers available at no cost, but to have endorsed Morgan's enterprise would have been comparable to giving Louisiana away.[41]

Still the governor did not wish to alienate the colonel, and he hoped to use him to gain immigrants, but only under the existing regulations. He approved the land grants Morgan made to the persons who followed him to New Madrid, offered him employment as an agent to conduct families to New Madrid, and assured him that the Spanish government would reward him liberally for his services. Morgan, on his part, apologized for his previous behavior and accepted the offer. When he returned to the United States, he published a brochure describing the New Madrid settlement in glowing terms. The colonel, however, resented Miró's refusal to entertain his project, and he blamed Wilkinson and the enmity between the governor and Gardoqui for its failure. It is probable that Morgan accounted for few settlers going to Spanish territory because he soon abandoned his role as immigration agent.[42]

In addition to what Morgan had proposed, Governor Miró received a number of other projects from persons offering to bring in colonists, and he commissioned some of them to act as agents under the established laws. Unfortunately, not one of them was responsible for many settlers arriving in Louisiana, and, certainly, those settlers who came did so in fewer numbers than the horde that the Spanish officials anticipated. The agent Miró favored from the time he submitted his first memorial in 1787 was Wilkinson, and yet as the governor's chosen representative the brigadier was not devoted to the concept of emigration from Kentucky because it was contrary to his other scheme of separating the West from the United States.

After Wilkinson's departure from New Orleans in September, 1787, Miró sent repeated reminders to him to send colonists. In August, 1788, the governor advised him to instruct the settlers to bring a year's supply of food because Louisiana's harvest was expected to be small. After receiving the royal order of December 1, 1788, that accepted Wilkinson's second proposal, in early March, 1789, Miró informed the brigadier to commence sending the families immediately. In order to make Louisiana more attractive and to promote better relations with the American settlements, the governor instructed his agent to advertise the new low duty of 15 percent, and he added privately that he could reduce that sum for the "notables"[43]

Meanwhile, Wilkinson was filled with jealousy and suspicion of any possible rival and worked only halfheartedly for immigration. After learning of Morgan's project and the d'Argès mission, in letters to Miró, Wilkinson maligned them both; and later he included Benjamin Sebastian, whom he had previously recommended to the governor, in his attacks. In the area of immigration, Wilkinson insisted that it worked against the larger enterprise of securing the independence of the West. He was also against lowering the duty on imports to Louisiana because it created the false assumption that it was a prelude to the removal of all trade restrictions, and because the settlers would prefer to wait rather than emigrate.[44]

In New Orleans the governor patiently urged his agent to send settlers; he dismissed the notion that emigration from Kentucky injured the other project. In 1789 he wrote to the brigadier: "And thus, my friend, I only add that you will do a great service to His Majesty, if you induce a large number of families to come down the river, who have some property, and who do not need additional help, other than land."[45] He refused to believe that only poor families would come because of the 15 percent import duty. He added, optimistically, that already a number of colonists had arrived with slaves, and that others too had been established without any cost to the government. While the numbers were still modest, he retained hope of increased immigration.[46]

In April, 1789, goods belonging to the brigadier arrived in New Orleans, followed by Wilkinson himself who presented some fresh ideas. By the summer of 1789, he had adopted the position that it was preferable for Kentucky, once independent, to establish a formal connection with Spain rather than to come directly under Spanish dominion. His views concerning trade and immigration were more pessimistic. He argued that, by restricting trade in Kentucky to only a few persons, the Spanish government could promote secessionist fervor there, and he stated that the new tariff hurt immigration because many would prefer to pay it rather than leave Kentucky, so that he recommended withdrawing the 15 percent duty. But realizing that Miró was committed to encouraging immigration, Wilkinson produced an alternate solution: he would send confidential agents to spread the news of the favorable advantages of living in Louisiana, and, at the same time, they would attempt to convert the notables to the separatist cause. He calculated that the project would cost 7,000 *pesos*. Another alternative was to increase the government purchase of tobacco to 10,000,000 pounds annually.[47]

The flaw in Wilkinson's proposals was that they required money, and the governor adamantly refused to spend any unnecessary money. Since Miró refused to loosen the purse strings, the brigadier pleaded excessive expenditures in his operations and thus managed to pry loose the 7,000 *pesos*. But Miró outlined his immigration policy more concretely, reiterated that no costs were to be incurred, and avowed his certainty that if information were dispersed throughout the West of the reception and the advantages that the colonists would receive in Louisiana they would be sufficiently motivated to come. Although Wilkinson accepted these conditions, on his return to Kentucky he continued to demonstrate very little enthusiasm for this unremunerative assignment.[48]

Wilkinson's attitude had greatly disillusioned Miró by the end of 1790, and he saw that the plans were not progressing as rapidly as earlier anticipated. Not only was the conspiracy in Kentucky producing no results, but nothing was changed in respect to immigration. The governor complained to Captain General Luis de Las Casas in Havana that Wilkinson ceased to mention the families and that he merely proffered advice where it was not needed.[49]

Soon after that, in a letter to Spain, Las Casas expressed concern about the policy of permitting Americans to enter Louisiana. He was thus one of the first to question its wisdom. He considered the Americans in Louisiana to be too close to their own territory and hinted that since they still retained their language, customs, and religion, the consequences would prove fatal. The captain general proposed instead that these families be interspersed with Spanish settlers. He recognized that it was costly and that it would reduce Spain's population, but it had the merit of promoting tranquility in the province and helping insure its permanence to Spain.[50]

In December, 1790, Wilkinson sent the governor a letter detailing the reasons for the lack of immigration, and he confessed that for the last two months it was completely stopped and doubted if it could ever be started. But in February, 1791, he suddenly became optimistic and conjectured that the obstacles to emigration would soon vanish when the people learned the genuine nature of the king's goodwill.[51] The next month he declared to the governor of Natchez, Manual Gayoso, that, "It is with the most sensible pleasure I can assure you that Emigration begins again to rear its languid head," and he claimed that he too thought of going to Louisiana soon. Still he persisted in recommending that the river be closed to Americans mainly because Spanish purchase of American tobacco would injure immigration.[52]

Contrary to the brigadier's expectations, the "languid head" of emigration refused to "rear" itself, and the flow of colonists remained a trickle rather than the expected torrent.[53] As the year 1791 drew to a close, and with it Miró's tenure as governor, the friendship between the Spaniard and Wilkinson had waned considerably. By now the governor saw little likelihood of the West's defection, but he continued to cling to the prospect that American colonization in Louisiana, under the system he outlined years earlier, was the possible salvation of the province, and more importantly, of Mexico. In a report made in Spain in 1792 upon his retirement, he emphasized that it was preferable to permit Americans to settle peacefully in the colony in supervised establishments with priests and commanders rather than to resist them. He pointed out that geographically the Americans were already within the confines of the province since the drainage of the vast Mississippi basin constituted a unified region and that no bulwark could contain them if they chose to descend on the colony.[54]

The principal hope for Spanish retention of Louisiana was that Americans could be used to build a barricade against more of their kind in the United States. Governor Miró cherished the belief that those within Spanish territory could eventually be assimilated, but an ambitious project of this magnitude required time, and time was not on Spain's side. His successor, the baron de Carondelet, in order to protect the colony, revived the conspiracy of separating the American West, intrigued with Indians, and preferred Europeans to Americans in his immigration policy. Officially, Americans could still enter the province, but they were not given the encouragement they had received previously, when Miró was governor.[55]

Perhaps Miró's greatest contribution in devising an immigration policy for Louisiana was his foresight in resisting the temptation of conceding land in large grants to immigration agents who pledged themselves to introduce sizeable numbers of colonists. It was this practice, which Miró avoided, that a generation later caused Mexico so much sorrow in Texas.. He recognized the impossibility of acquiring colonists elsewhere and sought, through a wise effort of assimilation, to use Amricans to create a buffer province. Because of Spain's worldwide commitments and the turmoil resulting from the French Revolution, this plan was not developed as thoroughly as it might otherwise have been, and the projected Hispanization never achieved impressive results. Had Spain retained Louisiana and implemented Miró's proposals, the outcome might well have been considerably different from the Mexican experience of American colonization in Texas.

Notes for "The Immigration Policy of Governor Esteban Miró in Spanish Louisiana"

[1]While Miró and immigration in Louisiana have previously been studied, no one has appreciated his part in determining royal policy. To cite two examples: Arthur Preston Whitaker, *The Spanish American Frontier: 1783-1795* (Boston, 1927), 97-107, attributes immigration policy to the count of Floridablanca, the Spanish secretary of state, while Mattie Austin Hatcher, in "The Louisiana Background of the Colonization of Texas, 1763-1803," *Southwestern Historical Quarterly,* 24 (1921): 169-94, gives an early survey that does little to trace the development of policy.

[2]Vicente Rodriguez Casado, *Primeros años de la dominación española* (Madrid, 1947), 104-6; Lawrence Kinnaird, ed., *Spain in the Mississippi Valley, 1765-1795,* 3 vols. (Washington, 1946), 2:xxiii; Joseph de Loyola to Antonio de Ulloa, September, Archivo General de Indias (Seville), Papeles procedentes de Cuba, legajo 109, hereafter cited as AGI, PC.

[3]*Yndice,* May 26, 1774, AGI, PC, leg. 174A (the royal order is missing); "Ynstrucción reservada al Coronel Bernardo de Gálvez para su dirección en el Gobierno de la Provincia de la Luisiana" (n.d.), ibid., leg. 174B; John Walton Caughey, *Bernardo de Galvéz in Louisiana, 1776-1783* (Berkeley, 1934), 69.

[4]Andrés de Tortosa to Bernardo de Gálvez, February 17, 1779, AGI, PC, leg. 119; Martín Navarro to José de Gálvez, March 24, 1778, ibid., leg. 1,232.

[5]Fernando Solano Costa, "La emigración acadiana a la Luisiana española (1783-1785)," *Cuadernos de Historia Jerónimo Zurita,* 2 (1954): 85-125. A total of 1,598 persons came from France. Navarro to José de Gálvez, "Estado que manifiesta los nobres de los Barcos, número de Familias, y personas Acadianas existentes, desde 29 qe. Llego la l[era] Expedición, hasta el día de la fecha," December 12, 1785, AGI, PC, leg. 2,360, copy attached to Navarro's letter to José de Gálvez of the same date in AGI, PC, leg. 85.

[6]For example, Caughey, *Bernardo de Gálvez,* 81, states that in 1779, Spain spent 128,568 *pesos* on immigration costs when only 40,000 had been budgeted. Also see Charles H. Cunningham, ed., "Financial Reports Relating to Louisiana, 1766-1788," *Mississippi Valley Historical Review,* 6 (1919): 385; and Jack D. L. Holmes, "Some Economic Problems of Spanish Governors of Louisiana," *Hispanic American Historical Review,* 42 (1962): 521-43.

[7]Alejandro de Cantillo, *Tratados, convenios y declaraciones de paz y de commercio . . . desde el año de 1700 hasta el día* (Madrid, 1843), 587-88; Caroline Maude Burson, *The Stewardship of Don Esteban Miró, 1782-1792* (New Orleans, 1940), 24-25.

[8]Memorial of Harris Alexander *et al.* to the count of Gálvez (Bernardo de Gálvez), March 1, 1785, AGI, PC, leg. 2,352; Bernardo de Gálvez to Miró, October 20, 1785, ibid.

[9]Miró to Bernardo de Gálvez, September 5, 1785, Archivo Histórico National (Madrid), Estado, leg. 3,888bis, no. 2, hereafter cited as AHN, Est. In 1784 a census of the Natchez District revealed a population of 1,619. AGI, PC, leg. 116.

[10]Count of Gálvez to José Gálvez, October 27, 1785, AHN, Est., leg. 3,888bis, no. 56.

[11]Royal order to the count of Gálvez, April 5, 1786, ibid., no 37; royal order to the bishop of Salamanca, April 5, 1786, ibid.; Andrés, bishop of Salamanca, to the marquis of Sonora, September 28, 1786, ibid. The Irish priests were Michael Lamport, Gregory White, William Savage, and Constantine MacKenna. Ibid.

[12]Miró to Sonora, February 10, 1787, AHN, Est., leg. 3,888bis, no. 182; ibid., June 1, 1787, no. 81. In 1785 the inhabitants numbered by families, as follows: Second Creek, 55; Cole's Creek, 40; and Santa Catalina Creek, 180. The Natchez District then had about 1,100 whites and 900 slaves. Jack D. L. Holmes, *Gayoso, The Life of a Spanish Governor in the Mississippi Valley, 1789-1799* (Baton Rouge, 1965), 20.

[13]Jack D. L. Holmes, *Documentos inéditos para la historia de la Luisiana, 1792-1810* (Madrid, 1963), 29-30, n. 20.

[14]"Memorial of Pierre Rezard de Wouves d'Argès," March 18, 1787, AHN, Est., leg. 3,889, expediente 6. For other accounts of d'Argès, see Whitaker, *Spanish American Frontier*, 78-89, and Charles Gayarré, *History of Louisiana*, 4 vols. (New Orleans, 1885), 3:197-201.

[15]*Minuta*, AHN, Est., leg. 3,889, exped. 6.

[16]D'Argès to the count of Aranda, February 18, 1787, ibid.; "Memorial of d'Argès," ibid.

[17]Aranda to the count of Floridablanca, April 2, 1787, ibid., no. 594.

[18]Ibid.

[19]Whitaker, *Spanish American Frontier,* 80, 104-7.

[20]Ibid., 80-81.

[21]Floridablanca to Sonora, May 10, 1787, AHN, Est., leg. 3,889, exped. 6; *Minuta*, June 1, 1787, ibid.

[22]Sonora to Floridablanca, June 2, 1787, ibid.; royal order to Aranda, June 28, 1787, ibid.

[23]Royal order to the governor of Louisiana, August 23, 1787, ibid., no. 38.

[24]Ibid.

[25]Royal order to Diego de Gardoqui, September 5, 1787, AHN, Est., leg. 3,889, exped. 6.

[26]D'Argès to Gardoqui, January 19, 1788, ibid., no. 1; ibid., January 27, 1788, no. 2; ibid., January 31, 1788, no. 4.

[27]Gardoqui to d'Argès, February 1, 1788, ibid., no. 5; Gardoqui to Floridablanca, ibid., February 16, 1788; ibid., April 18, 1788, leg. 3893, no. 19 *reservada;* ibid., July 25, 1788, no. 20 *reservada.*

[28]The extensive literature on James Wilkinson includes: William R. Shepherd, "Wilkinson and the Beginnings of the Spanish Conspiracy," *American Historical Review*, 9 (1904): 490-506; Samuel Flagg Bemis, *Pinckney's Treaty: America's Advantage from Europe's Distress, 1783-1800,* rev. ed. (New Haven, 1960), 121-24; Whitaker, *Spanish American Frontier*, passim; Juan Navarro Latorre and Francisco Solano Costa, *Conspiración español¿ 1787-1789: Contribución al estudio de las primeras relaciones histórica entre España y los Estados Unidos de Norteamérica* (Zaragoza, 1949); Manuel Serrano y Sanz, *El Brigadier Jaime Wilkinson y sus tratos con España para la independencia del Kentucky* (Madrid, 1915), 19-20; and James Ripley Jacobs, *Tarnished Warrior: Major-General James Wilkinson* (New York, 1938).

[29]"Memorial of James Wilkinson," September 3, 1787, AHN, Est., leg. 3,889bis, no 52.

[30]Ibid.

[31]Miró and Navarro to the court, September 25, 1787, ibid., no. 13 *reservada*; Whitaker, *Spanish American Frontier*, 103-6.

[32]Miró to Antonio Valdés, January 8, 1788, AHN, Est., leg. 3,888bis; Miró to Carlos de Grand-Pré, February 2, 1788, ibid.

[33]Miró to Valdés, May 15, 1788, ibid.

[34]Navarro to Valdés, November 11, 20, 1788, ibid.

[35]Royal order to the governor of Louisiana, December 1, 1788, ibid.

[36]D'Argès to Anderson, June 15, 1788, ibid., leg. 3,889, exped. 6; Miró to Floridablanca, August 17, 1788, ibid., leg. 3,889bis; d'Argès to Miró, August 12, 1788, ibid.; Miró to Valdés, September 30, 1789, ibid., leg. 3,889, exped. 6.

[37]Miró to d'Argès, March 4, 1789, ibid., leg. 3889bis; Miró to Wilkinson, March 1, 1789, AGI, PC, leg. 174A; Miró to Valdés, February 12, 1789, AHN, Est., leg. 3, 889, exped. 6.

[38]Among those presenting immigration proposals were Agustin Macarty, William Fitzgerald, Maurico Nowland, Bryan Bruin and his son, Peter Bryan Bruin, James Kennedy, William Butler, and Peter Paulus. Much of the documentation can be found in the AHN, Est., legajos 3,888bis, 3,889, 3,889bis, and 3,894; however, in the AGI, PC, the material is very scattered. Hatcher, in "The Louisiana Background," concludes that because several persons were commissioned as immigration agents, they introduced large numbers of settlers. My own investigation has revealed otherwise.

[39]The literature concerning George Morgan is extensive. See Max Savelle, "The Founding of New Madrid, Missouri," *Mississippi Valley Historical Review*, 19 (1932): 30-56, and *George Morgan, Colony Builder* (New York, 1932); Fernando Solano Costa, "La Fundación de Nuevo Madrid," *Cuadernos de Historia Jerónimo Zurita*, 4-5 (1956): 91-108; and Louis Houck, *A History of Missouri from the Earliest Explorations and Settlements until the Admission of the State into the Union*, 3 vols. (Chicago, 1908), 2:108-29.

[40]Morgan to Gardoqui, August 30, 1788, AHN, Est., Leg. 3,894; "George Morgan Plan for Settlement," September, 1788, ibid.; Gardoqui to Valdés, October 4, 1788, ibid.; Morgan to Miró, April 14, 1789, ibid., leg. 3,888bis; E. G. Swem, "A Letter from New Madrid, 1789," *Mississippi Valley Historical Review*, 5 (1918): 342-46.

[41]Miró to Valdés, May 20, 1789, AHN, Est., leg. 3,888bis, no. 39 *reservada*; ibid., June 12, 1789, no. 41 *reservada.*

[42]Miró to Morgan, May 23, 1789, ibid., leg. 3,888bis; "Commission from Stephen Miró to Colonel George Morgan," May 29, 1789, in Louis Houck, ed., *Spanish Regime in Missouri,* 2 vols. (Chicago, 1909), 1:308-9. A pamphlet on New Madrid is in the AGI, PC, leg. 2,364. In a census report of December 1, 1797, the population was given as 615. "Statistical Census of New Madrid of 1797," in Houck, ed., *Spanish Regime*, 2:393-97.

[43]Miró to Wilkinson, August 6, 1788, AGI, PC, leg. 2,372; ibid., March 1, 1789, leg. 174A.

[44]Wilkinson to Miró, February 14, 1789, AHN, Est., leg. 3,888bis, no. 218; ibid., February 12, 1789; Wilkinson to Miró, February 6, 1791, AGI, PC, leg. 2, 374.

[45]Miró to Wilkinson, April 11, 1789, AHN, Est., leg. 3,888bis.

[46]Miró to Valdés, April 11, 1789, AGI, PC, leg. 177A.

[47]"Wilkinson Memorial of 1789," September, 1789, AHN, Est., leg. 3,886, exped 1.

[48]Miró to Wilkinson, September 18, 1789, ibid., leg. 3,886, exped. 6; ibid., September 22, 1789.

[49]Miró to Captain General Luis de Las Casas; December 7, 1790, ibid., leg. 3,898.

[50]Las Casas to the count of Campo de Alange, February 17, 1791, ibid.

[51]Wilkinson to Miró, February 14, 1791, February 17, 1791, AGI, PC, leg. 2,374.

[52]Wilkinson to Manuel Gayoso, March 17, 1791, ibid., leg. 2,374.

[53]A census of June 14, 1792, showed that the Natchez District had approximately 4,691 inhabitants, but the next year the population dropped to 4,446. In 1796 Gayoso placed the district's residents at 5,318. Holmes, *Gayoso,* 116. By way of comparison, Kentucky's population leaped from 73,677 in 1790 to 220,955 in 1800, while Tennessee in the same period grew from 35,691 to 105,602. *World Almamac* (1968 centennial ed., New York, 1967), 260.

[54]Esteban Miró to the count of Campo de Alange, August 11, 1792, in Holmes, *Documentos inéditos*, 26-27. Miró also stated that, although immigration had not developed as had been anticipated, Louisiana's population had increased by 25,000 during his ten-year administration: in 1782 it was 20,000, and by 1792, it had passed 45,000, ibid., 24.

[55]Baron Francisco de Carondelet to Aranda, June 10, 1792, AHN, Est., leg. 3,898, no 1 *reservada*. For views regarding the unwillingness of Americans to emigrate and the assimilation of those who did, see Whitaker, *Spanish American Frontier,* 157-162, and Holmes, *Gayoso*, 196-97, 272.

SPAIN'S IMMIGRATION POLICY IN LOUISIANA AND THE AMERICAN PENETRATION, 1792-1803*

Gilbert C. Din

"I wish a hundred thousand of our inhabitants would accept the invitation. It may be the means of delivering to us peaceably what may otherwise cost a war."[1] With these words Thomas Jefferson, writing to President George Washington, greeted the Spanish invitation of 1788 to Anglo-Americans to settle in Louisiana. This change in Spanish policy signaled the beginning of Anglo-American penetration of Louisiana. Because settlement with Spaniards and European Catholics had proved to be too costly, Spain was resorting reluctantly to Anglo-American colonization. The government planned, in permitting entry of Anglo-Americans, to Hispanize them, convert them to Catholicism, and instill in them sufficient loyalty so that they would defend the colony against all invaders—even invaders from the United States.[2] However the implementation of this new and potentially dangerous policy required an era of peace, and peace did not exist in that region during the 1790s. Instead Louisiana experienced numerous crises as it was menaced in turn by the French, the British, and the Anglo-Americans. Concurrently, the rapid growth of the western settlements of the United States brought Anglo-Americans closer to Louisiana. As they entered and threatened to inundate the colony, worried Spanish officials began to doubt that the Anglo-Americans in Louisiana would defend the province against attack from the United States. As early as 1792, Louisiana governors sought ways to augment the colony's non-American population. For a decade local authorities struggled with the question of Anglo-American immigration and promoted colonization schemes to increase the province's loyal population. In the end, the war Jefferson thought might come was averted as Spain retroceded the colony to France, which in turn soon sold it to the United States.

The changed attitude toward Anglo-American colonization in Louisiana and West Florida began immediately after Francisco Luís Hector, baron of Carondelet, became

*This article first appeared in the *Southwestern Historical Quarterly*, 76 (1973): 335-76. Reprinted here with the kind permission of the author and publisher.

governor of these provinces on December 30, 1791.[3] Only two weeks after assuming the governorship, he recommended to Madrid that Europeans be encouraged to come to Louisiana and, contrary to earlier Spanish policy against making expenditures to bring in immigrants, he urged that they be assisted in their settlement, beyond being given free lands, a liberal commercial policy, and religious tolerance. While the baron did not suggest stopping Anglo-American immigration—believing it impossible to do—he and subsequent governors were very much concerned about becoming outnumbered by what they increasingly regarded as a subversive element.[4] Thus with Carondelet, immigration policy reverted to securing a loyal European Catholic population, one which would be compatible with Spanish rule and monarchical government.

Through the spring of 1792, Governor Carondelet continued to promote the immigration policy he thought was best for the colonies in his charge. He began issuing announcements which favored the admittance of French émigrés, and Irish, Flemish, and German immigrants. When he learned that growing numbers of these people were arriving in the United States, he exhorted the court to bring them to Louisiana and advised making "small expenditures," such as furnishing their transportation from New Madrid in Upper Louisiana to their new homes down river, and supplying them with food and seed. He believed that once the first settlers were established, the malicious lies that existed about the tyranny of the Spanish government would be dissipated. The governor warned against permitting Anglo-Americans to swarm into Louisiana and seize it without "unsheathing the sword." He scoffed at the oaths of allegiance Anglo-Americans took upon settling in the province, stating that they would easily turn against Spain despite the oaths. Because of their unreliability, Carondelet decided to exert every effort to impede their settlement on the west bank of the Mississippi and to admit them only with moderation on the east bank.[5] In accordance with this aim, he stopped the projected settlement of Alexander Fowler on the Maramec River in Upper Louisiana, but he still allowed Anglo-Americans to settle on the Amité River in Lower Louisiana.[6]

In order to attract European immigrants in the United States to Louisiana, the governor dispatched two agents there. The first to leave was Captain Henri Peyroux de La Coudrenière, who earlier had brought Acadian families from France. On April 6, 1792, Peyroux received a copy of the conditions under which French, German, Irish, or Flemish immigrants would be admitted into the province. Soon he departed for Philadelphia aboard the *Amable María* with the promise of promotion to lieutenant colonel and an increase in salary if he was successful in his mission.[7]

Meanwhile in Philadelphia the Spanish ministers to the United States, Josef de Jáudenes and Josef de Viar, were discreetly attempting to direct French royalists and German and Dutch Catholics to Louisiana. They purposely avoided advertising in the city's newspapers for fear of offending the United States government. With the arrival of Peyroux, they believed that a general exodus of persons bound for Louisiana would begin if the Crown provided their transportation and if Anglo-American merchants were permitted to send merchandise to Louisiana.[8]

Once in Philadelphia Captain Peyroux went to work. He commissioned a brigantine to take colonists to New Orleans. But when Jáudenes and Viar learned that the ship carried only twenty-five immigrants while taking 1,040 barrels of flour, they sternly warned him against allowing this to happen again. By letter Peyroux protested and informed the ministers they had misinterpreted his actions. He assured them he would soon go to Philadelphia and personally explain what had happened. However, the Frenchman departed for Delaware, instead, neither justifying his behavior nor attempting to acquire more immigrants.[9]

Carondelet's second agent was Thomas Wooster. Two years earlier Wooster had attempted to secure permission to take colonists to St. Augustine in East Florida. Although the proposal was rejected, he settled in Louisiana where he became a captain of militia. In June, 1792, he left for the United States to attend to private matters, at the same time agreeing to send colonists back.[10] In Philadelphia Jáudenes and Viar at first considered him better suited than Peyroux to the task inasmuch as he spoke English. But Captain Wooster's peculiar behavior soon disappointed the Spanish officials. Instead of openly soliciting for colonists, he posted a notice on a cafe wall announcing that anyone wishing a passport to New Orleans or desiring to become a Spanish citizen could obtain information from him. Appalled by this news, the ministers published in the local newspapers denials of their having any connection with Wooster and stated that only they were authorized to issue Spanish passports. Wooster's effectiveness as an immigration agent ended—and, in any case, he was soon jailed for debts.[11]

With the failure of the missions of these two agents, Carondelet abandoned this method of acquiring colonists from the United States. It probably would have been necessary to furnish them with transportation, and the Spanish government several years previously had determined not to spend money on immigration. Furthermore, since it did not want to be accused by the United States of stealing its population, Spain moved very cautiously. Consequently, the Crown issued a royal order which ended express commissions to individuals to acquire colonists in the United States.[12] However, Governor Carondelet did not give up his efforts to gain colonists and continued to listen to proposals he received in New Orleans.

In the summer of 1792, he learned from several sources that a substantial number of French émigrés were present in the western United States settlement of Gallipolis. The colony, established under the auspices of the Scioto Company, had foundered, leaving the royalists in considerable hardship and exposed to Indian raids. Since the settlement was dying, Friar Josef Didier, a Benedictine monk, and twenty others left Gallipolis in order to resettle in Spanish territory. In New Madrid the Frenchmen were well received by the Spanish authorities. Encouraged by the friendly reception, Didier wrote to the governor in New Orleans in June and applied for permission for other Gallipolis émigrés to enter Louisiana. Carondelet readily acceded to his request. Over the next several years a steady stream of Frenchmen arrived in Upper Louisiana.[13]

A month after Didier penned his letter to Carondelet, another Frenchman, Barthélemi Tardiveau, a merchant of fifteen years' residence in the United States, also wrote to the governor about securing for Louisiana the colonists of Gallipolis. From Kaskaskia, Tardiveau warned Carondelet against allowing Anglo-Americans to settle on Spanish lands and urged the fortifying of the west bank of the Mississippi with loyal settlers. Besides offering to bring the Gallipolis émigrés, he suggested that he travel to Europe and recruit colonists from among the French refugees to be found there in several nations. He asserted that merely through the nominal cost of his commission, Louisiana could gain some 300,000 French immigrants. Despite his exaggerated claim, the governor approved his suggestion and invited him to New Orleans. Carondelet authorized him to bring merchandise to defray the cost of his journey. The baron also promised Tardiveau two thousand *pesos* if he would go to Madrid to present his project personally at court.[14]

The governor was then enthusiastic about some German families which had recently arrived from Philadelphia and which he had settled at Galveztown, giving them houses and rations for a year. He informed the count of Aranda, the minister of state, that he would continue to establish German and Flemish families at Galveztown until they numbered a hundred. It was the governor's intention to distribute colonists along the length of Lower Louisiana, on both banks of the Mississippi, from the river's mouth to Nogales, over three hundred miles upstream.[15]

Although Tardiveau did not make the trip to Europe because of turmoil in France, he was in New Orleans the following spring, where he presented the governor with a memorial requesting a loan for the construction of a wheat mill in New Madrid. Carlos DeHault deLassus and Pedro Audrain were to be his partners in this venture. Besides their proposal for the mill, the partners volunteered to conduct the Gallipolis families to Louisiana, if the government would pay for the immigrants' transportation costs and rations until their first crop was harvested. The petitioners asked that the new settlement be named New Bourbon. Governor Carondelet made a contract with the three men, in which he loaned them 9,000 *pesos* with which to build two mills on the condition that they supply the province with 6,000 barrels of flour for ten years at a fair price. The Frenchmen also accepted the responsibility of bringing a hundred families from Gallipolis, for which they received an additional loan of 2,500 *pesos*, plus the cost of transporting the families to their new homes.[16]

Soon the partners left New Orleans in order to fulfill their contract. Audrian, charged with bringing the Gallipolis colonists, traveled by sea to Philadelphia and then overland to the American west while his two associates ascended the Mississippi. DeHault deLassus received the civil and military command of New Bourbon, which soon came into existence. Carondelet expressed much faith in this project and glowingly termed it "an epoch in the annals of this Province, and perhaps in Septentrional America." He hailed it as the start of halting the Anglo-American and English advance and the preservation of Louisiana intact.[17]

About the same time that Tardiveau made his proposal, Jacques Clamorgan of St. Louis made an offer to increase Upper Louisiana's population. His was the type of project which the Spanish Crown could not accept because of the heavy expenditures it required. Clamorgan wanted to charter ships to bring German colonists from Europe to Philadelphia and then overland to Spanish territory. The immigrants were to be provided with land, poultry, oxen, cows, implements, and rations for ten months, which technically the settlers were obligated to regard as purchased on credit and to pay for later. Clamorgan presumed that his enterprise could bring a thousand families to Upper Louisiana.[18] However, this proposal, like so many others of its kind, was not accepted.

From 1793 on, Louisiana's problems began to increase noticeably. A lull in the presentation of immigration proposals coincided with the threat of invasion. The danger stemmed from the activities of Citizen Edmond Genêt, the revolutionary French government's minister to the United States, who was scheming with American frontiersmen to attack the province. Moreover, Governor Carondelet faced internal turmoil as French Jacobins began cropping up in Louisiana. Despite his expulsion of a number of these overly zealous republicans and his restrictions on their entry into the province, he found tranquillity difficult to maintain. On one occasion Carondelet summoned the Anglo-American militia from Natchez to preserve order in New Orleans.[19] Besides the problem of unrest among the French Creoles, tension existed within the ranks of the slaves, who were about as numerous as the whites. The abortive slave insurrection of 1795 at Pointe Coupée led to the governor's ban on the importation of slaves. In the midst of all this unrest, Carondelet tried to promote a freer trade policy in order to reduce dissatisfaction among the established residents and in order to encourage new immigrants. However, since it was imperative that the new settlers be loyal to the Spanish government, European colonization was given even greater encouragement than had been the case in the past.[20]

In June, 1794, the baron emphasized the urgency of populating Louisiana and stressed the need to retain the colony and to safeguard Mexico. He suggested that each ship bound for New Orleans transport from six to eight German or Flemish settlers. He also advised opening the Mississippi to trade to obtain in this way the defection of the American West. Several months later, in November, he dispatched a lengthy *informe* to the court in which he reiterated the necessity to stimulate trade and to increase the colony's population.[21] Soon the governor received an immigration proposal which he actively promoted.

The plan Carondelet favored belonged to a refugee Frenchman, the marquis of Maison Rouge. Only shortly before, Maison Rouge had arrived in Louisiana, claiming to represent other *émigrés* in the United States. He brought with him several settlers, agricultural tools, and materials for a sawmill. In a proposal which the marquis soon made to the governor, he stated his plan to begin a wheat-growing settlement in Ouachita, which would also be useful in the defense of Louisiana.[22] Carondelet quickly endorsed the project, and he agreed to pay the transportation costs of Maison Rouge's settlers from

New Madrid to Ouachita and the cost of their rations as well. The governor also proposed to do this for all new settlers to Louisiana. Moreover, he reprimanded Commandant Thomas Portell of New Madrid for having temporarily detained the marquis's party, and instructed Portell to permit all French royalist, Dutch, Flemish, Irish, German, or any other European immigrants to enter and settle in Louisiana, including Anglo-American farmers and artisans. However, French republicans and Jacobins were to be kept out or expelled if they were already in the colony.[23]

Maison Rouge's contract obligated him to bring in only thirty agricultural families, each of which would receive a cash bonus of a hundred *pesos* once it had settled down in Louisiana. The Crown also agreed to pay the transportation costs for 3,000 pounds of baggage per family which came by sea to New Orleans and then was sent up to Ouachita. Thirty square leagues of land were set aside for Maison Rouge's colonists.[24] Although Carondelet believed the contract would bring in many of the right kind of settlers, it proved to be disappointing. Despite the governor's order excluding Anglo-Americans and Irishmen, some came in nonetheless.[25] After the court had approved the contract, the marquis brought fewer colonists than the governor had expected: thirty-one brought by Augustus de Breard in 1796, and twenty-two more the following year. Moreover, not all of them were agricultural workers: some were Anglo-Americans, and slaves made up about twenty of the total number.[26] Maison Rouge's failure to live up to the terms of the contract raised suspicion about his real purpose for being in the colony; Commandant Carlos de Grand-Pré at Avoyelles doubted that the marquis would remain long in the province.[27] Although he stayed in Louisiana until his death in 1799, Maison Rouge did very little to justify the great enthusiasm with which Governor Carondelet had initially greeted his proposal.

About the same time that Maison Rouge's settlement at Ouachita was beginning, several other proposals to bring in colonists reached the governor. In April, 1795, Joseph Piernas, a former officer in the Louisiana Regiment, offered to establish, at his own expense, five hundred loyal Irish and German agricultural families on the Calcasieu River, near the Gulf of Mexico and about thirty-six miles east of the Sabine River. Piernas pledged to construct within eight years a village of three hundred persons, which would have a church with a priest, a surgeon, and a schoolmaster. Besides this he would also maintain a guard at the mouth of the Calcasieu River. Piernas requested the duty-free entry of 30,000 *pesos* worth of merchandise for each fifty families that came, land for the settlement, and all the privileges entitled to him as the founder of the colony.[28] Although Carondelet endorsed the plan and the court approved it in 1798, no settlement resulted. In 1799 Piernas again attempted to promote his project. On this occasion, he authorized Calvin Adams to bring in two hundred Dutch and Irish Catholic families. Once more, however, his scheme failed and no settlement was founded.[29]

In July, 1795, Captain Luis de Vilemont, a Frenchman in Spain's service, also presented a plan for bringing in colonists. Vilemont had arrived in Philadelphia the previous year purportedly to study natural history. In Louisiana he talked with the governor and doubtlessly was influenced by him inasmuch as Vilemont's proposal called for bringing French, Dutch, German, and Flemish refugees. The baron gave the project his hearty approval. In his memorial, Vilemont pointed out the emptiness of Louisiana and the rapid increase in population of the United States's western settlements. He warned against letting in Anglo-Americans and non-Catholics, terming such action the settling of the Goths at the gate of Rome, and predicting that they would usurp the colony. Instead, preferred Europeans should be brought to Louisiana aboard Spanish naval vessels and a settlement made similar to that at Natchez, where Anglo-Americans resided. The Europeans could settle in villages similar to those in their native lands and could retain their customs and languages. Vilemont foretold that the increase in population would stimulate commerce greatly and convert Louisiana into the granary of the Spanish colonies.[30]

In Spain the Vilemont project was not considered until after the signing of the Treaty of San Lorenzo between Spain and the United States, which marked the start of Spain's retreat in the Mississippi Valley and the reduced importance of Louisiana. It was not surprising, therefore, that the Council of State on November 13, deemed the proposal impractical because of the great cost it entailed, the impossibility of allowing religious tolerance (which he asked for), the discontent it would engender in France, England, and Holland where the colonists would be recruited, and finally, Vilemont's incorrect assumption that Louisiana's defense was vital for Mexico. The rejection clearly reflected Louisiana's diminished importance in Spanish diplomacy.[31]

The last proposal of 1795 came in December and was presented by a Mr. Butler, who was a friend of Josef de Jáudenes, the Spanish minister, and who wished to become an immigration impresario. Butler desired Spanish approval of his ownership of land he sought to buy from the heirs of recently deceased Jonathan Bryan, who had obtained it from the Creek Indians. Butler was also prepared to journey, armed with maps, to Flanders where he would sell tracts of land. He proposed that the Spanish government obtain the Creeks' consent to the land exchange by providing them with gifts. The Crown was to pay for Butler's trip to Europe, the gifts to the Indians, maps, surveying expenses, all of which he calculated would cost 40,000 *pesos*.[32] The lack of further information about this project seems to indicate that the Spanish government did not show much interest in it.

However, a possible result of Butler's plan was one made by Josef de Jáudenes, which was very similar. Jáudenes also proffered a land-selling scheme to attract European immigrants to Louisiana, but one which would have entailed no cost to the Crown. Land agents were to be placed in the principal European cities and newspaper advertising was to induce the public to buy land. Spanish consuls would issue titles to the land. Once in Louisiana the settlers would take oaths of loyalty and vassalage to Spain. While Jáudenes stated that the United States government engaged in such practices without engendering any complaints from foreign nations, the Spanish government, nevertheless, refrained from entering into any land promotion schemes to gain settlers for its North American colony.[33]

Spain acted cautiously in the mid-1790s because it was at war with Britain. Even in the far-off Mississippi Valley, Spaniards feared invasion from the United States or Canada. In order to gain an ally and settle disagreements, Manuel Godoy, the minister of state, decided to reach an accord with the United States. By the Treaty of San Lorenzo of October, 1795, Spain accepted the thirty-first parallel as the boundary line from the Spanish Floridas, gave the Americans the use of the river, and granted them the right of deposit at New Orleans. The treaty resulted in the loss of the principal Spanish defenses in northern Lower Louisiana, which really mattered little to Godoy as he was now guided only by the wish to obtain the best possible terms in disposing of Louisiana. Inasmuch as the colony's interests were not being defended in Europe, it fell to local officials to protect the province as best they could. When news of the treaty reached New Orleans, Governor Carondelet held back surrendering the posts, an act which Madrid belatedly and temporarily sustained. But Spanish procrastination in giving up the posts combined with Anglo-American impatience produced the Natchez revolt of 1797. The next year Spain relinquished control of the lands stipulated in the 1795 treaty.[34]

Besides surrendering the Spanish forts, the Treaty of San Lorenzo decreased Lower Louisiana's security, because the Natchez District of West Florida, which contained many Anglo-Americans, passed to the United States. This population problem partially explains Carondelet's attempt to build up Ouachita, not far away, with a European population loyal to Spain. However, at about this time the governor temporarily shifted ground on Anglo-American immigration to Louisiana. After 1795 the immediate enemy was Britain. Consequently, the governor encouraged United States frontiersmen to come to Louisiana to build up the colony's defenses against possible invasion from Canada. He issued advertisements to Anglo-Americans to settle in the province; and when William Murray presented his proposal in New Orleans in 1796, Carondelet endorsed it.[35]

Murray represented a group of Kentucky speculators, who included Harry Innes, Benjamin Sebastian, and others involved in James Wilkinson's plot to separate Kentucky from the United States. While the real intent of Murray's group was to acquire a ten-million-acre land grant, they claimed discontent with the Untied States government as the motive for inquiring about the formation of a settlement of 4,000 families. The group believed that with a liberal trade policy the project could be realized within six years. Murray asked that the settlers be permitted to regulate their community and be permitted to select their own officials. The governor rejected this stipulation; but in all other respects he approved the project.[36] Carondelet's endorsement of this proposal raises a question about his motives inasmuch as the plan was obviously designed to acquire a huge land grant for purposes of speculation. Possibly his true reason in accepting the proposal was his wish to keep alive the Wilkinson conspiracy. However, since Murray's plan was so much at variance with previous immigration and land policy, there should not have been much expectation that Madrid would approve it.[37]

The immigration proposals Governor Carondelet most favored were those made by European noblemen, such as that of the spurious Dutch aristocrat the baron de Bastrop,

Philip Hendrik Nering Bögel. In his first communication to Carondelet, brought to Louisiana by Maison Rouge, Bastrop proposed bringing directly from Europe three hundred Dutch families. He wanted, by way of assistance, fifty *pesos* for each white working person he brought.[38] His proposal delighted the governor who quickly obtained Intendant Francisco Rendón's approval of it. Carondelet authorized Bastrop to bring in the families immediately without waiting for a time-delaying court approval. In 1795 the bogus baron came to Louisiana with the settlers that Augustus de Breard brought to Ouachita for Maison Rouge.[39] The following year he requested from the governor a land grant of twelve square leagues on which to establish the families he proposed to bring, granting each one a maximum of 400 arpents (336 acres) for the cultivation of wheat. Inasmuch as his settlers in this proposal were to come from the United States, he wanted their transportation and rations from New Madrid to be paid for by the Crown as well as rations for several additional months. Carondelet accepted these terms in a contract made on June 21, 1796, reserving the right to reclaim lands that had not been ceded after three years.[40] Soon Bastrop left Louisiana for Kentucky where he had business interests.

Over the next several years Bastrop's immigration efforts and business ventures achieved only modest success. In the spring of 1797, the baron descended the Mississippi with ninety-nine persons. By April 19 he was in Ouachita where he spent a few days settling the colonists he brought before continuing on to New Orleans to lay new plans before the governor. Carondelet approved Bastrop's plan to build up Ouachita with European settlers as a barrier against the Americans of Natchez and he was willing to spend money to do so. However, he was dependent on the intendancy to grant the funds needed. In June the governor made a lengthy exposition to the intendant of the advantages to be gained in supporting Bastrop's project. Carondelet also requested money to supply the baron's settlers with rations for six months and to reimburse him for his expenses in bringing them from New Madrid. The message was the first inkling the acting new intendant, Juan Ventura Morales, had of Bastrop's second project.[41]

Morales disapproved of Carondelet's plans for Bastrop. The intendant informed the governor that there were no funds for the project because of the war in Europe. Furthermore, Morales called a meeting of the Royal Treasury Council, and it also opposed acting on Bastrop's project until Madrid could either approve or reject it. Although the governor was disappointed by Morales's decision, he urged Godoy to accept Bastrop's plan, terming the cost modest and necessary to increase the production of flour and to prevent a slave uprising or an Anglo-American revolt. The intendant did allow the governor to pay for the colonists already in Ouachita and for their rations. However, the Bastrop commission was suspended. Morales warned that Bastrop would only bring Anglo-American Protestants, not Europeans or Catholics, and that Ouachita was unsuitable for the cultivation of wheat.[42]

After his initial effort to bring colonists failed to receive the proper authorization, Bastrop made two additional proposals. In October, 1797, he requested permission to bring in five hundred families aboard five or six ships. While the new governor, Manuel

Gayoso de Lemos, approved the project, Intendant Morales did not, and the baron soon abandoned it. Bastrop next tried to sell to Colonel Abraham Morhouse his "rights" to the land grant which had been set aside for the colonists he was to bring. However, the Spanish government rejected his claim to ownership and the Dutchman drew up a new offer to bring colonists. By this proposal made in 1800, he would bring five hundred families and pay for all their travel expenses, rations, and costs of settlement. He pledged to accomplish the project in five years. Bastrop also requested the land he had previously solicited from Carondelet. This time the baron intended to bring in slaves to raise cotton and to work in cotton gins. The new governor, now the marquis of Casa-Calvo, approved the plan.[43] Bastrop at this time proposed to sell part of his land grant to Morhouse, but the new intendant, Ramón López y Angulo, suspecting that Bastrop wanted to leave the colony after making the sale, refused to permit it. Furthermore, López y Angulo halted the sale of all land grants. He also blocked Bastrop's purchase of a cypress forest from Juan Filhio; the baron had intended to build a sawmill and supply the province with lumber.[44] Stymied in his efforts, Bastrop returned to Ouachita to construct a forge for the production of iron. The next year he obtained an exclusive license for trade with the Indians and a partnership in the New Orleans firm of Lille Sarpy Colsson and Company. Although filled with entrepreneurial spirit, Bastrop was plagued by business reverses. This was especially true after the United States took over control of Louisiana in 1803. Less than two years later the baron de Bastrop departed for Texas, following the withdrawing Spanish flag.[45]

In August, 1797, Carondelet's term as governor of Louisiana ended and he left for his new post as president of the Quito Audiencia. For five and a half years he had attempted to build the colony's population, particularly through the acquisition of European settlers. While he received a number of proposals to bring in Europeans, they usually required spending government money which was not available or not permitted by the Crown. Toward the end of his term, Anglo-American immigration to Louisiana increased considerably, stimulated in part by the governor's own efforts. But Spanish officials after Carondelet worried very much about this influx and feared that the Anglo-Americans would engulf the province. Therefore, not surprisingly, in the last years of Spanish rule local officials tried to deter such settlement. Desperately and in vain, they also sought to acquire the kind of colonists who would preserve the province for Spain.

When Manuel Gayoso de Lemos assumed the governorship in August, 1797, he was confronted by more problems with fewer resources than Carondelet had faced in 1792. Anglo-Americans were now in Natchez, across the river from Lower Louisiana. Spanish fortifications were virtually nonexistent and military strength was barely sufficient to maintain internal order. Moreover, in Spain there was little support for safeguarding Louisiana. By 1796 Minister of State Godoy was prepared to sell the province at the first opportune moment. In 1797, when the Spanish minister in Philadelphia, Carlos Martínez de Irujo, informed Godoy about William Blount's threat to invade Louisiana, the minister of state wrote on Irujo's dispatch, "You can't lock up the countryside."[46] Years earlier Spain had stopped spending money to foster immigration to the colony; now there was not even money to spend on its defense.

During his administration, Governor Gayoso was even more adamant in his opposition to American immigration than Carondelet had been. Undoubtedly the Natchez rebellion in 1797 had convinced him that most Anglo-Americans could not be relied upon to become loyal Spaniards. The oath of allegiance they took on entering Louisiana meant nothing to them. Therefore, for two years as governor, Gayoso attempted to acquire only selected American immigrants.

From September, 1797, Gayoso began issuing instructions to post commandants on the admittance of immigrants and on land grants. Unmarried and propertyless settlers could not receive land immediately; they first had to show their willingness to work for several years. Gayoso also abrogated the previous policy of religious tolerance and stated that henceforth tolerance would be granted only for the present generation; their children would be required to become Catholic. Those unwilling to accept this condition were to leave Louisiana immediately. Furthermore, anyone who was not a Catholic farmer, artisan, or a person of importance who had held a public office in the United States, would no longer be admitted in the province.[47]

Until his death Governor Gayoso remained preoccupied with the Anglo-American penetration of Louisiana. Using the "Natchez example," he pointed out to the commandant of New Madrid that an indiscriminate admittance of Anglo-American settlers would inundate the "old and good inhabitants of this country." He advised allowing only useful and trustworthy persons in the province. He realized how difficult the task would be inasmuch as Spaniards were few in the colony, but he hoped that future generations would become Hispanized. In numbers Spaniards ranked after the French and Americans. Because Louisiana's defenses were weak, he considered it imperative that a disloyal element not arise in the colony.[48] Upper Louisiana's small population was particularly susceptible to being overrun by the Anglo-Americans. Lieutenant Governor Zenon Trudeau of Upper Louisiana believed it desirable to acquire colonists from any available source, which for him was the Ohio Valley where Germans, Irishmen, and French *émigrés* resided as well as United States citizens disillusioned with their own government. Like Commandant James Mackay of St. Andrew on the Missouri, Trudeau recommended restoring religious tolerance. In mid-1798 he blamed the virtual halt of immigrants to Louisiana on Gayoso's new regulation on religion.[49]

However, the governor was unmoved by Trudeau's exhortation and believed that the danger extended beyond Louisiana to New Spain also. Gayoso counseled caution in building up the colony's population and felt it preferable to wait for the right kind of settlers rather than court disaster with the wrong ones. He also remained intransigent on the point that new immigrants be Catholic. Even if no colonists arrived, he considered it imperative that the king's orders be obeyed. However, he advised Trudeau to preserve the friendship of his settlers and remove any pretext they might have for complaint.[50]

Because he desired to obtain colonists from a new source, Gayoso suggested that Trudeau contact persons who traded in Canada and induce them to bring families from there to settle in Upper Louisiana. Any agent bringing in French Canadian families would receive ten arpents (8.4 acres) for each one hundred granted to new families. The agents could dispose of these lands in any way they wished, except by selling them to persons residing outside the province. Gayoso did not expect an immediate influx of French Canadians because Spain was then at war with Britain. Nevertheless, he did anticipate their coming after the war and advised Trudeau to continue his efforts to acquire them.[51]

In July, 1799, not long before he died, Governor Gayoso expressed his last thoughts on the question of immigration. He urged Intendant Morales not to permit any new settlements to be established until peace prevailed again. He rejected the idea of populating Louisiana with Anglo-Americans, and even showed doubt about letting in any settlers until the war ended. He was opposed to Anglo-American immigration because only those unhappy with the United States government would come, a group he described as disorderly, vice-ridden, and probable disseminators of new and unwanted ideas. He considered that present circumstances did not warrant allowing colonists in Louisiana. Gayoso, therefore, recommended to the court against innovation and the establishment of new settlements. He felt that the Crown could either make Louisiana a military bastion against Anglo-American immigration or permit United States settlers to come. However, if such settlers were allowed to come to Louisiana, he suggested that it be done in such a manner that Louisiana would not be lost nor the downfall of Mexico precipitated.[52]

Gayoso's last remarks clearly delineated the hazards Louisiana faced and the vexing problem of Anglo-American immigration. Virtually on their own resources, some Louisiana officials attempted to stem the flow of Anglo-Americans into the province, while in Spain the Crown thought only of getting rid of the colony, which it did in 1800. Gayoso's death in 1799 also ended the era of strong governors who were dedicated to the preservation of Spanish authority in Louisiana. After his death caretaker administrations followed which merely presided over the colony until the transfer to France was completed in 1803.

As interim governor the marquis of Casa-Calvo, who succeeded Gayoso, did very little to establish an immigration policy. He made only a slight effort to halt the Anglo-American advance into Louisiana. Although he advised commandants to eject from their districts such immigrants who had settled without proper authority, he appeared reluctant to prevent new settlements on the west bank of the Mississippi as earlier governors had done. The last governor of Louisiana, Manuel Juan de Salcedo, replaced Casa-Calvo in June, 1801. He, too, exerted little influence during his two-year term.[53]

In these last years of Spanish dominion over Louisiana, the intendancy came to exercise increased authority in matters of immigration and land grants. Morales was the first intendant to assert the prerogatives of his office during the Carondelet administration, and later he also plagued Gayoso with querulous opposition on even the most trivial matters. As Carondelet challenged the intendant's sole right to grant lands, the Crown intervened to settle this dispute. In 1798 the king sustained the intendant's competency in this area. Morales celebrated his victory by issuing elaborate instructions on the granting of land, which were aimed to make it difficult for Anglo-Americans to obtain land.[54]

In the time of Casa-Calvo, the new intendant, Ramón de López y Angulo, was even more militant about preventing Anglo-Americans from entering the province. In July, 1801, he asked the Crown to suspend the granting of land. His real purpose, which extended beyond his jurisdiction, was the desire to regulate Anglo-American entry into Louisiana. He declared that these settlers were coming to the province at too accelerated a pace. To prove it, he cited the names of those requesting free lands from the intendancy. He opposed the Anglo-Americans because they were establishing themselves everywhere. He recommended that until the Crown determined what course was to be followed land grants be halted. Echoing Gayoso's advice of two years before, he preferred to wait until more useful and less dangerous immigrants were available. New land grants should be limited to old settlers only and used for the promotion of industry. Complaining about a practice that was going on throughout the colony, López y Angulo pointed out that commandants and district syndics were making interim grants of land but were not submitting them to the intendancy for confirmation.[55]

The next year some steps were taken to restrain the flow of Anglo-Americans into Louisiana. In certain districts, commandants were instructed to oust all immigrants who did not have proper authority to settle; and in other districts, commandants were ordered not to let any Anglo-Americans settle at all. However, these last minute efforts, doubtlessly futile, were the final ones made in a desperate attempt to prevent the Anglo-Americans from overrunning Louisiana. On January 18, 1803, Spain belatedly dispatched a royal order informing the Louisiana authorities of the province's retrocession to France. The order was proclaimed in New Orleans in May and the transfer to French hands was completed on November 30. By then Napoleon Bonaparte had already sold Louisiana to the United States.[56]

When the United States acquired Louisiana, the colony still had not been overwhelmed by the Anglo-Americans, although their numbers were growing steadily.[57] By now Anglo-Americans could be found established in virtually every corner of the province, even west of the Mississippi and near the Texas border. In Lower Louisiana, the most densely populated region, where Frenchmen, Acadians, Germans, and Spaniards were present, Americans were not in a position to overwhelm these older established settlers, and in some respects this would never happen. It was in the thinly inhabited region of Upper Louisiana that Anglo-Americans had recently made their greatest gains. Nonetheless, even here with its scant population, they had not yet succeeded in becoming the dominant element. While the American settlers were primarily located on isolated farms, village life was in the hands of the French, who also controlled the industry, commerce, and even the majority of the mines of the region. The Americanization of Upper Louisiana, which would come in the near future, had still not begun in 1803.[58]

Contrary to its earlier efforts, Spain did virtually nothing to foster immigration in its final decade of control over Louisiana. When the Crown, in 1787 and 1788, permitted Anglo-Americans to settle there, it did so because it could no longer spend money to transport Spaniards or loyal Europeans to the colony. The only people obtainable at no cost to Spain came from the United States. But before long they came to be considered unreliable citizens. Nevertheless, Spain did not dare order their total exclusion to Louisiana for fear of invasion. Although Spanish officials in Louisiana sought to acquire Europeans, only a few, already in the United States, migrated to the colony. Because of Spain's inability to defend the province, Godoy came to terms with the United States in 1795, and then disposed of the colony to France in 1800.

Spain's removal from the Mississippi Valley resolved the problem of confrontation with the United States over Louisiana. The problem the Iberian nation faced here was, in reality, part of a larger issue. From 1790 on, Spain was in that final phase of its colonial period in the New World which Charles Chapman once called the "defensive defensive."[59] Challenged by more problems than it had solutions for, Spain found itself retreating along the periphery of its American empire. On the surface, the Spanish retrocession of Louisiana to France would have been a brilliant maneuver had France assumed the colony's defense. Instead France's sale of Louisiana to the United States surprised Spain; and while Spain protested the sale it did not actively attempt to regain the province. Unable to colonize Louisiana with a loyal population and faced with Anglo-Americans entering it at will, Spain probably averted an internal rebellion by its retrocession to France. Three decades later, Mexico, facing a similar crisis in Texas, lacked a solution to the same dilemma. Consequently, Mexico experienced an insurrection in Texas, led chiefly by Anglo-American immigrants from the United States.

Notes for "Spain's Immigration Policy in Louisiana and the American Penetration, 1792-1803"

[1]Quoted in Isaac Joslin Cox, "The New Invasion of the Goths and Vandals," *Proceedings of the Mississippi Valley Historical Association*, 8 (1914-1915): 183.

[2]For Spanish immigration policy in Louisiana before 1792, see Gilbert C. Din, "The Immigration Policy of Governor Esteban Miró in Spanish Louisiana," *Southwestern Historical Quarterly*, 73 (1969): 155-75; see also Mattie Austin Hatcher, "The Lousiana Background of the Colonization of Texas, 1763-1803," ibid., 24 (1921): 169-94.

[3]Arthur Preston Whitaker, *The Spanish-American Frontier: 1783-1795* (Boston, 1927), 162, states that Spanish policy against permitting Anglo-Americans to enter Louisiana changed as a result of the French terror and a reactionary government in Spain. However, archival documentation clearly indicates that Governor Carondelet initiated it. See also Lawrence Kinnaird, "American Penetration into Spanish Louisiana," in *New Spain and the Anglo-American West*, 2 vols. (Los Angeles, 1932), 1:220.

[4]Baron of Carondelet to the count of Floridablanca, January 13, 1792, no.9 reservada, Biblioteca Nacional, Madrid, "Documentos de la Luisiana," 3, 19, 246. The Archivo Histórico Nacional, Estado, is hereafter cited as AHN, Est. Governor Manuel Gayoso de Lemos of the Natchez District advised Floridablanca that it was impossible to prevent Americans from entering Louisiana. Gayoso to Floridablanca, January 26, 1792, AHN, Est. leg. 3,902, no. 4 reservada. On Carondelet's character see Whitaker, *Spanish-American Frontier*, 153-56.

[5]Carondelet to Floridablanca, February 25, 1792, AHN, Est., leg. 3,898, no.9 reservada; Carondelet to the count of Aranda, June 10, 1792, ibid., no. 1 reservada.

[6]Lawrence Kinnaird, ed., *Spain in the Mississippi Valley, 1765-1794,* 3 vols. (Washington, 1946), 3:xxv-xxvi. Fowler's project is described in "A Royal Invitation to the Industrious," ibid., 46-51. For Carondelet's instructions to stop the settlement, see Carondelet to Lieutenant Governor Zenon Trudeau of Upper Louisiana, June 8, 1792, ibid., 51-52. See also "Carondelet: Instructions to Trudeau, New Orleans, March 28, 1792," in Abraham P. Nasatir, ed., *Before Lewis and Clark: Documents Illustrating the History of Missouri, 1785-1804,* 2 vols. (St. Louis, 1952), 1:152.

[7]"Notes sur l'arrive et le séjour en Louisiane de M. Henri Peyroux de la Coudrenière," September 28, 1800, Archivo General de Indias (Seville), Papeles procedentes de Cuba, leg. 217; [Carondelet] to Josef de Jáudenes and Josef de Viar, April 17, 1792, ibid. leg., 104A, paquete A. The Archivo General de Indias, Papales procedentes de Cuba is hereafter cited as AGI, PC. Earlier Jáudenes and Viar had informed the Spanish court of the large numbers of immigrants arriving in the United States. Jáudenes and Viar to [court], September 21, 1791, AHN, Est., leg. 3,894bis.

[8]Jáudenes and Viar to Floridablanca, June 5, 1792, attached to AHN, Est., leg. 3,894bis, no. 110; ibid., June 14, 1792, no. 98.

[9]Jáudenes and Viar to Henri Peyroux, June 6, 1792, ibid., no. 110; Jáudenes and Viar to Floridablanca, July 31, 1792, ibid., no. 110. Peyroux eventually returned to New Madrid, his misconduct apparently forgiven. Jack D. L. Holmes, ed., *Documentos inéditos para la historia de la Luisiana, 1792-1810* (Madrid, 1963), 279.

[10]Carondelet to Jáudenes and Viar, May 31, June 20, 1792, AGI, PC, leg. 104A.

[11]Jáudenes and Viar to Floridablanca, July 31, 1792, AHN, Est., leg. 3,894bis, no. 113; Jáudenes and Viar to Aranda, October 29, 1792, ibid., no. 119 and 3 enclosures. Wooster gave out circulars listing the advantages of settling in Louisiana to interested persons. One such person, Midad Mitchel, traveled to Gallipolis, where some residents joined him on his journey to Louisiana. On his arrival there he was arrested, but was subsequently employed by Governor Gayoso at Natchez. "The Arrest of Mitchel–1793," in Louis Houck, ed., *The Spanish Régime in Missouri,* 2 vols. (Chicago, 1909), 2:4-8.

[12]Minuta, October 26, 1792, AHN, Est., leg. 3,895bis.

[13]Benedictine Monk of the Congregation of St. Mauro to Carondelet, June 22, 1792, Biblioteca Nacional, Madrid, "Documentos de la Florida," 2, 19,509, ff. 191-95. Friar Josef de Didier served as a priest at St. Louis from 1793 to 1799. He died in New Orleans on September 2, 1799. Holmes, ed., *Documento inéditos,* 273 n.

[14]Barthélemi Tardiveau to Carondelet, July 17, 1792, AHN, Est., leg. 3,898 (translated in Kinnaird, ed., *Spain in the Mississippi Valley*, 3:60-66); Carondelet to Aranda, October 1, 1792, ibid., no. 15 reservada. For a full-length biography of Tardiveau see Howard C. Rice, *Barthèlemi Tardiveau: A French Trader in the West* (Baltimore, 1938).

[15]Carondelet to Aranda, October 1, 1792, AHN, Est., leg. 3,898, no. 15 reservada. The Galveztown settlement in Louisiana arose during the American Revolutionary War when Governor Bernardo de Gálvez allowed Americans to settle there. Bernardo de Gálvez to José de Gálvez, January 15, 1779, no. 233, in Kinnaird, ed., *Spain in the Mississippi Valley*, 1:326-27.

[16]"Memorial of DeHault deLassus, Barthélemi Tardiveau, and Pedro Audrain," April 17, 1793, AGI, PC, leg. 2,363; Carondelet to the duke of Alcudia (Manuel Godoy), April 26, 1793, AHN, Est., leg. 3,898, no. 6 reservada. The partners never used the 9,000 *pesos* but returned the money to the Spanish treasury. They invested their own money and lost it in the venture. In 1796 they renewed their request for the loan. At that time their mill was two-thirds completed. Carondelet to the Prince of the Peace (Manuel Godoy), March 1, 1796, ibid., leg. 3,900, no. 74 reservada; Hatcher, "Louisiana Background," 183-85. The population of New Bourbon in 1795 was not over 153; in 1796 it was 383; and the next year it was 461. Holmes, ed., *Documentos inéditos,* 267 n.

[17]Carondelet to Alcudia, April 26, 1793, AHN, Est., leg. 3,898, no. 6 reservada; Louis Houck, *A History of Missouri from the Earliest Exploration and Settlements Until the Admission of the State into the Union,* 3 vols. (Chicago, 1908), 1:365. The quote is from Carondelet to Alcudia.

[18]"Plan of Population for Illinois," Kinnaird, ed., *Spain in the Mississippi Valley,* 3:208-215. For more information about Clamorgan's activites in Louisiana, see A. P. Nasatir, "Jacques Clamorgan: Colonial Promoter of the Northern Border of New Spain," *New Mexico Historical Review*, 17 (1942): 101-12.

[19]Carondelet to the Prince of the Peace, April 1, 1796, AHN, Est., leg. 3,900, no. 77; Whitaker, *Spanish-American Frontier,* 171-73, 187-92; Jack D. L. Holmes, *Gayoso: The Life of a Spanish Governor in the Mississippi Valley, 1789-1799* (Baton Rouge, 1965), 170-73; Ernest R. Liljegren, "Jacobinism in Spanish Louisiana, 1792-1797," *Louisiana Historical Quarterly*, 22 (1939): 47-97, hereafter cited *LHQ*; Frederick Jackson Turner, "The Origins of Genêt's Projected Attack on Louisiana and the Floridas,"*American Historical Review*, 3 (1898): 650-71; F. R. Hall, "Genêt's Western Intrigue, 1793-1794," *Journal of the Illinois State Historical Society*, 21 (1928), 359-81.

[20]Carondelet to Alcudia, March 27, May 1, 1794, AHN, Est., leg. 3,900, no. 30; elg. 3,899, no. 34 reservada; Carondelet to Eugenio Llaguno y Arriola, February 29, 1796, ibid., leg. 3,900, no. 16; Jack D. L. Holmes, "The Abortive Slave Revolt at Pointe Coupée, Louisiana, 1795," *Louisiana History*, 11 (1970): 341-62; François-Xavier Martin, *The History of Louisiana*, 2 vols. (New Orleans, 1827-1829), 2:31.

[21]Carondelet to Alcudia, June 3, November 24, 1794, AHN, Est., leg. 3,899, no. 36 reservada and no. 128. The November letter was published as Baron of Carondelet, "Carondelet on the Defense of Louisiana, 1794," trans. by W. F. Giese, *American Historical Review,* 2 (1897): 474-505.

[22]"Memorial of the Marquis de Maison Rouge," n.p., n.d., AGI, PC, leg. 2,364. For a detailed study of Maison Rouge in Louisiana, see Jennie O'Kelly, Mitchell, and Robert Dabney Calhoun, "The Marquis de Maison Rouge, the Baron de Bastrop, and Colonel Abraham Morhouse—Three Ouachita Valley Soldiers of Fortune," *LHQ*, 20 (1937): 289-368.

[23][Carondelet] to Gayoso, January 20, 1795, AGI, PC, leg. 22, no. 79; Carondelet to Thomas Portell, January 30, 1795, ibid.

[24]"Maison Rouge Contract," March 18, 1795, ibid. The contract was approved by royal order. Diego de Gardoqui to the Intendant of Louisiana, July 14, 1795, ibid., leg. 560.

[25]Carondelet to Juan Filhio, November 20, 1795, ibid., leg. 22, no. 898.

[26]Carondelet to Juan Ventura Morales, June 5, 7, 27, 1796, ibid., leg. 89, Morales to Carondelet, August 11, 1796, ibid.; Filhio to [Carondelet], May 6, 1797, ibid., leg. 214; O'Kelly, Mitchell and Calhoun, "Marquis de Maison Rouge," 325-26.

[27]Carlos de Grand-Pré to Carondelet, July 30, 1796, AGI, PC, leg. 2,354.

[28]"Memorial of Joseph Piernas," April 24, 1795, ibid.; Jack D. L. Holmes, "Joseph Piernas and a Proposed Settlement on the Calcasieu River, 1795," *McNesse Review*, 13 (1962), 59-80, contains a translation of the proposal. The Spanish text is in Holmes, ed., *Documentos inèditos,* 148-69.

[29]Jack D. L. Holmes, ed., "The Calcasieu Promoter: Joseph Piernas and His 1799 Proposal," *Louisiana History*, 9 (1968): 163-67.

[30][Luis de Vilemont] to Carondelet, October 31, 1794, AHN, Est., leg. 3,895bis, no. 265; Vilemont to [Carondelet], July 10, 1795, ibid., leg. 3,890, expcd. 34; "Petition of Luis de Vilemont," attached to Carondelet to Alcudia, July 30, 1795, ibid.; minuta, Novermber 12, 1795, ibid.

[31]Count de Montarco to the Prince of the Peace, November 14, 1795, ibid.

[32]Jáudenes to Alcudia, December 1, 1795, ibid., leg. 3,896, no. 320; "Butler Memorial," Novermber 30, 1795, ibid.

[33]Jáudenes to Alcudia, July 29, 1796, ibid., no. 299.

[34]Samuel Flagg Bemis, *Pinckney's Treaty: America's Advantage from Europe's Distress, 1783-1800* (revised ed., New Haven, 1960), 245-93; Arthur Preston Whitaker, *The Mississippi Question, 1795-1803* (reprint; Gloucester, MA, 1962), 51-67.

[35]Carondelet to Morales, June 11, 1797, enclosed in Ramón López y Angulo to Miguel Cayetano Soler, July 13, 1801, AGI, Santo Domingo, leg. 2,617. Carondelet still tried to exclude Anglo-Americans from Lower Louisiana and West Florida, where he favored European settlement. DeHault deLassus issued a pamphlet inviting immigration, "A Sketch of the Advantages that are made, and Quantities of land that are granted to farmers by the Spanish Government, in the District of New Madrid. . . . " (n.p., April 8, 1796), Louisiana Collection, Bancroft Library, Berkeley. See also Kinnaird, "American Penetration into Spanish Louisiana," 221-22; and Houck, *History of Missouri,* 2:183-84.

[36]"Petition of Benjamin Sebastian, John Hollingsworth, Harry Innes et al.," July 5, 1796, AGI, PC, leg. 674; Carondelet to William Murray, Novermber 24, 1796, ibid.; "Contract of William Murray," ibid.

[37]Whitaker, *The Mississippi Question,* 156.

[38]"Memorial of Baron de Bastrop," August 25, 1794, AGI, PC, leg. 2,364. For a survey of Bastrop's activities, see Charles A. Bacarisse, "Baron de Bastrop," *Southwestern Historical Quarterly*, 58 (1955): 319-30. Another proposal to form a Dutch or German settlement, made by Benjamin Fooy, one-time commandant of the Spanish post of Campo de Esperanza, received royal approval in 1798; but nothing came of it. Houck, ed., *The Spanish Régime in Missouri*, 2:114.

[39]Carondelet to Grand-Pré, September 16, 1795, AGI, PC, leg. 22, no. 712; [Carondelet] to Francisco Rendón, March 9, 1795, ibid., leg. 2,364; Rendón to Carondelet, March 17, 1795, ibid.

[40]Bastrop to Carondelet, June 20, 1796, AGI, Santo Domingo, leg. 2,580; "Bastrop Contract," June 21, 1796, ibid.

[41]Bastrop to Morales, June 20, 1797, AGI, PC, leg. 601; Carondelet to the Prince of the Peace, June 16, 1797, AHN, Est., leg. 3,900; Carondelet to Morales, June 11, 1797, ibid. Bastrop sought to build wheat mills in Ouachita and requested lands on both banks of Bayou Barthélemy and Bayou Siard on which to establish them; Carondelet approved the request and granted the land. Bastrop to Carondelet, June 12, 1797, AGI, Santo Domingo. leg. 2,580. Bastrop brought no more than ninety-nine persons to Ouachita: sixty-four on May 8, 1797, and thirty-five more on May 10, 1797. L. M. Perez, "French Immigrants to Lousiana, 1796-1800," *Publications of the Southern History Association*, 11 (1907): 106-12.

[42]Morales to Carondelet, June 13, 1797, AHN, Est. leg. 3,900; "Decision of the Junta," ibid.; Carondelet to the Prince of the Peace, June 16, 1797, ibid.; Morales to Carondelet, June 30, 1797, AGI, Santo Domingo, leg. 2,580, no. 129.

[43]Gayoso to Morales, October 5, 1797, AGI, PC, leg. 44; Francisco de Saavedra to the Prince of the Peace, February 23, 1798, AHN, Est., leg. 3,901; Bastrop to the marquis of Casa-Calvo, June 18, 1800, ibid.; Casa-Calvo to López y Angulo, July 10, 1800, ibid.

[44]Casa-Calvo to Luis de Urquijo, August 8, 1800, AHN, Est., leg. 2,901; López y Angulo to Urquijo, August 12, September 25, 1800, ibid., leg. 3,888, no. 94 reservada, no. 95 reservada. The Crown rejected Bastrop's commission in 1802. Soler to Pedro Cevallo, July 13, 1802, ibid., leg. 3,901.

[45]Martin, *History of Lousiana,* 2:180; Bacarisse, "Baron de Bastrop," 327-30.

[46]Martínez de Irujo to the Prince of the Peace, August 5, 1797, AHN, Est., leg. 3,891, no. 73, exped. 23, with Godoy's marginal notation, October 20, 1797; Holmes, *Gayoso*, 196.

[47]Two sets of immigration instructions issued by Gayoso in New Orleans are dated September 3, 1797, and February 20, 1798, AGI, PC, leg. 220, and leg. 2,365. See also Martin, *History of Louisiana,* 2:153; and Holmes, *Gayoso*, 227-28. Gayoso permitted some Americans to settle in New Feliciana, Concordia, and Bayou Boeuf, but he exercised caution in doing so.

[48]Gayoso to DeHault deLassus, September 9, 1797, AGI, PC, leg. 44.

[49]Trudeau to Gayoso, January 15, 1798, ibid., leg. 214; Santiago Mackay to Gayoso, Novermber 28, 1798, ibid., leg. 215B; Houck, *History of Missouri,* 1:332.

[50]Gayoso to Trudeau, July 9, 1798, AGI, PC, leg. 2,365.

[51]Gayoso to the Prince of the Peace, November 22, 1798, AHN, Est., leg. 3,900; ibid., August 20, 1798, AGI, PC, leg. 44; Gayoso to Trudeau, August 9, 1798, ibid.

[52]Gayoso to Morales, July 1, 1799, AGI, Santo Domingo, leg. 2,617. Gayoso disapproved a 144-square-league grant to M. Tardiveau near New Madrid and also objected to new settlements on the west bank of the Mississippi. Furthermore, he was against developing those already in existence. Gayoso to the Prince of the Peace, July 8, 1799, AHN, Est., leg. 3,901, no. 1. In the fall of 1798, Colonel Zacharias Cox arrived in New Orleans and offered to establish 600 Kentucky families near New Madrid. Gayoso told him to renew his proposal after the war ended. Gayoso to the Prince of the Peace, December 22, 1798, ibid., leg. 3,900.

[53]Casa-Calvo to V. Layssard, December 22, 1799, AGI, PC, leg. 3,900; Martin, *History of Louisiana,* 2:172.

[54]The Gayoso-Morales struggle is discussed in Holmes, *Gayoso*, 217-22; Morales's regulations are in Charles Gayarré, *History of Louisiana*, 4 vols., 3rd ed. (New Orleans, 1885), 3:632-40. The offices of governor and intendant were united between 1788 and 1793 and then separated when Francisco Rendón became intendant. Governor Carondelet found him congenial and cooperative. After Rendon was appointed to a post in Zacatecas, Juan Ventura Morales served as intendant ad interim until 1798. He became a watchdog of expenditures. A royal order of October 22, 1798, confirmed the intendancy's sole right to grant land. Holmes, *Gayoso*, 219.

[55]López y Angulo to Soler, July 13, 1801, AGI, Santo Domingo, leg. 2,617. For a study of Louisiana land laws, see Francis P. Burns, "The Spanish Land Laws of Louisiana," *LHQ*, 11 (1928): 557-81.

[56]Manuel Juan de Salcedo to V. Layssard, October 6, 1802, AGI, PC, leg. 138; Salcedo to Archinard y Poyres, October 6, 1802, ibid., Martin Duralde to Salcedo, July 31, 1802, ibid., no. 350 reservada; [Salcedo] to Duralde, August 13, 1802, ibid.; Whitaker, *The Mississippi Question*, 176-86; Arthur P. Whitaker, "Spain and the Retrocession of Louisiana," *American Historical Review*, 39 (1934): 454-76; Mildred Stahl Fletcher, "Louisiana as a Factor in French Diplomacy from 1763-1800," *Mississippi Valley Historical Review*, 17 (1930): 367-76.

[57]Louisiana's population has been estimated at over 50,000 in 1803; four-fifths of it was located in Lower Louisiana. Whitaker, *Mississippi Question*, 276 n. While Americans had entered Louisiana in growing numbers before 1803, contrary to the conclusion of Hatcher ("Louisiana Background," 194), they had not yet become the dominant group. Her figure of 27,000 for Louisiana's population in 1798 is also too low. Ibid.

[58]E. M. Violette, "Early Settlements in Missouri," *Missouri Historical Review*, 1 (1906): 38-52. In 1803 Upper Louisiana's population was estimated as 10,340; by the next year it was 25,000. Jonas Viles, "Population and Extent of Settlement in Missouri before 1804," ibid., 5 (1911): 189-213.

[59]Charles Edward Chapman, *Colonial Hispanic America: A History* (New York, 1933), 184-85.

PART VII

SLAVERY AND FREE AFRICANS

THE PROBLEM OF INDIAN SLAVERY IN SPANISH LOUISIANA, 1769-1803*

Stephen Webre[1]

The first Spanish colonists in the New World enthusiastically thrust the native peoples into bondage to work the mines and perform other necessary tasks the white men themselves disdained. So calamitous were the demographic consequences of this ruthless exploitation of the indigenous population, which was accustomed neither to the brutal work regime nor the unfamiliar diseases that its European masters imported, that protests soon spanned the Atlantic Ocean and reached the Spanish throne. Idealists, under the vigorous leadership of the Dominican friar Bartolomé de Las Casas, demanded that the king extend his royal protection to these most unfortunate of his subjects. This campaign was ultimately successful. With the so-called New Laws of 1542 it became an established principle in Spanish law that the native inhabitants of the Americas were free vassals of the Crown and that they were not to be enslaved.[2]

No such prohibition existed in the French colonies. The French experience in North America was different from that of the Spanish. Frenchmen came into New France and Louisiana chiefly as traders to exploit the established native economy and, therefore, had little need to reorient the allocation of labor. For their own limited domestic requirements, they acquired a few slaves from the Indians themselves.[3] It is true that, in the subtropical lower Mississippi Valley where the foundations for a plantation system were laid early, the French did initially seek to exploit Indians as slave laborers in commercial agricultural undertakings. But the first major shipments of slaves from Africa arrived during the second decade of the eighteenth century and blacks quickly became dominant among the servile labor force. From the beginning, the French settlers considered them more desirable as slaves than the Indians.[4]

Although never as important as African slavery, Indian slavery persisted in Louisiana throughout the French dominion and was a well-established institution by the time Spain took possession of the territory in the 1760s. The efforts of Spanish administrators to

*This article was first published in *Louisiana History*, 25 (1984): 117-35. Reprinted with the kind permission of the author and the Louisiana Historical Association.

reconcile this survival with the traditional Spanish prohibition of the practice constitute a brief, although revealing, chapter in the complicated story of the difficulties that Spain experienced governing the vast, strategically vulnerable, and sparsely settled former French colony.

Indian slavery in Louisiana clearly declined in comparative significance during the years of the French dominion. Early census figures present many problems of coverage and definition, but it is possible to derive from them a general idea of the numbers involved. A count taken for the entire colony in 1726 indicated the number of Indians held in slavery as 229. At the same time, the number of black slaves had already reached 1,540. Of these Indian bondsmen, the greatest numbers were concentrated in New Orleans, Mobile, and the Illinois country.[5] By the beginning of the Spanish period, the number of Indians remained approximately the same while that of blacks had increased substantially to perhaps 5,000. The most significant populations of Indian slaves were recorded at New Orleans and its neighboring river posts, as well as at Pointe Coupée, Natchitoches, and, far upriver in Spanish Illinois, at St. Louis, and Ste. Geneviève.[6]

Only scattered information remains regarding the tribal origins of Indians still held in slavery at the time of the cession to Spain. Official reports and judicial records used as documentation for the discussion of Spanish policy which follows mention a variety of tribes, but most frequently the Pawnees and Comanches. It is significant that many Indian slaves were described as "creoles" or "born in the country," suggesting that they were born into slavery of slave parents. By the Spanish period, in fact, many slaves were no longer pure-blooded Indians. *Mestizos* (*métis* in French), the mixed offspring of unions between Indians and whites, appeared frequently among the slave population as did *zambos* (*griffes* in French), the mixed offspring of Indians and blacks or mulattoes. These slaves' claims to special status as Indians were based on biological descent alone as they almost certainly had lost any meaningful contact with their native culture and adopted the language and values of their masters. For their part, whites were not overly fastidious about the ethnic identity of their slaves and tended to refer to any mixed-blood as a mulatto.[7]

In Louisiana, as in New France, the French seldom used the word "slavery" to describe the relationship that existed between Indian servants and their white masters. It is very common in records from the French period to see Indians referred to simply as "belonging to" someone.[8] Other than informal, often unwitnessed, bills of sale, French Louisianians seldom possessed title to their slaves. This was largely because master-slave relationships were frequently the product of gradual evolution from more informal relationships in which Indian children were taken in, reared, fed, and educated after a fashion, then converted into permanent servile members of white households.[9] Still, there can be no doubt that the legal status of these Indians was that of slaves. They were routinely bought and sold as such and, from almost the beginning, at least in Louisiana, they were considered to be no less subject to the provisions of the *Code Noir* than the blacks themselves.[10]

Although Spain acquired the province of Louisiana from France in 1762, the serious work of conversion to Spanish laws and institutions did not begin until August 1769, with the arrival from Cuba of Don Alejandro O'Reilly. Governor O'Reilly occupied New Orleans with an armed force in the wake of a 1768 settler revolt which had resulted in the expulsion from the colony of the first Spanish governor, Don Antonio de Ulloa. Acting on orders from the Spanish Crown, the new governor moved quickly to reestablish Spanish authority and to punish those responsible for the revolt. He also issued a number of proclamations designed to make practice in Louisiana conform to the laws of the Spanish empire in general.[11]

One important aspect of colonial life affected by the imposition of Spanish law was the institution of slavery.[12] Spanish slave law differed from the French *Code Noir*—and, for that matter, from English and Anglo-American slave law—in several important respects. Among these was the fact that Spanish law recognized the slave as a person endowed with certain rights, among them the right to own property and to appear as a party in a lawsuit. Under Spanish law, slaves were even permitted to sue their masters for redress in cases of ill treatment and, in some provinces, Louisiana included, it was even possible for slaves to sue to compel their own manumission.[13]

Spanish slave law was also unique in that it exempted the native inhabitants of America, the Indians, from chattel servitude. Governor O'Reilly took note of the fact that there was a substantial number of Indians held in slavery by the French colonists. As this practice was contrary to Spanish law, he published a decree outlawing it on December 7, 1769. O'Reilly's decree contained a definitive and general prohibition, from the date of publication, of the enslavement of Indians under any pretext whatever. While the decree temporarily confirmed the tenure of proprietors already holding Indian slaves, it prohibited their alienation (by any means other than manumission) until such time as the Spanish Crown should rule on their status. Finally, the decree directed all masters of Indian slaves to appear before the appropriate local authorities and declare the number of slaves held, their age, sex, tribe of origin, and market value.[14]

The officials charged with responsibility for the transition to Spanish rule faced many problems at once. From the beginning, they probably assigned a relatively low priority to the question of the Indian slaves. Little immediate effort was made to enforce the terms of O'Reilly's edict. When the problem reemerged, some twenty-five years later, the baron de Carondelet, governor of the province, complained to the Crown that he had been unable to locate among the local archives any evidence that administrative action had been taken or that the required declarations had been made.[15]

Carondelet's sweeping assertion notwithstanding, it is clear that some steps (however ineffective) were taken toward compliance, at least in Spanish Illinois. The declarations regarding Indian slaves held at St. Louis and Ste. Geneviève were duly made and have survived.[16] Although Pedro Piernas, who arrived at St. Louis in May 1770 to assume command of the Illinois post, apparently made a conscientious attempt to carry out the edict, there was much confusion among the populace regarding such a significant departure from traditional practice. In July 1770, upon transmitting the required declarations, Piernas informed Governor Luis de Unzaga that a number of local inhabitants had already engaged to purchase Indians at the time the decree was first published and that some had even advanced cash toward completing the transactions. Unzaga advised Piernas that such sales (there were fourteen Indians involved in all) might be recognized, even if consummated subsequent to the date of the decree, but that in future no Indian whatever was to be enslaved, purchased, or sold—pending, as always, a ruling from Spain.[17]

No official resolution of the Indian slave question ever came from Spain, so the status of those Indians held as slaves at the time of the cession remained in doubt; but the Spanish law courts in Louisiana clearly recognized that Indian slavery had been legal during the French regime and routinely enforced debts incurred in slave purchases prior to the cession and held parties liable for damages involving the loss of Indian slaves.[18] Further, it is clear from the record that Indians continued to be held, bought, and sold as slaves throughout the early Spanish period with very little show of concern by local authorities. Spanish law defined slaves as immovable, or real, property and required for their transfer a formal act executed before a notary and witnesses. Such an act must include, among other specific information, the source of the vendor's title.[19] Even so, the necessity of formalizing and publicizing an illegal transaction does not seem to have deterred many masters. Contracting parties frequently misidentified Indians in acts of sale as mulattoes, a practice which not only facilitated evasion of the law but also has probably obscured the full extent of such Indian slave transaction from historians.[20]

For more than twenty years, no serious effort was made to enforce O'Reilly's edict. However, a case arising at St. Louis in 1787, in which criminal proceedings were brought against a group of alleged runaway Indian slaves, did prompt Governor Esteban Rodríguez Miró to instruct the post lieutenant governor, Francisco de Cruzat, to republish the O'Reilly ordinance.[21] Cruzat's proclamation against the enslavement of Indians in Spanish Illinois was appropriately righteous and vigorous. Still, it is illustrative of the general disregard for this particular law that Cruzat himself, at the conclusion of his tour of duty, returned to New Orleans with at least two Indian slaves of his own.

Not long after his return from Spanish Illinois, Francisco de Cruzat died. Following his death, his slaves, Pierre and his sister Marie, brought suit against Cruzat's estate to obtain their freedom. At the same time, Pierre and Marie's half-brother Baptiste sued his own master, Manuel Bourgignon, a flatboatman from Ste. Geneviève. These three suits, heard at New Orleans early in 1790, are significant because they appear to have been the first instances of use in Louisiana courts by Indian slaves of the remedy inherent in the principle of Spanish law that an Indian could not be enslaved.[22]

Marie, Pierre, and Baptiste claimed to be the children of Catherine, a full-blooded Indian woman. How Marie came into Cruzat's possession is not clear from the documentation. Pierre stated that Cruzat had purchased him some eight years previously from Charles Charleville. This transfer having occurred well after the date of O'Reilly's proclamation, Pierre demanded his liberty under the "laws of the kingdom . . . which call upon all the magistrates of America to restrain those who, through ignorance or malice, seek to enslave the Indians."[23] Marie having already successfully sued for her freedom, the Cruzat heirs did not contest Pierre's action and he duly received his emancipation papers shortly thereafter.[24]

Baptiste's father had been a black man. In his response, the defendant Bourgignon claimed that he had purchased Baptiste only under the misapprehension that he was a mulatto and, therefore, subject to slavery under both French and Spanish law. Governor Miró ordered Baptiste freed and Bourgignon later brought an action of his own against the estate of the party from whom he had purchased the slave in 1788, charging that the vendor had deliberately misrepresented his race. He eventually succeeded in recovering the purchase price of 400 pesos.[25]

The cases of Marie, Pierre, and Baptiste marked the beginning of a new phase in the history of Indian slavery in Louisiana: one in which the Indians themselves sought to enforce the law by bringing suit against their masters.[26] For the years between 1790 (when the first suits were heard) and 1794 (when Governor Carondelet, reacting to intense pressure from white slaveowners, ordered a suspension of all such suits), we have been able to locate among the judicial archives of Spanish Louisiana a total of thirteen suits for freedom by slaves claiming Indian descent.[27] The overall significance of this admittedly small body of litigation is difficult to assess. All of these cases were heard before the governor himself at New Orleans (Governor Miró at first, then, after 1791, Governor Carondelet). Justice of this sort was essentially unavailable at the outlying posts, tiny communities where the commandants were often Frenchmen who had a poor understanding of Spanish law and were usually under the influence of the local white population.[28] Only with great difficulty could Indians living as slaves in Spanish Illinois, for example, expect to reach the capital in order to press their grievances.[29]

Although only a very small percentage of those eligible to seek their freedom under Spanish law actually did so, there were clearly enough cases to attract the anxious attention of the whites of the lower Mississippi Valley. White observers found it difficult to believe that the slave plaintiffs in these suits acted on their own account without the encouragement of some outside agency. In the context of a society profoundly affected, both demographically and psychologically, by the massive slave rebellion which erupted in the French sugar colony of Saint-Domingue in 1791, no challenge to the slavery system could be taken lightly.[30]

Other than the very fact that slaves were suing their masters for their freedom—a phenomenon that could not have occurred under the French regime—two factors, in particular, must have disturbed slaveholders. One was the apparent ease with which the Indians won their suits.[31] The other was the uncertainty of racial identity in a population where miscegenation was widely practiced. The typical plaintiff in an emancipation suit was not a full-blooded Indian but a mixed breed. If a slave, however African he might superficially appear, could prove to the satisfaction of the court that he was descended from Indians in the maternal line, then he might legally demand his freedom without compensation to his master. This introduced a new element of uncertainty into the ordinarily stable realm of property rights. It also threatened to swell the population of free persons of color precisely at a time when whites were beginning to view that population as a dangerous element within society. At the same time, it threatened to engender unwelcome ambitions and resentments among that portion of the slave population to whom this particular remedy was not available. For planters already convinced that the Spanish administration, particularly under Governor Carondelet, was too lenient towards the slave and free colored population, these developments were a source of great concern and even fear.[32]

The earliest freedom suits involved primarily slaves whose masters resided either at New Orleans or in Spanish Illinois. These plaintiffs had little trouble demonstrating their Indian ancestry and, in general, their masters did not vigorously resist their bids for emancipation. Later, however, suits began to originate on the part of plantation slaves at Pointe Coupée and on the German Coast. From the record, it appears that these slaves were not generally reputed, at least by the whites in their communities, to be Indians. These new demands encountered stiff resistance on the part of masters and ultimately led planters in the affected areas, under the leadership of Julien Poydras of Pointe Coupée, to petition Carondelet and the Crown for relief.

Crucial in provoking this white reaction were suits brought in 1793 by two slaves of Pointe Coupée planters.[33] In one action, Cécile, the daughter of a full-blooded Comanche woman and herself a recently freed slave, brought suit to compel the emancipation of her sister and her sister's five children and six grandchildren. This suit involved twelve slaves and four planters at three different posts (Pointe Coupée, Attakapas, and Opelousas), and apparently provoked considerable discussion among the rural white population.[34]

The second suit of importance, and that which caught the attention of Julien Poydras for he was named a defendant in it, was brought about the same time as Cécile's action by Marie Jeanne, a slave of the New Orleans merchant Manuel Monsanto but held at Pointe Coupée in the service of Monsanto's agent Isaac Fastio. Marie Jeanne claimed to be sixty years old and the daughter of a black man and a full-blooded Indian woman who had been a slave of Jean Rondeau. She also claimed to have two grown children, a "griffe" daughter named Marie and a "mestizo" son named Antoine Sarazin. The two children, at the time of the suit, were slaves of Poydras.[35]

Lacking documentary evidence to support her claim to Indian ancestry, Marie Jeanne presented the testimony of three elderly whites and a free black woman of Pointe Coupée. In his response, Monsanto declared that he had purchased the plaintiff in good faith in 1782, in the belief that she was a mulatto. He stated his willingness to abide by the court's decision should it find that she had been improperly held in slavery. Monsanto's co-defendant, Julien Poydras, on the other hand, was not inclined to submit. His spirited and audacious defense reduced the three essential points: that the "mulatto" (as he insisted upon calling her) Marie Jeanne could not prove her claim to Indian descent; that her son Antoine Sarazin had once before sued for his freedom and lost, thereby confirming as legal his status as a slave; and, most daring of all, that the Spanish law which prohibited the enslavement of Indians did not apply to the province of Louisiana.[36]

While Poydras's first two points dealt with the facts of the case, his third point dealt with the law.[37] Poydras argued that the Spanish law in question could not apply to Louisiana because the treaty of cession between France and Spain had guaranteed the property rights of those French settlers who elected to remain behind. He also argued that the law had never been intended to apply to a situation such as that which prevailed in the former French colony. Poydras contrasted the history of the Spanish conquest of Mexico and Peru with that of the French colonization of New France and Louisiana:

> The early conquistadores of those remote regions [Mexico and Peru] pursued the Indians with iron and fire in hand and reduced them to slavery without the consent of the government and in spite of the most express prohibitions, against which they even had the temerity to offer armed opposition. There was no alternative more just than that the government, having reduced them to the proper submission, place the natives in the enjoyment of that liberty that had been deprived them against the strictest orders. But the history of this colony [Louisiana] offers nothing similar. The inhabitants never made war against the Indians except in self defense. They fixed all their sights on commerce and concentrated all their forces on conciliation and friendship and finally succeeded in attracting them [the Indians].[38]

Thus, Poydras concluded that the prohibition against Indian slavery had been a necessary restraint on Spanish rapaciousness, a restraint which was not required in the case of the French who, according to Poydras, had always treated the Indians well. Any slaves the French held, Poydras declared, had been justly taken in wars provoked by the Indians themselves.[39]

Poydras's unflattering comparison of French and Spanish activities in the New World could hardly have been calculated to win the sympathy of a Spanish court. In any case, he did not long restrict his defense to legal arguments. In fact, he shortly moved to transfer the dispute from the judicial to the political arena. In February 1794, Poydras and twenty-six other whites, primarily residents of Pointe Coupée and the German Coast, petitioned Carondelet to transmit to the Crown a memorial in which they demanded an end to the liberation of Indian slaves. The planters complained of economic hardships general to the colony but aggravated for them, they claimed, by the "continuous unjust lawsuits, fomented by malignant seducers, of many slaves claiming exemption from servitude under the specious pretext of supposing themselves to be descendants of free Indians. . . ."[40]

Poydras and his associates argued that the Indian freedom suit phenomenon was not only economically harmful to the province but also politically dangerous as well. It made the entire slave population susceptible to subversion and encouraged slaves to flee to New Orleans to file suits against their masters. Once away from their plantations, the whites asserted, these slaves came under the undesirable influence of free blacks and mulattoes and abandoned themselves to drunkenness and theft.[41]

Given the political realities of the moment, Carondelet had little choice but to take the memorialists' position seriously. The execution of Louis XVI had led to war between Spain and Revolutionary France in 1793 and the governor felt he could not be certain of the French planter's loyalty in case of an invasion. He was equally distrustful of the slaves themselves and professed to share the whites' belief that the recent flurry of Indian freedom suits had been inspired by ill-intentioned agents of the sort who had brought about the ruin of the French colonies in the Caribbean. Still, Carondelet did not endorse the slaveholders' demands wholeheartedly. Instead, he proposed to the Crown an unrealistic compromise solution which would have gradually freed some Indian slaves after one year but would have required others to purchase their freedom. Carondelet believed the delay would permit owners sufficient opportunity to replace their Indians with blacks.[42]

While Governor Carondelet awaited a royal reply to his compromise proposal, he sought in April 1794 to defuse the local political situation by ordering an indefinite suspension of the hearing of Indian freedom suits. All affected slaves were directed to return to their masters who, in turn, were enjoined to refrain from punitive actions against them.[43]

Although it was in theory only an interim measure, many planters regarded the suspension as a definitive conclusion to the affair. At least one, in fact, even sought to reestablish claim to slaves who had previously been recognized as free.[44] Among the slaves, there were some individuals who were less inclined to accept this reversal as final. In some cases, plaintiffs sought to evade the suspension and return their cases to court by charging their master with mistreatment.[45] In others, slaves apparently lost confidence in Spanish justice altogether. In one particularly tragic instance, Antoine Sarazin, one of the plaintiffs in a recently suspended suit, enlisted in a conspiracy to raise the slave population of Pointe Coupée and massacre the whites. Arrested and interrogated, he confessed his role in the rebellion plot and died on the gallows at Pointe Coupée on May 29, 1795.[46]

In all, twenty-three slaves were hanged as a result of the discovery of the 1795 Pointe Coupée conspiracy. At least five signers of the memorial on the Indian slave problem had slaves implicated: Colin LaCour, Simon Croizet, Charles Dufour, Jean-Baptist Tounoir, and, significantly, Julien Poydras himself, upon whose plantation the conspiracy centered and sixteen of whose slaves received the death penalty. These events seemed to confirm the memorialists' most disturbing fears and certainly made them and other slaveholders even more resistant to innovations in the slavery system.

In Spain, meanwhile, the bureaucracy proceeded at its customarily lethargic pace. Carondelet's dispatch and the accompanying memorial of the planters had arrived in November 1794. It was not until a year later, however, that the Council of the Indies requested a search of the archives of the Ministry of the Indies for papers relevant to the question at hand. The ministry replied that it could find no evidence that Governor O'Reilly had ever submitted his decree of 1769 for approval. It was apparently for this reason that the Crown had never made a determination on the matter. The file returned to the council for action and presumably died there for nothing more was ever heard of it.[47] Local Spanish officials in Louisiana patiently awaited a royal response which never came and, in the interim, liberated no more Indian slaves.[48]

The Spanish colonial empire was the most widely dispersed political system the world had known. Its vast territorial expanse and the primitive means of communication available tended to hinder effective administration. Scholars today attribute the empire's general success and remarkable longevity in the face of such difficulties at least in part to the latitude enjoyed by local magistrates to disregard or modify the effect of written directives from the metropolis.[49] Governor Carondelet was an experienced colonial administrator and would have been aware, if only intuitively, of his mediative position between royal wishes and local realities. His primary responsibility was not to enforce any particular law, however just its original intent, but to preserve Louisiana for the empire.

Enormous difficulties faced colonial officials in the closing years of the eighteenth century. Carondelet, in particular, governed a frontier province inhabited chiefly by a non-Spanish population, which, while it had accustomed itself to foreign rule over the years, owed the Spanish Crown only the loyalty of convenience. French Louisianians were in close touch with events in their homeland where a major revolutionary upheaval was challenging many of the traditional assumptions upon which the Spanish monarchy and its worldwide empire was based. The French Revolution had already unleashed social forces that had destroyed one plantation colony, Saint-Domingue. It was not at all unreasonable to imagine that something similar might happen in Louisiana.

Louisiana's Indian slaves were, thus, the innocent pawns in a much larger game. Between the beginning of the Spanish period and the 1790s, the total slave population of the province of Louisiana increased from approximately 5,000 to approximately 20,000.[50] Of this number, it is likely that no more than two or three hundred were of identifiable Indian descent. Given their statistical insignificance within the total slave labor force, it is at first difficult to comprehend the outcry with which the French planters reacted to the freeing of a frankly tiny number of Indians. But, as is often the case when the heat of the controversy appears disproportionate to the cause, the ostensible issue here was not the real issue.

The planters, in opposing the Indians' freedom demands, were not defending their right to exploit Indian labor. What they objected to in Spanish slave law was not that it exempted Indians but that it recognized all slaves as persons endowed with certain rights, which, in turn, were enforceable by the slaves themselves in courts of law. Such a view of the slave was inconsistent not only with French legal tradition, as embodied in the *Code Noir*, but also with changing social, economic, and political conditions in Louisiana. The local French slaveholders, in bringing political pressure to bear on Governor Carondelet, were seeking to shape the enforcement of Spanish law to meet their own needs, needs which increasingly demanded a slavery regime which deemphasized the slave's quality as person in favor of his quality as property and which exchanged the existing, Spanish system of reciprocal rights and obligations for a new one, based on the older, French model characterized chiefly by dominion and control.

As a consequence of the extension of United States sovereignty to Louisiana in 1803, the large planters of the province suddenly found themselves in a position to make their own laws. Julien Poydras was himself, in fact, an important member of the first Legislative Council named in 1804.[51] The new legislators did not then deem it necessary, or even worthwhile, to stipulate in law the status of Indians, or persons of Indian descent, held in slavery. That comparatively minor problem they left to perplex the state courts.[52] But they did dedicate themselves energetically to the resurrection and reenactment of many restrictive features of the Old French *Code Noir*. The new Black Code of 1806, along with a measure, passed in 1807, severely limiting the practice of manumission, substantially dismantled the objectionable aspects of Spanish slave law.[53] These new laws disqualified slaves as parties in civil suits and as witnesses against white persons. They also made it difficult for a master to free slaves of his own volition. Particularly significant with respect to the preceding discussion of the Indian slavery controversy, they made it impossible for one to be compelled to do so against his will.

Notes for "The Problem of Indian Slavery in Spanish Louisiana, 1769-1803"

[1]A previous draft of this paper was awarded the Latin American History Prize at the 61st Annual Meeting of the Southwestern Social Science Association, Houston, Texas, March 1983. The author wishes to acknowledge the assistance and advice of Edward F. Haas, Joseph D. Castle, Morgan Peoples, and Thomas D. Watson.

[2]Lewis Hanke, *The Spanish Struggle for Justice in the Conquest of America* (Philadelphia, 1949), remains the standard introduction to the debate over Indian policy in the early Spanish colonial empire.

In general, the history of slavery, the plantation, and race relations in colonial Louisiana is an open field of opportunity for researchers. Valuable introductions include Thomas Marc Fiehrer, "The African Presence in Colonial Louisiana: An Essay on the Continuity of Caribbean Culture," in Robert R. Macdonald et al., eds., *Louisiana's Black Heritage* (New Orleans, 1979), 3-31; and James T. McGowan, "Creation of a Slave Society: Louisiana Plantations in the Eighteenth Century" (Ph.D. dissertation, University of Rochester, 1976). Almon Wheeler Lauber, *Indian Slavery in Colonial Times within the Present Limits of the United States*, Columbia University Studies in History, Economics, and Public Law, 54, no. 3 (New York, 1913), discusses Louisiana under both the French and Spanish regimes, but his emphasis is on English America.

[3]Marcel Trudel, *L'Esclavage au Canada français: Histoire et conditions l'esclavage* (Quebec, 1960).

[4]Daniel H. Usner, Jr., "From African Captivity to American Slavery: The Introduction of Black Laborers to Colonial Louisiana," *Louisiana History*, 20 (1979): 25-48; Dunbar Rowland and Albert Sanders, eds., *Mississippi Provincial Archives, 1701-1740*, 3 vols. (Jackson, MS, 1929), 2:574. On the African slave trade in early French Louisiana, see also John G. Clark, *New Orleans, 1718-1812: An Economic History* (Baton Rouge, 1970), 23-25.

[5]Charles R. Maduell, Jr., comp., *The Census Tables for the French Colony of Louisiana from 1699 through 1732* (Baltimore, 1972), 50; Nancy M. Miller Surrey, *The Commerce of Louisiana during the French Regime, 1699-1763*, Columbia University Studies in History, Economics, and Public Law, 71, no. 1 (New York, 1916), 230. The number of African slaves may have been greater than that shown in the 1726 census. Clark, *New Orleans*, 23-24, reports that the Company of the Indies imported more than 2,500 blacks in 1722 and that such imports totaled 6,000 by 1731. Under the French regime, Illinois referred to both banks of the Mississippi River north of the Ohio. At the close of the Seven Years' War, this area was divided between Britain and Spain. The term "Spanish Illinois" as used below refers to the west bank of the Mississippi, or roughly that

area now included in the state of Missouri. Abraham P. Nasatir, *Borderland in Retreat: From Spanish Louisiana to the Far Southwest* (Albuquerque, NM, 1976), 3-4.

[6]These approximate figures are synthesized from data found in various sources. A 1763 census of river communities from English Turn to Pointe Coupée indicated the total number of black and mulatto slaves as 4,652 and of Indian slaves as 60. See "Recapitulation générale des recensemens [sic] ci-joints faits à la Nouvelle Orléans et dans tous les quartiers qui en dependent depuis le bas du fleuve jusqu'à la jurisdiction de la Pointe Coupée, inclusivement, en l'année mil sept cent Soixante trois," Seville, Spain, Archivo General de Indias (hereinafter AGI), Santo Domingo, legajo 2595, folios 148-49. (Unless otherwise noted, documents cited from AGI are also available on microfilm at Loyola University, New Orleans, and the University of Southwestern Louisiana, Lafayette.)

The figure given for Indian slaves in the 1763 census is clearly too low. The so-called O'Reilly census, made in 1769, reported 61 Indian slaves in the city of New Orleans alone and a total of 112 for the city, its adjacent posts, and the posts of Natchitoches and Rapides. Lawrence Kinnaird, ed., *Spain in the Mississippi Valley, 1765-1794*, 3 vols. (Washington, DC, 1946), 1:196. The O'Reilly census omitted the entire slave population of Pointe Coupée, a serious oversight since that post was one of the most developed plantation communities in the colony and had always had a substantial unfree population. Pointe Coupée reported 20 Indian Slaves in 1745 and 12 in 1763. It would seem safe to assume that there must have been between 10 and 20 in O'Reilly's time. See, respectively, Bill Barron, ed., *Census of Pointe Coupee, Louisiana*, 1745 (New Orleans, 1978); and the 1763 manuscript census cited above. To these figures should be added a total of 98 Indian slaves reported at St. Louis and Ste. Geneviève in 1770-71. See the commandants' reports published in Kinnaird, ed., *Spain in the Mississippi Valley*, 1:167-70, 172-79.

A major difficulty in arriving at reliable figures is that, while the French routinely distinguished between Indians and blacks or mulattoes when counting the slave population, the Spanish did not. On the Spanish censuses of Louisiana, see the useful monograph of Antonio Acosta Rodríguez, *La población de Luisiana española, 1763-1803* (Madrid, 1979).

[7]Miscegenation was common in colonial Louisiana and complexion or physical appearance was no sure guide in the absence of certain knowledge of ancestry. To a large extent, ethnic identity among "creole" slaves depended upon self-estimation or local reputation. Whites could and did view a reddish complexion as characteristic of both Indians and mulattoes. See, for example, testimony in the case of Duvergés v. St. Martin, Louisiana Historical Center (hereafter LHC, Louisiana State Museum, New Orleans, Spanish Judicial Records, January 14, 1795 (2), in which the witness stated of the plaintiff that she was "rouge ou Mulâtresse ou Sauvagesse." On the imprecision of Spanish socioracial terminology, see Magnus Mörner, *Race Mixture in the History of Latin America* (Boston, 1967), 56-60. French terminology was no more precise. The word *griffe*, in fact, was also used to describe the offspring of the union between a black and a mulatto. The visible difference between these *griffes* and those who were born of unions between blacks and Indians was probably insufficient to provide infallible ethnic identification. On the problematic nature of racial labels in colonial Louisiana, see the comment on vital records in Elizabeth Shown Mills, comp., *Natchitoches, 1729-1803: Abstracts of the Catholic Church Registers of the French and Spanish Post of St. Jean Baptiste des Natchitoches in Louisiana*, Cane River Creole Series, no. 2 (New Orleans, 1977), xv.

For the purposes of this study, the word "Indian" is taken to mean both full-blooded and mixed-blooded persons of Indian descent.

[8]That is "sauvage appartenant à . . . ." Trudel, *L'Esclavage au Canada*, 9-10, 16-17. This formula appears frequently in the vital and judicial records of French Louisiana. See, for example, Mills, comp., *Natchitoches*, passim.

[9]Several such cases are described in the life histories of Indian plaintiffs to be found in the colonial judicial records of Louisiana. The laws which governed these relationships were local and customary. The French Crown eventually recognized them but otherwise declined to legislate on Indian slavery. Trudel, *L'Esclavage au Canada*, 9-10, 41-42.

[10]Opinion of Procureur Général François Fleuriau regarding the problem of runaway Indian slaves, LHC, French Judicial Records, August 1, 1726 (3). The *Code Noir*, introduced for the West Indies in 1685 and for Louisiana in 1724, was a response to the expansion of the black slave population in those areas and never applied to New France, where the vast majority of slaves remained Indian. Trudel, *L'Esclavage au Canada*, 37-38.

[11]John Preston Moore, *Revolt in Louisiana: The Spanish Occupation, 1766-1770* (Baton Rouge, 1976); Bibiano Torres Ramírez, *Alejandro O'Reilly en las Indias* (Seville, 1969), 97-179; O'Reilly to Arriaga, December 10, 1769, in Kinnaird, ed., *Spain in the Mississippi Valley*, 1:132-35.

[12]It is frequently reported that O'Reilly simply reenacted the French *Code Noir* and that, therefore, whatever other changes may have been wrought locally, the accustomed law of slavery remained the same. A recent

study has shown, however, that O'Reilly's reenactment of the *Code* was, at the most, an interim measure and that the laws that governed slavery in Louisiana during the Spanish dominion were, in fact, Spanish rather than French. Hans W. Baade, "The Law of Slavery in Spanish *Luisiana*, 1769-1803," paper presented at Louisiana's Legal Heritage, a symposium held at the Louisiana State Museum, New Orleans, April 23, 1981. Although too late for consultation in the preparation of the present study, a revised version of Baade's important essay has recently appeared in Edward F. Haas, ed., *Louisiana's Legal Heritage* (Pensacola, FL, 1983), 43-86. All citations below are to the transcript version.

[13]Ibid., 4-19. See also, Elsa V. Goveia, "The West Indian Slave Laws of the Eighteenth Century," *Revista de Ciencias Sociales*, 4 (1960): 75-105.

[14]Printed broadside (French text), December 7, 1769, LHC, Colonial Miscellany, 1966.40.705. An English translation appears in Kinnaird, ed., *Spain in the Mississippi Valley*, 1:125-26.

[15]Carondelet to Llaguno, May 17, 1794, AGI, Santo Domingo, legajo 2563, folio 964vo.

[16]Kinnaird, ed., *Spain in the Mississippi Valley*, 1:167-70, 172-79.

[17]Unzaga to Piernas, n.d., AGI, Papeles de Cuba, legajo 81. This letter appears in English translation in Kinnaird, ed., *Spain in the Mississippi Valley*, 1:189-92.

[18]See, for example, Bormé *v.* Brumeaux heirs, LHC, Spanish Judicial Records, May 20, 1776 (1); Jeanne *v.* Maroteau, LHC, Spanish Judicial Records August 21, 1783 (1). The latter was a case of *coartación*, or freedom purchase, a customary practice known in Cuba and introduced by the Spanish into Louisiana. It provided that any slave possessing the financial means to pay his own market value might compel his master to emancipate him in return for such compensation. Thus, the plaintiff Jeanne availed herself of a remedy that would have been available to her even had she not claimed Indian ancestry. *Coartación* was not universal to the Spanish empire. It was totally unknown under French law. For freedom purchase in Louisiana, see Baade, "Law of Slavery," 35-55.

[19]Hans W. Baade, "The Formalities of Private Real Estate Transactions in Spanish North America: A Report on Some Recent Discoveries," *Louisiana Law Review*, 38 (1977-78): 691-99.

[20]Not all slaveholders bothered with evasive tactics. In 1781, Guillaume Marre executed an act before the Spanish notary Andrés de Almonester y Rojas by which he sold to Joseph Verloin DeGrüy a sixteen-year-old Comanche girl whom he described as "una salvaje mi esclava nombrada Tereza." Years later, when the woman brought suit for her freedom and DeGrüy's title came under examination by the court, Marre claimed that he had been unaware of the prohibition. Marie Thérèse *v.* DeGrüy, LHC, Spanish Judicial Records, July 19, 1793 (1).

[21]Louis Houck, ed., *The Spanish Regime in Missouri*, 2 vols. (Chicago, 1909), 1:249-50.

[22]We have not located the record of Marie's suit. Some details of her case may be learned, however, from her letter of manumission issued by the executor of Cruzat's estate. Orleans Parish Notarial Archives, New Orleans (hereinafter OPNA), Acts of Rafael Perdomo, vol. 15, folios 243-44.

[23]Pierre v. Cruzat heirs, LHC, Spanish Judicial Records, May 4, 1790 (1), folio 6-6vo.

[24]OPNA, Acts of Rafael Perdomo, vol. 15, folios 154-55.

[25]Baptiste *v.* Bourgignon, LHC, Spanish Judicial Records, January 23, 1790 (2): Bourgignon *v.* Lalumendière heirs, LHC, Spanish Judicial Records, January 21, 1791 (1). The original act of sale, dated at Ste. Geneviève, October 24, 1788, described Baptiste as a mulatto. Bourgignon *v.* Lalumendière heirs, folios 1-2.

[26]This phenomenon is routinely noted in traditional accounts of the period but, perhaps because of the exaggerated nature of the eventual white reaction, there has been a tendency to overdramatize it. Most accounts are based upon that of Charles Gayarré, *History of Louisiana*, 4th ed., 3 vols. (New Orleans, 1903), 3:334-35: ". . . suddenly, in 1793 and 1794, they [the Indian slaves], almost in a body, startled Governor Carondelet by applying for their freedom." Gayarré offers no precise citation, but it appears beyond question that the sole source for his discussion is a single line from Carondelet's May 17, 1794, letter to Don Eugenio de Llaguno y Amirola, AGI, Santo Domingo, legajo 2563, folio 964vo.

[27]In addition to those cited elsewhere in this article, these include Jean Baptiste *v.* Morel, LHC, Spanish Judicial Records, January 13, 1791 (1); Marianne *v.* Pomet, LHC, Spanish Judicial Records, January 13, 1791

(2); Julien *v.* Tallon, LHC, Spanish Judicial Records, July 12, 1791 (1); Joseph *v.* St. Cyr, LHC, Spanish Judicial Records, July 12, 1791 (3); Ignacio v. Soubie, OPNA, Court Proceedings of Francisco Broutin, vol. 24, folios 125-46.

[28]Hans W. Baade, "The Administrative and Judicial Functions of the Lieutenant Governors and Post Commandants of Spanish Louisiana," paper presented before the Louisiana Historical Association, New Orleans, March 21, 1980.

[29]Even if one did so, he would still have to evade his master's vigilance long enough to make contact with the authorities or with sympathetic free persons. Such was the case, for example, of Baptiste, cited above, who accompanied his master, the flatboatman Bourgignon, downriver. Baptiste accused Bourgignon of seeking to remove him forcibly from New Orleans to prevent his pressing his case. He went into hiding and petitioned for the protection of the court. Baptiste *v.* Bourgignon, folios 6-7.

[30]On the impact of the Haitian Revolution—and the closely related matter of the French Revolution—on Louisiana in the 1790s, see, especially, Ernest R. Liljegren, "Jacobinism in Spanish Louisiana, 1792-1797," *Louisiana Historical Quarterly*, 22 (1939): 47-97; Thomas Marc Fiehrer, "The Baron de Carondelet as Agent of Bourbon Reform: A Study of Spanish Colonial Administration in the Years of the French Revolution (Ph.D. dissertation, Tulane University, 1977); Paul F. LaChance, "The Politics of Fear: French Louisianians and the Slave Trade, 1786-1809," *Plantation Society in the Americas*, 1 (1979): 162-97.

[31]In all seven cases of suits brought to judgment prior to the 1794 suspension, the governor found in favor of the Indian plaintiffs.

[32]French planters resented in particular Carondelet's efforts to enforce Spanish laws designed to protect all slaves from mistreatment by their masters. LaChance, "Politics of Fear," 173-75; Baade, "Law of Slavery," 16. See also the derogatory comments of a Pointe Coupée planter regarding the favorable reputation Carondelet enjoyed among the slaves, in Narcisse *v.* Croizet, LHC, Spanish Judicial Records, July 5, 1793 (1).

[33]Pointe Coupée was an indigo-producing district on the Mississippi River north of Baton Rouge and had been the scene of a slave insurrection scare in 1791.

[34]Cécile *v.* Tounoir, LHC, Spanish Judicial Records, August 7, 1793, (1); Cécile *v.* Émond, et al., OPNA, Court Proceedings of Francisco Broutin, vol. 24, October 17, 1793, folios 21-81.

[35]Marie Jeanne *v.* Monsanto and Poydras, OPNA, Court Proceedings of Francisco Broutin, vol. 21, September 4, 1793, folios 302-87. Antoine's father appears to have been a prominent white man of the district with the same name who had once been Marie Jeanne's master. See Antoine *v.* Deshôtels heirs, LHC, Spanish Judicial Records, March 7, 1774.

[36]Monsanto, possibly offended by the last assertion, dissociated his case from that of Poydras and declared his complete acceptance of the authority of the Spanish legislation in question. Marie Jeanne *v.* Monsanto and Poydras, folio 45-45vo. Monsanto's show of loyalty to Spain may have been politically motivated. He was a Jew of Portuguese and Dutch antecedents and remained in the colony by the governor's sufferance. Bertram Wallace Korn, *The Early Jews of New Orleans* (Waltham, MA, 1969), 10-40.

[37]It was certainly true, as Poydras asserted, that Marie Jeanne's case had its weaknesses. As far as proving her own Indian ancestry was concerned, she could present no baptismal certificate. Those she produced for her two children, located in the parish registers at Pointe Coupée, offered her case no support and one even showed evidence of tampering sufficient to render its contents equivocal. Marie Jeanne *v.* Monsanto and Poydras, folios 49-54. It was also true that Antoine had once sued unsuccessfully for his freedom. But that case, heard almost twenty years earlier, involved a completely different legal question, the validity of a verbal codicil to his mistress's will. The young slave made no appeal to any Indian ancestry at the time; in fact, he described himself as a mulatto. Antoine *v.* Deshôtels heirs.

[38]Marie Jeanne *v.* Monsanto and Poydras, folios 324-28vo.

[39]Specifically, Poydras maintained that most Indian slaves in Louisiana were descendants of the Natchez who had been ordered enslaved by the French Crown after their defeat in a campaign provoked by their massacre of white settlers at Fort Rosalie in 1729. Poydras's claim was not true, and it is inconceivable that he did not know it. Most of the slaves taken by the French in their early campaigns against the Natchez and the Chickasaw Indians were apparently shipped off to the sugar plantations of the French West Indies. John R. Swanton, *Indian Tribes of the Lower Mississippi Valley and Adjacent Coast of the Gulf of Mexico*, Bureau of

American Ethnology Bulletin No. 43 (Washington, DC, 1911), 186-257; Patricia D. Woods, *French-Indian Relations on the Southern Frontier, 1699-1762* (Ann Arbor, MI, 1980), 105.

[40]Poydras, et al., to Carondelet, New Orleans, February 28, 1794, AGI, Santo Domingo, legajo 2563, folios 968-69.

[41]"Representación de varios habitantes sobre esclavos indios Natchez, 1794-95," AGI, Santo Domingo, legajo 2532, folios 607-19.

[42]Carondelet to Llaguno, New Orleans, May 17, 1794, AGI, Santo Domingo, legajo 2563, folios 965vo-66.

[43]Ibid.; Cécile *v.* Émond, et al., folios 47-49.

[44]Duvergès *v.* St. Martin, LHC, Spanish Judicial Records, January 14, 1795 (2).

[45]Ibid.; Cécile *v.* Émond, et al., folios 63-79.

[46]On events in Pointe Coupée in 1795, see Jack D.L. Holmes, "The Abortive Slave Revolt in Pointe Coupée, Louisiana, 1795," *Louisiana History*, 11 (1970): 341-62; Juan José Andreu Ocariz, *Movimientos rebeldes de los esclavos negros durante el dominio español en Luisiana* (Zaragoza, 1977): 117-77 and passim. For Antoine's confession and execution, see "Procès criminel contre les négres de la P[te] Coupée sur le Crime de Révolution ou Conspiration contre les Blancs, 1795," LHC, Spanish Judicial Records, May 2, 1795 (1), folios 54-56vo, 103-103vo. In the trial record, the whites referred to Antoine as a mulatto. In his own testimony, he described himself as merely a "créole de se Poste. . . ." We will never know whether he took the claim to Indian ancestry seriously or not.

[47]Endorsements of November 24, 1794, December 18, 1795, and December 30, 1795, to "Representación de varios habitantes . . .," folios 614-15, 616-17vo, 618-19vo.

[48]This statement reflects the documentary record as we have been able to reconstruct it. We do have references, however, to an apparently isolated case in which the last Spanish governor of Louisiana, Manuel Juan de Salcedo (1801-1803), freed a mestizo woman and her children belonging to the estate of Francisco Bouligny. Our search for the record of this case has been unsuccessful. We cannot, therefore, be certain whether Salcedo acted on the basis of as yet undiscovered royal instruction or simply in ignorance, genuine or willful, of the earlier controversy. Gilbert C. Din, "The Death and Succession of Francisco Bouligny," *Louisiana History*, 22 (1981): 312-13. See also, intestate succession of Francisco Bouligny, LHC, Spanish Judicial Records, November 25, 1800 (1), folios 93-96; OPNA, Acts of Carlos Ximénez, vol. 18, folios 134-35vo.

[49]John Leddy Phelan, "Authority and Flexibility in the Spanish Imperial Bureaucracy," *Administrative Sciences Quarterly*, 5 (1960): 47-65.

[50]LaChance, "Politics of Fear," 196-97.

[51]Legal aspects of the transition to Anglo-American rule are treated in George Dargo, *Jefferson's Louisiana: Politics and the Clash of Legal Traditions* (Cambridge, MA, 1975).

[52]On at least two occasions, questions involving Indian slaves reached the Louisiana supreme court. In both cases, the court ruled on procedural grounds rather than consider arguments based on racial origin. It is interesting to note, however, that in each instance the local jury had found for the slave plaintiff and had placed great emphasis on his Indian ancestry in doing so. Séville *v.* Chrétien (1817) from St. Landry Parish; and Ulzère et al. *v.* Poeyfarré (1820 and 1824) from St. James Parish; both abstracted in Helen H. Tunnicliff Catterall and James J. Hayden, eds., *Judicial Cases Concerning American Slavery and the Negro*, 5 vols. (Washington, DC, 1926-34), 3:456-65, 476. In a similar case arising in Missouri, the supreme court of that state ruled directly on the question of Indian slavery, finding it unlawful as having been prohibited under the colonial regime. Harrison Anthony Trexler, *Slavery in Missouri, 1804-1865*, Johns Hopkins University Studies in Historical and Political Science, ser. 32, no. 2 (Baltimore, 1914), 80-81.

[53]Baade, "Law of Slavery," 27-31.

THE LAW OF SLAVERY IN SPANISH LUISIANA, 1769-1803*

Hans W. Baade

There is a tradition in Luisiana[1] that [Governor Alejandro] O'Reilly confirmed or perhaps even guaranteed the continued applicability of the French *Code Noir* in 1724[2] under Spanish rule. This tradition is already reflected in the classic nineteenth-century works of Judge Martin and Charles Gayarré.[3] Although squarely contradicted by the Supreme Court of Luisiana as early as 1816, it is still carried forward more or less routinely by authors with ready access to original Spanish-period sources.[4]

Closely allied with the notion that French *slave* law continued to be applied in Luisiana after O'Reilly's 1769 reorganizations[5] is the more general proposition that French *private* law, too, remained in effect. This proposition, as well, has had eminent supporters, from Thomas Jefferson to Gustavus Schmidt and, more recently, Col. John Tucker.[6] Such a radical "Francophile" view of the legal history of Spanish Luisiana cannot, however, still be maintained today. The original sources now accessible demonstrate, it is submitted, beyond doubt (1) that O'Reilly was authorized to change the law of the province if he deemed it advisable to do so;[7] (2) that he did, indeed, introduce the law of Castile and of the Indies;[8] (3) and crucially, that his actions in this respect received the express approval of his Majesty in Council;[9] (4), and finally, that the judicial authorities of Spanish Luisiana routinely applied Spanish rather than French law between 1770 and 1803.[10]

If "Spanish" rather than French *private* law prevailed (and was in fact applied) in Spanish Luisiana after O'Reilly's reorganizations, it seems unlikely that the situation as to slave law was different. For one thing, as the insurgents of 1768 were to find out rather quickly, the public law (including the penal law) of the new sovereign was applied more or less automatically,[11] and slave law tends to be, in the nature of things, more of a public-law than of a private-law character. (Legal restrictions on the freedom to manumit,

*This article was first published as the introduction in *Louisiana's Legal Heritage,* Edward F. Haas, ed. (Pensacola, FL: Published for the Louisiana State Museum by the Perdido Bay Press, 1983), 43-86. Reprinted with the kind permission of the author and the publisher.

to take the key factor, are *iuris publici* [sworn publicly] almost by definition.) Furthermore, even in the realm of "private" slave law, the two most significant transactions with slaves as objects: their sale and their mortgaging, were subjected to an elaborate set of regulations enacted by O'Reilly and Governor [Luis] Unzaga in 1770, and reflecting Castilian rather than French legal institutions.[12]

It is reasonably clear, therefore, that the slave law of post-1769 Spanish Luisiana operated in a "Spanish" rather than in a French legal environment, and that at least in part, it reflected the law of Castile and of the Indies rather than French colonial law. The white population of Luisiana, however, remained basically Francophonic and socially as well as culturally oriented towards metropolitan and especially overseas France during Spanish rule. It may be, therefore, that the "living" slave law of the province between 1769 and 1803 was French rather than Spanish in content. That possibility gains further in strength in direct proportion to remoteness from New Orleans, for as I have attempted to show elsewhere, Spanish Luisiana was essentially a "dual state," and the legal folkways at the posts remained French.[13]

The kind of ambivalent coexistence thus envisaged could, however, have existed only to the extent that there were no fundamental differences between French and Spanish slave law as actually enforced by the Spanish judicial authorities of the province. Wherever there was such a fundamental difference, on the other hand, pertinent Spanish judicial practice in Luisiana will readily inform us whether the Spanish authorities of the province applied French or Spanish slave law.

The present study therefore seeks, first, to identify the salient differences between Spanish and French prototypes of slave law in the latter part of the eighteenth century. As will be seen presently, this task is greatly facilitated by a lively and ongoing debate among historians of what might be called the comparative "living law" of slavery in the Americas. Secondly, an attempt is made to place O'Reilly's "confirmation" of the *Code Noir* into the general context of his reorganization of the administrative and judicial structure of the province. Thirdly, by examining some thirty judicial records and about three hundred notarial instruments, we will try to determine to what extent (if any) the Spanish authorities in Luisiana actually applied, in their day-to-day practice, those parts of "Spanish" slave law that were *directly contrary* to the *Code Noir* of 1724.

Spanish Law

Several key provisions of the French colonial law of slavery as codified in the late seventeenth and early eighteenth centuries are readily traced to Roman precedent. This applies, in particular, to disqualifications and incapacities of slaves: as witnesses, arbitrators, private litigants, and contracting parties.[14] Given the heritage of the French legal system, the fact of these borrowings is not nearly as remarkable as their one-sided selectivity to the detriment of slaves. No provision was made for the judicial sale of slaves cruelly abused by their masters, recognized in Imperial Rome.[15] *Peculium*, or the

Roman-law notion of quasi-property by sufference, was precluded by inference; and self-purchase (widely practiced in the Roman Empire) was inhibited by the *Code Noir* of 1724.[16] This one-sided legislative preference of masters over slaves and of slavery over liberty was further underlined by the speedy supression or restriction of two Roman-law borrowings in the 1685 *Code Noir* that were favorable to slaves: the power of masters twenty years of age to manumit, and implied manumission by testamentary institution.[17]

The Castilian legal system, too, was built in part on Roman foundations, and several provisions of Alfonso el Sabio's *Siete Partidas* on the subject of slavery are of Roman origin. The most famous of these is the initial sentence of Title 21 of the fourth *Partida*, which declares slavery to be contrary to natural reason. Law 6 of that title authorized slaves to file complaints of cruelty against their masters, and directed the judicial sale of such slaves when cruelty is established, so as to preclude their return to the same master. A third well-known provision is a law of the fifth *Partida* confirming the validity of guarantees by a slave as a natural obligation, "*por cuanto es ome* [sic]." As interpreted by the authoritative commentary of Gregorio López, this passage reflected the general Roman-law rule expounded by the Glossators and by Bartolus that slaves could contract natural obligations; and by the mid-seventeenth century, it supported standing to enforce self-purchase contracts.[18]

Perhaps even more importantly, until the Bourbon reforms of the late eighteenth century, Castilian secular law was taught almost entirely on the basis of Roman texts and Roman-law treatises, with the *derecho patrio* serving only as an occasional illustration. The university reforms initiated by Charles III ultimately reversed this pattern and made Castilian-language instruction in the laws of the land the rule rather than the exception.[19] These reforms, however, reflected a more pervasive policy reorientation based on the Enlightenment. Thus, when the Council of the Indies undertook to formulate a cohesive policy on the subject of slavery in the last decades of the eighteenth century, it could (and did) resort to those institutions and doctrines of the Roman law of slavery that were supportive of liberty rather than slavery, and that favored slaves rather than masters.

This process is best documented by a lengthy report, or *informe*, filed with the Council of the Indies at its request in January, 1782, and jointly prepared by the former intendants of Caracas, Havana, and Luisiana.[20] The Council was at that time considering the representations of the inhabitants of these intendancies, and of Santo Domingo, against the local promulgation of the famous *cédula* of May 31, 1789, on the Education, Treatment, and Employment of Slaves. After a brief summary of the law of slavery since antiquity, the *informe* noted that in modern times, slaves received "incomparably milder" treatment in Spanish overseas possessions than in the American colonies of France, England, or the Netherlands. One of the results of this mild treatment, they pointed out, was the much more favorable ratio of freedmen to slaves in Spanish possessions.[21]

The intendants attributed the mildness of the Spanish system of slavery as compared with other European slave systems then extant to three factors. These were the protective concern of the Spanish sovereigns for the Indians, which by analogy extended to slaves as well; the constant protection of these disadvantaged castes by judicial and ecclesiastical authorities; and finally, "*la sabiduría de nuestras leyes patrias, que adoptando únicamente la parte benigna de la legislación romana, ciñeron los derechos de la esclavitud a los precisos términos de la necesidad.* ["The wisdom of our native laws, which adopting only the benign part of Roman legislation, girded the rights of slavery to the precise terms of necessity."][22]

In particular, the *informe* pointed to three institutions of Spanish law that had "*suavizado la esclavitud hasta un grado desconocido en las demas naciones*" ["softened slavery to a point unknown in other nations"]. First, masters did not require official permission for the manumission of their slaves. Secondly, Spanish law enabled slaves to purchase their freedom, and that of their wives and children, by paying their purchase price to their masters. Thirdly, and finally, Spanish tribunals were open to slaves who complained of the cruelty of their masters, and where *mal trato* [mistreatment] was established, the judge was empowered to sell the slave to another master.[23]

These conclusions were incorporated into a *consulta* of a plenary session of all three *salas* of the Council of the Indies, dated March 17, 1794.[24] There is little doubt, therefore, that they expressed not only the views of seasoned senior officials with field experience in the Americas (including Luisiana) but also the legal position of the Council of the Indies itself. Nevertheless, a few qualifying remarks seem indicated.

First, the situation described by the intendants and by the Council was that prevailing at the very end of the eighteenth century. Spanish slave law as actually applied in the Indies had undergone considerable development in the course of that century, and this development had not been uniform. To take an example of the former factor: self-purchase was bitterly resisted by some slave owners in New Granada even in the latter part of the eighteenth century. Their lawyers argued that the *peculium* of slaves belonged in law to the master, who could repossess it at any time, and that in any event, no one could be forced to sell his property if he did not want to. These arguments were, as we have seen, contrary to a benign view of Roman law as received in Castile. They accordingly failed to prevail before the *Audiencia* of New Granada and tribunals subject to it, but the right of self-purchase had to be vindicated, even at that late date, by persistent litigation.[25]

As regards lack of uniformity, it will be recalled that even as late as 1785, the *Audiencia* of Santo Domingo had favored the *Code Noir* over a "libertarian" version of Spanish law. Conversely, Cuba practiced a system of self-purchase (known as *coartación*) even more advanced than that described in general terms by the intendants. Cuban slaves could purchase their freedom, as it were, on the installment plan, with the double advantage that their purchase price was fixed at the early stage, and more "free time" became available for outside employment to obtain funds for payment of the balance remaining. So far as can be determined, this type of limited self-purchase was not practiced outside of Cuba.

Finally, mention must be made of the self-laudatory tone of the *informe*, which stands in stark contrast with its ultimate recommendations. The question to be answered was, after all, if the *cédula* of 1789 should be promulgated in places where it had been suspended upon the protests of the local population, *i.e.*, of the slaveholders and their supporters. The intendants recommended *against* the enforcement of the *cédula*, arguing that its principles were entrenched in Spanish slave law then prevailing, while the rules as to implementation were too detailed for reasonable accommodation to local circumstances.[26] Given the acknowledged gap between theory and practice in legislation for the protection of slaves against their masters, this was hardly a further step in the direction of "*humano trato* [humane treatment].[27]

Nevertheless, it seems abundantly clear that eighteenth-century Spanish slave law was qualitatively different from the French law of slavery then prevailing. France had, as it were, codified those parts of the Roman law of slavery that were to the advantage of slaveholders: lack of legal capacity, of power to contract, and of property rights. To these, it had added the requirement of official approval for manumissions. Spanish law, on the other hand, had received, implemented, and expanded the rules and notions of Roman slave law favoring the well-being and the ultimate freedom of slaves: *peculium*, self-purchase, and judicial protection. Additionally, it had always favored rather than restricted voluntary manumission.

The results were there, for all to see. The proportion of freedom to slaves was highest in the Spanish ultramarine possessions. Slaves fled from the French to the Spanish part of Santo Domingo, not in the opposite direction, and even foreign observers opposed to the institution of slavery praised the mildness of Spanish slave law in comparison to other Western systems of slavery in America.[28]

O'Reilly's "Reenactment" of the *Code Noir* and the Reorganizations of 1769-70

A. The "Reenactment"

By royal *cédula* of April 16, 1769, Gen. Alejandro O'Reilly was commissioned to proceed to Luisiana with a force of arms to take formal possession of that colony. He was authorized to appoint an *asesor*, or legal adviser, and a *fiscal*, or prosecutor. With the assistance of these two *letrado* (university-educated) lawyers, he was directed to "institute prosecutions, and to punish in conformity with the Laws, the instigators and accomplices of the uprising" against Governor Ulloa, and to set up, "in the military as well as the political establishments, the administration of justice and the management of my royal *hacienda* [estate], the form of government, dependency and subordination which may be advisable according to the instructions you bear and those which may be issued to you later."[29]

On August 18, 1769, General O'Reilly took formal possession of New Orleans on behalf of Spain. He quickly moved to accomplish the legal and political objectives of his mission. His activities in this regard can be divided chronologically into three phases: the establishment and consolidation of Spanish power, the punishment of those responsible for the expulsion of Governor Ulloa in 1768, and the basic reorganization of the judicial and administrative system of Spanish Luisiana.[30] His "reenactment" of the *Code Noir* falls into the first of these three phases.

On August 27, 1769, or less than two weeks after having taken formal possession of Luisiana, O'Reilly issued a proclamation on the subject of the administration of justice.[31] After stating that nothing was more essential for good order than the observation of laws, and expressing admiration for the "wisdom and piety" of the *Code Noir* of 1724, O'Reilly directed that this code be "observed with exactitude." He then announced that his "other occupations" did not permit him to attend to litigation in person, and appointed two individuals, Sieurs Fleurieu and Ducros, to "*administrer la Justice dans cette Partie*." The proclamation then directed that the judgments to be rendered by Fleurieu and Ducros be followed and executed, and concluded by ordering all "officers and others" to lend all the aid and forceful support to this end that might be required of them.

O'Reilly's motives in making this proclamation (along with some others) are further explained in his report to the marqués de Grimaldi, dated August 31, 1769, on the taking of possession of New Orleans and acts connected therewith.[32] He wrote that these initial *providencias* [provisions] had been received with much favor locally, and had been of good effect. As a general proposition, he stated, no change was to be made unless it was "*necesaria y muy reflexionada*" ["necessary and well thought out"]. The next step, he continued, was the banishment of evil elements and the punishment of the ringleaders of the uprising. After that, provision would have to be made for the future government of the colony. O'Reilly expressed assurance that in four months, royal authority would be solidly established, and that he would then be able to return to Havana.

B. The Reorganizations

The "other occupations" referred to in the proclamation of August 27, 1769, we see, were the need to deal with subversives and to punish the ringleaders of the rebellion. This second phase of O'Reilly's activities in Luisiana was concluded with his judgment in the treason trials, dated October 24, 1769. That judgment imposed severe penalties, including sentences of death, on the principal ringleaders. It was expressly based on "*nuestras leyes*" ["our laws"],[33] thus giving a strong indication as to the nature of the legal system to be established in the third and ultimate phase of O'Reilly's activities in Luisiana.

That phase began on November 25, 1769, when O'Reilly issued a proclamation reciting the role of the Superior Council in the late insurrection, and stating that

> with a view to prevent hereafter evils of such magnitude, it is indispensable to abolish the said council, and to establish in their stead that form of political

> Government and administration of justice prescribed by our wise laws, and by which all the states of His Majesty in America have been maintained in the most perfect tranquility, content, and subordination.[34]

This policy was implemented by two sets of texts that are of decisive significance for the subsequent development of Luisiana law under Spanish rule.

The first set consists of two documents: Ordinances of the *Ayuntamiento* [municipal government] of New Orleans, and Instructions for adjudicating civil and criminal cases in Luisiana. These documents are collectively known today as "O'Reilly's Laws;" they are both dated November 25, 1769, and form the basis of the organization of the *cabildo* and the central administration of justice.[35] The Ordinances regulate the organization and functions, including the judicial functions, of the *Ayuntamiento* or secular *cabildo* of New Orleans, which replaced the Superior Council. The Instructions set forth the rules of civil and criminal procedure to be applied by the governor and the *cabildo* sitting judicially, but they also contain substantive rules, especially on criminal law and the law of both testate and intestate succession.

The second set of legal texts consists of a series of instructions issued to the two lieutenant governors at St. Louis and at Natchitoches on January 26, 1770, and on February 12, 1770, to the "lieutenants" or, in subsequent parlance, the commandants, of the nine original posts. They are, in substance, adaptations of the instructions of November 25, 1769, to the needs of judicial administration and legal recording outside New Orleans, and they incorporate these Instructions by reference where appropriate.[36]

In addition to these two sets of major tests, O'Reilly also promulgated a regulation on the subject of mortgages, dated February 12, 1770. Soon thereafter, on November 9 of that year, his successor, Governor Unzaga, enacted an ordinance regulating the sale of slaves, immovables, and ships.[37]

C. Courts and Lawyers

As described in greater detail elsewhere, Spanish Luisiana was a "dual state" so far as the administration of justice is concerned. There was a highly sophisticated Spanish-type judicial system at the capital, paralleling those of municipalities of similar size and importance elsewhere in Spanish America.[38] The posts, on the other hand, were administered by commandants with limited judicial powers comparable to those of justices of the peace. The judicial powers of the two territorial lieutenant governors at Natchitoches and St. Louis were somewhat more extensive but still limited, in civil matters, to controversies under one hundred *pesos*.[39]

In New Orleans and its immediate environs, the *alcaldes* [mayors] of the *cabildo* exercised general civil jurisdiction, subject only to immunities conferred by the military and ecclesiastical *fueros* [authorities]. The governor had exclusive jurisdiction in litigation where members of the military were defendants, and in cases arising outside of New Orleans where the object in controversy exceeded the jurisdictional powers of the commandants or lieutenant governors of the posts. As a practical matter, this included all slave cases arising outside of the New Orleans metropolitan area. Clerics with faculties as ecclesiastical judges and later, the bishop, had exclusive jurisdiction over civil actions against members of the clergy, but no freedom-purchase case in the *fuero ecclesiastico* has come to our attention.

The judicial decisions of the governor of Luisiana and of the *alcaldes* of New Orleans were subject to review by a special Tribunal of Appeals at Havana, composed of high officials of the Spanish administration of Cuba and convoked on an *ad hoc* basis as occasion arose.[40] While there were a number of appeals to that Tribunal from Luisiana,[41] none of these, apparently, involved a freedom-purchase question. Decisions of the Havana Tribunal of Appeals could be appealed, in theory, to the Council of the Indies sitting judicially, but diligent search has yielded only one Luisiana case which reached that Council in this manner.[42] At the turn of the century, the *ad hoc* appellate tribunal at Havana was replaced by the *Audiencia* of Santo Domingo, which had been evacuated from Hispaniola to Cuba.[43] There is, however, no known instance of a Luisiana appeal to that *audiencia.*

The slave-law jurisprudence of Luisiana, then, consists of decisions of the governor or one of the *alcaldes* of the *cabildo* of New Orleans sitting judicially. These officials were almost invariably not law-trained.[44] In most instances, however, they had the benefit of the advice of the *auditor de guerra*, or judge advocate, who also acted *ex officio* as the *asesor letrado*, or law officer, of the courts at New Orleans. Under the customary law of Castile and of the Indies codified by *cédula* late in the eighteenth century, lay judges were not liable for negligence in the exercise of their judicial functions if they conformed their decisions to the legal advice (or *dictamen*) of an *asesor letrado* holding a royal appointment.[45]

Records of judicial proceedings were kept by the appropriate *escribano*, or notary, who also issued citations to the parties and to witnesses, and received proof documentary and deposition testimony. Pleadings had to be in Spanish, and had to be filed through *procuradores del numero*, or pleaders. Initially, there were two *escribanos* and two *procuradores* in New Orleans, but this number was increased to three at a later date.[46] These notaries and pleaders were licensed after being examined as to the skills of these crafts,[47] but unlike the *asesor letrado*, they were not university-trained lawyers. Costs were taxed pursuant to a detailed fee schedule.[48] This made the legal system essentially self-financing.

Jurisprudence, Policy, and Notarial Practice, 1770-1803

A. The Impact of the Reorganization on the Law of Slavery.

We have seen further above that on August 27, 1769, General O'Reilly made provisional arrangements for the administration of justice, and directed the observance of the 1724 *Code Noir*. On October 24 of the same year, he passed sentence on the 1768 insurgents pursuant to *Spanish* law; and one month later, he abolished the *Conseil Supérieur* [Superior Council]. Within a year thereafter, he and his successor completely revised the judicial and administrative system of Luisiana, which became, in essence, a Spanish ultramarine province under the jurisdiction of the Council of the Indies. How did these fundamental changes in Luisiana's legal system affect the applicability of French slave law, which had been decreed at the very outset of this three-phase process?

To begin with the most obvious and immediate change, the abolition of the *Conseil Supérieur* did away with the necessity or indeed the possibility of obtaining a finding of "legitimate cause" and a manumission license from that body, both of which were necessary prerequisites for manumission under the French *Code Noir*. As readily verified by the numerous *cartas de libertad* [manumission papers] in the Spanish notarial archives of New Orleans, Spanish Luisiana did not continue the French requirement of government approval for voluntary manumissions. In 1775, for instance, the *escribania* [notarial office] of Juan (Jean) Garic passed 24 notarial acts of manumission, and that of Andrés Almonastér, nineteen.[49] None of these instruments refer to a governmental or judicial approval, and the minutes of the *cabildo* of New Orleans contain no reference to manumission petitions.[50]

It will be recalled that the slavery *informe* of 1792 was later to single out three features of Spanish slave law which, in the opinion of the three former intendants, made it "incomparably milder" than other slave systems then extant, including that of France. These were the freedom of voluntary manumission, the right of self-purchase, and judicial protection against the cruelty of slave owners.[51] The first of these humanitarian features, we just saw, became part of Luisiana law almost immediately with the abolition of the *Conseil Supérieur*. The third-mentioned of the key humanitarian features of Spanish slave law, remarkably, was introduced by O'Reilly's Instructions. These provided that slaves could ordinarily initiate proceedings only with the approval of their masters. Where, however, a master had exceeded the bounds prescribed by law in exercising his authority over a slave (*i.e.*, where he had acted cruelly as legally defined), the slave could secure judicial approval to proceed against his master. Upon establishment of the charge, the slave was "entitled to require either his liberty or to be sold."[52]

Thus, two of the three main humanitarian features of late eighteenth-century Spanish slave law, both of them directly contrary to the *Code Noir* of 1724, became effective in Luisiana as a result of O'Reilly's legislation. Another change, of a lesser nature, was brought about by the Spanish Luisiana mortgage and conveyance ordinances of 1770. This legislation classified slaves as immovables for purposes of sale and hypothecation; the *Code Noir* had provided that they were movables.[53] There can be no doubt that these changes in the law of Luisiana brought about by positive enactment of the Spanish authorities displaced preexisting French slave law at least *pro tanto*, for whatever the legal significance of O'Reilly's "reenactment," of the *Code Noir*, it could not have stood at a higher level than his subsequent legislation.

There still was the question, however, whether the *Code Noir* remained effective in Luisiana to the extent that its provisions were not abrogated or modified by Spanish legislation applicable to and in Luisiana. As we shall see further below in connection with the purchase-of-freedom jurisprudence of Spanish Luisiana, that was not the case: O'Reilly's reorganizations had introduced the law of Castile and of the Indies in its entirety, and the Spanish judicial authorities applied only that law. The point of the continued applicability of the *Code Noir* was, so far as our research indicates, specifically raised in only one of these cases.[54] There is, however, at least one Spanish Luisiana decision in a case not involving the purchase of freedom where that point was also put in issue.

In *Angelica* v. *Juan Perret Estate*, a free person of color sought to enforce a testamentary bequest to her by the decedent. Two of the heirs favored compliance with this bequest, but a third one objected. Acting on her behalf, her husband Luis Ranson argued that the testamentary bequest was void because O'Reilly had "ordered that the Edict of the King that serves as the Regulation for the Negroes be preserved, observed, and complied with." He then textually recited, in Spanish, article 52 of the *Code Noir*, which as we saw invalidated donations *mortis causa* or *inter vivos* from white persons to persons of color.[55] The objector concluded by requesting that the court accordingly declare the bequest to Angelica to be invalid. *Alcalde* Forstall ruled, with the assistance of *Lic.* Odoardo as *asesor*, that despite this *contradicción* [contradiction] by Luis Ranson, the movables of the decedent be handled over to Angelica as provided in his will.[56]

Exactly eleven months earlier, *Lic.* Odoardo had assisted the governor sitting judicially in a purchase-of-freedom case. This was the petition of Catalina, a mulatress thirty-six years of age, for freedom for herself and her five-year old daughter from the estate of J. B. Destréhan. Initially, the estate objected to the petition, but at a later stage, the dispute was over the price. On October 14, 1773, Governor Unzaga, with the advice of *Lic.* Odoardo, ordered the appointment of Santiago Beauregard as the official estimator, and his valuation of 320 *pesos* was paid by the petitioner. Thereupon, Estevan Boré as executor of the estate issued a letter of manumission to the petitioner and her daughter.[57]

It thus seems clear that when professionally advised, the courts of Spanish Luisiana did *not* apply the *Code Noir* even where there was no contrary Spanish legislation directly in point, and that they *did* apply the Spanish law of freedom-purchase which had not been expressly extended to Luisiana. On the other hand, as Angelica's case illustrates, O'Reilly's initial preservation of the *Code Noir* was well remembered under Spanish rule, and its text continued to be accessible. It should come as no great surprise, therefore, that a determined effort was made to return to the *Code Noir* as soon as opportunity presented itself.

B. Governor Gálvez and the Slaveholders' *Fronde*

Let us recall at this point the astute observation by Professor Davis that a Spanish governor of Luisiana had opposed the introduction of freedom-purchase into that province, claiming that "what was proper for Cuba was not necessarily suitable for other Spanish possessions." This refers to the judgment of Governor Gálvez in *Suriray* v. *Jenkins*,[58] an epic case which will require detailed attention here.

The key figure in that case was María Juana, a slave of Juan Suriray. She had filed a purchase-of-freedom petition in Governor Unzaga's court, and the appropriate initiating order had been made. In a new proceeding in the Governor's Court, she alleged that thereupon, she had been removed by her master to Juan Dubourq's plantation, inhibited in her efforts to secure her freedom, and treated with cruelty. She had fled to the city, and now sought to obtain her freedom. She asserted that her claim was unopposed by secular law, and supported by Divine law.[59]

When ordered to reply on penality of suffering judgment by default, Juan Suriray argued, first, that in the laws of Spain, there was no obligation for the master to free or to sell a slave, or to destroy his property. He also called attention to General O'Reilly's confirmation of the *Code Noir*, which recognized the absolute right of masters to dispose of their slave property at their own free will. As to the facts, he alleged that María Juana was trying to enter the possession of an Englishman, with whom she was in collusion.[60]

When Governor Unzaga came to rule on these submissions, Suriray had already filed proceedings against Jenkins, the master of a British vessel then in port, charging him with enticement and harboring a fugutive slave. For this reason, and on the supposition that María Juana's (second) petition was a smoke screen in the enticement case, Governor Unzaga revoked his prior dispositions in the petition-for-freedom case, and joined this matter to *Suriray* v. *Jenkins*.[61] In so doing, he had the benefit of advice from the *asesor letrado, Lic*. Odoardo.[62]

The litigation between Suriray and the British captain was fairly protracted and apparently somewhat lurid. When all proofs had been taken and the matter was ripe for adjudication, *Lic*. Odoardo was absent from the province and had not been replaced. Governor Unzaga, expressing his inability to arrive at a just decision without professional consultation, thereupon decided to refer the case for advice to a member of the Havana bar.[63] The advice tendered in due course by *Lic*. Veranes, a Cuban advocate, was to the effect that the plaintiff had not made out his case, and that the action should be dismissed with costs to be taxed against him. As regards María Juana, he advised that she be given her *carta de libertad* upon payment of the price of her acquisition by her master, as was customary in Cuba in like cases pursuant to a royal *cédula* of June 21, 1768. If the slave did not have the price of her redemption, on the other hand, her owner was to be compelled to sell her to another master.[64]

When this consultation reached New Orleans, Governor Unzaga had been replaced by Bernardo de Gálvez, but the new *asesor letrado* had not as yet arrived. On May 23, 1777,

Governor Gálvez, again without the aid of a legal adviser, disposed of *Suriray* v. *Jenkins* in accordance with the advice tendered by *Lic.* Veranes. In the *María Juana* case, however, he ruled differently. The governor assigned two reasons for departing from the *dictamen* [judgment] of the Havana *letrado.* First, he said, the *cédula* relied on (described by Gálvez as a *Real Ordén*) was addressed to Cuba, and thus not effective in the other domains of his Majesty, which as provided were governed by "*las leyes Generales del Reyno.*" Secondly, he added, customs and usages locally prevailing should not be changed without grave reasons known to the king.[65]

This ruling seemingly comes close to accepting the plaintiff's twin submissions that the general law of Spain did not recognize a right to self-purchase, and that such a right had no place in Luisiana in view of O'Reilly's confirmation of the *Code Noir.*[66] It overlooked, however, that the *Siete Partidas* provided, and that O'Reilly's Instructions had expressly spelled out, the right of slaves to be sold to new masters or obtain their freedom upon establishing cruelty, which had been very much at issue in the instant case. Moreover, it failed to reflect the local custom of Spanish Luisiana, which had already recognized an enforceable right to self-purchase.[67]

The error of Governor Gálvez in these respects may have been simply due to the lack of competent professional legal advice in New Orleans at the time. There is, however, another possibility. While in Luisiana, Bernardo de Gálvez contracted marriage with Feliciana de Saint-Maxent, a daughter of Gilberto de Saint-Maxent, who was one of the wealthiest merchants of New Orleans and owned 200 slaves. Some of these slaves were included in Feliciana's *dote* [dowry].[68]

Even in the absence of such a direct interest, the governor does not seem to have been immune to the charge of familial bias. His recommendations or trade policy, in particular, are said to have carried the "strong flavor of nepotism."[69] It is not unlikely, therefore, that the views of Governor Gálvez as to the slave law and policy appropriate for Luisiana were influenced to some considerable extent by his family connection to French slave holding New Orleans society, if not more directly by his own interests as a local slave owner.

That may also serve to explain the governor's participation in a contemporaneous attempt of the *cabildo* of New Orleans to secure the enactment of a slave code at utter variance with royal enactments of eighteenth-century Spanish slave law, and reflective of the most repressive features of the French *Code Noir.* This endeavor was initiated on October 10, 1777, when Governor Gálvez presented a royal communication relating to compensation for runaway slaves executed pursuant to judicial sentence.[70] Some time later, on February 13, 1778, the *cabildo* charged two of its officials, F. M. de Reggio and Joseph Ducros, with the task of preparing the regulations requisite for implementing the royal communication. Some eight months after that, the two commissioners submitted a draft "*reglamento dirigido por los negros mulatos y pardos,*" which the *cabildo* ordered to be communicated to the principal inhabitants of the province before its submission "*a los pies de Su Majestad.*"[71]

The *cabildo* minutes and records do not contain the text of the de Reggio-Ducros draft, but the printed text as communicated to the posts has survived. It is entitled, in full, *CODE NOIR OU LOI MUNICIPALE, SERVANT DE REGLEMENT POUR LE Gouvernement & l'administration de la Justice, Police, Discipline & le Commerce des Esclaves Négres, dans la Province de la Louisianne, entreprit par Délidération* [*sic*] *du CABILDO en vertu des Ordres du* **Roi**, *que Dieu garde, consignés dans sa Lettre faite à Aranjuez le 14 de Mai 1777.*[72] Since Ducros knew no Spanish,[73] it is highly likely that this is the version submitted by the two commissioners on October 16, 1778.

Ducros, it will be recalled, had been one of the two provisional judges appointed by O'Reilly's proclamation "confirming" the *Code Noir*. It is hardly surprising, therefore, that the de Reggio-Ducros draft *Code Noir* of 1778 closely follows the slave code enacted by Louis XV for French Luisiana in 1724. Many of its 73 provisions reflect literally, or substantially, those of the French *Code Noir*, which obviously served as the model.[74] The proliferation of sections is due, in the main, to three causes. First, a number of provisions of the French prototype were divided into individual sections. Secondly, the rules dealing with runaway slaves and their abettors were considerably expanded. Thirdly, and more significantly, there were a few substantive innovations, which may serve as indicators of the spirit inspiring this draft.

Most remarkable about these proposed innovations was the endorsement of racial discrimination of free persons of color as a guiding principle. Subject to a relatively minor exception, it had been a basic rule of French colonial law that lawfully manumitted freedom enjoyed "*les mêmes Droits, Privilèges et Immunités dont jouissent les personnes nées libres*."[75] This rule was now to be converted into its exact opposite: the *affranchis* were admonished not to insult, injure, or beat white persons, "*ni pretendre s'égaler à eux*," but to the contrary, to yield and to be respectful, on penalty of twice the punishment inflicted on white persons for like offenses.[76] For good measure, the final article of the de Reggio-Ducros draft provided that free Negresses and mulatresses were not to wear show pieces, nor garments ornamented with gold or silver, nor silk clothes, on pain of confiscation of these effects.[77]

Given this general orientation, it comes as little surprise that the 1778 *projet* of a black code for Luisiana faithfully reflected the major repressive features of the 1724 *Code Noir*. Thus, slaves were to be incapable of holding property, of contracting, and of receiving inheritance; subject to one exception, they were to be disqualified as witnesses; and they were generally deprived of standing in civil litigation.[78] Even the proscription of donations from whites to *free* blacks, which we saw had been held inapplicable in Spanish Luisiana, was to be re-introduced.[79]

Under the French slave code of 1724, we have seen, slaves could be manumitted only with license of the *Conseil Supérieur* upon a showing of legitimate cause.[80] This provision now had to be revised, if only because the Council had been abolished in 1769.[81] The 1778 draft provided, accordingly, that manumissions were to be effective only if approved judicially. Before granting his approval, the judge was to take testimony from four inhabitants of good repute, both as to life and morals of the slave and as to the legitimacy and truth of the master's motives. Manumissions made without observation of these formalities were to be void even if passed in notarial form, and the notaries were admonished to decline "absolutely" to pass such acts. And explanatory footnote to this provision added: "*Quand il s'agit de faire un Citoyen d'un Esclave, on doit prendre toutes les précautions possibles pour s'assurer de la Régularité de ses moeurs, de la docilité de son caractère & de sa disposition au travail*" ["When one acts to make a citizen out of a slave, one should take all possible precautions to assure the regularity of their customs, the docility of their character and their willingness to work."][82] For the selection of those destined to be second-class citizens forever, this was surely a wise precaution.

As already mentioned, a printed text of the de Reggio-Ducros draft *Code Noir* was communicated to the post commandants, with directions to ascertain the actions of local inhabitants. In February, 1779, the *cabildo*, with Governor Gálvez in attendance, devoted two full sessions to the reading of the *projet* and of the comments thereon. It thereupon decided to convoke an extraordinary session, to be attended by "*los mas notables habitantes y los mas distinguidos de esta Jurisdiccion*" ["the most noteworthy and most distinguished of this jurisdiction"], for the purpose of finalizing the text for submission to the Crown for appropriate action.[83] The extraordinary *cabildo* as thus augmented met in due course on March 1, 1779, and unanimously resolved to petition his Majesty for approval of the draft *Code Noir*. A large number of local notables signed this petition along with Governor Gálvez and the *cabildo*.[84]

The subsequent fate of the de Reggio-Ducros *projet* is somewhat obscure. The matter came up again before the *cabildo* more than five years later, on June 11, 1784, when Leonardo Mazange reported, in his capacity of *síndico procurador* (or city attorney) on the prosecution of runaway slaves and their accomplices then awaiting trial. The exemplary penalties required for the occasion, he stated, were not available, because the *código negro* [black code] prepared by the *cabildo* in cooperation with Gálvez and the notables had not been submitted to his Majesty for approval. The *cabildo* thereupon decided to charge the *alcalde* with the task of preparing the prosecution of the culprits and their accomplices "*con arreglo a las Leyes de estos reinos de Indias*" ["according to the Laws of these kingdoms of the Indies."][85]

Whether the decision not to submit the draft *Code Noir* of 1778-79 for royal approval was due to the arrival of the new *asesor letrado* in May, 1779, or to the cooling of relations between Gálvez and the *cabildo*, or to yet other causes, seems difficult to determine. Whatever the reasons, the *fronde* was over before it began. The episode just described is nevertheless of considerable significance, as it illustrates the enduring attachment of Francophonic notables (including both rural squirarchy and New Orleans officialdom) to a slave law system as well as a biological racism totally at variance with the eighteenth-century Enlightenment. We will see further below that these attitudes, expressed in virtually identical language, were to come to the fore again some two decades later, when Spanish authority was no longer there to protect the subject races.[86]

C. Spanish Freedom-Purchase Law in Operation

Pursuant to a decree issued by Governor Unzaga on November 9, 1770, all sales and donations of slaves had to be in notarial form, and the schedule of fees promulgated by General O'Reilly in 1769 prescribed a charge of twelve *reales* [1.5 *pesos*] for the passing of slave sale contracts by Luisiana *escribanos*.[87] While neither of these enactments dealt directly with the formal requisites of manumissions, it seems to have been assumed quite generally that these, too, should be in notarial form. Freedom-purchase cases decided for the plaintiff uniformly ordered the master to execute a notarial *carta de libertad*.[88]

Where freedom was purchased by bargain transaction, the buyer appears to have insisted regularly on the execution of such a notarial instrument. Random examination of the notarial archives shows several instances of the subsequent formalization of emancipations initially executed by private writing.[89] As a self-authenticating public document, the *carta de libertad* both perpetuated and facilitated the proof of freedom. Furthermore, it routinely contained boilerplate warranties and jurisdictional submissions by the master-vendor, including language as to the actual payment or waiver of the *exceptio non numeratae pecuniae* [exception without financial remuneration] so as to preclude future claims by the vendor on the ground that the purchase price had not in fact been paid.[90]

The following figures might give some idea as to the frequency of manumissions in notarial form. In 1775, Garic passed twenty-four *cartas de libertad*, and Almonester, nineteen, for a total of forty-three.[91] Twenty-five years later, the three *escribanos* then in practice executed a total of fifty-four such documents, and in 1803, that figure had risen to ninety.[92] On the average, there appear to have been about twenty acts of manumission per *escribano* per year. Thus, Garic's successor, Mazange, passed twenty-one *cartas de libertad* in 1780, and his successor, Pedesclaux, passed twenty-eight such acts in 1790.[93] Even without the benefit of a comprehensive calculation, it seems reasonable to assume that considerably more than one thousand instruments of manumission were executed by the New Orleans *escribanos* in the thirty-four years of direct Spanish rule.

More importantly for present purposes, the notarial acts of manumission regularly recite the objectives of the parties. It is possible, therefore, to determine the statistical incidence of freedom-purchase bargain transactions (both voluntary and judicially sanctioned) in relation to unilateral acts of manumission motivated by family considerations, charity, or desire to reward loyal services. Of the twenty-four instruments of manumission passed by Garic in 1775, for instance, eight evidence transactions in which the slave bought his or her freedom at a price agreed upon with the master.[94] Of the fifty-four *cartas de libertad* recorded by the three New Orleans *escribanos* in 1800, twelve were self-purchase agreements.[95] Another twenty-five were third-party transactions, in which a free person (typically a close family relation) bought the liberty of a slave or of a slave family.[96] Only one of the manumission acts passed by New Orleans *escribanos* in 1800 was executed pursuant to a judgment in a purchase-of-freedom case.[97] Of the ninety *cartas de libertad* passed by the same three *escribanos* in 1803, fifty-seven evidenced freedom-purchase transactions (27 self-purchase; 30 third-party), but there were only two notarial manumissions pursuant to judicial decree.[98]

This numerical disparity between purchase-of-freedom litigation and voluntary manumissions seems fairly representative for the last quarter of the eighteenth century in Luisiana. In 1780, for instance, there were only two purchase-of-freedom cases, but Mazange alone passed twenty-one acts of manumission.[99] Of the twenty-eight *cartas de libertad* recorded by Pedesclaux in 1790, only one was passed in compliance with judicial mandate.[100] Our own examination of the judicial archives indicates that in the sixteen years between June, 1773, and August, 1791, a total of seventeen freedom-purchase cases were filed; and Dr. Burson states in her carefully researched study that the total of such cases for the entire Spanish period is fifty-two.[101] On the cautious estimate of a rate of slightly less than two freedom-purchase cases and forty notarial manumissions including about fifteen to twenty freedom-purchase transactions per year during this period, it seems reasonably certain that in about nine cases out of ten, freedom did not have to be vindicated by litigation but was purchased at a price agreed upon by the parties.

That should serve to put into proper focus the function of freedom-purchase litigation in Spanish Luisiana. The law of Castile and of the Indies as there in effect, we have seen, permitted slaves to purchase their freedom at their appraised value, irrespective of the master's determination not to manumit.[102] Given a ready market for slaves, this meant in practice that the parties could negotiate with full assurance of the outcome and reasonable assurance as to its cost. The primary function of litigation was not to force the master to manumit the slave, but to determine the price at which he had to do so. All of the freedom-purchase actions examined in connection with this study[103] are, in essence, disputes over the monetary price of freedom—*i.e.*, the current market value of the slave.

Two cases, chosen more or less at random, illustrate the operation of this system. In 1780, Nicolas,[104] a slave of Mme. Prevost, petitioned for his freedom. The estimates of the experts nominated by the parties differed, 1,200 to 800 *pesos*. The expert appointed by the court agreed with the latter figure, and freedom was decreed at that price. Costs were assessed against the petitioner, as was customary. They came to 27.5 *pesos*, or 220 *reales*, of which 107 went to the *escribano*, and 32, to the *asesor* (*Lic.* Postigo). Early in 1789, Tonton, a *parda*, successfully petitioned to purchase the freedom of her sister Feliciana, a slave of Gravier Beltran.[105] The parties' experts came in at 600 to 1,200 *pesos*. Manumission was decreed by Governor Miró, with *Lic.* Postigo as *asesor*, at 800 *pesos*, the valuation of the court-appointed *tasador* [appraiser].

Only one instance of attempted slaveholder resistance to manumission at the judicially-approved appraisal value of a slave has been found. This is the 1789 case of Josefa,[106] a mulatto slave of Mme. Brazeau. The petitioner demonstrated substantial resourcefulness, starting by an inquiry as to her estimated value in the inventory of M. Brazeau's will. The widow objected to valuation at this sum (350 *pesos*), and appointed her own expert. She listed all the virtues of the slave, whom she described as a good cook, washerwoman, ironer, and pastry maker. The widow's expert, obligingly, came in at 1,000 *pesos*, and the petitioner's expert, at 600. The officially appointed expert's figure was 700 *pesos*, and Josefa now sought her freedom for that amount.

What followed then is highly instructive for present purposes. Governor Miró, sitting with *Lic*. Postigo, ordered the respondent to issue a letter of manumission upon payment of the 700 *pesos*. The widow Brazeau responded to this judicial order by stating that she should not manumit Josefa at such a price. Upon re-application and deposit of the 700 *pesos* in court, Mme. Brazeau was ordered by Governor Miró to issue a letter of manumission to Josefa within three days.[107]

Further description and analysis of freedom-purchase cases would be repetitive at this point. It should, however, be pointed out that the system as just outlined could operate efficiently only if a number of rules of Spanish slave law directly contrary to the *Code Noir* were routinely enforced. First, slaves had to possess judicial standing to bring freedom-purchase petitions against their masters. This right was never in doubt in Spanish Luisiana.[108] Secondly, again contrary to the *Code Noir* and its abortive 1778-79 offspring, slaves had to have the right to accumulate some property, or *peculium*. This, too, was recognized, as illustrated by the 1788 case of Juan Francisco Mangloar,[109] who petitioned to purchase his freedom from his owner, Carlos Olivares. The petitioner (a slave) was willing and able to purchase his freedom in cash at his estimated value of 1,050 *pesos*. Governor Miró, with *Lic*. Postigo as *asesor*, promptly inquired as to the source of the funds. It was established to the satisfaction of the court that Mangloar had made substantial savings in his business activities, and the execution of a letter of manumission was ordered.

Finally, freedom-purchase by relatives, which appears to have become the prevailing method by the end of the eighteenth century, would have been hampered seriously if persons of color had been legally incapacitated from receiving donations from whites as provided by the French *Code Noir*. We have already noted that in the 1774 case of *Angelica* v. *Juan Perret Estate*,[110] the validity of such donations had been upheld. Rather unsurprisingly, this jurisprudence, too, was followed in subsequent cases.[111]

Summary and Conclusion

The purpose of this study was to determine to what extent (if any) French slave law survived the introduction of the law of Castile and of the Indies in Luisiana after O'Reilly's reorganizations of November, 1769. That question presented itself because O'Reilly had, on August 27, 1769, reconfirmed the applicability of the *Code Noir* enacted in 1724 by Louis XV for French Luisiana. In view of that action, it more or less had become conventional wisdom that French slave law continued in force in Spanish Luisiana.[112]

A survey of the ongoing debate about the "living law" of slavery in the Americas showed that eighteenth-century French and Spanish slave law differed in three essential respects. Under Spanish law, the master could manumit his slaves without official or judicial license. The slave, if cruelly treated, could institute judicial proceedings for sale to another master, and much more importantly, his freedom could be compulsorily purchased by himself or by a third party at this judicially appraised market value. French slave law, on the other hand, denied the slave standing in court, capacity to contract, and capacity to own property. It also condemned the sale of freedom to slaves, and required an official license based on a finding of "legitimate motive" as a prerequisite for the validity of manumissions.[113]

In Luisiana, the requirement of official permission for manumissions was abolished with the suppression of the Superior Council in November, 1769. "O'Reilly's Laws" also expressly codified the right of slaves to seek new masters after a judicial determination of cruel treatment, but no legislative provision was made for a judicially enforceable right to purchase one's freedom.[114] That right was recognized and enforced, nevertheless, in a steady stream of judicial decisions, averaging somewhat less than two cases per year for the thirty-four-year period of direct Spanish rule.[115]

Since claims to freedom at the assessed current market value of slaves were judicially enforceable, there was a substantial volume of voluntary freedom-purchase transactions. A cautious estimate is that nine out of ten paid-for manumissions were obtained by agreement rather than litigation, and that 500 or more manumissions in the Spanish period were obtained by these two devices in combination.[116] It seems well established, therefore, that there is a direct causal relation between the legacy of Spanish slave law and the exceptionally high ratio of freedmen to slaves in early nineteenth-century Luisiana.

On the whole, the Francophonic population of Luisiana does not appear to have opposed the law of compulsory freedom purchase, since it was at least as profitable to sell a slave his freedom as it was to sell a slave. In 1778-79, however, an attempt was made by the *cabildo* of New Orleans (with the support of Governor Gálvez) to seek royal sanction for the restoration of French slave law and, as a new element, the codification of "white supremacy." For reasons not entirely apparent today, that effort proved to be abortive.[117]

Remarkably enough, the freedom-purchase features of Spanish slave law survived for the first four years of United States rule, although Laussat had been prevailed upon by the Francophonic notables to "reenact" the 1724 *Code Noir* during the brief interlude of French sovereignty. This was probably so because freedom purchase was viewed by that time as a profitable if minor branch of the slave trade.

Our general conclusion, then, is that Spanish slave law completely replaced the *Code Noir* of 1724 during the period of direct Spanish rule lasting from late 1769 to November, 1803; Judge Derbigny's decision in *Beard* v. *Poydras*[118] has stood the test of time. It has not been our purpose to pass judgment on the past, or to identify villains. We have, however, encountered some genuine heroes and (not to forget) heroines. These are the countless *gens de couleur* who literally slaved for their freedom or who, at the bottom of "free" society, hoarded their hard-earned *reales* to buy liberty for a loved one still in captivity. Their loyalty and industry were monumental, and deserve remembrance as well as admiration.

Notes for "The Law of Slavery in Spanish Luisiana, 1769-1803"

[1]Throughout this essay Professor Baade uses the Spanish rendition of Louisiana.

[2]Louis XV's Edit concernant les Nègres Esclaves à la Louisiane, of March, 1724, reprinted in *Louisiana Historical Society Publications,* 4 (1908): 75-90.

[3]François Xavier Martin, *The History of Louisiana from Earliest Period* (1827; reprint ed., 1963), 214; Charles Gayarré, *History of Louisiana,* 4 vols. (1854), 3:37

[4]Compare *Beard* v. *Poydras, 4 Mart.* (O.S.) 348 (1816) with, *e.g.,* J. D. L. Holmes, *A Guide to Spanish Louisiana 1762-1806* (New Orleans, 1970), 4.

[5]These are described below. See text at notes 35-39.

[6]Thomas Jefferson, Opinion in the *Batture* case, Mar. 7, 1808, in *American State Papers, Public Lands* (Washington, 1832-1837), 2:59, 65-66; Schmidt, "The Batture Question," *Louisiana Law Journal,* 1 (1841): 84, 98-99; "Exchange of Correspondence with Julien Seghers," *Louisiana Law Journal,* 1 (1842): 22, 27-38; J. Tucker, *Effect on the Civil Law of Louisiana Brought About by the Change in Its Sovereignty* (Soc'y of Bartolus, Juridical Stud., no. 1, 1975), 2-42

[7]Royal *cédula* of April 16, 1769, discussed and quoted in note 31.

[8]See text at note 36.

[9]Royal *cédulas* of August 17, 1772, Archivo General de Indias, Papales procedentes de Cuba, hereafter cited AGI, Cuba, leg. 180A, first bundle, items 1-12.

[10]See text at note 91, and *e.g., Landreux* v. *Cochrane & Rhea,* 43 N. Broutin 127, 267 at 268-29 (Forstall, *alcalde,* J. Martínez de la Pedrera, *asesor,* 1800) (New Orleans Notarial Archives), citing *Partida* 3, 28 §§ 4 & 9. Further instances of citation to Spanish legal sources are listed in Caroline M. Burson, *The Stewardship of Don Esteban Miró 1782-1792* (New Orleans, 1940), 204-5.

[11]The insurgents were convicted, and some of them were executed, pursuant to Spanish law, see text at note 35.

[12]These are discussed in Baade, "The Formalities of Private Real Estate Transactions in Spanish North America," *Louisiana Law Research,* 38 (1978): 655, 686-99.

[13]See Baade, "Marriage Contracts in French and Spanish Louisiana: A Study in 'Notarial' Jurisprudence," *Tulane Law Review,* 53 (1979): 1, 55-79.

[14]Louisiana *Code Noir,* articles 22, 24 & 25; William W. Buckland, *The Roman Law of Slavery* 82-87 (1908; reprint ed., New York 1969).

[15]In Imperial Rome, a slave complaining of ill treatment could seek sanctuary. The complaint had to be inquired into, and if it was found to be true, the slave had to be sold so as not to be returned to his old master. ID., 37-38; Inst. 1, 8, 2 & Dig. 1, 6, pr. (Ulpian).

[16]Under the *Code Noir* of 1685 (article 28) as well as that of 1724 (article 22) *all* of a slave's property belonged to his master. As to *peculium* under Roman law, see Buckland, *Roman Law of Slavery,* note 13.

[17]See text at notes 44 and 46; Buckland, note 49, at 537 & 462-64; C. 6, 27, 5, § 1 (Justianian, 531).

[18]Part. 4, 21, § 1, corresponding to Inst. 1, 3, § 2 & Dig. 1, 4, 5, § 1 (Florentinus); id., § 6, Part. 5, 12, § 5, with note 6 by Gregorio López. For a concise statement of the contractual capacity and legal standing of slaves, especially regarding the enforcement of self-purchase contracts, see Antonio Gómez, *Variae Resolutiones Juris Civilis, Communis, et Regii*, ch. 1, no. 3, with add. no. 4 (pp. 427 & 430 of the 1794 edition [3 vols.]; the additions, by J. de Cyllon Laynev, are dated 1653 [2 vols.]). The addition cites, among others, Gregorio López. Most of the pertinent laws of the *Partidas* on slavery and manumission are translated into English in L. Moreau Lislet & H. Carleton, *The Laws of the Siete Partidas which are still in Force in the State of Louisiana*, 2 vols. (New Orleans, 1820), 1:580-97. Roman law sources on these subjects are listed on 580 and 597.

[19]See generally Peset Reig, *Derecho Romano y derecho patrio en las universidades del siglo XVIII, Anuario de Historia de Derecho Español*, 45 (Habana, 1975): 273, 325-39.

[20]*Informe del Consejo de Indias acerca de la observancia de la Real cédula de 31 de Mayo de 1789 sobre la educación, trato y ocupaciones de los escalvos*, reprinted in J. A. Saco, *Historia de la Esclavitud de la Raza Africana en el Nuevo Mundo y en special en los Paises Americo-Hispanos*, 3 vols. (Habana, 1938), 3:247-78. We have failed to locate the original in Seville but the *consulta* corresponding to it is in *AGI, Indiferente General, leg. 802*. The signature of the former Intendant of Luisiana, consulted on that occasion, Martín Navarro, is lacking in Saco, *Historia*, 3:278, but it is clear from the *consulta* that he was one of the three authors of the *informe*.

[21]Ibid., 257-58.

[22]Ibid., 258.

[23]Ibid., 258. A royal *cédula* of February 8, 1790, which was received in New Orleans, specified that freedom purchases by slaves, whether by agreement or by operation of law, were not subject to the *alcabala*. *AGI, Cuba, leg. 180B.*

[24]*AGI, Indiferente General, leg. 802, ff. 5-7*

[25]Norman A. Meiklejohn, "The Implementation of Slave Legislation in Eighteenth-Century New Granada," in R. B. Toplin, ed., *Slavery and Race Relations in Latin America* (Westport, CT, 1974), 176, 183-88.

[26]Saco, *Historia*, 3:266-78.

[27]Ibid., 257. The three former intendants readily acknowledged that there was a gap between legal norms and their application in practice, 256-57, and that Spaniards were not free of sin in this respect. They were of the opinion, however, that Spain's faults in this connection were much smaller than those of other nations, 276-77.

[28]Most prominent among these was Alejandro von Humboldt, *Ensayo Politico sobre la Isla de Cuba*, 3 vols. (first written in 1807); Spanish ed. (Paris, 1827), 1:179-80; our citation is to the reprint in *Publicaciones del Archivo Nacional de Cuba*, 50 (1960). The "ameliatory measures" preceding the abolition of slavery in the British Empire were first implemented in Trinidad because the Spanish law there in force was "far milder" than the French *Code Noir* then still in effect in St. Lucia, see L. J. Ragatz, *The Fall of the Planter Class in the British Caribbean, 1763-1833* at 415 with further references (1928).

[29]*AGI, Santo Domingo, leg. 2594, f.* 58 (available on microfilm at Loyola University, New Orleans.)

[30]For details, see Hans W. Baade, "Marriage Contracts in French and Spanish Louisiana: A Study in 'Notarial' Jurisprudence," *Tulane Law Review*, 53 (1979): 3, 34-39.

[31]*AGI, Santo Domingo, leg. 2543, f. 195* (available on microfilm at Loyola University, New Orleans).

[32]Ibid.,, *ff.* 171 *et seq.*, 184.

[33]*AHN (Madrid), Consejos, leg.* 20, 854, at 595-96. For details, see Baade, "Marriage Contracts," 35-36, and sources there cited.

[34]English translation reprinted in *Louisiana Law Journal,* 1 (1841): 1-2.

[35]Ibid., 3-55.

[36]*AGI, Cuba, leg. 188A*. For details, see Baade, "Marriage Contracts," 37-39; Baade, "The Administrative and Judicial Functions of the Lieutenant Governors and Post Commandants of Spanish Luisiana" (unpublished paper presented at the 22nd Annual Meeting of the Louisiana Historical Association, New Orleans, March 21, 1980).

[37]These two enactments are discussed in Hans W. Baade, "The Formalities of Private Real Estate Transactions in Spanish North America," *Louisiana Law Review*, 38 (1978): 655, 686-99.

[38]See generally Baade, "Marriage Contracts," 37-39, 51-53. We have failed so far in our efforts to find a direct parallel in Spanish North America. Puebla is a good prototype of a non-*Audiencia* city, well described by R. Lieher, *Stadtrat und städtische Oberschicht von Puebla am Ende der Kolonialzeit (1787-1819)* (1971). It was, however, entirely Hispanic, much larger, and much more prosperous. Vera Cruz might furnish a better example for comparison, but apparently still awaits in-depth description.

[39]See the sources cited, note 35; Lieutenant Governors' Instructions, §§ 1 & 2; Post Commandants' Instructions, § 1. See also the descriptions of the Louisiana court system in the letters of Governor Claiborne to the President, August 24, 1803, Clarence E. Carter, ed., *The Territorial Papers of the United States*, 28 vols. (Washington, DC, 1934), 9:16, 20-21 and of Daniel Clark to the Secretary of State, n.d., 1803, ibid., 29, 36-37. Especially the latter report must be regarded as a major achievement, since it was written by a layman apparently without access to any of the sources here used.

[40]This tribunal was set up pursuant to O'Reilly's recommendations by a Royal *cédula* of August 17, 1772, *AGI, Cuba, leg. 180A.*

[41]See, *e.g., Aragon de Villega* v. *Perdomo*, May 28, 1788 (Gov. Miró, J.), Spanish Judicial Archives, Louisiana State Museum. Laura Porteus called this case "the best example of legal debate found in the Spanish Archives." Laura Porteus Papers, Louisiana State University, Baton Rouge.

[42]*Aragon* v. *Perdomo,* see note 40, was appealed from the Havana Tribunal to the Council of the Indies, which ordered, on March 10, 1790, the sequestration of Perdomo's *escribanía* pending the termination of the cause, id., *f.*51v-52v. Unsuccessful searches for further Luisiana appeals to the Council of the Indies have been made of *AHN (Madrid), Consejos, legs. 21696-21705*, containing judgments of the Council of the Indies rendered between 1761 and 1829; the Spanish Judicial Archives in the Louisiana State Museum, through June, 1791, and of the notes made by Miss Porteus (*supra* note 13) for the entire Spanish period, with like results. Luisiana controversies that would presently be classified as legal, but were then regarded as governmental, reached the Council of the Indies routinely, see, *e.g.*, note 43. Dispositions of the Council regarding Luisiana that are now in the *AGI (Seville)* are accessible through *Colección de documentos inéditos para la historia de Hispano-América*, vols. 7 & 12: *Catálogo de los fondos cubanos del Archivo General de Indias, Tomo I*, 14 vols. (*Consultas y decretos, 1664-1783 & 1784-1820)* (Madrid, 1929 & 1930), vols. 1 and 2. This collection, too, has been searched unsuccessfully for appeals to the Council's *Sala de Justicia.*

[43]Royal Order of August 6, 1800, *AGI, Santo Domingo, leg. 2531, f. 579*; Royal *cédula* of November 13, 1800, *AGI, Cuba, leg. 1806*; see also *AGI, Santo Domingo, leg. 1146, no. 20* of 1800.

[44]So far as can be determined, there are two exceptions from this. Dr. Vidal, the last *asesor letrado*, sat judicially in his capacity as acting governor after the death of Governor Gayoso and before the arrival of Governor Salcedo. *Lic.* Joseph Ortega served for a time as *alcalde* of the first vote and sat judically in that capacity. Elections of law officers of the Crown to positions on the *cabildo* were, however, later held to be irregular. A Royal *cédula* of December 26, 1798, invalidated the election of Manuel Serrano, then the *asesor*

letrado of the Intendant of Luisiana, as *Alcalde ordinario* of New Orleans, holding that office to be incompatible with his duties as a Royal official. *AGI, Cuba, leg. 180C.*

[45]Council of Castile, *cédula* of September 22, 1793, *recopilada* in N. R. 11, 16, 9, extended to the Indies by *cédula* of the Council of the Indies, July 2, 1800, *AHN, Consejos, leg. 51690*, with the proviso that in *asuntos gubernativos*, lay viceroys, *Audiencia* presidents, and governors were to be held to the same standards of liability as their *asesores*. This is perhaps the best illustration of the danger of generalizing about the effectiveness of the *Novisíma Recopilación* in Spain's ultramarine dominions.

[46]For details, see Baade, "Marriage Contracts," 50-52.

[47]See, *e.g.*, the examination of Pedro Bertonniere, *procurado* candidate, by J. Postigo, New Orleans 1783, *Louisiana Historical Quarterly,* 20 (1937): 1142, 1143-1144.

[48]The original fee schedule was enacted as an appendix to O'Reilly's Instructions of November 25, 1769, reprinted in English translation in *Louisiana Law Journal,* 1 (1841): 55-60. For application in slave freedom cases, see text at note 103.

[49]Compiled from Garic, Acts 6 (1775), and Almonester, Acts 1775, New Orleans Notarial Archives, Civil District Court, New Orleans.

[50]Minutes of the *Cabildo* of New Orleans, Books I & II, in Louisiana Collection, New Orleans Public Library. That collection contains the original, and excellent typed transcription, and an English translation. We have used the Spanish typescript but frequently consulted the holograph original.

[51]See text at note 22.

[52]Instructions, see note 34, Sec. I, § 2, *Louisiana Law Journal,* 1 (1841): 27, 28-29. This provision reflects *Partida* 4, 21, § 6, see note 17.

[53]See text at note 36; *Code Noir* of 1685, article 44; *Code Noir* of 1724, article 40.

[54]*Suriray* v. *Jenkins*, discussed below at 57-67.

[55]Louisiana State Museum, New Orleans, Spanish Judicial Records, May 25, 1774, f. 5, also abstracted in Porteus, "Index to the Spanish Judicial Records of Louisiana," 18, *Louisiana Historial Quarterly*, 10 (1927): 438, 445; hereafter cited *LHQ*. (All citations to Spanish Luisiana decisions hereinafter are to these two sources; the Spanish originals are arranged chronologically by initial filing date.)

[56]Ibid., f. 10.

[57]Louisiana State Museum, June 25, 1773; Laura L. Porteous, "Index to Spanish Judicial Records of Louisiana, XIV," *LHQ,* 9 (1926): 556.

[58]Louisiana State Museum, February 28, 1776; Laura L. Porteous, "Index to Spanish Judicial Records of Louisiana, XXI," *LHQ,* 11 (1928): 314, 338.

[59]María Juana, Louisiana State Museum, February 28, 1776, f. 1 & 3; 4, *LHQ,* 11 (1928): 339.

[60]Ibid., f. 7; 7v; Porteous, "Index to Spanish Judicial Records," *LHQ,* 11 (1928): 339.

[61]Louisiana State Museum, February 18, 1776; Porteous, "Index to Spanish Judicial Records," *LHQ,* 11 (1928): 340.

[62]See note 80, f. 9; Porteous, "Index to Spanish Judicial Records," *LHQ,* 11 (1928): 339-340.

[63]See note 128, f. 291v-292; Porteous, "Index to Spanish Judicial Records," *LHQ,* 11 (1928): 349.

[64]Ibid, f. 296-297; Porteous, "Index to Spanish Judicial Records," *LHQ,* 11 (1928): 350.

[65]Ibid., f. 297v-298; *LHQ,* 11 (1928): 350.

[66]See text at note 59.

[67]Part. 4, 21, §, *supra*, text at note 53; O'Reilly's Instructions, Sec. I, § 2, see text at note 51; Catalina's Case, see text at note 56.

[68]Ezquerra, "Un patricio colonial: Gilberto de Saint-Maxent, teniente de governador de Luisiana," *Revista de Indias,* 10 (1951): 429, 478, 496-97.

[69]J. W. Caughey, *Bernardo de Gálvez in Louisiana 1776-1783* (Berkeley, CA, 1934), 250.

[70]*Cabildo* Minutes, *supra* note 93, October 10, 1777, Spanish typescript, vol. I, 136B-137A (B = v; A = r of the Spanish holograph original).

[71]Ibid., I, 143A & B (February 11, 1778); 149A-150A (October 6, 1778).

[72]The copy here used was located in Parsons Collection, Humanities Research Center, University of Texas, Austin. For a facsimile reproduction of the title and last page thereof, see D. C. McMurtrie, *Louisiana Imprints* (Hattiesburg, MS, 1942), 102-3.

[73]*Cabildo* Minutes, Spanish Typescript, vol. II at 45A-46 (October 26, 1781). According to the minutes for July 31, 1778, id., I, 147B-148, the *Cabildo* bought the four volumes of the *Recopilación* of the Indies and a one-volume *Curia Philipica* on that day, not having been able to obtain them earlier despite repeated efforts. (This passage was called to my attention by Professor J. D. L. Holmes.)

[74]The first ten articles of the 1778 draft, for instance, correspond substantially to the first six provisions of the 1724 *Code Noir*. See also *infra*, note 123.

[75]Slave Code of 1685, article 591; Louisiana *Code Noir*, article 52.

[76]de Reggio-Ducros draft, article 72.

[77]Ibid., article 73. This provision was taken from the *Recopilación* of the Indies (9, 5, § 28) which had become available locally a few months earlier, see *supra* note 117. It was a sixteenth-century *recopilada*, in desuetude in the eighteenth century.

[78]Ibid., articles 22, 24 & 25. Articles 24 and 25 of the draft correspond almost literally to articles 25 & 26 of the 1724 *Code*.

[79]Reggio-Ducros draft, article 68(2) = 1724 *Code*, article 52(2); *Angelica* v. *Juan Perret Estate, supra* at notes 98 & 99.

[80]*Code Noir*, article 50.

[81]See text at note 33.

[82]Reggio-Ducros draft, article 70.

[83]*Cabildo* Minutes, see note 49, I, 155A-155B (February 19, 1779); id., 156A-156B (February 26, 1779).

[84]Ibid., 156B-157B. Those signing were (left to right and top to bottom), Bernardo de Gálvez, Pedro Piernas, Pierre Deverges, Franco. Ma. de Reggio, Francisco de la Barre, Joseph Ducros, Forstall, Arnoul, Chabert, Manuel Andrés Armesto, Menéndez Portico, Alberto Auvrin de Lamour, L. Vilte Paseur de Lamour, Bevazeur Waetbezuio, Lech Cacarty, Lason Deusouve, Francisco Deulle, Duparet, J. Mezcier, G. Levyroux, Guydo Dufossat, Sossier, J. Lacoste, Francisco Broutin, N. Bernardez, Deverges L. Boidor, Miou Monplaisier, Leonardo Mazange, Joseph Devalliere, Maxente, Lacou Dussouve, G. Leyroux, Delino Chalmet, and finally, as *escribano* of the *cabildo*, Juan Bautista Garic.

[85]*Cabildo* Minutes, II, 131A-132B (June 11, 1784).

[86]See text at note 144.

[87]See Hans W. Baade, "The Formalities of Private Real Estate Transactions in Spanish North America," *Louisiana Law Review,* 38 (1978): 655, 693-95; Fee Schedule, see note 47, *Louisiana Law Journal,* 1 (1841): 58. The fees for appraisers of slaves, incidentally, were 11 *reales*, ibid., at 59.

[88]See, *e.g.*, Josefa's Case, see text at note 106.

[89]See, *e.g.*, 9 & 10 Pedesclaux 286 (1790); 43 ibid., 749 (1803); 15 N. Broutin 11 (1807). 1 J. Lynd 150 (1805) is a transcription of a Maryland manumission dated 1799. (In the following individual notarial acts in the New Orleans Notarial Archives are cited by *escribano* or notary, volume, page, and year.)

[90]For details, see Baade, "Formalities," 715-16.

[91]These figures are compiled from Garic, Acts 6 (1775), and Almonester, Acts 1775. Unless otherwise noted hereinafter, all *cartas de libertad* ("emancipations") listed in the indices to notarial acts have been examined.

[92]Pedesclaux, Acts 36 & 27 (1800); N. Broutin, Acts 2 (1800); Ximinez, Acts 16 (1800 abstracted only); Pedesclaux, Acts 43, 44 & 45 (1803), N. Broutin, Acts 5 & 6 (1803); Ximinez, Acts 19 (1803 abstracted only).

[93]L. Mazange, Acts 1780; Pedesclaux, Acts 9, 10 & 11 (1769) (index count and spot checks only).

[94]Garic, Acts 6 (1775). At least nine of Almonester's nineteen *cartas de libertad* evidence freedom sales transactions, but the figure is probably greater, as slaves were also manumitted by those who had recently bought them for that purpose, see 1775 Almonester 259 & 298.

[95]Sources as see text at note 91,

[96]Sources as see note 91. In 2 N. Broutin 203 (1800) a slave mother appears to have bought freedom for her two-year old son without obtaining freedom for herself.

[97]36 Pedesclaux 102 & 44 id., 364 (1803).

[98]43 Pedesclaux 102 & 44 id., 364 (1803).

[99]Magloir, Louisiana State Museum, August 12, 1780; Laura L. Porteous, "Index to Spanish Judicial Records of Louisiana, XXXIV," *LHQ,* 14 (1931): 619; Nicolas, Louisiana State Museum, October 27, 1780; Porteous, "Index to Spanish Judicial Records, XXXV," *LHQ,* 15 (1932): 164; Mazange, Acts 1780 (index count).

[100]9 & 10 Pedesclaux 286 (1790).

[101]Burson, *Stewardship*, 191.

[102]See text at notes 22 and 56.

[103]For additional documentation, see Hans W. Baade, "The Law of Slavery in Spanish Luisiana, 1769-1803," unpublished paper presented at a conference on Louisiana's Legal Heritage, Louisiana State Museum, New Orleans, April 23, 1981, pp. 42-50.

[104]See note 98.

[105]Louisiana State Museum, January 17, 1789.

[106]Louisiana State Museum, March 6, 1789.

[107]Id., ff. 13v-14; 15-15v. Nevertheless Josefa was taxed the costs, amounting to 34 *pesos* 4 1/2 *reales*.

[108]Even in María Juana's case, discussed above, text at notes 58-61, the court did not deny the legal standing of the petitioner, although expressly requested to do so by the defendant slave owner.

[109]Louisiana State Museum, August 19, 1788.

[110]Discussed in text at notes 54 and 55.

[111]See, *e.g.*, *Mariana Dela* v. *Carlota Lalande Estate*, Louisiana State Museum, June 30, 1791; *Andrés Gombot Estate*, ibid., August 31, 1791. In the latter case, the court gave effect to the will of Andrés Gombot emancipating his slave María and leaving his estate to her.

[112]See text at notes 1-12.

[113]See text at notes 13-27.

[114]See text at notes 48-51.

[115]See text at notes 56; 101-6

[116]See text at notes 93-100.

[117]See text at notes 69-84.

[118]4 Mart. (O. S.) 348 (1816).

A PRIVILEGE AND HONOR TO SERVE: THE FREE BLACK MILITIA OF SPANISH NEW ORLEANS*

Kimberly S. Hanger

Free black militia units in New Orleans played a vital military role from the perspective of both the Spanish government and the free population of color itself.[1] Spain's primary interest in Louisiana—a colony it reluctantly accepted from France as part of the Treaty of Paris accords in 1763—was strategic: Louisiana would serve as a buffer zone between mineral-rich New Spain and the aggressive British North American colonies. Throughout the French and Spanish colonial periods, though, Louisiana's population remained sparse, and both metropolitan governments were faced with little option but to turn to the free population of color to assist in their defensive needs. Forming part of the strategic circum-Caribbean region, the colony lacked any realistic alternative to arming and organizing substantial numbers of free black males. Some colonial leaders even preferred free black militiamen to regular troops and white militias.[2] Spanish governors thus called upon the free black militia of New Orleans to serve in almost every military campaign, the most noteworthy ones being the North American War for Independence and the threatened repercussions stemming from the French Revolution.

This article examines the organization and role of New Orleans's free militia of color and places it within the context of the free black militias that functioned throughout Spanish America. During times of war this militia helped to defend the colony from external and internal foes, and during times of peace it chased runaway slaves (*cimarrones*) and repaired breaks in the levee. The four decades of Spanish rule witnessed an increase in the size and prominence of the free black militia. As can be ascertained from the constant struggle to maintain the militia's existence and integrity in the early years of United States rule, free militiamen of color in New Orleans viewed their organization as a corporate entity that allowed them to associate with whites on a theoretically equal basis

*This article was first published in *Military History of the Southwest*, 21 (1991): 59-86. Reprinted with the kind permission of the author and the publisher.

and that bestowed upon them the honor and privileges that the entire free black community aspired to attain.

The character and purpose of New Orleans's free militia of color closely resembled other Spanish free *pardo* (light-skinned) militias.[3] Demographic realities in most frontier or marginal regions necessitated the enlistment of free blacks in urban and provincial militias. There simply were not enough whites to fill the ranks, especially during the last quarter of the eighteenth century when Spain attempted to place the burden of defense on the colonies. In addition, most white colonials actively endeavored to shirk their obligation as ablebodied royal subjects to train for and fight in what they considered metropolitan squabbles that were of little concern to them. Administrators thus drew upon the lower, often mixed-blood, sectors of society, who were more cooperative because they were more easily coerced. In some areas, however, free men of color were the soldiers of choice. For instance, Leon G. Campbell found that in Peru "the best soldiers were the free Negroes and Indians, but the serious doubts which the Spanish held about their loyalty meant that they had to be carefully supervised."[4] The baron de Carondelet, governor-general of Louisiana from 1791 to 1797, considered militiamen, free black and white, superior to regular troops because the former were familiar with the terrain and also less expensive to the government.[5]

Throughout Spanish America, militia duty offered free blacks several opportunities. By belonging to the corporate military body, free blacks could potentially transcend race and class barriers. In many respects, "the military minimized racial and social differences—both legally and in practice—in favor of corporate unity," although the militia, more so than the *fijo* regiments (units stationed permanently in the colonies), reflected the hierarchical Spanish social structure.[6] The *fuero militar* comprised the most coveted of military privileges. A system of judicial administration in which members of the military corporate group judged accused personnel, the *fuero militar* was given to officers of the militia in full. In effect, according to the provisions of the military reorganization of the 1760s, militia officers would be tried by a military court rather than by an ordinary tribunal in all civil and criminal cases in which they were defendants. Enlisted personnel not on active duty were granted protection of the *fuero* solely in criminal cases, but when mobilized for active service, they too received the full *fuero*. In war-torn Cuba, where the number of eligible whites was insufficient for defense, General Alejandro O'Reilly, who spearheaded the reorganization, recruited numerous free *pardos*. Hoping to boost loyalty, performance, and morale among the large free black population, he extended the *fuero* to the free militia of color on the same basis as for the white. Many colonial administrators, especially those outside the strategic Caribbean, balked at granting free black militiamen equal privileges, but most of them eventually complied with at least portions of the O'Reilly measures.[7]

The *fuero militar* accorded free black militiamen, officers in particular, privileges many white persons were denied. A significant symbol of distinction, the *fuero* "placed the holder above and apart from the rest of society and in effect constituted the militia as a social elite."[8] Because free blacks coveted this distinctive badge and whites envied their having it, colonial administrators had to walk a thin line in appeasing both groups: they relied on free men of color to help defend their New World kingdoms, but they could not upset the traditional social order. Although the *fuero* and other privileges, such as pensions and exemption from taxes, fostered corporate over class unity, it could not completely dissolve the hierarchical social barriers that segmented colonial society by race and class.[9]

The militias of New Orleans reflected strong racial and class divisions within the society. In its formation of the free black militia, New Orleans evidenced even greater concern with color distinctions than did many regions of the New World and even of Louisiana. Colonial administrators in the viceroyalties of New Spain, New Granada, and Peru lumped Africans, *pardos*, *indígenas*, and *mestizos* together into free *pardo* units, and in New Granada these racial groups, along with whites, formed "all colors" integrated units. In Opelousas and Natchitoches, Louisiana, free blacks served in white militias.[10] New Orleans, however, created and sustained distinct free *pardo* and *moreno* militia companies throughout the Spanish period. Explanation for this organization based on strict racial differentiation can be found in the fact that Louisiana came under the jurisdiction of Cuba, and New Orleans, as administrative center of Louisiana, had the greatest contact with Havana. Cuba had established the pattern for separate free *pardo* and *moreno* units and would maintain them well into the nineteenth century.[11] But whether they were congregated into multiracial groups or divided into racially distinct units, the free militias of color in each region received equal pay, provisions, and treatment. The distinctions in Louisiana and Cuba were more idealist than materialist in nature.

Militia service was not without its drawbacks. It was compulsory for all ablebodied free black males, and white commanders often assigned free *pardo* and *moreno* companies the least desirable duties. Providing the first line of defense in battle, free blacks acted as scouts, flankers, and diversionary forces.

When the colony and metropolis were not embroiled in war, free black militias labored on public works and rode in slave patrols. For the rank and file, militia service was especially toilsome: it involved frequent travel away from family and community, possible danger, and infrequent promotion. Enlisted men were often taken away from lucrative civilian jobs in order to be pressed into lower-paying military duty. They also faced prejudice and disdain from white militiamen, many of whom doubted their loyalty.[12] Although free black militia officers also encountered social prejudice and discrimination, they reaped many more benefits than did enlisted personnel. Officers were more fully covered by the *fuero militar* and received higher pay and retirement benefits. Prestige accompanied military leadership; for outstanding feats of combat free black officers merited commendation in the form of praise, medals, and money. Militia officers commonly assumed positions of leadership within the community at large. They were called upon to testify as character witnesses, stand as godparents, and cosign for loans. In addition, they frequently were exempted from paying taxes, tribute, and licensing fees.

When white officials threatened to disband free militias of color or replace their black officers with white ones, members voiced their opposition and struggled to maintain their status as influential participants in the society.[13]

Organization of the white and free black militias of Louisiana was based on Cuba's 1769 "*Reglamento para las Milicias de infantería y Dragones de la isla de Cuba . . .*" codified by O'Reilly. This codification obligated all physically able men between the ages of fifteen and forty-five to serve. The reorganization plan converted several existing and almost all new militia companies from urban to provincial units. Although Louisiana's white and free black militias officially were classified as urban until March 28, 1796, they functioned in practice as disciplined units because of the colony's frontier character and purpose as a defensive bulwark of New Spain.[14]

In Louisiana, as in other Spanish American colonies, colonial administrators were torn between their distrust of the free black man's ability to command and the need to enhance morale and loyalty among free black troops. They partially resolved this dilemma by adopting the solution used by other officials, a dual system of command. Led by free black noncommissioned officers, second lieutenants, lieutenants, captains, and commanders, the free colored militia companies were supervised by white advisers who formed part of the *plana mayor* (headquarter command and staff group).[15] During the 1780s Louisiana created the post of *Garzón de Pardos y Morenos Libres* and promoted a white first sergeant, Juan Bauptista Mentzinger, to fill this post at the grade of second lieutenant. Mentzinger was the only person to hold this position; in the 1790s, organization of the free black militia reverted to its free black commander-white adviser pattern. By 1801, however, the free *pardo* and *moreno* militia battalions had both a white commander, who formed part of the *Plana Mayor de Blancos*, and two black commanders, who formed part of the *Plana Mayor de Pardos* and the separate *Plana Mayor de Morenos*.[16]

The "*Reglamento para las Milicias de Infantería de Pardos y Morenos, de Nueva Orleans*" promulgated by the marqués de Casa-Calvo on April 13, 1801, synthesized and recorded scattered ordinances that had been in practice for several years.[17] As was true of many of the provisions that governed Louisiana, the New Orleans *reglamento* was modeled on Cuban legislation, in this case the 1780 "*Reglamento de Milicias La Habana.*" It comprised nine chapters covering such subjects as: the foundation, strength, and make-up of the corps; governing and police regulation; discipline; penalties and punishments; promotion and filling of positions; marriage regulations; uniforms, badges, and emblems; and requisites for distinguished merit awards.

In order to obtain as many troops as possible, the *reglamento* ordered colonial officials to prepare a list of all free black individuals between the ages of fifteen and forty-five capable of carrying arms, compiled according to neighborhood residence or present station in other parts of the colony. The list was to detail the age, height, and general health (*robustez*) of each man within one hundred leagues (three hundred land miles) of the city, and the captain of each company was to keep this roster current. The structure of each *pardo* and *moreno* company consisted of one captain, lieutenant, second lieutenant, and sergeant first-class, one or two sergeants second-class, six corporals first-class, six corporals second-class, and seventy-four soldiers, although the actual numbers rarely followed these exact guidelines.[18] Each company also had drummers and fifers, who were to be free and of the same color as their unit and could begin service at age five. The physician Don Domingo Fleytas administered to both the disciplined white militia and the free *pardo* and *moreno* militias. For the Battalion of Free Pardos of New Orleans the uniform was composed of a white jacket with inlaid collar of gold buttons, trousers, round hat with a crimson cockade, and black half boots. Members of the free *moreno* battalion dressed similarly but in a green jacket with white buttons and lapels.[19]

Included in the qualifications for officers, sergeants, and corporals were knowledge of reading and writing, ability to command, honesty, and a proper lifestyle respective to the officer's social position. Even though the *reglamento* stipulated that administrators prepare service records (*hojas de servicio*) for each officer and noncommissioned officer (noncom), scholars have never found any such documents for free blacks in Louisiana or any other part of Spanish America. Given the same authority as commanders of other veteran and militia regiments, the commanders of *pardo* and *moreno* battalions had the power to arrest and punish any soldier or officer who disobeyed orders, took absence without leave, or displayed disrespect. Officers and soldiers alike could petition for redress of any presumed injustice; royal administrators encouraged them to do so even though the process might be long and expensive. The *reglamento* instructed all officers and noncoms to inculcate in their companions a love of royal service and military glory through both word and deed.

The *reglamento* also specified requirements for the recruitment of rank-and-file members. During times of war the age qualification of fifteen to forty-five years could be extended in order to recruit more soldiers. Although soldiers were to stand at least five feet tall, they could be slightly shorter as long as they were in good health.[20] No capable man was exempted from the obligation to defend his fatherland (*patria*) and king, but the rules stipulated that officers enlist lawyers, notaries, scribes, druggists, doctors, surgeons, priests and other ecclesiastical officials, school masters, and various local public officeholders only as a last resort. The exemption, however, did not apply to the individual's children, clerks, servants, or other dependents.

Required to pay some taxes like other subjects, militiamen did not have to pay licensing fees for operating stores, vending goods, or practicing a trade. While the free black militia units were obligated to drill one day each week (whichever day would be least burdensome on the poor) and were subject to a rigorous annual inspection, they could be mustered into active service only on the occasion of an emergency or with the concurrence of every local resident (*vecino*). They were to stay in the area for a period no longer than two hours. In all other cases the commander was to render the governor a precise account of the proceedings and pay each soldier two *reales* per day, each corporal three *reales*, and each sergeant four *reales*.[21] When a detachment marched through a region, the commander was held personally responsible for any damage caused. During bimonthly firing practices officials provided free black soldiers with ten cartridges, distributed at the time of the formation so that the bullets would not be lost or misused. The same practice held true for rifles; only in actual campaigns were they distributed for long durations of time. The overall philosophy of the Spanish Crown was that although vassals were born with a definite obligation to serve the king and defend the empire, the utility of any military force depended more on its quality, discipline, subordination, and honor than on its mere numbers.

According to this 1801 regulation all militiamen were granted the *fuero militar* on an equal basis with regular troops. This privilege was intended to augment their prestige as valuable members of the *Distinguido Servicio de las Armas*. In particular, free *pardo* and *moreno* militia officials were to be treated with respect; no one, including a white person, was permitted to provoke them through word or action. After twenty years of militia service free black officers could retire and continue to earn the *fuero* for the rest of their lives. Time served in actual battle counted double toward retirement. If a militiaman were crippled or mutilated in the line of duty, he would merit not only the *fuero*, but also the salary of an invalid (*sueldo de inválido*) for his remaining years; and if he died, his wife and children would receive an invalid's salary for four years, renewable with royal permission. Although officers merited a fixed salary, sergeants, corporals, and soldiers earned wages only during active combat. To become an officer, rank-and-file members had to advance through the hierarchy, except when war time offered opportunities for advancement through a distinguished act of valor.

For those militiamen who acted disgracefully rather than valiantly, retribution was swift and harsh. Punishment occasionally varied by rank, color, and social status. The *reglamento* carefully outlined the penalties incurred by non-commissioned officers for unsavory conduct, but rarely mentioned punishments for officers. Spanish administrators apparently trusted officers, even free black ones, more than enlisted men, or else they intended to deal with each case of officer misconduct on an individual basis. Noncoms and soldiers, regardless of color, were condemned to death if they deserted to the enemy and to two years of public work if they were absent without leave. Punishment for buying any personal effect, piece of clothing, or ornament associated with the militia varied according to social standing. A noble person (someone with a *don* before his name) paid two hundred ducats, while a plebeian or commoner suffered four years of forced labor for the Crown. A militiaman who upon retirement lost the *fuero militar* could not continue to use his uniform, staff, or any other military distinction. If he violated this regulation, he suffered a one-month jail sentence; for the second offense he served two months in jail and had to relinquish the staff and uniform. Colonial administrators applied the proceeds from sales of confiscated uniforms to support impoverished prisoners. Each militia member could marry whomever he chose without royal permission or license, with the only stipulation being that he notify one of his superiors. If the woman he married, however, became unworthy due to her scandalous behavior, the militiaman faced dismissal. The supreme disgrace that could befall an officer consisted of failure to control and discipline his troops or cowardice in actions of war. Such faults constituted incontestable proof of the officer's lack of esprit de corps and inability to command military forces.

The *reglamento* concluded with a description of ways in which free *pardo* and *moreno* militiamen could qualify for awards of distinguished merit. Rewards like punishments, varied by rank. Colonial administrators could recommend to the Crown commendation of an officer for: defeat of an enemy with only two-thirds the number of enemy troops; retreat with permission in the presence of a vastly superior, well-disciplined enemy; detainment of a superior force due to choice of a favorable position; capture of a battery that defended the post entrusted to it until through deaths and injuries two-thirds of the enemy forces were lost; seizure of the enemy's flank by means of talent, skill, and quick wit; attainment of a very advantageous position due to the discipline of one or many regiments and the molding of worthy officers; or being the first man to jump a trench, climb a breach, or scale a rampart of the enemy. A sergeant or soldier merited distinction by: performing his duty for long duration with one or more wounds; being the first to climb a breach, jump within a trench or fort, take a flag, break the enemy battalion or squadron, or take possession of an enemy battery; saving the life of one or many of his companions, in particular that of an officer; combating with two enemies and taking them prisoner; not surrendering to three enemies until wounds made further defense impossible; or taking prisoner some officer of note.

The *reglamento* represented the culmination of a long developmental process occurring in the free black militias of New Orleans. During a span of twenty odd years the size of free black forces burgeoned from 89 to 1779 to 469 in 1801. Due to the unreliability of population figures for free blacks in New Orleans, calculation of the size of the militia as a proportion of the free black population is presently almost impossible. Militia rolls, however, provide substantial evidence of a much more numerous free black population than has formerly been realized. For example, H. E. Sterkx stated that in 1769 the free population of color numbered 165 for all Louisiana, of whom 99 resided in the capital, and subsequent scholars have accepted Sterkx's figures. By contrast, roster of free *pardo* and *moreno* males eligible for military service and living within four leagues (twelve land miles) of New Orleans list 61 free *pardos* and 238 free *morenos*.[22] Obviously, the census taker undercounted *pardos*, but even so, the number of males between the ages of fifteen and forty-five far exceeds Sterkx's sum. When one takes into account that females usually outnumbered males two to one in the New Orleans free black population, the extent of undercounting is even more astounding.[23] As later censuses showed, not all these men actively served in the free black militia; nevertheless, Louisiana governors had large reserves upon which to call if the need arose.

The next substantial set of militia rolls came from the era of the American Revolution, when the Spanish government officially created two companies of free black militia for the first time. Returns from a general census of the province taken in 1777 indicated that there were forty-six free *pardo* males (fourteen to forty-nine years of age) and thirty-nine free *moreno* males in the same age group, once again revealing a blatant underrecording of the free black population.[24] This 1777 *resumen general* accompanied a statement of the number of men who could carry arms in all of Louisiana; this statement did not include any free black persons. By 1770, however, militia lists for organized companies of free *pardos* and *morenos* appeared, and they enumerated 56 *pardos* and 33 *morenos*, for a total of 89 men, 9 of whom were officers. In attacks on several English forts on the Mississippi River in the fall of 1779, Governor and General Bernardo de Gálvez led 1,427 men, 80 of whom were free *morenos* and *pardos* from New Orleans. The number of free black troops embarking from New Orleans rose to 107 for the Mobile campaign and to 143 free *pardos* (5 officers, 22 noncoms, and 101 soldiers) in the Pensacola attack.[25]

Following the American War for Independence colonial administrators in Spanish Louisiana did not compile any militia rosters until the early 1790s, when European wars once again prompted defensive concerns to flare. By 1791 the size of the free *pardo* adult male population had grown large enough to warrant the formation of a second company, and on July 3, 1791, the recently appointed governor Carondelet promoted several officers and noncommissioned officers from the original company to higher posts within the new company.[26] One of these promotions went to Francisco Dorville, who rose from lieutenant of the first company to captain of the second company. Dorville had a long and illustrious service record, beginning with the campaigns against the English at Baton Rouge, Mobile, and Pensacola. As a second lieutenant of the free *pardo* company, Dorville earned the distinctive medal of merit and monetary gratifications from the king for his acts of bravery at Baton Rouge and an award of three hundred *pesos* for courage displayed at Mobile and Pensacola. By the end of the Spanish period Dorville had risen to the position of commander of the Battalion of Free Pardos of New Orleans.[27]

To fill the lieutenant position Dorville left vacant, the governor promoted second-lieutenant Carlos Simón. Carlos was most likely the son of Pedro Simón, commander of the free *pardo* and *moreno* militia in 1770. Like Dorville, Carlos Simón had served valiantly in the American Revolution, during which time he had received his post as second-lieutenant. Simón did not appear in the 1801 militia roster; he most likely had retired by that date.[28] During the reorganization of 1791 the Spaniards also promoted first sergeant Juan Bautista Saraza (Sarrar, Sarrase) to lieutenant of the second company of free *pardos*. In the expeditions against the English in the American Revolution, Saraza had served as a sergeant. By 1800 Saraza held the position of captain; he is listed as such in a petition presented to the New Orleans *Cabildo* (municipal council) by the free militia requesting support for a dance to be held in their honor for commendable service during the attack made on Fort San Marcos de Apalache.[29]

During the 1790s free black militia numbers increased, and organization became accordingly more complex. Table 1 details the size and structure of the free *pardo* and *moreno* companies in 1793, and Table 2 does the same for 1801. In addition to the figures for 1801 presented in Table 2, each *pardo* and *moreno* battalion had one commander of the respective phenotype; he was listed as part of the general command staff. Throughout the decade disparity between the size of the *pardo* and *moreno* battalions was increasing. More accurate total population figures might someday make association between general demographic trends and those of the militia possible.

Table 1
Organization of the Free Black Militias of New Orleans, 1793

	Free Pardos 1st Co.	*Free Pardos 2nd Co.*	*Free Morenos*
Captain	1	1	1
Asst. Capt.	-	-	1
Lieutenant	1	1	1
2nd Lt.	1	1	2
1st. Sgt.	1	1	2
2nd Sgt.	2	2	2
1st. Cpl.	6	6	6
2nd Cpl.	5	5	3
Soldiers	98	98	66
TOTAL	115	115	84

*Sources: For the free *pardo* companies, AGI PC 191, November 6, 1793; for the free *moreno* company, AGI PC 159-B, November 7, 1793.

One of the militia rosters compiled on May 1, 1801, shortly after promulgation of the "*Reglamento para las Milicias. . .*," recorded returns on age, height, and health. Although there are no data for militiamen who were dispatched to other areas of the province or who were incarcerated, information on a fairly representative sample is presented in Tables 3 and 4.

Because most promotions were based on number of years of service, the positive linear correlation between an increase in age and an advancement in rank is expected. The age range for soldiers indicates that officials were complying with the lower limit of peacetime militia enlistment specified by the *reglamento* but that they extended the upper age limit a bit. Interestingly, height also tended to correspond to rank in a positive relationship. Free *pardo* and *moreno* militiamen seem to have been quite tall compared to their white contemporaries. In his work on the Canary Islanders who immigrated to Louisiana, Gilbert C. Din provides evidence for his assertion that Spaniards, and Europeans in general, were short in stature. Officials hired persons to procure recruits and compensated them according to the height of the prospective soldier/immigrant: 15 *reales* for a recruit 5 feet 1/2 inch tall, 30 *reales* for a recruit 5 feet 2 inches tall, and 45 *reales* for one over 5 feet 3 inches tall. The height requirement was similar to the army's. . ." standard.[30] The terms defining condition of "robustness" were vague, but they do point to a better-than-average rating for the free black militia.

Table 2
Organization of the Free Black Militias of New Orleans

	Battalions of Pardos				*Battalion of Morenos*	
	Grenadiers	*Co. 1*	*Co. 2*	*Co. 3*	*Grenadiers*	*Co. 1*
Captain	1	1	1	1	1	1
Lieutenant	1	1	1	1	1	1
2nd Lt.	1	1	1	1	1	1
1st Sgt.	1	1	1	1	1	1
2nd Sgt.	1	2	2	2	1	2
Drummer	-	-	-	-	1	-
1st Cpl.	3	3	4	4	4	5
2nd Cpl.	5	3	4	4	3	2
Soldiers	36	97	94	94	35	79
TOTAL	49	109	108	108	48	92

Source: AGI PC 160-A, May 1, 1801.

The New Orleans free *pardo* and *moreno* militias constituted a vital part of Spain's circum-Caribbean defense system, a role the free black community and colonial administrators recognized and rewarded. Independent military units commanded by officers of their own phenotype furnished critical support for free blacks and provided them with their most significant political institution. Military association offered free blacks in New Orleans and throughout the Spanish empire one more instrument through which to advance socially and to voice their claims as valuable, trustworthy subjects. As Roland C. McConnell so aptly states, "black troops left an enduring legacy to Louisiana," and "in fighting for France, Spain, and the U.S.A., [they] were freedom fighters fighting for themselves."[31]

This legacy originated in the French regime, when colonial leaders first employed black troops in the Natchez campaign of 1729-1730 and then again in the 1735 campaign against the Chickasaw Indians. After organizing a company of forty-five free blacks and slaves with free black officers, Governor Bienville led them into battle against the powerful Chickasaws. Although their performance was less than heroic, the French must have glimpsed some potential—especially given the shortage of free white males—because French authorities created a company of fifty free black militiamen in 1739. This company battled Amerindians at Fort Assumption into the next year but then dissipated. From 1740 until 1779 free black troops were not employed in active combat.[32]

Table 3
Age and Height of Free Black Militiamen, New Orleans, 1801

	Mean Age	*Age Range*	*Average Height**	*N*	*Percent*
PARDOS					
Officers	42.3	26-65	5'4"3	13	100
Noncoms	31.6	15-48	5'3"3	30	75
Soldiers	23.1	15-48	5'2"2	151	47
MORENOS					
Officers	44.4	21-65	5'5"2	7	100
Noncoms	38.5	22-46	5'4"5	18	90
Soldiers	33.8	15-49	5'3"3	59	52

*Height measured in French feet, inches, and *lineas*.

Source: AGI, PC, 160-A, May 1, 1801.

Table 4
Health of Free Black Militiamen, New Orleans, 1801

	Good	*Average*	*Total*	*Percent*
PARDOS				
Officers	1	3	4	31
Noncoms	16	6	22	54
Soldiers	137	32	169	53
MORENOS				
Officers	1	2	3	43
Noncoms	15	-	15	75
Soldiers	53	12	65	57
TOTAL	223	55	278	

Source: AGI, PC, 160-A, May 1, 1801.

The Spaniards, however, recognized the presence of a "ghost" free black militia. Following the French and Indian War and acquisition of Louisiana, the Spanish Crown assigned Alejandro O'Reilly to the enormous task of reorganizing defenses in the New World. During the 1760s he "dictated the regulations which came to govern not only the Caribbean, but also Louisiana and the Floridas." Of a total force of 2,056 accompanying O'Reilly on his journey to Louisiana, eighty were from the free *pardo* and eighty from the free *moreno* militias of Havana. Most of these forces returned to Cuba with O'Reilly in 1770.[33]

Upon arriving in Louisiana, O'Reilly compiled lists of free black men who could be called into military service, and he intended to create a company of free blacks along with the four white militia units that he did form. Some scholars have claimed that O'Reilly failed to organize free blacks because their numbers were too few, but the 1770 lists disprove this contention. Perhaps French colonials objected to organizing and arming free blacks—they had previously done so—and O'Reilly did not want to push his reforms too far and fast. Especially in the early to mid-1760s French colonial leaders had expressed concern regarding the dissatisfaction of the populace, both slave and free. According to Carl A. Brasseaux, "Between 1763 and 1766, Louisiana, suffering from fiscal instability and official bickering, became an isolated, highly unstable entity, a powderkeg waiting for a spark."[34] Well into the Spanish period food shortages, inflation, and lack of specie enhanced the possibilities of armed revolt among free black and white commoners and the servile population. Nevertheless, O'Reilly appointed Pedro Simón, a free *pardo* of New Orleans, captain and commander of the free *pardo* and *moreno* militia from the Acadian Coast to Balize on February 24, 1770, just days before he returned to Cuba. Spaniards were wary about arming free blacks, but the expanding embroilment of Louisiana in confrontations with France, England, and the United States necessitated this expediency.[35]

The existence in the 1770s of at least the skeletal remains of a free black militia can be ascertained from various documents. The "*Liste de la quantité des naigres libre de la Nouvelle Orléans, 1770*" acknowledged Nicolás Bacus, free *moreno* captain, as compiler. Simón's command was not of long duration, apparently. On November 2, 1772, the notary Don Andrés Almonester y Roxas recorded the emancipation of a black woman and her two-year-old son by Simón Calfat (a.k.a. Calafat and Calfa), *pardo libre* and commander of the free *pardo* and *moreno* militia. During the American Revolution and into the mid-1780s Calfat headed the companies of free men of color. A common peacetime responsibility for free colored militias throughout Spanish America was the capture of runaway slaves (*cimarrones*). On October 15, 1773, the New Orleans *Cabildo* paid eighteen free black men two *pesos* each for chasing and capturing *cimarrones*. The *cabildo* paid this amount free and clear of what the individual masters might pay the successful free blacks.[36]

Governor Gálvez rejuvenated the free black militia in 1778 and dispatched it to battle the British at Baton Rouge (1779), Mobile (1780), and Pensacola (1781). Several scholars have researched and written about free black armed participation in these campaigns.[37] When Gálvez departed New Orleans on August 27, 1779, on his way up the Mississippi River to Manchac and Baton Rouge, he took with him 667 men, of whom

80 were free *pardo* and *moreno* soldiers and 9 were free black officers. Along the way additional militiamen and Amerindian allies joined him to comprise a total force of 1,427. Gálvez's army also included twelve civilian craftsmen; two of these were free blacks (Carlos, a free *pardo* carpenter, and Francisco Fortie, a free *moreno* gunsmith) and one was a black slave (Antonio, a blacksmith). At Baton Rouge the white and free black militias, with Amerindians, performed a feinting action and drew fire from the British batteries. This division allowed Gálvez to construct his own batteries. Within twenty-four hours the English had surrendered unconditionally, not only Baton Rouge but also Natchez and other river posts.[38]

Gálvez roundly praised his courageous troops, and he submitted the following names to the Crown for the appropriate commendations: Simón Calfat, captain of the free *pardo* and *moreno* militias, Juan Bautista Hugón (Ogón), *pardo* lieutenant, and Francisco Dorville, *pardo* second lieutenant, all men of valor and good conduct; Felipe Rueben, *moreno* lieutenant, and Noël Manuel Carrière, *moreno* second lieutenant, who had performed sufficiently; and Nicolás Bacus and Luis la Nuit, *moreno* second lieutenants, both of whom had displayed much valor and energy. Gálvez asked that the Crown bestow upon these men favors similar to those distributed to militia officers of the same phenotype in Havana and elsewhere. On January 12, 1780, the Crown granted Gálvez's request, dispensing ten silver medals of honor to officers of the free black militia for their exemplary battle conduct in the Mississippi River campaigns. In addition, administrators promoted several free black officers.[39]

The New Orleans free black militiamen who accompanied Gálvez on his next expedition, against Mobile, numbered 107, plus officers. Although Simón Calfat was the free black commander and captain of the New Orleans forces, a white officer, Lieutenant Pedro de Marigny, held ultimate command power. Foul weather delayed the expedition, but finally by the end of February 1780 the New Orleans forces joined Cuban reinforcements, several of them free blacks, outside Mobile. Once again Gálvez employed free black troops in a feinting action. This tactic eventually succeeded, but the siege was longer and the casualties greater than at Baton Rouge. Among those injured was one free *moreno*.[40]

Gálvez directed his third and final campaign against the British at Pensacola. He could not launch this expedition until March 23, 1781, because of a hurricane, but when he did leave New Orleans, he took 271 free black militiamen with him. Most likely, many of these free blacks belonged to the Havana companies; that, or the Spaniards in New Orleans had done some impressive recruiting! By May 10, 1781, the British surrendered West Florida to Spain, and Gálvez's troops returned victorious to New Orleans. Gálvez again requested and the Crown granted rewards for the officers of the free black militia. From Pensacola on May 26, 1781, Gálvez put forward the names of Simón Calfat, who had commanded the Louisiana free black militias in all three expeditions and had suffered one son killed and another wounded at Mobile, for a pension; Carlos Calfat, *pardo* second lieutenant, who had been injured and had demonstrated merit at Mobile, for a medal; and Pedro Tomás, *moreno* lieutenant, who had served well in the Pensacola attack, for a medal. Eventually the Crown conferred an annual pension of 240 *pesos* on Simón Calfat, a salary he drew until at least 1785, but which ceased at his death and could not be granted to his successor. The king also awarded distinctive medals of honor to Calfat and Tomás, medals of honor and bonuses of three hundred *pesos* each to *moreno* lieutenant Carrière and *pardo* lieutenants Hugón and Dorville, and a medal of honor and bonus of 250 *pesos* to *pardo* second lieutenant Nicolás Bacus Boisclair for valiant conduct at Mobile and Pensacola.[41]

On February 15, 1781, Gálvez relinquished his position as colonel of the Louisiana Infantry Regiment in order to seek promotion to field marshal of the royal armies. He concurrently was named captain-general of Louisiana and West Florida. Gálvez served as governor of Cuba until 1785, when the Crown appointed him viceroy of New Spain. He died on November 30, 1786, in Mexico City. In March 1787 the militia corps of free *moreno*s and *pardos* addressed a letter to José de Gálvez, uncle of Bernardo and minister of the Indies, expressing their concern and sympathy upon the death of their former leader. The free black militiamen proclaimed Gálvez their venerated protector, and his sudden death pained them. Nothing could equal the love and gratitude in their hearts that his beneficent relationship had produced.[42]

From 1782 to 1791 Esteban Miró governed Louisiana, and during that period the free black militia did not engage in active combat with a foreign enemy. It did, however, participate in expeditions against runaway slaves, repair breaks in the levee, and fight the fires that plagued New Orleans, in particular the "Great Conflagration of 1788." The lack of rosters for this decade probably indicates that the free black militia did not meet very regularly or in an organized form. Nevertheless, Miró promoted Juan Bautista Mentzinger, a white sergeant, to the post of *Sargento Primero, Garzón de los Pardos y Morenos Libres* in 1784, a position he held until 1789. Mentzinger's task was to instruct the free militia of color in matters of discipline and military preparedness.[43] Because the free black militia constituted an organized entity, colonial administrators called on it in emergency situations.

In 1782 and 1784 Miró employed free black militia members to hunt runaway slaves in the swamps and bayous, a task for which he and his successor, Governor Carondelet, considered them well-suited because of their familiarity with the terrain. The free *moreno* captain Carrière, along with his *moreno* lieutenant Tomás and *pardo* sergeant Juan Medes, led a detachment of seven free *pardos* and seven free *moreno*s in search of *cimarrones* for two and a half days. The *cabildo* paid them thirty-five *pesos*, five *reales* for their efforts. Apparently the *cabildo* surrendered these funds reluctantly; seven months after the first promise of funds, Carrière was again appealing for payment.[44] For this expedition and the one of 1784 the governor combined free *pardos* and *moreno*s in one unit and, interestingly, appointed two free *moreno*s to the highest positions. Lieutenant Colonel Francisco Bouligny commanded the 1784 expedition against the infamous San Malo band, whose exploits and eventual capture have been detailed by Gilbert C. Din.[45]

Cimarrón gangs consistently menaced Louisiana settlements, but the San Malo band's power posed a serious threat to racial control in the countryside and towns. In addition to veteran troops and white militias, Bouligny utilized one detachment of free *pardo* volunteers, a combined detachment of free *pardos* and African slaves, and three free black militia detachments led by Carrière, Dorville, and Bacus. According to the expedition's payroll, free black lieutenants earned one peso per day, sergeants six *reales*, and soldiers and guides four *reales*. These daily rates were equal for *pardo* and *moreno* units; white soldiers earned the same pay, but white noncoms and officers were paid higher wages. Although Bouligny complained that his small force of free *pardos* and *morenos* offered a meager challenge to the growing numbers of *cimarrones* and that some of them engaged in commerce with the runaways, he and his men disrupted the band, captured fifty of its members, and brought to execution four of the ringleaders.[46]

When natural disasters struck New Orleans, civil leaders called upon members of the free black militia to provide aid. The fire that swept through most of the city on March 21, 1788, occasioned the use of all available men to rescue persons and property and bring the blaze under control. Once property damage had been assessed, free blacks along with their white neighbors petitioned the Crown for indemnification for their losses. Included in these petitioners were Josef Duplessis, Josef Favrot, and Carlos Brulé, free *pardo* militiamen, who claimed 500, 307, and 2,850 *pesos* respectively in losses; *pardo* sergeant Pedro Bailly, who lost 2,615 *pesos* in buildings and effects; and the officers Tomás, Carrière, and Dorville, who lost 500, 2,500, and 3,000 *pesos* respectively.[47]

Breaks in the levee also occurred frequently, and many free black militiamen worked to repair them. In the spring of 1790 the *cabildo* issued a proclamation announcing the demand for the free black and slave workers to repair recent ruptures in the river banks that threatened New Orleans and surrounding plantations. The city council offered to pay free black laborers and rented slaves at the daily wage of three *reales*. Due to revenue shortfalls caused by the 1788 fire, hurricanes, and additional levee inundations, the *cabildo* pleaded with the city residents to contribute funds to pay the workers. According to McConnell, "ninety-one free men of color—forty-two *morenos*, forty-five *pardos*, and four officers—responded for crevasse work," and "each group worked for a month or more."[48]

During the 1780s free black militiamen endeavored to free one of their members from captivity. Taking the free *moreno* soldier Juan Gros prisoner of war in the Mobile campaign of 1780, the British in turn sold him to a wealthy Indian named Enexaqui. The 1770 "*Etat de Mulâtres et négres libres*" identified Gros as being thirty-four years old and living below New Orleans at English Turn; he most likely had participated in the Mississippi River campaigns prior to Mobile. Enexaqui removed Gros to the village of Mecsuque. Over a nine-year interval Enexaqui came to regard Gros with much affection and was reluctant to part with him. Upon solicitation by the officers of the free *pardo* and *moreno* militias of New Orleans, who stressed Gros's valor and service to the king, the Spanish government attempted to ransom Gros. After much wrangling Enexaqui agreed to part with Gros for 177 *pesos*, payable in goods through the Panton, Leslie and Company store. Enexaqui subsequently withdrew his offer, but with additional convincing and the temptation of hard cash, he acquiesced. Once again listed as a soldier in the 1793 roster of the Company of Free Morenos of New Orleans, Gros did not appear in the 1801 rosters due either to death or retirement.[49]

When Carondelet succeeded Miró as governor in 1791, one of his primary goals was to reorganize and strengthen Louisiana's defenses. In the early 1790s Spain found itself in the unenviable position of mediator between France and England, and on January 21, 1793, Spain declared war on France in response to the execution of Louis XVI. As a former French colony and neighbor of the pro-Enlightenment, expansionist United States, Louisiana faced potential invasion by one or both powers, either by land or by sea. Impending war worried Spanish colonial administrators; Louisiana's primary role within the empire was as a defensive bulwark to New Spain. In addition, a combined French and United States invasionary force proclaiming liberty, equality, and fraternity stood a good chance of success in Louisiana due to the pro-French sentiments espoused by many colonists and to the growing numbers of American immigrant settlers and merchants. Fear of internal insurrection also plagued Spanish leaders, once again because of favorable opinions toward French and American revolutionary ideals that were intensified by wartime economic disruptions. According to Ernest R. Liljegren, most of the colony was ready and eager to rally behind the French republican flag. His account, however, appears exaggerated. Liljegren himself points out that the prospect of a massive slave uprising modeled on that taking place in Saint-Domingue raised the apprehensions of white colonials in Louisiana and throughout the Americas. This dread discouraged much revolutionary activity. During the 1790s the actions of free blacks came under even closer scrutiny, as the racial warfare sweeping Saint-Domingue augmented always present anxieties about sympathetic collusion between slaves and free blacks.[50]

In Louisiana—with the exception of the Pointe Coupée conspiracies of 1791 and 1795—the possibility of a massive joint slave-free black insurrection never materialized. Spanish leaders distrusted colonists of French descent as highly as they did free blacks; in particular they feared collusion between French settlers and avaricious Americans who had been stirred into rebellion by the words of the French minister to the United States, Citizen Genêt. Discontent with Spanish rule and desire for restoration of the French regime appeared in petitions to the new French Republic, Genêt's "Brothers of Louisiana" missive, and testimony from a conspiracy in 1794. Overall, the colonists expressed discontent more with Spain's economic policies than with its philosophy of government. Thus, liberalization of commercial regulations solved many of the colony's problems. Even Liljegren admits that in New Orleans "most of the inhabitants were well disposed toward the government and took an active part in the preparations for its defense."[51]

One group in particular drilled regularly in order to defend New Orleans and Louisiana in the event of an invasion: the free black militia. Upon assuming the governorship, Carondelet vowed to increase military potential and at the same time decrease expenses.

Not only were militias more economical, they also were more adept at traversing local terrain than were regular troops. To this end, Carondelet reorganized and expanded the militias, including those of free blacks. On July 3, 1792, he created a second company. During the 1790s promotions proceeded rapidly, enhancing the loyalty of free black militiamen to the Spanish government. Carondelet stationed free black troops at the recently erected fortifications surrounding New Orleans. Late in 1793 he also dispatched members of the free *pardo* and *moreno* militia to reinforce Fort San Felipe de Placaminas, where they guarded the colony against an anticipated French invasion from the Gulf of Mexico.[52]

Several tests of loyalty arose from this expedition to Fort San Felipe. While at Placaminas, a French soldier of the Louisiana Fixed Regiment named Roland befriended the free *pardo* militiaman Carlos Josef Lange. These friends developed into co-conspirators, scheming to overthrow the Spaniards. Back in New Orleans after the expedition, the two met again and over drinks at a tavern discussed their plans for rebellion. Lange was supposed to rally support from among the free black militia, but upon advice of his free *pardo* father-in-law, Francisco de Lange, also a militiaman, and a free *moreno* corporal, Raphael Bernabé, Lange instead reported Roland to the Spanish authorities. A military court eventually found Roland guilty of conspiracy and transferred him to Pensacola.[53] In this instance members of the free black community displayed strong loyalty to the Spaniards.

The case of free *pardo* lieutenant Pedro Bailly also revealed the dedication of free black to the Spanish government and to their former French masters and ancestors, the one major exception being Bailly. Bailly boasted an exemplary, though inconsistent, military record. He served in the expeditions against the British as a corporal, and in 1786 he was promoted to first sergeant of the free *pardo* company. Carondelet then appointed him second lieutenant of the newly organized second company of free *pardos*; in 1792 he rose to the rank of lieutenant. He held that position when he and his company were dispatched to Fort San Felipe de Placaminas in November 1793. While at Placaminas free black troops were under the command of Don Luis Declouet, second lieutenant of the regiment of Louisiana, adjutant of the *pardo* and *moreno* militias. Apparently, Bailly resented the treatment of free black officers that the white command evidenced, and he spoke out against the way all whites—Spanish and French alike—behaved toward free blacks. Other sources indicate that Bailly had challenged the social order through legal channels several times. In actively pursuing his rights as a citizen of Louisiana, he occasionally prevailed, but now and again judges ruled against him unfairly.[54] In general, these cases revealed Bailly's untiring, undaunted struggle to achieve equal, just treatment within a society stratified by race and class.

Accused of making speeches maligning the Spanish government and of advocating French rebel maxims, Bailly was brought to trial in February 1794.[55] As decreed by a royal ordinance of May 14, 1793, anyone who espoused ideas contrary to public order and tranquility was to be tried for treason and punished accordingly. During the trial several white and free black officers and enlisted men testified as to what transpired at Placaminas. Declouet's testimony offers the clearest, most poignant account of Bailly's words and actions. In November 1793 Bailly inquired of Declouet what his opinion concerning notices put out by the French enemy was. Declouet replied that he considered the French to be enemies of the state, religion, and all humanity; Louisiana troops should therefore be prepared to meet and defeat them with unsurpassed rigor. Bailly then responded with a tirade against Louisiana's social structure and treatment of free blacks. After praising the racial equality that recently prevailed in Saint-Domingue, he railed against Spanish discrimination and injustice, even toward the free black militia officers who nominally held the same rank as whites. He condemned Don Gilberto Antonio de San Maxent, commander of all forces at Fort San Felipe, for spurning free black militiamen. When the government depended on free blacks to defend the colony, it promised to deal with them on an equal basis with whites, implying that at other times discrimination constituted the accepted norm. Despite these promises, Maxent never supped at the free black officers' table, preferring instead to dine with officers of his own race.

Bailly advocated liberty, equality, and brotherhood among all men, irrespective of race. Both at Placaminas and at a dance for free *pardos* Bailly urged blacks to join the Saint-Domingue rebels if and when they exported their revolution to Louisiana. He prized the title of active citizen (*ciudadano activo*) and chastised free *pardos* for passively subjecting themselves to the scorn and ridicule of whites. He offered personal examples of white mistreatment, in particular at the hands of aristocratic French planters. Bailly believed that free blacks should be willing to die in the struggle for equality. For espousing such radical ideas Bailly was found guilty of sedition on March 28, 1794, and confined to a Havana prison along with a French merchant from New Orleans, Don Juan Dupuy. Although the Crown released Dupuy and other whites after short prison stays, it did not return Bailly to New Orleans until mid to late 1796.[56]

Testimony in the Bailly trial, however, expressed how intensely loyal most free blacks were to the colony. Free black witnesses included Francisco Dorville, *pardo* captain; Carlos Simón, *pardo* lieutenant and brevet captain; Carlos Brulé, *pardo* sergeant; Josef Duplessis, *pardo* corporal; Santiago Leduf, *pardo* soldier; and María Gentilly, *parda* widow of Esteban Lalande. None of these *pardos* libres spoke Spanish, and thus all required a French interpreter. María Gentilly described the scene at a dance for free *pardos* given at her house and during which Bailly and many of the trial witnesses engaged in a conversation, the topic of which was the French Revolution. Bailly asked his friends to give their opinions about French revolutionary ideals and actions; he himself encouraged free blacks to strive to obtain the same advantages that blacks had achieved in the French islands. Esteban Lalande replied that losing one's life was no advantage. He then asked Bailly how it would be possible for him and other free *pardos* to fight against the whites during French rule of the colony and liberty under the Spanish regime. When Brulé sided with Lalande, Bailly became incensed, and the debate moved inside where inquisitive whites could not overhear it.[57] Generally agreeing that they were incapable of murdering their white relatives and benefactors, the free black witnesses opted for peaceful paternalism rather than revolutionary equality.

Most members of the free black militia remained loyal to Spain throughout the 1790s and into the 1800s, when Spain transferred Louisiana to France and then France transferred it to the United States. For his particular merit at Fort San Felipe and his constant zeal, activity, and love of royal service, free *moreno* captain Noël Carrière received a commendation from the Crown. In 1801 he held the honorable position of Commander of the Battalion of Free Morenos of New Orleans and was part of the general command staff.[58] He and other free black militiamen engaged in active combat once more on behalf of the Spanish government during the attack on Fort San Marcos de Apalache, a Panton, Leslie trading post, in June 1800. Responding to the American adventurer William A. Bowles's capture of the fort, the Spaniards sent Vicente Folch, commander of Pensacola, to recapture it. The expedition was successful but expensive; part of the 20,000 *pesos* spent went to provision and pay free black troops from New Orleans. In October officers of the free *pardo* and *moreno* units petitioned the *cabildo* for permission to hold weekly dances and offered their loyal service as a guarantee of responsible conduct. Promotions and new commissions abounded in 1801, when Governor Casa Calvo once again reorganized the free black militia into four companies of free *pardos* and two companies of free *morenos*.[59] In addition, the *reglamento* of 1801 firmly established the rights, responsibilities, and privileges accorded to free black militiamen.

During the waning years of Spanish rule in Louisiana, colonial administrators augmented the size and status of the free *pardo* and *moreno* battalions, and the free blacks of New Orleans did not surrender their militia rights without a struggle. Militia officers often functioned as community leaders, and all these factors combined to produce a powerful free black group that achieved a high social position in New Orleans. Thus, when the Americans assumed control of Louisiana in 1803 and attempted to shed the free black militia of its distinctive status and even threatened to disband it, free black leaders protested. Proud of their heritage and determined to preserve it, the militiamen petitioned the United States territorial government, citing their right as free citizens to form a military organization. Under United States rule the free black militia remained intact but lost some of its prestige.[60]

Although militia service was often toilsome, especially for the rank and file, it provided free blacks in New Orleans and throughout Spanish America with an important instrument for political expression, an avenue for social advancement, and a means by which to gain honor, prestige, and recognition. Despite the obvious disadvantages created by prejudice and economic sacrifice, "the free colored community ultimately supported their militia units and their right to bear arms as a fundamental right of citizenship."[61] The second half of the eighteenth century constituted a period of extensive, momentous transformations occasioned by Crown policy, demographic conditions, and metropolitan and provincial military disturbances. It was during this era that free blacks advanced their position through the militia; colonial administrators depended on free blacks to help defend their provinces, and free people of color took advantage of the situation. Under Spanish rule the New Orleans militia of free men of color was established as an integral part of Louisiana's defenses, and its members cherished the honorable position they had earned.

Notes for "A Privilege and Honor to Serve: The Free Black Militia of Spanish New Orleans"

[1]The term "free black" is used here to apply to all free persons of African descent. For specific color distinctions the terms *pardo* (light-skinned) and *moreno* (dark-skinned) are used.

[2]Roland C. McConnell, *Negro Troops of Antebellum Louisiana: A History of the Battalion of Free Men of Color* (Baton Rouge, 1968), 24-25.

[3]Studies of the free black militias in Spanish America include Christon I. Archer, *The Army of Bourbon Mexico, 1760-1810* (Albuquerque, 1977); Leon Campbell, "The Changing Racial and Administrative Structure of the Peruvian Military under the Late Bourbons," *Americas*, 32 (1975): 117-33; Herbert S. Klein, "The Colored Militia of Cuba: 1568-1868," *Caribbean Studies*, 6 (1966): 17-27; Allan J. Kuethe, *Military Reform and Society in New Granada, 1773-1808* (Gainesville, 1978); Kuethe, "The Status of the Free Pardo in the Disciplined Militia of New Granada," *Journal of Negro History*, 56 (1971): 105-17; Lyle N. McAlister, *The "Fuero Militar" in New Spain, 1764-1800* (Gainesville, 1957); McAlister, "The Reorganization of the Army of New Spain, 1763-1767," *Hispanic American Historical Review*, 33 (1953): 1-32, (hereafter cited HAHR)

[4]Campbell, "Changing Racial and Administrative Structure," 188-19.

[5]McConnell, *Negro Troops*, 24-25.

[6]Kuethe, "Status of the Free Pardo," 117.

[7]For further discussion of the *fuero militar* see Campbell, "Changing Racial and Administrative Structure," 118-19; Jack D. L. Holmes, *Honor and Fidelity: The Louisiana Infantry Regiment and the Louisiana Militia Companies, 1766-1821* (Birmingham, 1965), 76; Herbert S. Klein, *African Slavery in Latin America and the Caribbean* (New York, 1986), 232; Kuethe, *Military Reform and Society*, 30; McAlister, "Reorganization of the Army," 25-27.

[8]Kuethe, "Status of the Free Pardo," 109.

[9]Klein, "Colored Militia of Cuba," 17-18; Kuethe, "Status of the Free Pardo," 105-17.

[10]Campbell, "Changing Racial and Administrative Structure," 127-31; Holmes, *Honor and Fidelity*, 55; Kuethe, *Military Reform and Society*, 28; McAlister, "Reorganization of the Army," 6, 14, 20, 27.

[11]January 16, 1783, Archivo General de Indias, Papeles Procedentes de Cuba, Seville (hereafter cited as AGI, PC) Legajo 182-A; August 21, 1797, Archivo General de Indias, Audiencia de Santo Domino, Seville (hereafter cited as AGI, SD) Legajo 2568; May 1, 1801, AGI, PC, 160-A; AGI, PC, 203.

[12]Campbell, though, finds that in Peru *pardos* were considered more loyal than mestizos. For information on social prejudice see Klein, "Colored Militia of Cuba," 25, and Kuethe, "Status of the Free Pardo," 112-15.

[13]Klein, *African Slavery*, 232; Klein, "Colored Militia of Cuba," 22, 24-27; Kuethe, "Status of the Free Pardo," 110-13; McAlister, "Reorganization of the Army," 27; McConnell, "Louisiana's Black Military History, 1729-1865," in *Louisiana's Black Heritage*, Robert R. MacDonald, John R. Kemp, and Edward F. Haas, eds. (New Orleans, 1979): 39-41.

[14]Holmes, *Honor and Fidelity*, 51. See McAlister's definition of urban and provincial militias in "Reorganization of the Army," 4.

[15]Kuethe, "Status of the Free Pardo," 113.

[16]June 12, 1789, AGI, SD 2553; September 1, 1801, AGI, PC, 160-A.

[17]"Reglamento para las Milicias de Infantería . . ," April 13, 1801, AGI, PC, 160-A. (The date of the document is April 13, 1801, not May 1, 1802, as McConnell states in "Louisiana's Black Military History," 37.) Some of these ordinances included royal orders found in December 12, 1796 and January 18, 1797, AGI, SD, 2566 and August 21, 1797, AGI, SD, 2568.

[18]For example, see tables of official and enlisted personnel, May 1, 1801, AGI, PC, 160-A.

[19]This description differs from the one given by McConnell, "Louisiana's Black Military History," 38.

[20]This measure was in French feet,which were slightly longer than English feet. One hundred French feet equaled 106 English feet.

[21]There were eight *reales* in one *peso*, at the time equivalent to one United States dollar.

[22]February 22, 1770, AGI, PC, 188-A; September 1779, AGI, PC, 193-A; October 16, 1779, Archivo General de Simancas, Guerra Moderna, Simancas (Hereinafter cited AGS, GM) Legajo 6912; May 1, 1801, AGI, PC, 160-A; H.E. Sterkx, *The Free Negro in Ante-Bellum Louisiana* (Rutherford, NJ, 1972), 33.

[23]June 1778, AGI, PC, 194; 1778, AGI, PC, 1425; 1791, AGI, PC, 2362; Antonio Acosta Rodríguez, *La población de Luisiana española* (1763-1803) (Madrid, 1979), 51, 121, 354, 387.

[24]Spanish censuses taken for military purposes grouped individuals into three age categories: (1) 0-13; (2) 14-49; (3) 50+.

[25]May 12, 1777, AGI, PC, 2351; September 1779, AGI, PC, 193-A; October 16, 1779, AGS, GM, 6912; January 11, 1780, AGI, PC, 2351; March 14, 1780, AGS, GM, 6912; Holmes, *Honor and Fidelity*, 33.

[26]July 3, 1791, AGI, PC, 159-A; Census of New Orleans, November 6, 1791, New Orleans Public Library, Louisiana Division, New Orleans. According to this census, the number of *pardo* males, age fourteen to forty-nine, was seventy-six; this census very likely undercounted all free persons of African descent, as did most censuses.

[27]January 12, 1780, AGS, GM, 6912; January 16, 1783, AGI, PC, 182-A; July 3, 1791, AGI, PC, 159-A; May 1, 1801, AGI, PC, 160-A.

[28]January 12, 1780, AGI, PC, 182-B; July 3, 1791, AGI, PC, 159-A; May 1, 1801, AGI, PC, 160-A; Holmes, *Honor and Fidelity*, 255.

[29]1779, AGI, PC, 188-A; March 26, 1781, AGI, PC, 184-B; July 3, 1791, AGI, PC, 159-A; Letter from the Free Black Militia to the *Cabildo*, October 24, 1800, Petitions, Decrees, and Letters to the *Cabildo*, New Orleans, Public Library, Louisiana Division.

[30]Gilbert C. Din, *The Canary Islanders of Louisiana* (Baton Rouge, 1988), 16.

[31]McConnell, "Louisiana's Black Military History," 32.

[32]For more information about the militia during the French period, see McConnell, "Louisiana's Black Military History," 32-35, and McConnell, *Negro Troops*, 3-14.

[33]Quoted in Holmes, *Honor and Fidelity*, 10. For a list of O'Reilly's troops see April 1769, AGI, SD, 2656.
[34]Carl A. Brasseaux, *Denis-Nicolas Foucault and the New Orleans Rebellion of 1768* (Ruston, LA, 1987), 35.

[35]Jack D. L. Holmes, *A Guide to Spanish Louisiana, 1762-1806* (New Orleans, 1970), 6; Holmes, *Honor and Fidelity*, 47, 67; McConnell, *Negro Troops*, 24. For problems plaguing Louisiana prior to Spanish rule, see Brasseaux, *Denis-Nicolas Foucault*, 75-90. Because this article is on Spanish New Orleans, I use the Spanish form of the name in order to be consistent; spelling of names varied depending on who recorded them.

[36]February 22, 1770, AGI, PC, 188-A; November 2, 1772, Acts of Andrés Almonester y Roxas, f. 287, Orleans Parish Notarial Archives, New Orleans; October 15,1773, Records and Deliberations of the *Cabildo*, vol. 1, f. 80, New Orleans Public Library, Louisiana Division.

[37]William S. Coker and Hazel P. Coker, *The Siege of Mobile, 1780, in Maps with Data on Troop Strength, Military Units, Ships, Casualties, and Prisoners of War Including a Brief History of Fort Charlotte (Conde)* (Pensacola, 1982); Coker and Coker, *The Siege of Pensacola, 1781, in Maps, with Data on Troop Strength, Military Units, Ships, Casualties, and Related Statistics* (Pensacola, 1981); Holmes, *Honor and Fidelity*, 29-36, 54-55; McConnell, *Negro Troops*, 17-22.

[38]August 28, 1779, and September 28, 1779, AGI, PC, 603-A; October 16, 1779, AGS, GM, 6912; Holmes, *Honor and Fidelity*, 30-31; McConnell, *Negro Troops*, 17-19; W. James Miller, "The Militia System of Spanish Louisiana, 1769-1783," in *The Military Presence on the Gulf Coast*, ed. William S. Coker (Pensacola, 1975), 46-50. Miller only fleetingly mentions that eight free *pardas* and *morenos* accompanied Gálvez, with no other references to free black troops.

[39]September 1779, AGI, PC, 193-A; October 21, 1779, January 12, 1780, AGI, PC, 182-B. In *Negro Troops*, McConnell states that Calfat was a white man (p. 18). Primary documents, however, convincingly indicate that Calfat was a free black man. For example, when he emancipated his black slave Gabriela and her son, Calfat was listed as a *pardo libre* and the *comandante de las milicias pardos de esta provincia* (November 2, 1772, Acts of Almonester y Roxas, f. 287, Orleans Parish Notarial Archives, New Orleans). In addition, Calfat's predecessor, Pedro Simón, also was a free *pardo*.

[40]January 2, 1780, January 11, 1780, and March 20, 1780, AGI, PC, 2351; March 14, 1780, AGS, GM, 6912; Holmes, *Honor and Fidelity*, 31-33; McConnell, *Negro Troops*, 19-20.

[41]May 26, 1781, and August 18, 1781, AGS, GM, 6913; August 9, 1781, AGI, PC, 182-A; January 18, 1782, AGI, SD, 2548; Holmes, *Honor and Fidelity*, 33-36; McConnell, *Negro Troops*, 20-22.

[42]March 1787, AGI, SD, 2657; Holmes, *Honor and Fidelity*, 23-36.

[43]August 1784, AGI, PC, 159-A; June 12, 1789, AGI, SD, 2553; Holmes, *Honor and Fidelity*, 208.

[44]February 15, 1782 and September 20, 1782, Records and Deliberations of the *Cabildo*, vol. 2, fl. 53-54, 78, New Orleans Public Library, Louisiana Division; 1784, Kuntz Collection, 2: Spanish Colonial Period, Howard-Tilton Library, Tulane University, New Orleans.

[45]Gilbert C. Din, "*Cimarrones* and the San Malo Band in Spanish Louisiana," *Louisiana History*, 21 (1980): 237-62.

[46]May 28, 1784 and June 4, 1784, Records and Deliberations of the *Cabildo*, vol. 2, f. 131; Payroll lists, 1784; C. C. Thompson Collection, Box 2, Folder 9, Louisiana and Lower Mississippi Valley Collections, Louisiana State University Libraries; Din, "*Cimarrones*," 237-62; McConnell, *Negro Troops*, 22-23.

[47]March 1788, AGI, PC, 201; September 30, 1788, AGI, SD, 2576.

[48]McConnell, *Negro Troops*, 23; May 1790, Records and Deliberations of the *Cabildo*, Vol. 3, no. 2, f. 134-135.

[49]February 22, 1770, AGI, PC, 188-A; May 28 1789, AGI, SD, 2553; November 24, 1789, AGI, PC, 184-A; September 10, 1789, AGI, PC, 196; March 29, 1791, AGI, PC, 202; November 7, 1793, AGI, PC, 159-B.

[50]Klein, *African Slavery*, 217-242; Ernest R. Liljegren, "Jacobinism in Spanish Louisiana, 1792-1797," *Louisiana Historical Quarterly*, 22 (1939): 37-97. Liljegren's account is very pro-French; he uses evidence

from Carondelet's correspondence to support his contentions but admits that Carondelet was prone to exaggeration.

[51]Quote from Liljegren, "Jacobinism in Spanish Louisiana," 51-56, 59-60. See also 1794, AGS, GM, 7235.

[52]November 7, 1793, AGI, PC, 159-B; November 6, 1793, AGI, PC, 191; Holmes, *Honor and Fidelity*, 45-51, 53-58, 60; McConnell, *Negro Troops*, 24-47.

[53]McConnell, *Negro Troops*, 27-28.

[54]March 24, 1786, AGI, PC, 184-B; March 31, 1788, AGI, SD, 2576; July 3, 1791 and November 6, 1792, AGI, PC, 159-A; April 20, 1792, Records and Deliberations of the *Cabildo*, vol. 3, no. 2, f. 182; November 6, 1793, AGI, PC, 191; McConnell, *Negro Troops*, 28-29.

[55]Documents dealing with the Bailly trial and subsequent action can be found in AGI, Estado, 14-60 and 5-107.

[56]McConnell claims that Bailly was released from prison and returned to New Orleans once peace between France and Spain was restored in July 1795 (*Negro Troops*, 28). Official correspondence, however, indicates that on May 21, 1796, Bailly was still in prison and that the king refused to hear his case (AGI, Estado, 5-107). He appeared once again in notarial records in December 1796 (December 21, 1796, Acts of Francisco Broutin, no. 40, f. 328, Orleans Parish Notarial Archives, New Orleans).

[57]February 17, 1794, AGI, Estado, 14-60.

[58]February 13, 1796, AGI, PC, 23; May 1, 1801, AGI, PC, 160-A.

[59]June 22, 1800, AGI, SD, 2617; Letter from the Free Black Militia to the *Cabildo*, October 24, 1800, Petitions, Decrees, and Letters of the *Cabildo*, New Orleans, Public Library, Louisiana Division; May 1, 1800, AGI, PC, 160-A; Holmes, *Honor and Fidelity*, 72; McConnell, "Louisiana's Black Military History," 37.

[60]Holmes, *Honor and Fidelity*, 57-59, 74; McConnell, "Louisiana's Black Military History," 37-62; McConnell, *Negro Troops*, chapter 3.

[61]Klein, *African Slavery*, 233.

"ALMOST ALL HAVE CALLINGS": FREE BLACKS AT WORK IN SPANISH NEW ORLEANS*

Kimberly S. Hanger[1]

This study concentrates on the occupational activities of free men and women of color in New Orleans during the period of Spanish rule (1763-1803), while placing them within the context of the larger society.[2] With few exceptions, persons of all colors and classes worked and played together, by choice and necessity. As one scholar notes, "however zealous [Louisiana] society was to maintain the European conventions and barriers, mutual interdependence tended to weaken class differences."[3] White New Orleanians depended on free people of color to provide transportation, provisions, skilled labor, and a variety of services.

Opportunities for free labor burgeoned during the rapid economic growth of the late eighteenth and nineteenth centuries. At the same time, demographic increases within the free black population outstripped that of whites (see Table 1). Over the four decades of Spanish rule in Louisiana, rising numbers of nonwhites hired themselves out, purchased their *cartas de libertad* (manumission papers), and continued to practice their trades as free persons. With the exception of the United States, in slave societies in the Americas (or the Western Hemisphere), including Louisiana, "the free coloureds helped supply the need for a middle stratum between the slaves and the white proprietary/professional class."[4]

Founded in 1718 on the site of a long-established Native American portage point where the Mississippi River comes closest to the shores of Lake Pontchartrain, New Orleans was colonial Louisiana's principal urban center and port. The furs, hides, timber, and agricultural products of the Mississippi Valley region flowed through the city en route to the West Indies, the British North American colonies (later the United States), New Spain, and occasionally Europe. New Orleans also served as the entrepôt for slaves and various goods such as flour and cloth that colonials could not supply or manufacture

*Kimberly S. Hanger, "'Almost All Have Callings': Free Blacks at Work in Spanish New Orleans," originally published in *Colonial Latin American Historical Review*, 3, no. 2 (1994): 141-64.

themselves. France held Louisiana from 1699 to 1763, when it ceded that part of the colony west of the Mississippi and New Orleans to Spain under provisions of the Treaty of Paris in that year. Spain, in turn, governed Louisiana until 1803, when the United States purchased it.

Table 1
Colonial New Orleans Population

Year	Whites	Blacks		Indian Slaves	Total
		Slaves	Free Blacks		
1721[a]	278	173		21	472
1726[b]	793	78		30	901
1732[c]	626	258		9	893
1771[d]	1,803	1,227	97	0	3,127
1777[e]	1,736	1,151	315	0	3,202
1788[f]	2,370	2,131	820	0	5,321
1791[g]	2,386	1,789	862	0	5,037
1805[h]	3,551	3,105	1,566	0	8,222

[a]Jay K. Ditchy, trans., "Early Census Tables of Louisiana," *Louisiana Historical Quarterly*, 13 (1930): 214-20.

[b]Daniel H. Usner, Jr., *Indians, Settlers, and Slaves in a Frontier Exchange Economy: The Lower Mississippi Valley Before 1783* (Chapel Hill, 1992), 48-49.

[c]Charles R. Maduell, comp. and trans., *The Census Tables for the French Colony of Louisiana from 1699 through 1732* (Baltimore, 1972), 75.

[d]Lawrence Kinnaird, *Spain in the Mississippi Valley*, 3 vols. (Washington, DC, 1946), 2:196.

[e]Archivo General de Indias, Papeles Procedentes de Cuba, leg. 2351, May 12, 1777.

[f]Ibid., leg. 1425, 1788.

[g]Census of the City of New Orleans, November 6, 1791, New Orleans Public Library.

[h]Matthew Flannery, comp., *New Orleans in 1805: A Directory and a Census* (New Orleans, 1936).

Under French and Spanish rule Louisiana's value was mainly strategic. Both Bourbon monarchies viewed it as useful primarily within the context of larger geopolitical considerations: neither wanted Britain to seize it. Although Spain, like France, considered Louisiana an economic burden, the Crown hoped to utilize it as a protective barrier between mineral-rich New Spain and Britain's increasingly aggressive North American colonies. Thus, Spain actively endeavored to attract settlers and slaves to the region, not only to defend it, but also to balance the somewhat hostile French population remaining in Louisiana, as well as to promote agricultural and commercial growth.[5]

Many races and nationalities contributed to the social, economic, and cultural milieu of colonial New Orleans, making it one of the most cosmopolitan cities of North America and the Caribbean area. Visitor Henry Troth confirmed this when in 1799 he wrote that "the Inhabitants [of New Orleans] are a Mixture of Spanish, French, American, with an Abundance of Negroes and Mulattoes I believe nearly if not quite three to one white."[6] Table 1 details the demographic character of the city by year and race/status. Although census figures conflict, measure geographic space differently, provide only approximate accuracy, and exclude or undercount significant groups (Louisiana Indians, women, and free blacks in particular), they point to a growing population. Between 1721, year of the city's first census, and 1805, New Orleans's population rose from 472 to 8,222, more than a seventeenfold increase.[7] Most of this surge occurred toward the end of the century and was due more to immigration than to natural increase.[8] During the years of Spanish rule the white population almost doubled and the slave population grew 250 percent. The number of free blacks increased sixteenfold, and this group was undercounted throughout the period.[9]

In Louisiana, as in many areas of Spanish America, the Crown fostered the growth of a free black population in order to fill middle sector economic roles in society, defend the colony from external and internal foes, and give African slaves an officially approved safety valve. Colonial policy makers envisioned a society in which Africans would seek their freedom through legal channels, complete with compensation for their masters, rather than by running away or rising in revolt. In turn, slaves would look to the Spanish government to *rescatarnos de la esclavitud* (rescue us from slavery), and subsequently protect their rights and privileges as freedmen.[10]

Like free blacks in other American urban areas, those in New Orleans labored at middle- and lower-sector tasks in which they sometimes competed with lower-class whites and slaves but offered little threat to prominent whites. Policy and practice excluded them from the professions, clergy, and government positions, and relegated most of them to manual or skilled labor. Throughout the Americas competition and hostility flared between unpropertied whites and free people of color, most frequently manifested in attempts to limit free black participation in certain trades. Although craft guilds developed in other colonies, trade restrictions were rare in colonial New Orleans.[11] The demand for labor consistently surpassed supply, a situation that reduced competition and augmented opportunities for nonwhites to acquire skills.

The work free blacks did reinforced their ambivalent position in the community. New Orleans's "society consisted of a small and exclusive aristocracy of higher officials, successful merchants, and prosperous planters" and "a larger middle-class grading from petty officials and small tradesmen and planters to a group which tended to merge itself with the free people of color, while these, in turn, drifted farther away from the ever increasing slave group without, however, becoming a recognized part of the other white castes."[12] Persistent dependency and even downward mobility plagued newly freed blacks, who often expended all their resources to gain liberty and then had to toil at the same tasks they had undertaken as slaves. On the other hand, blacks who had been free for many years or had been born free often attained economic independence as farmers, traders, business persons, and slaveowners. Economically successful free persons of color usually endeavored to distance themselves from their slave past and identify with values espoused by dominant whites.[13] In a frontier society such as New Orleans, however, racial and economic groups relied on each other for peace and prosperity.

Censuses for the period were often incomplete, and undercounted the free black population as well as its contributions. Nevertheless, census returns offer valuable information on a broad spectrum of occupational pursuits. In 1791 and 1795 officials in New Orleans compiled information on each household head, including his or her name, occupation, age category, and race. In addition, they indicated the number (but not the names or occupations) of persons residing in each household by age group, gender, race, and status.[14]

The 1791 and 1795 censuses furnish at least partial glimpses of the tasks at which free persons of color toiled. Table 2 separates data on the type of occupation by gender and age group solely for free black heads of household in 1795. Especially numerous were free black carpenters, shoemakers, seamstresses, laundresses, and retailers.[15] Among heads of household ten out of nineteen shoemakers, twenty-one of thirty-seven carpenters, thirty of fifty-nine seamstresses, and thirty-two of thirty-three laundresses were free people of color. Scanty data from the 1791 census of New Orleans further indicate the frequency of certain occupations among free black male household heads: seven carpenters, five shoemakers, three tailors, one blacksmith, one hunter, one cooper, one wigmaker, and one gunsmith. A 1798 census of household heads in the upriver suburb of St. Mary recorded three male wood dealers, two male carpenters, one male carter, one male gardener, two female settlers, one female tavernkeeper, and one female washer, out of a total free black population of ninety-six.[16]

Free blacks probably pursued those trades in which they had been trained as slaves, or in which there was less competition from white workers, and/or demand exceeded supply. Although few written regulations restricted access to jobs by race, custom and practice all too frequently relegated free persons of color to positions with low prestige, responsibility, and pay. One contemporary observer, Claude C. Robin, commented upon the lucrative trades of baker and butcher. A few years prior to his writing, half the city's butchers were free blacks, but there was only one free black out of fifteen bakers. Robin also noted that among tailors the "competition of Colored men practicing this trade does not noticeably cut down the profit of Europeans, who are assumed to be better acquainted with fashions."[17]

As in most colonial societies, gender, as well as race, helped define occupation.[18] With few exceptions free black females and males in New Orleans performed separate tasks, a practice reinforced by both African and European traditions. Men functioned as artisans and laborers, whereas women favored retail activity, running small commercial establishments, such as shops and stalls, and peddling their wares on the streets. Women monopolized such gender-specific tasks as seamstress and laundress, while male tailors supplied and repaired men's clothing. Interestingly, tavernkeepers among the white population were most commonly males, whereas among free blacks they were females. Among tavernkeepers licensed by the city in 1787 there were sixty-three white males, two white females, two free black males, and six free black females. These figures probably concealed male-female partnerships in which the man obtained the license but operated the business jointly with his female consort. For example, upon being imprisoned for debt, the free *moreno* Francisco Barba begged the court for leniency; he and his wife ran a tavern and boarded soldiers of the Mexican fixed regiment, and his wife faced difficulties managing the service by herself.[19]

Material from notarial registers and court cases, like the example above, adds color in the census' sketch. When visiting New Orleans in the early 1800s, Robin remarked that "almost all . . . have callings" and that the variety was astounding. He further observed that "in the New World, the cities still have few of those useless families who boast of the crime of doing nothing."[20] Constant labor shortages kept all hands busy and reduced competition. In New Orleans free *morenos* and *pardos* pursued numerous trades, as noted in 1801 by Pierre-Louis Berquin-Duvallon, a writer and planter from Saint-Domingue:

> A great number [of free blacks], men, women, and children, crowded together in the city, are busied some in the mechanical arts, for which they have great aptitude and little attachment, or in some little retail trade, and the others in the chase, the produce of which they bring into the city where they sell it.[21]

One of the most famous free persons of color to emerge from the Spanish period was Santiago Derom (James Durham), the former slave of the Scottish doctor Roberto Dow and himself a skilled *médico*. Born in Philadelphia in 1762, Derom acquired his medical talents from one of his masters, Doctor John Kearsley, who was an authority on sore throat distempers. Doctor Dow of New Orleans subsequently purchased Derom. Derom in turn purchased his freedom in 1783 for 500 *pesos*, and by 1788 the free *moreno*, "then 26 years of age, and speaking French, Spanish, and English fluently, had become the most distinguished physician in New Orleans, with a large practice among both races." Few physicians earned the designation "distinguished" in the eighteenth century, particularly a free black in a racially stratified society, but Derom did practice his craft with skill. These accomplishments, however, did not exempt him from financial difficulties, as a 1791 civil case shows. Derom successfully sued Doña Isabel Destrean to collect a debt of 100 *pesos* owed him from 1788, when he provided treatment and medicine to slaves on her plantation. An 1801 ruling from the *cabildo* (town council) limited Derom's practice to the treatment of throat ailments, his specialty. He was one of the few free black physicians in colonial Louisiana and the earliest known licensed African-American physician in what became the United States.[22]

Table 2
Occupations of Free Black Heads of Household by Gender and Age,
*New Orleans, + 1795

	Females			Males		
Occupation	**14-49**	**50+**	**NG**	**14-49**	**50+**	**NG**
PUBLIC SECTOR						
military				1		
SERVICE SECTOR						
midwife		1				
tailor				3		
seamstress	25	1	3			
baker	1					
pastry cook						1
butcher	1			1	1	1
blacksmith				2		
tavernkeeper	1		1			
laundress	25	4	3			
hunter				4	2	
MANUUFACTURING SECTOR						
cooper				2		
joiner				5		
carpenter				17	4	1
mason				1		
shoemaker				9		1
silversmith				2		
gunsmith				1		
mattress maker	1					
COMMERCE SECTOR						
wholesaler				1		
shopkeeper	11					
retail dealer	9	5	3			
MISCELLANEOUS						
farmer	1			1		
TOTAL	75	11	10	50	7	4

*No free black heads of household in Age Category One (0-13)/ +Returns for the fourth quarter missing. NG not given / Source: 1795 Census.

Free men of color often served as agricultural laborers, overseers, and managers; some even operated their own farms and plantations (*habitaciones*). According to traveler Berquin-Duvallon, "part of them [freedmen] who live in the country cultivate food products, especially rice, and some small fields of cotton."[23] In 1777 a white couple paid the free *pardo* Pedro 530 *pesos* for serving as an overseer on their plantation, although the document did not indicate how long Pedro worked to earn this amount.[24] Carlos, also a free *pardo*, operated a dairy farm belonging to Don Luis Allard, whose plantation now forms part of City Park in New Orleans. According to terms of the three-year contract, Allard supplied a *moreno* slave to assist the free black, and Carlos earned one-fourth the newborn calves and half the milk produced.[25] In addition to owning a large plantation twelve leagues above New Orleans, the free *pardo* Simón Calpha commanded the free *pardo* and *moreno* militia and was awarded an annual pension of 240 *pesos* for his heroic leadership in campaigns against the British at Baton Rouge, Mobile, and Pensacola during the American Revolution.[26] A 1796 census of Metairie, situated just outside New Orleans, listed seven free black families who in total possessed thirty-four slaves and land measuring forty-two by forty *arpents* (in linear measure one *arpent* is about 190 feet).[27]

The most common trades for free black males were those in the construction and shipbuilding industries.[28] They worked as skilled carpenters, joiners, masons, and caulkers and as unskilled manual laborers. In 1791 Adelaida Raquet, *cuarterona libre*, paid the free *pardo* carpenter, Pablo Mandeville, 903 *pesos* for building her a house fifty-five by nineteen feet with a gallery of four feet. The house probably replaced the one for which Raquet claimed a loss of 1,500 *pesos* in the great fire of 1788. By 1801 Mandeville was forty-four years old and a first corporal in the First Militia Company of free *pardos*.[29] The last will and testament of Andrés Cheval, *pardo libre* and natural son of the *morena libre*, Manon, stated that three white persons and one free black man owed him money for his work as a carpenter. Cheval owned a young slave whom he ordered exchanged for the freedom of his legitimate daughter by his slave wife. He also provided funds to purchase the freedom of his legitimate son, but not his wife. Although the will was dated 1790, in 1801, at age forty-six, Cheval held the position of second corporal in the *pardo* militia.[30]

Rafael Bernabé was another free black carpenter, more specifically a joiner, who served in the militia. In 1801 he was a forty-four-year-old first sergeant in the First *Moreno* Company. Freed *graciosamente* (gratuitously) by the priest Pedro Bernabé in 1775, Rafael earned respect for his competence and loyalty. In 1797 Don Andrés Almonester y Roxas, the philanthropist who built Saint Louis Cathedral, the Presbytère, and other landmarks in New Orleans, commissioned Bernabé to craft all the doors, windows, staircases, and other woodwork in the cabildo (building), completed in 1799 to house the town council. Almonester paid Bernabé 550 *pesos* up front, but the free *moreno* had to guarantee his work with the value of two houses he owned.[31]

Wood for burning and building was an important commodity in colonial New Orleans, where wood vendors gathered in the Plaza de Armas to market their product. A

1798 census of Faubourg Ste. Marie listed three free black wood dealers living outside the walls of the city. Native American women and free persons of color gathered wood from the forests and plantations surrounding New Orleans and then brought it to the city's central square. Inhabitants paid as much as four *pesos* per cord in order to heat their homes, cook their food, and operate their businesses. The trade was so profitable that some free blacks and slaves began to cut timber illegally from the forests of the city commons and privately owned cypress groves along Bayou St. John. In 1794 anxious planters petitioned the *cabildo* to remedy what they perceived as increasingly frequent incidents of pilfering and destruction to fences, livestock, and slaves caused by runaway slaves, wood dealers, and hunters. Several of the city's hunters were free people of color.[32]

Free black women also pursued a variety of trades and business enterprises. Several operated small stores or peddled goods that they had made themselves or had purchased wholesale from another merchant or producer through the streets of the city and along roads leading into New Orleans. City Treasurer Pedro Pizanie collected eighty-one *pesos* from "las negras y otros individuos que venden en la Conga del mercado" in 1787.[33] Early in the nineteenth century, traveler Thomas Ashe remarked that "people of color, and free negroes, [along with Spaniards, mainly Catalonians] also keep inferior shops, and sell goods and fruits."[34] According to the 1795 census of New Orleans (Table 2), seventeen free black female household heads were *revendeuses* (secondhand dealers) and eleven were *marchandes* (shopkeepers).

In response to increasing numbers of retailers and complaints that street vendors posed unfair competition, the *cabildo* in 1780 resolved to construct a central, permanent market near the levee. *Cabildo* members in part created this marketplace in order to tax and regulate New Orleans's growing retail industry. Such an arrangement benefited the town council, which received rents from the stalls; the shopkeepers, who could reduce costs and competition because their overhead expenses now more closely equalled those of stall renters; and the general public, who could purchase officially regulated products in a central location. Although the fire of 1788 consumed this marketplace, the *cabildo* authorized construction of a replacement which opened in 1790.[35]

Few free women of color elected or were allowed to rent stalls directly from the city council. Of the thirty-three persons licensed to sell goods from stalls on the levee in 1795, only two were free blacks, both males.[36] Apparently, however, holders of these licenses rarely sold items from these stalls, but sublet them instead to free women of color and slave women. Describing the market which "adjoins the levée at the lower end of the Town," New York merchant John Pintard wrote in 1801:

> Market hours commense at 6 & are mostly over by 8. Very few people go to the market in person. All is brought by domestics—especially the females—who seem to be the chief buyers & sellers of the place. One meets with wenches with large flat baskets containing all kinds of goods with a measure in her hand traversing the

> streets & country in all directions. They are experts in selling, wait upon the ladies with their wares and are very honest & faithful to their employers.[37]

Judging from the account above and the following case, it appears that hawkers, most of them women, continued to ply their wares through the city's streets long after establishment of a marketplace. In 1797 Don Fernando Alsar and Co. together with fifty other *mercaderes* (shopkeepers, retail merchants) asked the town council to prohibit the activities of increasing numbers of women, slave as well as free black, who daily sold merchandise on the streets and other parts of New Orleans and even on plantations in the countryside. Lamenting that such practices detracted from their livelihood, the suplicants appealed to the mercy of the *cabildo*: they had to pay exhorbitant rents for their shops and at the same time try to feed their families.[38]

Several free women of color operated taverns and boarding houses, most of them located on streets lining the levee where sailors, soldiers, and travelers could gain ready access upon disembarking from their boats or leaving the barracks. Like other port cities in the Americas, New Orleans catered to the needs of a large transient population that kept the numerous tavernkeepers, innkeepers, and billiard hall owners in business. Colonial governments taxed and regulated these institutions which relieved the thirst of travelers and residents alike. Local authorities tried to protect the public from adulterated or sour alcohol, to keep spirits out of the hands of Louisiana Indians and Africans, and at the same time to raise revenues from licensing fees.[39] As noted above, only six of the seventy-three persons licensed by the *cabildo* to operate a cabaret were free women of color, but as in the case of free black retailers, others probably ran taverns whose licenses were in another person's name.

According to the 1795 census, the *morena libre* Carlota Derneville was one such tavernkeeper who also owned several rental houses, despite losing 2,000 *pesos* worth of property in the 1788 fire. Both as a slave and a free person, Carlota had labored diligently and saved her earnings. At age thirty-seven she purchased her freedom from Don Pedro Henrique Derneville for 400 *pesos*. Two years later in 1775 she agreed to serve Santiago Landreau without running away as long as the court ordered, if he would free her twenty-one-year-old son Carlos. Carlota was among those persons who paid a thirty *peso* licensing fee to operate a cabaret for the year 1787 and a forty peso fee in 1799.[40]

Many New Orleans free women of color labored as seamstresses and, like their counterparts in Rio de Janeiro and elsewhere in the Americas, "sewed dresses and made lace in the households and dressmaking establishments of the period."[41] The free *morena* seamstress Prudencia Cheval, "*de nación Pular*," was given her freedom, along with that of her two *pardo* children, at age seventeen by Don Francisco Cheval. In his will dated three years later, Don Francisco designated Prudencia and her children (most likely his children as well) as his only heirs. The inheritance included a two-story house, which Prudencia promptly leased to a prominent white resident. Boarders and renters often provided free blacks like Cheval and Derneville with supplemental income.[42]

Some free black women performed more than a single occupation. The *cuarterona* Magdalena brought her master before the governor's tribunal in 1793 to obtain manumission at the price of her estimation. In determining her worth, the slaveowner emphasized that Magdalena had mastered various domestic chores: cooking, sewing, washing, ironing, and candy and pastry making. The slave, on the other hand claimed that she was old, ill, had given birth to many children, and could not work much. Nevertheless, both appraisers valued Magdalena at 700 *pesos*, 200 of which she had to borrow to obtain her *carta de libertad*.[43]

Upon the death of Don Santiago Constant, the *parda libre* Mariana San Juan sued his estate for 1,344 *pesos*, equivalent to what she considered a less than just salary of eight *pesos* per month for fourteen years. During this time Mariana had served as Don Santiago's wife, cook, and laundress and had sold goods from his store throughout the streets of the city. In addition, she had managed his personal business as a faithful servant and his best confidant. The court awarded her remuneration of five *pesos* per month for three years, for a miserly total of 180 *pesos*.[44]

Like most white persons and slaves, free people of color acquired their skills by observation and apprenticeship. With the exception of the Ursuline school for girls, the royal Spanish school, and some private classes given by "qualified" individuals, few institutions in New Orleans offered a formal education. Wealthy colonists sent their children to schools in Europe, but the majority relied on private libraries and the expertise of master tradespersons.[45] Free blacks in particular learned trades, because there was a demand for their skills and they were excluded from most professions that required formal learning. According to physician Paul Alliot in 1803:

> there are many workmen of all kinds at New Orleans. All the men of color or free negroes make their sons learn a trade, and give a special education to their daughters whom they rarely marry off.[46]

For example, Luison Santilly, a *parda libre*, apprenticed her son to José Joaquín Fernández, master carpenter, for five years. During that time Santilly agreed to feed, care for, and provide medical expenses for the eleven-year-old boy.[47]

Skilled free blacks also trained others. The free *moreno* carpenter Pedro Laviolet contracted with María Josefa Roy to teach his craft to her *moreno* slave, who was ten years old. According to terms of the contract, Roy agreed to lodge, maintain, and dress the slave during the first four years of the deal, and Laviolet did the same during the final two years. Over the full six years Roy paid for the slave's medical care and reimbursed Laviolet for any time lost to illness or truancy. Laviolet was only to work the apprentice half a day, and on days that the slave was not needed by Laviolet he could work for Roy.[48]

Many freed persons acquired skills during their enslavement, and they often used these talents to earn the money that purchased their freedom. For example, the hairdresser Pompé, *moreno* slave of Don Josef Antonio de Hoa, chief official of the royal customhouse, purchased his liberty for 600 *pesos*. Having already deposited 400 *pesos*,

Pompé was to make installments based on his monthly earnings of twenty *pesos*, from which Hoa subtracted five *pesos* for haircuts for himself and his brother. In addition, Pompé had to serve Hoa freely for eight months.[49] Andrés Nata, a *moreno* blacksmith, purchased his freedom for the arbitrated amount of 800 *pesos*. Unfortunately, he enjoyed liberty for only a short time; he was buried four years later at the age of forty.[50]

Women and men involved in the service sector most likely obtained their talents less formally than artisans or managers did. They watched other slaves and free persons sewing, hunting, washing, cleaning, and selling and imitated their actions. On May 21, 1803, Don Antonio Jung manumitted *graciosamente* his *pardita* slave María Clara, the seven-year-old daughter of his former slave Francisca. That same day Doña Margarita Landreau registered a note of obligation assuming responsibility for the education of María Clara. In exchange for the *pardita's* labor over a twelve-year period, Landreau agreed to teach her the arts of cooking, washing, and everything else necessary to manage a house. One day before he manumitted María Clara, Jung also freed María Clara's sister Virginia, a three-year-old *pardita*. In this case, the free *morena* Venus, who had purchased her *carta de libertad* from Jung at the same time, promised to educate and care for Virginia until she could do so for herself. Virginia brought to the household all her clothes and fifty *pesos* to help Venus with food and clothing, but love primarily motivated Venus' action.[51]

Although free blacks acted upon every opportunity, several factors, some of them beyond their control, influenced the capacity of free persons of color to acquire economic security or accumulate wealth that was then passed on to their heirs. First, free blacks who acquired marketable skills either before or after being freed tended to prosper. Throughout the Americas skilled blacks found it easier to purchase freedom and continue to earn as free persons. Many slaveholders rented out their slaves, taking a portion of the slaves' *jornales* (daily wages) and permitting them to keep the remainder.[52] The *morena libre* Helena poignantly revealed the impact that possessing a skill high in demand could have on attaining and retaining free status. Helena tried to convince the court that appraisals of her slave son were excessive because he knew no trade and his master had readily admitted that the slave was a thief and drunkard. In her plea she provided several examples of skilled slaves who had purchased their freedom at the amount her son was appraised at and pointed out that an unskilled *moreno* slave could never earn such an exorbitant sum.[53]

The free person of color's ties to and reputation in the white community constituted a second factor in the succeed-fail equation. A corporate society stratified by race and class prevailed in Spanish New Orleans primarily operated according to *parentela* (extended family) and *clientela* (patron/client) relationships. Advantages accrued to those free blacks who were linked by kin and patronage to leading white families. When a prominent white man, Don Luis de Lalande Dapremont, brought charges of criminal activity against the free *pardo* Pedro Bailly, he threatened the livelihood of Bailly and his family. Bailly claimed that the charges were false and entered out of spite. Dapremont had just recently lost a suit that Bailly had brought against him for collection of a debt. Bailly also stated that the mistrust engendered by these charges had seriously affected his retail business because white patrons from whom Bailly had borrowed funds and goods were beginning to harass him for payment and refused to extend him additional credit. A militia officer and loyal servant of the king, Bailly had earned the distinction of a *buen vasallo* (good subject) meriting the favor of local leaders. The court eventually dropped Dapremont's charges against Bailly, thereby restoring his favorable reputation.[54]

Free persons of color occasionally formed business partnerships with white individuals. Pedro Viejo jointly owned a small dry goods store with the *morena libre* Juana. A native of Guinea, Juana was a former slave and the daughter of two slaves who had been married in the Catholic church. Half the enterprise belonged to her, and she designated Viejo as her only heir.[55] Antonio Sánchez and the *cuarterona libre* María Juana Ester were partners in another retail business. A native of New Orleans, María Juana had one natural daughter named Francisca, also a *cuarterona libre*. In her will María entrusted Sánchez with selling her share of the partnership's goods and placing its proceeds in her daughter's possession. Included in the estate inventory were farm and carpentry implements, wagons, ox teams, cows, horses, lumber, a canoe, slaves, and two farms.[56]

Kinship ties to white persons as well as patronage gave some free people of color added economic leverage. Some white fathers publicly acknowledged their free black consorts and offspring and donated personal and real property to them.[57] In his 1794 will, Don Pedro Aubry declared that he was single but that he had two natural children–Pedro Estevan and María Genoveva–by the *morena libre* María Emilia Aubry, all his former slaves. As his only heirs, the children received a farm twenty-one miles from New Orleans, two slaves, livestock, furniture, and household goods.[58]

When Don Francisco Hisnard died on July 28, 1798, he left a will written three months prior in which he declared that he was single but recognized his three natural children by the free *morena* Mariana Grondel, more commonly called Hisnard. Don Francisco instructed his executors to divide the proceeds from the sale of his goods among his only heirs, his three natural daughters. In addition, the three women came into possession of their mother's estate, Grondel having died one year before Hisnard. They inherited property totaling 1,852 *pesos* from their mother and 468 *pesos* 5 *reales* from their father. One daughter, Eufrosina, had served as the former slave and long-time consort of Louisiana's *auditor de guerra*, Don Nicolás María Vidal, for whom she bore three *cuarterona* daughters. One of these daughters, María de la Merced, "caused an international incident in Pensacola when she appealed to Andrew Jackson as territorial governor to intercede with Spanish officials to recover documents regarding her late father's estate."[59] Kinship ties with propertied whites and free blacks enabled some free persons of color to wield greater influence.

A third factor that could help a free person of color succeed materially was that of being born free or having free kin. Second or third generation free blacks usually inherited the accumulated riches, no matter how meager, of past generations, and slaves who had well-established free black friends or relatives stood a better chance of being rescued from slavery than those with no ties to the free black population. For example, Juan Bautista Hugón, born free and a captain of the free *pardo* militia when he died in 1792, purchased the freedom of four out of five of his children and at least one of their mothers during his lifetime. At the time of his death Hugón's goods consisted of a house and land in New Orleans, one slave, furniture, and clothes. He donated to a *morena* slave named Magdalena a bed, a stoneware fireplace adornment, one pig, and the chickens on the patio of his house. Hugón also requested that his testamentary executor, a captain in the *moreno* militia, purchase his fifth child's *carta de libertad*. Hugón's goods sold at public auction for 1,095 *pesos*. After paying for the *carta*, outstanding debts, and burial and court costs, the executor turned over 227 *pesos*, 5 *reales* to Hugón's children.[58]

One final testament illuminates the extent of property a free person of color could accumulate during a lifetime and bestow upon relatives and friends when he or she died. It also reveals the intricate kinship and patronage ties among free blacks and whites. Perrina Daupenne, *parda libre*, drew up her will in August 1790. She was the natural daughter of a white man she confessed not to know and the *parda libre* María Daupenne, single, and without any children. Daupenne owned a house in the city and ten slaves, five of whom she freed *graciosamente*. She also instructed her executor to purchase the freedom of a *pardo* slave belonging to a white man. In addition to giving Charity Hospital ten *pesos* and a priest thirty *pesos* to say thirty masses for her soul, Daupenne donated slaves, livestock, clothes, furniture, linen, household goods, and a cypress grove to her friends, aunts, and cousins, all of them women. To her brother she gave her share of their dead brother's estate. Daupenne's white godmother received her most prized possessions: all her gold jewelry and a mahogany armoire. Daupenne appointed another white person and government official, Don Manuel Andrés Lopéz de Armesto, to be her executor. Finally, Daupenne named as her heir the *moreno libre* Cándido Tomás, legitimate son of her female cousin.[61] Few free people of color went to their graves so wealthy, but those who did usually raised the material level of at least some free blacks and slaves who remained behind.

Free women and men of color in Spanish New Orleans actively participated in the economic and social life of the society. Though not as prosperous or prominent as leading white persons, some free blacks successfully battled downward mobility and secured a stable niche in the middle stratum. They astutely availed themselves of legal, demographic, economic, and political conditions in Spanish New Orleans to attain economic stability, even prosperity, and at the same time advance their social standing. In Louisiana and other colonies metropolitan and local discrimination against non-whites both in the courtroom and on the street restricted access to resources needed to enter the upper echelons of the social hierarchy. Records for the Spanish period of New Orleans' history attest to the daily battle free blacks waged in order to fight off poverty, free their families, and acquire property and patronage.

Notes for "'Almost All Have Callings': Free Blacks at Work in Spanish New Orleans"

[1]Research for this paper was funded in part by the American Historical Association Albert J. Beveridge Grant for Research in the History of the Western Hemisphere, the Program for Cultural Cooperation between Spain's Ministry of Culture and United States Universities, the Spain-Florida Alliance, and the University of Florida Department of History.

[2]Throughout this work I use the inclusive somatic terms "free black" and "free person of color" to encompass anyone of African descent, be he or she pure African, part white, or part American Indian (*indio*). The exclusive terms *pardo* (light-skinned) and *moreno* (dark-skinned)—preferred by contemporary free blacks over *mulato* and *negro*—are utilized to distinguish elements within the nonwhite population. Occasional references delineate further between *grifo* (offspring of a *pardo(a)* or *indio(a)* and a *morena(o)*), *cuarterón* (offspring of a white and a *pardo(a)*), and *mestizo* (usually the offspring of a white and American Indian but in New Orleans sometimes meaning the offspring of a *pardo(a)* or *moreno(a)* and an *india(o)*).

[3]Caroline Maude Burson, *The Stewardship of Don Esteban Miró, 1782-1792* (New Orleans, 1940), 253.

[4]David P. Geggus, *Slavery, War, and Revolution: The British Occupation of St. Domingue, 1793-1798* (Oxford, 1982), 19. David W. Cohen and Jack P. Greene, "Introduction," in *Neither Slave nor Free: The Freedmen of African Descent in the Slave Societies of the New World* (Baltimore, 1972), 8, further note this link between the right and ability to purchase one's freedom and opportunities for artisans and traders: "Certainly the evidence suggests that where the 'pulling up' of wives and relatives by newly freed men was a relatively common practice it was a reflection of the opening of the economy to colored traders and artisans." In New Orleans many of these traders were females, who also purchased *cartas* for themselves and loved ones.

[5]For a survey of Louisiana's colonial history, see Bennett H. Wall, ed., *Louisiana: A History*, 2nd ed. (Arlington Heights, 1990).

[6]"Journal of Henry Troth, 1799," transcr. Clinton Lee Brooke and Tyrrell Willcox Brooke, July 1970, p. 7. Manuscript in the Louisiana State Museum Historical Center.

[7]Ditchy, "Early Census Tables of Louisiana," 214-20. As was true in many areas of the Americas, censuses for New Orleans were taken sporadically and for specific purposes that excluded or under counted some segments of the population. For example, Louisiana officials ordered population counts when they wanted to tax residents or enroll them in military service. Women, free persons of African descent, and Native Americans were poorly represented in these censuses, nor is there much detailed information on them. Such characteristics as name, occupation, and address were recorded only for heads of household, with few households headed by women or free blacks. In addition, census takers rarely provided specific ages, but rather grouped inhabitants into three age categories: 0-14, 15-49, and 50 plus. Extant censuses for Spanish New Orleans, some of them mere *resumens* (summaries), are from the years: 1763, 1769, 1777, 1778 (in restoration at the Archivo General de Indias, Seville), 1785, 1791, 1795 (fourth ward missing), 1799 (parts of second and third wards missing), and 1803 (third ward free blacks missing). The French took far fewer censuses (1721, 1726, 1732, and 1746) and grouped people as whites, blacks, and Indian slaves. Some free blacks were included in the totals for whites, others in those for blacks. They rarely included ages, merely distinguishing between men, women, and children. It appears that Indian slaves were increasingly included with black slaves following the early French population counts. The bottom line is that one can only use census records to approximate the number, age, race, and status of people in colonial Louisiana and to identify general trends.

[8]Economic developments at the close of the colonial period only hinted at the spiraling and sometimes stunning material prosperity that lay ahead for New Orleans and its hinterlands. Spurred by the expansion and intensification of sugar and cotton production, rapid economic growth and population increase changed a

small town into one of the leading commercial centers of the Americas. Dubbed "the grand mart of business, the Alexandria of America," New Orleans was the exchange point for natural and agricultural products flowing out of and manufactured goods and people coming into the budding Mississippi River valley. For the first time the region began to attract significant capital investment and labor. Nevertheless, high mortality rates continued to kill off much of the newly arrived labor force (primarily of German and Irish nationality) and restrain New Orleans' economic development for much of the nineteenth century (Quote from Zadok Cramer, *The Navigator . . . to which is Added, an Appendix, Containing an Account of Louisiana. . . .*, 6th ed. (Pittsburgh, 1808, original printed 1801); Carrigan, "Privilege, Prejudice, and Strangers' Disease in Nineteenth-Century New Orleans," *Journal of Southern History,* 36 (1970): 568-78; John G. Clark, *New Orleans, 1718-1812: An Economic History* (Baton Rouge, 1970).

[9]For example, a count of ninety-seven free persons of color in 1771 was ridiculously low, given that militia rosters for 1770 list sixty-one free *pardos* and 283 free *morenos* between the ages of fifteen and forty-five living within four leagues (twelve land miles) of New Orleans. "Liste de la quantité des naigres libre de la Nouvelle Orléans, 1770," Archivo General de Indias, Papeles de Cuba (hereafter cited AGI PC) 188-A, February 22, 1770. Gwendolyn Midlo Hall attributes this discrepancy to the tendency by the French to allow certain free blacks, especially mistresses of prominent whites, to pass as white, whereas the Spanish paid much more scrupulous attention to recording exact phenotypes, based primarily on appearance and sometimes reputation. See Gwendolyn M. Hall, *Africans in Colonial Louisiana: The Development of Afro-Creole Culture in the Eighteenth Century* (Baton Rouge, 1992), 258-64.

[10]Herbert S. Klein, *African Slavery in Latin America and the Caribbean* (New York, 1986), 217-41.

[11]Cohen and Greene, "Introduction," 16. Lyman Johnson ("The Impact of Racial Discrimination on Black Artisans in Colonial Buenos Aires," *Social History,* 6 (1981): 301-16) notes the development of guilds in colonial Argentina, whereas Mary C. Karasch, *Slave Life in Rio de Janeiro, 1808-1850* (Princeton, 1987), 200, finds few guild restrictions operating in early nineteenth-century Rio. The only restrictions this author has found for Spanish New Orleans were requirements for the licensing of doctors by a panel of their peers. In 1801 when licenses were reviewed, the free *moreno médico*, Santiago Derom, was limited to the curing of throat ailments and nothing else (Records and Deliberations of the Cabildo (hereafter cited RDC), vol. 1, May 8, 1772 and vol. 4, no. 4, August 14, 1801).

[12]Burson, *Stewardship*, 253.

[13]Examples of such behavior are presented in this article and in Kimberly S. Hanger, "*Personas de varias clases y colores*: Free People of Color in Spanish New Orleans, 1769-1803" (Ph.D. dissertation, University of Florida, 1991). Researchers have noted such a division among free blacks and alliances with whites or slaves throughout the Americas. For a summary see Cohen and Greene, "Introduction," 11-16.

[14]Census of the City of New Orleans, November 6, 1791, New Orleans Public Library; "Recensement du 1er, 2me, et 3me Quartiers," July 1795, AGI PC 211 (hereafter cited 1795 Census). Census takers grouped persons in one of three age categories: (1) 0-14; (2) 15-49; (3) 50+. See also Hanger, "*Personas*," Appendix A for data on occupation for all heads of household, white and free black, for both years.

[15]Karasch, *Slave Life in Rio*, also finds in early nineteenth-century Rio that the most common occupation among skilled slaves and freedmen was that of carpenter, or more generally, any construction craft, including joiner, caulker, and mason, 200. Most females served as domestics and/or vendors, 206-8.

[16]"Recensement du Faux-bourg Ste. Marie pour l'anée 1798," AGI PC 215-A, 1 February 1798. Organized and subdivided beginning in 1788, the Faubourg Ste. Marie (Arrabal Santa María) was located just outside the city walls upriver. By 1798 240 whites, ninety-six free persons of color, and 256 slaves resided in the suburb.

[17]Cohen and Greene, "Introduction," 16; Claude C. Robin, *Voyages dans l'interieur de la Louisiane. . . .*, 3 vols. (Paris, 1807), 2:59-61. In 1795 three of the city's free black male heads of household listed their occupation as tailor, as compared to fifteen white males. Fourteen whites and only one free black were bakers, but two of the four butchers were free African Americans.

[18]Karasch, *Slave Life in Rio*, 185-213, 335-69.

[19]RDC, vol. 3, no. 2, 1787; Court Proceedings of Carlos Ximénez, fols. 243-45, November 30, 1804.

[20]Robin, *Voyages*, 2:75.

[21]Pierre-Louis Berquin-Duvallon, *Vue de la Colonie Espagnole du Mississipi, ou des Provinces de Louisiane et Florida Occidentale, en l'Anée 1802* (Paris, 1803), 253 and Robin, *Voyages*, 2:75. Ironically, in another section of his account Berquin-Duvallon perpetuated the myth, 252.

[22]Acts of Leonard Mazange, no. 7(1), fol. 303, April 2, 1783; "Executivos seguidos por Santiago Derom, Negro libre contra Doña Isavel de Trean, sobre el cobro de *pesos*," Spanish Judicial Records, Louisiana State Museum Historical Center (hereafter cited SJR), April 30, 1791; RDC, vol. 4, no. 4, August 14, 1801; Charles B. Roussève, *The Negro in Louisiana: Aspects of His History and His Literature* (New Orleans, 1937), 9-10. In the eighteenth century doctors were not esteemed as highly as they are today and usually ranked well below government officials, planters, merchants, and even lawyers on the colonial social scale. In the New World colonies of many nations barbers often doubled as surgeons and dentists, many of whom were free people of color. For examples, see Karasch, *Slave Life in Rio*, 202.

[23]Berquin-Duvallon, *Vue*, 253.

[24]Acts of Juan Bautista Garic, no. 8, fol. 399, November 5, 1777.

[25]Acts of Francisco Broutin, no. 25, fol. 275, October 24, 1793.

[26]Acts of Andrés Almonester y Roxas, fol. 287, November 2, 1772; Court Proceedings of Esteban de Quiñones, no. 1, fols. 87-103, February 8, 1779; Archivo General de Indias, Audiencia de Santo Domingo (hereafter cited AGI SD), legajo 2548, January 18, 1782. Calpha's militia service is detailed in Hanger, "*Personas*," 169-72, 182-85.

[27]"Tableu des habitations . . . Metairie," AGI PC 211, March 12, 1796. The two white households included on the census together possessed fifty slaves and land measuring twenty-four by forty *arpents*.

[28]Karasch finds the same for Rio, *Slave Life in Rio*, 200.

[29]"Relación de la perdida que cada Yndividuo ha padecido en el Yncendio de esta Ciudad acaecido el 21 de Marzo del presente año. . . .," AGI SD 2576, September 30, 1788; Acts of Francisco Broutin, no. 7, fol. 222, May 7, 1791; AGI PC 160-A, May 1, 1801.

[30]Acts of Francisco Broutin, no. 7, fol. 20, September 17, 1790; AGI PC 160-A, May 1, 1801.

[31]Acts of Juan Bautista Garic, no. 6, fol. 171, June 26, 1775; Acts of Francisco Broutin, no. 46, fol. 125, June 19, 1797; AGI PC 160-A, May 1, 1801. Additional information concerning Bernabé's role in a joint white/free black conspiracy to overthrow the Spanish government in the 1790s is provided in Hanger, "*Personas*," 297. Bernabé remained loyal to the Spanish regime. Further discussion of militia members' occupations can be found in ibid., 181-83.

[32]"Recensement du Faux-bourg Ste. Marie pour l'anée 1798," AGI PC 215-A, February 1, 1798; RDC, vol. 3, no. 3, September 19, 1794. Among household heads in New Orleans in 1795 were one white and six free

black hunters. Slaves commonly earned extra money by cutting and selling wood to their owners or other free persons both in the city and on plantations. One temporary resident also noted that Native American women living on the outskirts of New Orleans "go into the forests to gather wood, which they carry into the city. They still sell the wood per day for thirty-six or forty sols" (Paul Alliot, "Historical and Political Reflections," in *Louisiana Under the Rule of Spain, France, and the United States, 1785-1807*, trans. and ed. James Alexander Robertson, 2 vols. (Cleveland, 1911), 83). Gwendolyn Midlo Hall finds much interaction between slaves, runaways (maroons), and planters in the Bas du Fleuve region, that area between the mouth of the Mississippi River and New Orleans where many of the cypress swamps (*ciprière*) were. According to Hall, "the lands on and behind the estates afforded excellent, nearby refuge to runaway slaves. . . . The maroons living in the *ciprière* maintained a symbiotic relationship with sawmill owners. They cut and squared cypress logs, dragged them to the sawmills, and were paid for each log delivered," Hall, *Africans in Colonial Louisiana,* 202, 207.

[33]City Treasury Accounts for 1787, Cabildo Records, box 1, folder 4, Louisiana and Lower Mississippi Valley Collections, Louisiana State University. In New Orleans, as well as in Rio, "one of the most important peddling operations was the vending of all types of foodstuffs, fresh and prepared," Karasch, *Slave Life in Rio*, 207.

[34]Thomas Ashe, *Travels in America Performed in 1806*, 3 vols. (London, 1808), 3:260. In addition to free people of color and poor whites, other marginal economic groups—"primarily city slaves engaged in selling the surplus of their gardens and loot from nocturnal activities, or Indians peddling vegetables, fish, blankets, and trinkets"—participated in the city's retail industry, Clark, *New Orleans*, 256.

[35]RDC, vol. 3, no. 1, September 10, 1784; PDLC, book 4079, doc. 234, September 2, 1794. Both French and Spanish local officials actively involved themselves in ordering daily living, their most vital task being regulation of colonial food supplies. Authorities attempted to provide adequate, edible foodstuffs to the population at fair prices for both producer and consumer. During the Spanish period, government regulation of the New Orleans market intensified as the *cabildo* began exercising "a direct and increasing influence upon the daily economic life of the town." In this capacity town council members "set prices, inspect[ed] for quality, assure[d] the use of standard weights and measures, and prevent[ed] recurrent food shortages from benefiting monopolists and forestallers at the expense of the public welfare," Clark, *New Orleans*, 257.

[36]Report from Juan de Castañedo, city treasurer, 1795, Cabildo Records, box 2, folder 6, LLMVC.

[37]John Pintard, "New Orleans, 1801: An Account by John Pintard," ed. David Lee Sterling, *Louisiana Historical Quarterly,* 34 (1951): 232, hereafter cited *LHQ*. United States officials increased restrictions on license holding with similar results: "In the month of January, 1823, thirty-two vending licenses were issued by authorities. Only free males could procure the licenses, but the license-holders seldom did the actual selling. That task was generally reserved for black slaves: many plantation owners regularly sent their slaves into town to hawk surplus produce in the street. Most of these hawkers were women" (Lilian Crété, *Daily Life in Louisiana, 1815-1830*, trans. Patrick Gregory [Baton Rouge, 1981], 64). Travelers to Rio imparted the general impression that city market stalls were the domain of African women. These women, however, actually owned the stalls. Karasch surmises that "since so many stall owners were freedpersons, perhaps they had acquired a stall and freedom," Karasch, *Slave Life in Rio*, 207.

[38]PDLC, book 4079, doc. 287, October 6, 1797. The merchants referred to the "crecido número de Mulatas y Negras tanto libres." The New York merchant Pintard wrote that "one finds however but very little interchange of courtesy among the merchants—too great jealousy of each other prevails," in "New Orleans, 1801," 232.

[39]"Proclamación por Governador Unzaga y Amezaga para regular las casas de Trujos, Posadas, y Tabernas," August 26, 1770, AGI PC 110; Jack D. L. Holmes, "Spanish Regulation of Taverns and the Liquor Trade in the Mississippi Valley," in *The Spanish in the Mississippi Valley*, ed. John Francis McDermott (Urbana, 1974),

149-82. In 1791 New Orleans boasted more tavernkeepers than any other occupation—a full seventy heads of household (Census of the City of New Orleans, November 6, 1791, New Orleans Public Library).

[40]Acts of Andrés Almonester y Roxas, f. 268, October 27, 1773, and fol. 85, February 16, 1775; City Treasury Accounts for 1787, Cabildo Records, box 1, folder 4, LLMVC; "Relación de la perdida. . . .," AGI SD 2576, September 30, 1788; 1795 Census; City Treasury Accounts for 1799, Cabildo Records, box 2a, folder 8, LLMVC.

[41]Karasch, *Slave Life in Rio*, 201.

[42]Acts of Francisco Broutin, no. 7, fol. 89, December 23, 1790; Court Proceedings of Francisco Broutin, no. 23, fol. 277-88, August 20, 1793; Acts of Carlos Ximénez, no. 6, fol. 162, April 25, 1794. Don Francisco also donated a house and land to the free *pardo* carpenter Pablo Cheval and Pablo's sister Luison Cheval, the mother of seven *cuarterones* by Don Carlos Vivant (Acts of Francisco Broutin, no. 25, fol. 169, June 9, 1793 and no. 40, fol. 177, May 31, 1796).

[43]Court Proceedings of Francisco Broutin, no. 16, fols. 48-115, January 12, 1793.

[44]Ibid., no. 22, fols. 518-27, September 23, 1793.

[45]Henry P. Dart, "Public Education in New Orleans in 1800," *LHQ*, 11 (1928): 24-52; Roger Philip McCutcheon, "Libraries in New Orleans, 1771-1833," *LHQ*, 20 (1937): 152-58; Minter Wood, "Life in New Orleans in the Spanish Period," *LHQ*, 22 (1939): 642-709.

[46]Alliot, "Reflections," 85.

[47]Acts of Francisco Broutin, no. 15, fol. 245, July 27, 1792.

[48]Ibid., no. 15, fol. 70, March 17, 1792.

[49]"Promovidos por Pompé, negro contro el Sr. Dn. Josef Antonio de Hoa, Admr. de Rl. Aduana sobre que le otorgue su livertad, por la cantidad de 400 ps.," SJR, January 7, 1793; Acts of Carlos Ximénez, no. 4, fol. 193, April 12, 1793.

[50]Acts of Andrés Almonester y Roxas, fol. 262, May 8 1779; Msgr. Earl C. Woods and Charles Nolan, eds., *Sacramental Records of the Roman Catholic Church of the Archdiocese of New Orleans*, 10 vols. (New Orleans, 1987-1995), 3:220, October 24, 1783.

[51]Acts of Pedro Pedesclaux, no. 44, fols. 421 and 423, May 20, 1803, and fol. 428, May 21, 1803. The sisters' mother, Jung's former slave, had either died or been sold to another person.

[52]For example, see Karasch, *Slave Life in Rio*, 362, 364.

[53]"Elena Negra libre sobre darle la Libertad a su hijo Esclabo de Dn. Henrique Despres por el precio de su estimación," SJR, August 12, 1780.

[54]"Criminales seguidos de oficio contra el Pardo libre Pedro Bailly," SJR, October 7, 1791. Bailly was tried and convicted on similar charges in 1794, see Hanger, "*Personas*," 288-329.

[55]Acts of Andrés Almonester y Roxas, fol. 389, September 1, 1775.

[56]Court Proceedings of Narciso Broutin, no. 53, fols. 225-98, June 11, 1802. Of interest is that the inventory recorded personal names for all the oxen, but not the other animals.

[57]Several white fathers manumitted their natural offspring and slave consorts along with donating property to them. The present writer agrees with Loren Schweninger, however, that "even with the advantage of inheritance, it took energy, industry, and business acumen for these people [free people of color in the lower South] to maintain their property holdings. In towns and cities, free men and women of color took advantage of the continued demand for service businesses, the relatively small numbers of skilled whites and immigrants, and the general appreciation in city property values to expand their estates" during the antebellum period ("Prosperous Blacks in the South, 1790-1880," *American Historical Review,* 95 [1990]: 36.)

[58]Acts of Francisco Broutin, no. 30, fol. 328, December 23, 1794.

[59]"Testamentaria de Don Francisco Hisnard que falleció en el Puesto de Opellousas," SJR, August 27, 1798; Acts of Pedro Pedesclaux, no. 40, fol. 81, February 6, 1802; Acts of Narciso Broutin, no. 4, fol. 544, December 31, 1802; Jack D. L. Holmes, "Do It! Don't Do It!: Spanish Laws on Sex and Marriage," in *Louisiana's Legal Heritage*, ed. Edward F. Haas (Pensacola, 1983), 23.

[60]"Autos fecho por fin y Muerte de Juan Bta Hugón," SJR, August 8, 1792.

[61]Acts of Francisco Broutin, no. 7, fol. 1, August 23, 1790.

PART VIII
Arts, Entertainment, and Medicine

MUSIC AND ART IN SPANISH COLONIAL LOUISIANA*

Alfred E. Lemmon

Music, art, and ceremony were major components of imperial Spain. A prime example is the 1519 visit of Carlos V (1500-1558) to Barcelona, which was highlighted by his formal entry and the commemorative ceremonies honoring his grandfather, the Emperor Maximilian of Austria.[1] Likewise, the Spanish colonies, by royal decree from Madrid and due to the weight of ecclesiastical tradition within the Roman Catholic Church, regularly mounted public ceremonies connected with patriotic celebrations and observances. In 1533, only forty years after the European discovery of Puerto Rico, celebrations were held on the island on March 12 commemorating Spain's victories over the Turks.[2] Carlos V's death in 1558 prompted both civil and church authorities throughout the realm to eagerly render his memory every possible homage. Officials in Mexico City set out to surpass their colleagues in other parts of the Spanish Empire. Francisco Cervantes de Salazar, a professor of rhetoric at the recently founded (1553) University of Mexico, vividly described in his *Tumulo Imperial de la gran ciudad de México* the pomp and circumstance of the 1559 Mexico City ceremonies in memory of Carlos V.[3] The commemorative ceremonies for Felipe II (1527-1598) in 1600 was another opportunity for ostentatious display of public grief in Mexico. Like the *Tumulo Imperial* occasioned by the death of Carlos V, printed accounts were prepared for distribution locally and in Spain.[4] Birthdays, weddings, and coronations were a source of a constant stream of accounts sent to Spain in both manuscript and printed format. The purpose of these reports was to invoke royal favor on the colonial officials who staged the celebrations.

The musical and visual artists mustered all their resources to make the events memorable. Indeed, some of the greatest musical compositions of the New World owe their existence to these efforts to gain royal favor. The first opera written in the New

*This article is published with the kind permission of the author.

World, *La Púrpura de la Rosa* by Tomás de Torrejón y Velasco (1644-1728), was composed to celebrate Felipe V's (1683-1746) eighteenth birthday in 1701.[5] Participation in such events was not limited to the Spanish population. María Luisa de Borbón (1751-1819), wife of Carlos IV (1748-1819), was honored on her birthday in 1790 by a festive cantata written by three Moxos Indians of Bolivia (Francisco Semo, Marcelino Ycho, and Juan José Nosa). The cantata, written in their native tongue, is both a linguistic and musical codex of stellar artistic importance.[6]

In light of this knowledge, there was nothing uncommon about the meeting convened on April 24, 1789, in New Orleans to review the commemorative act held on the occasion of the death of Carlos III. In an April 4 extraordinary meeting, the *cabildo* responded to the *real cédula* of December 24, 1788, that called for demonstrations of "the love and loyalty for the deceased monarch."[7] At 9 o'clock on the morning of April 22, officials gathered under the direction of Governor Esteban Miró (c. 1744-1795) to procede from the *Casa del Gobierno* to the chapel of Charity Hospital, as the parish church had been destroyed in the March, 1788, fire.[8] The site selected posed particular problems. The chapel can perhaps best be described as a "poor ruined church, very small and uncomfortable."[9] Nonetheless, the members of the *cabildo* agreed upon the construction of a *tumulo* [tomb] in the chapel appropriate to the size of the building, and that the funeral rites would be celebrated on two especially constructed altars.[10]

With the dignitaries dressed in full mourning regalia, they were led to the chapel by their mace bearers and a full military escort. The chapel had been prepared with the majestic *tumulo* crowned by a funeral urn. The urn was placed on the top of five steps and covered with bright red velvet in the form of a mantel, worthy of the deceased monarch. On a pillow of the same fabric, but trimmed with gold braid and tassels, rested a scepter and crown. The crown was richly decorated with imitation precious stones. A canopy descended from the top in four arched festoons. The funeral bier was further decorated with medals representing various royal honors. The pulpit displayed some sixty royal coat of arms.[11] Illuminated by candles, the chapel was the scene of a magnificent spectacle for which the parish singers provided the most solemn music. The report on the commemorative ceremony destined for Spain was prepared by Pedro Pedesclaux, notary of the *cabildo* on April 25, 1789. Pedesclaux duly noted that 2,216 *pesos*, 5 *reales*, had been spent on the event.[12] Antonio de Sedella (1748-1829), more commonly known as Père Antoine, preached a eulogy in honor of Carlos III that earned him the title of "His Majesty's Preacher."[13]

Once the *cabildo* had completed arrangements for the commemorative service for Carlos III, work began immediately on the celebrations honoring the new monarch, Carlos IV. The proclamation of the new monarch was to be executed with all the pomp and spectacle the city treasury would permit. Carlos de Reggio, royal ensign, would begin the celebration by carrying the royal banner and leading the officials to the chapel for the singing of the *Te Deum* in honor of the new monarch. After the blessing of the royal banner, all the participants would proceed to the *Casa del Gobierno*, where the proclamation of the new king would take place on the balcony of the building. Afterwards, the ritual proclamation would be repeated in the town plaza and major public places of the city.[14]

On May 8, 1789, the *cabildo* met to review the May 4 ceremonies held in honor of Carlos IV. They noted that the ceremony demonstrated the "love, zeal, and loyalty" of the new monarch's local subjects. The account notes that the ceremonies began at 4:00 p.m. when Miró led all public officials, the military, civil servants, and distinguished citizens, through the streets of the city to the accompaniment of music. Civil and military officials appeared in full ceremonial dress; the six-month period of official mourning in memory of Carlos III was suspended temporarily for the duration of the celebration of Carlos IV's coronation.[15]

The *cabildo* noted that attention was paid to do everything in accordance with the *Recopilación de Leyes de los Reynos de Indias*, a compilation of laws for Spain's New World colonies, first published in 1681. Specifically observed were the regulations outlined in Book 3, Title 15, Law 56 that deal with protocol of officials attending ceremonial celebrations and in particular the carrying of the royal banner in procession.[16] Upon arrival at the chapel of Charity Hospital, Antonio de Sedella and other ecclesiastic officials greeted the civil and military authorities. The civil officials were led to their positions of honor for the singing of the *Te Deum*. Returning to Government House, the name of the new monarch, Carlos IV, was proclaimed for the first time to the public, and portraits of the new monarch and Queen María Luisa de Borbón were unveiled. The portraits were displayed beneath a bright red damascus canopy.[17] The celebrations continued for three evenings with an illumination of the city, musical concerts given by a large orchestra, the presentation of two comedies, and a great *sarao* or dancing party. As he had done earlier with the commemorative ceremonies for Carlos III, Pedro Pedesclaux faithfully reported everything to officials in Madrid on May 9, 1789.[18] While the city rightfully took pride in its first celebrations upon the death and coronation of a Spanish monarch, the events pale in comparison to those of other colonies. For example, in Guatemala, the cathedral choir and orchestra performed music especially composed by native son Rafael Antonio Castellanos (d. 1791) in honor of the deceased monarch and music by peninsular composer Joseph Coll (fl. 1790),[19] with text adapted to the Guatemalan environs, in honor of Carlos IV.[20]

The account sent to Madrid, like the minutes of the *cabildo* meeting, is brief. One major fault of the accounts prepared about the ceremonies is that they fail to note the artists and musicians involved in the events. Fortunately, other documents provide information that help provide a more complete picture.

First, Governor Miró was an individual of some musical taste. A letter written by Alexandre de Clouet (1717-1789) from Opelousas on October 8, 1785, describes De Clouet's efforts to locate an individual referred to simply as Préjean. Reportedly a great player of the violin and *clavinette*, Miró had requested De Clouet to locate him. All De Clouet could report was that Préjean apparently resided near Baton Rouge. Nonetheless, the document indicates Miró's interest in the musical arts, the presence of a violin and a *clavinette,* and an accomplished performer of these instruments in the colony.[21]

Miró's fondness for music was first displayed at least two years earlier. During Spain's participation in the American Revolutionary War, many soldiers including musicians came to Louisiana for its defense. After the war ended, most of the troops were withdrawn to Cuba. As they left, Miró complained to Acting Captain General José de Ezpeleta that he no longer had enough musicians for the regimental orchestra. He asked for clarinetists, trumpeters, and a director for the unit.[22]

Miró was not the only governor of Spanish Louisiana with an interest in music. Indeed, both Carondelet (1747-1807) and Gálvez (1746-1786) strongly manifested their musical interests in other posts that they held. Francisco Luis Héctor, Barón de Carondelet's musical interests were made clear during his tenure in Quito. As president of the royal *Audiencia* of Quito, Carondelet was dedicated to restoring the cathedral's artistic glories. His interest resulted in a new *Plan de Música* being approved by the Cathedral chapter shortly after his arrival. As a result, over the next fifteen years, the musical structure of the Quito cathedral was substantially rebuilt.[23]

However, the governor of Spanish Louisiana with the greatest reputation as a supporter of the performing arts was Bernardo de Gálvez. An examination of his brief tenure (1785-1786) as Viceroy of New Spain reveals his passion for ballet. When he departed Spain for his post in Mexico, he took with him the leading dancer of the *Coliseo* of Cádiz, the Italian Gerónimo Marani. Once in Mexico City, he expressed an interest in the economic and artistic improvement of that city's *Coliseo*. Among improvements he made to the theater was the installation of practice halls for the dancers. He also promulgated a *Reglamento u Ordenanzas de Teatro*,[24] which were advanced for the period. Important spectators were not permitted to be seated on the stage, as was the customary practice in European capitals during the period. Other innovations included changing the time of performances from 4:30 p.m. to 8:00 p.m., and organization of the theater's employees into companies of singers, dancers, and orchestral musicians. In an effort to improve the orchestra, he asked ecclesiastical officials permission for the better cathedral musicians to perform in the orchestra of the *Coliseo*.[25]

The sacramental and financial records of St. Louis Church provide the most information about the practicing musicians in New Orleans during the Spanish period. Cantors include Jean Vualle, who first appears in the 1765 church sacramental records as a cantor,[26] and Hubert Sauvagin who is referred to "as cantor of this parish" in 1772,[27] 1774,[28] and 1775.[29] Francisco Gonzáles is identified as a "native of Castille," and a cantor in 1790.[30] Arnau Saramiac appears as a cantor in two 1793 marriage records.[31] His burial record notes that he had served the parish church for some thirty-eight years.[32] Financial records, beginning in 1747, provide additional information on the church's music personnel. M. Pretzer's tenure as a singer is learned through payments made to a seamstress for his choir robe in 1755.[33] In addition, A. Hubert is first listed as a singer in 1766. Both of these individuals appear in the yearly expense summaries through

1781.[34] In 1784, a new singer, Hipolite Palacios, is listed on the roster.[35] With St. Louis parish church being designated a cathedral in 1793, additional singers appear, such as Antonio Talabera y Muñoz,[36] M. Hebert, and Ambrosio Pardos.[37] An enclosure in the financial records lists other singers not mentioned elsewhere. Señores Esquilet,[38] Clausin,[39] Josef Ysita,[40] Antonio Ysita,[41] and Josef Benluso[42] are mentioned as paid singers in the service of the cathedral. An examination of the sacramental records during the American period reveals that there was a boys choir active during the Spanish period. Burial records provide the name of at least one choirboy during the Spanish period, Antonio Xerez.[43] Further financial data on the singers are in the papers of Pierre Clément Laussat (1756-1835), French Colonial Prefect of Louisiana, which contains a report for the cathedral that details their fees.[44]

Two organists have been identified as being associated with the church during the Spanish period. The first is Josepthe Martens, first mentioned in the 1784 financial records.[45] Vicente Llorca, organist, served as a witness for the marriage of Antonio Talabera y Muñoz and María Margarita Briset in 1798.[46] Llorca, a soldier and native of Oliva in Valencia, came to New Orleans after the Pensacola campaign of Bernardo de Gálvez in 1781. Initially, he served as "cantor interino" of St. Louis parish church, where his charge was to set sacred texts to music in the Spanish style.[47] The chimney tax census for 1797 sheds information on the personal life of the cathedral organist, Vicente Llorca. He resided in the fourth *barrio*, residence number 75 1/2, and owned a residence with one chimney.[48] The cathedral's financial records indicate that a new cassock was made for him in 1801.[49] His funeral record indicates he died on September 9, 1803, at the age of 52 or 53. It states that he was both organist and cantor, son of Esteban Llorca and Ana María Vidal of Valencia, and left no will.[50]

The sacramental records also provide some idea on the administration of sacraments. The pomp and solemnity surrounding the baptism of the daughter of Juan Antonio Lugar and María Juana Prudhomme on June 24, 1793, was "graced by the sound of organ music."[51] The sacramental records are important for the reconstruction of the church's musical life because the musicians frequently served as witnesses for the administration of sacraments and were so identified. In some cases, no other information about the musicians is available. Funeral records for the years 1796 to 1798 contain information on some 214 funerals for those years. In at least 50 percent of the funerals, a minimum of four singers were employed.[52]

In 1802 the same records indicate that Luis Duclot[53] was paid to bind two *Rituals*[54] and two large choir books.[55] Regrettably, specific information about the *Rituals* and choirbooks is not given. While no musical archive of the French or Spanish colonial period survives for St. Louis Cathedral, through the use of sources common in all cathedrals of Spanish America, existing sacramental and financial records of the cathedral identify the key musicians, as well as members of the boys choir, during the Spanish period. It is significant that there is no mention of an organist until the Spanish period, nor is there any documentation about an organ in the colonial period.[56] However, we learn from sacramental records that the Spanish musical presence in St. Louis Cathedral did not survive the Louisiana Purchase. By 1811, the church had an English organist known only as Thomas. He served as organist for six or seven months, dying suddenly on Sunday, August 10, 1811, at 9:00 p.m.[57] The next time an organist of Hispanic origin is found in the cathedral records is in 1828, when Juan Francisco Alcay briefly served as organist.[58]

Documentation about musicians active in New Orleans not associated with the church is more difficult to obtain. However, one document does reveal the names of five other musicians active in Louisiana. In 1785, five French army deserters, members of the Regimiento de Ybernia, arrived in New Orleans. The resulting investigation into their arrival provides their names—Lamberto Damelin, Guillermo Yanzen, Adam Bensenguer, Jaime Diel, and Juan Villiams—but it says nothing of their musical background or activities in New Orleans.[59]

Notarial records indicate that on June 4, 1791, Alexandre Henry purchased a site on St. Peter Street for the construction of a theater, which eventually opened on October 4, 1792. The city fathers carefully stipulated the time that the ticket office was to open and the curtain to rise. Behavior in the theater was to be proper, and interruptions, hissing, improper language, and smoking were prohibited. The opening performance was reportedly shaky at best; however, as Henry Kmen noted in his epochal *Music in New Orleans: The Formative Years, 1791-1841,* "bad theater is better than no theater."[60] The first definite reference to an operatic performance in New Orleans occurred in 1796. On May 22 of that year a performance of *Sylvain,*[61] a one-act *opéra comique* first presented at the Comédie Italienne in Paris on February 18, 1770, by the French composer of Walloon descent, André-Ernest-Modeste Grétry (1741-1813), was given.[62] On July 17, 1796, *Blaise et Babet ou La suite des Trois fermiers,*[63] a two-act *opéra comique* premiered at Versailles on April 9, 1783, by Nicolas [Alexandre?] Dezède (1740/1745?-1792) was presented in New Orleans.[64] *Renaud d'Ast* of Nicolas-Marie Dalayrac (1753-1809), first performed at the Comédie Italienne of Paris in 1787, was premiered in New Orleans on September 3, 1799. Dalayrac, a composer of some sixty operas popular in France and Europe and the son of an aristocratic counsellor to the king, survived changing political winds well by adapting popular operatic tunes to Republican words. His "Veillons au salut de l'Empire" was originally from his *Renaud d'Ast.*[65] The New Orleans theater was financially unstable, even though in 1792 loges were selling at steep prices. By December 12, 1803, the building was ordered closed since it was on the verge of collapse.[66]

The theater gained the attention of the *cabildo* on several occasions. Indeed, with the death of Manuel Gayoso de Lemos, the members of that illustrious body addressed the question of their seating arrangements in the small theater. The theater manager was ordered to construct a new box for their use. It was to be built in front of the stage, not on the side as it had been during Gayoso's governorship. Furthermore, the new box was to be constructed with ample space because as their former box had been small.[67] The discussion over seating arrangements continued well into 1802. The *cabildo* members noted that when the theater was established, Governor Carondelet had ordered the box in front of the stage be divided into two separate boxes. A larger and more prominent box was on the right side, and a smaller box for the governor was on the left side. When Gayoso assumed the governorship in 1797, the seating arrangement continued. However, the number of *cabildo* members increased as a result of a royal order. When Nicolas María Vidal assumed the position of acting civil governor, the box was enlarged in 1799, as noted above. However, in 1802 when the theater opened, the box was once again divided into two. The small box on the left side was now reserved for the municipal and judicial officials. This action insulted these officials since they were the authorities in charge when the governor did not attend. They, therefore, requested that the box be returned to the previous configuration and a certified copy of the 1799 instructions concerning the box be sent to Governor Manuel de Salcedo, along with a copy of the minutes of the meeting at which they discussed the 1802 change in seating arrangements.[68]

Over a period of years, the *cabildo* expressed its concern about the dances of the African community. The carnival season subjected the city to numerous thefts and for that reason measures were taken to prohibit masking, nightly dancing by Africans, and dance-halls where fees were charged (as gambling frequently went on in them).[69] Later, in response to a request by Gov. Esteban Miró concerning greater observance of religious holidays, the *cabildo* issued a ruling that African dances, ordinarily held in the main plaza, could not begin on holidays until after the evening religious services had concluded. He further emphasized that the slave nightly dances that often lasted until mid-night, were prohibited in the city and countryside without the proper permission of masters and the government.[70]

Ironically, the African population was later seen as a salvation for the economically endangered first theater of New Orleans. Bernardo Coquet and Joseph Antoine Boniquet, the theater's operators, saw economic salvation by holding public dances for the African-American population. It was stipulated that dances would be held only on Sunday evenings, except during carnival season when two dances a week were allowed. No slaves were to be admitted to them without the written permission of their masters. Finally, to insure their economic success no other dances were allowed for the black population. Their reason for being was highly less intriguing and romantic than the popular legends about the "quadroon balls" attest.[71]

While knowledge about music during the Spanish period is limited basically to the names of musicians and operas that are of more historic than musical interest today, the opposite situation exists in the field of painting. The names of fewer painters than musicians who worked in New Orleans during the Spanish period are known. The first Spanish painter known to visit Louisiana was Miguel García, who reportedly travelled in the company of Bienville, although no painting of his has survived.[72] Joseph Furcoty, Joseph Herrera, and José de Salazar are listed as painters in the census of 1791.[73] It is also reported that F. Godefroid and Ambroise Pardo were painting portraits in New Orleans during the last decade of the eighteenth-century.[74] Of these artists, Salazar's work has survived, A native of Mérida, Yucatán in Mexico, his full name is José Francisco Salazar y Mendoza (d. 1802). He is known to have worked in New Orleans at the end of the eighteenth and early nineteenth century. Included in his *oeuvre* are portraits of some of the more important Spanish colonial figures in New Orleans. Philanthropist and builder Don Andrés Almonester y Roxas (1725-1798), the first bishop of the diocese of Louisiana and the Floridas Luis Peñalver y Cárdenas (1749-1810), the previously mentioned Antonio de Sedella, and the royal surveyor Carlos Trudeau (c. 1750-1816), all had their portraits painted by him. It is believed that he painted at least sixteen portraits in Louisiana.[75] Besides painting important civic and religious leaders, his subjects included individuals such as Clara de la Mota, an immigrant whose parents were residents of Curaçao.[76] Salazar died in New Orleans of an unspecified illness without the benefit of *Extreme Unction.* He was buried by Pedro de Zamora, vicar St. Louis Cathedral on August 15, 1802.[77] His estate sheds light on his living habits with information about his clothing, furniture, slaves, and household utensils,[78] and it provides a glimpse of his tools as an artist. Shortly before his death, he purchased a dozen black crayons, eight pencils, and one box of colors from Mercier & Cie.[79] Salazar's daughter, Francisca (fl. 1802), followed in her father's footsteps as a painter. Commissioned by church authorities, she copied her father's portrait of Bishop Peñalaver y Cárdenas.[80]

A comparison of music and the visual arts in the Spanish colonial period quickly reveals that more musicians are known by name than artists, but far less is known about the work of musicians than artists. In fact, while Vicente Llorca is known to have composed music, not one of his compositions has been found. This is in stark contrast to the portraits by Salazar that have survived. One could speculate that because Bishop Peñalver y Cárdenas was a native of Havana, possibly he brought with him the music of the distinguished Cuban composer of the period, Esteban Salas y Castro (1725-1803).[81] In contrast to the French colonial period,[82] nothing is known about the music that circulated in the Spanish era other than the three operas earlier described. Indeed, Louisiana is unlike other Spanish New World possessions where significant colonial music archives survive.[83]

An examination of the more than 2,700 entries in the *Encyclopedia of New Orleans Artists, 1718-1918* reveals that while the Spanish colonial period boasted of a painter of Salazar's caliber, that only approximately thirty artists from Spain or former Spanish colonies worked in New Orleans during the nineteenth-century.[84] In contrast, more than 120 French artists labored at their profession in New Orleans during the same period. At the same time, nineteenth-century New Orleans' musical ties to the Hispanic world were strong; this has been amply demonstrated in the writings of Alfred Lemmon,[85] S. Frederick Starr,[86] Robert Stevenson,[87] and Mary Grace Swift.[88] Indeed, as Jack Belsom has noted, a goodly portion of Italian opera was introduced to New Orleans, and as a result to the United States, via the Havana stage.[89]

Notes for "Music and Art in Spanish Colonial Louisiana"

[1]Emilio Ros-Fábregas, "Music and ceremony during Charles V's 1519 to Barcelona," *Early Music*, 23 (1995): 374-92.

[2]Donald Thompson, "Music in Puerto Rican Public Ceremony: *Fiestas Reales, Fiestas Patronales, Ferias*, and *Exposiciones*: A Chronological List of Official reports and Similar Documents, 1746-1897," *Inter-American Music Review*, 10 (1989): 135.

[3]Francisco Cervantes de Salazar, *Tumulo Imperial de la gran ciudad de México* (Mexico City, 1560).

[4]Robert Stevenson, *Music in Aztec and Inca Territory* (Berkeley, 1968), 202.

[5]Robert Stevenson, *La Púrpura de la Rosa* (Lima, 1976), 99-109.

[6]Alfred E. Lemmon, *Royal Music of the Moxos* (New Orleans, 1987).

[7]Actas del Cabildo (April 4, 1789), Louisiana Division, New Orleans Public Library. Hereafter cited as AC.

[8]"Acta del Cabildo de Nueva Orleans sobre las exequias por Carlos III, Abril 24, 1789," in "Colección de documentos sobre Luisiana 1767 a 1792," Tomo 3, Documento 31, Biblioteca Nacional de España. Hereafter cited as "Exequias por Carlos III."

[9]AC, October 2, 1789.

[10]Ibid, April 4, 1789.

[11]Ibid., April 24, 1789.

[12]"Exequias por Carlos III."

[13]AC, May 22, 1789.

[14]Ibid., April 17, 1789.

[15]AC, May 8, 1789.

[16]*Recopilación de Leyes de los Reynos de las Indias, Mandadas imprimir y publicar por la Magistad Católica del Rey Don Carlos II.* Quarta Impresion (Madrid, 1791). The exact title of this section is *De las precedencias, ceremonias y cortesías*. This particular law is a result of laws promulgated by Carlos V (1530), Felipe II (1565 and 1582), and Felipe III (1607 and 1642).

[17]AC, May 8, 1789.

[18]"Acta del Cabildo de Nueva Orleans sobre la proclamación de Carlos IV," Colección de documentos sobre Luisiana 1767 a 1792, Tomo 3, Documento 33. Biblioteca Nacional de España.

[19]Director of music in the theaters of Extremadura, Spain in 1790 according to Baltasar Saldoni, *Diccionario Biográfico-Bibliográfico de Efemerides de Músicos Españoles* (Barcelona, 1879), 66.

[20]Rafael Antonio Castellanos, *Subvenite Sancti Dei* (in honor of Carlos III), and Joseph Coll, *Levanten Pendones* (in honor of Carlos IV) in Alfred E. Lemmon, *Eighteenth-Century Music from Guatemala*, (S.Woodstock, Plumsock Mesoamerican Studies, 1984), 124-39; 141-74.

[21]Archivo General de Indias, Papeles procedentes de Cuba, legajo 198-A. The credit for the discovery of this letter goes to Winston De Ville, who generously made the citation available to the author. De Ville has promised an annotated translation of the letter in the forthcoming second volume of his *Mississippi Valley Mélange*.

[22]Esteban Miró to José de Ezpeleta, New Orleans, October 1, 1783, Archivo General de Indias, Papeles procedentes de Cuba, legajo 1377. Information provided by Gilbert C. Din.

[23]Robert Stevenson, "Quito Cathedral: Four Centuries," *Inter-American Music Review*, 3 (1980): 33.

[24]Maya Ramos Smith, "La Danza en México durante la Epoca Colonial," unpublished manuscript dated 1978. Smith cites the following documents from Mexico's *Archivo General de la Nación*: Asuntos de Teatro, Vol. 1411, folio 257; Colegio de San Gregorio, Vol. 153, Expediente 21.

[25]Ibid., 102-3.

[26]Charles E. Nolan and Earl C. Woods, eds. *Sacramental Records of the Roman Catholic Church of the Archdiocese of New Orleans*, 10 vols. (New Orleans, 1987-1995), 2:276. Hereafter *Sacramental Records*.

[27]Ibid., 3:202.

[28]Ibid., 129.

[29]Ibid., 273.

[30]Ibid., 4:148.

[31]Ibid., 5:31, 329.

[32]Ibid., 6:247.

[33]"Parish Church of St. Louis, Financial Records, 1747-1800;" Expense summary for 1747. Archives of the Archdiocese of New Orleans (AANO). Hereafter cited "Financial."

[34]Ibid., Expense summaries, 1755-1781.

[35]Ibid., 1784.

[36]*Sacramental Records*, 10:60 identifies him as "first cantor of this parish."

[37]Ibid., 1793.

[38]Ibid., January 14, June 24, July 31, August 21, August 22, 1798.

[39]Ibid., January 13, January 24, 1798.

[40]Ibid., February 4, 1798. *Sacramental Records*, 8:319 states that he was a native of Mexico.

[41]Ibid., February 4, 1798.

[42]Ibid., May 6, June 14, 1798.

[43]St. Louis Cathedral Funerals (1832-1833), Archives of the Archdiocese of New Orleans, 10-54.

[44]"Schedule of Fees for the parish of the Cathedral Church of Louisiana and others under its jurisdiction," April 18, 1803, Papers of Pierre Clément Laussat, Historic New Orleans Collection.

[45]"Financial," Expense summary, 1784.

[46]*Sacramental Records*, 1:261.

[47]Antonio Mestre, "Un olivense en la Nueva Orleans del siglo XVIII," *Levante*, July 3, 1990, cited in Vicent Ribes, *Comerciantes, esclavos y capital sin patria* (Valencia, 1993), 20.

[48]"1797 Spanish Chimney Tax Records for New Orleans," Historic New Orleans Collection.

[49]"Libro que contiene los folios desde el n. uno al doscientos ochenta y dos que hemos rubricado con nuestro secretario de camara y gobierno para que en el se rexistren por el mayordomo de la Fabrica de esta Sta. Iglesia Cathedral de la Luisiana a sus cuentas que corran desde el dia de hoy en que comienza el siglo decimonono de la Era Christiana, y quede el anterior en que se hacia archivado en nuestra secretaria. Nueva Orleans primera de Enero de mil ochocientos y uno. Luis, Obispo de la Luisiana;" Archives of the Archdiocese of New Orleans; 15v. Hereafter cited as "Libro."

[50]St. Louis Cathedral Funerals (1793-1803), 130-1298.

[51]Kimberly S. Hanger, "Personas de varias clases y colores: Free People of Color in Spanish New Orleans, 1769-1803" (Ph.D. dissertation, University of Florida, 1991), 266.

[52]"Libro," August 28, 1798.

[53]Florence Jumonville, *Bibliography of New Orleans Imprints, 1764-1864* (New Orleans, 1989), 17.

[54]"Libro," 15v.

[55]Ibid., 23r.

[56]Alfred E. Lemmon, "Music in St. Louis Cathedral, 1725-1844," in *Cross, Crozier and Crucible* (Lafayette, 1993), 489-504. Hereafter cited as Lemmon, "St. Louis."

[57]AANO, St. Louis Cathedral Funeral Records, 1803-1815, 170-713bis.

[58]AANO, Expense Summary, September 11, 1828. In the same document Alcay's name is also spelled Alcayde.

[59]"Declaraciones, que justifican el motivo y de que manera, se quedaron en el Regimiento de Ybernia, los cinco musicos que estan destinados para este de la Luisiana," December 9, 1785, Archivo General de Indias, Papeles de Cuba, Legajo 2, f. 200-209.

[60]Henry Kmen, *Music in New Orleans: The Formative Years, 1791-1841* (Baton Rouge, 1966), 58.

[61]Ibid., 58-60.

[62]José Quitin, "Grétry, Andre-Ernest-Modeste," *New Groves Dictionary of Music and Musicians*, 8:704-712.

[63]Ibid., 58-60.

[64]Leland Fox, "Dezède, Nicolas [Aldexandre?], *New Groves Dictionary of Music and Musicians*, 5:412-413. Dezède was a composer in residence in Paris, whose place of birth was not known, although evidence indicates that he may have been the illegitimate son of a German prince (perhaps Frederick II of Prussia).

[65]David Charlton, "Dalayrac [D'Alayrac] Nicolas-Marie," *New Groves Dictionary of Music and Musicians*, 5:148-51.

[66]Ibid., 58-60.

[67]AC, July 27, 1799.

[68]Ibid., January 15, 1802.

[69]Ibid., January 19, 1781.

[70]Ibid., June 2, 1786.

[71]Kmen, *Music in New Orleans*, 42-45.

[72]José Montero de Pedro, *Españoles en Nueva Orleans y Luisiana* (Madrid, 1979), 142.

[73]Burson, *Stewardship of Don Esteban Miró*, 247-48.

[74]Charles van Ravenswaay, "The Forgotten Arts and Crafts of Colonial Louisiana," *Antiques*, 63 (1953): 195.

[75]Ibid., 143-44.

[76]Bertram Wallace Korn, *The Early Jews of New Orleans* (Waltham, 1969), 42.

[77]AANO, St. Louis Cathedral Funerals, 1802, 115-1027.

[78]New Orleans Notarial Archives, Nicolas Broutin, Volume 24 (renumbered 55), Number 23, "Autos hechos por fin y muerte de Don José Salazar, folios 9-12.

[79]Ibid., folio 20.

[80]John Burton Harter and Mary Louise Tucker, *The Louisiana Portrait Gallery* (New Orleans, 1979), 1:124.

[81]Pablo Hernández Balaguer, *Los villancicos, cantadas y pastorelas de Esteban Salas* (Havana, 1986).

[82]Lemmon, "St. Louis," 490.

[83]Robert Stevenson, *Renaissance and Baroque Musical Sources in the Americas* (Washington, DC, 1970); Alfred E. Lemmon "Toward an International Inventory of Colonial Spanish American Cathedral Music Archives," *Actas del XV Congreso de la Sociedad Internacional de Musicología*, 1, edited by Ismael Fernandez de la Cuesta and Alfonso de Vicente, published in *Revista de Musicología*, 16 (1993): 92-97.

[84]*Encyclopedia of New Orleans Artists, 1718-1918* (New Orleans, 1983).

[85]Alfred E. Lemmon, "New Orleans Popular Sheet Music to 1900: The Latin Tinge," *Southern Quarterly*, 27 (1989): 41-58.

[86]S. Frederick Starr, *Bamboula! The Life and Times of Louis Moreau Gottschalk* (London, 1995).

[87]Robert Stevenson, "The Latin Tinge 1800-1900," *Inter-American Music Review*, 2 (1980): 73-102.

[88]Mary Grace Swift, *Belles and Beaux on their Toes: Dancing Stars in Young America* (Washington, DC, 1980).

[89]Jack Belsom, "Reception of Major Operatic Premiers in New Orleans during the Nineteenth-Century" (M. A. thesis, Louisiana State University, 1972).

ALMONESTER: PHILANTHROPIST AND BUILDER IN NEW ORLEANS*

Samuel Wilson, Jr.

In the floor of St. Louis Cathedral of New Orleans in front of the old altar of St. Francis of Assisi (now dedicated to St. Joseph) is embedded a marble slab covering the burial place of the city's first notable philanthropist, a Spaniard whose benefactions have left an indelible imprint on the city of his adoption. The Spanish inscription upon the present slab, a replacement of the original, which was removed to the Cabildo many years ago, broken and indecipherable, may be translated as follows:

Here lies the remains
of
Dn. Andrés Almonester y Roxas
Native of Mairena
In the Kingdom of Andalusia
Died in the City of New Orleans
The 26 of April of 1798
At the age of 73 years.
Knight of the Royal and Distinguished Spanish
Order of Carlos III.
Colonel of the Militia of this Plaza
Alderman and Royal Ensign of this Cabildo
Founder of the Lepers' Hospital
Founder and donor of this holy Cathedral Church
Founder of the Royal Hospital of San Carlos and of its church.
Founder of the church of the Convent of the Ursuline Nuns.
Founder of the Classes for the Education of young children
and founder of the house for the Clergy
All which he has erected at his Expense in this City.

Requiescat in Pace.

*Samuel Wilson, Jr., "Almonester: Philanthropist and Builder in New Orleans," first published in John Francis McDermott, ed., *The Spanish in the Mississippi Valley, 1762-1803*.

Each of the institutions listed here as being founded by him received through his generosity a new building, each a building of some architectural importance that did much to enhance the appearance of the city. Almonester is thus remembered as the foremost builder of his day, although there is little evidence to indicate that he was an actual building contractor. He seems to have been rather a builder in the larger sense, as instigator, donor, and financier of great building projects.

This distinguished son was born at Mairena del Alcor in the province of Seville in Andalusia, Spain, about the year 1725, the son of Miguel Joseph Almonester and Doña María Juana de Estrada y Roxas, both Andalusians. In his native land Almonester married Doña María Martínez, by whom he had a son who died at birth. In his will he states that "we both came on equal terms to that marriage, without fortune or dowry."[1] It was probably after the death of his wife that Almonester decided to come to Louisiana, the former French province that Louis XV had given to Spain by the Treaty of Fontainebleau in 1762.[2]

Almonester first appeared before the members of the Illustrious *Cabildo* on March 16, 1770,[3] at a meeting held in the residence of the governor, the old French colonial capitol at the corner of Toulouse and Levee streets. The new home of the *cabildo* was then under construction adjacent to the parish church facing the Plaza de Armas, under a contract signed by O'Reilly on December 11, 1769, with the local French builder François Hery, called Duplanty.[4] At this meeting of the *cabildo* "a Royal Edict from His Majesty was read by me [J.B. Garic], the present Secretary, dated August 11, 1765, at San Ildefonso, in which His Majesty honors Andrés Almonester y Roxas with the position of Secretary for all His Kingdom, and at the same time I read the appointment as Public Secretary for the War in charge of the Royal Treasury, made in favor of the said Don Andrés, dated March 12th of this year by the said Governor-General [Luis de Unzaga y Amezaga]." Unzaga had been appointed to succeed O'Reilly as governor. In acknowledging Almonester's appointment and in respect to the king, the members of the *cabildo* enacted a curious ceremony, "taking the Royal Edict in their hands and placing it upon their heads."[5] Such a ceremony was repeated whenever a document signed by the king was received by the *cabildo.* With the royal appointment went "the amount of 500 *pesos* per year with the privileges, power and exemptions bestowed upon the said appointment."

This appointment seems to have been the beginning of Almonester's fortune in Louisiana. It was in effect an appointment as notary public, an important position in the colony under both French and Spanish rule. After the reading of the edict, Almonester made his entrance into the assembly room and was sworn into office by the *cabildo.* Royal confirmation of his commission was issued by the king at El Pardo on March 11, 1773.[6] Almonester succeeded José Fernández, whose notarial records cover the period between August 18, 1768, and March 8, 1770.

O'Reilly, during the period of his administration, decided to dispose of public lands within the city which were no longer in use. The site of the old governor's residence, two squares of ground bounded by Levee (Decatur), Bienville, Royal, and Iberville, he gave to Hery, contractor of the first Cabildo building, in part payment of his contract. He gave the lots formerly occupied by the barracks, on either side of the Plaza de Armas, and other vacant lots to the *cabildo*, or sold them to individuals in its name on a perpetual ground-rent basis. Most of the purchasers were members of the *cabildo*, some of whom quickly sold them while others built houses. One of the first such sales was made of a 70 1/2-foot lot on the St. Ann Street side of the plaza to Francisco Simars de Bellile, sold for the *cabildo* on January 23, 1771,[7] later acquired by Almonester. Almonester, however, was not among the original purchasers, but as his fortunes improved he began to buy up this valuable real estate until eventually he had obtained all the land on the two sides of the square, property now occupied by the Pontalba buildings, built in 1849-50 by his daughter Micaëla, Baroness de Pontalba. Almonester's purchases of the Plaza properties extended over a period from 1774 to 1782[8] or later, and by the latter year were probably all occupied by new houses. On August 31, 1778, he leased part of his large house at the corner of Levee and St. Peter to Pedro Buygas, an area composed of "a salon, a hall, and a room beneath the staircase that serves as a winecellar."[9] Rents from his extensive real estate holdings eventually made him one of the wealthiest men in the colony. The houses he built on his own properties introduced him to the problems of construction in Louisiana, although no records have been found of building contracts or other data concerning these, his first buildings. This, of course, may indicate that he was himself the contractor for them.

THE LEPERS' HOSPITAL

The first of the major philanthropic building projects undertaken by Almonester was the Lepers' Hospital. Leprosy seems to have first appeared in the colony soon after the arrival of the first Acadian exiles in 1765.[10] One of the accusations brought against Spain's first Louisiana governor, Antonio de Ulloa, in 1768 was of "removing leprous children from the town to the inhospitable settlement at the mouth of the river."[11] On July 14, 1780, a report was made to the *cabildo* that an African in the house of a Madame Wels, recently arrived from Mobile, seemed, according to Dr. Robert Dow, to be afflicted with leprosy. Orders were given that if this was found to be true, legal steps should be taken to have him isolated.[12] No further mention is made of lepers in the *cabildo* records until nearly five years later.

At its meeting of April 22, 1785, a letter addressed to the *cabildo* two days earlier by Almonester was read, "offering a house to lodge the lepers."[13] In this letter Almonester informed the members that he had constructed a hospital for lepers composed of four separate sections, "large enough to house many white families and other separate quarters for negroes." This structure had been erected at his expense in the rear of his plantation near the city, "a distance of about two gunshots—bounded by the lands of Joseph Cultia on one side and on the other by a canal which he has constructed for the bathing of sick people, which will serve as boundary to said hospital, which he graciously offers to your Lordships so that the lepers may be kept together, of whom there are large numbers, so the public may perpetually enjoy this. Therefore from now on and for all time, I will donate in form according to law and renounce all rights that I have or may have to the said buildings and lands which I have donated within the referred-to boundaries."

The *cabildo* immediately appointed two of its members "to visit said location and in the presence of the Secretary have it measured by the surveyor and have said land and building appraised by experts and take possession of same in the name of this illustrious Council, and file all documents in the archives of the Cabildo." The act of donation of this property to the city is dated April 20, 1785.[14]

Governor Miró, on August 10, 1790, addressed a letter to Antonio Porlier regarding Almonester's charitable works and his expectations of royal honor; he hoped "to obtain this from the piety of the King for having constructed [a chapel for the nuns] and a leper hospital on his own land, which he gave at a proper distance from the city. The latter had such a good effect that, since the death of the five lepers who were caught, no others have been seen in the province."[15]

The site of the Leper's Hospital was indeed a remote and dreaded one that came to be called "la terre des lépereux" or "lepers' land"[16] a place seldom seen or visited by any except the inmates and those who cared for them. The plantation perhaps included the four-arpent plantation on Bayou Road that Almonester purchased from Joseph Chalon in 1781.[17]

The building that Almonester built for the hospital was probably a simple house of brick-between-posts construction, elevated on brick piers or walls, with galleries, in the characteristic Louisiana plantation-house style of the day. It perhaps somewhat resembled the house known as "Madame John's Legacy" built just three years later, in 1788,[18] when an earlier house on the site had been destroyed, along with most of New Orleans, in the great conflagration of that year.

CHARITY HOSPITAL

Perhaps the most ancient institutions in New Orleans are the Ursuline Convent and Charity Hospital; both were to be recipients of the benefactions of Almonester. For both he erected substantial and important buildings.

In 1779 the city was struck by a severe hurricane that virtually destroyed Charity Hospital,[19] and in 1780 two more hurricanes completed its ruin. A kitchen and a storehouse, however, had remained standing after the first hurricane; in these a provisional hospital of six beds was established.[20] On September 14, 1781, a memorandum was presented to the *cabildo* "by the Attorney General in which he relates the miserable condition of the poor, with no mitigation or assistance in their sickness and needs, owing to the misfortunes suffered by the hospital in which they were gathered, cured, and cared for, which was destroyed by consecutive hurricanes."[21] It was then decided to "take the necessary steps toward rebuilding same, for the assistance of the poor unfortunate subjects of His Majesty, which they need on account of their sickness."[22] Nothing was accomplished because of problems relating to the hospital funds, and on February 15, 1782, a report was made to Don Bernardo de Gálvez, the governor, that the destruction of other buildings, the rents from which had supported the hospital, "makes its reconstruction impossible, leaving the miserable sick in a deplorable condition, to die in the streets, or in any corner, deprived of all assistance and help."[23] The *cabildo* also noted "the high and angry . . . spirit of the citizens who observe that no steps have been taken to remedy and help the lamentable condition of those affected."

The hospital administrator Don Manuel Andrés López de Armesto, who had been originally the director of the Spanish school, complained that his many other official duties made it impossible for him to "give the proper attention to alleviate the condition of the poor sick, which, perhaps, with zeal and charity someone else, in time, might procure for them."

In reply to the *cabildo*'s representations, a letter was received on December 13, 1782, that Gálvez, although absent from the colony, wrote on August 18, 1782. In it he stated that he regarded the hospital as a particular concern of the governor's office and the captaincy general, and said therefore that "under this date I am ordering the acting Governor [Don Esteban Miró] . . . to put into operation all necessary steps that he deems useful in order to have it repaired and re-established to its former condition."[24] Then ensued a controversy between the *cabildo* and the governor over the question of jurisdiction, Miró asserting his authority jointly with the church authority despite customs that had prevailed under French colonial rule.

It was thus to Miró and the parish priest that Almonester, late in 1782, made the offer to rebuild the hospital at his own expense. With their permission he took over the site of the old hospital and all the materials salvageable from the wrecked buildings. The *cabildo*, feeling its authority usurped, doubted Almonester's motives, and although not wishing to "dissuade the giver to such pious works . . . [and] without trying to penetrate secret intentions," questioned the way in which "disposition [was] made of all materials of the ruins of the primitive hospital for rebuilding it, obstructing the extension of a street of this city."[25] This latter reference was to the blocking of Toulouse Street by the new hospital building.

Miró replied to these complaints in a lengthy letter addressed to the *cabildo* on March 20, 1783:

> Since the hurricane in August, 1780, which caused suffering in this province and left the hospital building in ruins and the inhabitants of this capital in misery, unable to rebuild the same with alms, being left in a deplorable state until the end of last year, when Don Andrés Almonester presented himself and offered to rebuild at his expense, constructing it much larger and with more solid materials than before. He immediately began its reconstruction with the consent of the Ecclesiastical Judge [Father Cirilo of Barcelona, pastor] as well as mine, being allowed to use the

> materials belonging to said hospital. This is but very little help toward the heavy expenses he has to meet in the undertaking, which is worthy of praise and admiration.
>
> In what condition would the poor of the city have been if some pious citizen had not offered to rebuild the hospital, even adding extra room. I see in this citizen's action nothing else but his wish of doing a pious deed, being a benefactor deserving the most praise. . . . This unforseen gift . . . might not take effect if I would adhere to Your Lordships' pretensions, which in substance means to force this citizen to present himself to Your Lordships for permission to execute his philanthropic gift.[26]

Miró then referred to the *cabildo*'s objection to the location of the new building, practically on the axis of Toulouse Street. The land in question was part of the land dedicated for the city fortifications and therefore under the jurisdiction of the governor. To have left the prolongation of the street vacant would have necessitated "the demolition of the storehouse and kitchen which at present exist,"[27] which would have deprived the deserving poor of any assistance at all. Otherwise it would not have been possible, as proposed by Almonester, "to build the house and chapel larger than they were before."

The *cabildo*'s chief reason for objecting to the new building seems to have been Almonester's claim to the patronship of the hospital, a privilege in which the *cabildo* and the clergy had formerly shared.[28] Apparently only the king could grant such honors and privileges, and this he eventually did, by a royal decree issued on April 23, 1793, stating that Almonester should enjoy this patronship in the king's name and should be entitled to the use of the royal tribune or seat of honor in the hospital chapel. This decree was published in Madrid in 1793 together with a lengthy "Constitution for the new Charity Hospital, constructed at the expense of Don Andrés de Almonester y Roxas, Colonel of the Militia of the city of New Orleans, in the Province of Louisiana, and Perpetual Alderman of the same, approved by His Majesty."

In this printed document is the fullest description of the new hospital, the name of which Almonester changed from St. John to St. Charles, in honor of the Spanish monarch Charles III. Work was begun under Almonester's direction early in 1783 and completed in 1786 at a cost of over 100,000 *pesos*. The new building was entirely of brick construction whereas the old one had been only of wood, probably brick between posts, a common French colonial type of construction.

Charity Hospital, when it was moved to its location at the end of Toulouse Street in 1743, was placed directly facing the old cemetery, which had been established at about the time the city was laid out in the 1720s in the square bounded by Toulouse, St. Peter, Rampart, and Burgundy. When a new cemetery was established in 1788, it was located about a block beyond Rampart Street between Conti and St. Louis, "in the rear of the Charity Hospital about 40 yards from the garden."[29] This is now St. Louis Cemetery No. 1, more than a block away from the site of Charity Hospital. Pope must therefore have referred to the old cemetery, which had existed long before Charity Hospital was founded.

The hospital contained a church 52 feet long, a sacristy of 20 feet, a chapel of 24 feet, four wards for beds, the first of 80 feet, the second of 60, the third of 40, and the fourth of 20, with two rooms, one of 24 feet for the Hospitaler and the other of 20 for the pharmacy. A vestibule at the opposite side from the church served as entrance to the hospital. The chapel was placed under the invocation of the Virgin of Consolation and the wards were dedicated to St. Joseph, St. Matthew, St. Bernard, and St. James. These descriptions were set forth in Almonester's petition to the king dated May 1, 1784.[30]

To support the hospital, Almonester offered to give a 50-arpent dairy farm known as La Metairie, probably located on the bayou of that name beyond Bayou St. John and extending back to Lake Pontchartrain. Milk from the dairy was sold in the city and would also supply the hospital. He also offered a 22-arpent plantation on Bayou St. John with a quantity of lime for sale and quantities of timber. The farm could supply the hospital with vegetables, chickens, and milk. Another plantation just beyond the city gate on Bayou Road, adjacent to the land he gave for the Lepers' Hospital, was also offered by Almonester, with the brickyard that had been established there by the Company of the Indies in 1725 and granted to Charles de Morand in 1731.[31] In addition Almonester proposed to build fifteen houses, each 25 feet wide and 36 feet deep, including a 6-foot gallery, each on a lot 30 by 120 feet. The rent from these houses would be used for the maintenance of the hospital. Until they were constructed Almonester offered to bear these maintenance costs himself, mortgaging his houses facing the Plaza de Armas.

Finally he offered the revenues from the six stores that occupied the ground floor of his own residence at the corner of Levee and St. Peter streets next to Government House. Each of these stores was described in Almonester's petition to the king dated November 20, 1786.[32] The following day a group of leading citizens was appointed with the approval of Governor Miró to carry out the intent of Almonester's offer, including Father Antonio de Sedella, the pastor, and Don Martín Navarro, the intendant.

On November 25, 1786, this board met with the governor and Almonester at Government House.[33] The several proposals that the donor had made for the support of the hospital were discussed and all but the last rejected for various reasons. It was agreed that the rent of the stores on the Plaza would produce about 1,500 *pesos* annually and this was accepted. Almonester also offered to donate several slaves for the use of the hospital, one of whom "could take care of the vegetable gardens that Sr. Almonester has fenced in alongside the hospital for the good of the inmates."[34] He also repaired five houses that had been donated to the hospital through the years. It was specified that the patronship of the hospital, after his death, would be inherited by his nephews, sons of his sisters, since at the time Almonester had no children of his own.

No plans or sketches of the Hospital of St. Charles have been found and few descriptions of it have survived. Its location and form appear on Pilié's map of August 18, 1808,[35] which shows that one of the wings, probably the one containing the chapel, was located almost on the axis of Toulouse Street, terminating the vista from the river and Government House. A map of the city in 1793 contained in the journals of Mathias James O'Conway[36] also indicates the hospital but erroneously shows it outside the fortifications. It does, however, clearly indicate an H-shaped plan with a suggestion of an elevation, gabled ends to each of the two wings, and a pedimented central bay with a small circular attic window above an entrance doorway. The architect of the building is unknown but it may have been Gilberto Guillemard, who was in Louisiana at the time, having participated in Gálvez's campaigns against Manchac and Baton Rouge in 1779. Dr. John Sibley mentioned the hospital briefly in his journal on September 21, 1802: "Visited the hospital; tis a large old building in form of an H. Did not go through it. . . ."[37]

Major Amos Stoddard, in his *Sketches . . . of Louisiana*, mentions that "the Charity Hospital stands on the westerly or back part of the city. Poor Spanish subjects and sometimes strangers (provided they paid half a dollar per day), were admitted into this asylum. Those entirely destitute were admitted gratis. They had medicine, sustenance, and other aid afforded them."[38]

One of the most interesting events to occur in the chapel of Charity Hospital was the solemn funeral services held in commemoration of the death of the Spanish king Charles III, in whose honor the hospital had been named. He died on December 14, 1788, but the news was not received by the New Orleans *cabildo* until April 4, 1789. It was then decided

> to observe it with the greatest solemnity and propriety possible in the small church of the hospital which was not destroyed by the flames of the last disastrous fire, in which a sepulchral monument will be erected in proportion to its small capacity, the bier draped in mourning. . . . At 9 o'clock on the 22 day of [April, 1789] . . . the Illustrious Council forming in a body presided over by Don Esteban Miró . . . Governor . . . preceded by their mace bearers, all dressed in strict mourning . . . proceeded from the Government House . . . to the church of the Charity Hospital . . . in the center of which was placed a majestic sepulchral bier comprised of five steps in proportion to the height of the church, on top of which was placed a sepulchral urn covered with bright red velvet in the form of a royal mantle. The head pillow was made of the same material, both with gold braid, with edges and tassels of the same. Resting on it was a septre and gilt crown adorned with bright and beautiful enamel which resembled precious stones, with a good arrangement of the magnificent insignias of the King and medals of distinguished Royal Orders. All this was adorned by a beautiful canopy, which, forming a colorful crowning, descended from the top in four arched festoons with beautiful ornaments. This embraced the four corners of the monument, all of which was draped in mourning like the main chapel, the contour of the altar, its furnishings and pulpit adorned with sixty Royal Coats of Arms placed in symmetrical harmony, all illuminated by a large number of torches and candles placed in large torch holders and candlesticks, the large number of lights giving splendor to the mournful display.[39]

Almonester must have been highly gratified to see this splendid display of royal pomp and ceremony in his chapel. The cost of the entire affair amounted to 1,216 *pesos*, 5 *reales*, and it is not unlikely that Almonester, then junior judge in the Illustrious *Cabildo*, had had an active part in planning and carrying out the royal obsequies. A few days later the trappings of mourning were temporarily laid aside for the joyous ceremonies of formally proclaiming the new king, Charles IV. The religious rites connected with these ceremonies were not held in the hospital chapel but within the parochial church, which had probably been temporarily established in the hastily repaired *corps de garde* of the royal jail, for the cornerstones for the new church to replace the burned one had only been laid on February 14, 1789, and the building was not to be completed until December, 1794.[40]

THE SPANISH SCHOOL

On July 17, 1771, a letter was addressed from Madrid to Louisiana's Spanish governor, Luis de Unzaga, stating that the king desired "to establish schools and arrange for masters to teach them . . . in order that the Christian doctrine, elementary education and grammar be taught . . . and an opportunity be provided to acquire the knowledge and use of the Spanish language."[41] As a result, in 1772 the Spanish authorities established a public school in New Orleans under the direction of Manuel Andrés López de Armesto with teachers of Spanish grammar, Latin, reading, and writing.[42] This Spanish school was never too well accepted by the French population of the city, and according to Governor Esteban Miró, writing in 1788, "no pupil ever presented himself for the Latin class; a few came to be taught reading and writing only; these never exceeded thirty, and frequently dwindled down to six. For this reason, the three teachers taught nothing beyond the rudiments."[43]

No location or description of the schoolhouse in which these classes were held has been found, but it was probably not too distant from the Plaza de Armas beyond Chartres Street, for it was destroyed in the conflagration of March 21, 1788, which burned the Cabildo, the parish church and Presbytère, and a great number of other structures. Perhaps the site was the same one on Royal Street on which it was re-established after the fire.

Following the conflagration, Almonester "offered as a substitute, free of charge, and as long as it should be wanted, a small edifice containing a room thirteen feet in length by twelve in width, which would suffice for the present, because, since the occurrence of the fire, many families had retired into the country, so that the number of pupils had, by that event, been reduced from twenty-three to twelve."[44] Again, the location of this temporary schoolroom is unknown, but it was possibly in one of Almonester's buildings facing the sides of the Plaza de Armas that had escaped the fire.

The Spanish school was re-established in a new plastered-brick, tile-roofed, one-story building located at what is now 919 Royal Street, below Dumaine. This house was no doubt the one built as a result of Miró's proposal for "the construction of a more respectable schoolhouse, the cost of which he estimates at $6000."[45] It is not known whether or not Almonester had anything to do with the construction of this building, which was typical of the smaller structures being built during the Spanish colonial period in New Orleans. Old photographs[46] show it with gable ends and a fairly steep pitched roof covered with round Spanish tiles, the ridge parallel to the street. Along the left side of the house was apparently a carriage way, entered from Royal Street through a large, arched gateway. There were indications in the roof that this may have been an addition to the house after it had become a private residence. There were four other square-headed openings across the front, one of which was converted into a shop window. Across the facade was a typical plastered-brick cornice, above which a canopy or fixed awning, supported on projecting iron bars, extended over the sidewalk. In the front slope of the roof were two chimneys, a smaller one above the inner wall of the carriage way, probably a later addition, and a larger original one that served fireplaces in the two front rooms of the house. This suggests that the plan was typical of the period: four nearly square rooms, two in the front and two in the rear, each pair with a double fireplace served by a single chimney. Generally, behind the rear two rooms was a recessed porch or gallery with a small anteroom or *cabinet* at each end.

When Luis Peñalver y Cárdenas arrived as first bishop in New Orleans in 1795, the Spanish school was still in operation, and he made note of it in his dispatch of November 1 of that year, reporting that "the Spanish school, which has been established here at the expense of the crown, is kept as it ought to be. . . . Excellent results are obtained from the Convent of the Ursulines in which a good many girls are educated. . . . As to what the boys are taught in the Spanish school, it is soon forgotten . . . they leave the school when still very young, and return to the houses of their parents mostly situated in the country, where they hear neither the name of God nor of King, but daily witness the corrupt morals of their parents."[47]

THE ST. LOUIS CATHEDRAL

Almonester's last three major building projects left the greatest impact on the visual appearance of New Orleans and became his most enduring monuments. These were the St. Louis Cathedral, the Presbytère, and the Cabildo, three impressive public structures facing the Plaza de Armas, the public square, that caused the noted Anglo-American architect Benjamin Henry Latrobe to say in 1819: "New Orleans has at first sight a very imposing appearance beyond any other city in the United States, in which I have yet been."[48]

The great conflagration of March 21, 1788, destroyed the buildings that had stood on these three sites. Immediate rebuilding of each of them was an urgent necessity but no funds were available either from church or state. It was only through the generosity of Almonester that their reconstruction in larger and finer form became possible. The first of these projects to be started was the Parish Church of St. Louis, which before its completion was to become the cathedral of the Diocese of Louisiana when that area was separated from the Diocese of Havana by papal decree on April 25, 1793. The architect selected by Almonester to design this important building was Gilberto Guillemard, a native of Longuy in the kingdom of France,[49] where he was born about the year 1747.

He entered the service of Spain in January, 1770, as a cadet and served for a few years before being sent to Louisiana. He distinguished himself in the campaigns of the Spanish governor Don Bernardo de Gálvez against the British at Manchac, Baton Rouge, Mobile, and Pensacola in 1779-81.[50] He was a nephew of Doña Isabel de la Roche, his mother's sister, wife of the noted Gilbert Antoine de St. Maxent,[51] one of whose daughters was the wife of Governor Unzaga and another the wife of Governor Bernardo de Gálvez, later viceroy of Mexico.[52] Guillemard in 1786 held the rank of captain of infantry and town aide-major at New Orleans, "charged by commission of the government with the functions of Engineer and surveyor in this province."[53] In 1790 he drew plans for a church at Natchez as well as for several other buildings in that area for Governor Miró.[54] He was undoubtedly the most qualified architect in New Orleans at the time, and with his distinguished military career and family connections, it is not surprising that Almonester selected him to design the new parish church and rectory that he offered to rebuild at his own expense.

Almonester's offer was made soon after the fire, for in a letter to Antonio Porlier dated August 10, 1790, Miró reported "that a junta was held on March 22, 1788, as a result of the terrible fire in this city. . . . It was stated [in the report of these proceedings sent April 1, 1788] . . . that Andrés Almonester had promised to construct a new parish church of brick and wood, as large or larger than the one destroyed, and near by, a house suitable for lodging the Reverend Father Vicar, the priest's assistants and the chief sacristan.[55] Apparently nothing was done for almost a year, for a meeting of the *cabildo* on February 13, 1789, the following was recorded:

> Andrés Almonester y Roxas, ordinary Junior Judge of the city and its jurisdiction for His Majesty, made known his desire of beginning construction of the parochial church as he had offered and called upon this Illustrious Council to fix the day for placing the four cornerstones and at the same time to appoint two commissioners to place two of them. The first two will be placed by the Governor [Miró] and the Reverend Father Vicar [Père Antoine de Sedella?]. In consequence it was agreed that the said stones be placed tomorrow the 14th inst.; Don Joseph de Ortega, Senior Judge, and Don Carlos de Reggio were unanimously appointed for this ceremony.[56]

At the time of this formal ceremony the plans of the new church had not even been drawn, for Almonester had evidently made his offer to rebuild the church and rectory contingent upon the king's conferring upon him a title of Castile. When this royal honor was not forthcoming, Almonester's fervor seemed to cool and no work was done on the proposed new church.

Months passed and by the end of the summer the populace began to show signs of impatience and to urge that some action be taken. At the *cabildo*'s meeting on October 2, 1789, the attorney general, Valentin Robert Avart, presented a statement

> relative to the considerable inconveniences the public suffers, having been disappointed by the promises made by Andrés Almonester, actual Junior Judge, after

> the fire and at the public gathering of the most notable people of this city. He made this statement at the said meeting, motivated by the inexplicable suffering to the health of those who are obliged to go to the poor ruined church that serves as a parish church. It is very small and uncomfortable in the wretched rainy weather. The people who attend are compelled to be tightly packed or to suffer outside in bad weather, resulting in negligence and laxity in attending the Divine Services. . . .[57]

If Almonester had indeed changed his mind about rebuilding the church, the *cabildo* agreed that it would then appeal to the king to provide for the building "as he usually does under similar circumstances as Protector of all the Indies." The inhabitants also expressed a desire to contribute if the king could not provide the requisite funds. In consequence, a letter was written to Almonester, to which he replied on November 6, 1789, with a long discussion

> relative to ascertaining the intentions of Andrés Almonester y Roxas regarding the reconstruction of the parish church he had promised. Due to the urgency of the said work, to better conditions for those coming to worship God and for the comfort of the inhabitants . . . to obviate new delays and eliminate all evasive answers, it was unanimously decided to . . . have the annual Commissioners send a simple message to the said Andrés for the sole purpose of asking him to kindly state plainly whether he has decided to reconstruct the said Parish Church or not, so that in view of his final answer, in case of an unexpected refusal, other suitable steps might be taken to achieve this holy objective.[58]

The following day, December 12, 1789, Almonester gave his answer to the *cabildo* through its two representatives, Reggio and De La Barre, who reported at the session of January 15, 1790, that they had been informed by Almonester that "he promises that he will start the work of repairing [rebuilding] the church on the first of the coming month."[59]

In Miró's letter to Porlier of August 10, 1790, previously quoted, the governor recalls that in his letter of June 3, 1789, he had reported that "Almonester laid the first brick of the parish church according to the plan I have submitted." The plan he referred to is unknown, but in a later decree, issued by King Charles IV on May 7, 1798, it is stated that "Don Andrés offered to have it [the parochial church] rebuilt in accordance with the plan drawn in the year 1791 by Sergeant-Major Gilberto Guillemard, who at that time was acting Engineer."[60]

It is possible that the date for the plan, 1791, is not accurate, for on February 22, 1790, Almonester had already signed a contract with the master mason Joseph Duguet "to conduct the works of the parochial church that is being rebuilt by the Señor Don Andrés . . . [Duguet agreeing] that he will put on the said work three hired workmen and one laborer. . . ."[61] None of Guillemard's plans for the church have been found. There is, however, a plan drawn by Carlos Trudeau, dated June 12, 1801, entitled "Geometrical Plan of the Parochial Church of the City of New Orleans."[62] This plan shows a building with massive brick walls additionally strengthened by exterior buttresses. In front, facing the square, are two hexagonal bell towers with three entrance doors between them, the central entrance being embellished by double columns against the wall on each side. Within, the church is divided into a nave and side aisles by rows of columns forming colonnades of five bays each. The sanctuary is beyond this and in the rear is a narrow room, probably for use as a sacristy.

Miró's account of the construction of the church given in his letter to Porlier, dated April 10, 1790, cited above, is perhaps the best source of information on this important project. He mentions that since the 1788 fire many people were not attending mass due to the inconvenience and crowded conditions of the temporary churches. At first, services were held in Almonester's chapel at Charity Hospital, but his was too small and too far from the center of town. Then arrangements were made "to have the Holy Sacrifice celebrated in a gallery of the Government House and at other places in the city." Finally a temporary church was set up in the restored old French *corps de garde*, now part of the Cabildo building, which, said Miró, "has been adorned with great propriety." This served as the parish church until December 8, 1794, when it was again destroyed by fire and the church was moved to Almonester's chapel at the Ursuline Convent.

Miró had apparently encouraged Almonester in his quest for titles and honors, but added in his letter that even though "there was no hope of the success of the petition of Andrés Almonester for a title of Castile, under which condition he had promised to build a new church at his own expense, he requests that he be allotted twelve thousand *pesos* of the property which belonged to this mission. He proposes to construct a parish church and rectory with this assistance and with the timbers promised him by some citizens, also using the bricks from the wall of the old cemetery. . . ."[63]

After laying the first brick, according to Miró, Almonester continued the work: "He had the remaining ruins demolished, the refuse cleared away, the site enclosed, and prepared to begin the actual work. He did so on March 15, this year [1789], pursuing it with such vigor that at the present time the wall has reached a height of six feet above ground all around, with a thickness of five feet and the columns of the nave fifteen in height. If he continues, it may be expected that three years from now, as the work cannot be carried on in the cold season, it will be entirely completed and the divine services may be held in it."

Miró then continued, explaining that Almonester's petition for a title was not a condition for his undertaking the rebuilding of the church and rectory, but he hoped such honors would be forthcoming as a result of his other philanthropic works such as the Lepers' Hospital, Charity Hospital, and the Ursuline chapel. These works, said Miró, were "calculated without exaggeration at the sum of 112,868 *pesos*, 7 1/2 *reales*," besides disbursements for the maintenance of the buildings and the poor hospital patients. Almonester was not unmindful, however, of his title hopes, and Miró continues:

> I have known his fervor to abate at times and I have seen it revive when his attorney informed him that the matter of his title was discussed in the council, and on

> another occasion when the *Contaduría General* made a favorable report. This vacillation resulted in his suspending the work after laying the first brick, removing the ruins of the old church and clearing the ground. Whereupon the *Ayuntamiento* [*cabildo*] wished to reprimand him strongly, but I, having prevented this indiscretion, which would have exasperated him, convinced him in such a manner by assisting in his re-election as *Alcalde* this year, which I know he desired in order to gain merit, that he again took up the work with great vigor. He promised me that he would continue it to completion, despite the flood which caused a break in the river levee on his lands, entailing the loss of his harvest, washing away his fences and destroying a large brick kiln, which cannot be rebuilt for another month when the waters recede. For this reason he was on the point of suspending the work, but on my giving him the bricks of the walls of the old cemetery, as they are to be replaced by stakes, he is using them to continue the works. For this assistance, which saves him less than 200 *pesos*, I beg you Excellency to secure the approval of His Majesty.
>
> I do not know how the Reverend Auxiliary Bishop can imagine that the church and rectory could be constructed for twelve thousand *pesos*, even with the donation of the timbers which he says have been promised to him by some citizens. I know that they will not amount to one thousand *pesos*, as they are very cheap now because the lack of market which was experienced caused a fall of price.
>
> The cost of the church being built by Don Andrés is estimated at 72,350 *pesos* and 7 *reales* at the least, and I shall not be surprised if it costs him much more. . . . If he had contented himself with building the church entirely of wood, instead of brick as he is now doing, he could have constructed both [church and rectory] for less then seventy thousand *pesos*.[64]

In the meantime Almonester had given up his petition for a title of Castile and instead requested the post of colonel for the local militia battalion, which he received on February 10, 1791.[65] In his military service sheet, dated December 31, 1797, when he had reached the age of sixty-eight, it is stated that he was of robust health and "of inestimable usefulness because of his philanthropic spirit, supposed valor, good application—capacity and conduct." He had also attained a higher position in the *cabildo*, for on the resignation of Carlos de Reggio as royal ensign and perpetual councillor, Almonester purchased this rank in the customary manner. On March 18, 1790, Governor Miró issued the royal commission,[66] and Almonester was sworn into the new position in the *cabildo* which he was to retain for the remainder of his life.

As Almonester had hoped and expected, his liberality in rebuilding the church was brought to the attention of the Spanish king, Charles IV, whose decree of May 7, 1798, points out that Almonester had seen to it that "the work of reconstruction was performed with the required solidity, having added to the beauty of the Church's interior various decorations such as sculptures, paintings, a well-made marble floor, windows with glazed sashes, bells and other accessories necessary to the splendor of a church which was to serve as a Cathedral. In this work he spent not only the estimated cost, which was set at 72,350 *pesos*, 7 *reales*, but also an additional 25,635 *pesos*, 2 1/2 *reales*, so that when the said church was left in servicable condition, he had spent a grand total of 98,988 *pesos*, 1 1/2 *reales*. . . ."[67]

When the parish church of New Orleans was elevated to the rank of cathedral upon the creation of the new Diocese of Louisiana in 1793, Almonester had quickly changed his plans and added the embellishments mentioned above by the king, as well as a gallery on each side of the nave with a fine choir balustrade and the high altar. His health was beginning to fail and he feared he might not live to see the completion of the cathedral that was intended to be his most important monument as well as his tomb. On August 20, 1794, Almonester drew up his will before the notary Carlos Ximenes. In it he included references to the new church, and indicated that he had, before his marriage to Louise de la Ronde, set aside a sum of 400,000 *pesos* for his philanthropic works, from which fund the cost of the church was being paid. His will states:

> 8] I declare, that of the fund of four hundred thousand *pesos* which I have said that I had before my second marriage, for the pious works mentioned, one of which is the parish church of St. Louis in this city, some money remains at my disposal, wherefore I order and it is my will that the said church shall be finished with the said remainder and in consideration of its not being sufficient to finish the whole, [let them finish] the iron screen-work belonging to the large sanctuary [*Capilla*], the sacristy and the side chapel, the pulpit in Roman style, the stalls for the lower choir, the high altar in Roman style, and the screen-work toward the galleries.
>
> 9] I declare, that the gallery which I have built in the said church in front of the sanctuary, over the principal door of the latter, I have reserved for myself and my family, and I have solicited and petition should be made to His Majesty to obtain the assignment [approval] of this; and hoping that the King (whom God preserve) may be pleased to grant it, I order, and it is my wish that this privilege and favor which I hope for may descend to my successors.[68]

By the end of the year 1794 the new cathedral was nearing completion. On December 8 it almost met disaster, for on that day the city was struck by a second conflagration. Starting on Royal Street between St. Louis and Toulouse, the fire spread rapidly over many of the structures that had been rebuilt since the fire of 1788. The flames leaped across St. Peter Street and again destroyed the *corps de garde*, which was being used as the parish church, severely damaged the prisons in its rear, and destroyed the small fire-engine house that had been built on the site of the old Cabildo, across Orleans Alley from the new cathedral. At this point, almost as if by a miracle, the wind shifted, and the fire reversed itself and spread in the opposite direction, cutting a swath of destruction as far as the city fortifications, along present Canal Street. The new cathedral was saved and hastily completed in time for the Christmas services that year.[69]

An account of the dedication was recorded at the time by Father Joaquín de Portillo:

> In the year of our Lord 1794, in the twentieth of the Pontificate of our Holy Father, Pope Pius VI, and in the seventh year of the reign of His Catholic Majesty, Don Carlos IV, Don Luis Peñalver y Cárdenas being elected first bishop of the newly erected See of Louisiana; Baron de Carondelet, Brigadier General of the Royal Army,

being governor of this city and province, on the 23rd day of the month of December, the new St. Louis parochial church of this city was blessed.

This parochial church, which became the Cathedral church since the erection of Louisiana into a diocese distinct from that of Havana, owes it existence to the piety and zeal of Don Andrés Almonester y Roxas, a native of the city of Mayrena del Alcor, kingdom of Sevilla, in Spain, a knight of the illustrious Order of Carlos III, colonel of the militia of New Orleans and perpetual Regidor of the Supreme Court.

This knight, so commendable for his eminent piety, is almost without an equal; the three churches of this city in which are offered prayer and sacrifice to our Lord are monuments of his devotion and piety. At his own expense he built the Chapel of the Ursuline Convent, a school for young girls, the Charity Hospital and its chapel, and also donated ground to serve as a site for a lepers' home.

These works alone would suffice to make his name illustrious, and gain for him the esteem and friendship of all his fellow-citizens. Yet, he did more. A fire having destroyed the parochial church on the 21st of March, 1788, the grief of the people made him conceive the vast project, worthy of his great heart, of rebuilding this sanctuary at his own expense. The edifice was begun in March, 1789, and in spite of a thousand obstacles, Almonester succeeded within five years in giving it the perfection, grandeur, solidity and beauty which we now admire.

Finally, the parish being unable, for want of funds, to decorate the interior in a manner worthy of a cathedral, he took upon himself the necessary expense of building a gallery on each side of the nave and providing a beautiful balustrade for the choir, together with a main altar on which the workmen were still engaged when another terrible fire broke out on the 8th of December and destroyed the temporary chapel. The Blessed Sacrament was carried to the chapel of the Ursulines and the ornamentation of the main altar hastily completed to receive our Lord so that the people might with more facility assist at the offices of the Church.

The new edifice was blessed on the day and in the year before mentioned, in the presence of the ecclesiastical and civil authorities of this city. At the opening of the ceremony, our illustrious benefactor presented the keys of the church to the Governor, who then handed them over to me. Immediately afterwards, Don Patricio Walsh, an Irish priest, chaplain of the Royal Hospital, Foreign Vicar, Ecclesiastical Judge of the Province for the Bishop of Havana (the Bishop of Louisiana having not yet taken possession), blessed the church. The Holy Sacrifice of the Mass followed the blessing, and these magnificent ceremonies filled with joy the hearts of all the faithful.

The next day, December 24, the clergy assembled in the monastery of the Ursulines, to which the Blessed Sacrament had been carried after the fire of December 8. The Governor, with all the notable personages of the city, also met therein; a procession was formed and the Blessed Sacrament carried with the greatest solemnity to the new church, in which I sang the first Mass and preached the first sermon.

After the benediction of the Blessed Sacrament, the ceremony was closed by the chanting of the *Te Deum* for the greater glory of God, and this was followed by loud salutes of artillery. It is then but just that the people and the ministers of the church should render perpetual gratitude to their illustrious and noble benefactor, Don Andrés Almonester y Roxas, and it is to prevent his works from falling into oblivion that I mention his name here "Ad perpetuam rei memoriam."

Don Joaquín de Portillo December 30, 1794[70]

Almonester's friend Miró was succeeded as governor of Louisiana by François Louis Hector, Baron de Carondelet, who took the oath of office in the presence of the *cabildo* on December 30, 1791. It was he who by law enjoyed the privileges of vice-patron royal in the cathedral, an honor coveted by Almonester. The donor was, however, awarded a seat of honor by the bishop and the privilege of burial in the cathedral, these honors being conferred by the Spanish king in his above-mentioned decree of May 7, 1798:

> in consideration of the fact that the laws forbid that Andrés Almonester y Roxas be granted the patronage of the Cathedral Church as he petitioned, therefore, I have resolved that said Don Andrés may hold the right to the seat granted him by the Reverend Bishop in the Choir of the said Church, and also that he be assigned a chapel, outside of the main one, to serve as his tomb with an inscribed flat stone placed on the exterior of the chapel proclaiming his generosity, piety, and liberality in the reconstruction of the Cathedral Church as well as in the works of the Hospital, the school of the Ursulines, and others, in which he has spent very large sums, and for all of which he has merited my Royal gratitude, as well as that he be so informed in my Royal name, and also that his deeds shall be borne in mind in the event he may ask for any other particular grace that may not be in conflict with the laws, resting assured that my Royal will, always benevolent toward my loyal subjects, shall be prompted to grant it.[71]

In previous decrees dated August 14, 1794, and May 4, 1795, which Almonester presented to the *cabildo* at its session of November 6, 1795, the king had made most flattering references to Almonester's generosity and deplored local court actions against him and apparent local opposition and animosity toward him. The king also admonished Governor Carondelet to "distinguish, assist and attend in a very special way, the said Almonester in everything he might justly require, without giving him cause to complain, for he has endeared himself to my Royal Person . . . as a subject whose actions have so well distinguished him by donating a large part of his wealth for the construction of the cathedral. . . ."[72] As a reward for Almonester's "inspiring zeal . . . in the construction of the parish church of New Orleans, built and decorated at your expense," the king on March 30, 1795, told Almonester that he had "seen fit . . . to grant you the use and as your property, a special pew erected on the inside of the said church and over the principal entrance. . . ." The special pew was to bring about a controversy in later years when his daughter Micaëla, Baroness Pontalba, directed her agent, N. B. LeBreton, to write the church wardens on April 3, 1832, "to reclaim from you her tribune which is located in the cathedral church, facing the chapel, and to which she has the right of full ownership."[73] By that time, however, under the American democracy, such royal privileges had lost their meaning.

Almonester was evidently not on the same good terms with Carondelet as he had been with Miró and felt that the new governor did not appreciate his charitable works, but saw only his selfish aims of honors and patronage. In a letter to Miró written on April 26, 1792, Joseph Xavier Delfau de Pontalba said:

> . . . we dined at Almonester's, who regrets you from the depths of his heart. He told me frankly that he would never find anyone to rejoice in the good that befalls others as much as you. He is entirely disgusted with being beneficent. Under your reign it was a joy to him, for you knew how to appreciate it, but now he intends to be selfish. He has abandoned the church. He has not laid a brick on it since your departure, and he added that before he takes up the work again they will have time to render an account to the court. He laid it aside to enjoy the patronage of the hospital and of the nuns. The Baron [de Carondelet] told him that the King's approbation was necessary. He [Almonester] pretends that the approval the King gave for the work is sufficient. . . . He supposes that when he produces the inventory of the goods of the hospital, they will ask for remittal of the revenues with which he has endowed it. His intention is to answer that as the King's approval is necessary for the patronage, he also demands it for the endowment.
>
> If force is brought to bear to compel him to turn it over, he will give in under protest and declare that he renounces the continuation of the church. . . . He is inconsolably awaiting the outcome and is being tormented in his old age.[74]

Governor Carondelet himself was one of those who had reported local feelings against Almonester during the course of construction of the cathedral. In a letter to Captain General Las Casas of Cuba, dated August 20, 1792, Carondelet wrote:

> The said Colonel Andrés Almonester, having enriched himself in this colony while exercising the office of notary public, undertook the erection of several public works, which to his efforts were highly useful, such as the Charity Hospital, which was destroyed by the last hurricane that struck this city, and which he reconstructed. He built the chapel of the Ursuline Nuns, and at present the parochial church, which is well advanced.
>
> It seems as if these proofs of patriotism should have won for Andrés Almonester the good will of all the citizens, but it has turned out all to the contrary. The opposition that they have shown him, has arrived to such a degree, that they would sooner stop attending Mass than enter the church he is constructing. I believe that a great part of this hatred is due to the fact that almost the entire city was destroyed four years ago by a very fierce and disastrous fire, and that many unfortunates, finding themselves without shelter, turned to Don Andrés in order to rent some of the houses belonging to him, which had escaped being destroyed by the fire, and because of this he suddenly raised the rent of his clients. He took advantage of the unfortunate public in order to increase his capital. In the meanwhile he vacated the command of the militia battalion serving in this city.
>
> After I had made His Majesty acquainted in regard to the expenses Andrés Almonester had been put to in favor of the public welfare, he (His Majesty) deigned to promote him to the rank of colonel and in command of the militia. This news caused the greatest consternation among the populace, due to the aforementioned reasons. . . .[75]

Almonester lived for several years after the completion of the great church and enjoyed the privileges of his tribune of honor. He also had the distinction of being invested there with the Royal Order of Charles III on September 8, 1796. His neighbor,

Pontalba, commented as follows: "He was enveloped in the great mantle of the Order and his train was carried by three lackeys in red. An immense crowd followed him as he went in state from the cathedral to his dwelling. . . ." Pontalba, referring to Almonester as "the famous Knight of Charles III," added: "That poor man is never satisfied. As soon as he gets one thing he strives for another. Now his mind is full with the title of Brigadier and he can talk of nothing else."[76]

When Don Andrés wrote his will in 1794 he left specific instructions regarding his burial, stating that "my body I commit to the earth . . . and order that on my dying, it be dressed with my military insignia and given burial in the parish church of St. Louis in this city, built at my expense, in such place as may be designated by my executors." When he had finished writing the will, however, he changed this provision in a gesture of humility, stating "that it was his desire that he should be buried in the cemetery or ground consecrated to the burial of the faithful, for on further reflection he has decided it thus, as deeming it fit, and that it not be done in the church as he had resolved."[77] Thus it was that at his death his body was buried in the parish cemetery, from whence it was later removed by order of the king and buried in the cathedral,[78] where it still rests.

Almonester's cathedral, being the central element in the composition facing the public square, never failed to attract the attention of visitors. Francis Baily, an Englishman visiting New Orleans in 1797, said merely that "the church is a plain brick building of the Ionic order and is fitted up within nearly the same style that all Roman Catholic chapels are. It no farther attracts the attention than as being the best edifice in the place."[79]

Although practically nothing recognizable of Almonester's building remains in the present St. Louis Cathedral, the basilica on Jackson Square will always be associated with its benefactor, who lies buried beneath its floor.

THE CABILDO

The *cabildo* was the name applied to the governing body of most Spanish-American cities and to the one instituted by the Spanish governor Alejandro O'Reilly in 1769, after he abolished the rebellious New Orleans Superior Council that had governed the city since its founding.[80] He then had a new building constructed to house the *cabildo*[81] on the site of the front part of the prison that the French had built in 1730 adjacent to the parish church. In 1750-53 they also built a large *corps de garde* or police station, adjacent to the prison, at the corner of Chartres and St. Peter streets.[82] In the great fire of March 21, 1788, O'Reilly's Cabildo building, of brick-between-posts construction, was totally destroyed, as were the roof and other wooden parts of the *corps de garde*. Most of its massive brick walls, however, remained standing. A new roof was soon erected and the building repaired and put to use as a temporary church[83] until a new one could be built on the old site.

Following the fire, the *cabildo* for a time held its sessions in Government House (at Toulouse and Decatur streets). This was, however, contrary to the laws of the Indies, so the *cabildo* sought suitable rooms that might be rented as a meeting place until its building could be rebuilt. Rooms in the upper story of Almonester's own large residence at the corner of St. Peter and Levee (Decatur), overlooking the Plaza de Armas, were finally selected[84] and used until the new Cabildo was finished in 1799. Rents were paid annually to Almonester and, after his death, to his widow.[85]

Nothing was done about rebuilding the Cabildo for several years, as no funds were available in the city treasury and none were forthcoming from the king, as this was considered a city project—a city hall, not a royal property. Meanwhile the temporary church, in the old, repaired *corps de garde*, was destroyed in the second great fire that occurred on December 8, 1794, again leaving only its heavy brick walls standing. Fortunately the new cathedral that Almonester was building adjacent to the old Cabildo site escaped the 1794 conflagration and, a little over two weeks later, was dedicated. The completion of this, his major project, left Almonester free to continue the work on the Presbytère on the lower side of the church. To be certain that the Cabildo would be built in a style compatible with Guillemard's design that he had adopted for the new Presbytère, Almonester decided that he should also build the new Cabildo. If no funds were available he would provide the funds himself as a loan to the city.

Thus it was that at the session held in Almonester's residence on January 16, 1795, when the problems of rebuilding the Cabildo were discussed by its members, "Don Andrés Almonester y Roxas generously promised that he would reconstruct the Cabildo building following the same plan he is using in constructing the Presbytère. At the time the building shall have been completed, it shall be appraised and its value will be paid out of city funds, in installments, without detriment to the City Treasury nor causing delays in making other payments to which this office must attend. The commissioners, grateful for such a generous offer, accepted it, duly thanking Don Andrés Almonester y Roxas and they agreed to let this gentleman proceed to reconstruct it under the terms he has proposed, giving him sufficient authority to carry it out."[86]

Guillemard, who had designed the Presbytère and the cathedral and probably most of Almonester's other buildings as well, prepared plans for the new Cabildo and spent much of his time in supervising its construction. It was soon decided that the new building would occupy not only the site of the old one destroyed in 1788 but also should include the old *corps de garde* that had been so severely damaged by both fires. Governor Carondelet pointed out to the members of the *cabildo* that in accepting Almonester's offer they had failed to inform him that

> the said Cabildo should extend to the corner of the Plaza [to St. Peter Street] including 41 feet front by 60 feet in depth belonging to His Majesty and assigned to quarter the main troops, leaving the lower floor of this building for the same purpose, constructing therein the rooms that might be required for the officer and soldiers of the guard, the upper floor remaining for the use of the Cabildo forever.

> For this purpose, all the ruins and bricks remaining on the grounds would be left for Don Andrés and 2,000 *pesos* besides would be delivered to him from the Royal Treasury. The Intendant with whom His Excellency held a conference about this matter, gave his consent, finding the proposition profitable to the Royal interests. It would otherwise be necessary to construct another building in the same place at His Majesty's expense for the use of the said guard. . . .[87]

The 2,000 *pesos* were given to Almonester to cover the costs of repairing the *corps de garde* for the king's account. The brick walls were restored and the windows and doors replaced. Entirely new construction was required on the site of the old Cabildo, and the two units were then combined by the great arcaded galleries that Guillemard designed for the facades of both the Presbytère and the Cabildo. The spacing of the five casement windows on the St. Peter Street side of the *corps de garde* dictated the spacing of the windows of the council chamber or *sala capitular* above, the great room intended for the meetings of the *cabildo.*

No plans or specifications for the Cabildo have been found, though several of Guillemard's plans for repairs and additions to the prisons in the rear exist in the city archives. Few references were made to it in known contemporary documents during the four-year period of its construction. Work had, however, been started by December 4, 1795, for on that date the *cabildo* "agreed that the hangman could not continue living in the place where he now resides as it is the place where Don Andrés Almonester has started to build the *Casas Capitulares.*"[88]

While waiting for the completion of the new building, the *cabildo* continued to hold its sessions in the rooms it had rented in Almonester's residence. Each year he received the annual rental of 240 *pesos* on December 31 from Juan de Castañedo, the city treasurer, for which Almonester gave a signed receipt. Aside from this rent and the 2,000 *pesos* given him from the royal treasury, Almonester was given no payments during his lifetime for the work and expense he incurred in building the new Cabildo. Actually the intendant's action in advancing the initial 2,000 *pesos* was not officially approved until he received a royal order from the Spanish court dated June 8, 1796, signed by Diego de Gardoqui and addressed to the intendant of Louisiana in acknowledgment of his letter of January 30, nearly six months before.[89]

In his letter to Spain explaining the terms of his agreement with Almonester for building the *corps de garde* as part of the new Cabildo, the intendant, Francisco Rendón, said:

> Most Excellent Sir:
>
> In the conflagration of the 8 of December of the past year 1794, the flames consumed the royal prison of this capital and the principal *corps de garde* contiguous to it, that occupied a lot belonging to His Majesty of 41 feet of front by 60 of depth. The city government ordered the rebuilding of the most necessary cells for the security of the prisoners, and I equipped one at small cost for the guard. Meanwhile, determined to replace the ruins, but having discussed in the Cabildo the rebuilding of

> the *Casa Capitular* that formerly stood next to the same lot on which the *corps de garde* was situated, Colonel of Militia Andrés Almonester offered to take charge of its construction under the same plan as the presbytère that occupied the other side of the church, with the idea of unifying the front of the Plaza, which in truth would beautify it, for they would form two wings to the temple that has just been finished and used for the first time.
>
> The governor, Baron de Carondelet, thought it suitable to the interests of the king that the said Andrés Almonester should take charge of building the principal (*corps de garde*), uniting the lots, aligning the building to the same front as the one on the other side. He in fact made this proposition to him, which the said Almonester accepted (always ready to sacrifice a great part of his magnificent fortune in public works, as he did at his own expense for the Cathedral, Church of the Nuns, Charity Hospital, and the said Casa Curial [Presbytère]), with the sole condition that there be ceded to him, the brick ruins which are standing on the lot, and two thousand *pesos* that he believes must be spent to buy the requisite materials for the walls and partitions of the said *corps de garde*, taking it upon himself to finally deliver it in all its extent without the king having to make any other expenditure.[90]

The intendant concluded his account of his arrangements with Almonester by pointing out that, after careful study, he was convinced that to build an entirely new and separate building for the *corps de garde* would cost the royal treasury from 4,000 to 5,000 *pesos* besides the annual maintenance costs. By taking advantage of Almonester's offer, a larger and better finished building would be obtained by the king and most of the expenses for repairs would be borne by the *cabildo*, as the upper part of the building, including its roof, would be the property of the city.

Thus the Cabildo was built and financed almost entirely by Almonester. Although he was not always well liked by his contemporaries, including no doubt some of his fellow members of the *cabildo*, Almonester's generosity in the donation of public works to the city and his paying for the construction of the new Cabildo as the work progressed could not but be acknowledged and recognized. Thus at its session on July 21, 1797, the *cabildo* commended him for his public-spiritedness. After listing the various buildings he had built at his own expense, they mentioned that only for the Cabildo would he ever expect any repayment. The progress of the work, the generous terms of his agreement, and their gratitude were then explained as follows:

> Perhaps by the early part of the next year the Cabildo building will be completed in brick from top to bottom. No doubt its cost will be over 30,000 *pesos* . . . [for which] the city is only to make partial payments from what is left in the City Treasury after its annual expenses have been covered, to be applied to its appraised value after the said building is completed. This benefit is considered a great favor, for the cash on hand in the city treasury is usually pledged for public outlays, and if there should be a balance left, it is not of a considerable amount. The results therefore will be that several years will elapse before this amount can be paid, the actual benefit at the present time being in favor of this city and none in favor of the benefactor. . . . Without his liberality we could not have a Cabildo building in this city without

> having to implore His Majesty's mercy in order to obtain some means for this purpose. As it seems to the commissioners that the city is anxious to express to the said benefactor how grateful we are, in an honorable and creditable manner for said buildings, which is the only thing his modesty would accept, the commissioners agreed that with city funds, a portrait of the said Don Andrés be made and placed in the chambers of the Cabildo, with the proper inscription concerning his deeds and liberality.[91]

A life-size portrait of Almonester with such an inscription was painted, but dated 1796, a year before the resolution was passed. It is believed to be the work of José de Salazar y Mendoza, a native of Mérida, in Yucatan, Mexico, who is referred to by a contemporary in New Orleans, the Irishman Mathias James O'Conway, as "the celebrated, self-taught, portrait painter."[92] Perhaps Salazar painted a duplicate of the 1796 work, or possibly the *cabildo* purchased an already completed portrait to hang in its council chamber.

At the same meeting of the *cabildo* at which the portrait of Almonester was authorized, Don Andrés presented a document "in which he requests their Lordships to please order that the enclosed certificate be recorded and filed in order that it be returned to him, together with the coat of arms and blazon concerning his illustrious family's name so that he may make use of them and be shown the honors and preeminences he is entitled to as a nobleman and famous knight."

The coat of arms, which was duly recorded, appears in one corner of the Almonester portrait, now owned by the St. Louis Cathedral. In it he appears with a rather pompous air, ready to be shown the honors he so coveted, the insignia of the royal order of Charles III prominently displayed on the lapel of his coat. On a cartouche in another corner of the portrait is the "inscription concerning his deeds and liberality." This inscription is almost exactly the same as the epitaph on his tombstone in the St. Louis Cathedral.

Almonester's health had begun to fail several years before, as indicated by the writing of his will in 1794. It was after this, however, that he undertook the construction of the Cabildo, and he continued to play an active part in the affairs of the city and to attend to his duties as the perpetual commissioner and royal ensign of the *cabildo*, which duties included the inspection of the frequent repairs and improvements to the royal prison behind his new Cabildo building. But he was not destined to live to see the completion of his last and perhaps most important building project. On April 20, 1798, he attended his last meeting of the *cabildo*, which was still holding its sessions in his residence. Five days later, on April 25, 1798, he died. He was buried the following day in the parish cemetery behind his Charity Hospital building in accordance with the desire expressed in his will.[93] Later his body was transferred to his tomb in the cathedral.

Manuel Gayoso de Lemos, who had succeeded Carondelet as governor, suggested that if it was agreeable to Almonester's widow, the work on the Cabildo should be carried on under the direction of its architect Guillemard. An appraisal of the work on the new building was ordered to be made by two experts representing the *cabildo* and two representing the Widow Almonester in order to determine the amount due his estate for the project. Hilaire Boutté and Godefroy Dujarreau, prominent architect-builders, were appointed by the *cabildo*. Not until October did Madame Almonester appoint Nicolás de Finiels and Bartolomé Lafon to represent her in the appraisal, which was to be made in the presence of Guillemard.[94]

Meanwhile, on December 3, 1798, Madame Almonester had asked to be relieved of the obligation of completing her husband's project, stating to the governor "that my present condition, by virtue of various occupations, does not permit me to continue to supervise the completion of the Cabildo, and as there are a few small items to be finished, as the ceiling and staircase, requests your Lordships to please accept my withdrawal from continuing it, leaving the said building in its present unfinished condition. . . ."[95]

This withdrawal was agreed to by the *cabildo*, the building was finished entirely under Guillemard's direction, and the debt due Almonester's estate was paid off within a few years. The building was substantially completed and the first session held in the new *sala capitular* on May 10, 1799. On December 30, 1799, Louise de la Ronde, Widow Almonester, gave a receipt to the city treasurer for four months' rent "of rooms of my property that served as a council chamber, at the rate of twenty *pesos* per month, from the first of January until the end of April, when the *cabildo* moved to one of the rooms of the new *Casa Capitular*. . . ."[96]

The appraisers eventually completed their work, with Hilaire Boutté being replaced by Carlos Trudeau. They had spent more than five months and fifty-two sessions at the task, "sometimes from sunrise until midnight,"[97] for which they were offered in compensation by the *cabildo* only "eleven *reales* for each session, a price lower than the wages allowed a day laborer."[98] A fee of 22 *reales* for each session was recommended by Guillemard on June 3, 1803, but as late as August 10, 1804, at least one of the appraisers, Dujarreau, was still attempting to obtain "a payment due for a very long time" from the *cabildo*'s successors, the mayor and aldermen of the American city of New Orleans.[99]

The *cabildo*'s accounts with the Widow Almonester were also finally settled. The appraised value of the building had amounted to 32,348 *pesos*, 6 *reales*. On August 19, 1803, she petitioned the *cabildo* for "the balance due her for the final payment of the *Casas Capitulares*." It was pointed out by the city treasurer that up to that date she had received a total of 27,500 *pesos*, plus Guillemard's fee of 500 *pesos* for directing the work, leaving a balance due her of 4,348 *pesos*, 6 *reales*. This amount was ordered to be paid.[100] Thus when the colony was transferred on November 30, 1803, from Spain to France, the cost of the Cabildo had been fully repaid to Almonester's estate.

Thus it was that the title to the entire Cabildo as well as the prison and *corps de garde* was given to the city of New Orleans, even though parts of it had been built at the king's expense and would normally have passed to the ownership of the French government, to be transferred with the other royal properties to the United States. Almonester's great building continued to serve as the city hall until 1853, when the three municipalities that constituted the city at that time were consolidated. The city hall was then established in the newly completed Second Municipality Hall on Lafayette Square,[101] now known as Gallier Hall in honor of its architect, James Gallier. The Cabildo has recently (1969) been restored by the Louisiana State Museum, the *sala capitular* looking now as it probably did when the historic transfer of Louisiana Territory from France to the United States was signed in it on December 20, 1803. Almonester's portrait will again hang on the wall of this historic room for which it was ordered to be painted in 1797.

CONCLUSION

When Almonester died on April 25, 1798, he was buried in the parish cemetery near Charity Hospital as he had requested in his will. In the 1794 will he had at first specified that he be buried in the new cathedral, but changed this before signing the will to interment in the cemetery. So thus he was buried on April 26, 1798. This change of burial place appears to have been a gesture of humility on Almonester's part, but it may also have had something to do with obtaining the king's approval for such a church burial. In a decree dated at Aranjuez, February 17, 1799, the king said that

> owing to the late arrival of the Royal Decree of May 7 last (1798), whereby Almonester was granted the privilege of selecting a chapel (excepting the main one) in the Cathedral, to serve as his tomb, he (the king) feared that Almonester had been buried some other place. He asked that if this were so, the reverend bishop of that province be ordered to communicate with Almonester's widow and, together with her, to select a chapel to which Almonester's remains might be transferred and that the said bishop, jointly with the Friar Antonio de Sedella, priest of the cathedral of that city, inform me of the entire proceedings through private channels. . . .[102]

The royal decree of May 7, 1798, which of course had not been written before Almonester's death, did not arrive until long after his burial in the cemetery. His widow, however, presented a copy of it to the court on April 24, 1799, in the litigation with Bishop Peñalver over the completing of the Presbytère. In that decree the king had referred to Almonester's many generous gifts to the city, for which he

> has spent large sums of moneys for the benefit of the church and the state in the construction and endowment of the Royal Charity Hospital as well as in the construction of the buildings for school girls, which works, according to the information given by the authorities of that province, represented an expenditure of more than one hundred thousand *pesos* . . . and also bearing in mind the information which, in compliance with the Royal Decree of April 18, 1796, was furnished by the reverend bishop in the following month of August and by the governor on July 31, 1797, upholding and corroborating all the statements set forth by the said Don Andrés, which showed him as a public benefactor, as in the instance of the reconstruction of the city council (*cabildo*) buildings which show actual proofs of his

> generous liberality and honesty of purpose. . . . I have resolved that the said Don Andrés may hold the right to the seat granted him by the reverend bishop in the choir of the said church and also that he be assigned a chapel outside of the main one to serve as his tomb, with an inscribed flat stone placed on the exterior of the chapel proclaiming his generosity, piety, and liberality in the reconstruction of the cathedral church . . . for all of which he has merited my Royal Gratitude.[103]

Thus it was by royal decree of the king of Spain, Charles IV, that Almonester's remains were removed from the cemetery and ceremoniously buried in the cathedral. This event was recorded in the church archives as follows:

> Translation and interment of the bones of the Señor Don Andrés Almonester y Roxas, which have been buried at the foot of the marble step of the altar of the Most Holy Virgin of the Rosary of this Holy Cathedral Church.
>
> By order of His Catholic Majesty, the Señor Don Carlos IV (whom God guard) and at the solicitation of the most Illustrious Señor Diocesan, Don Luis Peñalver y Cárdenas, worthy first Bishop of this Province of Louisiana and the Floridas, was disinterred from the common cemetery of the faithful, the body of the notable benefactor of this Holy Cathedral Church of New Orleans, Andrés Almonester y Roxas, founder of the three churches which there are in the said city, which works of his piety are not only useful to religion, but likewise to humanity. A native of Mairena del Alcor, Province of Andalusia in Spain, Archbishopric of Seville: died the twenty-fifth of April of the year just passed of ninety-eight, and to-day eleventh of November of ninety-nine, with the assistance of the mentioned Illustrious Prelate and all his clergy, was given honorable sepulture, with all possible funeral pomp, to the memorable bones of the aforesaid deceased; and in evidence of which, I sign
>
> Fr. Antonio de Sedella
> curate of the sacristy[104]

It is interesting to note that Almonester was buried in front of the altar of the Virgin, which has always been the one to the left when facing the main altar. On April 9, 1802, the body of his four-year-old daughter Andrea Antonia was buried in front of the same altar, "at the side of the bones of her father."[105] The bodies of father and daughter have not remained undisturbed, for on May 16, 1849, during the rebuilding of the cathedral, they, with the remains of other notables, were removed from the crypts beneath the church and returned to the cemetery, where they remained until the new cathedral had been completed.[106] It is possible that at that time Almonester's tomb was placed on the other side of the sanctuary rather than in its former location.

In spite of the many public honors that were paid to Almonester in life and in death, he evidently left behind a number of bitter enemies who did much to tarnish his name and reputation. Perhaps they were persons whom he had bested in business transactions, or who were envious of his wealth and honors. Perhaps they were only annoyed at his pompous and probably sometimes arrogant attitude. Such ideas are reflected in some of the letters of Pontalba and in Carondelet's remarks regarding Almonester's construction of the parish church and the opposition of the citizens toward him for having raised the rents of his buildings after the fire of 1788.

In any event, quite a few visitors to New Orleans eagerly picked up, repeated, and no doubt elaborated on the derogatory remarks they had heard about the city's great benefactor, in written and published works. Perhaps the worst of these was that published by John Pope at Richmond in 1792, six years before Almonester's death. Pope apparently understood little of the French-Spanish Catholic town he had visited or of its Latin love of ceremony, processions, and pageantry. He made the following remarks concerning Almonester, undoubtedly based on tales he had picked up from local gossips:

Don Andrea, a Catalan, arrived in New Orleans about Twenty Years ago:

> Propt on a Staff, deform'd with Age and Care,
> And hung with Rags that flutter'd in the Air.

> For ten Years past he hath been the richest Subject in Louisiana or either of the Floridas. About three Years since, he got disgusted with his Lady, against whom he prayed and obtained a Divorce *a Vinculo Matrimonii*, and a Dispensation from the Archbishop of Toledo, Primate of Spain and great Chancellor of Castile, for an incestuous Marriage with her younger Sister. To procure an Indulgence of this Kind, required a considerable Largess from the Coffers of the old Mammomist. He is now erecting to the glory of god, and in Atonement of his Rascalities a superb Church and Hospital. No Doubt when these shall be completed, but that he will be reminded by the Priests, who will know how to excite the Passions of Hope and Fear; that some other expiatory Acts remain, and which he is indispensable bound to perform, under no less Penalty than of having his Soul everlastingly damned in the liquid Flames of Hell-fire. To soothe his Vanity, his Name and Pious Deeds, will be ensculptured over the Front Doors and other Parts of the Buildings.

> Who builds a Church to God, and not to Fame,
> Will never mark the Marble with his Name.
>
> POPE.[107]

The story of the divorce seems to be completely without foundation. Almonester's first wife had died before he left Spain[108] and he had remained a widower until his marriage to the twenty-nine-year-old Louise de la Ronde in 1787.[109] Four years before this second marriage, he had purchased a fine house and presented it to his intended bride "that she might have an establishment."[110] The act of donation is dated May 3, 1783.[111]

An anonymous "Memoir of Spanish Louisiana 1796-1802," attributed to James Pitot, who became the first elected mayor of New Orleans after the Louisiana Purchase, does not mention Almonester by name but declares that New Orleans "still owes to the French the greatest part of the Royal or public buildings . . . and if it has a church, a town hall, a charity hospital, it owes these honorable establishments to the superstition of an enriched Spaniard who assured himself by this means of blessings and of honors. . . ."[112]

The American major Amos Stoddard, in his memoirs published in 1812, had evidently also heard unflattering remarks concerning Almonester and attributes his generosity in public and religious works to motives other than simple piety and charity: "The church belonging to the convent is small and was the gift of a gentleman who died a few years ago at New Orleans. He was in early life a notary and, by various speculations amassed an immense property and failed at last to leave an unspotted name behind him. He likewise built the cathedral church and charity hospital and endeavored by acts of beneficence near the end of his days, to atone for the errors of his youth."[113]

Almonester's true motives and feelings can never be known, but his good works as evidenced in his buildings speak for him. Although only the Cabildo and the Presbytère remain substantially as he conceived them, his buildings around the Plaza de Armas and those added by his daughter, the Baroness de Pontalba, established the center of the Vieux Carré of New Orleans as one of the most notable civic centers in America. His contributions to the St. Louis Cathedral, the Ursuline Convent, and the Charity Hospital will always be remembered and cause his name to be held in respect and gratitude by these ancient New Orleans institutions.

Notes for "Almonester: Philanthropist and Builder in New Orleans"

[1]Henry P. Dart, ed., "Almonester's Will," *Louisiana Historical Quarterly,* 6 (1923): 21, (hereinafter *LHQ*).

[2]Charles Gayarré, *History of Louisiana: The French Domination* (New York, 1854), 111.

[3]Cabildo Minutes (translations), 1:22, March 16, 1770, New Orleans Public Library.

[4]Louisiana Miscellaneous Documents, 1599, Manuscript Division, Library of Congress; Dart, ed., "Almonester's Will," 521.

[5]Cabildo Minutes, 1:22, March, 16, 1770.

[6]Ibid., 185, May 13, 1774.

[7]Records of J.B. Garic, January 23, 1771, New Orleans Notarial Archives (hereafter NONA).

[8]Ibid., 5:1; 6:1; 8:119.

[9]Ibid., 10:400; Charles Gayarré, *History of Louisiana: The Spanish Domination* (New York, 1854), 35.

[10]C[13]A, 6:21, Archives Nationales, Paris (hereafter cited AN); Minter Wood, "Life in New Orleans in the Spanish Period," *LHQ,* 22 (1939): 679.

[11]George W. Cable, *Social Statistics of Cities: Southern States, New Orleans, Louisiana* (Washington, 1881), 224.

[12]Cabildo Minutes, 2:33, July 15, 1780.

[13]Ibid., 3:49, April 22, 1785.

[14]Spanish Documents, bk. 4083, City Council, no. 101, fol. 196, New Orleans Public Library.

[15]Lawrence Kinnaird, ed., *Spain in the Mississippi Valley, 1765-1794,* 3 vols. (Washington, 1946), 2:373.

[16]Gayarré, *History of Louisiana, Spanish Domination*, 167.

[17]Acts of L. Mazange, May 7, 1781, NONA.

[18]Acts of Pedro Pedesclaux, 2:427, April 1, 1788, NONA.

[19]Roger Baudier, *The Catholic Church in Louisiana* (New Orleans, 1939), 199.

[20]John Duffy, ed., *The Rudolph Matas History of Medicine in Louisiana*, 2 vols. (Baton Rouge, 1958), 1:250.

[21]Cabildo Minutes, 2:75, September 14, 1781.

[22]Ibid., 76.

[23]Ibid., 28, February 15, 1782.

[24]Ibid., 152, December 13, 1782.

[25]Ibid., 156.

[26]Ibid., 173, April 11, 1783.

[27]Ibid., 174.

[28]Stella O'Conner, "The Charity Hospital of Louisiana at New Orleans," *LHQ*, 31 (1948): 21.

[29]Leonard V. Huber and Samuel Wilson, Jr., *The St. Louis Cemeteries of New Orleans* (New Orleans, 1963), 8.

[30]"Constitution and By-laws for the New Charity Hospital, Constructed at the Expense of D. Andrés de Almonester y Roxas" (translation), 3, Cabildo Archives, Louisiana State Museum, New Orleans (hereafter LSM).

[31]C[13]A, 8:82, AN.

[32]"Constitution and By-laws for the New Charity Hospital," 6.

[33]Ibid., 7.

[34]ibid., 8.

[35]MS, map, Pontalba Family Papers, Mont l'Evêque, France; restricted microfilm copy in Tulane University Library, New Orleans.

[36]Laurence F. Flick, *"Mathias James O'Conway," Records of the American Catholic Historical Society of Philadelphia,* 10 (1899): 285.

[37]G. P. Whittington, "Dr. John Sibley of Natchitoches, 1751-1837," *LHQ*, 10 (1927): 479.

[38]Amos Stoddard, *Sketches Historical and Descriptive of Louisiana* (Philadelphia, 1812), 199.

[39]Cabildo Minutes, 3, no. 2, p. 55, April 4, 1789.

[40]Leonard V. Huber and Samuel Wilson, Jr., *The Basilica on Jackson Square* (New Orleans, 1965), 14-15.

[41]Wood, "Life in New Orleans in the Spanish Period," 682.

[42]Henry E. Chambers, *A History of Louisiana*, 3 vols. (Chicago, 1925), 1:314.

[43]Gayarré, *History of Louisiana, Spanish Domination,* 205.

[44]Ibid.

[45]Ibid.

[46]Vieux Carré survey, square 57, Tulane University Library.

[47]Gayarré, *History of Louisiana, Spanish Domination*, 378.

[48]Samuel Wilson, Jr., ed., *Impressions Respecting New Orleans, by Benjamin Henry Boneval Latrobe* (New York, 1951), 18.

[49]Marriage Register 2, act 186, June 1, 1787, St. Louis Cathedral Archives (hereafter SLCA).

[50]"Dispatches of the Spanish Governors of Louisiana—el Baron de Carondelet" (translations), 5:310, Louisiana State Museum, hereafter LSM; Archivo General de Indias, Seville, *Papeles de Cuba*, leg. 1443, fol. 730.

[51]Ibid., 13, bk. 3, 16, November 9, 1784; AGI, leg. 1394, fol. 71.

[52]James Julian Coleman, Jr., *Gilbert Antoine de St. Maxent* (New Orleans, 1968), 53.

[53]Spanish Documents, box 45, doc. 1073-3, no. 14, LSM.

[54]Acts of R. Perdomo, 15:162, March 30, 1790, NONA.

[55]Kinnaird, ed., *Spain in the Mississippi Valley*, 2:372.

[56]Cabildo Minutes, 3, no. 2, 50.

[57]Ibid., 76.

[58]Ibid., 87.

[59]Ibid., 91.

[60]"Proceedings Instituted by Doctor Don Luis Peñalver y Cárdenas, Illustrious Diocesan Bishop, against Doña Luisa Delaronde, Widow Almonester" (translation), doc. 3777, p. 12, LSM.

[61]Acts of Pedro Pedesclaux, 4:134.

[62]Baptismal Register 1 (photostat plans bound in back), SLCA.

[63]Kinnaird, ed., *Spain in the Mississippi Valley*, 2:371.

[64]Ibid., 374.

[65]Jack D. L. Holmes, *Honor and Fidelity: The Louisiana Infantry Regiment and the Louisiana Militia Companies, 1766-1821* (Birmingham, 1965), 163.

[66]Cabildo Minutes, 3, no. 2, 100.

[67]"Proceedings against Widow Almonester," 12.

[68]Louisiana Supreme Court Annals, "The Celebration of the Centenary of the Supreme Court of Louisiana," *LHQ*, 4 (1921): 21.

[69]Huber and Wilson, *The Basilica*, 467, 629.

[70]C.M. Chambon, *In and Around the Old St. Louis Cathedral of New Orleans* (New Orleans, 1908), 39.

[71]"Proceedings against Widow Almonester," 15.

[72]Cabildo Minutes, 4, no. 1, 60-63.

[73]Miscellaneous Cathedral MSS, SLCA.

[74]Pontalba Miscellaneous Correspondence (translations), letter 6, LSM.

[75]"Dispatches of the Spanish Governors," 2:12; AGI, *Papeles de Cuba, leg.* 1441, no. 179.

[76]Grace King, *Creole Families of New Orleans* (New York, 1921), 98.

[77]Dart, ed., "Almonester's Will," 28.

[78]Funeral Records, 1793-1803, no. 314, April 26, 1798; no. 642, November 11, 1799, SLCA.

[79]Francis Baily, *Journal of a Tour in Unsettled Parts of North America in 1796 and 1797* (London, 1856), 299.

[80]Gayarré, *History of Louisiana, Spanish Domination*, 3.

[81]Louisiana Miscellaneous Documents, 1599-1602; Dart ed., "Almonester's Will," *LHQ*, 6 (1923): 521.

[82]Ibid., 1086.

[83]Kinnaird, ed., *Spain in the Mississippi Valley*, 2:372.

[84]Cabildo Minutes, 2:155, October 21, 1791; 161, December 2, 1791.

[85]MS rent receipts in the collection of Samuel Wilson, Jr.

[86]Cabildo Minutes, 2:191.

[87]Ibid., 4, no. 1, 58, November 6, 1795.

[88]Ibid., 72.

[89]Ibid., no. 3, 188, December 7, 1798.

[90]Miscellaneous Spanish Documents, fol. 369, New Orleans Public Library.

[91]Cabildo Minutes, 4, no. 3, 3, July 21, 1797.

[92]O'Conway Journals, American Catholic Historical Society of Philadelphia Archives, St. Charles Borromeo Seminary, Overbrook, Pa.

[93]Funeral Records, no. 314, April 26, 1798.

[94]Cabildo Minutes, 4, no. 4, 99, October 8, 1799.

[95]Ibid., no. 3, 182, December 3, 1799.

[96]MS in the collection of Samuel Wilson, Jr.

[97]American Documents, 1804-1814 (4077), no. 482, November 20, 1802, LSM.

[98]Ibid., February 28, 1803.

[99]Ibid., August 10, 1804.

[100]Cabildo Minutes, 5, no. 1, 93, August 19, 1803.

[101]Leonard V. Huber and Samuel Wilson, Jr., *The Cabildo on Jackson Square* (New Orleans, 1970).

[102]"Proceedings against Widow Almonester," 42.

[103]Ibid., 12-15.

[104]Funeral Records, 1793-1803, no. 642.

[105]Ibid., no. 910.

[106]Huber and Wilson, *The Basilica*, 36.

[107]John Pope, *A Tour through the Southern and Western Territories of the United States of North-America; the Spanish Dominions on the River Mississippi, and the Floridas. . .* (Richmond, 1792), 39.

[108]Stanley Clisby Arthur and George Campbell Huchet de Kernion, *Old Families of New Orleans* (New Orleans, 1931), 27.

[109]Marriage Register 2, act 179, March 20, 1787.

[110]Dart, ed., "Almonester's Will," 24.

[111]Acts of L. Mazange, 7:412.

[112]From a copy of an unpublished manuscript furnished the author by Réné J. Le Gardeur, Jr., and Henry C. Pitot. See John Francis McDermott, ed., *Frenchmen and French Ways in the Mississippi Valley* (Urbana, IL, 1969), 73.

[113]Stoddard, *Sketches*, 155.

SPANISH REGULATION OF TAVERNS AND THE LIQUOR TRADE IN THE MISSISSIPPI VALLEY*

Jack D. L. Holmes

There is a small tavern in Seville, Spain, where the following sign appears:

> IS THERE SOMETHING BETTER THAN WINE?
>
> The act of drinking is an art that only races of ancient lineage possess. When one makes use of wine moderately, as with all precious things, it is health and medicine, it increases muscular power, it exalts the sexual drive, it stimulates the nervous and psychical system, it renders eloquence easy, it leads to benevolence, to good fellowship, to forgiveness, and to heroism.
>
> Wine exalts fantasy, makes the memory lucid, increases happiness, alleviates pain, destroys melancholy, reconciles dreams, comforts old age, aids convalescence, and gives that sense of euphoria by which life runs smoothly, tranquilly, and lightly.[1]

Given the Spanish propensity for imbibing wine, it is not surprising that certain patterns of drinking and control were brought to the Mississippi Valley during the Spanish domination (1766-1803). Regulation of the consumption of alcoholic beverages apparently is as old as man's interest in drinking, for the famous Hammurapi Code dating back to about 1670 B. C. provided the death penalty for wine-sellers who adulterated their products or who charged excessive prices. Convicted felons were barred from those ancient taverns.[2] In colonial English America tavern keepers were warned against selling

*Jack D. L. Holmes, "Spanish Regulation of Taverns and the Liquor Trade in the Mississippi Valley," first published in John Francis McDermott, ed., *The Spanish in the Mississippi Valley, 1762-1803*.

to minors, servants, or sailors, while a New York ordinance prohibited shuffleboards and bowling alleys in their taverns.[3]

During the Spanish domination of Louisiana and the Floridas the government sought to control the importation and consumption of liquor in various ways. In the laws, edicts, and decrees governing taverns, the Spanish theory and practice can be noted.

SPANISH LICENSING OF TAVERNS

The authority of the government to license the sale of liquor in the Spanish colonies was recognized in Spanish law, as it was in regulations passed by other colonial powers.[4] The famous *Recopilación de las leyes de los reinos de las Indias* and the Ordinances for the Intendancy of New Spain contain rules for licensing *pulperías*, or, as they were called in Louisiana, cabarets. By royal decree of February 5, 1730, the intendants were granted the power to fix the number of taverns and to collect license fees every six months. The license fees were usually set at between $30 and $40 a year. It was stated that the government opposed monopolies in supplying the people with such "necessities" as wine, bread, oil, and vinegar.[5]

One of the first measures made by Alejandro O'Reilly when he established Spanish power and dominion over Louisiana in 1769 was a decree governing the number of taverns in New Orleans because of the disorders originating therein.[6] On October 8, 1769, he issued a comprehensive set of regulations for tavern keepers, innkeepers, billiard parlor proprietors, and the master lemonade seller.[7] O'Reilly provided for six inns, twelve taverns, six billiard parlors, and one lemonade shop. License fees varied, but tavern keepers were expected to pay 200 *livres* or $40 per year on a quarterly basis, and O'Reilly expected the city would be assured of $840 per year from this source of revenue.[8]

In 1775 Pedro Moris appeared before the New Orleans *Cabildo* asking for the post of lessee for the tavern license. He was required to post a bond of $6,600, pay an annual fee of $840 to the city, draw up a list of all taverns within a distance of three-fourths of a league from New Orleans, report unlicensed taverns to the government, and donate $100 annually to Charity Hospital.[9] Apparently Moris expected to make a profit on his investment, and he persuaded the *cabildo* to increase the number of taverns from thirteen to twenty-four.[10]

The tavern license fee varied from an annual cost of $23 in 1771[11] to $30 in 1786[12] and $40 by 1794.[13] By way of contrast, under the American government in 1816, the tavern license cost $60 plus a $2.50 issuing fee.[14]

The number of taverns varied considerably and a perusal of the records indicates a large turnover in the persons who paid for the privilege of selling liquor in New Orleans. The number varied from thirteen in 1775 to ninety-four in 1789, and the revenues from tavern licenses varied from $360 in 1777 to $1,996.31 in 1789.

Free blacks and mulattoes were allowed to operate taverns in New Orleans and four names appear in the records. Of the 280 persons who held licenses from 1770 to 1796, twenty-five were women, including eight widows. Apparently there was a waiting list, and when Diego de Alva surrendered his tavern license on December 21, 1770, Simon Lorenzo was granted that tavern's number and paid the license fee for the balance of the year.[15]

Although Bourbon Street today is famous throughout the world for the number and variety of its taverns and bars, during the Spanish period only two taverns were listed on that street in 1791, while on the river side of Front Street (now Decatur) there were twenty-six taverns.[16]

Collecting license fees in New Orleans was not always easy. When tavern keepers left with the militia on the Baton Rouge campaign in 1779, they declined to pay their license fees, leaving the city with a deficit of $1,200.[17] City steward Luis Boisdore reported in 1781 that there was considerable trouble in collecting the license fees.[18] Soldiers from the Louisiana Battalion stationed in New Orleans frequently ran their own taverns and, when the licenses came due, switched taverns with each other to avoid paying. Because they came under the *fuero militar*, which exempted them from ordinary civil justice, they were able to avoid being called into court on the matter.[19]

O'Reilly had forbidden anyone to operate a tavern without a government license posted on the tavern door beside a sign giving the proprietors' names. Topers could be served liquor in the taverns, but the only food they could eat with the beverages was restricted to bread, butter, cheese, oysters, salad, sausages, and radishes. Taverns could serve wine, brandy, and rum, but no beer, cider, bottled liqueurs, or syrups. On the other hand, thirsty boarders at the New Orleans inns could buy wine and liquor only with their meals or if consumed off the premises. Billiard parlors could serve beer and cider but not wine, brandy, or rum.[20]

Anyone failing to abide by the rules established by O'Reilly and subsequent governors faced the loss of his license and the closing of his tavern. Juan Puche, who ran a tavern on Front Street as early as 1787, continually violated the rules, and the *cabildo* suspended his license at the end of 1792, replacing him with another tavern keeper.[21]

Thus the Spanish government licensed taverns for two reasons: to raise revenue and to curtail disturbances which might occur from the proliferation of unauthorized and unsupervised taverns. Those tavern keepers who violated any of the regulations established were often fined, and these fines put to good use. Antonio de Ulloa, Louisiana's first Spanish governor, forbade anyone to carry liquor up the Mississippi River for the purpose of selling, trading, or giving it away subject to a fine of $25 per quarter-cask, one half being given to the commandant of the post who had captured the guilty party, and one half devoted to orphans and hospitals of the settlement.[22] Esteban Miró, governor general of Louisiana, provided that $20 fines levied on tavern keepers guilty of a variety of violations would go to a fund for chamber and justice expenses.[23] Informers in Upper Louisiana who reported persons selling forbidden liquor were granted one-third of the $100 fine, while the balance was placed "at the discretion of the government."[24]

A number of uses for tavern licensing taxes appear in the records. O'Reilly intended for the New Orleans fees to be placed in the police fund of the city.[25] In 1795 the intendant of Louisiana, Francisco Rendón, claimed that he had the power to license additional taverns himself and consign the fees for the treasury department.[26] While license fees from six taverns during the French period were used to aid the city's poor,[27] in 1797 the *cabildo* decreed that tavern taxes were to be used to support the San Carlos Charity Hospital.[28] Justice Francisco Pascalis de la Barre wanted to create six new taverns in 1794, the proceeds from which would pay two or three additional constables for the city.[29]

In 1792 Governor General Carondelet decreed that the *cabareteros* of Louisiana and West Florida should pay a tax of 50 cents a month to be used for repairing the piers and wharves of the provinces.[30] In New Madrid, the annual license fee was used for public works.[31] In 1794 a man named Miguel bid $52 for a tavern license for the purpose of building a jail,[32] and the following year the fees collected from Jean Baptiste Olive, Edward Robertson, and Charles Guilbault went to the same fund.[33] Those operating taverns and gaming tables at Opelousas paid a fee which went for the building of a jail also.[34] Miró authorized two taverns in the Pointe Coupee settlements, the revenues from which were devoted to such public works as a jail and repair of the government buildings.[35] At Valenzuela Andrés de Vega bid $100 for the privilege of running the post's only tavern, and this money was set aside for the parish church there.[36] The $700 collected at the post of San Carlos of Missouri in Upper Louisiana was supposed to go for the support of the parish church there, but Father Diego Maxwell reported to Governor General Manuel Gayoso de Lemos that Zenon Trudeau, the lieutenant governor at St. Louis, had decided to give the money to the poor.[37] At Pensacola the thirteen tavern keepers who each paid $30 a year for licenses saw the money go to build an embarcadero with a wharf.[38] At Natchitoches half of the proceeds from the "trucks" gaming tables supported the militia drummer,[39] while two wine-sellers paid $80 a year to subsidize the salaries of two constables.[40]

The Spanish government also attempted to use its licensing power in a regulatory manner to prevent abuses generally associated with taverns in Louisiana. Brandy-sellers at Natchitoches paid 400 *livres* each year to keep the wine shops there closed.[41] In Upper Louisiana unlicensed tavern keepers who sold liquor were fined $2 and imprisoned for three days for the first offense; $50 and fifteen days for the second; and expulsion under guard to New Orleans for the third.[42]

In 1804 a settler complained to Governor Vicente Folch y Juan of West Florida that five unauthorized taverns were operating on the Tickfau River and its tributaries above Lake Pontchartrain, to the "great dissatisfaction of many quiet subjects," because they were the meeting places of deserters, thieves, wandering vagabonds, and Indians.[43] Governor Folch issued a regulation reiterating the ban on unlicensed taverns, providing a fine of $25 and confiscating of the liquor for the first offense; a $50 fine and confiscation for the second; and a $100 fine and expulsion from the province for a subsequent violation.[44]

At the post of San Fernando de las Barrancas on the Chickasaw Bluffs (Memphis, Tennessee), tavern keepers who failed to obey the regulations were punished for the first offense with eight days' imprisonment; for the second, one month; and for the third, the loss of the liquor in their taverns, a one month in prison, and permanent expulsion from the post.[45]

One of the primary duties of the tavern keeper was to maintain order within his establishment. Settlers at Opelousas were divided in their opinions regarding the tavern which the commandant, Louis Pellerin, had established within a short distance of the parish church, and Father Valentin appealed to acting French governor Charles Philippe Aubry to close the tavern in 1766. Other settlers insisted that there had been no disorders in the tavern and asked for its re-establishment the following year.[46]

O'Reilly's 1769 regulation required tavern keepers to report all disputes and rows immediately to the nearest police officer and to seek aid from the guard in arresting those guilty of provoking disputes. Criminals, vagabonds, and prostitutes were barred from frequenting the taverns. Swearing and blasphemy were forbidden.[47] At Natchez, the twelve tavern keepers agreed to report to the nearest guard any disturbances within their establishment,[48] but a brawl broke out between Charles King and Edward Carrigan at James Riley's tavern after an episode of name-calling.[49] At San Fernando de las Barrancas, Gayoso decreed that the "tavern" would serve people standing outside, but would not permit anyone to enter in order to "avoid the results of gathering at similar spots."[50] Tavern keepers in Upper Louisiana were also ordered to inform the nearest police officer so as to arrest the guilty culprits and maintain order.[51]

Spanish officials attempted to control taverns by fixing their locations and selecting those to whom the franchise would be given. For the convenience of the patrons, Miró decreed that the two taverns at Pointe Coupee be located at public places serving the settlements which stretched along the river for twenty-six miles. He recommended they be located near the plantations of "honorable settlers," who would report any violations of the rules of good behavior.[52]

In the provinces, tavern licenses were offered at public auction to persons of good character.[53] If a person who had operated a tavern decided to give up his license, someone else could bid for it, but this sometimes caused problems. At Valenzuela Miguel Homs kept the tavern in 1781, but apparently gave up his license because he could not collect debts from those to whom he had extended credit. Andrés de Vega bid $100 for the franchise, which was granted to him by Commandant Anselmo Blanchard, but in the meantime Homs had obtained from Governor General Miró an extension of his franchise, thus providing two taverns for the post, which was restricted to one. Blanchard asked that Miró approve Vega's license and cancel that of Homs.[54]

At San Fernando de las Barrancas, Commandant Elías Beauregard selected the sole tavern keeper from among those of good reputation, but there seems to have been no license fee collected.[55] Because settlers at New Madrid resented the tavern franchises, Carondelet authorized Commandant Tomás Portell to allow all persons to buy and sell at retail and wholesale, but provided that only the licensed taverns might sell liquor at retail. Licenses for the tavern were sold at public auction on an annual basis.[56]

Occasionally tavern licenses were granted to help out a worthy, but poor, settler. Agustín Richard, the ferryboatman at Placaminas below New Orleans, asked Governor General Gayoso for a license to run a cabaret. Gayoso extended provisional permission while he sought the views of the commandant and suggested that some taverns might be closed if they were not obeying the laws set forth and replaced by others whose proprietors would follow instructions.[57]

Illicit pawnbroking occurred frequently at the taverns. At Natchitoches, where Indians and blacks brought stolen horses and clothing to the taverns in exchange for liquor, the situation was acute, and the commandant reported that even the troops at the presidio of Los Adaes on the Texas frontier engaged in the illegal practice.[58] James Ross and John Olaverry operated taverns at Natchez, where stolen goods frequently changed hands for the price of a few drinks.[59]

Because gambling at taverns frequently resulted in disputes, Gayoso forbade such games as dice in the Natchez taverns.[60] Hours of opening and closing were also set to avoid trouble. O'Reilly had decreed that taverns were not to sell liquor on feast days or Sundays, or during High Mass or Vespers, when the Sacrament was blessed. Taverns in New Orleans were to close at 8 p.m.[61] Miró reiterated these restrictions in 1786.[62] At Natchez the hours for closing were 8 p.m. in winter and 9 p.m. in summer, but they could open at sunrise.[63] At San Fernando de las Barrancas the tavern was ordered closed during working hours.[64] Jacob Myers agreed to close his New Madrid tavern on holidays and Sundays and after tattoo in the evenings.[65] When Gayoso became governor general at New Orleans, he ordered taverns and billiard parlors closed at the hour of tattoo but made an exception by permitting wicket openings at the taverns through which liquor might be sold to "sick persons" at "unseasonable hours." As in earlier decrees, taverns were to be closed on Sundays and feast days until after High Mass, and workers were forbidden to enter taverns until after working hours.[66] These restrictions had little effect, however, due to the prevalence of crooked police, who, for a little palm-greasing, would allow the New Orleans taverns to remain open at all hours of the day and night.[67] Dr. Paul Alliot commented in 1803 that New Orleans policeman collected enough graft in this fashion to enable them to retire in a short time.[68]

Other abuses at the taverns included serving adulterated liquors and cheating on the weights and measures. O'Reilly forbade the sale of adulterated liquors or sour or stale wines under any pretext and ordered such beverages confiscated and thrown into the streets.[69] At the post of San Carlos de Barrancas, three leagues from Pensacola, it was the common practice to sell adulterated liquor to the troops in violation of the laws, and there it involved the adjutant Josef Noriega.[70] The City of New Orleans examined annually the weights and measures used, and if tavern keepers were discovered selling unmeasured liquor in bottles, the beverages would be confiscated and thrown into the street.[71]

SPANISH RESTRICTIONS ON SALES

There were laws established which forbade the sale or exchange of liquor for three classes of people in Spanish Louisiana: Blacks, military personnel, and Indians. O'Reilly forbade the sale of liquor to "Mulattoes, Mulattresses, Negroes, and Negresses" who lacked written permission from their masters or mistresses, subject to a fine of $20 and eight days in jail for the first offense.[72] Miró repeated the prohibition in 1786,[73] after he had already forbidden coasters to sell liquor to black slaves along the Mississippi River.[74] The New Orleans *Cabildo* in 1784[75] and Governor General Gayoso in 1798[76] condemned the practice of selling liquor to black slaves, but they were as unsuccessful as the French had been after issuing a similar ban as early as 1717.[77] The practice was forbidden throughout Louisiana at such widely scattered posts as New Madrid[78] and Natchez.[79]

Various restrictions were placed on the sale of liquor to military personnel. A custom in French Louisiana allowed the daily issue of brandy rations to troops and sailors, but Antonio de Ulloa attempted to halt the custom when an expedition left for Upper Louisiana in 1767. He claimed such a practice resulted in "intoxication and disorder" and ordered the *filet*, as it was called, stopped. He did permit those who were "habituated" to alcohol to buy their own, however.[80] Gayoso forbade the sale of liquor to sailors on the Mississippi squadron of galleys and gunboats on the grounds that they were issued a daily *filet* with their meals, thus indicating that Ulloa's prohibition was not followed by subsequent governors, but Gayoso was opposed to a special tavern ashore for the sailors because, leaving their ships and becoming intoxicated, they would fail in their duty.[81] Yet the sailors finally did get their own tavern at San Fernando de las Barrancas the following year.[82]

As can be noted from earlier remarks, a number of soldiers from the New Orleans battalion operated taverns in New Orleans,[83] but such practice was officially discouraged. At San Fernando de las Barrancas, non-working soldiers were entitled to buy a quantity of liquor not to exceed one-third of their monthly salary. Working soldiers could buy a maximum of two flasks of brandy or its equivalent each month, compared to the three flasks of brandy authorized for sale to civilian workers "in consideration that they habitually need more and that they enjoy greater wages than the soldier." If a tavern keeper at the post sold a greater amount to a soldier on credit, the latter was not obliged to pay his debts.[84]

Tavern keepers were warned not to extend credit to soldiers or sailors at New Madrid.[85] At Fort San Felipe de Placaminas below New Orleans, tavern keepers who extended credit to soldiers or accepted items in pawn faced the loss of the items, their money, and a $10 fine.[86]

Of all the restrictions placed on sales of liquor, the most confusing regarded the distribution to Indians. Here Spain followed a difficult policy of continuing the French practice of supplying the natives with liquor, to which they had become accustomed, while at the same time forbidding traders and tavern keepers to sell any alcoholic beverages to the Indians. While Antonio de Ulloa recognized that the one thing most desired by the Indians in Upper Louisiana was brandy, he ordered that none be distributed to them. Commandants who discovered illegal brandy being shipped northward were to confiscate it and pour it into the river.[87]

The French had banned the sale of liquor to Indians in 1717,[88] and the Spaniards followed suit: O'Reilly in 1769,[89] Miró in 1786,[90] Gayoso in 1798.[91] As for the commandants of the Louisiana posts, they, too, issued various decrees against selling liquor to the Indians: Coulon de Villiers at Natchitoches,[92] Francisco Cruzat at St. Louis,[93] Carlos Dehault Delassus at New Madrid,[94] Louis DeBlanc at Natchitoches,[95] Vicente Folch at Baton Rouge,[96] Gayoso de Lemos at Nogales,[97] to mention just a few.

Pedro Piernas, lieutenant governor of Upper Louisiana, had reported in 1769 that "if the Brandy trade were vigorously forbidden them, one could do with them whatever he pleased. But with the abuse of that trade," he added, "the Indians are found to be importunate, insolent, and perhaps murderous, because of the intoxication to which they are inclined. . . ."[98] Captain Philip Pittman, an English officer, observed at about the same time that the "immoderate use of spirituous liquors" had virtually decimated the Tunicas.[99]

The Indians obviously made spectacles of themselves when drunk. Not all of the incidents were as harmless as that described at New Orleans in 1799:

> Outside of the gate we saw a large circular shade for drying and manufacturing bricks, under which were upwards of fifty Indians of both sexes, chiefly intoxicated, singing, drinking, rolling in the dirt, and upon the whole exhibiting a scene very disgustful. We soon came to another company of ten men sitting in the middle of the road, all intoxicated, amongst them was one standing, with a bottle of rum in his hand, whose contents he alternately administered to the rest, first by shaking the bottle and then pouring part of its contents into their mouths.[100]

One wild night affair among Indians at the Avoyelles post resulted in the death of a brave, but the other members of the tribe were so drunk they could not give testimony regarding the incident.[101] At Nogales a drunken Indian killed another, and the following day the dead Indian's kinfolk used a shotgun to atone for the death, thus retaining their "honor."[102] When Ventura Orueta gave brandy and whiskey to a group of Abenaqui Indians near Fort Carlos III in 1787, the result was a near riot between the Abenaqui and Arkansas tribes.[103] A Cherokee and Choctaw had a drunken fight at Natchez resulting in a black eye and a dead horse.[104] Drunken Choctaws, supplied by the pro-Spanish trader Turner Brashears, broke up a conference with American commissioners at Muscle Shoals in 1792.[105] At Mobile the Alibamons raided farms, stole horses, and killed slaves due to the influence of liquor, according to Indian commissioner Juan de la Villebeuvre, but he reluctantly asked for more liquor to keep the natives content.[106]

Villebeuvre wrote that the Choctaws had become so addicted to the rot-gut, raw rum that they would go to the Americans to get it if Spain failed to keep them supplied.[107] He was probably correct, for two months later the Americans delivered 100 gallons of whiskey to the Chickasaws they were trying to win to their side.[108] Although Governor General Miró had discouraged the distribution of liquor to the Indians,[109] he reluctantly agreed to supply tafia to those chiefs and warriors he was courting for defensive alliances against the expansion of the United States.

His successor, the Baron de Carondelet, saw nothing wrong in yielding to the pleas of the Indians for a little tafia for "medicinal purposes."[110] Although traders were forbidden to give liquor to Upper Louisiana Indians,[111] in 1787 Francisco Cruzat reported he had given them 1,400 jugs of tafia and 14 casks of liquor.[112] At San Fernando de las Barrancas, where distribution of liquor to the Indians by the tavern or local soldiers was forbidden,[113] Chickasaws received annual presents from the Spanish government which consisted of 660 pots of tafia valued at 81 cents a pot.[114] Indians pleaded with Gayoso for brandy, wine, and tafia.[115] At Natchez Choctaw Indians received gifts of liquor from the commandant, Carlos de Grand-Pré.[116] Governor Gayoso, who personally preferred not to give them liquor, was forced to provide barrels of tafia for leading Choctaw chiefs in 1792,[117] and when he was governor general of Louisiana, he ordered the shipment of ten barrels of spirits for Upper Louisiana.[118] In the final analysis, it was the Spaniards' policy to provide moderate amounts of liquor at special occasions or designated times for the Indians, but they tried to discourage private traders or tavern keepers from adding to the problem.

Official Spanish policy discouraged intoxication, but, except for rare occasions, laws urged moderation rather than abstinence. Liquor was forbidden altogether along the Upper Missouri by agreement of the stockholders in the Missouri Trading Company.[119] Governor Gayoso was a great believer in banquet diplomacy, and when Colonel John Pope visited the Walnut Hills in 1791 he was regaled with "delicious Nuts and excellent Wines."[120] Gayoso considered that the moderate use of wine and other beverages was conducive to good health along the frontier.[121] Another visitor to Spanish Louisiana, Samuel S. Forman, was treated by Commandant Pierre Foucher to the hospitality of the New Madrid post, which included "an elegant dinner in the Spanish style, and plenty of good wine and liquors," including numerous toasts "to the health of the ladies."[122] A visitor to New Orleans remarked that the settlers were moderate in their use of wine, but that northern visitors preferred their grog, a "poison in this climate."[123] The same visitor commented that wine was served at breakfast, dinner, and supper without limit.[124]

Intoxication seemed to prevail at all levels and among all classes of society. Among the troops stationed in Louisiana and West Florida, the immoderate use of alcohol was notorious. Colonel John Pope wrote that the "inordinate use of Ardent Spirits and bad Wine" contributed to the poor health of the soldiers.[125] "The abominable vice of drunkenness" became so serious at the Nogales post that Gayoso was forced to warn the commandant that if he failed to check it, he would be severely reprimanded and punished.[126] Elías Beauregard, the commandant, was well known for his own affection for the bottle.[127]

It was the custom on the river to give three daily *filets* of "liquor breaks," a custom known to some as "smoking the pipe." Gayoso maintained this policy, which Governor Ulloa had attempted to curtail, but he hoped this would be an example of moderate use of liquor which would not lead to drunkenness.[128] Carondelet found that the commandant of Upper Louisiana's military detachments paid the men in brandy because of the lack of specie, and he ordered Lieutenant Governor Trudeau to stop the practice.[129]

Still, drunken soldiers were the rule rather than the exception. Stephen Minor claimed that he feared to call out the militia because the men were usually drunk.[130] When Captain Josef Portillo from the second battalion of the Louisiana Infantry Regiment complained of suffering from a "fever," Diego de Vega wryly commented that it was probably a "calentura de aguardiente" or rum fever.[131] Zenon Trudeau cited the prevalence of inebriation in Upper Louisiana in 1798,[132] and at the end of the Spanish regime, an officer wrote that so prevalent was drunkenness among the soldiers that they were whipped on bare backs daily for the "vice."[133] Nor were the Spanish soldiers on the frontier the only ones guilty of tippling too much. Andrew Ellicott disgustedly wrote that the American commander of troops at Natchez was subject to "frequent and outrageous fits of intoxication."[134] Recognizing the danger of such behavior, Governor Winthrop Sargent recommended that no liquor be distributed to American troops in Natchez.[135]

If the troops drank too much, so did the settlers. Zenon Trudeau wrote in 1798 about "passive idleness which gave them over to the tasting of spiritous liquors and drunkenness, a taste fatal to all the villages, and which has caused the total ruin in these new settlements of the greater part of the best families, upon which was placed the hope of prosperity of this country."[136] Francisco Bouligny observed a similar problem at Natchez:

> Every time that an inhabitant comes to present his complaint to the commandant he passes the entire day in the town of Natchez where it is the custom, particularly of the common people, to deliver themselves up to drink with the greatest excess. This gives rise to disputes and fights, which occasion great injuries and inspire in the vicious ones a greater desire to come to town in order to become intoxicated than does the importance of the complaint that they have to present.[137]

Governor Gayoso, who once decreed that workers who reported absent because of drunkenness would lose their wages for that day and be charged the value of the rations issued to them,[138] was forced to fire his own overseer for habitual drunkenness.[139]

Professional men also succumbed to the lure of "demon rum." Dr. Alexander Skirving of Baton Rouge ordered such large quantities of rum in 1799 that he began to vomit—he drank himself to death.[140] The American surgeon stationed at Fort Stoddard on the Spanish-American frontier in 1799 fell on a bottle of rum which he carried in his pocket and died as a result.[141]

Not even the clergy were immune to overindulgence. Irish priests in Natchez were particularly known as convivial topers. Father Malone was well liked by everyone but had a weakness for the bottle, particularly on St. Patrick's Day. Father Gregorio White was so drunk on one occasion that he could not baptize an infant who was in danger of dying. He was finally removed because he "was abandoned to the excessive habit of drink."[142] The priest of Galveztown dismissed the sacristan of that parish for a similar reason.[143] Ellicott claimed that a Baptist preacher named "Hannah" had become drunk, had proceeded to preach to the Irish Catholics of Natchez, had been thrashed, and, when arrested, had provoked a two-week revolt against Spanish rule.[144] Actually, the man referred to was Barton Hannon, a shoemaker by trade and a Baptist only by faith. But Ellicott was right in saying he was drunk—so much so that he could not remember at his trial what he had done.[145]

SPANISH REGULATION OF THE LIQUOR TRADE

Two motives determined the regulations passed concerning the liquor trade to Spanish Louisiana: revenue and protection. On February 22, 1770, Alejandro O'Reilly imposed a tax or tariff on imports of rum at $1 a barrel or $2 a pipe.[146] This product usually came from the West Indies and found a ready market in New Orleans. Cuban rum bound for the Crescent City paid an export tax at Havana of $2 a pipe in addition to the tariff imposed by O'Reilly.[147]

By checking the records it is possible to note the quantity of this product which was imported at New Orleans. Between 1778 and 1798 the annual shipment varied and the revenues ranged from $369 to $3,082.86. O'Reilly had expected an assured annual income from this source of $500.[148]

In the Spanish period authorities allowed a deduction of 10 percent for waste,[149] a policy carried on by the American government, which charged the same tariff rate.[150] Shippers noted that a cargo of tafia from Santo Domingo on arrival at New Orleans had shrunk considerably. A 1771 shipment, for example, started out with 130 *bariques* consisting of 65 pipes or 7,800 gallons of tafia, but on arrival at New Orleans, what with leakage and consumption during the voyage, only 120 arrived at the city and, after paying duties, only 100 were put up for sale.[151] It was natural to find that importers sought to avoid paying the duties.

Felix de Materre imported fifty-six barrels of tafia in 1785 but failed to pay the duties of $7, and the treasurer of New Orleans demanded that he be forced to make restitution.[152] Most shippers had the privilege of making their own declarations regarding the cargoes, and the *cabildo* sought to prevent fraud by appointing one of the city coopers to act as inspector for unloading, inspection, and taxing of the incoming tafia.[153] Still, abuses continued, and in 1795, of thc 809 pipes entering New Orleans, only 603 were taxed, the balance having been declared "leakage."[154]

The following year the *cabildo* considered the claims for exemption from paying duties by such shippers bringing Jamaica-refined rum into the city. Simon Tevenot, who brought a cargo from Charleston to New Orleans, insisted he need pay only the tariff on his Havana rum, but that rum from other ports was exempt. Samuel Moore claimed his fourteen barrels of Jamaica rum brought aboard the *Alfredo* were also exempt. The *cabildo* answered these claims by decreeing that all rum, whether refined or not, coming to New Orleans from any port in the Americas, was subject to the usual $2-a-pipe duty.[155]

The intendant, Martín Navarro, had suggested that all liquor imports would be taxed at the rate of 8 percent of the selling price.[156] Taxes were levied on shipments of French Bordeaux and brandy, which, after the commercial decree of January 22, 1782, were allowed to enter Louisiana.[157] On August 24, 1796, an extensive tariff list for Louisiana was issued by the intendant, Juan Ventura Morales.[158] In 1798, however, the *cabildo* asked the Crown to determine whether duties would be collected on quantity alone or whether the quality and selling price should be taken into consideration in fixing the internal revenue taxes.[159]

Americans migrating as settlers to Louisiana were forbidden to bring brandy with them,[160] but apparently this prohibition was not strictly adhere to. In 1792 there arrived at Natchez 728 *potes* of brandy in several barrels valued at $595.[161] Peach brandy was popular, and Robert R. Livingston claimed that Louisianians would prefer that to the best French brandy.[162]

Smuggling was a constant problem, and rum, wine, and brandy were among the products most frequently involved. A royal decree of October 20, 1792, provided that, when no actual culprit was involved in liquor confiscated in this illegal smuggling, the intendant could order the commandant to make an inventory of the goods, place a tax or tariff fee thereon, and then sell the goods at public auction. In 1797 seven *toneles* or *bocoes* of rum were seized at Mobile from the schooner *Havanera* because they were not included in the manifest of the cargo. After being valued, they were said to be worth $1.25 a gallon, and on April 22, 1797, an auction was held at Mobile during which the 743 gallons of rum were sold at a price of $918.50. The government realized a commission of one-sixth of the sale price on this English rum.[163]

Governor General Miró, who was charged with smuggling in his *residencia*, admitted that occasionally ships carrying Louisiana lumber to Havana returned with two or three hidden barrels of Bordeaux wine, but that the total amount of all smuggled goods never exceeded $6,000 a year.[164] Throughout the Spanish period the government officials sought, usually without success, to eliminate smuggling, but the Gulf Coast was too extensive to check the abuse completely.

After rum or tafia, the most important import was wine. At first the Louisiana settlers refused to drink the Spanish *riojas* which were sent to replace French Bordeaux, Burgundies, and clarets. Indeed, one of the alleged causes for the revolt of 1768 was said to be the "inferior" Spanish wines.[165] The San Sebastian firm of Larralde sent a ship in 1777 with ninety-eight casks of *rioja*, but it did not find a market in New Orleans, "for when the colonists tasted it, they manifested as much repugnance for it as if they had taken an emetic." The merchant declined to continue his efforts to market the Spanish wines in Louisiana as a result.[166] Intendant Martín Navarro agreed that the Spanish wine did not travel well and that the New Orleans tipplers would not have taken it "as a gift."[167]

The royal decree of March 23, 1768, had forbidden the importation of foreign wines into Louisiana,[168] however, and within a few years ships were bearing shipments from Cataluña and other Spanish regions to Louisiana. Apparently the forty-four cargoes of wines brought between 1773 and 1775 found some sort of market in New Orleans.[169]

Another royal decree of January 22, 1782, allowed French wines to enter Louisiana subject to duty, and the *Joven Josef* brought Bordeaux and brandy to New Orleans in 1787.[170] Spain's minister of the exchequer, Diego de Gardoqui, urged that Spanish merchants send such fine-quality *riojas* as those of Manuel Quintano to Louisiana because they closely resembled the Bordeaux wines in sweetness, color, and lightness.[171] New York ships occasionally carried wine to New Orleans,[172] and during 1798 the lack of wine in New Orleans has been remedied by a number of shipments,[173] notwithstanding the rise in price on Bordeaux wines during the undeclared naval war of 1798 from $40 to $100 a cask.[174] During 1798 Bordeaux and white wines arrived at Mobile, Pensacola, and St. Marks, in addition to New Orleans.[175]

The price of wine varied, of course, with the quality, supply, demand, and other factors. Gregorio Vergel, a tavern keeper at Baton Rouge, reported white wine sold at $1 a bottle.[176] At the estate sale of Gayoso in 1799, however, three bottles of white wine brought only $1.50.[177] At Natchez in 1792, 112 bottles of wine sold for an average price of 50 cents a bottle.[178] The same price prevailed with the sale of 3,000 bottles of wine at the death of Gilberto de St. Maxent.[179] During 1777 the average price for wine was 10 cents a bottle.[180]

Wine-drinking habits were noted by Dr. Alliot and C. C. Robin. Dr. Alliot commented:

> The great exports of wine which ship furnishers send to Louisiana, make that product very cheap. The captains and merchants sell very little of it in their stores. It is only those who can not pay cash for it who buy it of them. All wines are exposed at public sale. Some days it is sold for only eighteen or twenty piastres per barrel. Since the tavern-keepers only make their purchases at public sale, it happens that when they are all assembled at the market place, they agree among themselves that when any piece is fixed at a certain price by them, however little or much it be, the barrel will never be sold at a higher figure.[181]

Robin wrote:

> . . . Wines of different types are brought in, principally those of Madeira, Málaga and especially those of Bordeaux and the coasts.

> The English drink the Madeira and the Spaniards the Málaga, but the French, being the most numerous, insure that the greatest consumption is of French wines. Besides, the Spaniards have adopted our ways and also taken up drinking them and their greater abundance is more conducive to habitual use. It is hardly possible to ascertain the wholesale price of wine because it is so variable, but the consumption of French wines is so great that their abundance never lowers the price for long. One can always make a reasonable profit out of wine.[182]

Considering these comments, it is curious that Robert R. Livingston could write that French wines would not be pleasant to "the palates or the purses of the inhabitants" of Louisiana.[183]

Brandy was not as popular as other liquor because of its cost. Robin wrote that "if the price of brandy were lower, the people would become accustomed to it and would prefer it," but that tafia and rum were more popular in Louisiana.[184] In 1777 French brandy sold for $4 a cask,[185] but by 1796 the tariff had driven the price much higher.

Whiskey—sometimes known as "Monongahelie," "bald face," "bust head," or "the stranger"—was not as popular in New Orleans as along the vast Mississippi Valley frontier. The price of whiskey in the west varied from 50 cents to $1 a gallon, although in 1794 during General Anthony Wayne's campaign against the northwestern Indians a keg containing ten gallons sold for $80.[186] The tariff on whiskey imported into Louisiana was 31 cents a gallon.[187]

Although Athanase de Mézières, lieutenant governor at Natchitoches, had suggested that Louisiana rye be used to "manufacture whiskey which is used in Flanders and Holland,"[188] it was the United States which produced that product rather than Louisiana. A center of the industry was Knoxville, where Abraham Sittler and John Taylor advertised copper stills with "broad bottom, wide nick, large cap, and free access for the vapour into condensation, with my patent worm of copper, covered or lined with pewter.[189] During 1794 over 500 gallons of whiskey were shipped from these western settlements to Natchez and then reshipped to New Orleans.[190] With the repeal of the whiskey tax in 1797, trade between the Kentucky and Tennessee settlements and New Orleans increased.[191]

On occasion, the importation of whiskey presented problems to Louisiana commanders. Elías Beauregard, commandant of Nogales, kept more than one gallon of the whiskey coming downriver, and when Spain decided to evacuate that post, Gayoso humorously commented, "I dare say that the wisky Beauregard has at the Hills will offer greater difficulties to dislodge than the King's effects. . . ."[192] When Joseph Calvet brought eleven barrels of Kentucky whiskey to Natchez, they were confiscated by Grand-Pré and placed in the royal storehouse pending the decision on their disposition from Governor General Miró. Years later Calvet was still asking that his whiskey be returned to him or that he receive payment for its value.[193]

Gin was not overly popular, but bottles of Holland and Island gin sold at 20 and 30 cents respectively.[194] At Baton Rouge the price of a bottle of gin in 1799 had risen to $1.[195]

Cherry liqueur was sold at auction in 1799;[196] thirty bottles of absinth sold in 1777 for only $17.[197] Anisette and cider were also sold at varying times.

Beer was another popular beverage in Spanish Louisiana. In 1771 Athanase de Mézières had urged that the government support the manufacture of malt liquors and vinegar and the brewing of ale, which was already being produced at Natchitoches. He claimed that valuable foreign exchange would be saved if Louisiana produced its own malt products.[198] In 1782 Marcos Olivares bought thirty-one barrels of beer at New Orleans for $530.[199] Francis Baily noted that the porter was drunk at New Orleans in 1797.[200] At the sale of Gayoso's estate, fifty-five bottles of beer were valued at $20.56.[201]

Spaniards enjoy a wine punch called *sangría*, which features red wine, sugar, fruits, water, and ice. Baily thought the punch mixed with claret and water was weak,[202] and in 1775 it had been outlawed in New Orleans taverns.[203]

Domestic trade accounted for some of the liquor supply in Spanish Louisiana. James Rose carried a barge laden with rum, wine, and liquor from New Orleans to Natchez in July, 1793.[204] But domestic production was also an important source. Two Spaniards named Méndez and Solís experimented with the first tafia produced in Louisiana.[205] The *cabildo* was not sure whether to tax this tafia, which was so important in supplying the Indian trade, and asked the Crown for its opinion in 1798.[206] In 1799 a traveler brought a 1,500-gallon still to Mr. Delongua, who distilled tafia near New Orleans.[207] By the end of the Spanish dominion twelve distilleries turned out huge quantities of tafia near the Crescent City and it was estimated that one Parisian arpent could produce an average of 1,200 pounds of sugar and 50 gallons of tafia. Predictions were that Louisiana could produce, along its river plantations alone, 25,000 hogsheads of sugar and 12,000 puncheons of tafia.[208]

CONCLUSION

Spain, as France before her, attempted to solve the liquor question by licensing taverns and restricting the sale of alcoholic beverages. Violations of the regulations were a commonplace occurrence. Although tariffs were levied on incoming liquor, smuggling and other subterfuges denied Spanish officials the money they should have received. Efforts to prevent overindulgence were generally not successful, and Louisiana under Spanish domination would have applauded another ancient Spanish slogan: "Hermano, bebe, que la vida es breve"—"Brother, drink, for life is short."[209]

Notes for "Spanish Regulation of Taverns and the Liquor Trade in the Mississippi Valley"

[1]Sign in the "Bodega Puenta," Seville, copied by writer in 1962.

[2]Cyrus H. Gordon, *Hammurapi's Code, Quaint or Forward-Looking?* (New York, 1957), 9-10.

[3]Oscar Theodore Barck, Jr., and Hugh Talmage Lefler, *Colonial America* (New York, 1958), 358-59.

[4]For example, see Sidney and Beatrice Webb, *The History of Liquor Licensing in England, Principally from 1700 to 1830* (London, 1903); Leonard S. Blakey, *The Sale of Liquor in the South* (New York, 1912).

[5]Francisco Rendón to Francisco Luis Héctor, Baron de Carondelet, New Orleans, Apr. 15, 1795, AGI, *Papeles de Cuba, leg.* 31, citing the *Recopilación, ley* 12, *título* 8, *libro* 4, and the Ordinances for the Intendancy of New Spain (Dec. 4, 1786), arts. 160, 161.

[6]Jack D. L. Holmes, "O'Reilly's Regulations on Booze, Boarding Houses, and Billiards," *Louisiana History*, 6 (1965): 294. The decree is in the collection of the Louisiana State Museum, New Orleans. See Douglas McMurtrie, *Early Printing in New Orleans, 1764-1810, with a Bibliography of the Issues of the Louisiana Press* (New Orleans, 1929), 91.

[7]Holmes, "O'Reilly's Regulations," 293-300.

[8]Alejandro O'Reilly to Bailio Fr. Don Julián de Arriaga, no. 16, New Orleans, Dec. 10, 1769, in Lawrence Kinnaird, ed., *Spain in the Mississippi Valley, 1765-1794*, 3 vols. (Washington, 1946), 1:134.

[9]New Orleans *Cabildo* Minutes, Oct. 27, Dec. 1, 1775, New Orleans Public Library Archives.

[10]Ibid., Dec. 1, 1775.

[11]List of tavern keepers, New Orleans, Jan. 4, Sept. 1, 1771, AGI, *Papeles de Cuba, leg.* 110.

[12]Report of Francisco Blanche, 1786, New Orleans Municipal Papers, box 1 (1770-1806), Tulane University Archives, New Orleans.

[13]Report of Blache, 1794, ibid.; see app. 3.

[14]License to sell liquor, 1816, Kuntz Collection, Tulane University Archives.

[15]List of tavern keepers, New Orleans, Jan. 4, Sept. 1, 1771, AGI, *Papeles de Cuba, leg.* 110; New Orleans Municipal Records, folder 1 (duties for 1772), Louisiana State University Archives, Baton Rouge.

[16]New Orleans Census, Nov. 6, 1791, New Orleans Public Library Archives.

[17]New Orleans *Cabildo* Minutes, May 26, 1780.

[18]Ibid., Feb. 24, 1781.

[19]Ibid., Oct. 27, 1780.

[20]Holmes, "O'Reilly's Regulations," 294-99.

[21]New Orleans *Cabildo* Minutes, Jan. 25, 1793.

[22]Ulloa's regulations (New Orleans?), Mar. 14, 1767, in Louis Houck, ed., *The Spanish Régime in Missouri*, 2 vols. (Chicago, 1909), 1:15.

[23]Miró's *Bando de buen gobierno*, New Orleans, June 1, 1786, in New Orleans *Cabildo* Minutes.

[24]Art. 12, Proposed Trade Regulations for Spanish Illinois, St. Louis, Oct. 15, 1793, in Kinnaird, ed., *Spain in the Mississippi Valley*, 3:195.

[25]Holmes, "O'Reilly's Regulations," 295-96, 298.

[26]Rendón to Carondelet, New Orleans, Apr. 15, 1795, AGI, *Papeles de Cuba, leg.* 31.

[27]Charles E. A. Gayarré, *History of Louisiana*, 4th ed., 4 vols. (New York, 1903), 2:361-63.

[28]New Orleans *Cabildo* Minutes, Oct. 20, 1797.

[29]Letter of De La Barre, New Orleans, June 13, 1794, inserted in New Orleans *Cabildo* Minutes, June 27, 1794.

[30]Manuel de Lanzós to Francisco Belêtre, no. 29, Mobile, Aug. 8, 1792, letterbook in AGI, *Papeles de Cuba, leg.* 224-A.

[31]Carondelet to Tomás Portell, New Orleans, July 30, 1793, Mississippi State Provincial Archives, Spanish Dominion, 5:8, Mississippi State Department of Archives and History, Jackson.

[32]Carondelet to Portell, New Orleans, Aug. 5, 1795, AGI, *Papeles de Cuba, leg.* 22.

[33]General order of Carlos Dehault Delassus, New Madrid, n.d., in Frederic L. Billon, comp., *Annals of St. Louis in Its Early Days under the French and Spanish Dominations* (St. Louis, 1886), 333-34. Another New Madrid tavern keeper licensed on Aug. 24, 1795, was Jacob Myers, who bid $60 for the franchise at a Fort Celeste auction. Louis Houck, *A History of Missouri, from the Earliest Explorations and Settlements until the Admission of the State into the Union,* 3 vols. (Chicago, 1908), 2:274-75.

[34]Carondelet to Martin Duralde, New Orleans, Oct. 1, 1795, AGI, *Papeles de Cuba, leg.* 22.

[35][Miró] to Valentin LeBlanc, New Orleans, Sept. 4, 1789, draft, AGI, *Papeles de Cuba, leg.* 134-B.

[36]Anselmo Blanchard to [Miró], Valenzuela, Dec. 27, 1782, AGI, *Papeles de Cuba, leg.* 159.

[37]Luis [Peñalver y Cárdenas], Obispo [bishop], to Gayoso, New Orleans, Feb. 16, 1798, AGI, *Papeles de Cuba, leg.* 2365.

[38]Juan Ventura Morales to the secretary of state and treasury (Eugenio Llaguno y Amirola), no. 331, New Orleans, Oct. 15, 1799, AGI, *Audiencia de Santo Domingo, leg.* 2638.

[39]Athanase de Mézières to Luis de Unzaga y Amezaga, no. 402, Natchitoches, Feb. 16, 1776, in Herbert Eugene Bolton, ed., *Athanase de Mézières and the Louisiana-Texas Frontier, 1768-1780*, 2 vols. (Cleveland, 1914), 2:121.

[40]De Mézières to Unzaga, Natchitoches, Feb. 28, Mar. 14, 1771, ibid., 1:241, 243.

[41]De Mézières to Unzaga, no. 402, Feb. 16, 1776, ibid., 2:121.

[42]General order of Carlos Dehault Delassus, in Billon, comp., *Annals of St. Louis*, 333.

[43]T. Hutchins to the governor of West Florida (Folch), New Orleans, Aug. 12, 1804, AGI, *Papeles de Cuba, leg.* 59.

[44]"Regulations" issued by Folch, Baton Rouge, Oct. 30, 1804, AGI, *Papeles de Cuba, leg.* 2368.

[45]Jack D. L. Holmes, "The First Laws of Memphis: Instructions for the Commandant of San Fernando de las Barrancas, 1795," *West Tennessee Historical Society Papers*, 15 (1961): 104.

[46]Petition of Opelousas settlers to Aubry, New Orleans, Sept. 25, 1767, fragment, AGI, *Papeles de Cuba, leg.* 198.

[47]Holmes, "O'Reilly's Regulations," 298.

[48]Agreement of Natchez tavern keepers, Natchez, June 26, 1792, Natchez Chancery Court Records (7 vols., translations), vol. D, 109.

[49]King *vs.* Carrigan, Sept. 6, 1796, ibid., vol. E, 227.

[50]Holmes, "The First Laws of Memphis," 104.

[51]General order of Carlos Dehault Delassus, in Billon, comp., *Annals of St. Louis*, 333-34.

[52]Miró to Valentine LeBlanc, New Orleans, Sept. 4, 1789, draft, AGI, *Papeles de Cuba, leg.* 134-B.

[53]Ibid.

[54]Anselmo Blanchard to [Miró], Valenzuela, Dec. 27, 1782, AGI, *Papeles de Cuba, leg.* 195.

[55]Holmes, "The First Laws of Memphis," 104.

[56]Carondelet to Portell, New Orleans, July 30, 1793, Mississippi Provincial Archives, Spanish Dominion, V. 7-9. Miró also forbade liquor shippers to sell their goods at retail, preferring that alcohol be vended exclusively by licensed tavern keepers. [Miró] to Valentin LeBlanc, Sept. 4, 1789, AGI, *Papeles de Cuba, leg.* 134-B.

[57][Gayoso] to Lauretat Sigur, New Orleans, Mar. 12, 1798, AGI, *Papeles de Cuba, leg.* 251-A.

[58]De Mézières to Unzaga, no. 87, Natchitoches, Mar. 14, 1771, in Bolton, ed., *Athanase de Mézières*, 1:243.

[59]Jack D. L. Holmes, *Gayoso: the Life of a Spanish Governor in the Mississippi Valley, 1789-1799* (Baton Rouge, 1965), 112.

[60]Agreement of Natchez tavern keepers, vol. D, 108.

[61]Holmes, "O'Reilly's Regulations," 296-97.

[62]Miró's *Bando de buen gobierno*.

[63]Agreement of Natchez tavern keepers, vol. D, 108-9. On Natchez taverns see Holmes, *Gayoso*, 112.

[64]Holmes, "The First Laws of Memphis," 104.

[65]Bond of Jacob Myers, New Madrid, Aug. 24, 1795, in Houck, *A History of Missouri*, 2:274-75.

[66]Gayoso's *Bando de buen gobierno*, New Orleans, Jan. 1, 1798, Louisiana Collection, Bancroft Library, Berkeley; photostat in MS Collection, New York Public Library.

[67]Berquin-Duvallon, *Vue de la colonie espagnole du Mississippi, ou des provinces de Louisiane et Floride Occidentale* (Paris, 1803), 187.

[68]Quoted in James Alexander Robertson, ed., *Louisiana under the Rule of Spain, France, and the United States, 1785-1807*, 2 vols. (Cleveland, 1911), 1:79.

[69]Holmes, "O'Reilly's Regulations," 297.

[70]Folch to the Conde de Santa Clara, Pensacola, Aug. 18, 1798, AGI, *Papeles de Cuba, leg.* 154-A; Gayoso to Santa Clara, no. 18, confidential, New Orleans, Oct. 3, 1798, AGI, *Papeles de Cuba*, legs. 154-A, 1502-B.

[71]Holmes, "O'Reilly's Regulations," 297.

[72]Ibid.

[73]Miró's *Bando de buen gobierno.*

[74]Miró's regulation, New Orleans, Oct. 14, 1785, AGI, *Papeles de Cuba, leg.* 3. This has been translated in Kinnaird, ed., *Spain in the Mississippi Valley*, 2:150-51.

[75]New Orleans *Cabildo* Minutes, Apr. 30, 1784.

[76]Gayoso's *Bando de buen gobierno.*

[77]N. M. Miller Surrey, *The Commerce of Louisiana during the French Regime, 1699-1763* (New York, 1916), 273.

[78]Billon, comp., *Annals of St. Louis*, 333-34; Houck, *A History of Missouri*, 2:274-75.

[79]Agreement of Natchez tavern keepers, vol. D, 109.

[80]Ulloa's regulation of Mar. 14, 1767, in Houck, ed., *The Spanish Régime in Missouri*, 1:3.

[81]Holmes, "The First Laws of Memphis," 104.

[82]Jack D. L. Holmes, "Fort Ferdinand of the Bluffs, Life on the Spanish-American Frontier, 1795-1797," *West Tennessee Historical Society Papers*, 13 (1959): 47, citing Manuel García to Gayoso, San Fernando de las Barrancas, Aug. 24, 1796, AGI, *Papeles de Cuba, leg.* 48.

[83]New Orleans *Cabildo* Minutes, Oct. 27, 1780.

[84]Holmes, "The First Laws of Memphis," 104.

[85]Houck, *A History of Missouri*, 2:274-75.

[86]Pedro Favrot to Carlos Howard, no. 44, Fort San Felipe de Placaminas, Jan. 18, 1799, "The Favrot Papers," 12 vols., W. P. A. Louisiana Historical Records Survey (New Orleans, 1940-63), 4:79.

[87]Houck, ed., *The Spanish Régime in Missouri*, 1:11, 15.

[88]Surrey, *The Commerce of Louisiana*, 273.

[89]Holmes, "O'Reilly's Regulations," 297.

[90]Miró's *Bando de buen gobierno*.

[91]Gayoso's *Bando de buen gobierno*.

[92]Coulon de Villièrs's proclamation, Natchitoches, Nov. 29, 1767, MS, Natchitoches Parish Records; microfilm copy in Northwestern State College Library, Natchitoches.

[93]Cruzat's ordinance, St. Louis, Oct. 7, 1780, in Houck, ed., *The Spanish Régime in Missouri*, 1:240.

[94]Billon, comp., *Annals of St. Louis*, 333-34.

[95]Louis DeBlanc to Carondelet, no. 29, Natchitoches, Sept. 4, 1794, AGI, *Papeles de Cuba, leg.* 30.

[96]Folch's printed "Regulations to be Observed by the Syndics and Alcaldes of the Jurisdiction of Baton Rouge," Baton Rouge, Oct. 30, 1804, AGI, *Papeles de Cuba, leg.* 2368.

[97]Gayoso's instructions to the commandant of Nogales (Elías Beauregard), Nogales, Apr. 1, 1791, AGI, *Papeles de Cuba*, in Mississippi Provincial Archives, Spanish Dominion, 3:503-20.

[98]Piernas's description of Spanish Illinois, New Orleans, Oct. 31, 1768, in Houck, ed., *The Spanish Régime in Missouri*, 1:72.

[99]Captain Philip Pittman, *The Present State of European Settlements on the Mississippi, with a Geographical Description of That River* (London, 1770), 35.

[100]Anonymous narrative, 1799, in Fortescue Cuming, *Sketches of a Tour to the Western Country . . .*, vol. 4, *Early Western Travels, 1748-1846*, ed. Reuben Gold Thwaites (Cleveland, 1904), 365. Cf. Carondelet to Gayoso, New Orleans, Mar. 18, 1795, transcript in the Spanish Papers, North Carolina Department of Archives and History, Raleigh.

[101]Corinne L. Saucier, *History of Avoyelles Parish, Louisiana* (New Orleans, 1943), 19.

[102]Gayoso to Miró, no. 102, Natchez, May 16, 1791, AGI, *Papeles de Cuba, leg.* 41.

[103]Report of Vallière, San Carlos, May 19, 1787, in Kinnaird, ed., *Spain in the Mississippi Valley*, 2:203-8.

[104]Holmes, *Gayoso*, 157.

[105]Governor William Blount to the secretary of war (Henry Knox), Knoxville, Sept. 20, 1792, in Clarence E. Carter, ed., *Territory South of the River Ohio, 1790-1796*, vol. 4, *Territorial Papers of the United States* (Washington, 1936), 172-74.

[106]Juan de la Villebeuvre to Carondelet, Boukfouka, July 22, 1794, in Kinnaird, ed., *Spain in the Mississippi Valley*, 3:328.

[107]Juan de la Villebeuvre to Carondelet, Boukfouka, Feb. 4, 1793, AGI, *Papeles de Cuba, leg.* 208. This is translated in Duvon C. and Roberta Corbitt, eds., "Papers from the Spanish Archives Relating to Tennessee and the Old Southwest, 1783-1800," *East Tennessee Historical Society Publications*, 29 (1957): 149.

[108]War Department, Apr. 27, 1793, "Correspondence of General James Robertson," *American Historical Magazine*, 2 (1897): 363.

[109]Miró's *Bando de buen gobierno*; Miró to Alexander McGillivray, New Orleans, July 12, 1784, AGI, *Papeles de Cuba, leg.* 2360.

[110]Carondelet to Gayoso, New Orleans, Feb. 21, 1792, AGI, *Papeles de Cuba, leg.* 18.

[111]Carlos Dehault Delassus to [Gayoso], "Expenses of New Bourbon," 1797-98, tr. into Spanish by Pedro Derbigny, New Orleans, Aug. 9, 1798, AGI, *Papeles de Cuba, leg.* 215-A.

[112]Francisco Cruzat's list of presents for the Indians, St. Louis, Nov. 27, 1787, in Houck, ed., *The Spanish Régime in Missouri*, 1:268.

[113]Holmes, "The First Laws of Memphis," 104.

[114]Gregorio LaRosa to Carondelet, no. 49, Natchez, Aug. 13, 1795, AGI, *Papeles de Cuba, leg.* 32.

[115]Payamataha to Gayoso ("Abacan"?), Aug. 20, 1793, AGI, *Papeles de Cuba, leg.* 215-A.

[116]Carlos de Grand-Pré to Martín Navarro, Natchez, Dec. 1, 1781, AGI, *Papeles de Cuba, leg.* 590.

[117]Holmes, *Gayoso*, 157; Gayoso's list of presents, Natchez, Sept. 4, 1792, AGI, *Papeles de Cuba, leg.* 160-A.

[118]Gayoso to Morales, New Orleans, Mar. 5, 1798, enclosed in Morales to Príncipe de la Paz (Manuel de Godoy), no. 6, New Orleans, Apr. 30, 1798, Archivo Histórico Nacional, Madrid, *Estado, leg.* 3902.

[119]Art. 12 of proposed trade regulations for Spanish Illinois, St. Louis, Oct. 15, 1793, in Kinnaird, ed., *Spain in the Mississippi Valley*, 3:195.

[120]John Pope, *A Tour through the Southern and Western Territories of the United States of North-America; the Spanish Dominions on the River Mississippi, and the Floridas; the Countries of the Creek Nations; and Many Uninhabited Parts* (Richmond, 1792; New York, 1888), 29.

[121]Holmes, "The First Laws of Memphis," 101.

[122]Samuel S. Forman, *Narrative of a Journey down the Ohio and Mississippi in 1789-90* (Cincinnati, 1888), 49.

[123]William Johnson's journal, quoted in Arthur P. Whitaker, *The Mississippi Question 1795-1803* (New York, 1934), 44.

[124]Ibid.

[125]Pope, *Tour*, 44.

[126]Gayoso to Beauregard, Natchez, July 16, 1794, AGI, *Papeles de Cuba, leg.* 42.

[127]Holmes, *Gayoso*, 232.

[128]Gayoso to Beauregard, Natchez, Mar. 22, 1791, AGI, *Papeles de Cuba, leg.* 41.

[129]Carondelet to Zenon Trudeau, New Orleans, Oct. 19, 1795, AGI, *Papeles de Cuba, leg.* 22.

[130]Minor to Gayoso, Natchez, Nov. 29, 1797, AGI, *Papeles de Cuba, leg.* 2371.

[131]Vega to Arturo O'Neill, San Marcos de Apalache, Sept. 11, 1788, AGI, *Papeles de Cuba, leg.* 184-A.

[132]Report of Zenon Trudeau, St. Louis, Jan. 15, 1798, in Houck, ed., *The Spanish Régime in Missouri*, 2:251.

[133]Report of Ignacio Fernández de Velasco on the state of Louisiana and West Florida, Aranjuez, May 12, 1806, Archivo del Servicio Histórico Militar, Madrid, *leg.* 5-1-9-15.

[134]Andrew Ellicott to the secretary of state (Timothy Pickering), Natchez, Apr. 1, 1798, Southern Boundary, U. S. and Spain, RG 76, vol. 2, National Archives.

[135]James R. Jacobs, *Tarnished Warrior, Major-General James Wilkinson* (New York, 1938), 177.

[136]Report of Trudeau, St. Louis, Jan. 15, 1798, in Houck, ed., *The Spanish Régime in Missouri*, 2:251.

[137]Bouligny to Miró, Fort Panmure de Natchez, Aug. 8, 1785, in Kinnaird, ed., *Spain in the Mississippi Valley*, 2:138, 141.

[138]Holmes, "The First Laws of Memphis," 95-96.

[139]Gayoso to Peggy Watts Gayoso, New Orleans, Oct. 18, 1797, MS owned by Mrs. C. Grenes Cole, Houma, La.

[140]Spanish West Florida Records, 18 vols. (W. P. A. Louisiana Historical Records Survey, Baton Rouge, 1939), 3:87.

[141]Bartholomew Schaumburgh to Thomas Cushing, Fort Stoddart [*sic*], Dec. 1, 1799, in Jack D. L. Holmes, ed., "Fort Stoddard in 1799: Seven Letters of Captain Bartholomew Schaumburgh," *Alabama Historical Quarterly*, 26 (1964): 252.

[142]Jack D. L. Holmes, "Irish Priests in Spanish Natchez," *Journal of Mississippi History*, 29 (1967): 173-74.

[143]Luis, Obispo, to Manuel Gayoso de Lemos, New Orleans, Mar. 27, 1799, AGI, *Papeles de Cuba, leg.* 102.

[144]Andrew Ellicott, *The Journal of Andrew Ellicott* (Philadelphia, 1814; Chicago, 1962), 100.

[145]The trial of Hannon is in AGI, *Papeles de Cuba, leg.* 163-A. On this episode see Jack D. L. Holmes, ed., *Documentos inéditos para la historia de la Luisiana, 1792-1810* (Madrid, 1963), 318.

[146]O'Reilly's decree, New Orleans, Feb. 22, 1770, New Orleans *Cabildo* Minutes; copy in Kuntz Collection.

[147]Royal decree of Aug. 17, 1772, cited in Ruth Ameda King, "Social and Economic Life in Spanish Louisiana, 1763-1783" (Ph. D. dissertation, University of Illinois, 1931), 165.

[148]Ibid.; O'Reilly to Arriaga, no. 16, New Orleans, Dec. 10, 1769, in Kinnaird, ed., *Spain in the Mississippi Valley*, 1:134.

[149]Henry P. Dart and Laura L. Porteous, eds., "Account of the Credit and Debit of the Funds of the City of New Orleans for the Year 1789," *Louisiana Historical Quarterly*, 19 (1936): 585.

[150]Proclamation of Mayor James Mather, New Orleans, Mar. 24, 1807, Kuntz Collection.

[151]Report of Feb. 6, 1771, New Orleans Municipal Records.

[152]Report of Francisco Blache, New Orleans, Jan. 29, 1785, ibid.

[153]New Orleans *Cabildo* Minutes, Jan. 25, 1793.

[154]Ibid., Aug. 29, 1795; Carondelet to Rendón, New Orleans, Sept. 28, 1795, AGI, *Papeles de Cuba, leg*. 32.

[155]New Orleans *Cabildo* Minutes, May 13, 1796.

[156]Reflections of Martín Navarro, *c*. 1780-84, in Robertson, ed., *Louisiana*, 1:255.

[157]Hugo de Pedesclaux to Martín Navarro, Burdeos [Bordeaux], Aug. 16, 1787, AGI, *Papeles de Cuba, leg*. 550.

[158]Morales, "Tariff," New Orleans, Aug. 24, 1796, AGI, *Papeles de Cuba, leg*. 184-A; see app. 5.

[159]New Orleans *Cabildo* Minutes, May 18, 1798.

[160]Charles E. A. Gayarré, *History of Louisiana: The Spanish Domination* (New York, 1854), 185.

[161]Statement of Francisco Candel (*guarda-almacén* of Natchez), Natchez, May 16, 1792, AGI, *Papeles de Cuba, leg*. 1446.

[162]Memoir of R. R. Livingston to Secretary of State James Madison, Paris, Aug. 10, 1802, in U. S. Congress, *State Papers and Correspondence Bearing upon the Purchase of the Territory of Louisiana* (Washington, 1903), 43-44.

[163]Carondelet to Pedro Olivier, New Orleans, Feb. 7, 1797, AGI, *Papeles de Cuba, leg*. 24; Morales to Pedro Varela y Ulloa, no. 161, New Orleans, Oct. 16, 1797, Archivo Histórico Nacional, Madrid, *Estado, leg*. 3902.

[164]Miró to Campo de Alange, Madrid, Aug. 11, 1792, Museo Naval, Madrid, MS, vol. 569, fols. 108-164; printed in Holmes, ed., *Documentos Inéditos*, 33.

[165]King, "Social and Economic Life," 139, citing Louisiana General Correspondence, 1967, vol. 49, Louisiana Historical Society MSS, New Orleans.

[166]Arthur P. Whitaker, ed., *Documents Relating to the Commercial Policy of Spain in the Floridas, with Incidental Reference to Louisiana* (Deland, 1931), 7.

[167]Reflections of Navarro, in Robertson, ed., *Louisiana*, 1:256.

[168]Royal decree of Mar. 23, 1768, cited in King, "Social and Economic Life," 159.

[169]Royal decree, August 17, 1772, ibid., 165; see also ibid., 139.

[170]Pedesclaux to Navarro, Bordeaux, Aug. 16, 1787, AGI, *Papeles de Cuba, leg.* 550.

[171]Whitaker, ed., *Documents Relating to Commercial Policy*, 121.

[172]Gayoso to Stephen Minor, New Orleans, Sept. 6, 1798, Gayoso Papers, Louisiana State University Archives.

[173]Gayoso to Minor, New Orleans, Sept. 6, 19, 1798, Gayoso Papers; Gayoso to Peggy Watts Gayoso, New Orleans, Aug. 22, 1797, MS owned by Mrs. C. Grenes Cole.

[174]Robertson, ed., *Louisiana*, 1:170.

[175]Whitaker, ed., *Documents Relating to Commercial Policy*, 256, 257.

[176]Deposition of Gregorio Vergel, Baton Rouge, Aug. 6, 1799, Spanish West Florida Records, 3:109-10.

[177]*Causa mortuoria* of Gayoso, 1799, AGI, *Papeles de Cuba, leg.* 169.

[178]Statement of Francisco Candel, Natchez, May 16, 1792, AGI, *Papeles de Cuba, leg.* 1446.

[179]Caroline Maude Burson, *The Stewardship of Don Esteban Miró, 1782-1792* (New Orleans, 1940), 241.

[180]King, "Social and Economic Life," 140-41.

[181]Quoted in Robertson, ed., *Louisiana*, 1:79.

[182]C. C. Robin, *Voyage to Louisiana, 1803-1806*, ed. Stuart O. Landry, Jr. (New Orleans, 1966), 43.

[183]Memoir of Livingston, Aug. 10, 1802, *State Papers and Correspondence*, 43-44.

[184]Robin, *Voyage to Louisiana*, 43.

[185]King, "Social and Economic Life," 142.

[186]"Daily Journal of Wayne's Campaign, from July 28th to November 2d, 1794, Including an Account of the Memorable Battle of 20th August," *American Pioneer*, 1 (1842): 354; Gilbert Imlay, *Topographical Description of the Western Territory of North America . . .*, 3rd ed. (London, 1797), 545.

[187]Morales, "Tariff," Aug. 24, 1796, AGI, *Papeles de Cuba, leg.* 184-A.

[188]Athanase de Mézières to Unzaga, no. 200, Natchitoches, Feb. 1, 1771, AGI, *Papeles de Cuba, leg.* 110; translated in Bolton, ed., *Athanase de Mézières*, 1:147.

[189]*Knoxville Gazette*, Aug. 1, Sept. 14, 1796.

[190]Minter Wood, "Life in New Orleans in the Spanish Period," *Louisiana Historical Quarterly*, 22 (1939): 669, hereafter cited *LHQ*.

[191]*Knoxville Gazette*, May 1, 1797.

[192]Gayoso to Minor, New Orleans, Mar. 2, 1798, Gayoso Papers.

[193]Petition of Joseph Calvet, New Orleans, Mar. 23, 1793, AGI, *Papeles de Cuba, leg*. 206.

[194]King, "Social and Economic Life," 142.

[195]Deposition of Gregorio Vergel, Baton Rouge, Aug. 6, 1799, Spanish West Florida Papers, 3:109-10.

[196]Gayoso's *causa mortuoria.*

[197]King, "Social and Economic Life," 140-41.

[198]Athanase de Mézières to Unzaga, no. 200, Natchitoches, Feb. 1, 1771, AGI, *Papeles de Cuba, leg*. 110; translated in Bolton, ed., *Athanase de Mézières*, 1:147.

[199]Laura L. Porteous, tr., "Index to Spanish Judicial Records," *LHQ*, 19 (1936): 242-51.

[200]Francis Baily, *Journal of a Tour in Unsettled Parts of North America in 1796 and 1797* (London, 1856), 310.

[201]Gayoso's *causa mortuoria.*

[202]Baily, *Journal*, 310.

[203]New Orleans *Cabildo* Minutes, Oct. 27, 1775.

[204]Statement of James Hillen, Natchez, Aug. 6, 1793, in May Wilson McBee, ed., *The Natchez Court Records, 1767-1805* (Greenwood, 1953), 151.

[205]Gayarré, *Louisiana, Spanish Domination*, 347.

[206]New Orleans *Cabildo* Minutes, May 18, 1798.

[207]Anonymous narrative, 1799, in Fortescue Cuming and Rueben G. Thwaites, *Sketches of a Tour* (Cleveland, 1904), 364.

[208]Jack D. L. Holmes, ed., "Louisiana in 1795: The Earliest Extant Issue of the *Moniteur de la Louisiane*," *Louisiana History*, 7 (1966): 148n.

[209]Sign in the Spanish restaurant "Bilbao," Miami, Fla., Aug. 2, 1969.

"QUADROON" BALLS IN THE SPANISH PERIOD*

Ronald R. Morazán

With the influx of free blacks into Spanish Louisiana from the island of Santo Domingo, the Spanish authorities provided them with special privileges to hold public dances which eventually became known as "quadroon balls." Soon after the public dance hall for whites was established in 1792, Governor Carondelet granted Santiago Bernardo Coquet the privilege of giving a weekly public dance for the blacks.[1]

Preferring black women, as they were "less demanding,"[2] the white men began patronizing the dance hall for blacks. To correct this situation, Gabriel Fonvergné, the attorney general (síndico procurador general) of the *cabildo*, asked the city council to petition Governor Carondelet to prohibit slaves from entering the dance hall. The governor, because of numerous complaints and objections from slave owners, refused the request of the *cabildo* and the attorney general but decided instead to prohibit white people from going to the dances for blacks. Permission to continue the dances was given by the following administration, which was that of Don Manuel Gayoso de Lemos, but after his death, the new attorney general of the *cabildo*, Don Pedro Dulcido Barrán, asked the city council to petition Acting Civil Governor Nicolás María Vidal to abolish the dances once and for all; however, Governor Vidal refused.[3]

By the middle of 1800, the public dance hall, which belonged to the *cabildo*, was taken away from the partnership of Coquet and José Antonio Boniquet, and the dances for the black people were suspended. A petition by some of the black soldiers to the governor requested that Acting Governor Vidal continue the dances for blacks at the house of Coquet until the new governor decided on the matter. Vidal conceded, but the *cabildo* was once more displeased. In 1801, the new attorney general of the *cabildo*, Pablo Lanusse, once more had the city council petition Gov. Manuel de Salcedo to abolish the dances; but the governor, through a recommendation of his lieutenant governor and auditor of war (*auditor de guerra*), Nicolás María Vidal, refused the petition without further hindrances.[4] The dances for blacks were continued during the American period.[5]

*First published in *Louisiana History*, 14 (1973): 310-15. Reprinted with the kind permission of the author and the Louisiana Historical Association.

DOCUMENT 367[6]

A petition from Captain Juan Bautista Saraza[7] and Ensign Pedro Galafate[8] of the Battalion of Octoroons, and Captains Pedro Tomás[9] and Juan Bautista Bacusa[10] of the Battalion of Quadroons of the Disciplined Militia for Louisiana, requesting the *cabildo* to grant them permission to hold a weekly public dance.

October 24, 1800

MOST ILLUSTRIOUS CABILDO

Captain Juan Bautista Saraza and Ensign Pedro Galafate of the Battalion of Octoroons, and Captain Pedro Tomás and Captain Juan Bautista Bacusa of the Battalion of Quadroons of the Disciplined Militia of the Province of Louisiana, with the greatest reverence and due respect to Your Lordships, come before you and expound: That various individuals came in our company from the recent expedition executed in recapturing Fort San Marcos de Apalache where the men experienced bad times such as irregularity of weather and nourishment, blistering heat due to the harsh season in which the expedition was undertaken, mosquitoes, night air, humidity, and other nuisances harmful to human nature, and finally, shelling from the cannons which they expected to receive at any moment.[11]

The men give infinite thanks to the Most High for granting them their wish to come back to their homeland. To recompense them in some manner, to cheer up their spirit, so that they can forget the hardships of the expedition which they undertook— which some people compared them to irrational animals who are only led and take shelter under the hot sun which bakes their brains—we jointly solicit the permission of the president of the *cabildo* [the governor] and Your Lordships to give weekly a public dance on Saturdays until the end of the next Carnival, beginning on the day of our most august Sovereign Charles IV, which falls on the fourth of the coming month The dance will not interfere with the one the white people regularly have, for they have their dance on Sundays.[12]

Through the kindness of Don Bernardo Coquet,[13] we have his permission to use his house for the dances. We ask that you be kind enough to provide the petitioners with city guards who previously protected the house when dances were given to prevent disorders. When we were on the expedition, we were informed that some people came to the dances given there determined to disrupt the peaceful diversions—some by provoking fights, others by chewing vanilla and spitting it out for the purpose of producing an intolerable stench, others by putting chewed tobacco on the seats so that the women would stain their garments—in short, doing and causing as much havoc as they could. This example of maliciousness was never experienced in the innumerable dances that were given in the chosen house while the guards were present. The guards, once you give them orders to attend, will be anxious to come, owing to the special privileges we shall offer them on the nights the dance is given.[14]

Therefore, we humbly plead that Your Lordships be kind enough to concede this solicitation which has nothing to do with violence and consequently will not cause any harm. This is the season for such diversion, both in America and in Europe. We shall always keep in our hearts your renowned benevolence and kindness.[15]

New Orleans
[Rubrics] Capt. Jean Baptiste Sçarasse
Pierre Tomás
Pierre Calpha
Jean Baptiste Bacuse

Notes for "'Quadroon' Balls in the Spanish Period"

[1]John E. Harkins, "The Regulatory Functions of the New Orleans Cabildo, 1769-1803" (M.A. thesis, Louisiana State University, 1971), 95-102.

[2]Claude C. Robin, *Voyage to Louisiana,* trans. by Stuart O. Landry (New Orleans, 1966), 56-57; "William Johnson's Journal: A voyage from Pittsburgh to New Orleans and Thence to New York in 1801," *Louisiana Historical Quarterly*, 5 (1922): 38, hereafter cited *LHQ*.

[3]Actas Originales del Cabildo de Nueva Orleans, 1769-1803, typescript directed by Joaquín Barcenas for the Civil Works Administration and the Federal Emergency Relief Administration of Louisiana, 1937. There are five *Libros* (Books) of the proceedings of the *cabildo* which are divided into ten *tomos* (tomes). Hereinafter, the work will be cited as Actas del Cabildo, Libro 4, t. 1: 83-84, January 22, 1796; Ibid., 85-86, January 29, 1796; Ibid., 3, 130-31, February 7, 1800; Ibid., 137-40, February 8, 1800; Ibid., 142-43, February 24, 1800.

[4]Ibid., Libro 4:4, 128, Aug. 14, 1801; Ibid., 137-38, Sept., 18, 1801.

[5]Nathaniel Cox to Gabriel Lewis, Dec. 16, 1806, in "Letters of Nathaiel Cox to Gabriel Lewis," *LHQ*, 2 (1919): 182.

[6]This is one of the numerous documents included in Ronald R. Morazan, "Letters, Petitions, and Decrees of the Cabildo of New Orleans, 1800-1803: Edited and Translated" (Ph.D. dissertation, Louisiana State University, Baton Rouge, 1972), 1:204-10.

[7]Juan Bautista Saraza (Scarasse) must have migrated from Santo Domingo during the slave uprising there and joined the Spanish military service when he came to Louisiana. He is listed as sergeant first class in the New Orleans Mulatto Militia for 1792, and soon rose to the rank of captain in command of the Battalion of Octoroons (*Batallón de Octorones*). After Louisiana was ceded to France, he went with the troops to Florida and returned to New Orleans. Later the Mulatto Militia was sent to Cuba to be incorporated into the Havana Regiment. When he returned to New Orleans, he established his residence at 89 Dauphine Street and opened an upholstery shop. Jack D. L. Homes, *Honor and Fidelity: The Louisiana Infantry Regiment and the Louisiana Militia Companies, 1766-1821* (Birmingham, 1965), 255; John A. Paxton, *Paxton's New-Orleans*

Directory, 1822. List of Names, Containing the Heads of Families, and Persons in Business, Alphabetically Arranged (1822).

[8]Pedro Galafate (Calpha) joined the New Orleans Mulatto Militia in the early 1790s and became a corporal first class in 1793. His uncle was the captain and commandant of the Mulatto Militia. In the War of 1812, Pedro was a corporal in the 3rd Regiment of Louisiana Militia. He established his residence at 67 Toulouse Street and was employed as a lamplighter for the city. Holmes, ed., *Honor and Fidelity,* 236; Paxton, *Directory;* Marion John Bennett Pierson, comp., *Louisiana Soldiers in the War of 1812* (Baton Rouge, 1963), 21; Abraham P. Nasatir, "Government Employees and Salaries in Spanish Louisiana," *LHQ,* 24 (1946): 924.

[9]Pedro José Tomás was born in 1767. He was the son of Juan Tomás and Margarita Millot. When he came to Louisiana, he established his residence at 41 Rue St. Ann. He married María Francisca Benjamín Gespere. From this marriage, a daughter named Agata was born in 1797. Agata died the year following the death of her father on November 29, 1815, at the age of forty-eight. "Cemetery Records of St. Louis Cemetery No. I." Vertical files of the Louisiana State Museaum Library, New Orleans, Louisiana (1936); Holmes, ed., *Honor and Fidelity,* 256.

[10]Juan Bautista Bacusa (Bacuse) was born in Gonaïves, Haiti in 1738. He established his residence at 7 Levee North in New Orleans when he came to Louisiana. He married Luisa Catarina Landrony. From this union, a son was born whom they named Bartolomé. Juan Bautista entered the Spanish military service in the early 1790s, and, by 1793, he was a sublieutenant of the New Orleans Negro Militia. Eventually, he became a captain and commanded the Battalion of Quadroons (*Batallón de Cuarterones*). He died on February 11, 1817, at the age of seventy-nine. "Cemetery Records of St. Louis No. I," *New Orleans in 1805;* Holmes, *Honor and Fidelity,* 233.

[11]Free black men were a substantial minority of about two thousand in 1803 in Louisiana. New Orleans, with approximately one thousand three hundred fifty, had the largest number. They were usually involved in small business or engaged in some of the mechanical trades. There is also a record of one who was permitted to practice medicine, although he did not have a license. Actas del Cabildo, Libro 5:4, 127, Aug. 14, 1801; Minter Wood, "Life in New Orleans in the Spanish Period," *LHQ,* 22 (1939): 656-57; Edwin A. Davis, *Louisiana: A Narrative History,* 2nd ed. (Baton Rouge, 1965), 131.

Non-whites were racially classified into various groups. At the top of the social scale was the octoroon (*octorón*), who was a mixture composed of seven-eighths white and one-eight Negro blood. The second place was occupied by the quadroon (*cuarterón*), who was the offspring of a mulatto and a white person. The third category was the mulatto, who was the offspring of a white and a black person; and, finally, the Negro was at the bottom. In other Spanish colonies, where there was a large number of Indians, there were other categories composed of *pardos*, a mixture of white and Indian; *mestizos,* the offspring of whites and Indians; and, finally, the *castizos,* the offspring of whites and *mestizos.* Angel Rosenblat, *La población indígena y el mestizaje en América,* 2 vols. (Buenos Aires, 1954), 2:137; A. J. Navard, *Why Louisiana Has Parishes, Policejurymen, Redbones, Cajuns, Creoles, Mulattos, Quadroons, Octoroons, Griffes* (New Orleans, 1943), 7; Edgar F. Love, "Marriage Patterns of African Descent in a Colonial Mexico City Parish," *Hispanic-American Historical Review,* 51 (1971): 79-91.

[12]A dance hall for whites was established in 1792 by an act of the *cabildo.* The contract specified that a private individual was to construct the building on a piece of land belonging to the city, and he was to have a lease for three years. After this time, the person could either continue to lease the building or sell it to the city for its appraised value. The contract was given to Filiberto Farge, and he retained it until 1801. In that year the *cabildo* awarded the contract of the dance hall to Celestino Lavergné, but he held it for only a few months before transferring it to Francisco Larosa. By this time, however, the rent had increased from twenty *pesos* monthly to one hundred fifty *pesos.* Larosa complained that, since he was denied the exclusive right to hold all social functions at the dance hall, he either wanted the rent reduced or the contract cancelled. Refusing his request, the *cabildo* informed him that it would try to encourage the people to use the dance hall for their social functions. Actas del Cabildo, Libro 4, t. 1, ff. 95-96, March 11, 1796; Ibid., t. 4, f. 99, June 12, 1801; Ibid., 106, June 26, 1801; Harkins, "Regulatory Functions of the Cabildo," 98-100.

[13]Santiago Bernardo Coquet was born in Marseilles, France, in 1759. He was the son of Santiago Coquet and Dame Roberteau. Santiago Bernardo married Sofía Deharpe and together they came to New Orleans and established their residence at 27 St. Philip Street. From this marriage, several children were born, most of

whom died while they were still infants. Bernardo, however, outlived the surviving children and his wife as well.

After the dance hall was taken away from him and his partner, José Antonio Boniquet, but not the privilege of giving dances for blacks at his house, Santiago bought a building at 24 Conti Street from where he conducted his business. Then he bought the lots adjacent to his home and, in 1808, erected the Théâtre de la rue Saint Philippe, the third oldest theatre in New Orleans.

Coquet died on September 11, 1839, at the age of eighty. "Cemetery Records of St. Louis No. I"; Stanley C. Arthur, *Old New Orleans* (New Orleans, 1936), 87; *New Orleans in 1805*; Paxton, *Directory;* Stanley C. Arthur, comp., *New Orleans Directory, 1807-1809.*

[14]White men, both Creoles and North Americans, preferred to go to the "quadroon" balls which were held on Saturday night. These did not conflict with the ball given for the whites on Sunday. One traveler believes that the white men preferred the quadroon women because they were easier to please and less demanding than white women. Eventually, the poor whites, who had been given the sobriquet of "Cajuns" by the Creoles, retaliated and called the Creoles "Boug-a-lees" because of their preference for quadroon women. Governor Miró, who was married to a Creole woman, Marie Celeste Elenore de Macarty, was most probably "forced" to issue some regulations against the quadroons in his *bando de buen gobierno* (inaugural proclamation). He forbade concubinage, prostitution, and even prohibited quadroons from dressing in an ostentatious manner, wearing coiffures, French caps, plumes and *mantillas.* Henry E. Chambers, *A History of Louisiana,* 3 vols. (Chicago, 1925), 1:341-43; François Marie Perrin Du Lac, *Voyage dans les Deux Louisianes et chez les Nations Sauvages du Missouri* (Lyon, 1805), 393-94.

[15]At first the Spanish government in America prohibited blacks from entering the military service but, by mid-sixteenth century, they were permitted to join because they manifested better resistance than others to disease and had the ability to adjust to tropical climates. *Recopilación de Leyes de los Reynos de las Indias,* 4 vols., 5th ed. (1841), Libro 3, Título 10, Ley 10; Lyle N. McAlister, T*he "Fuero Militar" in New Spain, 1764-1800* (Gainesville, 1957): 43.

When Governor O'Reilly came to Louisiana, he brought two companies of black militiamen—one of mulattos and the other of blacks (*morenos*). During the American Revolution, the Negro militiamen served with distinction in the campaigns against Manchac, Baton Rouge, Natchez, Mobile, and Pensacola. When Carondelet reorganized the militia, he divided it into two battalions consisting of one hundred troops each. The militia had a commandant, with the rank of breveted captain of the infantry, two adjutants, and other officers. The militia sometimes served in expeditions against runaway slaves. After Louisiana was ceded to France in 1803, a large number of the black militia was transferred to Pensacola and later mustered into the Havana Battalion. Holmes, *Honor and Fidelity,* 54-57.

When the militia was organized during the American period, blacks were excluded. Governor Claiborne was apprehensive of the situation and informed the secretary of state, James Madison, that the black freemen who had distinguished themselves in the Spanish service were bitter towards the government of the United States because of their exclusion from service. It was in 1812, however, that by an act of the legislature of the state of Louisiana, the governor was empowered to organize a corps of black freemen to be composed of four companies of sixty-four men each. This act came at an opportune time because the black militiamen served well and with distinction in the War of 1812. One of them, Captain Joseph Savary, is given credit for having been the one who killed British General Packenham. Claiborne to Madison, Dec. 27, 1803, in Dunbar Rowland, ed., *Official Letter Books of W. C. C. Claiborne, 1801-1816,* 6 vols. (Jackson, 1917), 1:314; "An Act to Organize in a Corps of Militia for the Service of the State of Louisiana, as Well as for its Defense as for its Police, a Certain Portion of Chosen Men Among the Free Men of Color," *Acts Passed at the First Session of the State of Louisiana, 1812,* Chapter 23, 72-72; Charles B. Rousseve, *The Negro in Louisiana* (New Orleans, 1937), 28-29; A. E. Perkins, "Victor Séjour and His Times," *The Negro History Bulletin,* 5 (1941-1942), 163.

THE PESTILENCE OF 1796—NEW ORLEANS' FIRST OFFICIALLY RECORDED YELLOW FEVER EPIDEMIC*

Jo Ann Carrigan

The date of the first appearance of yellow fever in New Orleans long has been a subject for historical speculation and disagreement. The difficulties arise from a scarcity of medical records for colonial Louisiana. Those records which do refer to disease usually consist of little more than vague descriptions employing even more indefinite terminology for the ailments which plagued the inhabitants—such as the fever, the malady, the pestilence. Inadequate diagnostic procedures and the lack of uniformity in disease nomenclature which characterized medical practice down to the mid-nineteenth century also complicate the task of the medical historian.

Joseph Jones, an eminent nineteenth-century Louisiana physician and prolific medical historian, carefully sifted through the evidence and testimony available to him in an attempt to determine the earliest history of yellow fever in Louisiana. He became convinced that the disease had been transmitted occasionally in the very late seventeenth and early eighteenth centuries to points on the American Gulf Coast through contacts with the West Indies, where yellow fever prevailed. But he noted several factors which might have served to postpone its appearance as an epidemic in New Orleans: the long and tedious trip up the Mississippi to the city, the sparse population, and the limited commercial activity during the French colonial period. Nevertheless, Dr. Jones refused to declare positively that the "Saffron Scourge" had never visited New Orleans under French rule. The record of disease in the Crescent City for a half-century after its establishment (1718) was "very imperfect"; no medical journal or native medical work, which might have detailed the nature of prevailing diseases, ever appeared in French colonial Louisiana.

*First published in the *McNeese Review*, 13 (1962): 27-36. Reprinted with the kind permission of the author and publisher.

Jones wisely concluded that the mere absence of medical records failed to demonstrate the total absence of yellow fever.[1]

Various years suggested by medical men and historians for the first importation of the killer-disease to New Orleans include 1765, 1766, 1767, 1791, 1793, and 1796. Mobile and Pensacola suffered yellow fever attacks in 1765, and New Orleans experienced an exceedingly unhealthy fall season that year. It is entirely possible that yellow fever was present in the Crescent City during that sickly season, but there is no remaining record of the specific diseases involved. In 1766, the year Antonio de Ulloa arrived with troops from Cuba to take control of the Louisiana colony for Spain, New Orleans suffered from an epidemic said to have closely resembled yellow fever.[2] At least one historical work, without stating the source or supplying details, set forth 1767 as the date of yellow fever's initial appearance in New Orleans.[3]

A sketch of epidemics appearing in *De Bow's Review* of 1846 stated, "The Yellow Fever, according to tradition, was first introduced into the New Orleans in 1769, by a British vessel from Africa with slaves."[4] Dr. Joseph Jones, however, could find no evidence to indicate that yellow fever had been introduced into the city by slave ships.[5] Bennet Dowler, another outstanding nineteenth-century Louisiana physician and student of the history of yellow fever, doubted that the epidemic of 1769 had been yellow fever at all. It was impossible, he declared, to determine the character of the disease in question from available records. Furthermore, Dowler contended, within a single generation after 1769 the scourge had appeared in the unquestionable 1796 epidemic, and those persons writing soon after that time who called it the first appearance of the disease could have questioned living witnesses about any previous occurrences. And, he insisted, they "would have been contradicted, had they made erroneous statements as to the period of its invasion."[6] Dr. Jones, however, writing some twenty years after Dowler, felt that a careful consideration of all available testimony indicated that 1796 definitely was not the first appearance, but that the fever had been present to some degree in 1791, 1794, and 1795.[7]

Around 1840 Dr. Daniel Drake, distinguished mid-western physician, educator, and medical author, visited New Orleans, made personal inquiries about the first yellow fever invasion, and decided upon 1791 as the fateful year, basing his conclusion on the testimony of "a venerable citizen" of the city. As John Duffy has pointed out in *The Rudolph Matas History of Medicine in Louisiana*, the testimony in this case, based on memory forty or fifty years after the fact, is hardly infallible.[8] The researches of Erasmus Darwin Fenner, active nineteenth-century Louisiana physician, editor, and medical historian, led him to conclude that the yellow pestilence first prevailed in New Orleans in 1793. In the 1840s he discussed the problem with five elderly gentlemen who had settled in the Crescent City between 1797 and 1804, and all commented that the disease was "spoken of familiarly" when they first arrived. One of them told Fenner that he distinctly remembered having heard a prominent physician frequently remark in the early 1800s that 1793 was the first yellow fever year.[9] A commentator not far removed in time from the events at issue, Berquin-Duvallon, who traveled through Louisiana in 1802, wrote: "This disease has now for seven years, made every summer, great ravages at New-Orleans. . . ." On the basis of his inquiries, he stated that yellow fever previously had been unknown in that city,[10] that is, before 1796.

Varying accounts and opinions, conflicting evidence, and testimony could be cited further; the foregoing should be sufficient to demonstrate the basic problem. One can only say that *some* cases of yellow fever undoubtedly occurred at various points along the Gulf Coast and in the city of New Orleans in the years before 1796. The fact that the epidemic of that year affected newcomers so much more severely than native or long-resident New Orleanians indicates a fairly extensive period prior to 1796 during which a portion of the Creole population might have acquired immunity through mild attacks of the disease. Nevertheless, in the absence of clear records on the subject before that date, the appearance of yellow fever in previous years can only remain a matter for speculation. Suffice it to say that 1796 marks the first visitation of yellow fever in New Orleans widespread enough to attract considerable attention, to call forth official mention, and to be identified with the yellow pestilence of Philadelphia and other eastern and southern Atlantic seaport cities, where it had prevailed intermittently since the late seventeenth century.

Even for the indisputable yellow fever epidemic of 1796 the records are scanty. The brief official reports of the Spanish attorney-general and the intendant, together with a series of letters written by Baron Joseph Xavier Pontalba to his wife, constitute the only extant contemporary records describing that first extensive visitation of yellow fever in the Crescent City. From these three accounts, however, one can reconstruct a fairly good picture of the stricken city.

According to Intendant Juan Ventura Morales, the epidemic broke out in late August.[11] On September 6 Pontalba wrote his wife that "the maladies are increasing here, and they are now more dangerous than ever."[12] Throughout September, October, and early November his daily letters were filled with commentary on the raging pestilence. On several occasions the baron noted an apparent abatement of the epidemic only to correct himself a few days later when the disease flared again.

From the very beginning Pontalba observed that the fever singled out the so-called "unacclimated," the newcomers—especially Americans and Englishmen—in preference to the Creole and long-resident population. Repeatedly he reassured his wife that the disease presented little danger except to strangers who were its principal victims.[13] Intendant Morales also commented on the fever's peculiarity in so obviously preferring foreigners to the natives.[14] Such a noticeable distinction is a fairly reliable sign that yellow fever was not *entirely* new to the area.

Regarding the nature and origin of the fever, there was considerable discussion and disagreement among laymen and physicians as if confronting an essentially new problem. This uncertainty indicates that the appearance of yellow fever in epidemic proportions was something new. Pontalba asserted that "the maladies" resulted from an overflow of the river on the opposite shore, which caused "subsequent fetid exhalations to be given off by the earth" as it dried out. Attorney-general Don Gabriel Fonvergne in a report to the city council blamed "the stagnated waters that remain in the gutters . . . the little cleanliness and care given to them, the dead animals abandoned on them, and on the margin of the river" for the contamination of the atmosphere and the spread of infection.[15] This concept of "fetid exhalations" or noxious effluvia arising from animal and vegetable decomposition was a common epidemiological tenet of the period, and was to be echoed in medical and lay philosophy of fever causation for almost a century to come.

In mid-September Pontalba reported to his wife the opinion of New Orleans physicians that the sickness was "the yellow fever of Philadelphia," but expressed his disagreement with that explanation. A few days later he wrote, "In common accord, people now believe that it is the same yellow fever that has been breaking out every year in Philadelphia, and which the Americans have brought along with them." Apparently Pontalba refused to accept the majority opinion, for in late October he remarked, "I do not understand the nature of that deadly malady, but I think it to be a kind of pestilent fever."[16] In a dispatch of October 31 the intendant summed up the several views of the epidemic which "has terrified and still keeps in a state of consternation the whole population of this town." Some called the disease "a malignant fever"; others, "the black vomit"; and still others believed it to be the yellow fever of Philadelphia.[17]

Confronted by a relatively new and terrifying malady, the people of New Orleans employed a variety of measures in the hope of staving off the disease. Pontalba told of the great fear among the people, especially among the women, who carried bits of garlic in their clothing, and burned animal skins, horns, hoofs, and tar to ward off the pestilential effluvia. In one letter he gave a full description of his own precautionary measures: "I always had camphor on me," he wrote, "and also much vinegar; two demijohns of the latter were used to sprinkle my apartments. . . . My servants, themselves, were soaked all over with the vinegar. I often chewed the quinquinia . . . " and, he added thoughtfully, "I was doing all this for you. . . ." The baron attributed his own immunity and that of several friends to their regular chewing of "quinquinia" or quinine, which he thought helped to hold off the infection.[18]

In October the baron mentioned a recipe by Dr. Masdevall, physician to the king of Spain, which was being circulated among the people of New Orleans as a preventive against the sickness. He felt it had been largely unsuccessful. Intendant Morales, on the other hand, credited the recipe with "marvellous effects," attributing to it the relative immunity of the Spaniards and the Negroes.[19] Baronne Carondelet, the governor's wife, placed her faith in the preventive powers of herb-tea compound and sarsaparilla.[20]

Pontalba had little regard for the physicians' efforts at treating the fever victims. When it seemed on one occasion that the epidemic was abating, he wrote: "The doctors pretend having found a remedy. . . ." The baron, however, attributed the declining force of the disease to "the change in the weather." The physicians contended that only "the emetics and the vesicatories" had arrested the epidemic, but Pontalba refused to give any such credit to those gentlemen. He then cited several cases of successful recovery without any of the "so-called succors." Attorney-general Fonvergne reported to the city council that the "most up-to-date care and remedies" had been without results.[21]

The epidemic of 1796 was without question a rather severe one. However, exact mortality figures were not available; no bureau of vital statistics, no board of health, no systematic measures existed at that time for keeping such records. Prevailing from late August until early November, the Saffron Scourge levied a fairly heavy tribute on the Crescent City. In the second week of September Pontalba reported the mortality as eight or nine fever victims per day. Later he wrote, "The doctors and the monks had been keeping the true number of deaths secret." For a time he estimated the toll at fifteen to seventeen deaths per day. By mid-October the main force of the epidemic was spent, but as late as November 6 the fever still caused "some ravage." The following day, November 7, Pontalba wrote that "we are now predicting the near end of the epidemic," and after that date he made no further mention of the pestilence in his letters.[22] The arrival of cold weather obviously curtailed the activities of the yellow fever mosquito.

On October 31 the intendant stated that the parish registry listed nearly two hundred deaths from all causes since the outbreak of the epidemic. This figure did not include those who died outside the town limits or "the protestants who perished (and they were numerous)."[23] According to the attorney-general in a report dated October 21, the "cruel epidemic" had already "led to the grave more than 250 persons."[24]

The population of New Orleans in 1796 probably was about six thousand, representing a two-fold increase over the figure in 1769 and including large numbers of strangers particularly liable to the fever—that is, never having been exposed before.[25] Even if the Creole population possessed a degree of acquired immunity, New Orleans still provided a fertile field for a virulent epidemic. Raging from late August until early November, the epidemic covered a period of at least ten weeks, during which there must have been several deaths each day. On one occasion, Pontalba mentioned a daily death count of eight or nine victims, and on another, as many as fifteen to seventeen per day. Even if this rate prevailed for only a short period, one might conjecture at least five fatalities per day for the remaining time. On that basis, a total of 350 to 400 yellow fever deaths for the entire period is probably a fair estimate.

This first great visitation of the pestilence in its side-effects on the life of the community set a pattern which would become a repetitive process during a century of epidemics to come. A general exodus from the city, a moratorium on business, a vain appeal for sanitary measures, and the expression of a man's depravity as well as his humanitarianism invariably accompanied "Yellow Jack's" ravages in New Orleans.

As the fever gradually spread through the city in 1796, many persons hoping to escape its attack fled the community. The émigrés sought refuge in the back country or left the colony entirely for regions far to the north. Pontalba, in commenting on this flight of the unacclimated, revealed the sorry plight of business in New Orleans: "The city is almost deserted; my storehouses, which had all been rented, are now left vacant."[26]

In the following years New Orleans commercial interests suffered untold losses from visits of the fever, losses so acute that every effort was put forth to conceal the existence of the disease from the people of the city and the outside world until the epidemic could no longer be hidden.

Those persons who did not wish to leave the city altogether but desired some measure of safety for themselves and their families, or who simply wanted a temporary respite from the depression of a city in despair, retired to resorts across the lake or to homes in the country or across the river. Along with his account of the grim aspects of the epidemic of 1796, Baron Pontalba also described his social activities during the pestilence, which included frequent house-parties at a friends' plantation across the river. Escaping from the plague, a large group of people amused themselves with pranks, jokes, and games. It is all slightly reminiscent of Boccaccio's ten who sought diversion in the telling of tales while hiding from the Black Death. In one letter the baron described a party so boisterous and playful that on retiring to his room early he found it necessary to barricade the door with a large table to keep the crowd from dragging him out. He justified the pranksters by pointing out that they "needed the air of the country, the maladies in town having driven them all into a state of deep melancholy." While in the city one heard nothing but talk of the epidemic, but across the river "all news of that sort is taboo, and they give themselves up to play," which included riding, racing, and "other extravagant things."[27]

In another letter Pontalba described more specifically some of the amusing "pleasantries" engaged in at one of the house-parties: "The ladies, on one side, found pleasure in knotting my bed sheet together, [and] in throwing water at me . . . while I, on the other, smudged their bed clothes with lamp-black, so that they became smeared all over with it." In further retaliation he applied a foul-smelling drug powder to their pillows, threw water at them, dropped pieces of wood down their chimneys at night, made holes in their chamber-pots, and engaged in other forms of devilment. Probably realizing that such goings-on with the ladies might provoke a spark of jealousy in his wife, who was absent from the scene, the baron added that after paying them back in kind he had become bored with such things and ceased to participate—"since all such pranks, *mon-amie*, cannot fill the void of my days, being only amusing for a time."[28]

Undoubtedly in the course of every epidemic which ever occurred there were groups of individuals who sought relief from the pressures of fear and desolation by some means of diversion—drinking, joking, or playing lively games. Certainly no other account of this escape device in Louisiana is quite as delightful as Pontalba's!

The unsanitary condition of New Orleans, noted so often in travel accounts, was linked with the prevalence of all kinds of diseases from an early period, in conformity with the widely accepted theory of atmospheric contamination. Since filth was blamed as a basic cause of disease in the Crescent City, from time to time throughout most of the nineteenth century, appeals for sanitary reform came from the newspapers, medical societies, and medical journals. Almost nothing was accomplished, however, until the latter nineteenth century, largely because of public apathy and official negligence. Yellow fever is not a filth disease, but sanitary improvements relating to drainage and water supply, when they finally came, probably helped to eliminate the disease by removing the condition conducive to mosquito breeding. Suffice it to say here that the attorney-general in Spanish colonial New Orleans associated the epidemic of 1796 with the filth-clogged gutters and decaying animal bodies on the river bank, and furthermore suggested that the city council ameliorate those conditions to prevent future epidemics.[29] Then, as in later years, the recommendations resulted in little effective action.

The epidemic of 1796 and every epidemic which followed presented the opportunity for this question to be raised: Is man inherently good or bad, altruistic or depraved? Epidemics created conditions which gave men the chance to rise to the heights of heroism or to sink to the depths of callousness. And as might be expected from the paradox that is man, there were examples of both extremes. In the overall picture of a century filled with epidemics it seems that the people of New Orleans generally rose to the occasion and evidenced a high degree of benevolence, almost strikingly in contrast to the stereotyped picture of moral disintegration in plague-stricken cities. In that very first yellow fever epidemic, Pontalba recorded an incident which can be scored to the dark side of man's nature. He told about the discovery of five bodies "in the backways merely covered with leaves, the trouble not having been taken to even bury them." The baron declared indignantly: "Such terrible cases in which bodies of yellow fever victims were abandoned, sometimes even by relatives, also occurred in later epidemics. However, one may safely say that these cases represented the exception rather than the rule.

On the other side of the ledger, Pontalba indirectly recorded some examples of strength and humanitarianism. He himself in ministering to the needs of several friends victimized by the malady showed a considerable amount of benevolence and fearlessness. And Governor Carondelet, believing it might intensify the general panic if he left town, courageously resisted for a time the demands of his wife and his friends that he retire to the opposite shore.[30]

There is no evidence that any official or organized measures were adopted for the care and relief of indigent victims in this initial surprise attack. Later, as the population increased and yellow fever became a familiar enemy, both official and unofficial emergency measures occasionally were adopted for the relief of the indigent sick during an epidemic season.

New Orleanians could scarcely have suspected in 1796 that the pestilence they suffered would be only the first of a century-long series of epidemic visitations. Within a very few years, however, yellow fever had become a familiar phenomenon in that city. Early in the nineteenth century the recurring summer and fall invasions of yellow fever had earned for the Crescent City a nation-wide reputation for insalubrity and the title "Necropolis of the South." Not until the early twentieth century were New Orleans, Louisiana, and the South to be delivered from the burden of the Saffron Scourge. During the outbreak of 1905 in New Orleans, and elsewhere, the national, state, and local health officials applied the knowledge of the recently discovered mosquito vector, brought the disease under control, and successfully demonstrated the means for its future prevention.

Notes for "The Pestilence of 1796—New Orleans' First Officially Recorded Yellow Fever Epidemic"

[1]*New Orleans Medical and Surgical Journal*, New Series, 7 (July, 1879): 132-33, 146. Hereafter cited as *New Orleans Medical and Surgical Journal.*

[2]Charles Gayarré, *History of Louisiana*, 4 vols., 4th ed. (New Orleans, 1903), 2:133; *New Orleans Medical and Surgical Journal*, 146; George W. Cable, *The Creoles of Louisiana* (New York, 1889), 291; John Smith Kendall, *History of New Orleans* (Chicago, 1922), 1:174.

[3]James Alexander Robertson, ed., *Louisiana Under the Rule of Spain, France, and the United States, 1785-1807*, 2 vols. (Cleveland, 1911), 1:175n.

[4]*De Bow's Commercial Review*, 2 (1846): 73.

[5]*New Orleans Medical and Surgical Journal*, 132.

[6]Bennet Dowler, "Tableau of the Yellow Fever of 1853, with Topographical, Chronological and Historical Sketches of the Epidemics of New Orleans," *Cohen's New Orleans Directory . . . of 1854* (New Orleans, 1854), 8.

[7]*New Orleans Medical and Surgical Journal*, 146.

[8]Joseph Jones, *Medical and Surgical Memoirs* (New Orleans, 1876-1890), 3, pt. 1, cxxxv; John Duffy, ed., *The Rudolph Matas History of Medicine in Louisiana*, 2 vols. (Baton Rouge, 1958), 1:206.

[9]Erasmus Darwin Fenner, "The Yellow Fever Quarantine at New Orleans," *Transactions of the American Medical Association*, 2 (1849): 624.

[10]Berquin-Duvallon, *Vue de la Colonie Espagnole du Mississippi ou des Provinces de la Louisiane . . . en l'Annee 1802* (Paris, 1803), trans. by John Davis as *Travels in Louisiana and the Floridas, in the year, 1802* (New York, 1806), 114, 118.

[11]Gayarré, *History of Louisiana*, 3:375.

[12]Joseph X. Pontalba to wife, September 6, 1796, in "Letters of Baron Joseph X. Pontalba to his Wife, 1798" (W.P.A. trans. typescript, Louisiana State University Library, Baton Rouge), 274. Hereafter cited as Pontalba Letters.

[13]Ibid., September 6, 11, 24, 30. November 3, 1796, 274, 284, 312, 323, 393.

[14]Gayarré, *History of Louisiana*, 3:375.

[15]Pontalba Letters, September 6, 11, 1796, 274, 284; Records of the City Council of New Orleans, Book 4079, Document 259, October 21, 1796 (W. P. A. trans. typescript, Louisiana State Museum Library, New Orleans). Hereafter cited as Records of the City Council.

[16]Pontalba Letters, September 19, 24, October 30, 1796, 300, 312, 385.

[17]Gayarré, *History of Louisiana*, 3:375.

[18]Pontalba Letters, September 15, 28, October 30, 1796, 291, 321, 386.

[19]Ibid., October 10, 1796, 344; Gayarré, *History of Louisiana*, 3:375.

[20]Pontalba Letters, October 15, 1796, 358.

[21]Ibid., September 14, 1796, 290; Records of the City Council.

[22]Pontalba Letters, September 12, 15, 24, October 13, November 6, 7, 1796, 285, 291, 312, 353, 399, 402.

[23]Gayarré, *History of Louisiana*, 3:375.

[24]Records of the City Council.

[25]Dowler, "Tableau of the Yellow Fever of 1853," *Cohen's New Orleans Directory*, 9; *New Orleans Medical and Surgical Journal*, 147.

[26]Pontalba Letters, October 13, 1796, 353.

[27]Ibid., October 9, 342.

[28]Ibid., October 15, 1796, 358.

[29]Records of the City Council.

[30]Ibid., September 22, October 7, 30, 1796, 307, 338, 385-88.

PART IX
The Catholic Church in Spanish Louisiana

SPANISH LOUISIANA: IN THE SERVICE OF GOD AND HIS MOST CATHOLIC MAJESTY*

Alfred E. Lemmon

Anticipating the Treaty of Paris, which would end the Seven Years' War (the French and Indian War), the "Most Christian Monarchs" of France ceded Louisiana to the "Most Catholic Monarchs" of Spain. The Bourbon monarchs on both the French and Spanish thrones viewed the province of Louisiana as a means of preventing British expansionism. While acknowledging Louisiana as a sizeable buffer between New Spain and the westward-moving Britons, Spain did not rush to claim its bounty.[1] Authorities viewed the province "as little more than an inconsequential backwater far from the center of the empire."[2] This immense territory would stretch the limited Spanish manpower and financial resources in the Gulf of Mexico region. Moreover, the new possession had to be evaluated in light of the current political and economic policies of the Bourbon reforms, a movement dedicated to the revamping of the Spanish government.[3]

Catholicism in Spanish Louisiana over the following forty years, reflected the long-standing relationships between the Catholic Church and the Spanish Crown. The Catholic Church was the chosen medium of their "Most Catholic Majesties" to transmit Spanish culture. In that capacity, it was the handmaiden of conquest, colonization, and governance.[4] The home relationship between church and state was carried over to the colonies. A de facto national church, in New World affairs it was dependent upon the powerful Council of the Indies for personnel, directives, and finances. It served that same council as educator, cultural agent, and guardian of social welfare.[5]

Catholic Christianity since Gothic times had unified the great diversity of peoples and kingdoms that constituted Spain. The establishment of Catholicism in the Spanish

*First published in Glenn R. Conrad, ed., *Cross, Crozier and Crucible: A Volume Celebrating the Bicentennial of a Catholic Diocese in Louisiana* (Lafayette, LA: The Archdiocese of New Orleans in cooperation with the Center for Louisiana Studies, 1993). Reprinted with the kind permission of the Archdiocese of New Orleans.

New World can be viewed as an extension of the reconquest of the Iberian peninsula.[6] The Spanish monarchs, as an incentive to the conquest of the Moors, had been granted extensive powers by the Catholic Church. The "Most Catholic Monarchs" were given the authority to nominate all major prelates and to reap the rewards of tithes and endowments "assigned to the support of religion."[7] Therefore papal bulls, promulgated centuries earlier, are essential to an understanding of Catholicism in Spanish Louisiana. *Orthodoxiae fidei propagationem*, granted in 1486 by Innocent VIII to Fernando and Isabella, stated that "Hence it is that Catholic Kings and princes, athletes of Christ and tireless warriors battling in that cause, never fail to find in us their deserved assistance and favor." In 1493 a series of papal bulls addressed the relation of church and state in the New World. Beginning with the confidential *Inter caetera*, and followed by *Pius fidelium*, a second *Inter caetera*, *Eximiae devotionis*, and *Dudum siquidem*, Alexander VI gave Spain exclusive rights to all the islands and land (respecting Portuguese rights) and apostolic privileges for Christianizing the New World.[8] Julius II's *Universalis ecclesiae* of 1508, reinforced the bulls of Alexander VI.[9] The consent of civil authority was required for the establishment and functioning of every cathedral, parish church, convent, hospital, and charitable organization in the New World. The establishment of dioceses and the immigration of clergy to the New World were governed by agencies of the Crown. Archbishops and bishops were nominated by the Crown for formal appointment by the pope.[10] The special relation to the church that Spain enjoyed in the New World was nothing new. The workings of church and state had been so interrelated that they were basically inseparable.

The French residents of Louisiana, upon learning that they were Spanish subjects, felt betrayed by France. They did not mind showing their displeasure over the prospect of Spanish rule.[11] To further complicate matters, Antonio de Ulloa (1716-1795), the first Spanish governor, had far more experience as a naval officer and scientist than as an administrator or governor.[12] In 1769 to establish Spanish authority in the colony, Charles III dispatched Alejandro O'Reilly (1723-1794) to Louisiana as governor.[13] A soldier-administrator, credited with saving the king's life, the Irish-born O'Reilly wasted no time in fulfilling his mandate.[14]

When Alejandro O'Reilly arrived in New Orleans aboard the Spanish frigate *Volante* in August 1769, every effort was taken to make his entry as triumphant as possible. It was a calculated celebration designed to affirm the Spanish presence in the troubled colony. As representative of the king, His Most Catholic Majesty Charles III, O'Reilly was received with full religious and military ceremonies.[15] The vast province was no longer to look northward to Quebec for political leadership and orders, but rather to Cuba. Accordingly, the bishop of Santiago, Cuba, was entrusted with the spiritual affairs of the new colony.[16] While residents were uncomfortable with this new-found relation to Cuba, the transfer from France to Spain solidified the province's long-existing relation with its more southerly neighbors.[17]

O'Reilly, fully aware of his role as guardian of the faith, quickly realized that Spanish religious and civil officials were confronted by a new reality. Both a French population puzzled by Spanish religious practices and the immense geographical territory of Louisiana challenged O'Reilly and subsequent governors.[18] No time was wasted in announcing that a person found wanting in observance of religious regulations or guilty of moral turpitude would be punished.[19] Exercising almost complete authority over the Church, O'Reilly quickly communicated to authorities the lamentable lack of missionaries to care for the spiritual needs of the Catholics in the vast territory. In a letter dated November 10, 1769, he informed Antonio Bucareli, captain general of Cuba, that the battalion stationed in Louisiana needed a chaplain. He specifically requested a chaplain who could learn French quickly.[20] Realizing the French Capuchins would not be sending any more priests to Louisiana, he requested missionaries from Spain. While some Capuchins working in Louisiana chose to remain, others found Spanish rule unattractive and returned to France.[21]

The prominence of the Capuchins, and in earlier years the Carmelites and Jesuits in Louisiana, underscores the lack of secular clergy. The "spiritual conquest" of Louisiana, like the rest of the Spanish New World since the sixteenth century, was plagued by the absence of the secular or diocesan clergy. The lack of such clergy meant that the regular clergy, (religious orders such as Franciscans, Dominicans, Capuchins, and Jesuits), were granted powers normally reserved for the secular clergy.[22]

O'Reilly's instructions to Athanase de Mézières[23] at Natchitoches reflect the interrelations of church and state. O'Reilly not only ordered the post's church repaired, but made it clear that it was the responsibility of every parishioner to contribute. The parishioners heeded the word of De Mézières and the post's Capuchin missionary, Father Stanislas, and built a new church. O'Reilly's tenure in Louisiana ended prior to the completion of the church, but his handpicked successor as governor, Luis de Unzaga,[24] did see it completed. During the course of construction, Father Stanislas asked to be reassigned. Although his request was denied, by early 1774 Natchitoches was without a missionary.[25]

Unzaga's actions reiterated O'Reilly's commitment to the enforcement of the laws and regulations of the Catholic Church. He viewed the remaining French Capuchins as good and virtuous clerics but contended that some knew their duties and others did not.[26] He complained to Spanish officials that some churches were without priests. He was aware of O'Reilly's plan for eighteen priests for the province with some six for New Orleans alone.[27] All were to be assigned within the boundaries of the present state of Louisiana with the exception of the two priests assigned to the posts of St. Louis and Ste. Genevieve. The governor's reports alerted Bishop Echevarría of Cuba and appropriate Spanish officials that it was necessary to send more priests to serve the spiritual needs of the colonists. The arrival of Spanish Capuchins ushered in a new period, marked by long overdue expansion, for the Catholic Church in Louisiana.[28]

Unzaga also acknowledged that the missionaries would need assistance in more temporal affairs, such as housing. The dilapidated residence of the Capuchins in New Orleans was uninhabitable and immediately upon arrival Unzaga ordered the construction of a new rectory. If Unzaga realized the importance of a new rectory, it was his good fortune that Andrés Almonester y Roxas arrived shortly before Unzaga succeeded O'Reilly in 1770. Eventually Almonester would become the great builder of Spanish New Orleans.[29] Offering his Most Catholic Majesty the Royal Hospital (1783), the Lepers' Hospital (1785), and the church of the Ursuline nuns (1787), he assured himself a place in history. However, immediately after the great fire of 1788, Almonester promised to build a new rectory, parish church, and a structure for the *cabildo*. He was rewarded with special privileges, including a special seat of honor in the sanctuary of the cathedral when the diocese was erected.[30]

The Spanish Capuchins quickly realized that to achieve success they would have to adapt themselves to the reality of life in Louisiana. Father Cirilo de Barcelona, appointed superior of the newly arrived missionaries in 1772,[31] immediately began to learn French. He viewed it as an indispensable tool in the establishment of the Spanish Catholic Church in Louisiana. A tireless worker who followed an austere and rigid life style, he soon clashed with the French Capuchins. Living what Cirilo found to be a relaxed life style, the French Capuchins had become lax in their adherence to rules and regulations. He frowned on their owning slaves to work their plantation. The ownership of slaves by the Church had been addressed under French rule in November 1743. The Church was not allowed to accept slaves as part of a bequest, nor was it allowed to receive money that resulted from the sale of slaves.[32] Cirilo quickly communicated his views on the matter to officials in Cuba. However, the enormous popularity of the French Father Dagobert, pastor of the Church of St. Louis in New Orleans, tempered any enthusiastic cries for reform.[33]

Indeed, French customs and views remained well and alive in Spanish Louisiana. While Almonester's cabildo building, cathedral, and presbytère and his daughter's (the Baroness Pontalba) buildings constitute one of the great civic centers in the United States,[34] no striking innovations by Spanish administrators remain, and no distinctive social trends resulting from Spanish law or practice have yet come to light. Their desire was not to upset the French colonists unduly.[35] The Spaniards did, however, introduce laws governing the treatment of slaves. Slaves were granted a limited right to sue their masters in court when laws governing them were ignored.[36] More importantly, the right for slaves to purchase their freedom was introduced in 1769.[37] Indeed, from 1771 to 1805, the number of free people of color increased from 97 to 1,566, while the number of slaves increased less then threefold, from 1,227 to 3,105.[38]

Bernardo de Gálvez became governor in 1777.[39] A member of a family prominent in Spanish political affairs, he was the nephew of José de Gálvez, minister of the Indies and the embodiment of the Bourbon Reforms. Bernardo's father was captain general of Central America and soon became the viceroy of Mexico, a position Bernardo himself would eventually hold. Realizing his mission as protector of the faith, he reported that no bishop had set foot in Louisiana since the founding of the colony. As a result, the sacrament of confirmation had not been conferred on individuals. Both civil and religious authorities thought a visit to Louisiana by the bishop of Santiago, Cuba, would be too difficult, so five missionaries were authorized to grant the sacrament of confirmation.[40]

The lack of a visitation by the bishop of Santiago emphasized the ecclesiastical and spiritual problems resulting from governing the colony from afar and called for a change in ecclesiastical jurisdiction. Previously governed by vicars general, from 1784 to 1791 Louisiana was under the jurisdiction of an auxiliary bishop of Cuba (first of Santiago, then Havana upon the creation of that diocese) resident in the colony. Although the king approved Cirilo de Barcelona as auxiliary bishop resident in New Orleans, Pope Pius VI did not issue the bulls of appointment until 1784 and he was not consecrated titular Bishop of Tricali in Havana until March 6, 1785. Cirilo was to rectify such problems as the lack of proper observance of religious regulations by both clergy and laity.[41]

The relationship of church and state is pointed out clearly in a December 24, 1784, entry in the acts of the *cabildo* of New Orleans. It appears that Cirilo, as acting bishop, appointed a church warden without proper regard for the customs of the colony. The *cabildo* asked that the appointment be revoked. Bernardo de Gálvez instead requested that the *cabildo* apologize to Cirilo for their actions.[42]

In 1787 the newly created diocese of Havana assumed responsibility for Louisiana.[43] Cirilo had to inform Havana of bad news on several occasions, ranging from antagonism toward the Spanish missionaries, the 1788 fire which destroyed the parish church of St. Louis, and the lack of proper religious education for black slaves. News of such lax standards in Louisiana were not unusual. Therefore, a royal edict of May 31, 1789, established regulations for the direction, education, and occupation of slaves. To the dismay of plantation masters, chaplains were to exercise the role as spiritual leaders not only to the plantation owners, but also the slaves.[44]

International politics also helped to shape the development of Catholicism in Louisiana, as seen in the case of the Acadians and the refugees of Saint-Domingue, who were allowed to enter Spanish Louisiana. In permitting the Acadian and Santo Domingo immigrations, the Spaniards actually helped to preserve the French language.[45] New parishes were founded out of necessity, and soon Cirilo found himself repeating cries for additional priests.

Challenged by the Spanish conquest of West Florida, Cirilo was well aware that Spanish-speaking missionaries would be totally unacceptable in that former English possession. He, therefore, obtained the services of four Irish missionaries studying at the University of Salamanca. They served the English of West Florida and eventually were employed elsewhere in Louisiana.[46]

The best known Spanish cleric in New Orleans was Antonio de Sedella, best remembered as Père Antoine. Any person who simultaneously held several offices was destined to be controversial. Père Antoine managed always to be at the center of difficulties from the day he arrived in 1781 until his death in 1829.[47] However, the career of Père Antoine reflects the Catholic Church in Louisiana as part of the Spanish Catholic Church. He was appointed pastor of the parish of St. Louis by Bishop Echevarría of Cuba in 1787 upon the advice of Esteban Miró, governor of Louisiana.[48] The governor pointed out to the bishop that Sedella had served in an exemplary manner while pastor *pro tem* and should therefore be named pastor.

Unfortunately, difficulties began almost immediately after the Good Friday fire of 1788 that destroyed the parish church. Even though New Orleans lacked an appropriate church in 1789, Père Antoine led the memorial services for Charles III, and the religious ceremonies honoring the new monarch, Charles IV.[49] Conditions in New Orleans are quickly revealed when one realizes that music for full orchestra and choir was commissioned for those ceremonies in other New World cities,[50] while the most New Orleans had to offer its monarchs was the chapel of Charity Hospital.

The lack of appropriate facilities for such prominent ceremonies, the destruction of the Spanish school by fire in 1788 (and its subsequent dwindling enrollment), the infiltration of Americans into the colony, the fact that parents still preferred their children to attend French schools, and the French Revolution of 1789 were all indications of a situation which would only deteriorate. After numerous unsuccessful attempts to direct the religious affairs of the colony from distant points through first a vicar general and then an auxiliary bishop, a report, dated August 27, 1792, describing the deplorable condition of both religious and ecclesiastical affairs was forwarded to Madrid. It recommended the separation of Louisiana from the ecclesiastical jurisdiction of Havana and the erection of the Diocese of Louisiana and the Floridas with New Orleans as its see.[51] Ironically, it was Antonio de Ulloa, responding to economic and geographic concerns, who had first called for the creation of a diocese in Louisiana.[52] It was Francisco Luis Héctor, Baron de Carondelet's great pleasure to see a diocese established in New Orleans during his tenure as governor.[53] The career administrator served throughout the Spanish realm, from San Salvador to Quito. In Quito he concerned himself with artistic glories,[54] as opposed to more mundane tasks in New Orleans, such as the construction of sidewalks, levees, and Carondelet Canal.[55] With word of the creation of the Diocese of Louisiana and the Floridas, Cirilo de Barcelona returned to Cuba. Nearly two years, however, would pass before Luis Peñalver y Cárdenas (1749-1810) would assume his responsibilities as first bishop of the new diocese in 1795.

Peñalver y Cárdenas was exceptional among Spanish New World bishops, in that he was a native of the Western Hemisphere. Born in Cuba, he was an individual of exceptional talents.[56] He and his brother bishops in the Spanish New World were charged with the evangelization, education, and welfare of the colonials.[57] Until his arrival, Father Patricio Walsh, an Irish priest who had been educated in Spain, oversaw the religious affairs of the province. Carondelet and Walsh endured a variety of problems together, ranging from a declining number of priests to another major fire (which at least spared the new Church of St. Louis). The temporary church was destroyed in the

December 8, 1794, fire and the new church was pressed into service even before the first bishop could arrive. Thus the present St. Louis Cathedral was dedicated on Christmas Eve 1794–minus its bishop and with an Irish priest presiding.

When Luis Peñalver y Cárdenas did arrive, he was greeted with all proper religious and civic ceremony. A servant of both God and king, he was most likely unaware, at that time, that his appointment and term of office coincided with one last futile effort of Spain to hold on to Louisiana to protect more valuable possessions.[58] Returning at the same time, after several years of banishment, was Père Antoine. Relieved of his duties in New Orleans because of political intrigue, he had his case pled directly before the king, who issued an edict reinstating him as pastor of the Church of St. Louis.[59]

In an effort to revitalize the Catholic Church in Louisiana, the new bishop eagerly called for a diocesan synod. Holding such a meeting would have placed undue stress on the entire diocese because of the lack of clergy and amount of time required for all clergy to assemble from throughout the colony. Therefore, he prepared an extensive sixty-three paragraph "Instrucción para el Gobierno de los Párrocos de la Diócesis de la Luisiana" for clergy reminding them of the necessity of proper observance of all rituals, ranging from the number of wax candles needed for certain services, the proper way to kneel, to more important matters such as the right of the king to establish schools. Pastors were urged not only to fulfill all religious duties, but also to be especially careful of the rights of the Crown in ecclesiastical matters.[60]

The first bishop strove vigorously to administer the established parishes under his care, as well as those of the Illinois country, Mississippi, and the Floridas. Peñalver y Cárdenas has been described as a stern prelate "whose main goals in Louisiana were to preserve the purity of faith, drive out error, and correct sinful habits."[61] An indication of his activity on behalf of his territory is shown by his four visitations in the diocese. The first (1795) focused on the immediate area of New Orleans, the second (1796) covered the German Coast to Natchez, the third (1796) included Attakapas, Opelousas and Natchitoches, and the fourth (1797) was a relatively long trip to Mobile and Pensacola. Only the small establishments of St. Louis, New Madrid, and Ste. Genevieve were omitted.[62]

The importance of accurate record keeping by the Spanish is quickly revealed by the inspection of the sacramental registers of St. Louis Cathedral by Luis Peñalver y Cárdenas. The newly arrived bishop was distressed by the number of omissions and mistakes. He repeated that criticism during his visit to St. John the Baptist Parish in Edgard, Louisiana, during October, 1795,[63] and to Natchez in 1796.[64]

He quickly seized upon situations that could be used to promote the Church. Pierre Janin, a priest who fled the French Revolution, eventually settled in the Diocese of Louisiana and the Floridas, and not fond of larger cities, was sent by Peñalver y Cárdenas to clergy barren Arkansas. Sent to minister to the faithful at *Los Arcas*, he established the first parish in 1796. Janin was instructed by the bishop to construct a small house, where he was to administer the sacraments and maintain all necessary records. Peñalver y

Cárdenas seems to have taken a personal interest in attending to Janin's needs. He requested that churches give Janin supplies and himself sent needed items from his own chapel.[65]

The lack of sufficient clergy remained a constant theme until the final years of Spanish rule. The absence of priests well educated in moral and dogmatic theology, logic, and Latin was only one set of problems plaguing local education of young men for the priesthood. Students had not been taught Latin and were not inclined toward the study of theology. Rather, they were more apt to follow in the footsteps of their fathers who were navigators, fishermen, or hunters.[66] On July 24, 1800, a royal decree was issued establishing a position specifically for the instruction of such needed skills. In that royal order, insight is gained into Louisiana as part of the Spanish empire as funding was to come from the Mexican dioceses of Mexico City, Puebla, and Michoacán.[67]

Events during the first bishop's tenure reminded all that Louisiana served "His Most Catholic Majesty." Carondelet was transferred to Quito, where he served as president of the *audiencia*.[68] By 1801, Manuel Luis Gayoso de Lemos y Amorin, Sebastián Calvo de la Puerta y O'Farril, Marqués de Casa-Calvo, Francisco Bouligny, and Manuel Juan de Salcedo would serve Louisiana as governors. Bishop Peñalver y Cárdenas found the situation, particularly the climate, in the new diocese taxing and requested reassignment in 1799.[69] Two years later, in the service of God and king, he was selected to be the sixth archbishop of Guatemala, a far more prestigious post.[70]

Because of the cession of Louisiana to France, Francisco Porro, the chosen successor to Peñalver y Cárdenas, never took possession of his diocese. While waiting to depart, he was reassigned to the Diocese of Tarazona, Spain.[71] Thomas Hassett was charged with the operations of the province. He faced critical questions such as determining the diocese's relation with the American government, the fate of church records, and the future of the priests attached to the cathedral, the Ursuline nuns, and the regular and secular clergy.[72]

The Spanish period saw the growth of the Church: new parishes were established in St. Martinville (1765), St. James (1769), Donaldsonville and Edgard (1772), Opelousas (1777), Galvez Town and St. Gabriel (1779), St. Bernard (1787), Assumption and Baton Rouge (1793), and Avoyelles (1797). Many new colonists also arrived from Acadia (1765-1785),[73] the Canary Islands (1778-1783),[74] and St. Domingue (1790s).[75] Other colonists came from Mexico, Cuba, and Chile. In addition, English-speaking people came from New England, New York, Virginia, Maryland, Pennsylvania, and South Carolina.[76]

Sacramental records provide a fascinating view of Spanish New Orleans. During 1780, some 410 people (mostly children) were baptized in the Church of St. Louis. Approximately 300 were slaves or free persons of color, while just 110 were children of white parents. New Orleans was a cosmopolitan town according to the marriage records of the same year. Of the forty-three marriages, only nineteen of the brides and thirteen of the grooms were from New Orleans. The remainder of the parties contracting matrimony were from Acadia, the Canary Islands, Cuba, Ireland, Illinois, Italy, South Carolina, Virginia, Quebec, and Spain.[77] Ten years later (1790), some 585 persons were baptized. Again, the majority (450) of the baptized were either slaves or free people of color. Some 110 adult slaves were baptized on Holy Saturday alone.[78] Ten years later (1800), sacramental records again reveal the ethnic fabric of New Orleans. Fifty-two percent of the persons baptized in the cathedral were slaves, thirty-one percent were whites, and seventeen percent were free persons of color. The baptismal records demonstrate that eighty percent of the mothers were natives of Louisiana, in contrast to only forty-five percent of the fathers. Of the couples whose marriages were celebrated in 1800, eighty-two percent of the brides were natives of Louisiana, only forty percent of the grooms were born in the colony. Of the 242 individuals whose death was recorded at the cathedral, seventy-six were white, fifty-five were free persons of color and 111 were slaves.[79]

In 1802 the French colonial prefect of Louisiana, Pierre Clément de Laussat noted that missionaries were needed in the colony.[80] In a letter to Denis Decrès, minister of the Marine and the Colonies, he explained the need to reassure the clergy of the importance of their services and of the support that they could expect from the French government. His pronouncement was welcomed by the Louisiana clergy. He stressed that funds were needed to pay the salaries of the religious and asked that a sum be sent for that expense immediately.[81] As part of Laussat's effort to gain a firm grasp on religious affairs, Thomas Hassett (vicar general of Louisiana and the Floridas), prepared a report listing the religious parishes of Louisiana, and the names of the clergy, both secular and regular. The report included information on their salaries and subsidies received from the royal treasury.[82] At the same time, the Irish-born and Spanish-educated Hassett, one of Peñalver's two canons, prepared a new schedule of fees for the cathedral parish. Rules for the proper observance of religious ceremonies were explained in detail.[83]

In his letter to Bishop John Carroll of Baltimore, Laussat confided that in contrast to the French and Spanish governments, he believed that the new American government would take little or no interest in the religious affairs of the province.[84] With the completion of Laussat's responsibilities to oversee the Louisiana Transfer, he left for Martinique,[85] and the initial Americanization of the Catholic Church in Louisiana, accustomed to French and Spanish ways, would begin. That process, however, took almost a century.

Notes for "Spanish Louisiana: In the Service of God and His Most Catholic Majesty"

[1]Herbert Eugene Bolton, *Texas in the Middle Eighteenth Century* (Austin, 1970), 102-3.

[2]Light T. Cummins, "Antonio de Ulloa, 1766-1768," *The Louisiana Governors: From Iberville to Edwards*, ed. Joseph G. Dawson III (Baton Rouge, 1990), 56.

[3]Troy S. Floyd, *The Bourbon Reformers and Spanish Civilization: Builders or Destroyers?* (Boston, 1966), ix-xi.

[4]Richard E. Greenleaf, ed., *The Roman Catholic Church in Colonial Latin America* (Tempe, AZ, 1977), 1.

[5]William Eugene Shiels, *King and Church: The Rise and Fall of the Patronato Real* (Chicago, 1961), 18.

[6]Edwin Edward Sylvest, Jr., *Motifs of Franciscan Mission Theory in Sixteenth Century New Spain Province of the Holy Gospel* (Washington, DC, 1975), 4.

[7]Ibid., 11.

[8]L. Weckmann, "Alexandrine Bulls," *New Catholic Encyclopedia*, 18 vols. (New York, 1967), 1:306.

[9]W. M. Porras, "Patronato of Spain," *New Catholic Encyclopedia*, 10:1115-16.

[10]France V. Scholes, "Church and State in New Mexico 1610-1650," *New Mexico Historical Review*, 11 (1936): 9-19.

[11]"Noticias presentadas por Antonio de Ulloa sobre los acontecimientos de Luisiana en el año 1769, incluyendo la conspiración que se declaró el 29 de Octubre." Archivo General de Indias, Seville, Audiencia de Santo Domingo, legajo 2543, folios 31-124; hereafter AGI, Santo Domingo.

[12]John Preston Moore, "Antonio de Ulloa: Profile of the First Spanish Governor of Louisiana," *Louisiana History*, 8 (1967): 189-218.

[13]Eric Beerman, "Alexander O'Reilly, An Irish Soldier in the Service of Spain," *The Irish Sword: The Journal of the Military History Society of Ireland*, 15/59 (1982): 101-4; Jack D. L. Holmes, "Alexander O'Reilly, Colonial Governor, 1769-1770," Dawson, ed., *Louisiana Governors*, 56-60.

[14]"Sobre la llegada de Alejandro O'Reilly y providencias que tomó para arrestar las principales cabezas de la sublevación, etc." AGI, Santo Domingo, legajo 2543, folios 125-262.

[15]Actas de Cabildo, Volume I, Book I, f. 1; New Orleans Public Library, Louisiana Division. "Alejandro O'Reilly sobre su viaje y llegada a Nueva Orleans, con las 22 embarcaciones del convoy, recibimientos y entrevista con el gobernador francés y ceremonias de la toma de posesion por parte de España de aquella colonia, 31 agosto, 1769. [Julián Paz, *Catálogo de Manuscritos de América existentes en la Biblioteca Nacional* (Madrid, 1933), Entry 275, document 22.

[16]J. M. Pérez Cabrera, "Santiago de Cuba, Archdiocese of," *New Catholic Encyclopedia*, 12:1073.

[17]"Résumé annoté par le ministre de diverse lettres de M. de Bienville, April 10, 1706. France. Archives Nationales, Archives des Colonies, Série C13a, 1, ff. 502-13; hereafter ANF.

[18]Alexandre O'Reilly, lieutenant général espagnol, à Charles Philippe Aubry. Demande des noms des instigateurs de la révolte d'octobre 1768 contre Ulloa. ANF, C13a, 49, ff. 37-38r.

[19]Roger Baudier, *The Catholic Church in Louisiana* (New Orleans, 1939), 181.

[20]David Ker Texada, "The Administration of Alejandro O'Reilly as Governor of Louisiana, 1769-1770" (Ph. D. dissertation, Louisiana State University, 1969), 240.

[21]Baudier, *Catholic Church*, 180.

[22]Charles Edwards O'Neill, *Church and State in French Colonial Louisiana: Policy and Politics to 1732* (New Haven, 1966). Jean Delanglez, S.J., *The French Jesuits in Lower Louisiana (1700-1763)* (Washington, DC, 1935). New Orleans Public Library, Louisiana Division, Actas de Cabildo. In the session of March 4, 1774, Governor Luis de Unzaga presented the royal edict, dated October 12, 1773, of Clement XIV, dissolving the Jesuits.

[23]Herbert Eugene Bolton, *Athanase de Mézières and the Louisiana-Texas Frontier, 1768-1780* (Cleveland, 1914), 75-92.

[24]Light T. Cummins, "Luis de Unzaga y Amezaga," Dawson, ed., *Louisiana Governors,* 52-56.

[25]Athanase de Mézières to Luis de Unzaga, Natchitoches, February 1, 1770. AGI, Papeles de Cuba, legajo 110, f. 96; Baudier, *Catholic Church,* 182.

[26]"Relación del Gobierno actual de la provincia de la Luisiana en lo espiritual y noticias de su constitución y establecimiento por don Luis de Unzaga. Nueva Orleans, November 14, 1772. (Sobre el modelo que ha dado el Gobernador de Luisiana Unzaga a aquel Diocesano para el gobierno espirituel, 1772-1774), AGI, Santo Domingo, legajo 2594, ff. 748-97.

[27]Texada, "O'Reilly," 241.

[28]Baudier, *Catholic Church,* 188-89.

[29]Samuel Wilson, "Almonester: Philanthropist and Builder in New Orleans," in John Francis McDermott, ed., *The Spanish in the Mississippi Valley, 1762-1804* (Urbana, 1974), 183-84.

[30]"Royal Order that Andrés Almonester y Roxas be granted the use of a special tribune in the Church of New Orleans," May 4, 1795, Archives, Archdiocese of New Orleans; hereafter AANO.

[31]Baudier, *Catholic Church,* 185.

[32]Declaration du Roy concernat les Ordres Religieux establis aux Colonies françois de l'Amérique, November 25, 1743, The Historic New Orleans Collection, MSS 352; hereafter HNOC.

[33]Baudier, *Catholic Church,* 187.

[34]Wilson, "Almonester," 247.

[35]Thomas Ingersoll, "Old New Orleans: Race, Class, Sex and Order in the Early Deep South, 1718-1819" (Ph. D. dissertation, University of California, Los Angeles, 1990), 515.

[36]Ibid., 570.

[37]Ibid., 584, and Kimberly S. Hanger, "Personas de Varias Clases y Colores: Free People of Color in Spanish New Orleans, 1769-1803" (Ph. D. dissertation, University of Florida, 1991).

[38]Hanger, "Personas," 41.

[39]Jack D. L. Holmes, "Bernardo de Gálvez, Colonial Governor, 1777-1783," in Dawson, ed., *Louisiana Governors,* 56-61. Ralph Lee Woodward, Jr., trans. and ed., *Tribute to Bernardo de Galvez: Royal Patents and Epic Ballad Honoring the Spanish Governor of Louisiana* (New Orleans, 1979).

[40]María del Carmen Cerbián González, "El Obispado de Nueva Orleans," *Hispania Sacra,* 40 (1988): 781-82.

[41]Ibid., 782-83.

[42]Actas de Cabildo, Book 3, Volume 1, f. 13. Louisiana Division, New Orleans Public Library.

[43]J. M. Pérez Cabrera, "Havana, Archdiocese of," *New Catholic Encyclopedia,* 6:951. Gonzàlez, "Obispado," 782.

[44]Baudier, *Catholic Church,* 204-7, 215.

[45]Carl A. Brasseaux, *The Founding of New Acadia: The Beginnings of Acadian Life in Louisiana, 1765-1803* (Baton Rouge, 1987), 73-89.

[46]Jack D. L. Holmes, "Irish Priests in Spanish Natchez," *Journal of Mississippi History,* 29 (1967): 169-80. AGI, Papeles de Cuba, legajos 594 and 601 contain further information on the question of Irish priests in Spanish Louisiana.

[47]Richard E. Greenleaf, "The Inquisition in Spanish Louisiana, 1762-1800," *New Mexico Historical Review,* 50 (1975): 45-72. Charles Edwards O'Neill, S.J., "'A Quarter Marked by Sundry Peculiarities': New Orleans, Lay Trustees and Père Antoine," *Catholic Historical Review,* 76 (1990): 235-77.

[48]Caroline Maude Buison, *The Stewardship of Don Esteban Miró, 1782-1790* (New Orleans, 1940).

[49]Actas de Cabildo, Book 3, Volume 2, ff. 113-119. Louisiana Division, New Orleans Public Library.

[50]Alfred E. Lemmon, *Music from Eighteenth-Century Guatemala* (S. Woodstock, 1986), 8.

[51]"Informe sobre si será conveniente segregar las Provincias de la Luisiana y la Florida de la Diocese de la Habana y establecer un obispo proprio en aquella ciudad [Nueva Orleans], AGI, Santo Domingo, legajo 2674, ff. 83-84.

[52]Bibiano Torres Ramez, *Alejandro O'Reilly en las Indias* (Sevilla, 1969), 173-77.

[53]Thomas Fiehrer, "The Baron de Carondelet as Agent of Bourbon Reform: A Study of Spanish Colonial Administration" (Ph. D., dissertation, Tulane University, 1977), 367-77.

[54]Robert Stevenson, "Quito Cathedral: Four Centuries," *Inter-American Music Review,* 3 (1980): 33.

[55]Receipt for work by Francisco Dorcillia and Roberto Monplaisir, February 18, 1793. HNOC, MSS 54.

[56]Eric Beerman, "A Genealogical Study of Luis Peñalver y Cárdenas: Spain's First Bishop of Louisiana and the Floridas," *Records of the American Catholic Historical Society,* 84 (1978): 33-34. Also consult Josefina Alonso de Rodríguez, "El Illmo. S. D. D. Luis Peñalver y Cárdenas, VI Azobispo de Guatemala" (M.A. Thesis, Universidad de San Carlos de Guatemala, 1972).

[57]Antonine Tibesar, "Latin America, Churches in" *New Catholic Encyclopedia,* 8:451.

[58]Michael J. Curley, C.SS.R., *Church and State in the Spanish Floridas (1783-1822)* (Washington, DC, 1940), 260.

[59]Baudier, *Catholic Church,* 225-26.

[60]Ibid., 209-12; Curley, *Spanish Floridas,* 261-64.

[61]Charles E. Nolan, *St. Mary's of Natchez: The History of a Southern Catholic Congregation, 1716-1888,* 2 vols. (Natchez, 1992), 1:72.

[62]Curley, *Spanish Floridas,* 262-63.

[63]Earl C. Woods and Charles E. Nolan, eds., *Sacramental Records of the Roman Catholic Church of the Archdiocese of New Orleans,* 7 vols. (New Orleans, 1987-1992), 6 (1796-1799): xviii.

[64]Nolan, *St. Mary's,* 1:72-73.

[65]Morris S. Arnold, *Colonial Arkansas, 1686-1804: A Social and Cultural History* (Fayetteville, 1991), 90-91.

[66]El Obispo de la Luisiana sobre la necesidad de fundar un seminario conciliar en aquella capital, AGI, Santo Domingo, legajo 2531, ff. 556-57.

[67]"Al Gobernador de la Luisiana. Participándole haberse resuelto se erija una cátedra de Gramática, Lógica, Moral y Dogma y ordenándole auxielie al obispo dela Luisiana," AGI, Santo Domingo, legajo 2529, f. 13.

[68]Fiehrer, "Baron de Carondelet," 584-94.

[69]El Opispo Peñalver al Rey, Nueva Orleans, July 21, 1799 (Varias representaciones de Luis Peñalver, Obispo de Luisiana), AGI, Santo Domingo, legajo 2589, ff. 499-540.

[70]Agustin Estrada Monroy, *Datos para la Historia de la Iglesia en Guatemala,* 30 vols. (Guatemala, 1972), 2:185-97.

[71]El Obispo Porro, Aranjuez, 28 de octubre de 1803 (Sobre nombramiento de Francisco Porro, para Obispo de Luisiana), AGI, Santo Domingo, legajo 2672, ff. 113-235.

[72]Cerbrian González, "Obispado," 788.

[73]John Howard Young, "The Acadians and Roman Catholicism: In Acadia from 1710 to the expulsion, in exile, and in Louisiana from the 1760s until 1803" (Ph. D. dissertation, Southern Methodist, 1988), 252-54.

[74]Gilbert C. Din, "Canary Islander Settlements of Spanish Louisiana: An Overview," *Louisiana History,* 27 (1986): 353-74; *The Canary Islanders of Louisiana* (Baton Rouge, 1988).

[75]Gabriel Debien and René Le Gardeur, "Les colons de Saint-Domingue Réfugiés à la Louisiane, 1792-1804," *Revue de Louisiane/Louisiana Review,* 10 (1981): 11-49.

[76]*Sacramental Records,* 3:xix.

[77]Ibid., xx.

[78]*Sacramental Records,* 4:xx-xxi.

[79]*Sacramental Records,* 7:xix-xx.

[80]"Report of Laussat on matters pertaining to Louisiana," October 21, 1802, HNOC, MSS 125.

[81]Letter from Pierre Clément de Laussat to Denis Decrès, minister of the Marine in Paris, April 13, 1803, HNOC, MSS 125.

[82]Report on the parishes and the clergy serving in the province of Louisiana, April 18, 1803, HNOC, MSS 125.

[83]Schedule of fees for the Parish of the Holy Cathedral Church of Louisiana, April 18, 1803, HNOC, MSS 125.

[84] Letter from Pierre Clément de Laussat to Bishop John Carroll, Baltimore, January 28, 1804, HNOC, MSS 125.

[85]Pierre Clément de Laussat, *Memoirs of My Life. . .,* trans. and intro., by Agnes-Josephine Pastwa, ed. and fwd. Robert D. Bush (Baton Rouge, 1978), 105-6.

CHURCH COURTS, MARRIAGE BREAKDOWN, AND SEPARATION IN SPANISH LOUISIANA, WEST FLORIDA, AND TEXAS, 1763-1836*

Light Townsend Cummins

The phenomenon of marital breakdown is clearly reflected in the records of church courts in Spanish colonial Louisiana and Texas from the 1760s through the 1830s.[1] At first glance, the chronological and geographic boundaries of this historiographical focus may appear to be somewhat unorthodox.[2] Historians seldom link these two provinces, except in the broadest definitional sense, as being parts of the Hispanic frontier of North America. Spanish and Mexican Texas are also treated herein as an entity.[3] The restricted geographical orientation of much scholarship on these areas obscures significant points of common reference for the various parts of the North American Hispanic frontier. The conceptualization of social history does not always follow the traditional way in which we view political history. In particular, the day-to-day social and cultural experiences of residents in Spanish Louisiana and Texas in matters of family life, religion, material culture, personal economy, and folkways created a commonality just as remarkable as their dissimilar governmental institutions and administrative structures.

This commonality is certainly the case in considering the family. Louisiana and Texas during the period examined shared the tenets of Hispanic law and the Roman Catholic Church. The study of marriage breakdown, therefore, provides an appealing opportunity to focus on the family for both areas as common parts of a cultural imperium reflecting the same normative social values as embodied in civil and canon law. The records of church court proceedings regarding marital disputes in Spanish Louisiana (including its post-1783 West Florida district) and Texas contain much information about family values. Such records, however, are anecdotal, limited in number, and therefore statistically unrepresentative.[4] Moreover, as Richard Boyer has observed, divorce records

*First published in the *Journal of Texas Catholic History and Culture*, 4 (1993): 97-114. Reprinted with the kind permission of the author and publisher.

deal with atypical spouses who were "engaged in the politics of marriage in which power and resentment, alliances and isolation, practicality and idealism were jumbled up."[5] Nonetheless, church court cases do provide a window through which some everyday experiences of family life can be viewed, albeit in a negative sense.

The Roman Catholic Church in Texas and Louisiana, as elsewhere throughout the Spanish empire, permitted marriage to be terminated by annulment or suspended by separation (*divorcium a mensa et thoro* or "divorce from bed and board" as it was called). Annulment falls beyond the focus of this essay, but it deserves limited mention. A myth perpetuated from earlier eras of historical writing implies that annulment was a popular and frequent way to end a marriage, especially among the elite classes of western society. Recent research has called this assumption into question and now many historians of marriage argue that such was not the case. Evidence from Louisiana and Texas supports the contention that annulment was rarely used as mechanism to end marriage and, when it did occur, it was not a symptom of marital breakdown. Only two cases in this study involve annulments. Both were related to the special historical circumstances created by Louisiana's proximity to and contact with British areas to the northeast. Annulments could be granted on the "precontract" condition when one of the partners in the union had already been married at an earlier time.

These two cases arose in Louisiana when local residents married immigrants from the Atlantic Coast arriving as part of the Anglo-American influx into the province. Both of these actions were brought by men who found that their wives had contracted earlier unions. For example, in 1784 Pedro Boydant brought suit before the ecclesiastical court at New Orleans seeking an annulment of his marriage of six years. He had recently learned that his wife, Susanna, had been married in a Protestant ceremony to an English subject during her earlier residence in New England. Susanna had supposed that her first husband had died and, presumably for that reason, she never informed the trusting Pedro. The first husband, however, had recently surfaced in Jamaica with the result that Boydant filed suit "to bring into the record" his wife's first marriage under the terms of precontract.

The second case was brought to the church court by Antonio Marmillon, who sought an annulment on behalf of his daughter Margarita. The young woman had been married to John Joseph Dorquingny for almost two years and, during that time, Don Antonio reported officially that the marriage had never been consummated. The husband had immigrated from Philadelphia, where he had lived before his residence in Louisiana. News from the Atlantic Coast indicated that Dorquingny also had a wife living in the Pennsylvania port city. The husband, however, denied the accusation after being confronted by Margarita and her father. John Joseph's refusal to confess to bigamy forced the ecclesiastical judge, Father Cirilo de Barcelona, to conduct a full-scale inquiry into the matter.

The judge ordered John Joseph to be incarcerated in the public jail until the case was heard by the court, while Margarita was remanded to the protection of the Ursuline Convent for the duration of the proceeding. The judge held formal hearings at which he questioned several Anglo-American ship captains and sailors. All of them reported that it was widely known that John Joseph had two wives, one in Philadelphia and one in New Orleans. Indeed, witnesses reported that the accused even bragged of his sexual exploits with these two women and boasted to compatriots frequenting the New Orleans docks that his "Philadelphia" wife was even more beautiful than his local one. After hearing graphic testimony, the judge speedily annulled the marriage of Margarita Marmillon and remanded the bigamist to the prison at Havana where he was bound over for criminal trial by the authorities.[6]

Apart from annulment, *divortium* (divorce) as a term can mean several things to the historian and therefore must be clarified according to its popular usage during the eighteenth and early nineteenth centuries in the Hispanic world. Today, divorce generally means the total dissolution of a marriage. Both partners are free and unfettered in the negotiation of a new, legal conjugal relationship. Historically, the word divorce was popularly used in Spanish Texas and Louisiana to mean something else: separation from bed and board.[7] This legal action, a judicial separation, did not constitute absolute divorce as we know it today. Separation from bed and board merely released couples from the conjugal obligations of the marital bond and permitted them to live apart as legally independent persons. In so doing, civil and ecclesiastical law still recognized the validity of the ruptured marriage as a union of enduring status. Spouses so separated were not free to remarry and, at least in theory, were required to practice sexual abstinence. Significantly, women so divorced did regain control over their dotal property along with their share of community assets. Separation from bed and board constituted the primary legal mechanism by which broken marriages were dealt with in Texas and Louisiana under the regime of Spanish law.[8] It was sanctioned by the Council of Trent and was introduced into Hispanic custom as early as the twelfth century.[9]

A judicial separation could be secured on one of three grounds. First, cruel and violent treatment or abuse of partner by a spouse was a ground for suspending a marriage. In general, this ill treatment was usually by the husband directed against the wife. Such abuse had to threaten "her life, her sanity or her tranquility to such a degree that cohabitation became impossible."[10] Second, adultery was a ground for separation because it threatened the conjugal union at the most fundamental level. Third, separation from bed and board could be granted if the husband refused to provide necessary food, clothing, or shelter for his wife. Individuals seeking a judicial separation "needed a strong case against their consorts."[11] Ecclesiastical authorities granted a separation most sparingly, usually only in those cases that involved the most blatant and irreparable of circumstances. "Neither was it sufficient to prove that the offenses were real," Sylvia Arrom has noted for Mexico City during this era, "the plaintiff had to convince the judge both that the danger posed by continued cohabitation was extremely serious and that the delinquent spouse was incapable of reform."[12]

The process that plaintiffs followed in securing a judicial separation from bed and board was simple and direct. Legal jurisdiction for such cases in Texas and Louisiana rested solely with ecclesiastical courts, although the civil courts sometimes meddled in such matters. This jurisdiction was reaffirmed and upheld when the Crown issued a royal order stipulating that all divorce cases in Texas and Louisiana remained exclusively under the church courts and canon law.[13] Such courts usually were composed of one person sitting as judge. The judge of the court (generally the bishop or his designated agent) received the initial complaint filed by the plaintiff, conducted an investigation of the facts, gave the accused spouse the opportunity to file a written rejoinder countering the charges filed, and—if the case was seen as valid—solicited the testimony of at least three independent witnesses before rendering a decision. If the judge decided to grant the judicial separation after considering all of this evidence, he sent his recommendation to the governor who officially certified the result. At times, the judicial authorities of the civil government in Texas and Louisiana also heard marital disputes, usually when wives brought criminal complaints against their husbands in domestic discords or when property or other economic assets carried into marriages as part of marriage contracts had to be disposed of.[14]

My survey of the ecclesiastical and judicial records for Texas and Louisiana has located almost three dozen cases involving formal legal requests for separation from bed and board from the 1760s to the 1830s. Approximately one-third of these cases dealt with family violence, another third with adultery, while the final third were grounded in desertion or failure to provide. In about one-third of the total cases the records were incomplete or the judge terminated the dispute before the full circumstances of the particular action could be read into the record of the proceedings. The picture presented by these cases indicates that the phenomenon of marriage breakdown—especially in the areas of family violence, desertion, and adultery—was generally consistent with such occurrences in other parts of the western European world for the late eighteenth and early nineteenth century.[15]

More than any other circumstance relating to marriage breakdown, family violence and wife abuse were the reasons that brought women before the judge as plaintiffs.[16] Typical of such cases was that of María Antonia Rodríguez who appeared before the Louisiana ecclesiastical tribunal in 1782 because of the violent nature of her marriage. She asked for a divorce and noted that she had been married to José Molina for five years. During that time, he had been "continually drunk" and given to all manner of excess. He routinely beat her and, on several occasions, forced himself sexually on her when she did not desire it. At various times during their marriage, José had become so violent that María hid in her mother's house where she sought refuge from his abuses.[17]

Witnesses from María's neighborhood provided the court with stark testimony of José Molina's abusive behavior. Antonio Junque, for example, recounted that Molina treated his wife "no better than a slave" and was known to beat her with regularity. Antonio Delgado told the court that he used to live in the same building as the Molinas, whose fighting often disturbed the neighbors. Molina was "a vagrant without employment" and was "given over to drink." On one occasion, Delgado recalled that Molina came home very drunk, hit his wife repeatedly as they stood in the street, pushed her to the ground, and then roughly dragged her inside, where he forced her to have sex with him against her will. Leon Casteon, another neighbor, recalled an evening when he was in the Molina's kitchen. José, again in a drunken state, attacked his wife. He threw her to the floor, kicked her repeatedly, ripped her clothes, and pushed her crying into the street. María further adding to the catalog of her husband's misbehavior, told the divorce court that Molina had taken most of her clothing, her other personal possessions, and many of their household items out of their residence, presumably to sell them in order to buy drink. The court immediately granted María separation from bed and board. She also gained control of her antenuptial possessions and the small amount of community property remaining in the Molina home.

Ecclesiastical judges usually had sympathy for wives who were clearly the victims of flagrant physical abuse. In 1784 Margarita Prudome desired a separation from her husband under circumstances similar to those of María Molina. Margarita, who had been married for six years, complained that her husband Pedro Duranton led a completely disorganized life. Habitually drunk, he often beat her, tore her clothes, and took whatever property she had of value in order to trade for wine and spirits. Margarita told the judge that she had tried to live with Pedro and be a good wife but that she could no longer stand the violence. Witnesses who appeared on her behalf supported her petition for separation, which the court granted.[18]

Some of the requests for separation from abused women had a plaintive tone, as was the case with Catalina Toupar, who told the court

> the horrible treatment and deranged conduct of my husband and by which he has spent everything of value which I and my children have, without helping us or providing for us, and because of this I am obliged to live with my children in the most ultimate misery and am thus of the necessity of asking Your Excellency that you be served to divorce us so that we will no longer be married.[19]

Domestic violence and wife abuse were not limited to the unemployed and vagrant classes. At San Antonio de Béxar, María Jiménez requested a divorce from her husband, Bernardo Castillo; she complained that she was the victim of "*mal tratos*" by her husband, who physically abused her. The ecclesiastical tribunal, upon investigating her claims, was not entirely convinced that she was without fault. In fact, the judge ruled that both María and Bernardo shared equal blame for the fighting and refused to grant a divorce. Instead, the court instructed both parties about proper deportment in a marriage and admonished them to behave in the future.[20] They presumably managed to behave since no record has been found of additional appearances before the court by this couple.

At Baton Rouge, a prominent and wealthy Anglo-American planter, James Mullin, found himself the object of an abuse-based divorce action in 1794 when his wife accused him of having beat her repeatedly. Leonor Miller contended that her husband "abused her badly and tore her clothes off her back, sold her property and deserted her, leaving her penniless."[21] In a similar case, Miguel Eslava (the royal quartermaster and supply officer for the garrison at Mobile) was sued for separation from bed and board by his wife, who also claimed abuse. Miguel had "abused her and thrown her out of the house." She sought both a separation from him and a separate financial settlement for her children. The tribunal granted the separation and oversaw a property settlement that protected her interests.

Abused wives occasionally sought redress from civil authorities even when they did not seek divorce from the Church courts. For example, Marie Theresa Leiville attempted to give away much of her separate property before her death so that her husband would not get it. She had long been the victim of beatings and abuse by her husband, Philippe Flotte, but had never sought a separation. Suffering in the final stages of a terminal illness, she decided to give friends all of her antenuptial property in an effort to deprive her husband of it. He brought a civil suit attempting to stop her from doing so. The resulting trial offered her the opportunity to make public the family violence which had plagued her marriage. François Bertin, a Louisiana surgeon, testified on her behalf that he had treated Marie over the years for "many fractures and injuries as much on the arms as on the head which were very dangerous." He recalled that she had said these injuries "had come from the bad treatment she had received from her husband." The surgeon also informed the court that "Flotte during his wife's [current] illness had maltreated her by injuries and threats so frightful that he was obliged to put him out of the sick room for fear of some injuries to the patient."[22] Governor Luis de Unzaga, sitting as the judge of the court, found for Marie and permitted her to dispose of the property.[23]

The civil authorities also became involved in legal proceedings when divorced spouses failed to execute property settlements resulting from decrees of the ecclesiastical tribunals. For example, Margarita Meilleur sued her husband Claudio La Coste, from whom she had been judicially separated. She demanded a return from him of her dowry and her share of their common property in addition to seeking protection from his revenge. The two had been married in 1768 and, after several years of marriage, Margarita secured a separation based on abuse. In her suit before the civil court, she noted "that for many years her husband has maltreated her, even to the extent of striking her, which gave rise to scandal in the neighborhood." As a result of the previous separation decree, however, she feared that her former husband apparently planned to punish her. As Margarita reported:

> She has now heard that La Coste is prepared to sell all of his property and go to France, and has said that when Father Cirilo will be absent from this city he will take her by violence with him and make a servant of her, and after he gets her in his country he will feed her on bread and water and shut her up in a place where she will never see the sun, in revenge for the grievances he says he has received from her.[24]

Thus, resolution of property disputes was sometimes as great a problem for some women as the securing of the divorce from bed and board itself. Elizabeth Villiers took her separated spouse, Francisco de Volsay, to civil court in an effort to secure restitution of her dowry and her share of their common property. The judge ordered a settlement, to which Francisco agreed. He gave his wife the ownership of a slave, two thousand pounds of deerskins, and 160 *pesos* in currency. In return, Elizabeth agreed not to make any claims upon his estate after his death.[25] Occasionally, wives also sought legal action against their husbands to resecure control of antenuptial property even when separation was not contemplated. Feliciana Furgangin sought a civil judgement in 1787 against her husband Joséf Duget because "he has not only wasted the little means he had, but has squandered a part of her dowry." She requested the civil authorities to issue a decree "so as to enable her to save the property that belongs to her." This the court did.[26]

Adultery, along with physical abuse and family violence, also brought a number of couples before the ecclesiastical tribunals. Spanish law had long addressed the crime of adultery within the patriarchal value system of the Hispanic family. For that reason, adultery was both a civil and a religious crime, "which a man commits knowingly by having intercourse with a married woman, or one betrothed to another man."[27] In practice culpability for adultery, therefore, rested largely with the woman. Few wives accused their husbands of adultery. The majority of actions for separation in Texas and Louisiana grounded in adultery were sought by husbands against their wives.[28]

Judges seemed reluctant to grant separations from bed and board based solely on the grounds of adultery. Instead, the clerics who sat on ecclesiastical tribunals usually attempted to reconcile the erring partners by encouraging them to restore their conjugal fidelity. Texas clerics, to and even greater extent than those in Louisiana, reacted to adultery cases by attempting to effect a reconciliation. At San Antonio de Béxar, María Casimira Benítez and Juan José Flores reconciled while their case was pending before the tribunal.[29]

The church's reluctance to grant a judicial separation from bed and board solely on the basis of adultery rested in part on the difficulty of documenting indisputably a specific offense, since adultery usually occurred secretly. A 1795 Louisiana case at Opelousas stands as testimony to such difficulties. Daniel Callaghan had long suspected his wife of having an adulterous affair with Charles Peck, a neighbor. Charles Peck visited the Callaghan home on numerous occasions when Daniel was away on business. Servants and other neighbors reported that Charles and the wife often secluded themselves in the bed chamber of the Callaghan home, but both parties disclaimed any wrong doing. Daniel Callaghan confronted his neighbor, who vigorously denied the accusations. The irate husband thereupon recruited one of his friends, Thomas Fletcher, to spy on the suspected paramours during one of his regular absences from the district. Thomas Fletcher laid at wait in the night, observed Charles's arrival at the Callaghan home, and peeked through the windows, whereupon he saw the two apparently "in the appearance of enjoyment, one of the other" on the bed. Nonetheless, when Thomas testified before the ecclesiastical tribunal, he was obliged to report honestly that it had been too dark to see if illicit intercourse had actually taken place. In her defense the wife explained that she was ill and that Charles Peck had been treating her malady. The tribunal therefore took no action on the matter.[30]

Benito Allon had a similar experience when he accused his wife, María Buenaventura, of adultery. Benito complained to the church court that he had contracted a venereal disease from María. He testified that he could not have been exposed to the illness by anyone else since he had been faithful to María. Benito believed that his wife had become diseased from an illicit union with Vicente Cola. The husband told the court that it was a well-known fact that Vicente suffered from the disease. Benito, moreover, produced witnesses who told the tribunal that they had observed María entering Vicente's home and remaining inside the building all night, not leaving until morning. Nonetheless, the court refused the separation and ordered María to live faithfully with her husband and to stop seeing Vicente.[31]

The problem in sorting through adulterous relationships is further illustrated by a long-running case that lasted from the 1760s until the early 1790s. Luis Forneret, the public interpreter for the Spanish government at Mobile, had married Isabel Alexandre in 1767. Shortly thereafter, Luis traveled to France for an extended residence occasioned by the death of his father and the necessity of settling the estate. According to Luis, he found upon his return to the Gulf Coast that his wife had moved to Pensacola and had become the mistress of Daniel Ward. Adultery suits and countersuits followed for years in the ecclesiastical courts of Spanish Louisiana. She claimed that she had merely worked for Daniel Ward as a domestic servant and governess and charged Luis of having a sexual relationship with one of his female slaves, by whom he had fathered several children. After several unsuccessful attempts at reconciliation, the court finally ordered in 1793 that the two warring spouses stop bickering and live together without further accusations of adultery.[32]

On some occasions aggrieved husbands sought a separation from their adulterous wives while they had strong personal feelings of attachment. At Nacogdoches, for example, Francisco López reluctantly filed for separation from his wife, Juana Antonia Ocona, because of her illicit relationship with José Manuel. Francisco wrote his wife a loving and painful letter explaining that he had no recourse other than to ask that God pardon her marital offenses, for he apparently could not.[33]

As they were with physical abuse, ecclesiastical judges were much more likely to grant separations from bed and board occasioned by desertion (grounded on failure to provide support) than they were for adultery. Desertion was sometimes a reality in Texas and Louisiana because a significant number of residents were military or civil employees of the government whose postings involved assignment to remote or undesirable locations. The demands of frontier life and the hardships which ensued from such an existence also insured that trailing spouses could not or would not always follow their partners. In 1793, for example, a Spanish soldier at New Orleans sued his wife for separation because she refused to live with him at his new assignment at the Balize fort. Balize, situated in the deep delta of the Mississippi River near its mouth, was a swampy, remote, and unhealthy place according to the reluctant wife, who flatly refused to leave New Orleans and continue residence with her husband.[34]

The mobility and anonymity of frontier life created an opportunity for spouses to move with relative ease and, in so doing, to subvert their marriages. Church courts sometimes prosecuted such occurrences with vigor. For example, in 1792 Genova Goder, a resident of the Illinois country of Spanish Louisiana, reported to the church tribunal that her husband of eight years, Joseph Lubierre, had moved to the vicinity of Baton Rouge and was living there with a widow. The court acted speedily, ordering the arrest of the husband and decreeing that he henceforth reside with and support his lawful wife.[35]

The circumstances of desertion were not always easy to resolve. Fernando Rodríguez de Meza, a resident of the Canary Islands, had left Santa Cruz in 1772 and moved first to Havana and then to New Orleans where he eventually established his permanent residence. His wife, Antonia Aguilar, did not emigrate with him but remained at Santa Cruz. Although Rodríguez did not attempt to remarry, he apparently lost contact with his wife. By the 1780s she had become impoverished and, learning of his location, began to send Fernando requests for money. He refused to support her. She eventually contacted the ecclesiastical court at New Orleans, asking that the judges order Fernando to send her money. He appeared before the tribunal and explained that he had not deserted his spouse. Instead, Antonia had refused to follow him as his wife. He said that she was free to move to New Orleans at any time and resume her residence with him. He also told the court that he had earlier sent her one thousand *pesos*. This was all she would get unless she reunited with him. In the light of this testimony, the ecclesiastical court refused to be further concerned with the matter.[36]

For the most part, however, church courts exhibited little hesitancy to become involved in petitions for separation from bed and board, especially those grounded in abuse, adultery, or desertion. Although it is impossible to quantify the number of failed marriages out of the total population, the manner in which the authorities in Louisiana, Texas, and West Florida aggressively resolved marriage breakdown cases, nonetheless, provides a clear picture of family values and social expectations. The church saw protection of the family unit as perhaps the most important assumption underlying separation hearings.

The thoroughness with which these tribunals approached the cases that came before them permits four general conclusions to be drawn. First, separation from bed and board was difficult to obtain because ecclesiastical courts attempted to ensure the viability of marriages rather then legitimating their rupture. These tribunals were, therefore, an important agency in combating marriage breakdown. Separations from bed and board were granted with regularity only in cases of physical violence of husbands against their wives. Except for abuse cases, ecclesiastical judges were reluctant to grant separation, preferring instead to preside over enforced reconciliations. Adultery and, to an extent, desertion were therefore less often accepted as compelling reasons to end a marriage.

Second, separation (reflecting common practice throughout the Hispanic legal world of the eighteenth and nineteenth centuries) was often used by women as a protection against the violent excesses of their husbands. It was the last resort for battered, abused, or deserted women. Hence, in an overwhelmingly patriarchal culture, separation for bed and board represented (albeit in an inherently negative sense) one of the few aspects of social organization weighted in favor of women as victims. At the same time, men who sought divorce from their spouses because of the wife's adultery were often refused relief by the courts. These cases usually resulted in a court decree for reconciliation. This condition lends itself to an interesting speculation that, although supported by the cases examined, is beyond proof because of the limited documentary record. Women who sought separation grounded on abusive treatment actually desired to end cohabitation. On the other hand, men who sought divorce based on the wife's adultery did not seek to end the relationship but were seeking the assistance of church authority in reasserting conjugal control over their spouse.

Third, most divorce cases brought by women as plaintiffs also involved the wife's desire to control her antenuptial possessions or her share of the common property. All the examined cases that were grounded in physical abuse also attempted to substantiate the husband's misuse of property. Courts were careful to make awards of property to wives who successfully secured separation under such circumstances. Separated married women sometimes appeared before civil authorities to compel compliance with orders concerning property. This circumstance raises questions about whether these cases reflect the concerns of the entire society. Did married poor women bother to seek a separation from bed and board when their marriages degenerated into violence? Perhaps they did not. Perhaps poor couples used cheaper, less formal, and more expedient solutions, such as extralegal separation, a simple return to the wife's family, a move to another locality, or other similar strategies in response to solving marital breakdown. Securing of separation from bed and board before the church court might well have been as much an economic phenomenon of social class as a symptom of marital breakdown for abused women on the Hispanic frontier.

Fourth, the study of marital breakdown as reflected in the records of Louisiana, West Florida, and Texas holds a historiographical lesson for the Hispanic frontier of North America. The experience of settlers there, at least in terms of family values, had great similarity in Hispanic law and religion from region to region across differing eras of administration and government sovereignty. Like the mission, the presidio, and the *villa*, the nuclear family was an important and integral institution essential for understanding the sociology of the Hispanic frontier of North America.[37] It too deserves serious and considerate study by historians.

Notes for "Church Courts, Marriage Breakdown, and Separation in Spanish Louisiana, West Florida, and Texas, 1763-1836"

[1]Marital breakdown occurred when physical abuse, domestic violence, adultery, incompatibility, spousal failure to provide the necessities of life, or the failure to consummate or maintain the conjugal union rendered the family unit disfunctional. Not all marriage breakdowns resulted in suits for separation from bed and board because there were many extralegal ways to end a marriage, especially for the nonelite social classes. Many of these strategies, ranging from mutually agreed informal separations to bigamy, probably escaped notice of the authorities. The social history of such phenomena is difficult to research because manuscript and archival sources which have been preserved generally do not document the commonplace realities of daily life. Instead they provide documentation of deviations from standard normative practices. This study is based on material related to separation contained in the Spanish Judicial Records of Louisiana located at the Louisiana State Museum in New Orleans, the Ecclesiastical Notary records of that province in the Civil District Courts Records of Orleans Parish located in the District Courts Building of New Orleans, and the Archivo de Béxar located at the University of Texas at Austin. The latter is widely available in a microform reproduction. The citations in this essay are to the microform edition. For a general discussion of these records, see Henry Putney Beers, *French and Spanish Records of Louisiana: A Bibliographical Guide to Archive and Manuscript Sources* (Baton Rouge, 1989), 30-31, 34-35, 150-80; and Adán Benavides, Jr., comp, and ed., *The Béxar Archives (1717-1836): A Name Guide* (Austin, 1989), xi-xxii.

[2]The period concerned here is the mid-1760s to the mid-1830s. During these decades Texas was a Spanish province until 1821, and then part of independent Mexico. In terms of civil, judicial, religious, and military jurisdiction, it was never linked with Louisiana—although an imperial province of strategic importance to the Indies during the late eighteenth century—had a much greater geographical extent and a more diverse ethnic population than did relatively more homogeneous Texas. The territory of colonial Louisiana included most of the western Mississippi valley and, during the 1780s and 1790s, extended across the northern Gulf Coast to encompass parts of the modern states of Mississippi, Alabama, and Florida. This latter area was known as West Florida, first having been a British colony from 1763 to 1781, and Spanish from 1781 until 1819. Louisiana's large Gallic population, coupled with an increasing Anglo-American migration, gave the province a greater cultural and demographic variety than that found in Texas during that period. For recent historical literature on these provinces, see Light T. Cummins, "Texas Under Spain and Mexico," in *A Guide to the History of Texas*, Light T. Cummins and Alvin R. Bailey, Jr., eds. (Westport, CT, 1988), 3-16; Cummins, "Spanish Louisiana," in *A Guide to the History of Louisiana*, Cummins and Glen Jeansonne, eds. (Westport, CT, 1982), 17-25; and Cummins, "Colonial Louisiana," in *Louisiana: A History*, Bennett H. Wall, et al., 2nd ed. (Arlington Heights, IL, 1990), 52-67.

[3]The institutionalization of Hispanic frontier scholars into two schools, those of the southeast and the southwest, is historiographical reality, heightened by the fact that the manuscript records for Louisiana and Texas are generally maintained as parts of different archival collections. Such separation is an appropriate historiographical distinction, but only as long as historical analysis focuses on the institutional aspects of the Spanish imperium in the Indies: studies of government and colonial administration, international rivalry and Native American relations, methods of frontier organization and expansion, and commercial development. In these aspects of political and economic institutions, Hispanic Texas and Louisiana probably show more historical disparities than similarities. For a fuller discussion, see David J. Weber, "Turner, the Boltonians, and the Borderlands," *The American Historical Review,* 91 (1986): 66-81; Michael C. Scardaville, "Approaches to the Study of the Southeastern Borderlands," *Alabama and the Borderlands: From Prehistory to Statehood*, R. Reid Badger and Lawrence C. Clayton, eds. (University, AL, 1985), 184-96.

[4]Silvia M. Arron, *The Women of Mexico City, 1790-1857* (Stanford, CA, 1985), 206-7.

[5]Richard Boyer, "Women, *La Mala Vida*, and the Politics of Marriage," in *Sexuality and Marriage in Colonial Latin America*, Asunción Lavrín, ed. (Lincoln, NE, 1989), 258-59.

[6]Roderick Phillips, *Putting Asunder: A History of Divorce in Western Society* (Cambridge, England, 1988), 3; "Información de Pedro Josef Boydant para hacer constante el primer matrimonio subsistente de su mujer." July 1784, Acts of S. de Quiñones, Vol. 3, Orleans Parish Notarial Archives, Civil District Court Building, New Orleans, Louisiana; "Memoria de Don Antonio Marmillon," Acts of S. de Quiñones, Vol. 1, ibid.

[7]Phillips, *Putting Asunder*, 12-13; Arrom, *Women of Mexico City*, 208.

[8]Arrom, *Women of Mexico City*, 208.

[9]Phillips, *Putting Asunder*, 13.

[10]Vaughan Baker et al., "Le Mari et Seigneur: Marital Laws Governing Women in French Louisiana," in *Louisiana's Legal Heritage*, Robert R. Macdonald and Edward F. Haas, eds. (New Orleans, 1983), 12-13.

[11]Arrom, *Women of Mexico City*, 209-10.

[12]Ibid., 209.

[13]"Royal Decree on divorce case of Josefa Castañeda," Archivo de Béxar, roll 18, folios 92-94.

[14]For a full discussion of marriage contracts, see Hans W. Baade, "Marriage Contracts in French and Spanish Louisiana: A Study in Notarial Jurisprudence," *Tulane Law Review*, 53 (1979): 1-93. See also: Joseph W. McKnight, "Spanish Law for the Protection of Surviving Spouses in North America," *Anuario de historia del derecho español*, 57 (1989): 367-406.

[15]For representative examples of this literature, see: Nancy Cott, "Eighteenth Century Family and Social Life Revealed in Massachusetts Divorce Records," *Journal of Social History*, 10 (1976): 20-43; Sheldon S. Cohen, "'To Parts of the World Unknown': The Circumstances of Divorce in Connecticut, 1750-1797," *The Canadian Review of American Studies*, 11 (1980): 275-93; María Beatriz Nizza da Silva, "Divorce in Colonial Brazil: The Case of Sao Paulo," in *Sexuality and Marriage in Colonial Latin America*, Lavrín, ed., 313-40.

[16]This finding is consistent with Arrom's study of early nineteenth-century Mexico City. She notes that "physical abuse was the primary reason women gave for seeking divorce." Arrom, *Women of Mexico City*, 232.

[17]María Antonia Rodríguez contra Josef Molina, su marido, sobre divorcio," Acts of S. de Quiñones, Vol. 1, Orleans Parish Notary Archives.

[18]"Informacion producida por Margarita Prudome de los malos tratos que Pedro Duranton, alias Lecouture, su marido le da." Acts of S. de Quiñones, Vol. 3, March 29, 1784, Orleans Parish Notary Records.

[19]"Doña Catalina Toupar contra Don Luis Lorsel, su marido, sobre separación," Acts of S. de Quiñones, Vol. 5, Orleans Parish Notary Archives.

[20]Action of Bernardo Castillo and José María Jiménez, Archivo de Béxar, February 19, 1829, Roll 169, folio 689.

[21]The court granted the separation. See Jack D. L. Holmes, "'Do It, Don't Do It:' Spanish Laws on Sex and Marriage," in *Louisiana's Legal Heritage*, Macdonald and Haas, eds., 32.

[22]"Phillipe Flotte v. Marie Theresa Leiveille, his wife, to prevent her from giving away her property," May 25, 1773, "Index to Spanish Judicial Records of Louisiana," trans., Laura Porteous, *Louisiana Historical Quarterly,* 9 (1926): 543-44, hereafter cited *LHQ*.

[23]Ibid., 544.

[24]Margarita Mellieur v. Claudio La Coste, her husband, to demand from him her dowry and community property. February 10, 1784. "Index to Spanish Judicial Records of Louisiana," trans., Porteous, *LHQ*, 20 (1937): 529.

[25]Elizabeth de Villiers v. Francisco de Volsay, her husband, January 27, 1780, "Index to Spanish Judicial Records of Louisiana," trans. Porteous, *LHQ,* 15 (1932): 548-49.

[26]Feliciana Fourganger v. Josef Duget, her husband. October 28, 1787, "Index to Spanish Judicial Records of Louisiana," trans. Porteous, *LHQ,* 25 (1942): 284-85.

[27]Holmes, "Do It! Don't Do It!," 19-20.

[28]Arrom, *Women of Mexico City,* 240-41.

[29]Case for Separation, María Casimira Benítez and Juan José Flores, March 5, 1808, Archivo de Béxar, Roll 37, folio 809.

[30]"Suit for Separation of Daniel Callaghan," Acts of S. de Quiñones, May 17, 1785, Vol. 4, f. 81, Orleans Parish Notary Archives.

[31]This verdict was acceptable to Allon, who apparently wanted his wife back. "Benito Allon contra su Mujer," Acts of Quiñones, October 1796, Vol. 8, f. 515, Orleans Parish Notary Archives.

[32]"Isabel Alexandre contra Luis Forneret." May 1793, Actos of Quiñones, Vol. 6, f. 134, Orleans Parish Notary Archives.

[33]"Francisco López to Juan Antonio Ocona," July 23, 1812, Archivo de Béxar, roll 51, folios 962-64.

[34]"Joseph Molina contra su mujer," May 9, 1793, Acts of S. de Quiñones, Vol. 6, f. 130, Orleans Parish Notary Archives.

[35]"Genova Goder contra Joseph Lubiere sobre renunciar al matrimonio," Acts of S. Quiñones, May 1788-July 1793, f. 117, Orleans Parish Notary Archives.

[36]"Testimonio de diligencias sobre deunar de Don Fernando Rodríguez, residente en esta, con su mujer Antonia Aguilar, residente en Islas Canarias," January 19, 1786, Acts of S. de Quiñones, Vol. 4:573.

[37]In his 1990 Presidential Address to the American Historical Association, the late David Herlihy made an impassioned plea for the study of the family as an important object of historical analysis. As he explained his purpose: "I want to examine the emergence of the family in the West as a moral unit and a moral universe: a unit in the sense that it is sharply differentiated from the larger associations of kin and community, and a universe in the sense that human relations within it are very different from human relations outside its limits." Herlihy, "Family," *American Historical Review,* 96 (1991): 1. For a general overview of the family in western culture, see Tamara K. Hareven, "The History of the Family and the Complexity of Social Change," *American Historical Review,* 96 (1991): 95-124.

THE INQUISITION IN SPANISH LOUISIANA, 1762-1800*

Richard E. Greenleaf

During the eighteenth century Louisiana, French and Spanish, provided one of the major channels for penetration of Enlightenment philosophy and of Protestantism into the Spanish Empire in North America. While the Bourbon kings of Spain never were willing to establish a formal Tribunal of the Holy Office of the Inquisition in Louisiana, the Spanish government and the tribunals in Mexico City and Cartagena did encourage and commission inquisitorial investigations in Louisiana.[1]

At the time France ceded Louisiana to Spain, the Spanish state was tolerant of French political philosophy, social ideas, and French Protestantism. Immigration of non-Catholics and foreigners was encouraged. Non-Spanish soldiers served in the Louisiana Regiment, and after 1782 the port of New Orleans was opened to free trade with France and with the rest of Spain's empire. The new governors in Louisiana and the Church adopted a posture of liberalism and flexible orthodoxy, and there were no known inquisitorial investigations in Spanish Louisiana until the 1790s. Spanish religion and Spanish Catholic culture were protected in other ways.

Political officialdom attempted to curb sedition and seditious ideas, a function that Mexican viceroys and the Inquisition usually shared after 1760. The usual jurisdiction of the Inquisition (preserving religious orthodoxy, supervising the moral conduct of layman and clergy, and attacking blasphemy and bigamy) was the purview of the ordinary in Louisiana, and since there was no bishop this power was delegated to an auxiliary vicar. A perusal of the records of the Diocese of Louisiana and the Floridas from 1576 to 1803 reveals that vicars took this responsibility seriously.[2]

What is often evident from the Mexican and Spanish Inquisition records is that there was a close circum-Caribbean surveillance of Catholics and foreigners alike who flouted

*First published in *New Mexico Historical Review*, 50 (1975): 45-72. Reprinted with the kind permission of the author and publisher.

religious orthodoxy and the power of the Spanish state. Inhabitants of Louisiana who talked heresy or sedition—and often they were the same thing—were arrested and tried by the Inquisition once they left home on business or other travel. Cuban authorities, the Mexican Inquisition Commissaries, and officials in Yucatán and Central America were informed of the culprits in question by an effective communications network. Very often the *comisarios* sought out such travelers, and on occasion the accused were persuaded to mend their ways.

From the trial record we learn that Enrique Extempli was a twenty-four-year-old Englishman from Fellin who had been a merchant in the British Natchez area for ten years. At the age of fourteen he had left home and his Lutheran parents to seek his fortune in the New World. He was in and out of jail in Spanish territory many times, usually charged with illegal trading. He had spent a year in prison in New Orleans before being deported, first to Havana and then to Cádiz as an undesirable alien. From Cádiz he and his partner Stephen Howard returned to the Gulf Coast. There he was apprehended again and sent to San Juan de Ulúa. The boy said he first encountered Catholicism and went to Mass during his stints in New Orleans, Havana, and Spain. It was when he began to learn Spanish and to find his place among Spaniards that he had realized the superiority of Spanish religion and culture. He had known other "heretics" in the Caribbean but he eschewed their ways and he truly wished to convert.

In his lengthy interrogation, Dr. Laso de la Vega followed the prescribed formulary for those who wished to renounce their previous beliefs and to become Catholics.[3] Laso de la Vega skillfully learned of the young man's Lutheran background, his early education in England, and his travels in the New World. Extempli believed in the virginity of Mary, before, during, and after the birth of Christ, but he had been taught that she was the mother of other children. He believed in the sacrament of baptism, but not in penance or the Eucharist. He denied the existence of Purgatory, the efficacy of indulgences, and the intercession of saints. He held the usual unacceptable Lutheran views on the power of the Pope, veneration of images, authority of bishops, and salvation through good works. Dr. Laso de la Vega certified to the Mexico City Tribunal of the Inquisition that Extempli was sincere in his desire to convert. The judges instructed Laso to make very sure that his prisoner was not a Jew in disguise and that he was not making his peace with the Church out of sheer expediency. A group of Veracruz clergy were appointed to instruct Extempli in Catholicism. When they certified that he was ready, a simple ceremony in the portico of the Veracruz cathedral, on September 29, 1780, absolved him of previous sins and errors and admitted him to the body of believers. One of the frustrating aspects of trials of this sort is that the record leaves off at this point, and the Natchez merchant fades from historical view.

It is obvious that some of the information gathered about Extempli probably came from clergy in New Orleans. There was one formally accredited *Comisario* of the Inquisition in New Orleans in the late 1780s and probably other informal agents who collected and dispatched information to the south and east by sea, and to the west through the chains of missions and presidios.

The Commissary of the Holy Office in Louisiana was the famous and controversial Capuchin friar Antonio de Sedella who had arrived in New Orleans with a group of Andalusian Capuchins in 1781.[4] Owing to his conflicts with ecclesiastical superiors and with the Spanish governor a decade later, there exists a body of data on "Père Antoine's" career as an Inquisitor. Most Louisiana historians have mentioned these events, but few have seen them in the perspective of Caribbean Inquisition history. What is clear from diocesan records is that long before his clashes with Governor Esteban Miró in 1790 over his status as Commissary of the Holy Office, Père Antoine was acting as judge in cases normally handled by the Inquisition in New Spain. During May of 1786 Governor Miró acknowledged reports Sedella sent him about investigations of faith and morals conducted under his jurisdiction as Auxiliary Vicar of New Orleans.[5] These prosecutions dealt with blasphemy, bigamy, reading of books on the Index, and lack of orthodoxy among the Indian population of Spanish Louisiana. In an official communication dated May 8, 1788, Sedella used the title "Vicar and Ecclesiastical Judge of New Orleans."[6] The records show that Père Antoine was conducting heresy investigations under the episcopal jurisdiction of Ordinary, and often circumvented proper judicial channels within the hierarchy, thereby netting himself criticism from his Florida and Cuban superiors. The difference between such prosecutions and Inquisition business was merely semantic, and they were designed perhaps to allay the fears of foreigners and non-Catholics in Louisiana.

On February 10, 1786, the Tribunal of the Holy Office of the Inquisition at Cartagena officially notified Fray Antonio de Sedella of his appointment as Commissary of the Holy Office in Louisiana.[7] This was the culmination of a century of effort on the part of Cartagena Inquisitors to extend their jurisdiction onto the mainland of North America. Contrary to the opinion of earlier writers on Spanish Louisiana, Sedella's appointment as *comisario* did not imply the establishment of an Inquisition court in New Orleans. Rather it meant that Père Antoine was to be the accredited representative of the Cartagena Tribunal there and he was to behave, as all *comisarios* did, only as an investigatory agent. When the Auxiliary Bishop of the Spanish Floridas, Sedella's superior, heard of the commission he protested the action vigorously.[8] Cirilo de Barcelona enlisted the support of the Captain General of Cuba and of his ecclesiastical superior in Havana, Bishop Santiago Echevarría. All three functionaries pointed out that the population of Spanish Louisiana was composed largely of Frenchmen and foreign merchants, many of whom were non-Catholics. Bishop Echevarría suspended Sedella's patent as commissary until a ruling regarding formalized Inquisition activity in Louisiana could be obtained from Spain. In a petition dated July 13, 1787, Cirilo de Barcelona requested Charles III to decide the matter. Charles upheld the suspension of Sedella's appointment on January 9, 1788, and the Cuban hierarchy so notified Père Antoine.[9] Sedella acknowledged receipt of the king's order and there the matter rested for two years.

Conflict between Sedella and his auxiliary bishop in Florida over the Inquisition patent led to hard feelings between the two men. Animosities intensified when Sedella polarized the New Orleans clergy into Andalusian and Havana groups. Partially as a result of this factionalism, but largely owing to reports of the deplorable state of religious life in the colony, Auxiliary Bishop Cirilo de Barcelona journeyed to Louisiana and launched a personal investigation. His episcopal visitation began on August 30, 1789, and continued throughout 1790. The Cuban superior had empowered Cirilo to send Sedella back to Havana if his findings would warrant it. The auxiliary bishop brought charges against Sedella for mismanagement of his vicariate in New Orleans and determined to relieve him of office.[10]

Because Père Antoine had a large popular following in New Orleans and public scandal was imminent as the proceedings unfolded, Cirilo was willing to strike a compromise with the rebellious Sedella. The arrangement, as the bishop reported it in his letters to Havana and to Spain was that he had agreed to withdraw charges in exchange for Sedella's promise to return to Spain "of his own free will." Cirilo claimed that as the ship was waiting to take him away, Père Antoine reneged on the deal avowing "that if he went at all it would be as a prisoner under official guard."[11] Exasperated, he complained to Governor Esteban Miró about Père Antoine's behavior and requested that Miró arrange for deportation. Meanwhile Sedella's ship set sail for Spain without its illustrious passenger.

At this juncture the real controversy over Antonio de Sedella's status as Inquisition commissary began. Governor Miró was aware that Sedella's 1786 appointment had been nullified, and he was flabbergasted when Père Antoine confronted him with a document which seemed to reinstate him as Inquisitor of Spanish Louisiana. As the French Revolution gained momentum and as a spate of books and revolutionary tracts issued forth from France, the Spanish Inquisition felt constrained to curtail their circulation in the empire. Consequently the Inquisitor General of Spain issued specific instructions to Holy Office Tribunals in the New World and to their commissaries to confiscate all subversive literature. Ignoring the revocation of Sedella's authority in 1787, the Spanish Tribunal sent Père Antoine a direct order on December 5, 1789, to search for and to seize suspected materials.[12] By April 1790 the order had arrived in New Orleans, and Sedella used it as a lever in his developing controversy with Governor Miró and Bishop Cirilo and one suspects with great bravado. Père Antoine went to the governor's residence at nine o'clock on the evening of April 29, showed him the order from Spain, and tried to give Miró instructions on how the order was to be enforced:[13]

> To carry into effect instructions of December 5 in conformity with His Majesty's wishes expressed in the instructions . . . it is necessary that I have recourse at any hour of the night to the Corps de Garde from which I may draw the necessary troops to assist me if they are necessary to carry on my operations. To this end Your Lordship will please issue the necessary instructions to the military commander that he must furnish me immediately the soldiers whom I may request to carry out my duties.

Sedella left the residence before the governor could finish reading the documents.

The next day Père Antoine escalated the controversy and kept the pressure on Governor Miró. He issued another formal order to Don Esteban at six o'clock in the afternoon of April 29, 1790.[14] Reviewing the contents of the request he had delivered twenty-one hours earlier, he threatened:

> Since at the time of this writing I have not received any communication from Your Lordship . . . I deem it necessary to warn you that the success of my mission is imperiled by such tardy measures, and since this matter is of the gravest concern and of the utmost importance to the service of the King, Your Lordship will please inform me without further delay what steps you intend to take so that I may proceed promptly to accomplish my task.

Perhaps, as he claimed later, Governor Miró feared that Sedella might trigger insurrection and economic disaster in Louisiana if he carried out his Inquisitorial functions. Certainly Père Antoine had strong support from large numbers of the colonists and among the Louisiana clergy; and both Miró and the bishop feared that Sedella was further polarizing an already divided clerical establishment. The Capuchin also had powerful allies on the governor's staff. Miró later confided to the Crown that his own auditor was one of the Sedella's confidants and chief supporters. At any rate the governor decided to use the occasion to justify ridding his government of a rebellious and intriguing friar who was vicar of New Orleans and a pretender to inquisitorial authority. After duly consulting with his legal counselor, Manuel Serrano, Colonel Manuel Gayoso of Natchez, and others, Miró empowered Cirilo de Barcelona to order the arrest of Antonio de Sedella. On the night of April 29, 1790, Père Antoine was secretly arrested and "forcibly marched to a ship" bound for Cádiz.[15]

Because of Sedella's popularity in New Orleans, and formal protests lodged in Cuba and in Spain, the issue became a political cause célèbre. Both Bishop Cirilo de Barcelona and Governor Miró were called to account for their actions. Each seemed to blame the other for the actual decision to deport Père Antoine. The Reverend Michael J. Curley, who examined the canonical process against Sedella, found it "strangely unconvincing" and came to the same conclusion that the auxiliary bishop's superior did when he reprimanded the visitor for exceeding his powers, violating proper legal procedures, and arranging for Sedella to be deported.[16] Governor Esteban Miró defended his actions in a lengthy dossier sent to the Spanish Minister of Justice and Pardons, Antonio Porlier, in 1790. On the surface his defense was an able one. He recounted, with adequate documentation, the auxiliary bishop's recommendations for Père Antoine's forced departure and then focused on the more serious issue of Sedella's intended inquisitorial activities. The governor wrote that when he read Sedella's nocturnal demand for troops to search for and to seize heretical literature, "I trembled at such an attempt to ignore the prerogatives of the Royal Patronage, but above all because it happened at such a critical time in these provinces."[17]

Governor Miró argued convincingly to Minister Porlier that Antonio de Sedella's attempt to extend the Inquisition's activities into Louisiana endangered the policies dictated by the monarchy for the purpose of encouraging immigration and stimulating commerce with foreigners—who were apt to be non-Catholics. The governor contended that any hint of Inquisition operations in Louisiana would be injurious to trade and future settlement:[18] "these foreigners are imbued with, and very frightened of the power of the Holy Office which they consider absolutely despotic and discriminatory, notwithstanding the uprightness, stature, and circumspection of its most just proceedings."

Certainly Miró was correct in his assessment of the religious temperament of foreigners in the Louisiana colony, but just as surely he exaggerated the extent of Père Antoine's machinations. The documentary record shows that Sedella had no intention of establishing an Inquisition, nor was he trying to install himself as chief inquisitor. He merely hoped to use his status as *comisario* of the Holy Office and its immunities in order to avoid deportation. Neither Governor Miró nor subsequent historians of Louisiana have seen these incidents in their correct light:[19] a conflict between Spanish civil authority and the institution known as the *Familiatura*, that corpus of privileges and immunities from civil jurisdiction enjoyed by commissaries of the Inquisition and familiar under Spanish legal codes.[20]

Père Antoine's deportation did not end his Inquisitorial activities, for he was allowed to return to New Orleans in 1795. It appears that this time he carried some secret commission from the Mexico City Tribunal. He supplied information on heretics and prohibited literature which often led to arrest and trial of Louisianians when they traveled the Caribbean in trade and commerce. Even after the purchase of Louisiana by the United States in 1803, Sedella continued as an agent. Letters from him to the governor of Yucatán and to the Mexican Inquisition are dated as late as 1806. They describe heretical literature in New Orleans destined for shipment to Mexico and give information about the seditious plots of fugitives from the Mexican Inquisition in New Orleans.[21]

The underlying issue in the jurisdictional dispute had been Sedella's commission to confiscate seditious literature. From the Holy Office's standpoint, fear of French literature and other Enlightenment tracts was well founded. Inventories of plantation libraries, discovered and published in modern times, attest to the presence of all manner of *avant-garde* reading matter from the 1730s onward. Allegations that colonial Louisiana was a provincial backwater, culturally destitute, are simply not true.[22] The 1769 inventory of the estate of M. Prévost, agent of the Company of the Indies in New Orleans for thirty years, listed some three hundred titles of books, primarily works of social and political philosophy with a decidedly radical tint. Prévost and his family read Montesquieu, Locke, Voltaire, Rousseau, and many other authors who were prohibited in Mexico and Spain.[23] After 1789, proscribed French political and economic tracts, as well as pamphlets against the Spanish state, infiltrated New Spain from the free ports of Louisiana and Cuba. Governors and clergy in New Orleans wrote letters to the Mexican Inquisition in the 1790s warning about the influx of prohibited books, and the inquisitors in Mexico City expressed concern about New Orleans as a center for political intrigue.[24] From 1794 onward the governors of Florida, Louisiana, and Cuba were instructed by the viceroy of New Spain and by the Council of the Indies in Spain to prohibit the book trade which had developed from Philadelphia via New Orleans and the United States border.[25]

In 1791 Felipe Santiago Puglia published in Philadelphia a particularly damning indictment of the *ancien régime* and the Spanish monarchy entitled *El Desengaño del Hombre*. Copies of the tract were circulated in New Orleans. The Holy Office condemned the book in 1794 in no uncertain terms.[26] The censors said Puglia was taking cheap shots at the Spanish monarchy and fomenting "rebellion of the most infamous sort." His attempt to induce loyal Spaniards to use the French Revolution as a model was attacked with great vehemence. The censor tried to show that liberty and happiness had not resulted from the French uprisings, but only desolation and spiritual "pestilences."[27] Concern with sedition and seditious literature from upriver was also evident in the documents of the diocesan archives from the 1790s. For instance, on September 30, 1796, Fr. Paul de Saint Pierre wrote a disquieting letter from Ste. Genevieve, in upper Louisiana, to Bishop Peñalver in New Orleans. He had just heard that mobs of "mad Frenchmen" had been demonstrating in Saint Louis during the last few days, "shouting Long Live Liberty, Long Live Equality, and singing songs against religion." Fr. Paul reported that American agitation in Spanish Illinois was reaching a dangerous peak.[28]

While the Spanish monarchy was attempting to Hispanicize the stubbornly French Louisiana colony, each year the French population grew. A large influx of émigrés from Santo Domingo and elsewhere bolstered the population, and New Orleans alone received some four thousand of these people in 1791. The population in the rest of the Louisiana country also grew. Arthur P. Whitaker studied a census taken by the bishop of Louisiana in 1797 which reported the population of lower Louisiana and Natchez as 43,087.[29] These Frenchmen, British traders, and American merchants added to the Francophile and Hispanophobe feelings in the colony. It was difficult, if not impossible, to contain the spread of heresy and sedition. In these difficult times of ideological conflict the governor of Louisiana was the coolheaded and tolerant Manuel Gayoso de Lemos who from 1789 to 1797 had governed the largely Protestant and American section of Natchez before he assumed his post in New Orleans in 1797.[30] Widely read, well-informed on political and economic issues in North America and Europe, Gayoso continued to promote the tolerant administrative environment necessary for political stability but damaging to orthodoxy. When Governor Gayoso died in 1799 his extensive library was auctioned off in New Orleans.[31] The four hundred and eleven volumes on the inventory have been analyzed in depth by Irving A. Leonard, who judges them to be "the working library of a practical man of affairs . . . reflecting Gayoso's varied experience and cosmopolitan culture." Quite a few of the books were on the Spanish Index of 1790 as "prohibited" or "subject to expurgation."[32] It appears that Governor Gayoso both created and was influenced by the tolerant environment which he engendered.

As the Mexican Inquisition revitalized itself to combat philosophe ideas translated into practice by French revolutionary activists after 1789, Spanish Louisiana clergy determined to pursue their previous policy of having heretics and blasphemers arrested after they departed from the colony. By far the most distinguished citizen of New Orleans tried by the Mexican Inquisition was Don Juan Longouran, a native of Bordeaux who had married into the distinguished and respected Fortier family.[33] Longouran had migrated to Louisiana sometime in the late 1760s and at the time of his trial in Mexico City in 1793, he was fifty-eight years old. For over twenty years he had been married to Marie Fortier, who lived in New Orleans with four of their children. The two eldest, Honorato and Mariana, were living in France with Longouran's brother while they completed their education. Longouran had graduated from medical school and had gone into the family business in Bordeaux when he was twenty-eight years old. In order not to marry a girl chosen by his father, Juan had gone to Haiti with a Captain Renart. After that he settled in New Orleans. With his wife he returned to Haiti where he bought a coffee plantation and forty slaves. Longouran and Marie returned to New Orleans to live because of an epidemic which decimated the labor force and because of business reverses. There he practiced medicine and engaged in trade. After the disastrous fire of 1788, which destroyed their property, Longouran began a career as merchant and army doctor all over the Caribbean—in Havana, Honduras, Nicaragua, Mexico. He traveled a great deal, leaving his family in New Orleans. A gregarious and an opinionated man, he talked too much about religion and politics. Baron Carondelet's staff had dossiers on him in Central America, where the baron had served prior to his Louisiana post.

The Mexican Inquisition amassed some five hundred pages of data from Louisiana and Central America during the years 1790 to 1795 on Juan Longouran. On a trip to Santa Cruz Yoro, Honduras, in 1790, Longouran was house guest of a business associate when he blatantly expounded heretical ideas. His host made him leave the house, and the next morning he denounced him to the Inquisition. Soon thereafter Longouran was jailed in Honduras and his properties embargoed. Perhaps owing to political influence in Tegucigalpa, he was later released. He then proceeded to Mexico City where his iconoclastic views again got him into trouble. It is evident the Dr. Longouran's rationalistic medical view of the universe and the nature of man had led him to question religious phenomena.[34] Evidence showed that Don Juan was a practicing Catholic when it was good for business, but that in his private life he was, to quote one report, an "obscene and lascivious" man who scoffed at religion. The Inquisition charged him with denying the validity of the sacraments of marriage and baptism. Don Juan said fornication was not a sin, and that when men took the women they desired, they simply followed natural law, which was, after all, the guiding motivation of the world. He claimed that Hell was nothing more than the labors and sufferings men undergo in their mortal lives. He opined that a God of mercy could not save only Christians, for there were only three and one half million of them in a world of thirty-three million souls. Such a situation, he explained, would make for a "small Heaven and very great Hell." He furthermore questioned the doctrine of the incarnation, the adoration of images, and various other mysteries of the Faith, saying he would not kiss the hands of bishops and popes or call for a priest at the hour of his death. He had spoken at length in favor of the French Revolution, and claimed it was legal and just to deny obedience to the Papacy.

The Holy Office of the Inquisition made a secret investigation of the Longouran affair, quietly gathering testimony and keeping the accused under serveillance as a "Protestant" and "secret spy." Perhaps he escaped immediate censure because the Holy Office wished to receive more data on his background from Cuba, Honduras, and Louisiana. As the Reign of Terror in France intensified, and as the Spanish were preparing to expel Frenchmen from the viceroyalty, the Holy Office arrested Longouran in Mexico on July 17, 1793, and confiscated his property. After a long judicial procedure, Juan Longouran was convicted of heresy and sedition. After he was reconciled in the auto de fe of August 9, 1795, he made lengthy penance in the Monastery of the Holy Cross at Querétaro and was finally deported from Veracruz on April 24, 1798, to serve eight years of exile in a Spanish prison. Juan Longouran was the typical example of the learned man who had separated religion and science in his thinking.

Another member of a prominent New Orleans family, the Saint-Maxent, almost had serious problems with the Inquisition in 1795. Francisco Maximiliano de Saint-Maxent, son of the famous Gilbert Antoine de Saint-Maxent, brother of the Condesa de Gálvez, wife of the Mexican viceroy, was serving as military commander of New Santander in 1795. The whole San Luis Potosí and Coahuila populace were gossiping about the trials of Frenchmen by the Mexican Inquisition, especially the case of Juan Marie Murgier formerly military commander of the province. Murgier had been jailed by the Holy Office as a heretic and had committed suicide in order to escape interrogation and punishment.[35] The Commissary of the Holy Office in New Santander, Fray Manual Díaz, was investigating other Frenchmen in the area when he happened to take testimonies about the conduct of Manual Maliban, whose case was pending. Witnesses against Maliban connected Saint-Maxent with Francophile sentiments and irreverent remarks about Spanish Catholicism. Furthermore Saint-Maxent had criticized the Inquisition for its handling of the Murgier affair. As a result the *comisario* alerted the Mexican Tribunal and a dossier on Saint-Maxent was opened.[36] The Commissary was ordered to gather additional evidence, even though the suspect had been transferred to Louisiana by the time the investigation got started.

It all began on April 14, 1795, when Manuel Morales Balbuena told Comisario Díaz that Maliban and Captain Saint-Maxent held similar views on religion and politics. Morales Balbuena had heard this from a Fray Francisco López, who had disputed with the captain about the ultimate worth of religious sects and political systems. López quoted Saint-Maxent as saying only on Judgment Day would it be clear who were right and who were wrong—the French or the Spanish. As the provincial commissaries continued gathering data more suspicion was focused on the captain, particularly as gossip intensified. In San Luis Potosí on May 21, Lt. Col. Silvestre López Portillo appeared before the commissary to give testimony which had not been solicited. He told of an incident related to him by one of Saint-Maxent's officers, which had occurred while they were on a reconnaissance. They had stopped to hear Mass and the Captain had jeered at the others: "Why are you doing this [ridiculous] thing? What do you think Mass is, anyway? It is nothing more than a ceremony." Scandalized by this story, López scurried to tell the Inquisition. On the margin of López's testimony, the commissary wrote an interesting comment: "This gentleman is known to be a man of more than usual piety, but he has the defect of a very lively imagination, and he tends to exaggerate." Obviously the *comisario* questioned whether López Portillo was an enemy of Francisco Saint-Maxent, and at the very least he felt that López was backbiting.

But the investigation of Saint-Maxent continued. On May 21, 1796, Vicente Santa Cruz, Captain of the Militia of New Santander, was induced to testify. The deposition makes it clear that López Portillo had discussed the Saint-Maxent affair with him and had, in a sense, recruited Santa Cruz to further inculpate the Frenchmen. Santa Cruz had been present at the Villa de Aguayo when Saint-Maxent ridiculed the Holy Mass. There the matter rested for almost ten years. In the meantime Francisco Maximiliano de Saint-Maxent had been transferred to Louisiana, and later served as governor of Pensacola, from 1811 to 1816. Perhaps as the result of new cycles of Francophobia in the Spanish world after 1800, and most probably because of colonial creole animosities toward the Gálvez family and its policies, the Saint-Maxent dossier in the Holy Office archive in Mexico City was reactivated between 1805 and 1809. On March 4, 1805, the prosecutor of the Holy Office instructed his staff to gather up-to-date information on Saint-Maxent's career since 1795 and to find out more about the original denunciations.

As a consequence the bureaucracy of the Inquisition finally located the only surviving witness in the Querétaro area. On September 18, 1809, the Reverend Father Fray Francisco López, who was serving as First Preacher of the Convent of San Antonio de Querétaro, testified about events of a decade before. Until he was specifically prompted by Commissary Dr. Rafael Gil de León, Fr. López could not recall the Saint-Maxent incidents. Within the context of gossip about the scandalous trial and suicide of Juan Marie Murgier, López did remember how Saint-Maxent had criticized the Mexican Inquisition for its anti-French prosecutions in the mid-1790s. He also remembered that Francisco Saint-Maxent had remarked that everyone was preoccupied with religious arguments in the province and that they were losing all sense of perspective. Then he made his oft-quoted statement that the arguments would be resolved on Judgment Day when mankind would know for sure which religion and which political system, French or Spanish, was the true one. As far as Saint-Maxent's life style and conduct were concerned, Father López said he had never heard him attack religion or the Church per se. Indeed, he had observed that Francisco Maximiliano Saint-Maxent was always among the first at church to hear Mass, and that he treated the clergy with esteem and respect.

Fray Simón Francisco Coronel, the chaplain of Saint-Maxent's regiment when he was stationed in New Santander, wrote from the Villa Nueva de Croix to say that he remembered the captain as a man who led a normal existence and whose religious sentiments gave no indication of scandal or wrongdoing. With these reports the second investigation of Francisco Maximiliano's orthodoxy ended in October of 1809. While the dossier contains no clues to the Holy Office's motivations in 1809, it seems safe to assume that the second investigation was somehow related to a security check prior to Saint-Maxent's appointment as governor of Pensacola in 1811. It is interesting to note that the fiscal of the Holy Office, when he suspended the proceedings, lamented that the evidence against Saint-Maxent was "very weak."

In line with the attempt to avoid open Inquisitorial activity within Louisiana proper, the Mexican Holy Office often compiled dossiers on suspected heretics within the military establishment and then waited for them to go on leave or be transferred to another locale before taking any action. This was the case with Antonio Ventura Carrión, a thirty-seven-year-old grenadier from Ciudad Rodrigo in Spain in the Louisiana Regiment. Carrión's comrades denounced him while they were on leave in Puebla. Carrión was investigated for heresy and obscene language in April 1797.[37] Before the trial ended almost two years later, perhaps a dozen of Ventura Carrion's comrades in arms had offered proof of his blasphemies and heresies. The testimonies are so thoroughly scatological that the worst of them cannot be analyzed here. That Antonio was a foul-mouthed and loud braggart about his own sexual exploits and a jeering critic of the righteous cannot be counted, but in the end the reader comes to distrust the motives of the "comrades" who denounced him.

Of those elements of the trial record which can be recounted with any delicacy the following are representative of Antonio Ventura Carrión's character. He had a mocking irreverence for saints, images, and the priesthood, which he considered an unnatural state. Many times he "talked to" religious sculptures in a very obscene way. He placed little pieces of bread in front of a carving of Christ and said: "Take it and eat. Don't you want to eat?" He told the Christ, "I am as good as you or better, and *I* eat," and "how whipped and bleeding you are—but better you than me!" Antonio ridiculed religious processions and funerals and jeered at the passerby and spoke to the corpses. On one memorable occasion during Holy Week he shouted at an image of Christ being carried through the streets, "Why don't you get down and walk like everyone else?" and "What fine raiments you wear. Didn't they used to be my own shirt and pants?" More offensive to his upright colleagues, and to the Holy Office of the Inquisition, were Ventura Carrión's Freudian allusions to Christ, the Virgin Mary, and the saints. He used religious literature, devotions, and broadsides torn from the walls of public buildings, as toilet paper. At great length and many times he disputed the virginity of the Virgin calling her a common Hebrew woman, and he made derisive comments about the sex life of Christ and the apostles. He referred to parts of his anatomy as "Saint this" and "Saint that." When his critics threatened to denounce him to the Holy Office for his deeds, Ventura Carrión had said "[expletive] the Inquisition." And so the testimony went. Let the reader understand that what is recounted here is only the milder part of the trial record. Real questions arise from the biographical part of Ventura Carrión's *proceso*. The astonishing and probably accurate picture of a young man, more picaresque than evil, brutalized by the society in which he lived, a thief, liar, and blasphemer who spent over half of his thirty-seven years in jail and large part of the rest as a draftee or "forced volunteer" in the military, does much to mitigate his behavior.

Antonio Ventura Carrión was born in Ciudad Rodrigo in Old Castile around 1760. He knew little of his parents because his father died when he was seven years old and he was sent to live in a miller's house and to work for his keep until he reached the age of fourteen. Antonio told the Inquisitors that he was a baptized Catholic but that he was not sure whether he had ever been confirmed. However, he had gone to confession and communion and he had heard Mass at regular intervals. When he was fourteen Ventura Carrión ran away and "fell in with bad company." He was arrested one night in Ronda and the judge declared him a vagrant and sentenced him to five years in prison at the Presidio of El Ferrol. In 1779 Spain was at war with England and there was a shortage of sailors. Somehow Ventura Carrión was pressed into the navy, but on the way to Cádiz he deserted and roamed around Extremadura until he got a job in Portugal with a band of roving bullfighters. Soon, however, he got drafted into the army and spent a tour of duty in Mallorca. After he extricated himself from this situation, he spent a year and a half in Zamora as servant to a colonel. One night one of the colonel's soldiers robbed his master's house and Antonio was blamed. This time he was condemned to a ten-year stretch in the presidio at Oran in North Africa. While he was there he got overly familiar with a lady and said insulting things to her. As a result he was flogged, and he tried to kill one of the guards after wresting a musket from him. Thereafter they transferred him to prison in Almanza Castle and lengthened his sentence. It was then that he was allowed to volunteer for military service in Louisiana.

Antonio pictured his life as a grenadier in Louisiana as hard but permissive in discipline. He became dissolute, irreligious, and obscene. Ventura Carrión and his friend, a Corporal Francisco Romaña, who was also tried for blasphemy in 1797, had the same attitudes: "In this life one must eat, drink and enjoy oneself because after death there is nothing." Antonio claimed that this was the philosophy of life of everyone in Louisiana. When the two soldiers, accompanied by other disapproving comrades, went on leave to Puebla in April 1797, one of the soldiers, who was from Puebla, Juan Francisco Bujanos, denounced them to the Inquisition. Other Louisiana soldiers gave evidence and some testimony was solicited by mail from New Orleans. After it had been evaluated by the Inquisition attorneys, Ventura Carrión was formally arraigned. The prosecutor charged that he was "a man alienated from God, obscene, scandalous, blasphemous, and a heretic. His utterances were offensive, impious, libertine, iconoclast, and Calvinist."[38] On September 11, 1797, he was removed from the Puebla jail and conducted to the Inquisition jail in Mexico City. There he languished for months while the wheels of justice turned. By January 1798 the staff of the Holy Office had spent considerable time counseling Antonio and showing him the error of his ways. He made a statement to the

Tribunal on January 11 which was full of contrition and penitence. Antonio admitted to being a weak and miserable sinner but he contended that he had never renounced the Catholic religion. He had always maintained an inner reverence for sacred images although he publicly mocked them. He realized that he had committed crimes against the Faith but he swore they were without malice and without knowledge of their gravity.

Whether from fear of punishment or true regeneration, Antonio Ventura Carrión humbled himself before the Inquisitors and begged for mercy. He now swore that he unreservedly believed in the omnipotence of God, the perpetual virginity of the Virgin, and all the other dogmas of the Church. He was renewing his knowledge of the catechism, the credo, and the sacraments, and he pled only to be allowed to live and die as a good Christian. He recognized his faults and dubbed himself as a "poor Gachupín" who would never again deviate from his faith "even if he were tortured" by those who hoped to lead him astray. Evidently the Holy Office of the Inquisition did not consider Ventura Carrión incorrigible, and most probably the judges were swayed to leniency by his contrition and by the dreadful circumstances of his formative years. On July 7, 1798, the *proceso* ended with the hint that Antonio Ventura Carrión was to be re-educated and reconciled with the Church. The final records are fragmentary and do not contain data after 1798. But the judges decided to send an extract of the proceedings to the Supreme Council of the Inquisition in Spain in order that the inquisitor general and Spanish officialdom might inform the king of problems faced in enforcing orthodoxy in Spanish Louisiana.

A case similar to Carrión's was the 1799 probe into the life and morals of Juan Braschi, captain of the brigantine *Sta. Gertrudis* out of New Orleans.[39] Since he often traveled to Mexico it seemed advisable to arrest him there to avoid scandal. If Carrión was a blasphemous and obscene soldier, Braschi was his nautical counterpart. His remarks about the pope and the morality of the clergy rankled the religious establishment. He read prohibited books and bragged about it, and his relations with a multitude of women were a New Orleans scandal. He openly espoused French political philosophy. Because the trial record is fragmentary we do not know the results of the investigation.

The diocesan records show a like concern for enforcing moral conduct among the Louisiana colonists. In June of 1797 Father Pierre Joseph Didier reported to the bishop's office on measures to curb blasphemy in upper Louisiana, and in February 1797 records of the ecclesiastical judge in New Orleans contain proceedings against another soldier, Miguel Solivella, for sexual immorality.[40] This same "Soldevilla" was investigated by the Inquisition commissary in Querétaro, Mexico, in 1799 when residents denounced him as a heretic and blasphemer while he was touring the bajío area recruiting soldiers for the Louisiana regiment.[41] While he was trying to convince a young boy from her father's household to join the army, Soldevilla visited with María Petra Suesnabar and her friends in Querétaro on three separate occasions. He said such shocking things that she decided to inform against him to the Commissary of the Holy Office on June 8, 1799. María Petra never found out his first name and knew the accused only as "Soldevilla." He had told her that the belief in immortality of the soul was false because after death the body was returned to dirt and the soul was converted into smoke. Consequently, he argued, there was no such thing as heaven or hell or saints. To prove his point he suggested to María Petra that she beseech a statue of San Antonio in her house to perform a miracle. Soldevilla proceeded to tell her and her girl friends not to believe what the clergy preached because all religious beliefs were nothing but folk customs. On his third visit to their home Soldevilla told María Petra he believed only in God and the Holy Virgin, but he did not believe in plural representation of the Virgin, for she was only one person and not many as some people believed. The girls were scandal-ized by Soldevilla's statements, and the other women, in separate appearances before the *comisario*, substantiated what María Petra had said. Meanwhile Soldevilla and his troops had left Querétaro and the commissary forwarded his investigation to the Mexican capital. The staff of the Holy Office searched its files for any additional information that might pertain to Soldevilla to no avail, but they had no recourse to the Louisiana diocesan papers, where "Soldevilla" did indeed have a record.

By 1799, the Mexican Tribunal of the Holy Office had amassed a body of data on heresy in Louisiana. Perhaps the judges had begun to feel that the province was so permeated with moral laxity and foreign ideas that it was virtually impossible to contain the spread of heresy and to discipline proscribed conduct. Inquisition records showed that even the Catholic citizenry were liberal, iconoclastic, and often anticlerical. This was the environment promoted by the Spanish state to further its political and economic goals in Louisiana.

Notes for "The Inquisition in Southern Louisiana, 1762-1800"

[1]As is the case with most Spanish Louisiana topics the documentary sources for Inquisition activity are widely scattered among the Spanish archives in Sevilla, Archivo General de Indias, hereafter cited AGI, and Madrid, Archivo Histórico Nacional, hereafter cited AHN); among the *ramos* of Inquisición, Civil, Historia of the Mexican Archivo General de la Nación, hereafter cited AGN; in what remains of the fragmented Cartagena papers; and among *Microfilm Edition of the Records of the Diocese of Louisiana and the Floridas 1576-1803*, ed. by Thomas T. McAvoy and Lawrence J. Bradley (Notre Dame, 1967), 12 reels (DLF). For a listing of Mexican and Caribbean Inquisition papers in AHN and AGI, see Richard E. Greenleaf, "Mexican Inquisition Materials in Spanish Archives," *The Americas*, 20 (1964): 416-20.

[2]DLF.

[3]See the formulary for "reconciliation" of foreign heretics who wished to convert to Catholicism in AGN, Inquisición, tomo 777, exp. 67. For an essay on how the procedures worked consult Richard E. Greenleaf, "North American Protestants and The Mexican Inquisition 1765-1820," *A Journal of Church and State*, 8 (1966): 186-99.

[4]Michael J. Curley, *Church and State in The Spanish Floridas* (1783-1822) (Washington, DC, 1940), 166.

[5]DLF, reel 2, May 6, 1786.

[6]DLF, reel 2, May 8, 1788.

[7]AGI, Audiencia de Santo Domingo. leg. 2673, Letter of February 10, 1786. Curley, 121-29 *passim*, has used parts of the Audiencia de Santo Domingo and Papeles de Cuba manuscripts listed below in his treatment of Sedella's conflict with visitor and Auxiliary Bishop Cirilo de Barcelona. See also the brief note on Sedella by S.L. Gassler, "Père Antoine, Supreme Officer of the Holy Inquisition of Cartagena, in Louisiana," *Catholic*

Historical Review, 8 (1922): 59-63, which depends on the Papeles de Cuba. For more information, consult the microfilm edition of selected Spanish Louisiana documents undertaken by Loyola University of New Orleans by José María de la Peña y Cámara, Ernest J. Burrus, and Charles Edwards O'Neill, *Catálogo de Documentos del Archivo General de Indias, Sección V, Gobierno Audiencia de Santo Domingo sobre la Época Española de Luisiana*, 2 vols. (Madrid and New Orleans, 1968).

[8]AGI, Audiencia de Santo Domingo, leg. 2673, Letter of July 13, 1787.

[9]AGI, Audiencia de Santo Domingo, leg. 2673, royal Order of January 9, 1788.

[10]For a detailed examination of the canonical process against Sedella see Curley, 122-29.

[11]AGI, Audiencia de Santo Domingo, leg. 2686, Letter of December 6, 1790.

[12]AGI, Audiencia de Santo Domingo, leg. 2686, Order of December 5, 1789.

[13]AGI, Papeles de Cuba, leg. 102, Letter of April 28, 1790.

[14]AGI, Papeles de Cuba, leg. 102, Letter of April 29, 1790. See also Gassler, 61.

[15]AGI, Audiencia de Santo Domingo, leg. 2686, Letter of December 6, 1790.

[16]For the reprimand see Curley, 129.

[17]AGI, Papeles de Cuba, leg. 102, Report of April 30, 1790.

[18]Ibid.

[19]See, for instance, Charles Gayarré, *History of Louisiana*, 4 vols. (New Orleans, 1879), 3:269-71; Alcée Fortier, *History of Louisiana*, 4 vols. (Paris, 1904), 2:62, 140, 327.

[20]For the most complete coverage of the Familiatura see Charles H. Lea, *A History of the Inquisition of Spain*, 4 vols. (New York, 1908), 2:263-83. The institution as it operated in Mexico is examined in Richard E. Greenleaf, "Antonio de Espejo and The Mexican Inquisition 1571-1586," *The Americas*, 27 (1971), 271-92.

[21]AGN, Inquisición, tomo 1430, exp. 8. See also the *Boletín del Archivo General de la Nación, Primera Série*, 2 (1931), 641-706, 828-62 *Passim.*

[22]Inventories of furnishings and books are described in Roger P. McCutcheon, "Books and Booksellers in New Orleans 1730-1830," *Louisiana Historical Quarterly*, 20 (1937): 606-18.

[23]Roger P. McCutcheon, "Inventory," ibid., 9 (1926): 429-57.

[24]AGN, Inquisición, tomo 1389, exp. 2.

[25]AGN, Historia, tomo 401, exp. 1.

[26]AGN, Inquisición, tomo 1389, exp. 2. See also the *Gaceta de México*, November 13, 1794.

[27]Consult Greenleaf, "The Mexican Inquisition and the Enlightenment 1763-1805," *New Mexico Historical Review*, 41 (1966): 185, for a translation of the Edict.

[28]DLF, reel 5, September 10, 1796.

[29]Arthur P. Whitaker, *The Mississippi Question, 1795-1803* (New York, 1934), 276, n. 24.

[30]See the biography by Jack D. L. Holmes, *Gayoso, The Life of a Spanish Governor in the Mississippi Valley, 1789 to 1799* (Baton Rouge, 1965).

[31]AGI, Papeles de Cuba, leg. 169, exp. 101.

[32]Irving A. Leonard, "A Frontier Library, 1799," *Hispanic American Historical Review*, 23 (1943): 21-51.

[33]AGN, Inquisición, tomo 1320, exps. 1, 2, 3; AHN, Inquisición de Méjico, leg. 2292, exp. 3.

[34]The following general description of Juan Longouran's heresies relies on Greenleaf, "The Mexican Inquisition and The Enlightenment," 187-89. The one thousand pages of trial records contained in AGN, Inquisición, tomo 1320 are to be examined in depth in Greenleaf, *The Mexican Inquisition of the Sixteenth Century* (Albuquerque, 1969).

[35]AGN, Inquisición, tomo 1331, exp. 14

[36]AGN, Inquisición, tomo 1382, exp. 25.

[37]AGN, Inquisición, tomo 1390, exp. 9.

[38]"Proceso contra Francisco Romaña, Corporal del Regimiento de Luisiana por proposiciones y blásfemo, 1797," AGN, Inquisión, tomo 1379, exp. 5.

[39]AGN, Inquisición, tomo 1368, exp. 4.

[40] DLF, reel 6, February 24, 1797 and June 19, 1797.

[41]AGN, Inquisición, tomo 1339, exp. 13.

Index